# Contemporary France

Essays and Texts on Politics, Economics and Society

**Longman Contemporary Europe Series**

*Series Editor*: Professor Jill Forbes, Queen Mary and Westfield, University of London

*Published titles*:

CONTEMPORARY SPAIN
Teresa Lawlor and Mike Rigby

CONTEMPORARY GERMANY
Mark Allinson, Jeremy Leaman
Stuart Parkes and Barbara Tolkiehn

# Contemporary France

## Essays and Texts on Politics, Economics and Society

SECOND EDITION

**Jill Forbes**
**Nick Hewlett**
**François Nectoux**

*An imprint of* Pearson Education

Harlow, England · London · New York · Reading, Massachusetts · San Francisco
Toronto · Don Mills, Ontario · Sydney · Tokyo · Singapore · Hong Kong · Seoul
Taipei · Cape Town · Madrid · Mexico City · Amsterdam · Munich · Paris · Milan

**Pearson Education Limited**
Edinburgh Gate
Harlow
Essex CM20 2JE
England

and Associated Companies around the World.

*Visit us on the World Wide Web at:*
*www.pearsoneduc.com*

---

First published 1994
**Second edition 2001**



ISBN 0 582 38159 2

*British Library Cataloguing-in-Publication Data*
A catalogue record for this book can be obtained from the British Library

*Library of Congress Cataloging-in-Publication Data*
A catalog record for this book can be obtained from the Library of Congress

10 9 8 7 6 5 4 3 2 1
04 03 02 01 00

Typeset by 35 in 9½/12 Palatino
Printed by Ashford Colour Press Ltd., Gosport

# Contents

# List of figures and tables

## Figures



## Tables

# List of texts

# List of abbreviations

| | |
|---|---|
| AC | Agir contre le chômage |
| AGF | Assurances générales de France |
| AIDS | Acquired immune deficiency syndrome |
| ANPE | Agence nationale pour l'emploi |
| APD | Appel de préparation à la défense |
| ASSEDIC | Association pour l'emploi dans l'industrie et le commerce |
| BEP | Brevet d'études professionnelles |
| BNP | Banque nationale de Paris |
| BTP | Bâtiment et travaux publics |
| BTS | Brevet de technicien supérieur |
| CAP | Certificat d'aptitude professionnelle |
| CAP | Common Agricultural Policy |
| CD | Centre démocratie |
| CDP | Centre démocratie et progrès |
| CDS | Centre des démocrates sociaux |
| CDU | Christlich-Demokratische Union |
| CECA | Communauté européenne du charbon et de l'acier |
| CEE | Communauté économique européenne |
| CEP | Certificat d'études primaires |
| CEPREMAP | Centre d'études prospectives d'économie mathématique appliquées à la planification |
| CERC | Centre d'étude des revenus et des coûts |
| CERES | Centre d'étude, de recherches, et d'éducation socialistes |
| CES | Collège d'enseignement secondaire |
| CFDT | Confédération française démocratique du travail |
| CFE–CGC | Confédération française de l'encadrement–Confédération générale des cadres |
| CFI | Crédit formation individuel |
| CFM | Compagnie générale maritime |
| CFTC | Confédération française des travailleurs chrétiens |
| CGT | Confédération générale du travail |
| CGT–FO | Confédération générale du travail–Force ouvrière |
| CIC | Crédit industriel et commercial |
| CIF | Cost insurance freight |
| CIRAD | Centre de coopération internationale en recherche agronomique pour le développement |
| CJD | Creutzfeldt-Jakob disease |
| CMU | Couverture maladie universelle |
| CNCL | Commission nationale de la communication et des libertés |
| CNI | Centre national des indépendants |

| | |
|---|---|
| **CNIL** | Commission nationale de l'informatique et des libertés |
| **CNIP** | Centre national des indépendants et paysans |
| **CNJA** | Centre national des jeunes agriculteurs |
| **CNP** | Caisse nationale de prévoyance |
| **CNPF** | Conseil national du patronat français |
| **CREDOC** | Centre de recherches pour l'étude et l'observation des conditions de vie |
| **CSA** | Conseil supérieur de l'audiovisuel |
| **CSG** | Contribution sociale généralisée |
| **DATAR** | Délégation à l'aménagement du territoire et à l'action régionale |
| **DDE** | Direction départementale de l'équipement |
| **DEUG** | Diplôme d'études universitaires générales |
| **DL** | Démocratie libérale |
| **DRE** | Direction régionale de l'équipement |
| **DUT** | Diplôme universitaire de technologie |
| **EC** | European Communities |
| **EDF** | Électricité de France |
| **EEC** | European Economic Community |
| **EMS** | European Monetary System |
| **EMU** | European Monetary Union |
| **ENA** | École nationale d'administration |
| **ENS** | École normale supérieure |
| **ERM** | Exchange Rate Mechanism |
| **EU** | European Union |
| **FEN** | Fédération de l'éducation nationale |
| **FGDS** | Fédération de la gauche démocratique et socialiste |
| **FHAR** | Front homosexuel d'action révolutionnaire |
| **FLN** | Front de libération nationale (Algeria) |
| **FN** | Front national |
| **FNSEA** | Fédération nationale des syndicats d'exploitants agricoles |
| **FO** | Force ouvrière |
| **FOB** | Free on board |
| **GAN** | Groupe des assurances nationales |
| **GATT** | General Agreement on Tariffs and Trade |
| **GDF** | Gaz de France |
| **GDP** | Gross Domestic Product |
| **GNP** | Gross National Product |
| **HIV** | Human immunodeficiency virus |
| **HLM** | Habitation à loyer modéré |
| **IFOP** | Institut français de l'opinion publique |
| **ILO** | International Labour Organization |
| **INED** | Institut national des études démographiques |
| **INSEE** | Institut national de la statistique et des études économiques |
| **IUT** | Institut universitaire de technologie |
| **JAC** | Jeunesse agricole chrétienne |

| | |
|---|---|
| **JEC** | Jeunesse étudiante chrétienne |
| **JOC** | Jeunesse ouvrière chrétienne |
| **LO** | Lutte ouvrière |
| **MATIF** | Marché à terme international de France |
| **MDSF** | Mouvement démocrate socialiste de France |
| **Medef** | Mouvement des entreprises de France |
| **MLAC** | Mouvement pour la libération de l'avortement et de la contraception |
| **MLF** | Mouvement de libération des femmes |
| **MNR** | Mouvement national républicain |
| **MPF** | Mouvement pour la France |
| **MRP** | Mouvement républicain populaire |
| **NATO** | North Atlantic Treaty Organization |
| **OECD** | Organization for Economic Cooperation and Development |
| **OFCE** | Observatoire français des conjonctures économiques |
| **ONI** | Office national de l'immigration |
| **ONISEP** | Office national d'information sur les enseignements et les professions |
| **OPCVM** | Organismes de placement collectif en valeurs mobilières |
| **ORTF** | Office de la radiodiffusion-télévision française |
| **OS** | Ouvrier spécialisé |
| **OTAN** | Organisation du traité de l'Atlantique Nord |
| **PAC** | Politique agricole commune |
| **PACS** | Pacte civil de solidarité |
| **PAF** | Paysage audiovisuel français |
| **PCF** | Parti communiste français |
| **PIB** | Produit intérieur brut |
| **PIL** | Programmes d'insertion locale |
| **PLIF** | Programmes locaux d'insertion pour les femmes |
| **PME** | Petites et moyennes entreprises |
| **PRG** | Parti radical de gauche |
| **PS** | Parti socialiste |
| **PSBR** | Public sector borrowing requirement |
| **PSU** | Parti socialiste unifié |
| **RATP** | Régie autonome des transports parisiens |
| **RER** | Réseau express régional |
| **RFA** | République fédérale d'Allemagne |
| **RFF** | Réseau ferré de France |
| **RI** | Républicains indépendants |
| **RMI** | Revenu minimum d'insertion |
| **RPF** | Rassemblement du peuple français |
| **RPF** | Rassemblement pour la France |
| **RPR** | Rassemblement pour la République |
| **RTF** | Radiodiffusion-télévision française |
| **SECAM** | Séquentiel couleur à mémoire |
| **SFIO** | Section française de l'Internationale ouvrière |

| | |
|---|---|
| **SICAV** | Société d'investissement à capital variable |
| **SIVP** | Stages d'insertion à la vie professionnelle |
| **SME** | Système monétaire européen |
| **SMIC** | Salaire minimum de croissance |
| **SMIG** | Salaire minimum interprofessionnel garanti |
| **SNCF** | Société nationale des chemins de fer français |
| **SNPMI** | Syndicat national des petites et moyennes industries |
| **SOFRES** | Société française d'études par sondages |
| **SPD** | Sozialdemokratische Partei Deutschlands |
| **SRA** | Stages de réinsertion en alternance |
| **SUD** | Solidaires, unitaires, démocratiques |
| **TGV** | Train à grande vitesse |
| **TP** | Travaux pratiques |
| **TUC** | Travaux d'utilité collective |
| **UAP** | Union des assurances de Paris |
| **UDC** | Union du centre |
| **UDF** | Union pour la démocratie française |
| **UDR** | Union pour la défense de la République |
| **UDT** | Union démocratique du travail |
| **UDVeR** | Union des démocrates pour la cinquième République |
| **UNEF** | Union nationale des étudiants de France |
| **UNR** | Union pour la nouvelle République |
| **UPF** | Union pour la France |
| **URSS** | Union des Républiques socialistes soviétiques |
| **VAT** | Value added tax |
| **ZAC** | Zone d'aménagement concerté |
| **ZUP** | Zone à urbaniser en priorité |

# Acknowledgements

All books based on university courses owe a large debt to those on whom they were first inflicted. The authors therefore wish to extend their gratitude to several generations of students of French at South Bank University, Oxford Brookes University, Queen Mary and Westfield College, and the University of Strathclyde, with a particular mention for Michael Agnew and Alisdair Gray. Lew Lewis has some claim to having been the originator of this book; Michèle Dickson brought her eagle eye to bear on many points of detail, as did Emmanuel Godin; Julia Henderson offered much encouragement as well as expert advice on matters of style, and Martin McKeand, as ever, provided indispensable moral support. Our first editor, Chris Harrison, was an enthusiastic and erudite reader of our work and much of the book's initial success came from his firm support, while the second edition would not have seen the light of day had it not been for Brian Place's technical assistance. Their help is gratefully acknowledged here.

We are grateful to the following for permission to reproduce copyright material:

*Alternatives Economiques* for an extract from 'Le Commerce extérieur français reste excédentaire' by Sandrine Trouvelot in *Alternatives Economiques* No. 170 May 1999 © *Alternatives Economiques*; Éditions Autrement for an extract from 'Décadence du repas bourgeois' by Henri Mendras from *Mots de passe* © Éditions Autrement, collection Ciel Ouvert 1985; *Cahiers Français* for an extract from 'Doit-on réorienter la logique du système de protection sociale?' in *Les Cahiers Français* No. 292 July–September 1999; CFDT for an extract from 'La CFDT: progresser vers l'autogestion des entreprises' in *CFDT: textes de base; La Croix* for '"Consommez", le nouveau mot d'ordre' by Robert Rochefort in *La Croix* 10 July 1999; La Découverte for extracts from '1952–1998: le cycle long de l'inflation' by Philippe Sigogne in *L'Économie française* 1999, and 'L'Éclatement du système des partis politiques' by Colette Ysmal in *L'État de la France* 1999–2000; *L'Expansion* for 'Le tourment agricole de la France: allons-nous vers une agriculture à deux vitesses?' by Jean-Pierre Tuquoi in *L'Expansion* 3–16 October 1991, extracts from 'La Fin du chômage?' by Lionel Steinmann and Walter Bouvais in *L'Expansion* 21 October–3 November 1999, and 'Les entreprises françaises ont fait le pari de la mondialisation' by Christian David in *L'Expansion* 4–17 November 1999; Librairie Arthème Fayard for an extract from *Politique* 2: 1977–1981 by François Mitterrand © Librairie Arthème Fayard 1981; Flammarion for an extract from 'Le rôle du Président de la République selon la constitution de la IV$^{e}$ République' in *Les constitutions de la France depuis 1789* edited by J Godechot; Éditions Gallimard for an extract from *La France des chômages* by

Olivier Mazel © Éditions Gallimard; *L'Histoire* for an extract from 'Les lois de décentralisation de 1982–83: la revanche des régions' in *L'Histoire* No. 143; *Libération* for 'Reconversion des vieilles régions industrielles: une usine textile sur les ruines de la mine de la Mure' by Sylvaine Villeneuve in *Libération* 6–7 April 1991, 'TGV: une décennie qui a changé la France' in *Libération* 22 September 1991, and 'La transhumance des aoûtiens' by Nadyn Charvet in *Libération* 15–16 August 1992; *Le Monde* for 'Quand la France s'ennuie' by Pierre Viansson-Ponté in *Le Monde* 15 March 1968, 'La politique industrielle de la sidérurgie: de plan en plan, une gestion désastreuse' by Eric Boucher in *Le Monde* 1 May 1988, '1982–1988: des nationalisations aux privatisations' by Claire Blandin in *Le Monde* 1988, 'Monsieur Mitterrand, modernisateur du capitalisme français?' by Erik Izraelewicz in *Le Monde* 8 May 1991, 'Lâchetés' by François Léotard in *Le Monde* 24 September 1991, 'Don Quichotte et les dinosaures' by Bertrand Poirot-Delpech in *Le Monde* 20 October 1993, 'L'extension du prolétariat' by Michel Cahen in *Le Monde* 7 October 1995, 'Des conflits sociaux d'un nouveau type' in *Le Monde* 26 January 1997, 'La tchatche des rappeurs marseillais' by Stéphane Davet in *Le Monde* 9–10 August 1998, 'Les mots vieux garçons' by Paul Garde in *Le Monde* 11 August 1998, 'Internet, ou la fin de la vie privée?' by Mathieu O'Neil in *Le Monde* September 1998, 'Cherche consommateur unique et unifié' by Serge Marti in *Le Monde* 31 December 1998, 'La France et ses langues' by Catherine Trautmann in *Le Monde* 31 July 1999, extracts from 'Le patrimoine des Français augmente, les inégalités aussi', by Laurent Mauduit in *Le Monde* 7 October 1999, and 'Le capitalisme français s'émancipe de l'État et obéit à de nouvelles régles du jeu' by Laurent Mauduit in *Le Monde* 1 January 2000; Front National for an extract from 'Le Pen: l'espérance française face à l'aube du IIIème millénaire' from http://www.front.nat.fr/discours/udt99.html; The *New York Times* Syndicate for 'Les foulards de la discorde' by Marie-Laure de Léotard in *L'Express* 30 October 1989, 'Le problème FN est derrière nous' by Romain Rosso in *L'Express* 1 July 1999, 'Jacques Chirac: le Président et le fantôme du Général' in *L'Express* 15 July 1999; *Le Nouvel Observateur* for an extract from 'Le retournement socialiste de 1982: de la relance à la rigueur' by Martine Gilson in *Le Nouvel Observateur* 2–9 May 1991, the articles 'La France en avait besoin' by Jean Daniel in *Le Nouvel Observateur* 16–22 July 1998, 'Lettre ouverte à Bernadette Chirac' by Dominique Fernandez in *Le Nouvel Observateur* 12–18 November 1998, 'Un remède pire que le mal' by Élisabeth Badinter in *Le Nouvel Observateur* 14–20 January 1999, all © *Le Nouvel Observateur*; Association Parité for an extract from 'Les Députées de la nouvelle législature en 1997' by Françoise Gaspard and Claude Servan-Schreiber in *Les Élections Législatives des 25 Mai et 1er Juin 1997: Les Femmes Dans la Compétition Électorale en France;* Librairie Plon SA for an extract from 'Discours prononcé par le général de Gaulle' by Charles de Gaulle in *Discours et messages Vol 2 1946–58; Le Point* for 'Les limites de la tolérance' by Claude Imbert in *Le Point* 30 October 1989; Éditions du Seuil for extract from 'Travail, capital et État pendant la période de croissance de l'après guerre' in *Abrégé de la Croissance Française* by J-J Carré et al. and the article 'Plus français que moi, tu rentres chez toi' by Hervé Le Bras in *Le Genre Humain* February 1989.

*Le Monde* for Figure 3.2 "pyramide des âges française" in *Le Monde* 13 April 1989; Éditions La Découverte for Tables 3.2 and 3.3 from *L'État de la France* © Éditions La Découverte.

We have been unable to trace the copyright holders of the articles 'Pourquoi la France a-t-elle trois millions de chômeurs en 1992?' by Philippe Eliakim and Olivier Drouin in *L'Événement du Jeudi* 4–10 July 1992 and 'Vivre en France avec un bas salaire: pas la peine de rêver' by Philippe Eliakim in *L'Événement du Jeudi* 5–12 July 1990, and would appreciate any information which would enable us to do so. Whilst every effort has been made to trace the owners of copyright material, in a few cases this has proved impossible and we take this opportunity to offer our apologies to any copyright holders whose rights we may have unwittingly infringed.

# Preface to the first edition

This book is based on courses taught by the authors at South Bank Polytechnic (now South Bank University), London, for an undergraduate degree in Modern Languages and International Studies, and it is therefore designed primarily for use by university students of French and European Studies. However, the essays in English will provide useful material even for those with little knowledge of French.

The book is divided into three parts devoted to politics in contemporary France, the post-war French economy and contemporary French society. Each part consists of an essay in English which surveys and analyses the major changes and developments since 1945, and a set of French language texts chosen to illustrate some of the principal themes discussed. The French texts have been selected with a view to both their historical and linguistic interest and are accompanied by language exercises intended to help students develop their awareness of lexical, grammatical and stylistic features of French and to extend their reading and comprehension skills. Each set of exercises also includes at least one essay or discussion question which can serve as a basis for written work or for further debate.

Suggestions for further reading are included at the end of each part and an appendix contains a chronology of significant events in post-war France.

# Preface to the second edition

This book has been widely adopted in modern languages and European studies departments both in the UK and abroad, but much has changed since it was first published and this new edition has therefore been thoroughly updated.

The English language essays have been revised to take account of the many political, economic and social changes in France during the last six years. They include some entirely new material, such as an examination of the fragmentation which now characterizes the party system, a discussion of the impact of globalization and of the so-called 'new economy', and a section on cultural policy and the mass media; they also attempt to look forward to the trends which are emerging in the new millennium.

Similarly, about half the French language material has been replaced with new texts and exercises which respond to changes in the French environment. Our selection has been guided by our own experience in the classroom as well as the many helpful comments we have received from colleagues, and we believe that these new texts will prove as intellectually stimulating and linguistically interesting as those they replace. The texts that have been removed can, however, be found on the Pearson Education website at www.booksites.net.

Finally, the suggestions for further reading take account of new material published since 1994 and for the first time incorporate pertinent websites, while the chronology has been extended to the year 2000.

*London and Oxford, February 2000*

# Introduction

In this book we explore both conventional and less conventional ways of looking at politics, economics and society in France since 1945. For a long time analysts would discuss political life in terms of overt conflict, revolt and extreme ideology up to 1968, followed by a calmer period thereafter. Economists would discuss reconstruction and the rapid growth of the economy for about thirty years after the war, followed by crisis in the 1970s, then partial, although not full, recovery. In the sphere of social analysis it was commonplace to characterize the nature of the boom years in terms of urbanization, more widespread access to consumer durables and to education, greater equality, followed by slower progress since the mid-1970s. All this was often summed up in one word, 'modernization'.

In the English essays we explore these themes and recognize that they help understand what took place in France – and in many other advanced capitalist countries – in the first thirty or so years of the post-war period. However, as another writer on France put it, 'if France . . . had energetically stepped onto the train to modernity, by the 1990s it had to face the fact that there was no longer any such station'.* In other words, post-war growth and modernization were not part of a process by which France moved ever nearer to a state of perfection, as it once had seemed, but represented instead one particular stage in the history of the post-war era, a stage from which France has now moved on. As we move into the twenty-first century, French politics, economics and society appear far more complex than they did during the long aftermath of the Second World War.

In the realm of politics, it seemed that France gradually became more moderate (a process which culminated in the mid-to-late 1980s) and began to resemble other industrialized nations more closely in this respect. But developments since the late 1980s have pointed to a growing crisis of confidence in party politics, particularly as practised by professional politicians, and to a fragmentation of the party system, which is in some ways reminiscent of the Fourth Republic. As regards the French economy, the various crises of the 1970s, 1980s and 1990s appear to be an inherent feature of the capitalist system, rather than exceptional phenomena, and have produced long-term mass unemployment and high rates of inflation, which make the prosperity of the *Trente glorieuses* seem like a distant memory. Finally, the re-emergence of widespread poverty, conflict over issues of immigration and ethnicity, and urban unrest have obliged commentators to rethink the thesis of increasing social harmonization and convergence. Another theme of this book is therefore the need to come to grips

* G. Ross, 'Introduction: Janus and Marianne', in J. Hollifield and G. Ross, *Searching for the New France* (Routledge, 1991), p. 13.

with political, economic and social developments in France and elsewhere which are symptoms of an era which is quite distinct from (and less easy to define than) the era of 'modernization'.

Developments in many other industrialized countries tend to confirm that touchstones so long taken for granted are now disappearing and that we are living in an era of greater uncertainty. Politically, the post-war consensus – or post-war 'settlement' as some have described it – is certainly over, with small, almost single-issue or nationalist, parties rising up in many West European countries to break the post-1945 mould of domination of centre-right and centre-left. Economically, neither state intervention nor market forces have been able to cure unemployment and other increasingly widespread socio-economic problems since the early 1970s. State intervention was blamed for lack of economic dynamism, but market-driven economics have patently failed to cure any of the ills which Keynesianism was supposed to have produced. Socially, profound inequalities, partly a result of uncaring market forces, are becoming commonplace in many countries where forty years ago they seemed to be heading for extinction.

France was a country which was solidly – if sometimes reluctantly – part of the uneasy peace which the cold war offered. But in the late 1980s and early 1990s it became abundantly clear that the post-war era was over in this respect as well. The Eastern bloc disintegrated and Germany was unified. The break-up of the old Soviet bloc gave rise to a bloody civil war – the first fully-fledged war in Europe since 1945 – in what was previously Yugoslavia, and relations between industrialized and less developed countries deteriorated rapidly as less developed countries became more defiant, sometimes with the most tragic of consequences for their own people.

One enduring element of political, economic and social stability since the war has been the European Community, with France as a key player right from the start. But here, again, it is far from clear whether the European Community can provide stability for France and other states in an increasingly unstable world, or whether, as it grows stronger, it will be a source of controversy and discontent both within and between member states.

France is once again proving to be a fascinating case study in this rapidly changing world. It is a country whose uneven social, economic, political and cultural development over the centuries, in part a result of its geographical position, has meant that it is particularly sensitive to wider conflict and contradictions. Looking at France, as with the wider world it responds to so sensitively, we can still only guess at the shape of things in fifty years' time; will late modernization and a long-unstable political situation in the post-war years mean that it is more vulnerable to the effects of the international turmoil? Or will France cope with uncertainty better because it experienced so much uncertainty itself?

One thing is certain. In order to make sense of events as they develop, students of political, social and economic aspects of France will need to look back at what has gone before. The object of this book is to encourage such an exercise and therefore to play a small part in allowing an informed view of events as they unfold in the future.

PART I

# Politics in France

Nick Hewlett

# Introduction

France was for a long time a country whose politics were dominated by conflict, where radicalism was prevalent and where political parties and pressure groups were often influenced by controversial ideologies. Strongly identified with a tradition of revolution and counter-revolution, class antagonism was expressed particularly clearly; Friedrich Engels commented in 1885 that 'France is the land where, more than anywhere else, the historical class struggles are each time fought out to a decision, and where, consequently, the changing political forms in which they move . . . have been stamped in the sharpest outlines'.[1] Between the revolution of 1789 and the end of the Second World War, all political regimes without exception had been brought to an end by revolution, *coup d'état* or war. In the period between the Second World War and the 1980s, France still retained its radicalism, with a strong Communist Party, frequent revolts by forces of both right and left, governmental crises and de Gaulle's authoritarian populism which firmly left its stamp on the constitution of the Fifth Republic. In contrast to many other advanced capitalist countries during the post-1945 period, France did not see the emergence of more consensual politics where dominant parties of the left and right were broadly in agreement. The last twenty years of the twentieth century, however, stand out in striking contrast to the past. The Communist Party has been seriously weakened, as has the communist-oriented trade union confederation, the *Confédération générale du travail*; Gaullism has a severe identity problem; the constitution of the Fifth Republic is now accepted by almost all forces of both left and right as the best way for France to order its formal politics; and the governmental scene has been largely dominated by a centre-oriented Socialist Party which has sought to be pragmatic and catch-all rather than to effect far-reaching transformations; centre-right governments have taken a similar approach; 'cohabitation' between a government of one complexion and a president of the Republic of another is now taken for granted; industrial relations in general are calmer than at any time since 1945, with trade unions suffering a serious drop in membership and a decline in rank-and-file militancy, and employers are more conciliatory than has long been their practice.

In this part we first analyse conflictual aspects of the 'old' political situation between the Second World War and 1981 and then go on to examine the left, the right, trade unions and foreign and defence policy, with special reference to the 'normalization' period of the 1980s and the 1990s. Some analysts have perhaps been over-hasty, however, in concluding that conflict, revolt and indeed class struggle are entirely a thing of the past in France. There remain some important manifestations of the old style of politics, in particular the persistence of the extreme right and a fragmentation of electoral allegiances. There is a solid, if diminished, core of support for the Communist Party, not to mention the emergence of significant support for ecology parties, but communists and ecologists have become fully part of the more moderate approach to government. In the concluding section of this part we briefly examine these exceptions to and problems with the general rule of moderation.

## 1945–81: instability, conflict and revolt

In order to understand the nature of French politics after the Second World War, it is necessary to look briefly at the French experience of the war itself. French defences against German military attack failed in 1940 and the occupying army entered the capital on 14 June, as millions of Parisians fled their homes and their city as best they could. Germany occupied the north and the west of France and a retired French military man, Marshal Philippe Pétain, became head of the remaining *État français* in the south and east, with a government based in Vichy. Pétain soon established that Vichy would pursue a policy of full cooperation with the Nazi regime and many ordinary French people supported him, particularly at first, because his apparent policy of damage limitation appeared to many to be the best way of surviving, both in a literal, personal sense and as a people.

Political reality is never that straightforward, however. Pétain and Vichy promoted an ideology of hard-right patriotism which abolished parliament in favour of a military Veterans League, dissolved trade unions and replaced the French Revolution's watchwords *Liberté, Égalité, Fraternité* with the slogan *Travail, Famille, Patrie*, reminiscent of the philosophy of fully-fledged fascism elsewhere in Europe. Indeed, the National Revolution, as Vichy described its programme, included widespread persecution of anti-clericals, Protestants, Freemasons and above all Jews, many thousands of whom were sent to their deaths in concentration camps in Germany. In November 1942 Germany extended the Occupied Zone to the whole of France and Vichy continued to cooperate to the full; huge numbers of French workers were forcibly sent to work in Germany for the Nazi war machine and France became an important supplier of agricultural produce and industrial products, including arms, to the Reich.

An ever-increasing number of French people resisted the occupation in a myriad of different ways, ranging from passive non-cooperation with the occupying force, to passing on information concerning the struggle against German activities, to acts of sabotage and assassination of German soldiers. Charles de Gaulle, an army general who had played an important part in the First World War, broadcast an appeal from London on 18 June 1940 calling for widespread participation in the Resistance and he became one of the principal leaders of the movement. After the German attack on the Soviet Union in Summer 1941 and thus the entry of the Soviet Union into the war, the French Communist Party joined the Resistance in strength and as the years passed the movement gained more and more support.

When Liberation finally came to Paris in August 1944 de Gaulle became head of state, supported by diverse elements of the Resistance, but the massive rifts and profound bitterness which had developed between resisters and collaborators meant widespread and often summary punishment – in many cases by death – of alleged collaborators.[2] The bitterness and divisions live on in some communities to this day and certainly had a substantial effect on the nature of post-war politics, as we shall see.

In many advanced capitalist countries after the Second World War, there emerged agreements between capital, labour and the state which were, in an immediate sense at least, mutually beneficial. In return for higher wages, welfare protection, basic trade union rights and virtually full employment, labour leaders agreed to limit strike and other protest action and in general accepted that it was the right of employers to make the pursuit of profit their driving principle. This helped governments, in the meantime, to implement programmes of economic reconstruction, often following the Keynesian policy of expanding the public sector, creating jobs and offering higher wages in order to stimulate demand. This set the tone for a more consensus-oriented pattern of politics and industrial relations from then on. In France, however, attempts to establish an enduring pattern of relations along these lines were unsuccessful. From September 1944 to May 1947 there was broad-based government with the participation, among others, of Socialists, Communists and the Christian Democratic *Mouvement républicain populaire* (MRP), during which time communist and other trade union leaders instructed their membership to be moderate in their demands and the pursuit of these demands. But the Communists were excluded from government in May 1947 and abandoned their previous policy of not rocking the boat. The Communist Party was the most popular political party at the time and attracted well over 25 per cent of votes in national elections, in part because of its central role in wartime resistance against Nazi occupation.[3] The communist-oriented *Confédération générale du travail* (CGT), meanwhile, was the most influential trade union confederation and from 1947 onwards held solidly class-against-class positions, which often meant a refusal to enter into negotiations with management unless terms seemed particularly favourable to the union side. The cold war climate of the late 1940s and 1950s, when the United States and its allies pursued a propaganda offensive against communist eastern Europe, meant that any party or trade union with any sympathy for the Soviet Union was treated as a pariah by other political forces, including the Socialists. French employers, meanwhile, were particularly intransigent and often refused even to embark upon negotiations with trade unionists, preferring an old-fashioned paternalistic approach to employee relations. Added to this was the more general tradition of revolt in France and a profound interclass mistrust born partly out of the war years when the employers, or *patronat*, were deeply involved in Pétain's National Revolution. There was little scope for consensus.

The Fourth Republic, from 1946 to 1958, was a period of tremendous political instability, and ultimately failure, whereas the programme of economic modernization during this period was very successful. The nature of the constitution of the Fourth Republic was in part a reaction against the highly authoritarian Vichy regime and thus gave substantial powers to members of parliament (*députés*) over both the ministerial composition and the actual programme of government. Legislative elections were carried out using a system of proportional representation, which gave smaller parties the chance to be represented in parliament as well as larger ones, but this tended to lead to the existence of more and more parties and no single party was large enough consistently to form the backbone of governments during this period. Cabinets came and went with alarming frequency; between 1946 and 1958 there were twenty-five different governments and fifteen prime ministers, of whom only two were in power for more than a year (Guy Mollet and Henri Queuille). For much of this period it was a case of trying to find ways of governing without the more militant parties of both left and right who between them often represented a majority in parliament: the *Parti communiste français* (PCF), the Gaullist *Rassemblement du peuple français* (RPF), which was anti-parliamentary and often highly obstructive, and (for a short period) extreme-right Poujadists.

A major and highly divisive problem during the whole of this period was colonial war. After its humiliating defeat in Indo-China in 1954 France withdrew its army, only to become involved in attempting to quell the Algerian independence movement later the same year. At first there was a considerable degree of consensus over the Algerian question, with virtually all major parties in favour of defending French Algeria against independence; the Communist Party alone campaigned systematically against the war and it even voted in favour of special powers to rule Algeria in 1956, in an unsuccessful attempt to win over the Socialists to a position of ongoing joint work. As time went by and as French casualties increased (including young men doing military service and reservists), the conflict had more and more impact on domestic politics. By the end of 1957 it was patently clear that policy on the Algerian question was bankrupt and, when Prime Minister Bourgès-Maunoury resigned at the end of September that year after losing a vote over the future of Algeria, no one was able to form a government for thirty-five days. Meanwhile the army, already humiliated and politicized by its defeat at the hands of the Germans in 1940, further defeat in Indo-China, and a fruitless attempt at asserting France's might during the Franco-British Suez adventure in 1956, was acting more and more as an autonomous force in relation to Algeria. Frustrated with fighting for weak governments whose commitment to French Algeria they thought could not be trusted, the army in Algeria appeared to be on the point of attempting a *coup d'état* in domestic France. After a revolt by soldiers and French Algerians on 13 May 1958, it seemed to many that the only person able to reconcile the army with some semblance of democratic politics was General de Gaulle, who had resigned from the provisional government in January 1946 amid inter-party bickering and after it had become clear that his proposals for a more authoritarian type of constitution, with more power for the president and government, and less for parliament, would not be accepted.

De Gaulle certainly came to power with the support of the army, but it would be inaccurate to speak of an actual *coup d'état*, for there were apparently no direct, conspiratorial contacts between him and the army. He became head of state on the understanding that the existing constitution would be abolished and a new one drawn up which would increase the power of the president and the government and reduce the power of parliament. The new constitution was approved by a large majority in a referendum in September 1958.

The Gaullist regime between 1958 and 1969 was a political expression of France's half-way position between an old-fashioned, rural country with backward social relations, and a more liberal, urban-based, advanced capitalist consumer society like many of its trading and diplomatic partners. Back in 1946 de Gaulle had insisted that his ideas with regard to the appropriate constitution for France were a response to 'notre vieille propension gauloise aux divisions et aux querelles' [see Text 1.1] and that its strong executive was the recipe for political stability. After Algerian independence in 1962 (strongly opposed by some people who had been ardent supporters of de Gaulle in 1958), France did indeed see a period of stability during which it seemed to many that de Gaulle's wish to bypass the divisiveness of political parties and to appeal directly to the French as a united people was an effective way of going about politics. De Gaulle restored some of the country's wounded national pride by paying great attention to France's supposedly independent place in the world, for instance by championing the development of the *force de frappe* nuclear deterrent and voicing his anti-Americanism. De Gaulle also pushed the economic modernization of France forward considerably and the average standard of living rose substantially during the 1960s. However, the Gaullist regime oversaw changes in these respects at great cost to others; French society was stiflingly bureaucratic and over-centralized and the social structure and social culture were frustratingly inflexible. This is what sociologist Michael Crozier described as 'la société bloquée' [see Text 1.2]. Political activist and analyst Régis Debray, meanwhile, described France of the 1960s as a 'la France à deux vitesses' with the economy cruising in a high gear and social aspects of France stuck in a low gear. On the one hand, economically France had undergone tremendous modernizing changes since the Second World War, which included an impressive growth in Gross National Product (GNP), the concentration of capital, the 'feminization' of the labour force and the vast increase in the number of graduates, whose historical task it was to oversee further economic development (see Part II). On the other hand, there was still a backward, paternalistic system of industrial relations where the *patronat* virtually refused to talk to the trade unions, an education system where relations between teachers and students were archaic, despite the massive expansion of student numbers, the traditional model of the family where patriarchy reigned, cultural and legal constraints on relations between the sexes which were out of date and, last but not least, the paternalistic and authoritarian nature of Gaullism itself.

It was in part the contradiction between these two – economic and social – aspects of de Gaulle's France which led to the explosion of May 1968. Students, frustrated at the education system's inability to cope physically with vastly increased numbers and its failure to respond to the changing moral climate, took to the streets, occupied universities, built barricades and fought violent battles with the riot police [see Text 1.3]. Then the combination of the sight of police violence against students and, for the working class, years of frustration at being faced with an intransigent *patronat* and a hostile government, persuaded working people also to take to the streets and to occupy factories and offices. France witnessed a 'revolutionary moment', like so many in the country's turbulent history, which was an expression of the deep conflicts in French society and political life; there was a three-week general strike, a virtual governmental power vacuum at the end of May, and economic paralysis. De Gaulle only managed to stay in power by the skin of his teeth and, despite winning an increased majority in the emergency legislative elections in June due to a right-wing backlash, he was obliged to leave office in April 1969 after staking his reputation on support in a referendum and failing to win it [see Text 1.4].

There is no doubt that the events of May 1968 launched a new era in French politics, although the right stayed in power until 1981. First, President Pompidou, for many years de Gaulle's prime minister, then President Giscard d'Estaing (from May 1974) introduced reforms which did bring France more socially and politically into line with other advanced capitalist countries, to a state which Debray might have described as at least approaching 'single-speed'. Pompidou, in contrast to de Gaulle, realized that the events of May were for a large part a result of certain social and political archaisms rather than a communist plot. His presidency therefore began with his prime minister Jacques Chaban-Delmas promising 'une nouvelle société' which he believed would provide the solution to such problems. Drawing inspiration directly from Michel Crozier, Chaban-Delmas later said before parliament on 16 September 1972: 'De cette société bloquée, je retiens trois éléments essentiels, au demeurant liés les uns aux autres de la façon la plus étroite: la fragilité de notre économie, le fonctionnement défectueux de l'État, enfin l'archaïsme et le conservatisme de nos structures

**Charles de Gaulle** (1890–1970)

One of the best-known politicians of the twentieth century, de Gaulle fought in the First World War and campaigned for the modernization of the French army in the following twenty years; he was made general in 1940. When Nazi Germany invaded France in 1940, he went to London to lead the Free French, and became head of the provisional government in France from the time of the Liberation in August 1944. He resigned in 1946, in part because of the adoption of what he regarded as a weak constitution, founded the *Rassemblement du peuple français* (RPF) in 1947, but withdrew from politics in 1953 with the intention of concentrating on writing. In 1958, in the midst of the Algerian crisis, de Gaulle came back as head of state with the support of the army, in what many saw at the time as a coup d'état. He introduced a new constitution which received overwhelming support in a referendum and which gave the president a great deal of power, consolidated still more in 1962, when the election of the president by universal suffrage was approved in a referendum. De Gaulle presided over the rapid modernization of French industry, Algerian independence, the development of an independent, French nuclear deterrent (the *force de frappe*) and consolidation of close ties with Germany. In his foreign policy he claimed to be independent of both the American and Soviet superpowers. He was re-elected president in 1965, but left office less than a year after the events of May 1968, when a majority voted against his proposals for minor constitutional reforms in a referendum. He was author of a number of books, including *Le fil de l'épée* (1932), *Vers l'armée de métier* (1934), and five volumes of *Mémoires* (1954–71).

sociales.'[4] The government encouraged a sort of company-level social contract between nationalized firms and trade unions, which gave improvements in pay in return for a guaranteed level of productivity and a new law extended the right to training leave. The employers' federation, the *Conseil national du patronat français* (CNPF), was encouraged to negotiate more widely with trade unions and the years 1969–74 did indeed see the signature of at least ten major, national collective agreements. But this reforming zeal on the part of government was relatively short-lived, partly because of differences in outlook between Chaban-Delmas and Pompidou, who was after all de Gaulle's *dauphin*, and he replaced Chaban with the more conservative Pierre Messmer in July 1972.

After the death of Pompidou in April 1974, however, the new President of the Republic Valéry Giscard d'Estaing implemented reforms which were more significant than Pompidou's and which reflected his particular brand of liberal conservatism, involving an emphasis on the rights of the individual, pluralism and social reform, as described in his book, *Démocratie française* [see Text 1.5]. Giscard's presidency began with a series of reforms, the main ones being reduction of the age of majority (including the right to vote) from twenty-one to eighteen years, wider availability of contraception, legalization of abortion, legalization of divorce by mutual consent, reform of the social security system, lowering of the age of retirement, new laws on equal pay and employment opportunities for women, new measures protecting employees from unfair dismissal and the attempt to restore credibility to the state broadcasting system. However, this period of liberal reform also turned to more conservative politics, prompted partly by the deepening of the economic crisis, provoked in part by the oil crisis of Winter 1973–4. In August 1976, after the resignation of Prime Minister Jacques Chirac amid quarrels with the president, Giscard appointed economics professor Raymond Barre as prime minister, almost exclusively because of his faith in Barre's ability to manage the economic crisis. The Giscard presidency thus turned into one dominated by the needs of economic crisis management.

Thus the period between 1968 and 1981 already hinted at the more consensual politics from the mid-1980s onwards and, significantly, May 1968 is the last major revolt which France has known. But during the early 1970s the effect of May was also to radicalize a large number of young people who believed that the overthrow of capitalism was necessary in order to emancipate humankind. The far left grew, the CFDT trade union became the focus for many long and militant industrial relations struggles [see Text 1.6], and women's and ecology movements flourished. The *Parti socialiste* (PS) radicalized and allied with the PCF in a new *Union de la gauche* unseen since the Popular Front of 1936, and the parties co-signed a *Programme commun de gouvernement* [see Text 1.7]. But the effects of the economic crisis from 1973 onwards meant that more radical political elements fared less and less well and the availability of more information on human rights abuses in the Soviet Union badly tarnished the image of all parties whose principal ideological point of reference was Marxism.

The *Parti socialiste*, however, went from strength to strength during this period, as we shall see in the next section.

## The left: swords into social democracy

When François Mitterrand was elected on 10 May 1981 people took to the streets in their tens of thousands to celebrate this significant victory. For the first time since the Popular Front of 1936, a predominantly socialist government was to be formed and since the great French revolution of 1789 France had only known three years of truly left-wing government. Moreover, the programme on which President Mitterrand had been elected was a radical one which drew much from the PCF/PS *Programme commun* of the 1970s. The new president and his colleagues had spoken unequivocally of a 'break with capitalism' where emancipation of the ordinary French person was the guiding principle and where the demands of the hitherto ruling class were to be brushed aside. The day after Mitterrand's victory capitalist dismay was expressed by the value of shares on the Paris Bourse going into free fall and the value of the franc dropping to the lowest point the European Monetary System would allow. It seemed as if a new era was dawning in French political history, and indeed it was. But by the time of his re-election in 1988 it was clear that the most significant point about the Mitterrand revolution was that it had actually sought to make and had succeeded in making peace between the dominant forces of the left and capitalism, rather than achieving a break with capitalism. How could this be so?

Between 1981 and 1984, the socialist government, which included four PCF ministers, did achieve three major structural reforms which had been heralded as crucial steps towards the building of a socialist France and which have had a profound and lasting effect, in spite of subsequent developments. First, they nationalized five major industrial groups (Saint-Gobain, Compagnie Générale d'Électricité, Pechiney, Rhône-Poulenc and Thomson-Brandt), thirty-nine banks and two financial institutions. This meant that sales from public firms went from 17 per cent to 30 per cent of total sales, while the proportion of all employees working for the state went from 11 per cent to 25 per cent. Second, they introduced substantial industrial relations reform in the shape of the *lois Auroux* (named after Minister of Labour Jean Auroux), which sought to legitimize the role of trade unions in the firm and in particular to make annual collective bargaining compulsory. Third, the Socialists undertook the most substantial decentralization programme in France's history in an attempt to remedy a situation where there had long been little scope for mediation between the individual citizen and the state [see Text 1.8].

Because of the importance of decentralization, which Minister of the Interior and Decentralization Gaston Defferre called the 'grande affaire' of Mitterrand's first period as president, it is worth dwelling on some aspects of it. For hundreds of years, France had maintained a highly centralized system of government and political administration for a variety of reasons, including regular threats from abroad to its territorial integrity, a will to ensure nationwide provision of certain basic rights and obligations (such as education, voting, taxes) and Parisian prejudice against the provinces. However, France in the late twentieth century was decidedly out of step with major allies such as West

Germany, Britain, Italy, Spain, Switzerland and the United State of America, where strong local government had come to be taken for granted. This is not to say that local politics were regarded as unimportant by ambitious politicians, as they were used not only as a springboard to higher things in Paris, but also – particularly in the case of large towns – as local power bases in their own right, albeit often to complement national responsibilities; Jacques Chaban Delmas, for instance, prime minister between 1969 and 1973, was mayor of Bordeaux from 1947 to 1995 and Gaston Defferre himself was mayor of Marseilles from 1953 until his death in 1986.

Under the decentralization programme, the twenty-two regional councils (*conseils régionaux*) were for the first time elected by universal suffrage, thus creating an additional directly elected body alongside those in the 96 *départements* and 36,000 *communes*. Perhaps more importantly, executive power was given to elected representatives in regions and *départements*, thus reducing the role of the *préfet* who until 1982 was the government's ever-present and very powerful voice, eyes and ears in the provinces (the *préfet* was given the new name *Commissaire de la République*). Not only were more resources poured into local government, but many new powers as well, in such areas as health, education, road maintenance and professional training. Care needs to be taken not to exaggerate the revolutionizing potential of decentralization, which still leaves France very far indeed from the federal structure of Germany, for example. It is also worth pointing out that with so many different bodies acting for citizens at the local level their various types and the extent of their responsibility remain opaque to many an ordinary voter. However, unusually for the Socialists' first reforms, decentralization came to be broadly supported by the right as well, in part informed by hope of successes in local elections, a hope amply realized in election results in the 1980s and early 1990s.

There were many other subsidiary reforms in the first two years of socialist government, which included a reduction of the legally defined working week from 40 to 39 hours, increasing statutory holiday entitlement from four to five weeks per year, the creation of many thousands of jobs in the public sector, reducing the age of retirement from 65 to 60 years for all, creating a ministry for women's rights, substantially increasing welfare benefits and the minimum wage, abolishing the death penalty, regularizing the status of 130,000 previously illegal immigrants and introducing a wealth tax.

Problems came very early in the life of the new government, however, when the economic crisis hit France hard and the government decided to devalue the franc in October 1981. Unemployment was rising fast and in mid-1982 the government implemented a simultaneous pay and prices freeze, a step which the right had never dared take. Taxation was increased. From this point onwards, the government concentrated on measures which it hoped would both save the economy from the worst effects of the crisis and in particular appeal to employers, who it had decided were still not particularly desirable allies, but were the only ones who would help France escape further decline and in particular electoral catastrophe for the PS. Socialism thus became far more pragmatic and the winds of change which blew strongly in 1981 had given way to the icy calm of 'realism' by mid-1983. In 1984 the Communists left government, as did the prime minister who had been the symbol of 1981 optimism, Pierre Mauroy. In his place came the more technocratic, pragmatic Laurent Fabius, who remained in power until the legislative elections of 1986.

It was largely economic problems and high levels of unemployment that meant the right won the 1986 legislative elections and Mitterrand, whose presidential term lasted until 1988, was faced with a choice between resigning and therefore almost certainly handing over his post to the right, or staying with a right-wing prime minister and government. That Mitterrand decided he could fruitfully 'cohabit' with a right-wing prime minister and government was another token of his new-found pragmatism and he was indeed able to share power without major conflict with the right until his re-election in 1988. As it turned out, *la cohabitation*, as it became known, was a godsend as far as Mitterrand's presidential credibility was concerned, for the period between 1986 and the presidential elections of 1988 allowed him to create an image of himself as a president representing national unity, to establish a distance between himself and the right's increasingly unpopular programme of reforms and thus to recover the enormous amount of personal ground lost in the opinion polls in the early to mid-1980s. Mitterrand won the presidential elections of 1988 on the strength of an election manifesto which contrasted starkly with his *110 propositions pour la France* of 1981 [see Text 1.9] and speaks volumes as to the ideological distance travelled by Mitterrand and the PS between 1981 and 1988. Entitled *'Lettre à tous les Français'* and subtitled, significantly, *'La France unie'*, the 1988 manifesto contains nothing of the optimism and certainly none of the radicalism of 1981 and outlines a safe, centrist set of positions. One of the few real innovations of the programme was the promise of a new guaranteed minimum income for all those in dire need (including the long-term unemployed and the young *nouveaux pauvres*), the *Revenu minimum d'insertion* (RMI). But the RMI was, typically, so uncontroversial that it was broadly approved of by the right as well. Mitterrand took his re-election as a mandate to set up government of the centre and this heralded an era of consolidation of the consensus politics he had adopted. The legislative elections which followed Mitterrand's re-election did not offer an absolute majority for the PS, however, so the new government, led by Michel Rocard, needed to juggle with PCF or centre-right backing according to the quarter from which new legislation was likely to attract support. Mitterrand and Rocard pursued a policy of *ouverture* which meant promoting participation in government by the centre-right and by people who were not career politicians, but this had only limited success. Recourse to constitutional devices to force through legislation in the absence of an obvious parliamentary majority became commonplace. So consensus government of the early 1990s was an uneasy business.

In May 1991 Mitterrand announced that prime minister Michel Rocard was to be replaced by Édith Cresson, the first woman prime minister in France's entire political history. This was a bold move, designed to polish up the tarnished image of the PS in the eyes of the electorate, with the local elections of 1992 and legislative elections of 1993 in mind. But Cresson was not a popular prime minister and by the end of 1991 both she and President Mitterrand had fallen greatly in public esteem, according to opinion polls. After local elections in Spring 1992 where the Socialists did particularly badly, Cresson was replaced as prime minister by Pierre Bérégovoy, who was of solidly working-class origins, had a reputation for a distinctly unsentimental approach to economics and was seen as the best hope as prime minister in the run-up to the Spring 1993 legislative elections. After the Socialists' resounding defeat in March 1993, Mitterrand nominated Gaullist Edouard Balladur as prime minister. As this second period of *cohabitation* began, Pierre Bérégovoy took his own life in an act which was tragically symbolic of the fortunes of the PS.

As France watched the physically ailing socialist president end his second *septennat*, it seemed as if the PS had given all it had to offer and was likely to be in opposition for a long time. But the 1995 presidential election brought the party a pleasant surprise when the PS candidate, Lionel Jospin, received 23.3 per cent of the vote in the first round, ahead of Jacques Chirac. Jospin lost to Chirac in the second round, but the PS took heart and from this point onwards the left gathered strength. So much so, in fact, that when President Chirac dissolved the *Assemblée nationale* and thus provoked a legislative election in 1997, with a view to consolidating the position of the right, the left won, to the great surprise of politicians, commentators and analysts. Jospin became prime minister and thus began the period of government by what became known as *la gauche plurielle*, composed of Socialists, Communists, Radical Socialists and the *Mouvement des citoyens*. This third period of *cohabitation* since 1986 was by now far from experimental and, indeed, almost the norm. The *gauche plurielle* coalition had been elected on a platform which was intended to appear realistic but caring, and alongside some public expenditure cuts and continued privatization came job creation and reduction of the working week to 35 hours in all companies by the first few years of the new millennium. This cautious but caring approach was represented especially by Minister for Employment and Solidarity Martine Aubry, as well as by Jospin himself. In these times which seemed so remote from the excitement of having a new socialist president and government almost twenty years previously, the PS still seemed the natural

**Martine Aubry** (b. 1950)

Minister of Employment and Solidarity in the Jospin government formed in 1997, Martine Aubry's background was as a senior civil servant and PS activist. She was educated at both the prestigious *Institut d'Etudes Politiques* in Paris and the *Ecole Nationale d'Administration* before holding numerous posts and responsibilities in the Ministry of Labour, including a first stint as labour minister under Prime Minister Édith Cresson, 1991–3. After the Socialist defeat in 1993, Aubry set up the *Fondation Agir contre l'exclusion* and worked with Socialists, Communists, trade unionists and company directors. Second in command in the Jospin government, Aubry has been associated in particular with negotiations over and legislation on the reduction in working time. She has never held a position as *député*, but has been deputy mayor of Lille since 1995. Her books include *Le Choix d'agir* (1994), *Petit dictionnaire pour lutter contre l'extrême droite* (with others, 1995) and *Il est grand temps . . .* (1997).

leader of the left, partly due to the years of effort and leadership by François Mitterrand. Under the leadership of Lionel Jospin, the PS in government came back from the brink of policies espousing wholesale, market-led pragmatism, where it teetered for a period in the early and mid-1990s, and began to pursue reforms which were to an extent influenced by traditional social-democratic principles, particularly in the realm of labour issues and more generally on the question of state intervention. The PS-led government was, arguably, still exceptional compared with the so-called 'Third Way' policies which influenced the Blair government in Britain and the Clinton administration in the United States. But these were still very much policies of the centre and ones which were not very distant from those of the French centre-right (perhaps in part because of the strong tradition of state intervention under governments of the right up to 1981). The PS's slight left turn by no means represented a return to the more traditional leftism of the *Programme commun*, or the first eighteen months of the Mitterrand presidency.

A key to the consolidation of the PS's image as a credible long-term party of government during the 1980s and 1990s was the fact that the PCF's popularity had plummeted and the Communists had lost roughly half their votes in successive elections. The four communist ministers' position as second fiddle in a rapidly rightward-moving government between 1981 and 1984 had caused the PCF much damage, but refusal to shake off the mantle of Stalinism had eroded its credibility as well; since the late 1970s the PCF had abandoned the more social-democratic, eurocommunist path adopted by it and many of its west European counterparts in the 1970s and returned to a virtual blind faith in the correctness of all things Soviet. Its dim view of people within its own ranks who publicly expressed any deviation from the official party line often led to disciplinary action and in some cases expulsion from the party. Thus the PCF's image was far from democratic.

However, when Robert Hue became leader of the PCF in 1994, the party soon seemed less of a spent force than under the stewardship of the traditional Stalinist Georges Marchais, who was general secretary from 1969 to 1994. The new leader took the party in a far more moderate direction, even supporting some privatizations, and after becoming leader he spelt out his views in two books, stressing the importance of internal democracy in particular. With thirty-seven seats in parliament from June 1997, compared with a previous twenty-four, and with 10 per cent of the vote in 1997, the PCF remains weakened but still a significant player on the left, with three government ministers from within its ranks in the late 1990s. But how should the PCF now be categorized? Did the 2.5 million people who voted for it in 1997 still vote in order to protest against the mainstream? From the moment it entered government in 1981, and in particular as it remained in government during the implementation of austerity measures at the end of 1982 and beyond, the PCF was bound to be viewed as a more mainstream, less protest-oriented party than it had been before, and indeed it was more moderate. It became slightly more associated with protest politics again in the later 1980s and early 1990s, when its relationship with the *Parti socialiste* became more ambiguous. But the fall of the Berlin Wall in 1989

**Robert Hue (b.1946)**

Robert Hue was a nurse at the *Centre de santé d'Argenteuil*, joined the *Jeunesse communiste* in 1962 and the *Parti communiste français* a year later. He has been on the central committee of the PCF since 1987, the politbureau since 1990 and has been leader of the party since 1994. Since 1994 he has taken the PCF in a far more moderate direction and it was in the left/green *gauche plurielle* coalition government in the late 1990s and early in the new century. Hue is known for his good humour. He has been mayor of Montigny-les-Cormeilles since 1977 and *député* for Argenteuil-Bezons since 1997. He was the communist candidate in the presidential elections of May 1995, when he received 8.6 per cent of the vote. He is author of a number of books, including *Histoire d'un village du Parisis des origines à la Révolution* (1981), *Montigny pendant la Révolution* (1989), *Communisme: la mutation* (1995) and *Communisme: un nouveau projet* (1999).

followed by the break-up of the Soviet Union and the rest of the eastern bloc, then the replacement of Georges Marchais by Robert Hue as leader, all helped to further undermine the party's image as a protest party working uncompromisingly against capitalism and for the interests of the traditional (in particular blue-collar) working class. Of course the continued decline of the blue-collar working class, the PCF's traditional membership and voting base, also contributed to the decline and change. The logic of this trajectory was indeed that the PCF should become an established part of the centre-left and the governmental *gauche plurielle*. So although the PCF has retained its old name, by contrast with many other European communist parties, and although it continues to win the support of some traditional working-class voters, it is no longer a party of protest in the traditional sense of one which systematically campaigns for a fundamental change in the social and political order of things. It is a party which has become associated with reform in the context of firmly governmental and moderate politics, although it is perhaps still the left-wing conscience of *la gauche plurielle*.

## The left pre-1981

If a young PS activist had fallen into a deep sleep in May 1981 and woken twenty or even ten years later, the change in the party's attitude towards government might have been surprising, or even shocking. But if the sleeper had some knowledge of the political scene since 1945, the surprise would have been less great. For a start, François Mitterrand, the major architect of change, had already enjoyed a long, non-socialist political career – including eleven ministerial posts under the Fourth Republic – before joining the ranks of the French Socialists. In addition, he had long had a reputation for being more of an opportunist than someone with a profound belief in socialism. Understanding his own particular evolution during the 1980s and early 1990s is helped by understanding this. In order to make sense of the rapid ideological and programmatic shift on the part of the PS itself during the 1980s and 1990s it is important to roll back history and look firstly at the 1970s and then more generally at the post-war era. The behaviour of the PS in the 1970s helps explain the PS's early 1980s radicalism and the Socialists' behaviour in the Fourth Republic helps remind one of the history of compromises – despite Marxist influences – which were characteristic of an earlier incarnation in the shape of the *Section française de l'Internationale ouvrière* (SFIO).

## The 1970s

The dominant position of the PCF on the left of the French political scene was long a formidable obstacle to the construction of a large socialist party; the Communists occupied a position of hegemony on the left in terms of ideological credibility, size of membership, degree of activism and electoral support. In the 1970s, however, the PS embarked on a course that would eventually crack this particular nut. In 1971, at the landmark Congrès d'Épinay, the PS was relaunched in a new and unified form under the leadership of François Mitterrand. Capitalizing on the climate of the early 1970s after the events of May had shown that left radicalism could be expressed along other lines than through the PCF, the newly-formed PS allied with the Communists in a move which was far more astute than any socialist or independent analyst realized at the time. The two parties signed a *Programme commun de gouvernement* which promised widespread nationalizations, constitutional reform (including curbing presidential powers), industrial relations reform, higher wages, more individual liberties and a foreign policy which would seek to curb the power of international capital [see Text 1.7]. Together the PS and PCF represented a formidable force, but it became increasingly clear that the PS was gaining far more from the pact than the PCF. As the joint candidate of the left in the 1974 presidential elections, Mitterrand came within a hair's breadth of beating Giscard d'Estaing, and the PS did particularly well in local elections in 1976 and 1977. In 1977 the PCF effectively sabotaged the union by demanding concessions which it knew the PS would not make and the left lost the 1978 legislative elections as a result. To an extent, the PS's strategy with respect to the PCF was cynical all along and Mitterrand publicly expressed this when he said in June 1972: 'Notre objectif fondamental, c'est de refaire un grand parti socialiste sur le terrain occupé par le PC lui-même, afin de faire la démonstration que, sur cinq millions d'électeurs communistes, trois millions peuvent voter socialiste.'[5]

This aspect of the strategy was certainly successful beyond the dreams of any PS leader, for the PS eventually built and consolidated its own party at the expense of the PCF. The ability of the PS to govern at first very much as the senior coalition partner between 1981 and 1984 and later on in the 1980s and 1990s as the major party of government is further proof of the success of its death-embrace strategy in relation to the PCF.

## 1945–1970

Understanding the PS's 180-degree turn during the 1980s is made easier by looking further back into the post-war history of the left. Under the Fourth Republic the Socialists behaved very differently in relation to the Communist

Party, largely falling in with the anti-communist, cold war ethos of the time. The socialist SFIO played an important role in many of the coalition governments of this period and indeed was closely associated with some of the least noble moments: during the miners' strike of 1948, it was the socialist interior minister, Jules Moch, who sent in troops against striking miners, which resulted in at least two deaths; the SFIO was intimately involved in formulating policies which resulted in the torture and death in French custody of members of the nationalist community in Algeria; and it was socialist Prime Minister Guy Mollet who collaborated with the British in sending troops to Egypt in an attempt to impose their will on President Nasser after he had nationalized the Suez canal. The general orientation of the SFIO under the Fourth Republic has been described by Michel Winock as 'le socialisme expéditionnaire'.[6]

In 1958 the SFIO was deeply split over the issue of whether de Gaulle should be supported as the only person able to avoid armed conflict in France itself as a result of the Algerian question. This set the tone for the rest of the decade and much of the 1960s as well. The Republic with which the Socialists had been so much associated had failed miserably. The new constitution of the Fifth Republic was approved by a large majority and the SFIO's behaviour under the Fourth Republic came to be seen by many progressive French people as deeply reactionary. Indeed a significant aspect of politics under the Fourth Republic was that participation in government had earned the socialist current a very bad reputation, whereas the PCF, excluded from power, emerged in far better shape.

The period of de Gaulle's presidency between 1958 and 1969 was of course dominated by the right and the left was relatively weak. Moreover, although the PCF still received at least one in five votes at elections during this period, the Algerian war had become the overwhelmingly dominant issue of the time and thus dampened the militancy of the trade union movement and made the PCF more isolated, at least in the late 1950s and early 1960s. The Socialists were divided during the 1960s and support for them was low. De Gaulle's authoritarian populism, together with claims that political parties were divisive and detracted from all-important national unity, apparently carried substantial weight, at least in the first years of his presidency. But signs were already emerging in the mid-1960s that the non-communist left was rising from its ashes. In 1965 François Mitterrand stood as candidate for a united left in the presidential election and received enough votes to force de Gaulle to a second round, which de Gaulle nevertheless won comfortably.

In 1968 there was no major political party both willing and able to take immediate advantage of the tremendous radical impulse. The PCF felt distinctly upstaged by the events and roundly condemned the student activists for adventurism, a criticism which was felt implicitly by many of the workers who were infected with the same enthusiasm in the struggles at their place of work. At the end of May the *Accords de Grenelle* offered substantial gains to the working class, but gains which were insignificant in relation to the size and radicalism of the May movement. The socialist current, meanwhile, was still too divided and it was not until the early 1970s, as we have seen, that the PS could embark on its road to government.

## The right: from standard bearer of the Republic to ordinary political actor

Both the character and the fortunes of the right during the last two decades of the twentieth century were highly mixed. On the one hand, the mainstream, parliamentary right was in terms of programme and ideology probably less exceptional and more like the conservative right in other western countries – thus less exceptional – than during the period from 1945 to 1980. This was largely to do with the decline of Gaullism as a separate ideology and is in keeping with the argument that French politics now conforms more to the west European model. However, the growth of the extreme right *Front national* (FN), albeit in crisis in the late 1990s, very obviously runs counter to this trend and is one which we shall seek to explain towards the end of this section. Despite a general ideological confluence, the mainstream right has experienced electoral failure, much frustration in terms of strategy, fragmentation and a major split for the Gaullist RPR. The victory of the left in 1981 was of course a major blow. Subsequently the PS's and in particular Mitterrand's lurch towards the centre right allowed the Socialists to claim in the mid-to-late 1980s that Mitterrand and the PS represented the politics of national interest which the right had claimed to embody in its years of exclusive government between 1958 and 1981. Following this, the period of cohabitation between right and left from 1986 to 1988 led to frustrations during, and electoral failure at the end of, this two-year period. But the greatest problem for the parliamentary, non-extreme right was the existence of deep divisions within its own camp which had troubled it for many years and which the rise of the *Front national* compounded. Conclusive victory for the right came in legislative elections in 1993, but it was a victory explained more by the weakness of the left than by widespread popularity of the right. Presidential victory in 1995 was followed by surprise defeat in the parliamentary elections of 1997, and a weakened President Chirac.

In this section we will begin by briefly considering the right under the Fourth Republic, so that we may understand the deep-rooted nature of its divisions. Next we look at the period of Gaullist dominance between 1958 and 1974 and then the post-Gaullist period between 1974 and 1981. Finally we return to the fortunes of the right during the 1980s and 1990s.

### The Fourth Republic

Backward socio-economic conditions, collaboration with the Germans on the part of elements of the right during the Second World War, strong anti-communism within the right as a result of the success of the PCF and finally the war with Algeria prevented the establishment of a stable, moderate right in the form of a large conservative or Christian democratic party similar to those in Italy and

Germany, or resembling the Conservative Party in Britain. Elsewhere such parties were often an important part of a more stable political situation. Attempts to set up a dominant centre-right party at first seemed promising with the formation of the MRP, which received 26 per cent of votes in elections to the Constituent Assembly in October 1945. The MRP's leaders were mainly Christian Democrats who were keen to defend the legacy of the Resistance and who were also at the time quite close to de Gaulle.

But in mid-1947 de Gaulle launched the RPF in order to express mass opposition to the constitution of the Fourth Republic and in support of the ideas expressed in his *Discours de Bayeux* in June 1946 [see Text 1.1]. Supposedly above the petty squabbles of party politics, the RPF soon developed a hard-right image and its appeal for many of its supporters was its virulent anti-communism. The RPF soon recruited large numbers of militants and in the legislative elections of June 1951 it received 22.5 per cent of the vote. The effect of RPF activity on the MRP was disastrous, with many former MRP voters lending their support to the Gaullists, so in the same legislative elections the MRP received only 13.4 per cent of the vote. The RPF soon came to grief as well, however, after de Gaulle left the RPF to its own devices in May 1953, partly in disgust that his group had begun to act like an ordinary, sectarian political party. The Gaullists received less than 4 per cent of the vote in the legislative elections of 1956.

The extreme right under the Fourth Republic was most effectively represented by the Poujadists. Pierre Poujade's party mainly sought to defend the interests of the small businessman against threats both from the state and from big business and the predominantly petit-bourgeois character of its electorate reflected this. As the leader of what was very much a party of reaction against both the growth of the state and the growth of big business, which were key factors in the economic modernization of the time, Poujade defended a romantic image of rural France, the glory of the Empire, and warned that Jews were attempting to take over French business. More concretely, Poujade won many votes on a straightforward campaign against the taxation of small firms [see Text 1.10].

The Poujadist movement reached its apogee at the elections of 1956 where it won 11.6 per cent of the vote, giving it 52 *députés* in the Assemblée nationale. The improving fortunes of a group of conservative right parties during the Fourth Republic seemed to suggest, not only that this section of the right had recovered from many of its supporters' earlier backing for Pétain, but also that it was to have a substantial influence on parliamentary politics in years to come. In 1949 the conservative *Centre national des indépendants* (CNI) was formed in order to halt the success of the RPF (the group became CNIP in 1951) and gained considerable influence. Indeed the years from 1951 to 1955 were dominated by conservative coalitions of the CNIP, the MRP and the Radicals.[7] However, the Algerian war and the consequent victory of de Gaulle in 1958 were to postpone the rise of this more traditional right until the 1970s. (See Table 1.1.)

**Table 1.1 Legislative elections, 1945–56 (percentage of votes cast for each party, metropolitan France only)**

| | PCF | Soc. | Rad. & Ass. | MRP | Ind. Cons. | Gaull. | Other |
|---|---|---|---|---|---|---|---|
| 1945 | 26.5 | 24 | 11 | 25 | 13 | — | 0.5 |
| 1946 June | 26 | 21 | 11.5 | 28 | 13 | — | 0.5 |
| 1946 Nov. | 28 | 18 | 11 | 26 | 16 | — | 1 |
| 1951 | 26 | 14.5 | 10.5 | 13 | 12 | 22.5 | 1.5 |
| 1956 | 26 | 15 | 15.5 | 11 | 15 | 4 | 13.5* |

* mainly Poujadists.
*Source*: J. Blondel, *The Government of France* (Methuen, 1974).

## The Fifth Republic

In order to understand developments on the right under the Fifth Republic it is useful to refer to René Rémond's now classic definitions of the different elements within the right.[8] According to Rémond, the history of the French right is best understood as the evolution of three main strands which are bonapartist, liberal and counter-revolutionary. These terms will become clear as we discuss each strand.

As we have seen, de Gaulle rode to power on the crest of a wave of unrest and conflict in 1958 and remained president of the Republic until 1969. For the whole of this period de Gaulle and the Gaullists dominated the political scene. The most lasting significance of governmental Gaullism was to use a strong, centralized state not only to establish political stability, but also to push forward the modernization of the economy. According to René Rémond and many others, Gaullism is a type of bonapartism, a reference to the populist–authoritarian rule of both Napoleon Bonaparte between 1799 and 1815 and Louis Napoleon from 1848 to 1870. The parallels are only approximate, and de Gaulle's regime certainly had more to do with liberal democratic principles than the regimes of either of the two Napoleons, but the elements of bonapartism were certainly all there. They are as follows:

(1) Rallying around the notion of national unity. De Gaulle insisted that national politics should be based on the common interests of the French as a nation, rather than on the principle of defending one social class against another or some other sectional interest.
(2) The association of capital and labour. This was part of the same principle and from time to time de Gaulle rather unsuccessfully attempted to develop the notion of *participation* between capital and labour both in terms of profit sharing and in terms of participation of the work-force in company decision making. De Gaulle's contempt for the traditionally more conflictual nature of management–union relations was informed by this.
(3) The importance of the national leader. The entire period between 1958 and 1969 was testimony to the importance of this particular bonapartist characteristic, with the figure of de Gaulle towering high above any other in

national politics. Recourse to referenda in order to appeal over the heads of 'divisive' political parties and reinforce the bond between leader and led was in part designed to reinforce his authority, and the constitution itself is imbued with the notion of the importance of the president of the Republic [see Text 1.11]. These aspects of Gaullism have had a profound effect on the style of politics in France since 1958 and have deeply affected every president of the Fifth Republic.

As we have seen, resolving the Algerian question was one of the most important achievements of the de Gaulle presidency. Other aspects of his all-important foreign policy, including a belief in the necessity for a strong and independent system of defence, are discussed below. As far as domestic policy was concerned, de Gaulle and his colleagues considered that modernizing the French economy was a priority and his presidency is intimately associated with this. Far from the preoccupation of today's right with the free market, economic change was achieved by intervention on the part of the state (see Part II). Law and order was all-important and in fact a galvanizing factor in the May 1968 revolt, which sounded the death knell of de Gaulle's rule, was strong feeling against police brutality.

The constitution of the Fifth Republic is one of the most enduring legacies of the de Gaulle era and parties of the mainstream left as well as the mainstream right now accept most elements of this constitution as an essential prerequisite for democracy in France.[9] Its most significant feature is that it allows for much executive (presidential and governmental) power and relatively little parliamentary power, in stark contrast with the constitution of the Fourth Republic. The president is elected by universal suffrage (although this was only introduced – by referendum – in 1962) and is responsible for the choice of prime minister and his or her dismissal. He (never yet she) nominates the rest of the cabinet (*conseil des ministres*) in consultation with the prime minister. The president may submit proposed changes in legislation to the French people in the form of a referendum and may dissolve the *Assemblée nationale* (the lower house), thus provoking an election. But perhaps the most controversial presidential power of all, and the one which comes closest to parting company with liberal democratic tradition, is that described in Article 16, which allows the head of state 'pouvoirs exceptionnels' (defined very generally as being those 'required by the circumstances') for a certain period during a time of crisis. This provision has been used only once since 1958, by de Gaulle, between 23 April and 30 September 1961, after a putsch by four generals in Algeria. But it is a highly significant provision in that it is a – now virtually unchallenged – symbol of the power of the president and is indeed always there, to be used if necessary. Although the constitution gives substantial powers to the president, there is nevertheless a degree of ambiguity which allows room for interpretation. Although the president chairs cabinet meetings, the government 'détermine et conduit la politique de la nation' (Article 20) and 'dirige l'action du gouvernement' (Article 21), and although the president is 'chef des armées' (Article 15), the government 'dispose de l'administration de la force armée'

(Article 20) and the prime minister is 'responsable de la défense nationale' (Article 21). In the text, then, it is nowhere clearly laid out who actually governs, but in practice it has been the presidents of the Republic who have dominated the legislature, the government, the civil service, the judiciary, the army, foreign policy and defence. This dominance prompted Maurice Duverger to call the Fifth Republic 'une monarchie républicaine'.[10]

During the period between 1958 and 1969, the liberal or moderate right was very much overshadowed by the figure of President de Gaulle and his party, at first called the *Union pour la nouvelle république* (UNR).[11] Partly because of the bi-polarizing effects of the constitution of the Fifth Republic, where national-level elections have two rounds and where there is a system of majority voting, the various elements of the liberal right joined the governmental coalition, which by 1978 included all of the liberal right (see Table 1.2). In 1962, the largest and most influential component of the liberal right, Giscard d'Estaing's *Républicains indépendants* (RI), which had its roots in the CNIP under the Fourth Republic, joined the UNR *députés* in support of the Fifth Republic and President de Gaulle. Indeed, Giscard occupied the important position of finance minister between 1962 and 1966, and then again under President Pompidou from 1969 to 1974. In 1969, after the election of Pompidou as president of the Republic, the governmental coalition broadened again to include the Christian-democratic *Centre démocratie et progrès* (CDP), by far the most significant other grouping on the centre-right. Pompidou's presidency was less bonapartist than de Gaulle's, and represented a move towards the centre-right ideologically as well as in terms of alliances. After the death of Pompidou in 1974 there was no obvious successor for leadership of the Gaullist movement, which was extremely dependent on the prestige and authority of its leader. In the 1974 presidential election the Gaullist candidate was Jacques Chaban-Delmas, but some Gaullist *députés*, led by Jacques Chirac, supported Giscard d'Estaing, and Chaban-Delmas received only 15 per cent in the first round, compared with Giscard's 33 per cent. The liberal right's time had come at last and Giscard d'Estaing was narrowly elected president of the Republic in the second round. However, the right alliance, which broadened again after Giscard's election, was an uneasy one, for the *Assemblée nationale* was dominated by Gaullist *députés* who were mistrustful of Giscard, and some liberal right parties in the coalition were anti-Gaullist. Jacques Chirac was nominated prime minister because of the continued weight of Gaullism in the *Assemblée nationale*, but he resigned in August 1976 in order to relaunch the Gaullist movement and was replaced by Raymond Barre, an economics professor with a firm belief in market economics. As we have already seen, in the first years of Giscard's presidency, France went a certain way to becoming a less exceptional country, particularly in the sphere of social affairs. But Raymond Barre's appointment as prime minister signalled a turn towards increased pragmatism, particularly as far as economic policy was concerned.

Chirac relaunched his party under the name *Rassemblement pour la République* (RPR) with new structures which gave him greater power and which made the party a more activist organization. Shortly afterwards, in February 1978, Giscard set up the liberal right electoral alliance, the *Union pour la démocratie française*

**Table 1.2 The growth of the right-wing ruling coalition**

| | |
|---|---|
| Legislative elections 1958 | Gaullists (UNR) |
| Legislative elections 1962 | Gaullists (UNR-UDT) + Independent Republicans (RI) |
| Presidential elections 1969 | Gaullists (UDR) + Independent Republicans (RI) + Centre Démocratie et Progrès (CDP) |
| Presidential elections 1974 | Gaullists (UDR) + Independent Republicans (RI) + CDP + Centre Démocratie (CD) + Radicals + Centre National des Indépendents et Paysans (CNIP) + Mouvement Démocrate Socialiste de France (MDSF) |
| Legislative elections 1978 | Gaullists (RPR) + Union pour la Démocratie Française (UDF) + Republican Party (ex-Independent Republicans) + Radical Party + Centre des Démocrates Sociaux (or CDS, fusion of CDP and CD) + Mouvement Démocrate Socialiste + Clubs Perspectives et Réalites + Young Giscardians + CNIP |

*Source*: V. Wright, *The Government and Politics of France* (Unwin Hyman, 1989).

(UDF) and virtually the whole of the liberal right was now working together in order to counter the threat of a left victory at the legislative elections the following month. The right won the elections, partly because of the deep rifts over policy which had developed within the left. But the presidential elections of 1981 were a disaster for the right: there were three Gaullist candidates (Chirac, Michel Debré and Marie-France Garaud) and also Giscard d'Estaing for the UDF. François Mitterrand was elected president and the left swept the board in the ensuing parliamentary elections.

## The 1980s and 1990s

The 1980s were to be a testing time for the right in several ways. To be catapulted into opposition after twenty-five years of right-wing government was of course a major blow. At that time Mitterrand and his socialist colleagues, far from being hampered by the constitution which some thought the left could not work with, appeared to use the governmental rules laid down by de Gaulle with the greatest of ease. As the 1980s went by and as the influence of the PCF declined and the PS moved to the right, the left majority increasingly appeared to represent the centre ground, which once only Giscard's centre-right coalition of the 1970s seemed capable of doing. Finally, the right was plagued with divisions which had greatly helped the left's victory in the first place.

The 1980s were not entirely barren as far as right-wing government was concerned, of course. When in 1986 it won a majority of seats in the legislative elections and thus had an opportunity to try to show that it had a better set of policies than the PS, Mitterrand nominated Jacques Chirac as prime minister and hampered his choice of ministers relatively little. Chirac's programme was based firmly on free-market economics and the politics of law and order. He set about denationalizing some of the companies nationalized in the early 1980s and even some nationalized just after the Second World War. He cut taxes, abolished the Socialists' wealth tax and in general passed legislation to encourage free enterprise, such as the deregulation of the financial sector, the relaxation of protection against redundancy and the introduction of flexible working hours. The government planned to reform the law on immigration, drawing up a new nationality code making entry into the country and residence in France more difficult to achieve and expulsion more easy for the authorities to carry out, but this was shelved, as it was clear that it was a particularly unpopular piece of proposed legislation (see Part III). There were also plans to privatize certain aspects of prison administration and a strong-arm campaign against drugs and terrorism. Overseas, the government sought aggressively to quell the growing movement for independence in French New Caledonia.

One area of dramatic defeat for the government of cohabitation from 1986 to 1988 was its policy on higher education. It published a bill which sought to introduce a greater element of selection into university entry and to increase university fees. At the end of 1986 hundreds of thousands of school and university students went on strike and demonstrated against the proposed reforms in a movement with enough similarities with the events of May 1968 to be taken very seriously and to persuade the government to withdraw its plans. By New Year 1987 public sector strikes over pay and working conditions had gripped the country and undermined the government's confidence. The result was that the reform programme was substantially slowed down in the hope of retaining enough support for the right to win the presidential elections of 1988. The right hoped in vain, however, and the French voted again for President Mitterrand, who had come to represent almost non-partisan statesmanship, as opposed to what were perceived as Chirac's highly partisan politics.

In 1993 the right emerged from the legislative elections with a massive parliamentary majority of over 350, although they received fewer votes than in 1981. There was certainly no need for a coalition and this enabled the new prime minister, Edouard Balladur, to begin implementing a programme which included widespread privatizations, tough measures on immigration and a strong emphasis on law and order, reinforced by Chirac's presidential victory in 1995. However, the huge wave of public sector strikes and demonstrations in November and December 1995 once again put the right on the defensive and contributed to its downfall in the 1997 legislative elections. This not only made Chirac look foolish for having called the election, but put him in a weaker position than Mitterrand had been vis-à-vis his governmental partners in *cohabitation*. If our thesis about the 'normalization' of politics in France were to be wholly valid, during the 1980s and 1990s we would have seen the emergence of a unified, liberal right. As far as programme and ideological orientation is concerned, this is partially true, but as far as organization is concerned the right has certainly remained as divided as in the 1970s and often more so.

The evolution of the RPR during the 1980s and 1990s was ambiguous. On the one hand, the RPR became far less intent on stressing the importance of state intervention than traditional Gaullism had been, and subscribed to the widespread consensus for creating the best conditions for the efficient functioning of widespread free enterprise. In this respect, there was increasing confluence with centre-right policy. Likewise, on Europe, the RPR also moved with the times and in favour of an expanded and more powerful European Union, even expressing interest in a common European defence programme.[12] In many ways, there is therefore now less to distinguish the majority of Gaullists from the rest of the right than there was during much of the period between 1945 and 1981, and Jérôme Jaffré has gone as far as saying that, 'en réalité, il convient de parler de disparition du gaullisme comme force électorale autonome au profit d'un bloc conservateur imparfaitement uni'.[13] However, the RPR at times gave in to the temptation – particularly during the first period of *cohabitation* – of adapting aspects of its programme to the extreme right positions of the FN. Particularly as far as issues of immigration are concerned, this caused considerable internal conflict in the party, with a leading opponent of capitulation to the extreme right, Michel Noir, publicly condemning electoral alliances between the FN and the RPR. The RPR, which became the first major party to have a woman as its leader (Michèle Alliot-Marie, since December 1999), might thus be said to have moved away from bonapartism towards the liberal right, but at times with a degree of accommodation to the extreme right, which is after all not something new for the Gaullist movement when one thinks of the RPF under the Fourth Republic.

However, a dramatic result of the many trials and frustrations for the Gaullists over two decades came in 1999, when the RPR split and Charles Pasqua set up the *Rassemblement pour la France* (RPF), reminiscent of the post-Second World War Gaullist party in political orientation as well as in acronym (de Gaulle's party set up in 1947 was called *Rassemblement du peuple français*, also RPF). With a strong right wing and highly patriotic orientation, intent on defending France from the ravages of a more integrated Europe, Pasqua told the founding congress of the new RPF, in highly fundamentalist–Gaullist fashion: 'Nous sommes le parti qui a toujours surgi des profondeurs de notre pays, du cœur de notre peuple, de l'âme de notre histoire, dès lors que ceux qui avaient en charge son destin l'avaient abandonné, trahi, déserte ou tout bonnement délaissé.'[14]

At the same congress the arch anti-European and new RPF vice-president Philippe de Villiers declared in a clear bid to attract FN voters, 'La France que nous aimons n'est pas celle dans laquelle les dealers et les récidivistes tiennent la rue . . . dans laquelle certains étrangers voudraient venir nous imposer leurs mœurs et leurs lois.'[15]

For the more truly liberal right during the 1980s and 1990s, there were increasing problems of fragmentation. After the elections of 1981 the parliamentary representation of the UDF was greatly weakened, with only 62 seats instead of 137 after the legislative elections of 1978. Electoral unity with the RPR helped in 1986, but one of the UDF's leaders, Raymond Barre, was strongly opposed to *cohabitation* with Mitterrand. After the low vote for Raymond Barre as UDF candidate in the 1988 presidential elections (16.5 per cent compared with Chirac's 19.9 per cent) Raymond Barre and the Christian democratic *Centre des démocrates sociaux* (CDS) formed their own parliamentary grouping in June 1988, the *Union du centre* (UDC). The centre-right did not enter the 1990s wholly divided, however, for the UDC, the UDF and the RPR formed a parliamentary intergroup, the *Union pour la France* (UPF) in June 1990, which meant approaching the 1993 legislative elections as a unified, or semi-unified, force, and which proved successful. Two major problems remained, however, for this organizationally volatile liberal right. First, there was – and still is – no leader with enough authority and charisma to pull the various strands together. The other major problem for both the liberal and the Gaullist right is the steady success of the *Front national*.

These two factors, added to electoral defeat in 1997, caused the liberal right great problems in the mid- and late 1990s. In 1994, Philippe de Villiers left the PR and UDF and set up the *Mouvement pour la France* (MPF), with a programme which promised to defend national sovereignty and fight corruption. After unsuccessful attempts by UDF leaders in 1995–6 to create a large, unified centre-oriented party modelled on the German CDU, defeat in the 1997 legislative elections, followed by further defeat in the regional elections of 1998, brought further problems. The regional elections once again raised the question of alliance with the FN, when the Front offered support, where necessary, for the election of centre-right regional presidents in return for a minimal common programme. Three regional presidents from *Démocratie libérale* (DL, the ex-*Parti républicain* renamed after being taken over by Alain Madelin in July 1997) and one other centre-right (*divers droite*) candidate were elected in this way. However, the UDF effectively disintegrated in May 1998 when DL left the group. Later that year, what was left of the UDF merged in order to become a political party, with card-carrying members.

The rise during the 1980s and consolidation during the 1990s of the counter-revolutionary, or extreme, right in the form of the *Front national* is a fascinating and alarming phenomenon. The FN advocates repatriation of large numbers of immigrants, more forceful law and order measures, including the reintroduction of the death penalty, a strong-arm campaign against drug pushers and users, is strongly anti-European and condemns the 'corruption' of all other political parties and politicians [see Texts 1.12 and 1.13]. The only well-developed and widely-known aspect of its programme, however, is its policy on immigration and immigrant workers. France has for a long time had a small but active extreme right like the Poujadists during the 1950s, but during the 1980s and 1990s the FN gathered more support and had more effect on the rest of the political spectrum than had been seen for many years.

The 1980s did not start well for the FN, however, and in 1981 its leader Jean-Marie Le Pen was unable to obtain the 500 signatures from *notables* which would have allowed him to stand as a presidential candidate. In 1983 a leading political analyst, Jean-Christian Petitfils, wrote convincingly that the extreme right was 'émiettée en une myriade d'îlots minuscules, de cénacles impuissants, de cercles fantomatiques [et] elle n'existe plus qu'à l'état de vestige historique'.[16] But in the 1983 municipal elections at Dreux, near Chartres, the FN attracted 16.7 per cent of the vote. In the legislative elections of 1986 it received 9.6 per cent and, due to the new system of proportional representation, the FN had 35 *députés*, the same number as the PCF. In the 1988 presidential elections Jean-Marie Le Pen received 14.4 per cent and in the legislative elections which followed the FN received 9.7 per cent. In December 1989 FN candidate Marie-France

Stirbois won a legislative by-election in Dreux. The 1990s began fairly well for the FN when in local elections in March 1992 it received 13.9 per cent of the vote and in the 1993 legislative elections it received 12.4 per cent. The 1997 presidential election saw the most successful result ever, when Le Pen received 15 per cent. The most convincing explanation for the rise and consolidation of the FN is that the existence of high unemployment together with a highly identifiable and often unintegrated immigrant population allowed the party's leaders, and Le Pen in particular, to capitalize on the fear or experience of unemployment combined with already existing racism. The FN has been able to convince its voters that immigrants are largely responsible for unemployment and other economic ills, as well as many other social problems such as the spread of Aids and more generally 'moral decline', such as the increase in drug taking and overt homosexuality. Lingering resentment towards ethnic minorities of North African extraction (a legacy of colonial days and the Algerian war) has thus been fuelled by Le Pen and other FN leaders who maintain that 'la France aux Français' would be a major step towards helping poor and marginalized *Français de souche*. The FN has done particularly well in the southern Provence-Alpes-Côte d'Azur area, where there is a large immigrant population, high unemployment and large numbers of *pieds noirs*, former French Algerians who fled Algeria in 1962. In local elections in June 1995 the FN emerged with political control of Toulon, Marignane and Orange, and subsequently took control of Vitrolles in February 1997. The FN has also done well in areas in the north and north-east where there have been job losses in traditional industrial sectors and where there are large numbers of immigrants.

A subsidiary and by no means mutually exclusive explanation for the rise of the FN is that, because politics in general has become more moderate and because the left no longer represents a current which systematically protests against the established order (even the PCF participated in government between 1981 and 1984), a vote for the extreme right is now seen as an effective way of expressing opposition to the political mainstream. For those who feel

**Jean-Marie Le Pen** (b. 1928)

Extreme right leader of the *Front national* who served in the parachute regiment in Indo-China in the mid-1950s, then in Algeria, Le Pen was elected to the *Assemblée nationale* as a Poujadist in 1956, then as an independent from 1958 to 1968. He has been president of the *Front national* since 1972 and was a candidate in presidential elections in 1974, 1988 and 1995, when he received 15 per cent of the vote. An accomplished orator and highly controversial figure who once described the gas chambers in Nazi Germany as 'a detail', he presided over the rise of the *Front national* from a tiny party in the early 1980s to a far larger and more enduring feature of the political landscape from the mid-1980s. He was a *député* for Paris 1986–8, and elected to the European parliament in 1984, 1989 and 1994. In 1998 he was found guilty of assault, stripped of the right to hold or seek public office for two years, and given a three-month suspended sentence. After a lengthy quarrel over the direction of the *Front national* with his second in command, Bruno Mégret, the party split in 1999. He is author of *Les Français d'abord* (1984), *La France est de retour* (1985), *L'Espoir* (1986) and *J'ai vu juste* (1998).

this political mainstream has passed them by, joining or voting for the FN seems a way of expressing protest, or, in the words of Colette Ysmal, the FN has become 'Le dernier recours pour les Français qui vivent ou craignent l'exclusion'.[17] Indeed, it seems as if there is a direct link between the decline of the PCF and the rise of the FN, although there is little evidence that large numbers of former PCF voters now vote FN. Rather, former PCF voters have switched their allegiance to another more mainstream party (like the PS) or abstain, but for people who wish to vote 'anti' and who did not vote before, the FN has become a logical option.

For the Gaullists and the UDF the rise of the FN has been problematical and has arguably dominated the fortunes of these parties since September 1983 when the Front had its first major electoral breakthrough. Since then supporters of the right have been split in three directions. The RPR quite openly adopted large chunks of its governmental programme during the first period of cohabitation in an attempt to win back votes from the Front, in particular in relation to immigrant workers and more generally to questions of law and order. This has had the effect of the RPR at times being identified more with the hard right than previously, but without its having the extra-parliamentary charisma of the FN. In the late 1990s both the Gaullists and the UDF split, also in part because of the influence of the FN.

But fragmentation also hit the extreme right in the late 1990s. For some time there had been open disagreement between Le Pen who, with his brand of crude populism, sought to split the more moderate right from without, and Bruno Mégret who, with an appearance of greater sophistication, wished to ally with sections of the moderate right in order to enlarge the FN. During the 1997 election campaign Le Pen punched a Socialist candidate and was barred from standing in elections, and in August 1998 he declared that his wife would stand instead of him in the 1999 European elections. Mégret took this opportunity to embark upon open warfare and by the end of 1998 there were two parties of the extreme right. In the June 1999 European elections Le Pen's list received under 6 per cent and Mégret's just over 3 per cent, so, whilst it would be wrong to speak of autodestruction on the part of the extreme right, it had certainly badly injured itself.

From this brief look at the fortunes of the right during the 1980s and 1990s it should be clear that it is highly fragmented and its predicament is still different from that of the right in some other countries in the west where a unified liberal right dominates and has relatively few problems with extremism to its right. In France the Gaullists are split, the rest of the centre-right is split, and the real source of hope for these parties is perhaps the fact that the extreme right is also split. However, the decline – but not yet disappearance – of bonapartism or Gaullism as an ideology and current distinct from the liberal right means that there is more common ground in terms of policy than there was in the past, despite these deep organizational rifts. Precisely because of this fragmentation, small parties can have a disproportionately large influence, as their votes can tip the balance and create a working majority in parliament.

## Protest: trade unions and beyond

The classic post-1945 route for European countries where politics were less conflict-dominated was one where trade unions played an important part in building a political climate of relative national unity. The role of trade unions was thus highly ambivalent. In an immediate sense they fought to defend the rights of their members against the interests of their employers, whether they worked in the public or private sector. In a broader sense, however, trade unions often had a dampening effect on class conflict, for they acted as a buffer to dissatisfaction and arrived at compromises with employers before unrest was expressed in terms of widespread direct action. Thus trade unions often served to prevent small conflicts from growing into larger ones and sometimes prevented large-scale changes from taking place. In many instances, moderate socialist or social-democratic parties of government after 1945 had close links with trade unions and formal or implicit agreements between government, union leaders and employers emerged on pay and working conditions, which made for a relatively calm industrial relations climate. This was the case in Scandinavia, Austria, the Netherlands and Britain, for instance.

As we have already seen, this was not the scenario in France, where trade unionism has long been associated with head-on collision with both employers and governments. In contrast to the situation in these other countries, particularly in northern Europe, in France there have for a long time been several mutually antagonistic trade union confederations, split along ideological lines. The rate of unionization is low and collective bargaining, particularly at individual company level was, until the 1980s, weak. Instead of a situation in which trade unions systematically negotiate with management and establish a code of behaviour, employees' terms and conditions – and since 1982 rules governing collective bargaining – are more regulated by law than in many countries, by legislation which has been passed at times when the balance of forces has swung in favour of the working class. Thus in 1936, after the formation of the Popular Front government, the *Accords de Matignon* established a legal right to paid holiday, a 40-hour week and the legitimacy of collective agreements; in 1946 there were laws on staff representatives, works councils and collective bargaining; in 1968 the *Accords de Grenelle* established the right for trade unions to organize at the place of work; and in 1982, soon after the formation of the PS-dominated government, the *lois Auroux* were passed which notably obliged employers at firm level to negotiate each year with trade union reprentatives and increased the power of the works council.

Although all the confederations have long explicitly or implicitly accepted the legitimacy of the capitalist system, France still displays few, if any, of the characteristics of trade unionism in countries well known for their more consensual politics, namely:

(1) a dominant, unified, moderate union confederation;
(2) a large proportion of their working population in trade unions;

**Table 1.3 Main union confederations in France**

| Confederation | Membership* | Political orientation |
|---|---|---|
| Confédération générale du travail (CGT) | 630,000 | Fairly close to PCF |
| Confédération française démocratique de travail (CFDT) | 560,000 | Moderate |
| Confédération générale du travail–Force ouvrière (CGT–FO) | 300,000 | Moderate, prioritizes collective bargaining |
| Confédération française des travailleurs chrétiens (CFTC) | 95,000 | Catholic |
| Fédération de l'éducation nationale (FEN) | 100,000 | Left-leaning |
| Confédération française de l'encadrement–Confédération générale des cadres (CFE–CGC) | 95,000 | Supervisory and managerial |

* The figures given here are estimates, taken from D. Labbé, 'Les principales organisations syndicales des salariés', *L'État de la France* (La Découverte, 1999), pp. 509–517.

(3) widespread and systematic negotiations with employers who are in general willing to talk;
(4) close relations between a large union confederation and a social-democratic-oriented Socialist Party.

A glance at the characteristics of the main organizations involved in industrial relations (Table 1.3) shows that it is an area where France in the 1990s still remained at odds with more consensual systems of politics in other countries. Indeed, one can safely assert that the trade union movement in France is in crisis. The point about large, relatively moderate and unified union structures elsewhere is that unrest among employees can be identified at an early stage, is clearly expressed and can in many cases be negotiated away at relatively little cost to employers. With a structure and practice such as the one found in France, this has rarely been the case. Indeed, there is a long history of industrial struggle taking place which is out of the control not only of management but also of the trade union leadership: during the time of the Popular Front government the rank and file rose up to push the union leadership far further in its pressure on government than the leadership had intended; in 1968 the leadership of the unions was taken by surprise by the breadth and militancy of rank-and-file support for the May movement; more recently, albeit on a smaller scale, in the 1986 and 1995 public sector strikes, rank-and-file trade unionists and even non-union members were highly militant. The public sector strikes of winter 1995 certainly spilled out of the control of trade union leaders at certain points.

The 1980s already saw a break with the past in some important respects, however. First, after the victory of the left in 1981, there was no mass movement on the part of the working class which sought to push a progressive government further in its objectives, as there had been in 1936 and 1947. Certainly, there was no actual pact between union leaders and government to limit industrial action, but informally the labour movement leadership allowed the government a substantial period of grace and went out of its way to avoid industrial disputes. The 1980s saw the number of days lost per annum in strike activity fall to the lowest level since 1945 (as shown in Figure 1.1), although this was to fall further in the 1990s, with the important exception of 1995. Significantly, the usually highly-militant *Confédération générale du travail* (CGT) organized no national day of action at all until after July 1984, when the PCF ministers left government. It was indeed significant that the only real mass demonstrations in the first few years of socialist rule were organized by the right, in protest against education minister Alain Savary's 1984 bill which, among other things, planned to reduce the autonomy of private schools (see Part III). In June 1984 there was a demonstration of over a million people (including many parents of private school students) and the government was obliged to back down.

This relative lack of activism on the part of the labour movement was a crucial factor in allowing the PS to implement austerity programmes and generally to bring about reforms which the right would have dearly loved to implement, but would probably have been stopped from doing by a militant labour movement. These included breaking the informal indexation of salaries to prices which had existed since the Second World War, asserting the legitimacy of the private firm as a crucial actor in the French economy, radically reducing the number of employees in traditional sectors, asserting the legitimacy of market forces in shaping the economy, and in general persuading the business community that the PS was a business-friendly government.[18] If the labour movement had risen up against the PS U-turn of 1982–3, the history of Mitterrand's France might have been very different indeed.

French trade unions in the 1980s became numerically far weaker, with the rate of unionization falling from about 19 per cent of the active population in 1980 to nearer 10 per cent in 1990, then to under 10 per cent by 2000. Many of the causes of this decline in union membership are also found in other industrialized countries. First, the number of blue-collar workers, who were always the most heavily unionized, has fallen considerably and the PS governments actively encouraged – or at least did nothing to prevent – the decline of steel, shipbuilding, coal mining and the car industry. Next, technological change meant that jobs were often 'rationalized' and this was also a cause of the high unemployment which has been a consistent feature of the French economy. But the French trade union movement was hit particularly hard because of its already weak and divided nature before industrial restructuring. The CGT, for a long time by far the largest and most militant of trade unions, was hardest hit by the decline, which compounded the already substantial problems caused by its association with the Stalinist politics of the PCF. *Force ouvrière* (FO) has gained support, as has the *Confédération française des travailleurs chrétiens* (CFTC), and non-union representatives now account for more than a quarter of all members of works councils. Nevertheless, it must be stressed that figures for elections to works councils and for staff representatives show that the union movement still has an influence which goes well beyond what raw union membership figures suggest; for example, in 1996 almost three-quarters of employees voting in works council elections chose to vote for trade union candidates.

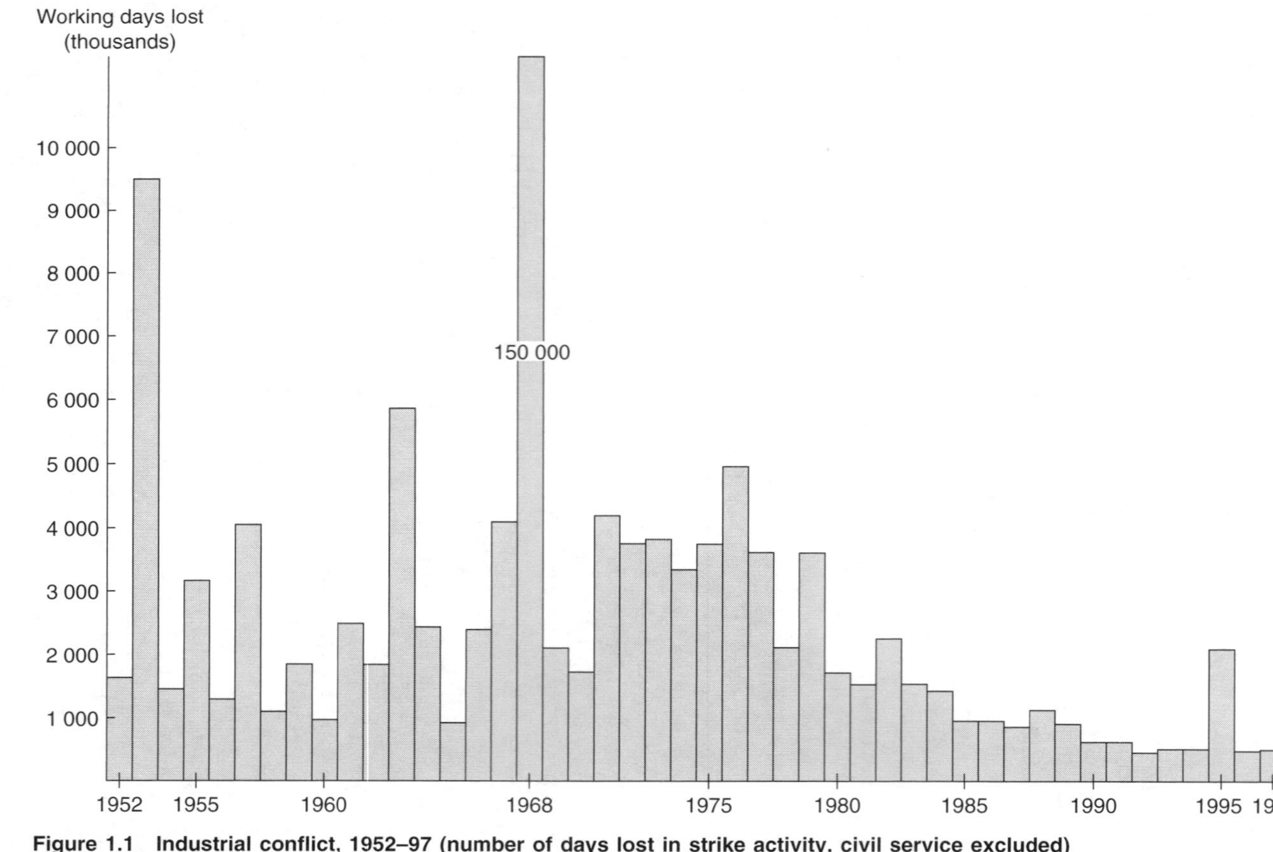


**Figure 1.1 Industrial conflict, 1952–97 (number of days lost in strike activity, civil service excluded)**
*Source:* Ministère du Travail et des Affaires sociales.

When the government introduced the *lois Auroux* in the early 1980s, this seemed to be a clear sign to the unions that it wished to shift the balance of power away from the *patronat* and in favour of labour, since the laws were designed to correct the hitherto severe lack of dialogue at company level between employers and employees. Employers were now obliged to discuss pay, working conditions and working time every year, although there was no obligation to actually reach agreement with trade unions. Unions were also allowed greater access to company information and nationalized firms admitted worker representatives to their boards. There was a new form of company-level dialogue in the shape of *groupes d'expression* which allowed workers and management to discuss issues which one side or the other wished to raise. On the whole the *lois Auroux* have proved positive for the unions and the trade union is certainly seen as a more legitimate social actor than was previously the case. Since 1983, when the legal obligation to negotiate annually first came into force, the number of workers covered by collective agreements has grown dramatically. However, most analysts are agreed that the introduction of *groupes d'expression* into the work place has meant that some employees have viewed these non-union entities as an alternative channel of communication with management, rather than an additional one, and management has been keen to do the same. Ironically, then, these laws which the unions very much welcomed and the *patronat* vehemently opposed have probably contributed towards weakening the trade union movement.

The divided nature of the trade union movement is due partly to the highly politicized nature of unions in France and also to the fact that no large, moderate socialist party emerged to be the natural ally of the movement. The fact that the working population was for long predominantly rural was also an important factor. This has greatly hampered the trade union movement's ability to play a more formal part in national politics. There have certainly been times when there was more unity of action than at others, such as during the period of the PS–PCF *Programme commun* in the 1970s, but the general rule has been fierce antagonism. More recently there has been little improvement in this situation, despite rumours at one time that the *Fédération de l'éducation nationale* (FEN) and FO might unite to form the core of a larger, moderate confederation committed to defence of its members' interests through collective bargaining above all else and close to the PS.

## Beyond conventional trade unionism?

Whilst the trade union movement remains small, fragmented and very uneven in strength between different sectors, it seems that there are two major developments taking place which continue to suggest that in France old conflictual habits die hard. First, there are signs that there is a radicalization which has been taking place within – or partially within – the trade union movement since the strikes of Winter 1995, followed by lorry drivers' action regarding working conditions the following year. There are pockets of new militancy which often represent a break with more traditional forms of trade union action and in some cases union structures. For example, after 1995 the left but loose grouping *Solidaires, unitaires, démocratiques* (SUD) gathered strength, with some Trotskyists within the group becoming distinctly more influential. Also, as managerial and supervisory workers, or *cadres*, have become proletarianized, there is now more militancy within this group [see Text 1.14]. Second, the decline of the trade union movement has been accompanied by a growth in the number and strength of other pressure groups which are prepared to take direct action, often against government policy. Farmers have become famous for taking direct action of various kinds, including dumping produce in front of town halls and herding cows down the Champs Élysées in Paris. But the organization *Agir contre le chômage* has also had a high profile, for example, as have various organizations set up to combat the FN, like *Ras le Front*, or to defend the rights of immigrants, particularly illegal immigrants, *les sans papiers*.

Returning to our general theme of consensus versus conflict, it should now be clear that a small trade union movement does not necessarily make for a more stable political situation than a large one. The most stable liberal democracies in post-1945 Europe have been those with large but moderate trade union movements. France has now a very small movement which is more moderate than it used to be, but trade unions and industrial militancy more generally are still unpredictable, partly precisely because of the smallness of the officially organized working class.

## Foreign relations and defence: from colonial imbroglio to quasi-consensus

If we look generally for a moment at France's more conflictual and ideological days, it is clear that France's place in the world and relations with other countries played an important part in maintaining this state of affairs. In a general sense, France was for many centuries at the geographical, cultural and diplomatic centre of a highly volatile international order, a position which often affected domestic affairs. To mention but the most obvious examples of the effect of international turmoil on domestic politics, the 1871 Commune of Paris (hailed by Karl Marx as the first proletarian revolution) was closely linked with the Franco-Prussian war; the formation of the PCF with both the First World War and the Russian Revolution; both the growth of the PCF and the popularity of de Gaulle with the Second World War; the governmental and extra-governmental instability of the Fourth Republic and the beginning of the Fifth Republic with colonial wars and decolonization. Finally, even the events of May 1968 were linked with foreign relations to the extent that one of the causes of the events was neglect by de Gaulle of certain important domestic considerations in favour of a grandiose foreign policy. After decolonization, however, foreign and, particularly, defence policy were among the first areas of near consensus among the main political parties and pointed the way towards a future, more 'modern', political system in general. Another factor to take into account is that, since 1945, western Europe has in general become a more stable political entity, in part because of the construction and development of the European Union, and this has eased France's foreign relations within Europe, a process which has had a direct effect on the domestic political scene.

In this section we look firstly at the situation under the Fourth Republic, when foreign relations were dominated by colonial war. Next we examine the de Gaulle era, when foreign relations, although dominated by the peculiarities of Gaullist ideology, not only attracted support from the greater part of the population as well as politicians, but also helped rid France of the strife-ridden question of colonial war. We then consider the post-de Gaulle era under Pompidou and Giscard d'Estaing which, despite still being strongly influenced by de Gaulle, represented a less grandiose approach which was more akin to that of other western powers than de Gaulle's all-out quest for French glory. Next, we consider the socialist period of presidency from 1981 to 1995, when there is no doubt that François Mitterrand took the more sober approach of Pompidou and Giscard a significant step forward, although signs of Gaullist influence were still there. Finally, we look at Jacques Chirac's presidency since 1995.

## The fourth republic

As the historian Jacques Fauvet has pointed out, one of the major errors of the politicians of the Fourth Republic was not to have pursued a different foreign policy.[19] In 1944 France held a conference in Brazzaville, capital of French Equatorial Africa, on the future of relations with its African colonies, and, although there was a commitment to reform, the conservative overall outcome of the conference was neatly summed up in one of the resulting recommendations: 'Les fins de l'œuvre de civilisation accomplie par la France dans les Colonies écartent toute idée d'autonomie, toute possibilité d'évolution hors du bloc français de l'empire; la constitution éventuelle, même lointaine, de self-governments dans les colonies est à écarter.'[20]

This reflected the views of most politicians at the beginning of the Fourth Republic and was a position which influenced the creation of the *Union française* in 1946, which put many former colonies in a slightly more autonomous but still highly dependent position; the most significant innovation of the Union was to grant (strictly limited) parliamentary representation to former colonies. This traditional colonial policy had in practice to be moderated in relation to some parts of French Africa and many colonies gained independence in the late 1950s or early 1960s, but it informed much of France's attitude overseas up to 1958.

Explaining France's intransigence in its colonial policy is not easy, given that the Second World War had substantially strengthened the hand of independence movements and that other colonial powers adopted a more reforming approach. But many felt that without its colonies France could not have counted itself among the victors of the Second World War. Just as importantly, a large proportion of France's trade after the war remained imperial, with the colonies accounting for a quarter of all French imports and receiving well over a third of French exports.

In Indo-China, France took up arms against the Viet Minh liberation movement after negotiations over independence with its communist leader, Ho Chi Minh, broke down in 1946. There ensued a long and bloody war and the loss of life of a total of 90,000 soldiers. But the French public remained largely apathetic in relation to the war, partly because only professional soldiers were sent to fight and not conscripts. This attitude rapidly changed, however, when in May 1954 the Viet Minh defeated the French at Dien Bien Phu, with the loss of one-tenth of all French troops in Indo-China, and posed a stark choice between total withdrawal or deeper involvement. The latter option would almost certainly have implied conscription, and with the war already mopping up 40 per cent of the French defence budget, the government decided on withdrawal, leaving the 'fight against Communism' in Indo-China in the hands of the Americans. The writing was already on the wall for the Fourth Republic.

The Algerian war began the same year and was to become by far the most divisive issue in the whole of the Fourth Republic. The Algerian *Front de libération nationale* (FLN) published a declaration of independence in November 1954 [see Text 1.15] and the movement gathered considerable support, in the end successfully driving the French, after tens of thousands of casualties on either side, out of the country. Crucially, the French decided in 1955 to send in conscripts, which well and truly brought the war back home. It is perhaps difficult to understand why France did not pull its troops out of Algeria sooner, or even why it engaged its troops in the first place, given its previous humiliating withdrawal from Indo-China in a similar war. But it must be remembered that, although the one million plus colonials in Algeria had lived there for several generations, they still considered themselves to be as much French as Algerian. In addition, Algeria was politically far more integrated into French life than were most other colonies, it being defined as three French administrative *départements* with *députés* representing them in the domestic parliament, rather than an overseas territory. In any event, the colonial question not only dominated the politics of the Fourth Republic, but in large part caused its downfall as well.

In the midst of the Algerian war there came another major humiliation for French policy overseas when in 1956 Franco-British forces attacked Egypt after the Egyptian President Nasser nationalized the Suez Canal, an important trade route to the East. America refused to support this attempt to defend western interests in the Middle East and Britain and France had to withdraw and allow Nasser to maintain the nationalized status of the canal. For both France and Britain the Suez adventure was a heavy blow to any lingering hopes of maintaining traditional influence over the Third World.

Conflict, humiliation and, in the end, deep divisions among politicians over colonial policy prevailed during this period. But developments were already taking place in another domain which were to help counter the conflictual tendencies not only in French political life but also in the international arena, namely the construction of the European Union. The creation of the Union was, in the long term, certainly to be an issue on which many French politicians and ordinary French people were to concur and, along with the development of the *force de frappe* nuclear strike force, an issue which helped the French accept decolonization. There were many reasons for the establishment of the European Union, but among the most important were the desire to facilitate intra-European trade (partly in response to the increasingly dominant position of the United States in world trade) and the desire to ensure lasting peace between west European nations. French politicians Jean Monnet and Robert Schuman played an important part in laying the foundations for the European Union, and France was one of the six original signatories of the Treaty of Rome which established the EU (or the EEC as it was then called) in 1957.

## De Gaulle

When de Gaulle came to power in 1958, French colonial policy desperately needed attention, and the achievement of formal independence of Algeria without major bloodshed in domestic France was in no small part due to the rallying nature of Gaullism. Indeed, this rallying owed much to de Gaulle's concept of the correct foreign policy for France, which was one of the most particular but also one of the most enduring features (along with the constitution of the Fifth Republic) of Gaullism. The notion that the nation was all-important was at the heart of Gaullist foreign policy and de Gaulle constantly stressed the importance of France's autonomy in relation to other countries. So appealing was de Gaulle's foreign policy that it has very strongly influenced all heads of state since de Gaulle.

De Gaulle's belief in the necessity of *grandeur* for France led him to believe – or so he claimed – that his country should play a leading role in international politics [see Text 1.4]. By 1958, the world was divided into two spheres of influence, one led by the USSR and the other by the United States. De Gaulle sought to avoid falling in with a typical western attitude towards the superpowers and he often took fiercely anti-American positions and developed more friendly relations with the Soviet Union than did most countries in the west. This independent approach led de Gaulle to develop France's own nuclear deterrent and to withdraw France from the integrated command structure of the North Atlantic Treaty Organization (NATO), which had been set up in 1949 to defend America and its allies in the west against the supposed threat of Soviet attack. De Gaulle sought to forge alliances which would shield Third World countries from the influence of the superpowers and would encourage them to look to France as their ally. This orientation often led to military intervention and during the de Gaulle years France notably fought in Gabon, Chad, the Ivory Coast, the Cameroons and Niger. De Gaulle had between 10,000 and 15,000 troops permanently stationed in various parts of Africa and a similar number of troops based in France as part of a *force d'intervention rapide* which was ready to strike at a moment's notice.

De Gaulle's belief in the special – almost spiritually inspired – role which France should play in the world meant that he was highly ambivalent in relation to the construction of a greater Europe, which might, he thought, swamp French interests. By the time he came to power the Treaty of Rome was already signed and he respected, in a general sense, the legitimacy of the EEC, but he was highly suspicious of any organization which seemed to encroach upon national sovereignty. In a famous incident, France boycotted the meetings of the Council of Ministers of the European Union in Brussels between June 1965 and January 1966, because of proposals to take certain important decisions (some concerned, for instance, with the Common Agricultural Policy) by majority voting on the Council of Ministers, rather than by discussing and compromising until there was consensus. With this tactic, which became known as 'la politique de la chaise vide', France won that particular battle and the status quo prevailed.

The final point we need to make about de Gaulle's foreign policy is that its formation was overwhelmingly shaped and its implementation supervised closely by de Gaulle himself. It was far too important an area to allow anyone but the president to influence it in anything but the most trivial fashion.

Thus the first ten or so years of the Fifth Republic saw tremendous changes in the domain of foreign policy, most notably in the form of decolonization. France went from being a nation with deep and often traumatic divisions over the question of foreign relations to one where there was generally agreement. Philip Cerny has developed a convincing thesis that 'the purpose of de Gaulle's foreign policy was not the attainment of glory and power for France for its own sake . . . [but] to create a new and more profound sense of national consciousness, capable of transcending the national issues which have characterized the French polity'.[21] So if we view de Gaulle's foreign policy mainly as a means to the end of consensus building, although he was not wholly successful (witness the events of May 1968), he certainly laid the basis for greater consensus both in domestic and in foreign affairs.

## Pompidou and Giscard d'Estaing

It would be wrong to claim that there was a clean break between the foreign policy of de Gaulle and that of his immediate successors, but Pompidou and especially Valéry Giscard d'Estaing were more pragmatic and less grandiose in their approach. Pompidou continued to make foreign policy speeches which were reminiscent of de Gaulle's, but, while using some decidedly Gaullist turns of phrase, the underlying message was more down-to-earth:

> Une France forte économiquement est seule en mesure de permettre la prospérité et le progrès social. Une France forte est seule en mesure de participer à la construction européenne sans y perdre sa personnalité et sans y sacrifier ses intérêts essentiels. Une France forte est seule capable d'avoir des alliés . . . et pas des maîtres.[22]

The one substantial foreign policy initiative which Pompidou took was to call a referendum on the enlargement of the European Union, and he made it clear that he was in favour of Britain's entry. De Gaulle had blocked Britain's entry, in part for fear of Britain acting as the Trojan Horse of American interests. With regard to NATO, official policy remained unchanged, although Pompidou was less anti-American than de Gaulle, and the Soviet Union's invasion of Czechoslovakia in 1968 had in any case already meant a little less friendliness between France and the USSR than during most of de Gaulle's presidency. In short, Pompidou's presidency represents a period of transition, in the realm of foreign policy as in other spheres, between de Gaulle's *régime d'exception* and subsequent presidential periods when politics were more akin to those of other advanced capitalist countries.

Giscard d'Estaing was elected president in the immediate aftermath of the massive 1973 oil price rise and in the midst of the ensuing world economic crisis, and his foreign policy orientation was even more obviously determined by practical constraints than Pompidou's. In the Middle East, Giscard developed a highly pro-Arab stance which had much to do both with the provision of oil and with nurturing a vast market for French manufactured arms. France under Giscard was the third largest producer of arms in the world (after the United States and the USSR) and between 1974 and 1978 the value of French arms exports rose from 4.8 milliard F to 8.4 milliard F. As far as the EEC was concerned, economic considerations were again uppermost in Giscard's mind and he played an important part in setting up the European Monetary System. He was also responsible for establishing regular summit meetings of leaders of member states, but perhaps the most significant and enduring element in Giscard's European policy was the consolidation of the special relationship between France and West Germany, a process already begun by de Gaulle and Chancellor Konrad Adenauer. There was a particular affinity between Giscard d'Estaing and Chancellor Helmut Schmidt, who had both been finance ministers, were both influenced by the liberal tradition in politics, and who had both come to power in May 1974. More importantly, France sought to benefit from West Germany's strong economy and there was close cooperation on the Rhône–Rhine canal, the aircraft Airbus, the space rocket Ariane, nuclear power and communications satellites. France and Germany were each other's principal trading partners. Meanwhile, Germany benefited politically from close association with its erstwhile arch-enemy in a Europe which had far from forgotten the traumas of the Second World War.

In the domain of Franco-African relations, Giscard was arguably even more interventionist than de Gaulle. Motivated by a desire to defend France's economic and strategic interests and to promote French language and culture abroad (its *rayonnement*), Giscard earned an ultimately damaging reputation for economically and particularly militarily propping up corrupt regimes. Some 14,000 French soldiers were stationed in Africa and there were, notably, military interventions in Mauritania, Morocco, Chad and Zaire. The close relationship between Giscard and the highly corrupt Emperor Bokassa of the Central African Republic played a part in Giscard's defeat in 1981 because of a substantial gift of diamonds (made public by the satirical newspaper *Le Canard enchaîné*) from the man who thought of the president of France as a close personal friend as well as a political ally.

## Mitterrand

As in so many other domains, the Mitterrand era in the end brought France closer to the foreign policy positions of other western countries, rather than further away, as many had predicted. At first, it seemed as if the new socialist government was set to pioneer a radical break with the past in certain areas, in order to shape foreign policy along more socialist lines. In a pre-election document published in 1980 entitled *Projet socialiste*, the PS stated that a new attitude was needed in relation to underdeveloped countries, in order, for instance, to break with the imperialist attitude of governments under the Fifth Republic. In October 1981, during a trip to Mexico, newly-elected President Mitterrand declared:

> Il n'y a pas et ne peut y avoir de stabilité politique sans justice sociale . . . L'antagonisme Est-Ouest ne saurait expliquer les luttes pour l'émancipation des damnés de la terre, pas plus qu'il n'aide à les résoudre . . . A tous les combattants de la liberté, la France lance son message d'espoir.[23]

France even sent 15 million dollars of military aid to Nicaragua in 1981 to support the Sandinistas in their struggle against American-backed Contras and, by way of attempting to demonstrate remorse for past relations with Algeria, the new Mitterrand government agreed to buy Algerian gas at a price which was substantially above the market rate. Aid to developing countries increased sharply and Jean-Pierre Cot, well known for progressive views on relations with Third World countries, was made minister for cooperation and development. Very soon, however, this very different approach gave way to a more Gaullist – or perhaps Giscardian – approach to the question of underdeveloped countries, where France sought diplomatically, economically and sometimes militarily to defend existing regimes, particularly in Africa, with little regard for their degree of respect for liberal democratic principles. There was thus a return to protection of French allies in francophone Africa regardless of their political complexion. Significantly, Jean-Pierre Cot was dismissed in December 1982.

In some other respects, it was clear virtually from the start that the Mitterrand presidency was to introduce a *rapprochement* with foreign policy of other nations, rather than a clear shift to the left or even the continuation of purer Gaullist policies. He soon made it clear, for instance, that he intended to be more pro-American than any previous president of the Fifth Republic and there were six meetings between Presidents Mitterrand and Reagan between May 1981 and May 1982. Mitterrand's enthusiasm for the deployment of American Cruise and Pershing missiles in Europe – though not in France – led him to take the extraordinary step of using an appearance before the West German parliament (*Bundestag*) in January 1983, just before West German legislative elections, to lend his support to placing these weapons in West Germany. He thus implicitly called for a vote against the German Social Democratic Party, the SPD, and in favour of the right. Later in the 1980s the French attitude changed somewhat towards the United States, as demonstrated in April 1986, when Mitterrand (with the approval of Prime Minister Jacques Chirac) refused to allow US planes to fly over French air space on their way to a bombing raid on Tripoli, Libya.

As far as relations with the Soviet Union were concerned, there were several different stages. At first, Mitterrand was decidedly cool towards the USSR, in contrast with the attitude of Giscard d'Estaing. This was partly because of the Soviet invasion of Afghanistan in 1979 and the imposition of martial law in Poland. It also served to reassure the United States that the presence of communist ministers in the government did not imply an endorsement of Soviet policy. In 1984 (the year of the departure of PCF ministers) relations between France and the USSR improved and both Foreign Minister Claude Cheysson and François Mitterrand visited the country. Finally, Mitterrand was one of the first to condone the post-communist politics of Mikhail Gorbachev, and subsequently of Boris Yeltsin and the break-up of the Soviet Union, although Mitterrand's first reaction to the *coup d'état* in the Soviet Union by communist hardliners in August 1991 was apparently to recognize them as the country's new leadership.

There was also a change of attitude towards the Middle East. Instead of carrying on the established practice of coolness towards Israel, Mitterrand became the first French president to make an official visit to the state, in March 1982, and he made a significant speech before the Knesset, the Israeli parliament. In the speech he confirmed the legitimacy of the state of Israel, whilst defending the rights of Arabs to dwell in the same region. France also set up a programme of economic, scientific and cultural cooperation with Israel. This was a significant new direction in French foreign policy which nevertheless did not prevent the government from maintaining close relations with the Arab world, a region which continued to supply much of France's oil and also to buy large quantities of French arms. However, France's relations with Iraq changed out of all recognition during the 1991 Gulf war, during which Iraq went from being a close ally and faithful purchaser of arms to being arch-enemy, thus

**François Mitterrand** (1916–96)

Trained as a lawyer, Mitterrand became the longest-serving president of the Fifth Republic. He was emprisoned by the Germans in 1940, escaped in 1941, served in the Vichy government in 1942 and joined the Resistance in 1943. *Député* in the Nièvre after the Second World War and one of the leaders of the centre-left, he occupied a number of ministerial posts under the Fourth Republic, including Minister for the Interior under Mendès-France (in 1954) and Minister for Justice under Guy Mollet (in 1956). In 1958 he opposed the return of de Gaulle and also the new constitution, and led the *Fédération de la gauche démocratique et socialiste* (FGDS) from 1965 to 1968. He joined the recently-formed *Parti socialiste* in 1971 and immediately became leader, signing the *Programme commun* with the *Parti communiste* in 1972. After two unsuccessful attempts to become president (in 1965 and 1974), he won the presidential elections in 1981 and formed France's first wholly left government for many years. He 'cohabited' with the right government between 1986 and 1988, was re-elected against Jacques Chirac in 1988 and cohabited again between 1993 and 1995. He died of cancer just after the end of his second presidential term. Mitterrand was known for his opportunism and predilection for political manoevres, and there were revelations in the mid- and late 1990s about ongoing friendships with former sympathizers with the extreme right. He published many books, including *Le Coup d'État permanent* (1964), *Ma Part de la vérité* (1969), *L'Abeille et l'architecte* (1978) and *Mon Testament* (1995).

falling into line with the policy of other powerful western nations. By the same token, Iran went from being enemy to ally.

In 1981 the Mitterrand government had continued to speak against the domination of European multinationals which it said the EEC represented. But for several reasons the Socialists in power evolved in a direction that was highly pro-European and strongly in favour of the single market of 1992 in particular. First, the socialist government felt obliged, in May 1983, to ask the EEC for a substantial loan in order to bail out a domestic economy in crisis. Second, cooperation with other EEC nation states seemed necessary if France was to encourage the placing of Cruise and Pershing missiles in some of these other countries. Third, the new, market-oriented economic policy which the Socialists had adopted seemed better served by the freer market offered by the Single European Act whose full force was timetabled for the beginning of 1993. In most respects, then, French socialism in government became almost synonymous with a stronger (and enlarged) Europe, with Mitterrand even very much in favour of close cooperation among EEC member states as far as foreign policy and defence are concerned. Mitterrand's position in favour of the Maastricht treaty, representing still greater political and economic cooperation, narrowly won the day at the referendum on Maastricht in September 1992.

Having pointed to areas in which Mitterrand's France became particularly conventional as far as foreign relations are concerned, it must be said that France maintained other areas where foreign policy was more Gaullist. In the realm of defence, France maintained a commitment to its own *force de frappe* nuclear strike force and continues to gain much popular support for an independent defence policy. But even here substantial cracks have appeared and the (1991) Gulf war against Iraq brought home to the French how difficult it was to maintain a stance independent of the United States and its allies, either from a traditional Gaullist point of view or from a socialist point of view. During this conflict Mitterrand attempted to distance France somewhat from the United States and its allies but it was clear that there was very little room for manoeuvre. Indeed, Mitterrand's Atlanticism meant that there was more cooperation with NATO than had been seen before under the Fifth Republic. Mitterrand certainly carried on in the Gaullist tradition of personally dominating the formulation of foreign policy and defence; and it was notable that during the first period of cohabitation one of the areas in which he gave way very little was that of foreign relations and, in particular, defence. Indeed, during the period of cohabitation between 1986 and 1988 one saw not only the extent to which the constitution allowed the president to dominate foreign relations but also the extent to which Mitterrand wished to do so.

## Chirac

Since the beginning of Jacques Chirac's presidential term in 1995, France's foreign policy and defence have on the whole continued to resemble more closely those of other western nations, and ironically have been on the whole less traditionally Gaullist than under Mitterrand. As far as Europe is concerned, for example, the major political parties agreed that it was important to meet the economic convergence criteria of the Maastricht treaty, although this meant some immediate pain in return for the promise of longer-term gain. Although the question of Europe was certainly divisive in some parties on the right (as it was in the British Conservative Party), general support for further European political and economic integration seemed to reinforce the 'normalization' of French politics.

In a landmark change of policy in December 1995, there came the associated announcement that France would re-integrate into the military command structure of NATO, thus reducing the distance from the United States in the realm of defence, which had been so important to de Gaulle. The decision to phase out military service was another significant change, presented as a necessary modernization, affecting the lives of many thousands of young men. In this bold, post-cold war development, military service would not be entirely phased out until 2002, and even then there would be contingency plans lest it be needed again at short notice, but it was seen as a decidedly modernizing step forward. Far less popular, however, was the announcement in summer 1995 that France was to resume nuclear tests in the South Pacific, three years after a moratorium initiated by Mitterrand. In France and Polynesia there were vigorous protests, and other EU member states made formal complaints, but, although Chirac reduced the number of tests, he did not stop them completely.

Relations with the United States, although in some ways closer, were at times tense. At the end of Mitterrand's presidency, foreign minister Alain Juppé held out against certain measures and eventually won concessions from the United States and Europe in GATT (international trade) negotiations, which meant audiovisual products were not included in the new GATT treaty, and it was agreed that there could be compensation for losses as far as agricultural produce was concerned. Some Franco-US tensions persisted, however, and in summer 1999 there was an unofficial boycott of US imports – and attacks on McDonald's restaurants – in response to American restrictions on imports of Roquefort cheese.

One clear change since the beginning of the Chirac presidency has been a policy of partial withdrawal on the part of France from Africa, at least in the military sphere. France was for many years regarded as the *gendarme* of Africa, but with the withdrawal of French soldiers from Africa between 1997 and 2002 the number will have fallen from 8,000 to 5,600. Various military bases which were previously regarded as being of high strategic importance were abandoned in 1998, including two in the Central African Republic. Instead of a bilateral relationship with various countries of Africa, France is beginning to reinforce its links from within the frameworks of international organizations such as the EU and the United Nations. Indeed, French policy in general is increasingly mediated through international organizations.

To sum up, in stark contrast to the situation under the Fourth Republic, French foreign policy is an area which, since de Gaulle, has become less and less disputed among the political parties. At first this relative consensus was formed round a highly peculiar and ideology-laden foreign policy as conducted by de Gaulle. But as time has passed, although some of the peculiarly nationalistic trappings of Gaullist foreign policy can still be seen, foreign policy has on the whole become less extraordinary and has come more and more to resemble that of other western nations. During the period of cohabitation between Chirac and Jospin, there was even some evidence that foreign policy was less the exclusive preserve of the president than it had been, precisely because it was more pragmatic and less grandiose.

## Conclusion: the death of conflict – a much exaggerated rumour?

Throughout Part I, it has been argued in a qualified fashion that French politics during the 1980s and 1990s were less conflict-dominated than during any other period since 1945. In order to avoid temptations to oversimplify, however, it is necessary to temper this argument further. First, it should not be thought that, in countries where politics have long been more centre-oriented, or consensual, this indicated a complete absence of political and social conflict. This is clearly not the case. If we take Britain, West Germany or Sweden, for instance, despite many years of relatively moderate parliamentary politics in the post-war period,[24] there have sometimes been long and bitter industrial conflicts which have in some cases even brought down governments. It is a question of degree. Whereas in countries of more moderate politics, overt, national-level conflict has been relatively rare and large parties of fundamental protest have often been absent, for a long time in France these factors were a way of political life. We have already seen how the rise of the *Front national*, with its protest orientation and anti-status quo ideology, is itself a strong reminder of political times past and represents a counter-tendency to the general direction in which politics have been moving.

Here we need also to mention the phenomenon of abstentions, which have reached record levels for the Fifth Republic in recent years. Abstentions in elections can be interpreted in two very different ways. They can be viewed as an indicator that the section of the electorate which abstains believes that all is well with parties and government and that they therefore do not need to vote (this would tend to confirm that we are witnessing consensualization of politics). Alternatively, higher levels of abstention may be interpreted as indicating disillusionment with politics and politicians and an inclination to protest against them. It is likely that in the recent high levels of abstentions there is a mixture of these two phenomena. These trends, along with popular disenchantment with politicians (partly because of instances of serious corruption among both right- and left-wing politicians), the resurgence of extra-parliamentary protest since 1995 and, arguably, a withdrawal of government from important areas have prompted analysts to coin numerous terms to describe politics which certainly have the potential, at least, for plenty of conflict: *fracture politique*, *malaise* and *morosité* are among them [see Text 1.16].

We must also briefly consider the rise of ecology politics. Ecology became popular during the 1970s after the events of May 1968, but it did not at this point become successful as a political party. Rather, the ecology movement engaged in single-issue campaigns such as protest against the construction of a nuclear power station or attempts to stop the army from using large tracts of land as training ground. During the 1980s, however, as elsewhere after the nuclear reactor accident at Chernobyl, in the Soviet Union, and discoveries about the erosion of the ozone layer, green politics became far more popular and more party political and the *Verts* received 10.6 per cent of the vote in the European elections in June 1989 and a total of 14.4 per cent (for the *Verts* plus *Génération Ecologie*) in regional elections in March 1992, although this figure fell to 7.6 in the 1993 legislative elections. By 1997, although they only received 3.6 per cent of the vote in the legislative elections of that year, ecologists were part of the *gauche plurielle* governmental coalition, and ecology leader Dominique Voynet was a very well known and well-respected politician. The influence of the ecology parties should not be exaggerated, but there is certainly a degree of ongoing support for this current which is still, partly, a movement of protest against more mainstream politics.[25] In addition, although the far left (which is largely Trotskyist or influenced by Trotskyism) is not and never has been very strong, the parties of the far left regularly receive between 1 and 3 per cent of the vote, and achieved a record 5.6 per cent in the 1995 presidential elections which, added to other votes against the mainstream parties, helps to qualify our thesis about the normalization of French politics. Arlette Laguiller has been a particularly important figure on the far left.

To conclude, we will mention the most important points made in the various sections of Part I. At the outset, we explained that in France, in contrast to many advanced capitalist countries after the Second World War, there was no pact between the state, the *patronat* and trade unions, as was seen in other, more moderate western countries and which helped create a more consensual political situation. Although this tri-axial arrangement is today regarded as less important in our cultures of free enterprise, it still remains a useful point of reference and was indeed achieved – albeit imperfectly – under left-wing governments during the 1980s. The *Parti socialiste*, representing the state, became

**Arlette Laguiller** (b. 1940)

Arlette Laguiller became a bank employee with the Crédit Lyonnais in 1956, where she remained until the late 1990s. She has been a Trotskyist activist since 1960 both in her own bank and in the banking sector more generally, and was one of the national leaders of the bank employees' strike of March–April 1974. She has been in the leadership of *Lutte ouvrière* since 1968 and still writes the editorial of the party's newspaper, also called *Lutte ouvrière*. She was presidential candidate for LO in 1974, when she was the first woman to stand in such an election, and then in 1981, 1988 and 1995, when she received her highest ever share of the vote, at 5.3 per cent. In the late 1990s LO worked more closely than in former times with the other Trotskyist organization, the *Ligue communiste révolutionnaire*, and also appeared frequently on television. Her books include *Moi, une militante* (1973), *Il faut changer le monde* (1988) and *C'est toute ma vie* (1996).

reconciled with the *patronat* during the 1980s and there was no longer a fear of sea change under a government of the left; on the contrary, the left came to be seen by many as the vessel through which a lasting stability could be achieved. Likewise there emerged more harmony between government and the labour movement, although no formal 'non-aggression' pact was signed. But perhaps one of the most important changes (not only under the Socialists but generally since 1981) has been the advent of more harmony between the *patronat* on the one hand and the working population on the other. The Socialists certainly helped this situation, notably with the introduction of the *lois Auroux* which encouraged dialogue. The trade unions, and industrial conflict more generally, still remain a potential rogue element in the French political scene, as was clear in Winter 1995; and their very smallness (and therefore their lack of 'control' of the working class) could be a factor leading to conflict in future.

Most importantly, however, despite the persistence of substantial minority protest politics mentioned above, mainstream parliamentary politics have been captured by forces which are more centre-oriented. This is expressed in the shift towards the centre-right on the part of the PS and the decline of the PCF, but also the more moderate nature of the PCF. On the right, France has seen the decline of traditional Gaullist ideology and confluence of the ideological paths of the UDF and the RPR, despite serious organizational divisions. It remains to be seen what the role of the new Gaullist RPF will be.

One reason for the decline of conflict politics is the gradual change in France's foreign relations. Decolonization removed a potent source of conflict and the rise of Europe added an obvious source of popular appeal, or at least lack of contention in terms of the overall project. De Gaulle worked hard at making foreign policy work in favour of national independence in order to unite the French and since de Gaulle successive presidents have gradually let go of the more extraordinary aspects of Gaullist foreign policy and have moved closer to the foreign policy of other advanced capitalist nations. Mitterrand was no exception to this rule, despite indications in 1981 that he would follow a more left-wing, radical path in some important areas of foreign policy, and Chirac certainly confirmed it.

Bearing in mind the very different situation at the beginning of the new millennium it is useful to think back, finally, to some of the more conflict-dominated events and periods since the Second World War. For the ruling class the victory of the left and PCF participation in government in 1981 came as a great shock; the near victory of the ex-Union of the Left in 1978, with a more even balance between Communists and Socialists than in 1981, was almost as great a shock; May 1968 profoundly rocked the existing political and economic order; de Gaulle's authoritarian populism was an extreme, political expression of the fact that France's economy and polity was in transition; colonial turmoil after the Second World War, including the near *coup d'état* in domestic France in 1958, speaks for itself; as do the election results under the Fourth Republic, where, between 1947 and 1956, parties opposed to the existing order consistently received about 40 per cent of the vote.[26] It is clear that the present situation is a very different one, although not without dangers for governments and presidents of either left or right.

# Notes

1 F. Engels, Preface to the third German edition of K. Marx, *The Eighteenth Brumaire of Louis Bonaparte* (1885) in K. Marx and F. Engels, *Selected Works in One Volume* (Lawrence and Wishart, 1968) p.94.
2 The complexity of the issues surrounding resistance and collaboration is enormous. In the confusion immediately following the Liberation decisions about who should be punished for collaboration were often based on flimsy evidence and the definition of collaboration was questionable. For a brilliant study of the complexity of the issue of wartime collaboration and resistance, which shows how fine a line there sometimes was between the two, see Marcel Ophuls's documentary film, *Le Chagrin et la pitié*, which was not at first shown by the state broadcasting network ORTF, which had commissioned it in the first place.
3 Political parties at the time were many and varied and none attracted anything like an absolute majority. In the parliamentary elections of November 1946, the three most popular parties were the PCF (28.8 per cent of votes), the MRP (26.3 per cent) and the socialist SFIO (18.1 per cent).
4 Quoted by R. Mouriaux and J. Capdevielle, *Mai '68: l'entre-deux de la modernité. Histoire de trente ans* (Presses de la Fondation nationale des sciences politiques, 1988) p.228.
5 Speech to the congress of the Second International in Vienna, 28 June 1972, quoted by O. Biffaud in 'Parti communiste. Le piège et le déclin', *Bilan du septennat* (*Le Monde, Dossiers et Documents*, 1988) p.71.
6 M. Winock, *La République se meurt* (Gallimard, 1985).
7 The Radicals were a centre party who had supported the Popular Front in the 1930s, but who were in right-leaning coalitions in the early 1950s.
8 R. Rémond, *Les Droites en France* (Aubier-Montaigne, 1982).
9 François Mitterrand made public remarks about changes to the constitution, but in the end he left it virtually untouched.
10 M. Duverger, *La Monarchie républicaine* (Laffont, 1974).
11 Since 1947 the main Gaullist party has had seven different names, none of them actually using the word *parti*, in keeping with de Gaulle's idea that conventional political parties represented partisan, and therefore not *French* interests. The RPF (*Rassemblement du peuple français*) was established in 1947 and on de Gaulle's return to power in 1958 the UNR (*Union pour la nouvelle république*) was set up. This became UNR-UDT (*Union démocratique du travail*) in 1962 and UDVeR (*Union des démocrates pour la cinquième république*) in 1967 and UDR (*Union pour la défense de la république*) in 1968. In 1971 the name became *Union des démocrates pour la république* (keeping the same initials, UDR) and since 1976 it has been RPR (*Rassemblement pour la république*); since 1999 there is also a new RPF (*Rassemblement pour la France*).
12 Deep divisions over the future of Europe emerged during the campaign for ratification of the Maastricht Treaty in September 1992, which sought amongst other things to set up a common foreign and defence policy. Jacques Chirac campaigned for a 'yes' vote, whereas two other RPR leaders, Philippe Séguin and Charles Pasqua, campaigned vigorously against the treaty. (Chirac's position, which was also that of President Mitterrand, narrowly won the day.)
13 J. Jaffré, 'Trente années de changement électoral', *La Ve République, Pouvoirs*, No 49, 1989, p.18.
14 *Le Monde*, 23 November, 1999, p.7.
15 Ibid.

16 J.-C. Petitfils, *L'Extrême droite en France* (PUF, 1983) p.123. Quoted by M. Charlot, 'L'Emergence du Front National', *Revue française de science politique,* Vol 36, No 1, February 1986, p.14.
17 C. Ysmal, 'Communistes et Lepénistes: le chassé-croisé', in *Histoire,* No 143, April 1991, p.53.
18 This point is made clearly by Alain Vernholes in 'Fermeture du tout-État et ouverture sur l'étranger', *Bilan du septennat* (*Le Monde, Dossiers et Documents,* 1988) p.92.
19 J. Fauvet, *La Quatrième République* (Fayard, 1960).
20 A. Ruscio, *La décolonisation tragique* (Editions sociales, 1987) p.28.
21 P. Cerny, *The Politics of Grandeur* (Cambridge University Press, 1980) p.4.
22 P. Couste and F. Visine, *Pompidou et l'Europe* (Libraires techniques, 1974) p.149.
23 Quoted by M.-C. Smouts, 'La France et le Tiers-Monde, ou comment gagner le sud sans perdre le nord', in *Politique étrangère,* No 2, 1985, p.339.
24 Consensus in Britain is thoroughly discussed in D. Kavanagh and P.Morris, *Consensus Politics from Attlee to Thatcher* (Clarendon Press, 1989).
25 The green electorate tends to be well to the left of centre, according to opinion polls, but many people voting ecologist see themselves as neutral in relation to the left–right axis and some (about one in five) place themselves on the right of the political spectrum.
26 H. Ehrmann, *France* (Little, Brown, 1968) p.16.

# Suggestions for further reading

## General

The sources on French politics are many and varied and are often very good. In French the three main journals are *Revue politique et parlementaire* (Presses universitaires de France), *Revue française de science politique* (Presses de la Fondation nationale des sciences politiques) and *Pouvoirs* (Presses universitaires de France). In English, there is *Modern and Contemporary France* (Longman), which has not only full-length articles, but also shorter items on recent developments, conference reports and a wealth of book reviews. The American equivalent is *French Politics, Culture and Society*, produced by the Center for European Studies at Harvard University. *West European Politics* (Frank Cass) often has articles on France. Two useful annual reviews are *Année politique et économique* (PUF) and *L'État de la France* (La Découverte). The daily newspaper *Le Monde*, as well as being an unbeatable day-to-day source of news about political developments, produces *'dossiers et documents'* on national elections and other major political events.

J.-J. Becker, *Histoire politique de la France depuis 1945* (A. Colin, 1996) provides a useful introductory survey of the post-war period, whilst J. Charlot, *La politique en France* (Livre de poche, 1994) is very good on the period since 1958. In English, R. Gildea, *France since 1945* (OUP, 1996) is an excellent general history, and V. Wright and A. Knapp, *The Government and Politics of France*, 4th edn (Unwin Hyman, 2000) is the best introduction in French or English to the theory and practice of French government itself. A. Stevens, *The Government and Politics of France*, 2nd edn. (Macmillan, 1996) is also very good, as is A. Cole, *French Politics and Society* (Prentice-Hall, 1998).

P. Hall, J. Hayward and H. Machin (eds), *Developments in French Politics*, 2nd edn. (Macmillan, 1994) surveys the political scene in a thought-provoking fashion. More specifically on the political parties, there is P. Ignazi and C. Ysmal (eds), *The Organization of Political Parties in Southern Europe* (Praeger, 1998) and C. Leyrit, *Les Partis politiques, indispensables et contestés* (Le Monde Editions/Marabout, 1997).

## General political history since 1945

M. Larkin, *France since the Popular Front* (Clarendon, 1997) is a good survey which situates politics in its social and economic context. The best general history of the Fourth Republic is J.-P. Rioux, *La France de la Quatrième République*, 2 vols (Seuil, 1980 and 1983) and has been translated into English as *The Fourth Republic 1944–1958* (Cambridge University Press, 1989). More specifically on governmental politics there is the excellent P. Williams, *Crisis and Compromise: Politics in the Fourth Republic* (Longman, 1964) and J. Fauvet, *La Quatrième République* (Fayard, 1959) is also very good. Also see J. Julliard, *La Quatrième République* (Hachette, 1980).

On the Fifth Republic there is M. Duverger, *La Cinquième République*, 5th edn (PUF, 1974), M. Duverger, *Le système politique français*, 19th edn (PUF, 1986), J. Chapsal, *La vie politique sous la Cinquième République* (PUF, 1984), S. Sur, *La vie politique en France sous la Cinquième République* (Montchrestien, 1982) and P. Avril, *La Cinquième République: histoire politique et constitutionnelle* (PUF, 1987). In English, one of the most thought-provoking books on politics in the Fifth Republic is J. Hayward, *Governing France: the One and Indivisible Republic* (Weidenfeld & Nicolson, 1983).

Politics in the Mitterrand era have been analysed in the very useful collection of essays in G. Ross, S. Hoffmann and S. Malzacher (eds), *The Mitterrand Experiment* (Polity, 1987). More journalistic but still very full accounts are found in S. Gras and C. Gras, *Histoire de la Première République mitterrandienne* (Robert Laffont, 1991) and P. Favier and M. Martin-Roland, *La Décennie Mitterrand*, 3 vols (Seuil, 1990, 1991 and 1996). In English, there is S. Mazey and M. Newman (eds), *Mitterrand's France* (Croom Helm, 1987), H. Machin and V. Wright (eds), *Economic Policy and Policy-making under the Mitterrand Presidency* (Pinter, 1984), A. Daley (ed.), *The Mitterrand Era* (Macmillan, 1996) and M. Maclean (ed.), *The Mitterrand Years: Legacy and Evaluation* (Macmillan, 1998).

For an informative and highly entertaining account of Mitterrand's attitude towards politics in the 1980s see F.-O. Giesberg, *Le Président* (Seuil, 1990).

For reflexions on the 'normalization' of French politics since the election of Mitterrand in 1981 see A. Duhamel, *Les habits neufs de la politique* (Flammarion, 1989), F. Furet, J. Julliard and P. Rosanvallon, *La République du centre* (Calmann Lévy, 1988), M. Duverger, *La nostalgie de l'impuissance* (Albin Michel, 1988) and R. Rémond, *La politique n'est plus ce qu'elle était* (Calmann Lévy, 1993). For a more critical account, see N. Hewlett, *Modern French Politics. Analysing Conflict and Consensus since 1945* (Polity, 1998).

J. Hollifield and G. Ross (eds), *Searching for the New France* (Routledge 1991), is an in-depth but accessible dissection of social and political developments in France since the publication of S. Hoffmann (ed.), *In Search of France* (Harvard University Press, 1963) which is itself still highly instructive.

### The left

There are many very good sources in both English and French on the left in France. J. Touchard, *La gauche en France depuis 1900* (Seuil, 1981) is a good starting point, as is G. Lefranc, *Les gauches en France 1789–1973* (Payot, 1974). In English, R. W. Johnson, *The Long March of the French Left* (Macmillan, 1981) is good on the left's slow road to power and J. Jenson and G. Ross, 'On the Roller Coaster: The French Left 1945–88', *New Left Review*, No 171 (Sept./Oct., 1988) is a good historical overview from a viewpoint which is critical both of the turn to the right on the part of the *Parti socialiste* and of the Stalinist nature of the *Parti communiste.*

More specifically on the *Parti socialiste*, H. Portelli, *Le socialisme français tel qu'il est* (PUF, 1980) is thought-provoking on the history of the party, where he argues that the PS is really a new incarnation of the *Parti radical*, but not a true socialist party. For a Marxist history of the PS see J. Kergoat, *Le Parti socialiste* (Sycomore, 1983). In English, D. Bell and B. Criddle, *The French Socialist Party*, 2nd edn (Clarendon, 1988) is a very thorough history and for an analysis of the Marxist-leaning wing of the PS see D. Hanley, *Keeping left? CERES and the French Socialist Party* (Manchester University Press, 1986). See also A. Cole, *François Mitterrand. A Study in Political Leadership* (Routledge, 1994) and H. Portelli, *Le parti socialiste*, 2nd edn (Montchrestien, 1998).

On the Communist Party, J. Fauvet, *Histoire du parti communiste*, 2nd edn (Fayard, 1977) is a comprehensive account and M. Aradeth, *The French Communist Party. A critical history (1920–1984)* (Manchester University Press, 1984) is useful as well. T. Judt, *Marxism and the French Left* (Clarendon, 1986) deals with the PCF and A. Kriegel, *Les Communistes français* (Seuil, 1970) contains all the insight of an ex-Communist. For party policy during the 1970s Union of the Left period, it is well worth looking at Parti communiste français and Parti socialiste, *Programme commun de gouvernement* (Editions sociales, 1972). Because of the crisis and decline of the PCF since 1981 there has been less published on it, but see the article by J. Ranger, 'Le déclin du parti communiste français', in *Revue française de science politique*, Vol 36, No 1, February 1986 and G. Ross, 'Organisation and Strategy in the Decline of French Communism', in *Socialist Register 1988* (Merlin Press, 1988). Communist leader Robert Hue has written several books, including *Communisme: un nouveau projet* (Stock, 1999).

There is relatively little published on the far left in France, but on the *Parti socialiste unifié* see J-P. Kesler, *De la gauche dissidente au nouveau Parti Socialiste, les minorités qui ont rénové le PS* (Bibliothèque historique Privat, 1990) and also V. Fisera and B. Jenkins, 'The Unified Socialist Party since 1968', in D. Bell (ed.), *Contemporary French Political Parties* (Croom Helm, 1982). More generally there is T. Pfister, *Tout savoir sur le gauchisme* (Filipacchi, 1972) and C. Hauss, *The New Left in France* (Greenwood Press, 1978). On Trotskyism, see Y. Craipeau, *Le mouvement trotskiste en France* (Syros, 1971). H. Hamon and P. Rotman, *Génération*, 2 vols (Seuil, 1987 and 1989) looks in detail at the rise and decline of the New Left before and after 1968 and in particular at the individuals associated with it.

## The right

The classic study of the history of the right in France is R. Rémond, *Les droites en France* (Aubier Montaigne, 1982) where the author explains his thesis as to the three different right-wing currents (bonapartist, liberal and counter-revolutionary). A newer, but now also classic, history is J.-F. Sirinelli (ed.), *Histoire des droites en France*, 3 vols (Gallimard, 1992). An examination of the various parties on the right during the 1980s appeared in the December 1990 *Revue française de science politique*, Vol 40, No 6. Also see C. Ysmal, *Demain la droite* (Grasset, 1984) and D. Calderon, *La droite française* (Éditions sociales, 1985).

On Gaullism there are many good sources, including J. Charlot, *Le Gaullisme* (A. Colin, 1970), A. Hartley, *Gaullism; The Rise and Fall of a Political Movement* (Routledge, 1972) and J. Touchard, *Le Gaullisme 1940–1969* (Seuil, 1978). By far the best biography of de Gaulle is J. Lacouture, *De Gaulle*, 3 vols (Seuil, 1984, 1985, 1986). Publications on the Gaullist movement in the 1980s include T. Desjardins, *Les Chiraquiens* (Table Ronde, 1986) and A. Knapp, 'Un parti comme les autres: Jacques Chirac and the Rally for the Republic', in A. Cole (ed.), *French Political Parties in Transition* (Dartmouth Publishing, 1990). A. Knapp, *Gaullism since de Gaulle* (Dartmouth, 1994) is very thorough and informative. See also the special issue of *Pouvoirs*, No 28, 1984, 'Le RPR'. On the RPR leader, F. O. Giesbert, *Jacques Chirac* (Seuil, 1987) is well worth reading.

A thorough history of the centre-right is given in M. Anderson, *Conservative Politics in France* (Allen and Unwin, 1974) and on Giscard d'Estaing and fellow Republicans see 'Le Giscardisme', special issue of *Pouvoirs*, No 9, 1979, B. Lecomte and C. Sauvage, *Les Giscardiens* (Albin Michel, 1978) and D. Séguin, *Les nouveaux giscardiens* (Calmann Lévy, 1979). From the horse's mouth, V. Giscard d'Estaing, *La démocratie française* (Fayard, 1976) is a clear guide to his liberal right ideology.

On the extreme right, J.-C. Petitfils, *L'extrême droite* (PUF, 1983) was the best overview before the rise of the *Front national*; see also S. Hoffmann, *Le mouvement Poujade* (Presses de la Fondation nationale des sciences politiques, 1956). Since then there has been S. Dumont, *Le système Le Pen* (Editions ouvrières, 1985), P. Milza, *Fascisme français passé et présent* (Flammarion, 1987), the rigorous N. Mayer and P. Perrineau (eds), *Le Front national à découvert* (Presses de la Fondation nationale des sciences politiques, 1989) and the fascinating A. Tristan, *Au Front* (Gallimard, 1988) where the author posed as a FN militant and then exposed the party in this book. See also M. Winock, *Histoire de l'extrême droite en France* (Seuil, 1993). Analyses from the 1990s include N. Mayer and P. Perrineau (eds), *Le Front national à découvert* (Presses de Science Po, 1996), A. N. Mayer, *Ces Français qui votent Front national* (Flammarion, 1999), P. Perrineau, *Le symptôme Le Pen. Radiographie des électeurs du Front national* (Fayard, 1997), P.-A. Taguieff and M. Tribalat, *Face au Front national. Arguments pour une contre-offensive* (La Découverte, 1998) and P. Fysh and J. Wolfreys, *The Politics of Racism in France* (Macmillan, 1998).

### Greens

In-depth publications on the green movement are rather few and far between, but see F. Faucher, *Les habits verts de la politique* (Presses de Science Po, 1999). See also P. Hainsworth, 'Breaking the mould: the Greens in the French Party System', in A. Cole (ed.), *French Political Parties in Transition* (Dartmouth Publishing, 1990), V. Hoffmann-Martinot, 'Grüne and Verts: Two Faces of European Ecologism', *West European Politics*, Vol 14, No 4, October 1991, and G. Saintenay, 'Écologistes: la désunion fait la force', *Revue politique et parlementaire*, No 2, 1992.

### Trade unions

Thorough publications comprising an overview of trade unions tend to be some years out of date, but see S. Béroud, R. Mouriaux and M. Vakaloulis, *Le mouvement social en France* (La Dispute, 1998), M. Borrel, *Conflits du travail, changement social et politique en France depuis 1950* (L'Harmattan, 1996), D. Labbé, *Syndicats et syndiqués en France depuis 1945* (L'Harmattan, 1996) and J.-F. Amadieu, *Les syndicats en miettes* (Seuil, 1999). See also G. Geledan, *Les syndicats* (Hatier, 1978), L. Last, *Les organisations du mouvement ouvrier aujourd'hui* (Editions Ouvrières, 1977) and J.-D. Reynaud, *Les syndicats en France* (Seuil, 1975), which are all well worth consulting. René Mouriaux has established himself as the foremost expert on French trade unions and among his other invaluable contributions there are *La CGT* (Seuil, 1982), *Les syndicats dans la société française* (Presses de la Fondation nationale des sciences politiques, 1983), *Le syndicalisme face à la crise* (Éditions de la Découverte, 1986) and *La CFDT* (Economica, 1989). In English, there is G. Ross, *Workers and Communists in France: From Popular Front to Eurocommunism* (University of California Press, 1982). For an analysis of conflict since 1995 see G. Groux, *Vers un renouveau du conflit social* (Bayard, 1998).

On the CNPF see J.-M. Martin, *Le CNPF* (PUF, 1983) and H. Weber, *Le parti des patrons: le CNPF 1946–1986* (Seuil, 1986).

### Foreign policy

The best overview of foreign policy since 1945 is found in A. Grosser, *Affaires extérieures: la politique de la France 1944–1984* (Flammarion, 1984) and there is also '1936–1986, 50 ans de politique étrangère de la France', special issue of the excellent journal, *Politique étrangère*, No 1, Spring 1986 and A. Dulphy, *La politique extérieure de la France depuis 1945* (Nathan, 1994).

On decolonization see H. Grimal, *La décolonisation, 1919–1963* (A. Colin, 1965) and the very interesting J. Ambler, *The French Army in Politics 1945–1962* (Ohio State University Press, 1966). More specifically, on Indo-China there is J. Lacouture and P. Devilliers, *Vietnam: de la guerre française à la guerre américaine* (Seuil, 1969) and R. Irving, *The First Indo-China War* (Croom Helm, 1975). On Algeria see B. Droz and E. Lever, *Histoire de la Guerre d'Algérie* (Seuil, 1982), C. Ageron, *Histoire de l'Algérie contemporaine* (PUF, 1980) and A. Horne, *A Savage War of Peace. Algeria 1954–1962* (Macmillan, 1977). For the Suez episode see H. Azeau, *Le piège de Suez* (Laffont, 1984) and H. Thomas, *The Suez Affair* (Weidenfeld & Nicolson, 1986).

On the construction of Europe see R. Mowat, *Creating the European Community* (Blandford Press, 1973) and, more specifically, D. Bahu-Leyser, *De Gaulle, les Français et l'Europe* (PUF, 1981).

More generally on de Gaulle's foreign policy, E. Kolodziej, *French International Policy under de Gaulle and Pompidou* (Cornell University Press, 1974) is excellent and much can be learned from de Gaulle's *Mémoires*. For Giscard d'Estaing's foreign policy, S. Cohen and M.-C. Smouts (eds), *La Politique extérieure de Valéry Giscard d'Estaing* (Presses de la Fondation nationale des sciences politiques, 1985) is very good, as is H. Simonion, *The Privileged Partnership: Franco-German Relations in the European Community, 1964–84* (Clarendon, 1985).

On Mitterrand, see F. Mitterrand, *Réflexions sur la politique étrangère de la France* (Fayard, 1986), A. Levy, 'Foreign Policy: Business as usual?', in S. Mazey and M. Newman (eds), *Mitterrand's France* (Croom Helm, 1987) and S. Cohen, *François le gaullien et Mitterrand l'européen*, in *L'Histoire*, No 143, April 1991.

## Useful websites

Banque de données sociales et politiques: http://solcidsp.upmf-grenoble.fr

Science Po Paris: http://www.sciences-po.fr

CEVIPOF: http://www.msh-paris.fr/centre/cevipof

CFDT: http://www.cfdt.fr

CGT: http://cgt.fr

FO: http://www.force-ouvrière.fr

PCF: http://www.front-nat.fr

PCF: http://www.pcf.fr

RPR: http://www.rpr.asso.fr

UDF: http://www.udf.org

Les Verts: http://www.verts.imaginet.fr/toutvert.html

TEXT 1.1

## Discours prononcé par le général de Gaulle à Bayeux, le 16 juin 1946

Au cours d'une période de temps qui ne dépasse pas deux fois la vie d'un homme, la France fut envahie sept fois et a pratiqué treize régimes, car tout se tient dans les malheurs d'un peuple. Tant de secousses ont accumulé dans notre vie publique des poisons dont s'intoxique notre vieille propension gauloise aux divisions et aux querelles. Les épreuves inouïes que nous venons de traverser n'ont fait, naturellement, qu'aggraver cet état de choses. La situation actuelle du monde où, derrière des idéologies opposées, se confrontent des puissances entre lesquelles nous sommes placés, ne laisse pas d'introduire dans nos luttes politiques un facteur de trouble passionné. Bref, la rivalité des partis revêt chez nous un caractère fondamental, qui met toujours tout en question et sous lequel s'estompent trop souvent les intérêts supérieurs du pays. Il y a là un fait patent, qui tient au tempérament national, aux péripéties de l'Histoire et aux ébranlements du présent, mais dont il est indispensable à l'avenir du pays et de la démocratie que nos institutions tiennent compte et se gardent, afin de préserver le crédit des lois, la cohésion des gouvernements, l'efficience des administrations, le prestige et l'autorité de l'État.

C'est qu'en effet, le trouble dans l'État a pour conséquence inéluctable la désaffection des citoyens à l'égard des institutions. Il suffit alors d'une occasion pour faire apparaître la menace de la dictature. D'autant plus que l'organisation en quelque sorte mécanique de la société moderne rend chaque jour plus nécessaires et plus désirés le bon ordre dans la direction et le fonctionnement régulier des rouages. Comment et pourquoi donc ont fini chez nous la I$^{re}$, la II$^{e}$, la III$^{e}$ Républiques? Comment et pourquoi donc la démocratie italienne, la République allemande de Weimar, la République espagnole, firent-elles place aux régimes que l'on sait? Et pourtant, qu'est la dictature, sinon une grande aventure? Sans doute, ses débuts semblent avantageux. Au milieu de l'enthousiasme des uns et de la résignation des autres, dans la rigueur de l'ordre qu'elle impose, à la faveur d'un décor éclatant et d'une propagande à sens unique, elle prend d'abord un tour de dynamisme qui fait contraste avec l'anarchie qui l'avait précédée. Mais c'est le destin de la dictature d'exagérer ses entreprises. A mesure que se font jour parmi les citoyens l'impatience des contraintes et la nostalgie de la liberté, il lui faut à tout prix leur offrir en compensation des réussites sans cesse plus étendues. La nation devient une machine à laquelle le maître imprime une accélération effrénée. Qu'il s'agisse de desseins intérieurs ou extérieurs, les buts, les risques, les efforts, dépassent peu à peu toute mesure. A chaque pas se dressent, au dehors et au dedans, des obstacles multipliés. A la fin, le ressort se brise. L'édifice grandiose s'écroule dans le malheur et dans le sang. La nation se retrouve rompue, plus bas qu'elle n'était avant que l'aventure commençât.

Il suffit d'évoquer cela pour comprendre à quel point il est nécessaire que nos institutions démocratiques nouvelles compensent, par elles-mêmes, les effets de notre perpétuelle effervescence politique. Il y a là, au surplus, pour nous une question de vie ou de mort, dans le monde et au siècle où nous sommes, où la position, l'indépendance et jusqu'à l'existence de notre pays et de notre Union française se trouvent bel et bien en jeu. Certes, il est de l'essence même de la démocratie que les opinions s'expriment et qu'elles s'efforcent, par le suffrage, d'orienter suivant leurs conceptions l'action publique et la législation. Mais aussi, tous les principes et toutes les expériences exigent que les pouvoirs publics: législatif, exécutif, judiciaire, soient nettement séparés et fortement équilibrés et qu'au-dessus des contingences politiques soit établi un arbitrage national qui fasse valoir la continuité au milieu des combinaisons.

Il est clair et il est entendu que le vote définitif des lois et des budgets revient à une Assemblée élue au suffrage universel et direct. Mais le premier mouvement d'une telle Assemblée ne comporte pas nécessairement une clairvoyance et une sérénité entières. Il faut donc attribuer à une deuxième Assemblée, élue et composée d'une autre manière, la fonction d'examiner publiquement ce que la première a pris en considération, de formuler des amendements, de proposer des projets. Or, si les grands courants de politique générale sont naturellement reproduits dans le sein de la Chambre des Députés, la vie locale, elle aussi, a ses tendances et ses droits. Elle les a dans la Métropole. Elle les a, au premier chef, dans les territoires d'Outre-mer, qui se rattachent à l'Union française par des liens très divers. Elle les a dans cette Sarre à qui la nature des choses, découverte par notre victoire, désigne une fois de plus sa place auprès de nous, les fils des Francs. L'avenir des 110 millions d'hommes et de femmes qui vivent sous notre drapeau est dans une organisation de forme fédérative, que le temps précisera peu à peu, mais dont notre Constitution nouvelle doit marquer le début et ménager le développement.

Tout nous conduit donc à instituer une deuxième Chambre, dont, pour l'essentiel, nos Conseils généraux et municipaux éliront les membres. Cette Chambre complétera la première en l'amenant, s'il y a lieu, soit à réviser ses propres projets, soit à en examiner d'autres, et en faisant valoir dans la confection des lois ce facteur d'ordre administratif qu'un collège purement politique a forcément tendance à négliger. Il sera normal d'y introduire, d'autre part, des représentants des organisations économiques, familiales, intellectuelles, pour que se fasse entendre, au-dedans même de l'État, la voix des grandes activités du pays. Réunis aux élus des assemblées locales des territoires d'Outre-mer, les membres de cette Assemblée formeront le Grand Conseil de l'Union française, qualifié pour délibérer des lois et des problèmes intéressant l'Union: budgets, relations extérieures, rapports intérieurs, défense nationale, économie, communications.

Du Parlement, composé de deux Chambres et exerçant le pouvoir législatif, il va de soi que le pouvoir exécutif ne saurait procéder, sous peine d'aboutir à cette confusion des pouvoirs dans laquelle le Gouvernement ne serait bientôt plus rien qu'un assemblage de délégations. Sans doute aura-t-il fallu, pendant la période transitoire où nous sommes, faire élire par l'Assemblée Nationale

Constituante le Président du Gouvernement provisoire, puisque, sur la table rase, il n'y avait aucun autre procédé acceptable de désignation. Mais il ne peut y avoir là qu'une disposition du moment. En vérité, l'unité, la cohésion, la discipline intérieure du Gouvernement de la France doivent être des choses sacrées, sous peine de voir rapidement la direction même du pays impuissante et disqualifiée. Or, comment cette unité, cette cohésion, cette discipline, seraient-elles maintenues à la longue, si le pouvoir exécutif émanait de l'autre pouvoir, auquel il doit faire équilibre, et si chacun des membres du Gouvernement, lequel est collectivement responsable devant la représentation nationale tout entière, n'était, à son poste, que le mandataire d'un parti?

C'est donc du Chef de l'État, placé au-dessus des partis, élu par un collège qui englobe le Parlement mais beaucoup plus large et composé de manière à faire de lui le Président de l'Union française en même temps que celui de la République, que doit procéder le pouvoir exécutif. Au Chef de l'État la charge d'accorder l'intérêt général quant au choix des hommes avec l'orientation qui se dégage du Parlement. A lui la mission de nommer les ministres et, d'abord, bien entendu, le Premier, qui devra diriger la politique et le travail du Gouvernement. Au Chef de l'État la fonction de promulguer les lois et de prendre les décrets, car c'est envers l'État tout entier que ceux-ci et celles-là engagent les citoyens. A lui la tâche de présider les Conseils du Gouvernement et d'y exercer cette influence de la continuité dont une nation ne se passe pas. A lui l'attribution de servir d'arbitre au-dessus des contingences politiques, soit normalement par le Conseil, soit, dans les moments de grave confusion, en invitant le pays à faire connaître par des élections sa décision souveraine. A lui, s'il devait arriver que la patrie fût en péril, le devoir d'être le garant de l'indépendance nationale et des traités conclus par la France.

Des Grecs, jadis, demandaient au sage Solon: 'Quelle est la meilleure Constitution?' Il répondait: 'Dites-moi, d'abord, pour quel peuple et à quelle époque?' Aujourd'hui, c'est du peuple français et des peuples de l'Union française qu'il s'agit, et à une époque bien dure et bien dangereuse! Prenons-nous tels que nous sommes. Prenons le siècle comme il est. Nous avons à mener à bien, malgré d'immenses difficultés, une rénovation profonde qui conduise chaque homme et chaque femme de chez nous à plus d'aisance, de sécurité, de joie, et qui nous fasse plus nombreux, plus puissants, plus fraternels. Nous avons à conserver la liberté sauvée avec tant et tant de peine. Nous avons à assurer le destin de la France au milieu de tous les obstacles qui se dressent sur sa route et sur celle de la paix. Nous avons à déployer, parmi nos frères les hommes, ce dont nous sommes capables, pour aider notre pauvre et vieille mère, la Terre. Soyons assez lucides et assez forts pour nous donner et pour observer des règles de vie nationale qui tendent à nous rassembler quand, sans relâche, nous sommes portés à nous diviser contre nous-mêmes! Toute notre Histoire, c'est l'alternance des immenses douleurs d'un peuple dispersé et des fécondes grandeurs d'une nation libre groupée sous l'égide d'un État fort . . .

(C. de Gaulle, *Discours et messages, vol. 2, 1946–58,* Plon, 1970, pp.649–52.)

## Exercices

### Lexique

Expliquez les mots et expressions suivants:

tout se tient (ll.2–3)
une propension à (l.4)
la situation . . . ne laisse pas de (ll.6–8)
tenir compte de (l.14)
se garder de (l.14)
les rouages (l.22)
se faire jour (l.31)
la clairvoyance (l.54)
au premier chef (l.61)
le mandataire (l.95)
mener à bien (l.116)
sous l'égide de (l.128)

### Grammaire et stylistique

(a) Trouvez les quinze occurrences du subjonctif dans ce texte en justifiant chaque fois le mode et le temps. 'Il est clair et il est entendu que le vote . . . revient' (l.52): pourquoi n'emploie-t-on pas le subjonctif dans cette phrase? Récrivez la phrase à la négative ('il n'est pas clair que'). 'les obstacles qui se dressent sur sa route' (l.121): subjonctif, ou non? 'des règles de vie qui tendent à nous rassembler' (ll.124–5): subjonctif ou non? Donnez la règle des subjonctifs en propositions relatives.

(b) 'Sans doute aurait-il fallu . . .' (l.84): expliquez l'inversion du sujet. Donnez une alternative en style plus parlé. Et faites vous-même des phrases commençant par peut-être, ainsi, sans doute, etc.

(c) 'C'est du Chef de l'État . . . que doit procéder le pouvoir exécutif' (ll.96–9). Pourquoi la phrase est-elle ainsi renversée? Quel est le mot mis en relief? Dans quelle intention? Analysez d'autres procédés de mise en relief dans le reste du paragraphe.

### Compréhension

(a) Comment de Gaulle explique-t-il les divisions qui dominent d'après lui la vie politique française?

(b) Quelles sont les différences entre le pouvoir législatif, le pouvoir exécutif et le pouvoir judiciaire?

(c) Décrivez le rôle (i) de la Chambre des Députés et (ii) du Président, selon le projet exposé dans ce texte.

### Questions orales ou écrites

(a) 'Dans le Discours de Bayeux, de Gaulle décrit une constitution peu démocratique.' Commentez.

(b) Faut-il avoir des constitutions différentes pour des peuples et des époques différentes (l.113)? Ou peut-on définir un système démocratique valable pour toute société et toute époque?

(c) Dans quelle mesure François Mitterrand aurait-il approuvé le Discours de Bayeux? Aurait-il changé d'avis? Si oui, pourquoi?

TEXT 1.2

## Le modèle bureaucratique français: la société bloquée

Résumons brièvement les caractéristiques essentielles de ce système. C'est naturellement un système *extrêmement centralisé.* Mais le sens profond de cette centralisation, que tous les observateurs s'accordent à reconnaître, n'est pas du tout de concentrer un pouvoir absolu au sommet de la pyramide, mais de placer une distance ou un écran protecteur suffisant entre ceux qui ont le droit de prendre une décision et ceux qui seront affectés par cette décision. Le pouvoir qui tend à se concentrer effectivement au sommet de la pyramide est un pouvoir surtout formel, qui se trouve paralysé par le manque d'informations et de contacts vivants. Ceux qui décident n'ont pas les moyens de connaissance suffisants des aspects pratiques des problèmes qu'ils ont à traiter. Ceux qui ont ces connaissances n'ont pas le pouvoir de décision. Le fossé entre les deux groupes, ou plutôt entre les deux rôles, se reproduit presque fatalement. Il constitue un excellent moyen de protection pour les supérieurs qui n'ont pas à craindre de pâtir des conséquences de leurs décisions et pour les subordonnés qui n'ont pas à redouter l'intrusion de leurs supérieurs dans leurs problèmes.

Cette tradition de centralisation est liée à une autre caractéristique moins souvent reconnue, mais tout aussi essentielle, *la stratification.* Les administrations françaises sont très fortement stratifiées selon les lignes fonctionnelles, mais surtout hiérarchiques. Les passages de catégorie à catégorie sont difficiles et les communications entre catégories mauvaises. A l'intérieur de chaque catégorie, la règle égalitaire prévaut et la pression du groupe sur l'individu est considérable . . .

*La société bloquée*

La société bloquée, en effet, est fondée sur une opposition constante entre des groupes toujours négatifs et toujours conservateurs et des individus – les membres de ces groupes –, à qui la protection que leur donne leur appartenance permet de manifester en toute irresponsabilité leur créativité personnelle. Révolutionnaire comme individu, conservateur comme membre d'un groupe, le citoyen de la société bloquée gagne sur les deux tableaux. Mais les institutions dont il fait partie seraient condamnées à l'immobilisme si des crises ne survenaient pour assurer les indispensables réajustements. Alors, dans de brefs moments où l'effervescence créatrice des individus peut briser les barrières de groupe, un nouvel équilibre s'établit dans une mêlée en général aveugle. Les résultats sont sans commune mesure avec les vœux des participants, et l'énergie dépensée, les traits fondamentaux du système demeurent, mais un certain nombre de problèmes ont été résolus.

Ce phénomène est particulièrement net dans notre système politique. Quand un système se trouve aussi parfaitement intégré et rendu aussi rigide par le caractère monolithique de son instrument administratif, de sorte qu'il n'y ait rien qui compte (sauf des protections) entre l'État et le citoyen, ce système a une force d'inertie considérable, il résiste très longtemps aux pressions avec la force de sa surdité et de son aveuglement. Mais quand il se trouve mis en mouvement à travers une crise, il est très difficile de l'arrêter. Quelques douzaines d'étudiants peuvent, par une réaction en chaîne imprévue, mettre en danger le régime tout entier . . .

*Les problèmes de la société française*

Le poids de la centralisation bureaucratique, l'impact d'une longue tradition de commandement militaire, le développement d'organisations industrielles qui ont adopté le modèle d'organisation que leur offrait l'État ou l'Armée nous ont habitués à un modèle général de centralisation que tempère seulement l'anarchie des privilèges et les bons sentiments du paternalisme. Un tel système s'accompagne naturellement de l'existence d'un fossé entre dirigeants et exécutants, d'un style rigide de relations entre groupes humains, d'un modèle contraignant de jeu fondé sur la défense et la protection et d'une passion générale de tous les individus pour la sécurité . . .

(M. Crozier, *La société bloquée,* Éditions du Seuil, 1970, pp.94–5, 172–3, 89.)

## Exercices

### *Lexique*

Expliquez les mots et expressions suivants:

un pouvoir formel (ll.7–8)
pâtir (l.14)
prévaloir (sur) (l.21)
sur les deux tableaux (l.29)
une mêlée (l.33)
sans commune mesure avec (l.34)

### *Compréhension*

(a) Précisez la notion de 'catégorie' administrative (ll.19–21).
(b) Ll.43–45: 'Quelques douzaines d'étudiants peuvent, par une réaction en chaîne imprévue, mettre en danger le régime tout entier.' Précisez l'allusion.
(c) Donnez les caractéristiques du modèle bureaucratique français, ses forces et ses faiblesses.
(d) Expliquez comment 'la protection que leur donne leur appartenance [au groupe] permet [aux individus] de manifester en toute irresponsabilité leur créativité personnelle' (ll.26–27).

### *Questions orales ou écrites*

(a) Comparez les systèmes administratifs français avec ceux de votre pays en montrant – comme le fait l'auteur dans le texte – dans quelle mesure ces systèmes reflètent les peuples qu'ils servent.
(b) Comment 'débloquer' le modèle bureaucratique français?

TEXT 1.3

## Trois tracts de mars–juin 1968

*Des incidents éclatent, le 14 mars, au cours de R. Francès, professeur de psychologie. Des étudiants en sociologie mettent en cause les résultats du dernier examen partiel, résultats qu'ils attribuent – sans aucun doute à tort – à des pressions administratives; ils demandent que l'examen fasse appel 'moins à la mémoire qu'aux qualités d'initiative et de recherche personnelle'. Le professeur répond qu'en première année le travail doit consister avant tout 'dans l'acquisition d'habitudes de formulation précise des idées, de compréhension exacte des lois et des recherches fondamentales . . . L'utilisation sérieuse et approfondie d'une bibliographie ne* [*lui*] *semble possible qu'à la suite d'une initiation de ce genre . . .' Un tract est distribué à cette occasion, celui des* Oies gavées, *texte en tout point remarquable, même si la revendication est utopique et certaines attaques personnelles injustes.*

*Nanterre ou la formation d'oies gavées*

Léthargie, déception, dégoût forment l'atmosphère quotidienne de tout amphithéâtre, et cela n'est pas particulier à la 1ère année. Écroulement de la vocation profonde, manque de débouchés et de considération, métier qui se réduit en général à faire compter des boules rouges et des boules bleues à des enfants, sont pour des psychologues et sociologues l'aboutissement d'années d''études' où toute valeur réelle, où tout dynamisme intellectuel s'est fait peu à peu ronger par les exigences d'un enseignement plus ou moins brillant en sa superficie, mais illusoire et même sclérosant en son substratum. Que nous propose en effet la faculté, alors que nous venons y chercher des voies d'ouverture d'esprit? Un paternalisme primaire qui, en favorisant l'élevage 'd'oies gavées' (expression du professeur Leprince-Ringuet), nous maintient dans la stérilité intellectuelle.

Les problèmes nous apparaissent clairement s'enraciner dans la structure de l'enseignement qui nous est donné, d'une part, dans le mode de passer et de corriger les examens, d'autre part:

L'ENSEIGNEMENT

1. Actuel.

Tout d'abord cet enseignement nous lasse avant de nous dégoûter par son caractère mécanique, figé et mort, par la banalité et l'extrême fadeur avec lesquelles il est dispensé. L'étudiant, non concerné par la fadeur et maintenu dans la passivité d'esprit, n'est plus qu'un scribe qui calque la terne parole de l'instituteur; et ces calques lui seront précieux puisqu'il les projettera, à la virgule près, comme l'instituteur, lui, l'exige, sur ses feuilles d'examens!

2. Exigé.

Nous exigeons la fin d'un enseignement illusoire et sclérosant, la fin du paternalisme primaire, la fin de la faculté des 'oies gavées'. Nous exigeons la naissance d'un réel dialogue, d'une véritable coopération professeurs-étudiants. Nous exigeons que la vie, l'ardeur, la recherche, le vrai travail en commun remplacent enfin la fadeur et la léthargie des amphithéâtres. Nous exigeons que les cours soient polycopiés bien avant les réunions – ils seront ainsi mieux élaborés – et qu'ils comportent enfin une incitation à la réflexion, à la recherche par des données bibliographiques correspondant à des problèmes précis. Les étudiants pourront alors travailler enfin intelligemment de vrais problèmes, étudier les relations bibliographiques, débattre déjà entre eux, lors de 'groupes de travail', tous les fruits de leurs recherches personnelles. Ils arriveront ainsi avec ardeur aux cours puisque ces cours seront enfin des réunions, des débats (méthode inaugurée avec fécondité par M. Ricœur, à qui nous demandons en passant trois sujets au choix aux examens et de ne pas nous poser de sujets tels: 'Jugement, erreur, volonté' qui ne peuvent être traités que comme questions de cours ou alors comme pur bavardage stérile) où le dialogue sera établi entre le professeur et les étudiants tel que ces derniers qui connaîtront déjà leurs cours puissent demander l'éclaircissement de questions délicates.

LES EXAMENS

1. Actuels.

Le calquage: de toute évidence, un élève de 4$^{e}$ de collège exulterait devant de telles épreuves qui lui rappelleraient ses plus faciles interrogations écrites. Il excellerait à ces examens, car il se prêterait parfaitement à ces contrôles du pouvoir mnémonique primaire. Il se ferait un plaisir de répondre à la perfection sous forme de réflexes conditionnés, à la demande de la définition de la société industrielle par Aron, à celle des lois de Hume sur l'attraction des idées, à celle de la date d'invention de tel test, à celle de l'utilisation d'un test ou de définitions de la psychologie génétique. En effet, il retracerait intégralement sur la feuille d'examen, à la virgule près, le passage précis du livre d'Aron ou ceux des cours de MM. Francès et Anzieu qui traitent de ces questions, et il agirait ainsi comme beaucoup d'entre nous ont agi parce qu'ils avaient compris comment satisfaire aux exigences de l'examen, comment recevoir l'approbation de l'enseignement ou tout au moins des assistants. Car il est clair que pour ces derniers, sous l'alibi de la validité de correction, la 'valeur' de la réponse est proportionnelle au degré de qualité du calque du cours, suivant les méthodes dont usaient les instituteurs d'antan pour corriger les fameuses 'copies'.

2. Exigés.

Livre ouvert, justice: nous exigeons que l'examen soit à livre ouvert et tienne ainsi compte avant tout de la capacité d'initiative intellectuelle, du pouvoir d'analyse et de réflexion en profondeur et non comme maintenant d'un simple pouvoir mnémonique primaire et stérile.

Sans doute ce réel examen mettra-t-il en question, de par sa nature, la compétence même de certains assistants d'aujourd'hui trop habitués dans leur correction hâtive et superficielle à ne pas déceler cette capacité d'initiative intellectuelle mais à ne comprendre le donné que par la 'vérité' du calque.

Pour les notes de correction, nous exigeons les mêmes barèmes pour tous les groupes de T.P., c'est-à-dire la double correction obligatoirement et sincèrement effectuée (nous ne devons plus être les boucs émissaires d'assistants frustrés par un manque de rétribution).

Enfin nous exigeons qu'après chaque examen les copies nous soient restituées pour la journée afin que nous puissions discuter de leur valeur lors des 'groupes de travail' qui s'organisent actuellement.

Ces exigences de base sont pour nous vitales, aussi devons-nous en toute urgence les présenter aux enseignants.

*Ce second tract appelle à une manifestation. Il a été produit par les comités d'action étudiants du centre universitaire de Censier à Paris, et est typique de l'esprit révolutionnaire de l'époque.*

*'Producteurs sauvons-nous nous-mêmes'*
*A dix millions de grévistes, à tous les travailleurs*

– Non aux solutions parlementaires, où de Gaulle s'en va et le patronat reste.

– Non aux négociations au sommet qui ne font que prolonger le capitalisme moribond.

– Assez de référendum. Plus de cirque.

– Ne laissons personne parler à notre place. Maintenons l'occupation de tous les lieux de travail.

– Pour continuer le combat, mettons tous les secteurs de l'économie touchés par la grève au service des travailleurs en lutte.

– Posons dès maintenant les jalons de notre pouvoir de demain (ravitaillement direct, organisation des services publics: transports, information, logement, etc.).

– Dans la rue, dans les comités de base, où que nous soyons, ouvriers, paysans, travailleurs, étudiants, enseignants, lycéens, organisons et coordonnons nos luttes.

POUR L'ABOLITION DU PATRONAT
POUR LE POUVOIR DES TRAVAILLEURS

Tous à la manifestation
Points de départ: 17 heures,
– Clichy
– Stalingrad, métro
– Porte de Montreuil
– Porte des Lilas
– Denfert-Rochereau

*Ce troisième tract provient de Rennes, en Bretagne, ville dans laquelle se trouvent une université et un certain nombre d'industries. Début juin, le mouvement de grèves commence à perdre son souffle et les syndicats sont divisés. Ce tract appelle à continuer le mouvement.*

*Continuons la lutte*

Le grand mouvement de grève engagé semble maintenant, d'après la presse gaulliste, se ralentir, se terminer!

Dans quelques entreprises et dans certains secteurs, en effet, le travail reprend. Mais ces entreprises se font sous la *contrainte policière* (Chèques postaux de Rennes où les flics ont forcé le piquet de grève à coups de grenades), sous *l'intimidation patronale*, et ne traduisent pas la volonté de l'immense majorité des travailleurs.

Nous voulons toujours

– l'abrogation des Ordonnances;
– la garantie des libertés syndicales;
– l'échelle mobile des salaires;
– les 40 heures immédiates;
– le S.M.I.G. à 1 000 F;
– le contrôle des travailleurs sur la gestion des entreprises.

POUR QUI NOUS PREND-ON?

– *Nous savons* que depuis dix ans, ce que le gouvernement nous 'donne', il l'a toujours repris (hausse des prix).

– *Nous savons* que la reprise inconditionnelle du travail nous ferait entrer dans un marché de dupes car le patronat pourrait toujours faire appuyer ses positions par le gouvernement et sa police.

Le gouvernement effrayé de l'ampleur du mouvement national de revendication se livre à un double chantage:

– appel à la violence fasciste (mobilisation de la population non laborieuse appuyée par la police et l'armée);

– manœuvre d'intimidation des masses laborieuses (reprise du travail posée comme préalable au 'dialogue').

ORGANISONS LA GRÈVE.

Unis dans la même lutte, les ouvriers, paysans et étudiants ont organisé un front d'entraide: il faut le renforcer, mais cela ne suffit pas.

Utilisons notre force, organisons nous-même la reprise du travail dans les entreprises de première nécessité pour:

– répondre aux besoins de la population;
– permettre aux grévistes de tenir;
– éviter que ce travail ne profite au patronat.

A Nantes, les grévistes de l'usine alimentaire Saupiquet ont remis les machines en route et ont distribué la production aux ouvriers de la région.

Partout faisons comme eux!

– *pas de reprise du travail sur de vagues promesses;*
– *non au piège des négociations;*
– *non aux élections législatives sous la pression policière.*

Nos usines, nos facultés, nos services publics, *gardons-les*: Faisons-les tourner *nous-mêmes* et *pour nous*!

Comité d'action travailleurs-étudiants de Rennes.

(Présentation d'A. Schnapp et P. Vidal-Naquet, *Journal de la commune étudiante. Textes et documents, novembre 1967 – juin 1968*. Éditions du Seuil, 1969, pp.125–7, 281–2, 783–4.)

## Exercices

### *Lexique*

Expliquez les mots et expressions suivants:

mettre en cause (l.2)
un examen partiel (l.2)
à tort (l.3)
la déception (l.13)
un débouché (l.15)
se réduire à (l.15)
sclérosant (l.20)
le substratum (l.20)
un paternalisme primaire (l.22)
une oie gavée (l.22)
la fadeur (l.32)
calquer (l.33)
à la virgule près (ll.34–35)
un polycopié (l.42)
une question de cours (ll.51–52)
une copie (l.72)
un examen à livre ouvert (l.74)
un T.P. (l.83)
un bouc émissaire (l.84)
un jalon (l.104)
un piquet de grève (l.126)
un marché de dupes (l.140)
un chantage (l.143)

### *Grammaire et stylistique*

(a) 'Plus de cirque' (l.99): l'expression est-elle positive ou négative? Comment peut-on le savoir?
(b) Le texte fait référence à 'l'instituteur' (l.35): quel est l'effet? Précisez le ton.

### *Compréhension*

(a) 'une 4^e^ de collège' (l.57): quel est l'équivalent dans votre pays?
(b) Avez-vous le sentiment que 'léthargie, déception, dégoût forment l'atmosphère quotidienne de tout amphithéâtre' (ll.13–14)? Discutez le mode d'évaluation (c'est-à-dire les examens) que vous propose l'université où vous étudiez en ce moment, et précisez s'il y a lieu, l'évolution des sensibilités et des circonstances depuis les années 60.
(c) Ouvriers, paysans et étudiants peuvent-ils vraiment s'unir dans la même lutte (l.149)? Qualifiez le ton du tract 'Continuons la lutte'. Dégagez ses buts politiques, ses propositions économiques. Des étudiants des années 90 pourraient-ils l'écrire? Justifiez votre réponse.

### *Question orale ou écrite*

(a) Estimez-vous que vos études et en particulier les examens qui les sanctionnent, fassent excessivement appel à la mémoire et insuffisamment à la réflexion? Vous sentez-vous une 'oie gavée'?

TEXT 1.4

## De Gaulle parle

*Une certaine idée de la France*

Toute ma vie, je me suis fait une certaine idée de la France. Le sentiment me l'inspire aussi bien que la raison. Ce qu'il y a, en moi, d'affectif imagine naturellement la France, telle la princesse des contes ou la madone aux fresques des murs, comme vouée à une destinée éminente et exceptionnelle. J'ai, d'instinct, l'impression que la Providence l'a créée pour des succès achevés ou des malheurs exemplaires. S'il advient que la médiocrité marque, pourtant, ses faits et gestes, j'en éprouve la sensation d'une absurde anomalie, imputable aux fautes des Français, non au génie de la patrie. Mais aussi, le côté positif de mon esprit me convainc que la France n'est réellement elle-même qu'au premier rang; que, seules, de vastes entreprises sont susceptibles de compenser les ferments de dispersion que son peuple porte en lui-même; que notre pays, tel qu'il est, parmi les autres, tels qu'ils sont, doit, sous peine de danger mortel, viser haut et se tenir droit. Bref, à mon sens, la France ne peut être la France sans la grandeur.

Cette foi a grandi en même temps que moi dans le milieu où je suis né. Mon père, homme de pensée, de culture, de tradition, était imprégné du sentiment de la dignité de la France. Il m'en a découvert l'Histoire. Ma mère portait à la patrie une passion intransigeante à l'égal de sa piété religieuse. Mes trois frères, ma sœur, moi-même, avions pour seconde nature une certaine fierté anxieuse au sujet de notre pays. Petit Lillois de Paris, rien ne me frappait davantage que les symboles de nos gloires: nuit descendant sur Notre-Dame, majesté du soir à Versailles, Arc de Triomphe dans le soleil, drapeaux conquis frissonnant à la voûte des Invalides. Rien ne me faisait plus d'effet que la manifestation de nos réussites nationales: enthousiasme du peuple au passage du Tsar de Russie, revue de Longchamp, merveilles de l'Exposition, premiers vols de nos aviateurs. Rien ne m'attristait plus profondément que nos faiblesses et nos erreurs révélées à mon enfance par les visages et les propos: abandon de Fachoda, affaire Dreyfus, conflits sociaux, discordes religieuses. Rien ne m'émouvait autant que le récit de nos malheurs passés: rappel par mon père de la vaine sortie du Bourget et de Stains, où il avait été blessé; évocation par ma mère de son désespoir de petite fille à la vue de ses parents en larmes: 'Bazaine a capitulé!'

Adolescent, ce qu'il advenait de la France, que ce fût le sujet de l'Histoire ou l'enjeu de la vie publique, m'intéressait par-dessus tout. J'éprouvais donc de l'attrait, mais aussi de la sévérité, à l'égard de la pièce qui se jouait, sans relâche, sur le forum; entraîné que j'étais par l'intelligence, l'ardeur, l'éloquence qu'y prodiguaient maints acteurs et navré de voir tant de dons gaspillés dans la confusion politique et les divisions nationales. D'autant plus qu'au début du siècle apparaissaient les prodromes de la guerre. Je dois dire que ma prime jeunesse imaginait sans horreur et magnifiait à l'avance cette aventure inconnue. En somme, je ne doutais pas que la France dût traverser des épreuves gigantesques, que l'intérêt de la vie consistait à lui rendre, un jour, quelque service signalé et que j'en aurais l'occasion . . .

*De Gaulle et l'Algérie*

Deux jours avant le référendum, le Général de Gaulle s'adresse aux Français.

ALLOCUTION RADIODIFFUSÉE ET TÉLÉVISÉE
PRONONCÉE AU PALAIS DE L'ÉLYSÉE, LE 6 AVRIL 1962.

Dimanche, va s'accomplir en France un événement d'une immense portée. Chaque Français en sera personnellement l'artisan si, comme je le lui demande, il vote: 'Oui'! au référendum.

Car la très grave question algérienne sera tranchée au fond et le sera par la nation elle-même. Ainsi, trouvera, enfin, sa solution humaine et raisonnable un problème qui, en restant posé depuis 132 ans, a entraîné pour l'Algérie, à côté de réalisations qui lui furent souvent favorables, des drames périodiquement renouvelés et dont le dernier en date fut le plus douleureux de tous, tandis que l'unité de la nation française, son action internationale, les conditions de sa défense, ses possibilités économiques, sociales et financières, en étaient finalement altérées. Ainsi, pourront s'établir dans la paix et l'association, c'est-à-dire conformément au bon sens et à l'amitié, les rapports nouveaux de l'Algérie et de la France.

Déjà, par le référendum, nous avons, en quatre années, réalisé trois changements capitaux, qui n'avaient pu jusqu'alors aboutir malgré d'innombrables épreuves et d'interminables débats. C'est par cette voie, en effet, que nous nous sommes donné des institutions telles que la stabilité, l'autorité, la continuité de l'État ont remplacé un régime de crises, d'impuissance et de confusion. C'est par la même voie que nous avons transformé en rapports de coopération avec douze Républiques africaines et la République malgache les rapports de colonisation que nous appliquions naguère à leurs territoires, d'où résulte dans ce vaste ensemble une situation de paix, de progrès, de compréhension, véritablement exemplaire et qui contraste de saisissante façon avec les troubles, les conflits, les rivalités, dont sont actuellement agitées tant de régions africaines, asiatiques et américaines. C'est par la même voie que nous avons, au moment voulu, reconnu le droit de l'Algérie à l'autodétermination et, du même coup, déclenché l'apaisement, déterminé les dirigeants de la rébellion à en venir aux pourparlers, fait en sorte que toutes tentatives de forcer en sens opposé la volonté du pays ne pouvaient être et ne sont qu'aventures aussi vaines que criminelles.

Mais, dimanche, en rendant définitive et solennelle une décision qui renouvelle le présent et dégage l'avenir, nous, Français, allons, en même temps, consacrer décidément la pratique du référendum, la plus nette, la plus franche, la plus démocratique qui soit. Prévu par la Constitution, le référendum passe ainsi dans nos mœurs, ajoutant quelque chose d'essentiel à l'œuvre législative du Parlement. Désormais, sur un sujet vital pour le pays, chaque citoyen pourra être, comme il l'est à présent, directement appelé à en juger pour sa part et à prendre sa responsabilité. Nul doute que le caractère et le fonctionnement des institutions de la République n'en soient profondément marqués.

Enfin, Françaises, Français! pour le Chef de l'État, qui est en charge de l'intérêt supérieur de la France et qui, à ce titre, demande à chacune et à chacun de vous d'approuver l'action menée dans un domaine dont tout dépend, le témoignage de votre confiance sera le nombre de celles et de ceux qui répondront en votant: 'Oui'!

Toutes ces voix encourageantes, ce seront les chances de la France!

Vive la République!

Vive la France!

*Le dernier Référendum de de Gaulle*

Le Général de Gaulle s'adresse aux Français, deux jours avant la date fixée pour le référendum:

ALLOCUTION RADIODIFFUSÉE ET TÉLÉVISÉE PRONONCÉE AU PALAIS DE L'ÉLYSÉE, LE 25 AVRIL 1969.

. . . Votre réponse va engager le destin de la France, parce que la réforme fait partie intégrante de la participation qu'exige désormais l'équilibre de la société moderne. La refuser, c'est s'opposer dans un domaine essentiel à cette transformation sociale, morale, humaine, faute de laquelle nous irons à de désastreuses secousses. L'adopter, c'est faire un pas décisif sur le chemin qui doit nous mener au progrès dans l'ordre et dans la concorde, en modifiant profondément nos rapports entre Français.

Votre réponse va engager le destin de la France, parce que, si je suis désavoué par une majorité d'entre vous, solennellement, sur ce sujet capital et quels que puissent être le nombre, l'ardeur et le dévouement de l'armée de ceux qui me soutiennent et qui, de toute façon, détiennent l'avenir de la patrie, ma tâche actuelle de Chef de l'État deviendra évidemment impossible et je cesserai aussitôt d'exercer mes fonctions. Alors, comment sera maîtrisée la situation résultant de la victoire négative de toutes ces diverses, disparates et discordantes oppositions, avec l'inévitable retour aux jeux des ambitions, illusions, combinaisons et trahisons, dans l'ébranlement national que provoquera une pareille rupture?

Au contraire, si je reçois la preuve de votre confiance, je poursuivrai mon mandat, j'achèverai, grâce à vous, par la création des régions et la rénovation du Sénat, l'œuvre entreprise il y a dix années pour doter notre pays d'institutions démocratiques adaptées au peuple que nous sommes, dans le monde où nous nous trouvons et à l'époque où nous vivons, après la confusion, les troubles et les malheurs que nous avions traversés depuis des générations. Je continuerai, avec votre appui, de faire en sorte, quoi qu'il arrive, que le progrès soit développé, l'ordre assuré, la monnaie défendue, l'indépendance maintenue, la paix sauvegardée, la France respectée. Enfin, une fois venu le terme régulier, sans déchirement et sans bouleversement, tournant la dernière page du chapitre que, voici quelque trente ans, j'ai ouvert dans notre Histoire, je transmettrai ma charge officielle à celui que vous aurez élu pour l'assumer après moi.

Françaises, Français, dans ce qu'il va advenir de la France, jamais la décision de chacune et de chacun de vous n'aura pesé aussi lourd!

Vive la République!

Vive la France!

(C. de Gaulle, *Mémoires de guerre, l'appel, 1940–1942*, Librairie Plon, 1954, pp.1–2; *Discours et messages*, 'Avec le renouveau (mai 1958 – juillet 1962)', Librairie Plon, 1970, pp.398–9; *Discours et messages*, 'Vers le terme (1966–1969)', Librairie Plon, 1970, pp.405–6.)

## Exercices

### *Lexique*

Expliquez les mots et expressions suivants:

le génie (l.9)
la relâche (l.34)
le prodrome (l.38)
la prime jeunesse (ll.38–39)
le référendum (l.60)
l'autodétermination (f.) (l.72)
déclencher (l.73)
la participation (l.100)
faute de laquelle (l.102)

### *Grammaire et stylistique*

(a) Justifiez les deux imparfaits du subjonctif (ll.32 et 40).
(b) 'Chaque Français en sera personnellement l'artisan si, comme je le lui demande, il vote: "Oui"! au référendum' (ll.48–49). Récrivez la phrase en commençant par 'Tous les Français'. Analysez les différences, en particulier en ce qui concerne l'effet obtenu.
(c) Le mot 'France'. Combien de fois apparaît-il et à quels endroits stratégiques du texte?

### *Compréhension*

(a) 'Rien ne me faisait plus d'effet que la manifestation de nos réussites nationales' (ll.23–24): exprimez l'idée en d'autres termes.
(b) 'Petit Lillois de Paris' (l.20): quelle atmosphère, quelle vie, suggère cette expression?
(c) Expliquez les allusions des lignes 25 à 31: 'revue de Longchamp, merveilles de l'Exposition . . . abandon de Fachoda, affaire Dreyfus, conflits sociaux, discordes religieuses . . . vaine sortie du Bourget . . . Bazaine'.
(d) 'la création des régions et la rénovation du Sénat' (ll.116–17): dans quelle mesure les successeurs de de Gaulle ont-ils rempli ce programme?

### *Questions orales ou écrites*

(a) La France est comparée à 'la princesse des contes ou la madone aux fresques des murs' (ll.4–5). Quels commentaires vous inspirent ces expressions?
(b) La pensée gaullienne a-t-elle évolué entre les trois textes?
(c) Qu'est-ce que le bonapartisme? En trouve-t-on quelque manifestation dans les trois textes donnés?

TEXT 1.5

## La France des années 1970 vue par Valéry Giscard d'Estaing

Depuis deux ans, une œuvre a été entreprise. Parcourons-la:

L'âge de la majorité abaissé à 18 ans;

L'indépendance donnée aux chaînes de télévision; le droit reconnu à l'opposition, et utilisé par elle, de déférer les lois au Conseil constitutionnel; les écoutes téléphoniques supprimées; la censure politique au cinéma abandonnée;

Le même collège rendu obligatoire pour tous les jeunes Français, égalisant davantage leurs chances; un effort d'adaptation des universités à la préparation de la vie active;

L'augmentation du minimum vieillesse de 63%;

Le maximum légal de la durée du travail ramené de 54 à 50 heures; l'âge de la retraite abaissé à 60 ans pour deux millions de travailleurs manuels; la politique contractuelle orientée vers la revalorisation des salaires de ces mêmes travailleurs; les principes d'une réforme progressive de l'entreprise présentés au Parlement.

Les plus-values constitutives d'un revenu imposées, les tantièmes abolis;

L'égalité effective des femmes et des hommes recherchée dans tous les domaines de la vie politique et sociale; l'interruption de grossesse humanisée, la contraception facilitée, l'adoption encouragée;

Notre législation en faveur des handicapés portée au niveau des plus avancées;

Le cours de la justice rendu plus rapide dans les grandes agglomérations; la détention provisoire plus étroitement limitée, la condition pénitentiaire humanisée; le contrôle de l'exécution des peines renforcé;

Un coup d'arrêt donné, dans les villes, au gigantisme destructeur et niveleur; l'amélioration de la qualité de la vie retenue comme objectif essentiel de l'action gouvernementale; l'écologie introduite dans l'étude de tous les grands projets; une politique d'ensemble mise en place pour les espaces verts autour des grandes villes; le sport doté d'un statut moderne; les métiers d'art protégés;

L'impôt des patentes réformé; les collectivités locales progressivement créditées par l'État de l'équivalent de la TVA qui pèse sur leurs investissements; une réflexion entreprise en vue de permettre, dans notre pays de vieille centralisation, l'exercice d'un véritable pouvoir local, et d'abord communal . . .

Une collectivité humaine consciente doit conduire elle-même son évolution. Il appartient aux hommes de notre temps de guider la marche de notre société vers une plus complète unité.

Les mesures propres à accentuer cette évolution sont nécessairement de nature et de portée très diverses. Il ne s'agit pas ici de les détailler, mais d'en fixer le but et d'en définir l'esprit.

Des mots simples suffisent à exprimer l'un et l'autre: justice et solidarité.

Le contenu concret de l'exigence de justice et l'étendue de la solidarité ne sont pas les mêmes d'une époque à l'autre. Le rôle des élus, celui des pouvoirs publics est d'exprimer et d'accomplir, à chaque période, ce qu'appelle la justice dans la conscience collective.

Aujourd'hui, au-delà des doctrines, un corps de convictions communes peut être dégagé sur ce sujet: *la justice consiste en l'élimination de la misère, la disparition des privilèges et la lutte contre les discriminations . . .*

Notre société est fondée sur l'*épanouissement individuel.*

Les pays du tiers-monde n'ont guère le choix. Ils doivent nécessairement penser et agir en termes de masses. Nourrir, vêtir, éduquer, loger les masses, constitue leur tâche prioritaire et ne laisse que peu de place pour la considération de l'individu. Nous devons le garder à l'esprit, pour juger équitablement certaines de leurs décisions.

La société démocratique française doit prendre en compte, elle aussi, les besoins généraux de la collectivité. Mais, en même temps, elle peut désormais se tourner vers l'épanouissement individuel.

Favoriser le développement de chaque personnalité, permettre à chacun de conduire sa vie: cet objectif correspond au stade d'évolution économique libératrice que nous avons atteint. Il répond aux aspirations profondes des Français et à ce qu'il y a de plus caractéristique dans notre culture nationale: le sentiment de la valeur de l'individu et le goût de la liberté.

Une conception collectiviste de l'organisation sociale, dominée par la notion de masse, est à l'opposé de l'évolution souhaitée par notre société. Ceci touche le fond des choses. Il ne suffit pas de poser une couche de peinture, serait-elle tricolore, sur un projet collectiviste pour le rendre approprié au tempérament et aux besoins du peuple français. Il n'y a de projet social valable pour la France que s'il vise à donner un contenu toujours plus large et plus vivant à la liberté individuelle de chacun.

Ceci concerne, bien entendu, les libertés fondamentales chèrement acquises par la nation et que, de façon risible, certains nous invitent à conquérir comme si nous ne les possédions déjà et comme si nous n'étions pas une des très rares fractions de l'humanité à en disposer aujourd'hui.

Ceci concerne également des libertés plus modestes, dont chacune est en contradiction avec une conception collectiviste de l'organisation sociale. Libertés de la vie privée; libertés de la vie professionnelle.

(V. Giscard d'Estaing, *Démocratie française*, Fayard, 1976, pp.16–17, 58, 71–2.)

## Exercices

### *Lexique*

Expliquez les mots et expressions suivants:

| | |
|---|---|
| le collège (l.6) | une plus-value (l.15) |
| la politique contractuelle (ll.11–12) | le tantième (l.15) |

un coup d'arrêt (l.23)
un gigantisme niveleur (l.23)
une patente (l.28)
Ceci touche le fond des choses (ll.61–62)

### Grammaire et stylistique

(a) (L.19): 'au niveau des plus avancées': expliquez l'accord.
(b) 'Il ne suffit pas de poser une couche de peinture, serait-elle tricolore, . . .' (ll.62–63). Récrivez la phrase en utilisant un autre temps du verbe être.
(c) 'Il ne s'agit pas de . . . mais de . . . et de . . .' (ll.36–37); 'le rôle des élus est de . . . et de . . .' (ll.40–41); 'Il répond aux . . . et à . . .' (ll.57–58). Etudiez ces structures et faites des phrases sur le même modèle.

### Compréhension

(a) Ll.58–59: 'ce qu'il y a de plus caractéristique dans notre culture nationale: le sentiment de la valeur de l'individu et le goût de la liberté.' Est-ce vraiment spécifique à la France? Comparez, à l'aide d'exemples, avec votre pays.

### Questions orales ou écrites

(a) Caractérisez la *Démocratie française* du point de vue politique.
(b) 'épanouissement individuel' (l.54): est-ce la même chose que 'démocratie'?
(c) Des années Giscard, quels éléments vous paraissent avoir duré, quelles réformes vous semblent temporaires?

TEXT 1.6

## La CFDT: progresser vers l'autogestion des entreprises

La condition première de cette progression est l'extension du secteur socialisé de l'économie. Mais si l'expropriation du capitalisme, c'est-à-dire la suppression de ses pouvoirs de décision et de gestion à tous les niveaux, est une condition indispensable, elle n'est pas suffisante. L'appropriation réelle des moyens de production par les travailleurs est inséparable d'un développement progressif de l'autogestion dans les entreprises socialisées. Là où les entreprises resteront privées, des moyens seront pris pour limiter l'arbitraire patronal et développer le pouvoir de négociation et de décision des travailleurs et de la collectivité.

Les secteurs clés à socialiser en priorité seront: les établissements de crédit, les groupes dominants de chaque branche, les entreprises industrielles stratégiques, les grands moyens de culture, d'information et de formation.

*1 – La gestion des entreprises socialisées*

• But

Les entreprises socialisées doivent être gérées par les travailleurs selon des modalités qui prennent en compte à la fois:

– le respect des orientations cohérentes du plan démocratique en matière de politique des rémunérations, de maîtrise de l'investissement, d'aménagement du territoire, d'équilibre des échanges extérieurs;

– la décentralisation de la gestion. Le découpage des unités décentralisées où s'expriment les décisions démocratiques doit tenir compte de ce qu'une trop grande dimension peut être un obstacle à la démocratisation.

– la nécessité pour le collectif des travailleurs ou pour l'instance à laquelle ce collectif délègue, sous son contrôle, une partie de ses pouvoirs, de répondre de sa gestion devant la collectivité publique locale, regionale ou nationale.

Les structures à mettre en place tiendront compte des confrontations inévitables à toute vie sociale où la lutte d'influence pour le pouvoir est une réalité permanente:

– au sein des entreprises en fonction du niveau de connaissance des travailleurs, de leurs orientations politiques;

– entre les besoins de la collectivité et la tendance des travailleurs de l'entreprise de conserver la plus large part possible des résultats de la production;

– entre les besoins de la collectivité et la tendance à la prise de responsabilité d'un grand nombre de travailleurs que rien n'a préparé à prendre en main leur avenir et les minorités militantes qui risquent de se sentir seules concernées par les responsabilités de gestion.

Le choix de la prise en charge de la gestion par les travailleurs, le refus de l'étatisme, de la bureaucratie et de la technocratie est un choix lucide, car il tient compte de ces contraintes, de cette complexité pour progresser vers l'autogestion.

• Mesures

**a.** Création d'un conseil d'entreprise composé de représentants élus par les travailleurs, à partir des différents établissements ou services.

Ce conseil assumera à la fois les fonctions d'un conseil d'administration et d'un comité d'entreprise. Par contre, face à lui, les sections syndicales dont les pouvoirs seront étendus, conserveront un rôle d'expression, de contrôle, de contestation centré sur la défense des intérêts des travailleurs. Elles ne devront donc pas être partie prenante des décisions de gestion.

Le conseil d'entreprise:

– élit et contrôle la direction de l'entreprise;

– négocie avec les sections syndicales;

– répond de sa gestion, au nom des travailleurs, devant les instances adaptées représentant la collectivité.

Pour répondre de sa gestion sur des bases saines, le conseil d'entreprise passe un contrat:

– si l'entreprise a une dimension nationale, le contrat est établi avec le plan démocratique national et contrôlé par une instance désignée par le Conseil économique et social;

– si l'entreprise a une dimension locale, le contrat est établi avec l'échelon régional du plan et contrôlé par une instance désignée par le Conseil économique et social régional, ou une structure décentralisée du même type.

Des procédures devront être mises en place, en vue de sanctionner le non-respect des engagements pris et de dénouer des situations de crise.

**b.** Au niveau des établissements, des conseils d'établissement dont la composition sera identique à celle des conseils d'entreprise seront mis en place. Dans le cadre du plan de l'entreprise, le conseil d'établissement jouira de toute l'autonomie possible. Toutefois, le chef d'établissement sera nommé par le conseil d'entreprise. Le conseil d'établissement dispose d'un droit de veto par rapport à cette nomination.

**c.** Un système de confrontation sera mis en place entre les conseils d'établissement d'une même unité géographique et l'instance territoriale la plus adaptée et la plus opérationnelle (commune, district . . . ) sur tous les problèmes concernant à la fois les entreprises et la commune ou l'unité territoriale appropriée: transport – pollution – logement – équipement . . .

**d.** Dans ces structures, les élus des travailleurs ont un rôle important à jouer en vue d'une réelle démocratisation:

– mise en place de mécanismes qui limitent les risques de voir les élus se réserver le monopole des décisions, ou s'ingénier à contourner les risques liés à la révocabilité du mandat;

– création de conditions pour que ces élus soient le plus possible les agents qui diffusent l'information, organisent la discussion et la décision des travailleurs;

– démocratisation du système éducatif, enjeu essentiel, dont l'effet ne peut se faire sentir que sur le long terme;

– transformation du contenu et des méthodes de la formation des adultes permettant aux travailleurs de participer activement à tous les débats concernant leur vie de travail et la vie de l'entreprise;

– accès aux actions de formation leur permettant de faire face à leurs responsabilités, en exerçant un contrôle réel technique et politique, sur la gestion;

– réinsertion professionnelle des élus afin de limiter les freins à la rotation des responsabilités électives.

*2 – La gestion des entreprises privées*

• But

Si la socialisation progressive de toute l'économie est un but, celle-ci ne pourra se réaliser que progressivement. Pendant longtemps, probablement, il faudra compter avec l'existence d'entreprises privées. Toutefois, celles-ci seront soumises à de nouvelles règles en conformité avec les objectifs du plan. Un contrôle des investissements s'impose. Il n'en reste pas moins qu'on ne peut attendre la socialisation de toutes les entreprises pour modifier la situation de pouvoir des travailleurs. Un très large droit de contrôle, limitant l'exercice du pouvoir patronal, devra donc être mis en place dans les entreprises privées.

• Mesures

**a.** Les pouvoirs d'intervention et de contrôle des comités d'entreprise et d'établissement seront élargis. Toute information demandée, concernant l'entreprise, devra leur être communiquée.

**b.** Des instances de contrôle seront mises en place au niveau des groupes et des holdings.

**c.** Un contrôle syndical sera institué sur tous les aspects individuels de la condition salariale et du contrat de travail.

**d.** Bénéficiant d'un rapport des forces global modifié, la négociation verra son champ élargi aux conditions de travail et à l'organisation du travail avec droit de contrôle syndical sur ces points.

**e.** Un système de confrontation sera mis en place entre les comités d'établissement de la même localité et l'instance politique communale sur les problèmes communs.

**f.** Lorsque la direction d'une entreprise envisagera des licenciements collectifs pour raison économique, le comité d'entreprise, le syndicat ou la collectivité publique territoriale pourront faire appel à une instance compétente qui établira un diagnostic public dans le but de rechercher les solutions les meilleures pour les travailleurs. Cet appel sera suspensif de toute décision.

**g.** Si les travailleurs d'une entreprise demandent majoritairement la socialisation de leur entreprise, un débat public devra s'instaurer avec la collectivité publique territoriale concernée, la décision finale revenant aux instances politiques.

('Des objectifs de transformation conduisant au socialisme autogestionnaire', adopté par le Conseil National de la Confédération française démocratique du travail en avril 1974, in *CFDT: textes de base* (2), Montholon–Services, 1977, pp.81–5.) *Note*: This text does not reflect the current position and thinking of CFDT.

## Exercices

### *Lexique*

Expliquez les mots et expressions suivants:

assumer des fonctions (l.42)
être partie prenante de (l.46)
une instance (l.50)
un échelon (l.57)
dans le cadre de (l.64)
par rapport à (l.66)
un groupe (l.104)
un holding (l.105)
un licenciement collectif (l.114)
un appel suspensif (l.118)

### *Grammaire et stylistique*

(a) Quelle différence faites-vous entre 'répondre à' et 'répondre de' (l.52)? Faites des phrases avec ces deux constructions.

### *Compréhension*

(a) Décrivez les aspects principaux de l'autogestion.
(b) Expliquez l'expression 'secteur socialisé de l'économie' (ll.1–2) et expliquez son importance dans le texte.
(c) Expliquez le rôle du conseil d'entreprise (l.40).

### *Questions orales ou écrites*

(a) Autogestion, rêve utopique ou possibilité pratique?
(b) L'autogestion, une idée dépassée? Expliquez bien votre réponse.

## TEXT 1.7

# Programme commun de gouvernement du Parti communiste français et du Parti socialiste, 1972

*Préambule*

En présentant un programme commun de gouvernement, le Parti communiste français et le Parti socialiste ont conscience d'accomplir un acte politique de grande importance. Ils affirment ensemble leur volonté de mettre fin aux injustices et aux incohérences du régime actuel. Pour y parvenir et pour ouvrir la voie au socialisme, des changements profonds sont nécessaires dans la vie politique, économique et sociale de la France.

Les perspectives ouvertes par l'union de la gauche et le rassemblement de toutes les forces du peuple, les propositions développées dans ce programme sont les moyens qui permettront aux Françaises et aux Français de vivre mieux, de changer leur vie. La préoccupation fondamentale du programme est de satisfaire leurs besoins et leurs aspirations.

Ce programme est un programme d'action; il constitue un engagement des deux partis l'un à l'égard de l'autre comme à l'égard du pays; il crée une situation nouvelle permettant d'instaurer une véritable démocratie politique et économique.

Le Parti communiste français et le Parti socialiste conservent naturellement leur personnalité. Ils se réclament l'un et l'autre de principes qui fondent leur existence propre. Certaines de leurs appréciations politiques sont différentes. Ceci ne met pas en cause leur volonté et leur capacité de gouverner ensemble.

L'accord qu'ils constatent aujourd'hui entre eux est suffisamment large pour leur permettre de proposer au pays un programme commun de gouvernement pour la prochaine législature.

Le Parti socialiste et le Parti communiste français sont convaincus que ce programme répond aux aspirations de millions de Français et aux exigences du développement de la démocratie.

Ils appellent les Français à le soutenir et à le faire triompher. Ils le soumettent aux autres partis et organisations démocratiques en les invitant à les rejoindre dans cette action . . .

*La démocratisation et l'extension du secteur public*

Pour briser la domination du grand capital et mettre en œuvre une politique économique et sociale nouvelle, rompant avec celle qu'il pratique, le gouvernement réalisera progressivement le transfert à la collectivité des moyens de production les plus importants et des instruments financiers actuellement entre les mains de groupes capitalistes dominants.

Le secteur public sera étendu, démocratisé et restructuré. Les entreprises nationales, dotées d'une large autonomie de gestion, respecteront, dans leurs activités, les orientations du Plan.

Le changement des formes juridiques de la propriété doit permettre aux travailleurs d'accéder effectivement aux responsabilités. Lorsque les travailleurs de l'entreprise en exprimeront la volonté et en accord avec le gouvernement, de nouvelles structures de gestion fixeront les conditions de leur intervention dans la désignation des conseils d'administration, l'organisation du travail, la gestion du personnel, les rapports avec le Plan.

A côté des nationalisations, l'appropriation collective revêtira des formes diverses: sociétés nationales ou d'économie mixte, coopératives, mutuelles, services publics locaux, etc.

Dès le début de la législature, un seuil minimum de nationalisations sera franchi. Cette politique de transfert à la collectivité doit donc viser d'emblée l'ensemble du secteur bancaire et financier et les groupes et entreprises industriels qui occupent une position stratégique vis-à-vis des secteurs clés de l'économie, c'est-à-dire:

– les entreprises qui répondent directement à des fonctions collectives ayant le caractère de service public et donc à des besoins sociaux fondamentaux;

– les sociétés vivant sur fonds publics, qu'il s'agisse de marchés publics, de subventions, de crédits de faveur, etc.;

– les principaux centres d'accumulation capitaliste qui dominent la plus grande partie, voire la totalité de certaines productions réduisant la concurrence à celle de quelques firmes géantes;

– les entreprises qui contrôlent des branches essentielles pour le développement de l'économie nationale (niveau technique, échanges internationaux, rôle régional, etc.).

Le franchissement du seuil minimum doit permettre de limiter et de circonscrire les bases monopolistes. Il laissera subsister un important secteur privé.

Les restructurations de l'appareil de production devront s'effectuer de façon progressive et souple, en fonction d'une stratégie industrielle adaptée aux nécessités du progrès économique et social et du caractère international de la vie économique. La nationalisation ne doit pas être étatisation. La progressivité des nationalisations sera liée au développement économique et aux exigences des masses, dont il est déterminant qu'elles prennent les plus larges responsabilités. C'est pourquoi, au cas où les travailleurs formuleraient la volonté de voir leur entreprise entrer dans le secteur public ou nationalisé, le gouvernement pourra le proposer au Parlement . . .

*Les institutions nationales*

L'existence d'un système électoral assurant une représentation aussi juste que possible des électeurs constitue une condition du fonctionnement démocratique du Parlement.

La loi électorale instituera la représentation proportionnelle pour les élections à l'Assemblée nationale et aux assemblées régionales.

*Le président de la République*

Dans le régime actuel, le chef de l'État détient, dans la conduite de la politique intérieure et extérieure, des pouvoirs exorbitants qu'il exerce sans contrôle.

Les dispositions du texte constitutionnel qui ont servi à l'instauration et aux abus du pouvoir personnel doivent être supprimées ou corrigées.

Il appartient au gouvernement, responsable devant l'Assemblée nationale, de déterminer et de conduire la politique de la nation.

L'article 16, qui permet au président de la République de s'arroger tous les pouvoirs, sera abrogé. Le pouvoir de décision sans contreseing sera limité à la désignation du Premier ministre, aux messages au Parlement, aux rapports avec la Cour suprême et à la dissolution; l'article 19 de la Constitution sera modifié en ce sens.

Le référendum ne pourra être utilisé comme un moyen de faire plébisciter la politique présidentielle contre le Parlement; l'article 11 de la Constitution sera précisé en ce sens.

La durée du mandat du président de la République sera fixée à cinq ans, un délai suffisant entre son élection et celle des députés à l'Assemblée nationale évitant toute simultanéité . . .

(*Programme commun de gouvernement du Parti communiste français et du Parti socialiste*, Éditions sociales, 1972 pp.49–50, 113–15, 150–1.)

## Exercices

### *Lexique*

Expliquez les mots et expressions suivants:

mettre en cause (l.20)
le grand capital (l.32)
un instrument financier (l.35)
le secteur public (l.37)
le conseil d'administration (l.44)
la société d'économie mixte (l.47)
d'emblée (l.50)
vis-à-vis de (l.52)
voire (l.59)
s'arroger (l.88)
abroger (l.89)
le contreseing (l.89)

### *Grammaire et stylistique*

(a) 'les sociétés vivant sur fonds publics, qu'il s'agisse de marchés publics, de subventions etc' (ll.56–57). Traduisez la phrase en anglais. Utilisez l'expression 'qu'il s'agisse de' dans d'autres phrases.

(b) 'La progressivité des nationalisations sera liée au développement économique et aux exigences des masses, dont il est déterminant qu'elles prennent les plus larges responsabilités.' (ll.69–72). Quel est le temps/mode de 'prennent'. Justifiez-le.

### *Compréhension*

(a) Comment comprenez-vous la phrase suivante: 'la nationalisation ne doit pas être étatisation.' (l.69)?
(b) Qu'est-ce que le Plan dont il est question à la ligne 39?
(c) Selon le texte, quel était le caractère des rapports entre le Parti communiste et le Parti socialiste en 1972?
(d) Qu'entendent les auteurs du texte par 'la démocratisation et l'extension du secteur public'? (l.31)
(e) Qu'est-ce que la représentation proportionnelle (l.79)?

### *Questions orales ou écrites*

(a) Pensez-vous qu'il y avait beaucoup d''injustices et incohérences' (l.5) dans le régime politique du début des années 70? Justifiez votre réponse.
(b) Dans quelle mesure le Parti socialiste a-t-il appliqué depuis 1981 les réformes mentionnées dans ces extraits?
(c) Dans quelle mesure le PS a-t-il changé les 'institutions nationales' conformément à ses intentions de 1972? Comment peut-on expliquer son comportement à ce sujet?

TEXT 1.8

## Les lois de décentralisation de 1982–83: la revanche des régions

*Introduction*

La loi du 2 mars 1982, dite 'loi Defferre', est relative aux droits et libertés des communes, départements et régions. Elle contient trois ruptures: la suppression de tous les contrôles de l'État a priori, le transfert du pouvoir exécutif des préfets au département et à la région, la reconnaissance du droit à l'intervention économique.

1. Les actes des collectivités locales sont exécutoires une fois notifiés à l'autorité compétente, c'est-à-dire le préfet, qui n'est plus autorité de tutelle. Disparaît le contrôle a priori des actes des Conseils municipaux et de leurs maires, des Conseils généraux et de leur président. Cependant, en cas de désaccord, le représentant de l'État peut procéder à un recours auprès du tribunal administratif. De même, le citoyen peut procéder à un recours pour suspendre une décision d'une collectivité territoriale auprès du préfet ou du tribunal administratif si le motif est jugé sérieux et de nature à justifier l'annulation. Les actes à caractère financier sont contrôlés par la Cour régionale des comptes.

2. Autre changement considérable, le transfert du pouvoir exécutif du préfet au président du Conseil général. Chaque transfert de compétences s'est accompagné des moyens financiers correspondants et des transferts de services de la préfecture vers le Conseil général. Enfin, les services extérieurs de l'État sont à la disposition du président pour la préparation et l'exécution des délibérations.

La région est consacrée collectivité territoriale de plein droit. Cette assemblée est désormais élue au suffrage universel direct. Le président est détendeur du pouvoir exécutif en lieu et place de l'ancien préfet de région. Aux côtés du Conseil régional est installé un Comité économique et social, au rôle consultatif.

3. Les communes, les départements et les régions disposent désormais de trois formes d'intervention économique: aides directes, aides indirectes, création de services publics locaux. Les aides directes ont été souvent contestées car jugées trop onéreuses au regard de leur efficacité. La loi de janvier 1988, dite d''amélioration de la décentralisation', recadre d'ailleurs les interventions économiques. La commune ne peut plus intervenir directement, sauf en milieu rural pour le maintien des services nécessaires à la satisfaction de la population.

La répartition des compétences entre les communes, les départements, les régions et l'État a été fixée par les lois de janvier et juillet 1983. Il n'y a aucune superposition de compétence et donc de tutelle entre les collectivités territoriales. Ce principe conditionne les transferts par blocs de compétences: à la commune, l'urbanisme et la gestion des sols; au département, l'action sociale et la santé, les collèges de l'enseignement public, les transports scolaires; à la région, la formation, les lycées et l'aménagement du territoire.

Il y a simultanéité du transfert des compétences et du transfert des ressources. Mais les charges confiées aux régions sont telles que les impôts des collectivités territoriales ont augmenté (en moyenne de 15% en 1990).

L'HISTOIRE: *La décentralisation a souvent été présentée, surtout à ses débuts, comme 'la grande affaire' du premier septennat de François Mitterrand. Était-ce la révolution annoncée ou l'État omnipotent a-t-il encore de beaux restes?*

BÉATRICE GIBLIN-DELVALLET: Il y a un peu des deux. C'est une révolution dans la mesure où ce sont les élus qui maintenant exercent les responsabilités de l'aménagement du territoire. Les maires des grandes villes sont devenus très puissants, de même que les présidents des Conseils généraux, qui disposent de budgets importants. Les régions aussi, avec moins d'ampleur, ont pris leur place dans cette redistribution des pouvoirs. Mais l'État est tout de même là, bien présent, par l'intermédiaire, par exemple, de ses représentants à la DDE (Direction départementale de l'équipement) ou à la DRE (Direction régionale de l'équipement).

Cela dit – et là on retombe dans les vieilles pratiques d'autrefois –, les 'grands' élus, qui cumulent toujours plusieurs mandats, ont tendance à ignorer ces délégués ou les préfets pour contacter directement à Paris le cabinet du ministre, sinon le ministre lui-même, dans l'espoir de faire avancer leurs dossiers. S'il y a donc eu décentralisation, celle-ci ne s'est pas accompagnée d'une déconcentration du pouvoir de l'État.

L'HISTOIRE: *Ces nouveaux pouvoirs, ce sont autant de nouvelles baronnies qui apparaissent . . . ?*

BÉATRICE GIBLIN-DELVALLET: Et quelles baronnies dans certains cas! Observez ce qui se passe dans la région parisienne. Est-il normal qu'il y ait si peu de structures intercommunales, qu'il n'y ait pas de communauté urbaine, que la capitale, ville-département riche, soit si nettement séparée de la petite couronne morcelée en une myriade de communes? Situation qui rend difficiles les politiques d'aménagement.

L'HISTOIRE: *La décentralisation a généré de fortes tensions entre ces nouveaux centres de décision.*

BÉATRICE GIBLIN-DELVALLET: Oui, mais ces rivalités existaient aussi avant la décentralisation, elles sont plus visibles aujourd'hui. Vous en avez un bel exemple avec la Zone d'aménagement concerté du tunnel sous la Manche. Voilà une ZAC de 300 hectares concédée par l'État à la société Eurotunnel et qui est l'objet d'enjeux et de visées contradictoires. Eurotunnel a envisagé d'implanter une infrastructure qui bénéficiera surtout à Calais. Mais à Dunkerque, où l'État a déjà investi des sommes considérables, on n'a pas renoncé à être le port 'locomotive' du littoral nord.

Et qui, entre-temps, est devenu maire de Dunkerque? Michel Delebarre, ministre de l'Équipement, des Transports, du Logement et de la Mer jusqu'en décembre dernier, qui conçoit une logique de l'aménagement du territoire, en conformité, bien sûr, avec les ambitions légitimes qu'il nourrit pour sa ville. Il faut poursuivre le développement de Dunkerque, plaide-t-il, si l'on se met à privilégier maintenant Calais, c'est ni plus ni moins défaire ce qu'on a commencé à bâtir. De cette opposition d'intérêts est née une situation d'impasse qui, à deux ans de l'inauguration du tunnel, ne profite à personne.

L'Histoire: *Pour les simples citoyens, qu'est-ce que la décentralisation a changé au fond?*

Béatrice Giblin-Delvallet: Ils ont vu leurs élus, surtout dans les grandes villes, se mobiliser pour la réalisation d'équipements en vue de rénover certains quartiers et, au niveau régional, pour financer remises en état ou constructions scolaires. Les contribuables se sont rendu compte aussi qu'ils ont dû payer parfois 10 à 15% d'impôts locaux en plus. Ce qui m'amène tout naturellement à évoquer les dérives budgétaires de certains maires et, d'une manière générale, l'extrême opacité des finances publiques locales. Mais, à la suite de quelques 'affaires', les maires sont en train de suivre les budgets de près! . . .

L'Histoire: *La décentralisation, c'est plus de pouvoir pour les régions. Mais les vingt-deux régions françaises ne sont pas, vous le rappelez, sur un même pied d'égalité. Dans la perspective d'une Europe sans frontières, que peuvent-elles contre les quinze* Länder *de l'Allemagne réunifiée, riches, pour la plupart, d'une longue histoire, celle de l'ex-RFA?*

Béatrice Giblin-Delvallet: La question ne se pose pas en ces termes parce que l'Europe des régions – tant pis pour ceux qui s'obstinent à y croire –, ce n'est pas pour demain. Il est vrai que l'histoire n'est pas la même des deux côtés de la frontière. L'Allemagne est un État fédéral, organisation politique imposée par la France et la Grande-Bretagne. La région – le *Land* – n'a rien à voir avec l'idée qu'on se fait de la région en France, où l'on a – faut-il toujours le rappeler? – une tradition bien ancrée de centralisme. Ici, le pouvoir régional est donc perçu, depuis les années soixante-dix, comme un instrument contre l'État jacobin qui vous a trop longtemps dépossédé de votre destin. Chez les Allemands de l'Ouest, où la division du pays a entraîné une conscience très aiguë de la nation, le *Land* est, au contraire, un outil au service de la nation tout entière . . .

L'Histoire: *Le développement d'une ville ou d'un département tient aussi à la personnalité de ses élus. N'y a-t-il pas là une autre source d'inégalité?*

Béatrice Giblin-Delvallet: Vous avez des maires efficaces et compétents, et vous en avez des plus timorés, des plus passifs. Mais je vois d'autres risques. Face à un grand maire aujourd'hui, quelle est la force d'opposition? La presse régionale, qui pourrait tenir un rôle de contre-pouvoir, se tait (par prudence?). Dans les grandes décisions d'aménagement, en dépit des efforts d'information qu'il faut saluer, le débat parmi les citoyens est inexistant. Il faut reconnaître que les dossiers ne sont pas simples et que le citoyen lambda qui veut suivre une séance municipale ne peut que décrocher devant la complexité technique d'un projet dont il aura vu la superbe maquette exposée dans un salon de l'hôtel de ville.

Les Français restent favorables à la décentralisation. Mais, pour autant, leur a-t-elle conféré cette 'nouvelle citoyenneté' qu'on avait gravée à sa naissance comme en exergue?

(Entretien avec Béatrice Giblin-Delvallet, *L'Histoire*, No 143, April 1991.)

## Exercices

### *Lexique*

Expliquez les mots et expressions suivants:

de beaux restes (l.45)
les 'grands' élus (ll.55–56)
la petite couronne (l.66)
une politique d'aménagement (l.68)
une ZAC (l.74)
un port 'locomotive' (l.78)
les contribuables (l.92)
la dérive (l.94)
une 'affaire' (l.96)
l'État jacobin (l.110)
un contre-pouvoir (l.119)
un dossier (l.122)
un citoyen lambda (l.122)
en exergue (l.128)

### *Grammaire et stylistique*

(a) Ll.63–67: justifiez les subjonctifs et faites des phrases sur le même modèle.
(b) 'ce que' (l.84). Dans quels cas utilise-t-on 'ce que' ou 'ce qui', dans quels cas utilise-t-on 'qu'est-ce que', 'qu'est-ce qui'? Faites des phrases pour illustrer la règle.
(c) 'Les contribuables se sont rendu compte' (l.92). Dans quel cas les participes passés de verbes réflexifs ne s'accordent-ils pas avec leurs sujets? Justifiez la règle dans ce cas-ci et inventez d'autres exemples.

### *Compréhension*

(a) Quelle différence voyez-vous entre la Direction départementale de l'équipement et la Direction régionale de l'équipement (ll.52–54)? Soyez aussi précis que possible. Que mettez-vous sous l'expression 'les structures intercommunales' (l.65)?
(b) Expliquez dans vos propres termes la situation de Dunkerque et Calais (ll.71–78).
(c) Expliquez ce qu'est le 'cumul des mandats' (l.56). Quelles conséquences peut avoir le fait que la décentralisation ne s'accompagne pas d'une déconcentration du pouvoir de l'État (ll.58–60)?
(d) Précisez la différence que l'auteur fait entre Länder et régions (ll.105–113). Pensez-vous comme B. Giblin-Delvallet que 'l'Europe des régions, ce n'est pas pour demain' (ll.103–104)?

### *Question orale ou écrite*

(a) Concrètement, qu'est-ce que la décentralisation a changé dans la vie des Français?

TEXT 1.9

## Que faire du progrès? Manifeste du Parti socialiste, janvier 1981

Partout s'élève cette interrogation: que faire du progrès? On pensait au XIX$^{e}$ siècle que la machine, en relayant la force physique de l'homme au travail, avancerait sa libération, mais les détenteurs du capital en ont fait l'instrument de leur domination. La machine moderne, qui ne se substitue plus seulement au muscle de l'homme, mais à sa mémoire et à son jugement, contribuera-t-elle à cette libération manquée? Il dépend de nous de ne pas laisser passer cette chance. Toute évolution scientifique entraîne une mutation des idées et des mœurs, suscite de nouvelles formes d'expression et prépare l'autre révolution, celle des structures économiques et des rapports sociaux. Nous vivons l'une de ces époques. Non seulement les socialistes ne craignent pas le progrès, mais ils le désirent. Il n'est pas de socialisme sans la science. La peur de l'acte créateur est le propre des sociétés perdues. Le danger n'est pas que l'homme invente, mais qu'il ne maîtrise pas (dans les domaines notamment de la biologie et de la génétique, de l'informatique et du nucléaire) ce qu'il crée. D'où la nécessité de le rendre responsable et, par le développement du savoir et le mécanisme des institutions, de lui en donner le moyen.

Accordons-nous sur ce point: quelque idée qu'on ait de l'avenir, rien ne changera si les inégalités, l'accès au savoir, le partage du pouvoir restent ce qu'ils sont. Regardons autour de nous. La société capitaliste asservit l'homme. La société communiste l'étouffe. Capitaliste ou communiste, la société industrielle, par ses entassements dans les centres urbains, par la dégradation des équilibres naturels et par ses critères scientifiques, se ressemble plus qu'elle ne diffère. La technique triomphe mais l'homme fiché, informatisé, médiatisé, manipulé, perd son autonomie. Objet ou sujet, la marge est étroite. La volonté des socialistes, au contraire, est que 'l'homme fasse lui-même sa propre histoire'.

Écoutons Jaurès: 'L'histoire humaine ne commencera véritablement que lorsque l'homme, échappant à la tyrannie des forces inconscientes, gouvernera par sa raison et sa volonté la production elle-même. Ce sera le jaillissement de la vie, ardente et libre, de l'humanité qui s'appropriera l'univers par la science, l'action, le rêve.'

Mais balayer les inquiétudes et réveiller l'espoir, mobiliser les énergies, retrouver confiance en nous-mêmes, conduire le progrès, asseoir la paix sur des bases solides, combattre l'égoïsme et le repli sur soi, essayer de rendre la société plus juste et les hommes plus solidaires, qui le fera sans un projet audacieux et sans le soutien de forces vives du pays, de ses travailleurs, de sa jeunesse, de ses intellectuels, de ses savants?

C'est ce projet que nous soumettons aux Français. Il n'offre pas un modèle de société toute faite. Il ne décrète pas à l'avance les étapes de sa transformation.

Il ne codifie pas le futur. Fidèle aux enseignements des luttes ouvrières, il esquisse une démarche, propose des objectifs et en détermine les moyens. Les socialistes, assurés qu'il n'est pas, dans la société industrielle, de libération de l'homme qui ne commence par sa libération des structures économiques imposées par le capitalisme, refusent pour autant d'enfermer l'homme dans les mécanismes de tout autre système – comme celui du marxisme-léninisme, théorie officielle des régimes communistes – dont l'idéologie cherche sans eux, et malgré eux, à pourvoir aux besoins matériels, spirituels, culturels de tous et de chacun. Le problème de notre société se pose désormais en termes de civilisation . . .

*La liberté*

Exprimons cette double conviction: il n'est de socialisme que celui de la liberté; il n'est de liberté réelle et vécue que celle qu'apporte le socialisme dans lequel nous croyons.

D'immenses espaces de liberté restent à conquérir. Sur le système en place, sur sa classe dirigeante, sur ses rapports de production et son modèle de croissance, sur son organisation, ses cadences, sa durée du travail, sur son détournement du temps libre, sur sa bureaucratie et sa fiscalité injuste et tatillonne, sur ses critères culturels, sa presse, sa radio, sa télévision, sur l'inégale condition de l'homme et de la femme.

Que signifie la liberté du travail pour le chômeur, la liberté pour la femme victime d'une ségrégation juridique, politique, professionnelle et sociale? La liberté des jeunes devant lesquels la société se ferme? Que devient la liberté de la presse quand le pouvoir contrôle les grands moyens d'information, quand les maîtres de l'argent s'approprient les techniques modernes de communication? Où est la liberté de l'exploitant agricole obligé de s'endetter pour survivre, celle de l'entrepreneur suspendu à la décision de son banquier?

Si l'on nous oppose, comme l'a fait le gouvernement avec la loi Peyrefitte, que la sécurité des Français justifie la réduction du champ des libertés traditionnelles, nous répondrons que l'insécurité est d'abord sociale: insécurité de l'emploi, du pouvoir d'achat, du revenu, de l'épargne, du logement. Quand l'iniquité corrompt le corps social, le désordre n'est pas loin.

Liberté et sécurité, nous voulons préserver l'une par l'autre. Non pas à la manière de M. Giscard d'Estaing qui spécule sur la peur pour que dure son pouvoir, mais en assurant, partout et à tous, une vie mieux respectée, mieux remplie et plus libre. Nous pourrons alors appliquer la loi sans faiblesse.

La défense de la liberté commence avec le respect de la démocratie. Démocratie politique dont les socialistes se veulent les héritiers naturels, démocratie économique et sociale dont ils sont les artisans. Or, sous tous ses aspects, la démocratie est menacée.

Il nous paraît dangereux, par exemple, que le chef de l'État concentre dans ses mains, comme c'est le cas aujourd'hui, la totalité des pouvoirs. Il nous paraît plus dangereux encore qu'un tel état de chose puisse durer plus longtemps. Nous ne sommes déjà plus tout à fait en République. Où en serons-nous dans sept ans si, par malheur, M. Giscard d'Estaing était réélu le 10 mai?

D'où ces propositions:

– la durée du mandat présidentiel sera réduite à cinq ans, une seule fois renouvelable. Ou bien la durée du mandat sera maintenue à sept ans, mais non renouvelable;

– les membres du Conseil supérieur de la magistrature cesseront d'être nommés par le chef de l'État;

– dans sa définition des relations entre le gouvernement et le Parlement, la Constitution sera strictement appliquée;

– les modifications constitutionnelles prévues par le programme socialiste seront soumises au Parlement;

– la représentation proportionnelle sera instituée pour les élections législatives, régionales et, à partir de 9 000 habitants, communales.

(F. Mitterrand, *Politique 2 1977–1981*, Fayard, 1981, pp.307–8, 310–11.)

## Exercices

### *Lexique*

Expliquer les mots et expressions suivants:

relayer (l.2)
le détenteur (l.3)
les mœurs (f.pl.) (ll.7–8)
être le propre de (l.12)
être fiché (l.23)
esquisser une démarche (l.40)
pourvoir à (l.46)
tatillon (l.57)
l'iniquité (f.) (l.70)

### *Grammaire*

(a) 'Le danger n'est pas que l'homme invente, mais qu'il ne maîtrise pas . . . ce qu'il crée' (ll.12–14). Écrivez la phrase à l'imparfait en identifiant précisément les temps/modes utilisés.
(b) en (l.16 et l.40). Que représente ce pronom dans chacun de ces cas?

### *Compréhension*

(a) 'La machine moderne, qui ne se substitue plus seulement au muscle de l'homme mais à sa mémoire et à son jugement . . .' (ll.4–5). Exprimez l'idée autrement, illustrez-la avec précision, et commentez.
(b) Expliquez et commentez la phrase: 'Nous ne sommes déjà plus tout à fait en République' (l.83).

### *Questions orales ou écrites*

(a) '... il n'est de socialisme que celui de la liberté; il n'est de liberté réelle que celle qu'apporte le socialisme dans lequel nous croyons' (ll.50–52). Etes-vous d'accord?

(b) Évaluez les propositions mitterrandiennes concernant la démocratie politique. Où en est la France sur ce tableau?

## TEXT 1.10

# Tract de recrutement poujadiste, 1953–55

Union de Défense des Commerçants & Artisans
MOUVEMENT DE SAINT-CÉRÉ
26, RUE DE LA RÉPUBLIQUE – TEL. 125
SAINT-CÉRÉ (LOT)

NOTRE PROGRAMME

1° RÉFORME FISCALE impliquant essentiellement l'imposition à la base: seule formule honnête permettant la juste perception de l'impôt en évitant la fraude et les inquisitions qui en découlent;

2° En attendant: égalité devant l'impôt, quel que soit le régime de distribution adopté. C'est pourquoi nous dénonçons les sociétés anonymes, les coopératives de distribution et plus particulièrement celles des organismes d'État;

3° Abattement à la base égal au salaire d'un employé ou d'un ouvrier qualifié;

4° Aménagement d'un système de sécurité sociale, d'allocations familiales et de retraites basé sur un esprit d'égalité entre tous les Français.

Repoussant toute collusion avec les groupements d'intérêts, les synarchies, les abâtardissements politiques, l'Union de Défense, consciente de ses devoirs et de ses charges, s'engage à rendre à ce peuple de petits et moyens commerçants et artisans l'existence digne qui leur est due, en les soulageant de l'obsession monstrueuse des exactions fiscales.

L'Union de Défense entend mener dans la France entière une action énergique pour relever le défi de l'augmentation des patentes, en retournant aux préfets les patentes de tous les adhérents, en décidant de ne les payer que sur la base de 1953.

NOS MOYENS D'ACTION

1° SURVEILLER avec une extrême vigilance l'indépendance totale du Mouvement. Elle repousse toute ingérence, qu'elle provienne de politiciens tentaculaires, de chefs de syndicats rémunérés outre leurs services administratifs, de groupements financiers et de leurs chèques paralysants, de sociétés déclarées ou occultes. Elle entend déjouer toute manœuvre qui tendrait à engager politiquement tout responsable du Mouvement.

2° SOUTENIR une action effective par la présence jusqu'à la complète réalisation de son programme. L'Union s'engage donc, dans l'ordre et la dignité, mais avec une fermeté invincible, à s'opposer par tous les moyens à n'importe quel système d'inquisition fiscale, tant que les pouvoirs publics n'auront pas reconnu et consacré les légitimes revendications des commerçants et artisans.

3° CONSERVER dans sa pureté et dans son intégralité les points du programme sur lesquels commerçants et artisans sont unanimes.

(E. Cahm, *Politics and Society in Contemporary France (1789–1971). A Documentary History*, George Harrap & Co., 1972, pp.349–50.)

## Exercices

### Lexique

Expliquez les mots et expressions suivants:

| | |
|---|---|
| un abattement fiscal (l.12) | une exaction (l.19) |
| une collusion (l.15) | une ingérence (l.26) |
| une synarchie (l.15) | occulte (l.28) |

### Grammaire et stylistique

(a) 'Qu'elle provienne' (l.26): justifiez le subjonctif.
(b) Certains puristes répugnent à l'usage de l'expression 'basé sur' (l.14): que peut-on dire à sa place?
(c) Relevez le vocabulaire émotionnel dans ce texte, et surtout sa première partie, 'Notre Programme'.

### Compréhension

(a) Que comprenez-vous par 'politiciens tentaculaires' (l.26), 'inquisition fiscale' (l.34)? Qualifiez le ton employé.
(b) Précisez la revendication exprimée aux lignes 25–30. Que pensez-vous des moyens d'action envisagés dans le tract?

### Question orale ou écrite

(a) En vous replaçant dans le contexte social, économique et politique de la France du début des années 50, comment expliquez-vous le succès d'un tract comme celui-ci?

TEXT 1.11

# Le rôle du Président de la République selon la constitution de la IV$^{e}$ République et de la V$^{e}$ République

*1 La Constitution de la IV$^{e}$ République* (extrait)

DU PRÉSIDENT DE LA RÉPUBLIQUE

ART. 29. – Le Président de la République est élu par le Parlement.

Il est élu pour sept ans. Il n'est rééligible qu'une fois.

ART. 30. – Le Président de la République nomme en Conseil des Ministres les Conseillers d'État, le Grand Chancelier de la Légion d'Honneur, les ambassadeurs et les envoyés extraordinaires, les membres du Conseil supérieur et du Comité de la Défense Nationale, les recteurs des Universités, les préfets, les directeurs des administrations centrales, les officiers généraux, les représentants du Gouvernement dans les territoires d'outre-mer.

ART. 31. – Le Président de la République est tenu informé des négociations internationales. Il signe et ratifie les traités.

Le Président de la République accrédite les ambassadeurs et les envoyés extraordinaires auprès des puissances étrangères; les ambassadeurs et les envoyés extraordinaires étrangers sont accrédités auprès de lui.

ART. 32. – Le Président de la République préside le Conseil des Ministres. Il fait établir et conserve les procès-verbaux des séances.

ART. 33. – Le Président de la République préside, avec les mêmes attributions, le Conseil supérieur et le Comité de la Défense Nationale et prend le titre de Chef des armées.

ART. 34. – Le Président de la République préside le Conseil Supérieur de la Magistrature.

ART. 35. – Le Président de la République exerce le droit de grâce en Conseil Supérieur de la Magistrature.

ART. 36. – Le Président de la République promulgue les lois dans les dix jours qui suivent la transmission au Gouvernement de la loi définitivement adoptée. Ce délai est réduit à cinq jours en cas d'urgence déclarée par l'Assemblée Nationale.

Dans le délai fixé pour la promulgation, le Président de la République peut, par un message motivé, demander aux deux Chambres une nouvelle délibération, qui ne peut être refusée.

A défaut de promulgation par le Président de la République dans les délais fixés par la présente Constitution, il y sera pourvu par le Président de l'Assemblée Nationale.

ART. 37. – Le Président de la République communique avec le Parlement par des messages adressés à l'Assemblée Nationale.

ART. 38. – Chacun des actes du Président de la République doit être contresigné par le Président du Conseil des Ministres et par un ministre.

ART. 39. – Trente jours au plus, quinze jours au moins avant l'expiration des pouvoirs du Président de la République, le Parlement procède à l'élection du nouveau Président.

ART. 40. – Si, en application de l'article précédent, l'élection doit avoir lieu dans une période où l'Assemblée Nationale est dissoute conformément à l'article 51, les pouvoirs du Président de la République en exercice sont prorogés jusqu'à l'élection du nouveau Président. Le Parlement procède à l'élection de ce nouveau Président dans les dix jours de l'élection de la nouvelle Assemblée Nationale.

Dans ce cas, la désignation du Président du Conseil des Ministres a lieu dans les quinze jours qui suivent l'élection du nouveau Président de la République.

ART. 41. – En cas d'empêchement dûment constaté par un vote du Parlement, en cas de vacance par décès, démission ou toute autre cause, le Président de l'Assemblée Nationale assure provisoirement l'intérim des fonctions de Président de la République. Il sera remplacé dans ses fonctions par un vice-président.

Le nouveau Président de la République est élu dans les dix jours, sauf ce qui est dit à l'article précédent.

ART. 42. – Le Président de la République n'est responsable que dans le cas de haute trahison.

Il peut être mis en accusation par l'Assemblée Nationale et renvoyé devant la Haute Cour de Justice dans les conditions prévues à l'article 57 ci-dessous.

ART. 43. – La charge de Président de la République est incompatible avec toute autre fonction publique.

ART. 44. – Les membres des familles ayant régné sur la France sont inéligibles à la Présidence de la République.

### 2 *La Constitution de la Ve République* (extrait)

#### LE PRÉSIDENT DE LA RÉPUBLIQUE

ART. 5. – Le Président de la République veille au respect de la Constitution. Il assure, par son arbitrage, le fonctionnement régulier des pouvoirs publics ainsi que la continuité de l'État.

Il est le garant de l'indépendance nationale, de l'intégrité du territoire, du respect des accords de Communauté et des traités.

ART. 6. – Le Président de la République est élu pour sept ans au suffrage universel direct.

Les modalités d'application du présent article sont fixées par une loi organique.

ART. 7. – Le Président de la République est élu à la majorité absolue des suffrages exprimés. Si celle-ci n'est pas obtenue au premier tour, il est procédé, le deuxième dimanche suivant, à un second tour. Seuls peuvent s'y présenter les deux candidats qui, le cas échéant après retrait de candidats plus favorisés, se trouvent avoir recueilli le plus grand nombre de suffrages au premier tour.

Le scrutin est ouvert sur convocation du Gouvernement.

L'élection du nouveau Président a lieu vingt jours au moins et trente-cinq jours au plus avant l'expiration des pouvoirs du Président en exercice.

En cas de vacance de la Présidence de la République pour quelque cause que ce soit, ou d'empêchement constaté par le Conseil constitutionnel saisi par le Gouvernement et statuant à la majorité absolue de ses membres, les fonctions du Président de la République, à l'exception de celles prévues aux articles 11 et 12 ci-dessous, sont provisoirement exercées par le président du Sénat et, si celui-ci est à son tour empêché d'exercer ces fonctions, par le Gouvernement.

En cas de vacance ou lorsque l'empêchement est déclaré définitif par le Conseil constitutionnel, le scrutin pour l'élection du nouveau Président a lieu, sauf cas de force majeure constaté par le Conseil constitutionnel, vingt jours au moins et trente-cinq jours au plus après l'ouverture de la vacance ou la déclaration du caractère définitif de l'empêchement.

Il ne peut être fait application ni des articles 49 et 50 ni de l'article 89 de la Constitution durant la vacance de la Présidence de la République ou durant la période qui s'écoule entre la déclaration du caractère définitif de l'empêchement du Président de la République et l'élection de son successeur.

ART. 8. – Le Président de la République nomme le Premier Ministre. Il met fin à ses fonctions sur la présentation par celui-ci de la démission du Gouvernement.

Sur la proposition du Premier Ministre, il nomme les autres membres du Gouvernement et met fin à leurs fonctions.

ART. 9. – Le Président de la République préside le Conseil des Ministres.

ART. 10. – Le Président de la République promulgue les lois dans les quinze jours qui suivent la transmission au Gouvernement de la loi définitivement adoptée.

Il peut, avant l'expiration de ce délai, demander au Parlement une nouvelle délibération de la loi ou de certains de ses articles. Cette nouvelle délibération ne peut être refusée.

ART. 11. – Le Président de la République, sur proposition du Gouvernement pendant la durée des sessions ou sur proposition conjointe des deux assemblées, publiées au *Journal officiel*, peut soumettre au référendum tout projet de loi portant sur l'organisation des pouvoirs publics, comportant approbation d'un accord de Communauté ou tendant à autoriser la ratification d'un traité qui, sans être contraire à la Constitution, aurait des incidences sur le fonctionnement des institutions.

Lorsque le référendum a conclu à l'adoption du projet, le Président de la République le promulgue dans le délai prévu à l'article précédent.

ART. 12. – Le Président de la République peut, après consultation du Premier Ministre et des présidents des assemblées, prononcer la dissolution de l'Assemblée Nationale.

Les élections générales ont lieu vingt jours au moins et quarante jours au plus tard après la dissolution.

L'Assemblée Nationale se réunit de plein droit le deuxième jeudi qui suit son élection. Si cette réunion a lieu en dehors des périodes prévues pour les sessions ordinaires, une session est ouverte de droit pour une durée de quinze jours.

Il ne peut être procédé à une nouvelle dissolution dans l'année qui suit ces élections.

ART. 13. – Le Président de la République signe les ordonnances et les décrets délibérés en Conseil des Ministres.

Il nomme aux emplois civils et militaires de l'État.

Les conseillers d'État, le grand chancelier de la Légion d'Honneur, les ambassadeurs et envoyés extraordinaires, les conseillers maîtres à la Cour des comptes, les préfets, les représentants du Gouvernement dans les territoires d'Outre-Mer, les officiers généraux, les recteurs des académies, les directeurs des administrations centrales sont nommés en Conseil des Ministres.

Une loi organique détermine les autres emplois auxquels il est pourvu en Conseil des Ministres ainsi que les conditions dans lesquelles le pouvoir de nomination du Président de la République peut être par lui délégué pour être exercé en son nom.

ART. 14. – Le Président de la République accrédite les ambassadeurs et les envoyés extraordinaires auprès des puissances étrangères; les ambassadeurs et les envoyés extraordinaires étrangers sont accrédités auprès de lui.

ART. 15. – Le Président de la République est le chef des armées. Il préside les conseils et comités supérieurs de la Défense Nationale.

ART. 16. – Lorsque les institutions de la République, l'indépendance de la Nation, l'intégrité de son territoire ou l'exécution de ses engagements internationaux sont menacées d'une manière grave et immédiate et que le fonctionnement régulier des pouvoirs publics constitutionnels est interrompu, le Président de la République prend les mesures exigées par ces circonstances, après consultation officielle du Premier Ministre, des Présidents des assemblées ainsi que du Conseil Constitutionnel.

Il en informe la Nation par un message.

Ces mesures doivent être inspirées par la volonté d'assurer aux pouvoirs publics constitutionnels, dans les moindres délais, les moyens d'accomplir leur mission. Le Conseil Constitutionnel est consulté à leur sujet.

Le Parlement se réunit de plein droit.

L'Assemblée Nationale ne peut être dissoute pendant l'exercice des pouvoirs exceptionnels.

ART. 17. – Le Président de la République a le droit de faire grâce.

ART. 18. – Le Président de la République communique avec les deux assemblées du Parlement par des messages qu'il fait lire et qui ne donnent lieu à aucun débat.

Hors session, le Parlement est réuni spécialement à cet effet.

ART. 19. – Les actes du Président de la République autres que ceux prévus aux articles 8 (1er alinéa), 11, 12, 16, 18, 54, 56 et 61 sont contresignés par le Premier Ministre et, le cas échéant, par les ministres responsables.

(J. Godechot (ed.), *Les constitutions de la France depuis 1789*, Garnier-Flammarion, 1970, pp.397–429.)

## Exercices

### *Lexique*

Expliquez les mots et expressions suivants:

accréditer (l.13)
le droit de grâce (l.23)
proroger (l.44)
dûment (l.49)
le cas échéant (l.76)

### *Grammaire et stylistique*

(a) Justifiez l'usage de 'du' dans le titre 'Du Président de la République'.
(b) Sur le modèle de 'rééligible' (l.4), faites des adjectifs en 'ible'.
(c) Etudiez la langue contractuelle. Notez en particulier l'usage intensif du passif. Trouvez des expressions particulières à cette langue et cherchez les équivalents en anglais.

### *Compréhension*

(a) Donnez la différence entre 'la vacance' (l.92) et 'les vacances'.
(b) Qu'est-ce que *Le Journal officiel*?
(c) Quand on parle d' 'empêchement' (l.83) de la Présidence, de quoi s'agit-il exactement? Donnez des exemples.
(d) Comparez les Articles 29 et 30 de la Constitution de la IV^e^ République et les Articles 5 et 6 de la Constitution de la V^e^ République. Quelles différences apparaissent? Montrez leur importance.
(e) Écrivez deux 'petites annonces' comprenant la description des fonctions pour le poste de Président sous les deux régimes.

### *Questions orales ou écrites*

(a) En quoi l'article 11 de la V^e^ République (sur le référendum) est-il particulièrement significatif?
(b) Comparez le rôle du Président sous les deux constitutions.
(c) Était-il nécessaire de changer le rôle du Président en 1958?

## TEXT 1.12

# 'L'espérance française à l'aube du IIIème millénaire', selon Jean-Marie Le Pen

La France est-elle sortie de l'Histoire? Elle, qui pendant plus de mille ans lui imprima sa marque. Les autres nations d'Europe qui depuis plus de deux millénaires rayonnent sur le monde, qui avec elle ont bâti la civilisation, vont-elles accepter de voir disparaître leur souveraineté, leur langue, leur âme. Vont-elles livrer leur peuple au Moloch, se résigner à n'être plus que des États «floridiformes» ou «californoïde» aux ordres de Washington ou de New York, comme ceux qui composent la colonie d'Amérique du Nord, sujet devenu tyran.

Si le mondialisme n'annonce pas les jours ultimes, s'il n'est qu'un avatar de l'histoire, peut-être oublié ou honni dans cinquante ans, s'il n'est qu'une conséquence de l'abandon des règles morales et civiques qui nous ont gouverné pendant des siècles, alors il nous appartient de le traiter comme ce qu'il est, une idéologie matérialiste à l'instar du communisme, contre lequel on peut, contre lequel on doit lutter, pour lui échapper. Il dépendra des plus lucides, des plus courageux et des plus sages de mobiliser les peuples pour assurer dans le monde de demain non seulement la défense des Droits de l'Homme, mais celle des Droits de l'Âme en s'inspirant des succès et des échecs de trois millénaires et plus de civilisation. Car ce sont bien, aujourd'hui, à l'aube du 3ème millénaire notre civilisation et ses valeurs qui sont menacées par la mise en place du Nouvel Ordre Mondial. Les dix dernières années ont été marquées par une explosion des relations internationales dans les domaines économiques et financiers. Les marchés n'aiment pas les frontières. Ils sont pour eux, sources de perte de temps, de contrôle et de régulation. Il fallait donc les abattre et organiser le vaste marché mondial que les mondialistes appellent de leurs vœux. C'est essentiellement pour cette raison que les nations sont le verrou à faire sauter en priorité. En effet, la Nation, cadre traditionnel d'exercice du pouvoir des pays occidentaux est en train de subir une véritable révolution. Les bouleversements économiques, démographiques et sociaux à l'échelle planétaire, mais aussi l'idéologie «du nouvel humanisme» organisent une mutation du monde qui conduit inexorablement à la disparition de la Nation en tant qu'entité constituée. Un territoire, une population et une volonté de partager un avenir commun constituaient les fondements d'une Nation. Aujourd'hui, la tendance est à la création de grands ensembles qui avalent les frontières et tentent de mixer les populations. Plus de barrières, plus de contrôle, la liberté d'échange devient la règle. La Nation, dans sa spécificité, dans sa substance, subit l'assaut du mondialisme avec la complaisance des gouvernants de droite et de gauche qui, tels les moutons de Panurge, suivent, sans mot dire, les diktats des gourous de la finance internationale. C'est vite oublier que l'ensemble des sociétés politiques de l'Europe a été marqué pendant tout le XIXème siècle et une partie du XXème par l'unicité, le regroupement et la concentration des entités politiques et administratives. Le renforcement de l'autorité de l'État s'était affirmé par les sacrifices consentis et partagés par l'ensemble de la communauté nationale. La révolution industrielle, mais aussi l'école, l'église, l'armée, les guerres, avaient contribué à un sentiment fort d'appartenance et à un effacement progressif des disparités locales au profit de la Patrie et de la Nation. Cette fin de siècle est, au contraire marquée par la division et l'émiettement. La construction européenne nous a été imposée par des traités scélérats qui ont comme seule finalité de dissoudre la France dans un ensemble supranational et fédéral. Depuis le Traité de Rome, l'Acte Unique, Maastricht, Amsterdam et la mise en place de I'EURO ont en quelques années mis en pièce plus de quinze siècles d'histoire. Ce démantèlement organisé de la Nation se conjugue aussi avec la promotion de petites entités régionales qui parcellisent un peu plus le cadre national. L'Euro-régionalisme sera l'aboutissement du projet, jamais avoué, d'États-Unis d'Europe. La Nation est ainsi désagrégée en amont par le pouvoir fédéral et en aval par l'autonomie de nouvelles régions constituées. Son harmonie, son homogénéité et son existence sont remises en cause sans que personne, mis à part le Front National, ne s'oppose à cette mort lente. Un jour ou l'autre, l'histoire jugera les criminels qui ont trahi l'indépendance nationale et ont contribué à affaiblir la France. L'imbécillité n'est pas, en histoire, une circonstance atténuante.

(Discours de Le Pen, université d'été, Orange, 3 septembre 1999, http://www.front-nat.fr/discours/udt99.htm – 11/10/99. Extract.)

## Exercices

### *Lexique*

Expliquez les mots et expressions suivants:

livrer leur peuple au Moloch (l.5)
un avatar de l'histoire (ll.8–9)
les marchés n'aiment pas les frontières (l.21)
les moutons de Panurge (l.36)
l'unicité (l.39)
un effacement progressif des disparités locales (ll.43–44)
un traité scélérat (l.46)
L'Euro-régionalisme (ll.51–52)

### *Grammaire et stylistique*

(a) Conjuguez 'subit' (l.34) au présent, à l'imparfait, au futur, au passé composé et au subjonctif présent.
(b) Examinez les exemples de langage passionnel dans ce texte. Inventez d'autres exemples vous-même.

### *Compréhension*

(a) De quelle façon, selon Le Pen, la France est-elle 'sortie de l'histoire' (l.1)?
(b) Pourquoi Le Pen est-il contre 'la création de grands ensembles qui avalent les frontières et tentent de mixer les populations' (ll.32–33)?

(c) 'L'imbécillité n'est pas, en histoire, une circonstance atténuante' (l.58). Expliquez le sens de cette phrase.
(d) Trouvez les parties du texte où Le Pen présente la France en tant que victime des actions des autres. Quel est son but en présentant une telle position?

### *Questions orales ou écrites*

(a) Analysez la perspective lepéniste sur l'Europe. Est-ce une perspective patriote, xénophobe ou autre?
(b) Le Pen présente-t-il un point de vue pratique ou purement polémique?

## TEXT 1.13

# «Le problème FN est derrière nous»

***Un entretien avec l'antilepéniste Eric Osmond, porte-parole du Manifeste contre le Front national.***

*Après l'éclatement du FN, les européennes confirment le déclin de l'extrême droite française. Allez-vous vous dissoudre?*

Bientôt, j'espère! La dynamique du FN est brisée. Avec 5,7% des voix, Jean-Marie Le Pen a perdu sa puissance, tandis que Bruno Mégret, à 3,2%, a été incapable de la récupérer et d'en développer une autre. Pas de vainqueur, donc, mais deux grands perdants. Il faut avoir le courage et l'honnêteté de le dire: la page du FN est en train de se tourner et le problème est derrière nous. Toutefois, si le FN a diminué, le racisme demeure. Et les raisons – colères sociale et politique – qui ont poussé certains électeurs à voter Le Pen n'ont pas miraculeusement disparu, même si la situation sociale s'améliore. Troisième élément, l'implosion du FN, au moment où la droite, elle, explose, fait des municipales de 2001 un moment politique dangereux: ce sont des élections très localisées où des individus sans foi ni loi seront prêts à tout pour garder leur fauteuil. Le Manifeste n'annoncera donc pas sa dissolution immédiate. Nous resterons vigilants.

*N'est-ce pas une façon de sauver votre fonds de commerce?*

Dès que nous aurons la conviction que tout danger est écarté, nous en tirerons les conséquences. Nous ne prolongerons pas artificiellement le combat. Toutes les associations antifascistes ne semblent pas être sur cette ligne. A entretenir, contre l'évidence, le mythe d'une «bête immonde» sans cesse renaissante, le risque est grand de jeter le discrédit sur la pertinence passée du combat mené en commun.

*Finalement, quelle a été l'utilité des associations anti-FN?*

Indéniablement, le FN a fait sa scission tout seul. Et celle-ci est déterminante dans la volatilité et la désertion électorales. En revanche, nous avons institué une chose, qui n'est pas indifférente dans les motifs de la rupture: la diabolisation. Cette digue démocratique qui, pendant des années, a maintenu à l'écart ce parti pas comme les autres et, finalement, créé les conditions de son blocage à 15%. Notre militantisme a ainsi contribué à provoquer la lassitude, l'énervement et l'impatience des mégrétistes, qui ont conduit le Front à se disloquer.

(Propos recueillis par Romain Rosso, *L'Express*, 1 July 1999.)

## Exercices

### *Lexique*

Expliquez les mots et expressions suivants:

la dynamique du FN est brisée (l.5)
l'implosion du FN (l.13)
sur cette ligne (l.21)
la diabolisation (ll.28–29)
se disloquer (l.33)

### *Grammaire et stylistique*

(a) 'ce sont des élections très localisées où des individus sans foi ni loi seront prêts à tout pour garder leur fauteuil' (ll.14–16). Qu'est-ce qui explique l'impact de cette phrase, du point de vue du choix des mots?
(b) Le langage du texte est 'parlé'. A quels égards diffère-t-il du langage écrit? Donnez des exemples.

### *Compréhension*

(a) De quelles élections européennes s'agit-il (l.3)?
(b) Qui est Bruno Mégret (l.6)?
(c) Résumez le texte en vingt mots.

### *Questions orales ou écrites*

(a) Eric Osmond dit que 'si le FN a diminué, le racisme demeure' (l.10). Dans quelle mesure le FN crée-t-il le racisme et a quel point le FN profite-t-il du racisme?
(b) Faites une mise à jour de la situation en ce qui concerne les organisations d'extrême droite en France. Commentez la pertinence actuelle des propos d'Eric Osmond dans le texte.

TEXT 1.14

## Des conflits sociaux d'un nouveau type

L'apparition de nouveaux types de conflits en France pourrait avoir une origine simple: l'influence, de plus en plus faible, de la tradition du mouvement ouvrier. Tandis que les syndicats sont en perte de vitesse, au point de s'appuyer sur le plus modeste taux de syndicalisation des pays industrialisés, de l'ordre de 8 à 10% selon les experts, c'est la relation à une histoire et à ses rites établis qui ne se retrouve pas nécessairement dans les dernières illustrations fournies par l'actualité sociale, du Crédit foncier de France aux intermittents du spectacle, des chauffeurs-routiers aux actions menées par les chômeurs. Les modalités surprennent, parfois, et les catégories mobilisées, différentes, ne s'inscrivent plus ou peu dans une continuité.

Insensiblement, une page a été tournée au cours de ce dernier quart de siècle. Si l'on a pu écrire et prétendre que l'homérique bataille des Lip avait coïncidé avec la fin des «trente glorieuses», il faut aussi admettre que les sursauts actuels n'ont plus rien à voir avec cette fameuse «conflictualité productive» d'alors. Les conflits du passé répondaient à des objectifs d'émancipation ou de progrès. Ceux d'aujourd'hui, dos au mur le plus souvent, se justifient davantage par l'instinct de survie ou par la réaction de la dignité bafouée, et ne font donc pas appel aux mêmes ressorts collectifs. Ils n'empruntent pas les mêmes voies ou, s'ils le font, semblent les redécouvrir dans une forme d'improvisation spontanée.

Pareillement, des salariés ou des travailleurs qui n'avaient pas de traditions de lutte bien ancrées se sont révélés. On a pu être étonné, dans le cas du Crédit foncier, de voir les cadres, non seulement s'associer à une occupation, mais cautionner une séquestration. C'était oublier que, au-delà d'un «malaise» fréquemment commenté, ce passage à l'acte signifie que les frontières devaient fatalement se déplacer un jour ou l'autre pour correspondre au développement des activités tertiaires dans le monde du travail. Les poids sociologiques évoluant, il est logique que des catégories socioprofessionnelles, considérées comme privilégiées, finissent par entrer en lice. D'autant que leur statut se banalise et que, démographiquement, dans le secteur bancaire, les employés sont devenus une minorité en comparaison des gradés, hiérarchie intermédiaire, qui savent de plus en plus ce qui les différencie des cadres supérieurs. Une forme de prolétarisation ou de paupérisation des classes moyennes amène celles-ci à se rapprocher des techniques de contestation qu'elles dédaignaient jusqu'à présent.

Que les chauffeurs-routiers fassent la démonstration de leur combativité extrêmement organisée, comme à la fin de 1996, va dans le même sens. Ce que confirme leur capacité à provoquer le phénomène identitaire de «grève par procuration», apparu pour la première fois lors de la puissante mobilisation sociale de novembre-décembre 1995. En d'autres temps, Lénine avait, paraît-il, pour coutume d'affirmer que, si les garçons-coiffeurs descendaient dans la rue, la révolution ne serait pas loin. Nous n'en sommes certes pas là, mais l'image parle. Il est évident que, en quelques années, une profession est passée d'un mode de protestation anarchique à une maîtrise orchestrée de sa colère, grâce à un apprentissage, favorisé par l'apport technique de syndicalistes chevronnés, venus de la RATP ou de la SNCF.

Haute en couleur, la guérilla des intermittents du spectacle montre, de la même façon, que la scène sociale est désormais occupée par de nouveaux acteurs qui représentent d'autres enjeux, et que ce sont ceux-là qui s'amplifieront. L'émergence des chômeurs eux-mêmes n'est sans doute plus qu'une question de temps. Les occupations d'ANPE ou d'Assedic, menées avec le soutien militant d'Agir contre le chômage (AC!) ou de l'APEIS, prouvent que le climat change. Mais il faudrait aussi regarder de plus près les actes isolés et désespérés de chômeurs dont la violence verbale, mais surtout physique, parfois suicidaire, annonce la fin de la résignation.

A la différence des années 80, par exemple, les coordinations ou les pulsions corporatistes velléitaires ne paraissent plus dominer et, mieux, semblent être en passe d'être oubliées. A leur tour, elles ont été supplantées par des organisations plus structurées qui ne cessent d'élargir leur influence à la faveur de l'émiettement syndical. A savoir, par tous les courants contestataires que, par commodité ou ignorance, les DRH nomment «trotskistes» et qui rassemblent, pêle-mêle, toutes les nuances de l'extrême gauche ou, plutôt, ce qui ne rentre plus dans les lignes traditionnelles, depuis l'émergence du syndicat SUD jusqu'à la résistance interne de Tous ensemble au sein de la CFDT.

Désormais, et c'est ce qui intéressera pour l'avenir, ces mouvances-là sont présentes partout, et pas seulement au sein de Force ouvrière où elles contribuent au flou organisationnel. On les retrouve au cœur de la CFDT, qui éprouve de plus en plus de difficultés pour s'en dépêtrer, mais s'épanouissent également dans une CGT qui les avait longtemps pourchassées et doit maintenant les accepter. Après la désintégration sociale et l'émiettement syndical, de nouvelles lignes de force sont en train d'apparaître.

(Alain Lebaube, *Le Monde*, 26 February 1997.)

## Exercices

### *Lexique*

Expliquez les mots et expressions suivants:

un intermittent du spectacle (l.7)
une homérique bataille (l.12)
bafouer (l.17)
un ressort collectif (l.18)
une séquestration (l.23)
RATP (l.45), SNCF (l.45), ANPE (l.50), Assedic (l.50), APEIS (l.51), DRH (l.60), SUD (l.62), CFDT (ll.63, 66), CGT (l.68).

un passage à l'acte (l.24)
entrer en lice (l.28)
la prolétarisation ou paupérisation des classes moyennes (l.32)

### *Grammaire et stylistique*

(a) Conjuguez 'établis' (l.5) au présent, à l'imparfait, au futur, au passé composé et au subjonctif présent.
(b) Comment décrire le style et le ton de ce texte?
(c) Quel est le point de vue de l'auteur, à votre avis, et ce point de vue s'exprime-t-il dans le choix du langage? (Donnez des exemples.)

### *Compréhension*

(a) Expliquez la phrase: 'Les modalités surprennent, parfois, et les catégories mobilisées, différentes, ne s'inscrivent plus ou peu dans une continuité' (ll.8–10).
(b) Trouvez des informations sur Lip (l.12). Quelle est la signification de Lip dans l'histoire des conflits sociaux depuis la Deuxième Guerre Mondiale?
(c) Qui est Lénine (l.39)? Quelle a été son influence sur la France?

### *Questions orales ou écrites*

(a) Trouvez des exemples récents de conflits sociaux. S'agit-il de conflits traditionnels ou 'd'un nouveau type'? Quelle est la différence entre les deux?
(b) Dans votre pays, comment les structures sociales ont-elles changé depuis trente ans, et les conflits sociaux ont-ils aussi changé? Pourquoi?

TEXT 1.15

## La proclamation du Front de libération nationale pour l'indépendance du pays

Au peuple Algérien,

Aux militants de la Cause nationale,

A vous qui êtes appelés à nous juger, le premier d'une façon générale, les seconds tout particulièrement, notre souci, en diffusant la présente proclamation, est de vous éclairer sur les raisons profondes qui nous ont poussés à agir, en vous exposant notre programme, le sens de notre action, le bien-fondé de nos vues dont le but demeure l'INDÉPENDANCE NATIONALE dans le cadre nord-africain. Notre désir aussi est de vous éviter la confusion que pourraient entretenir l'impérialisme et ses agents: administratifs et autres politicailleurs véreux.

Nous considérons avant tout qu'après des décades de lutte, le Mouvement national atteint sa phase finale de réalisation. En effet, le but du mouvement révolutionnaire étant de créer toutes les conditions favorables pour le déclenchement d'une action libératrice, nous estimons que, sur le plan interne, le peuple est uni derrière le mot d'ordre d'indépendance et d'action, et sur le plan externe, le climat de détente est favorable pour le règlement des problèmes mineurs dont le nôtre avec surtout l'appui diplomatique de nos frères arabes et musulmans. Les événements du Maroc et de Tunisie sont à ce sujet significatifs et marquent profondément le processus de lutte de libération de l'Afrique du Nord. A noter dans ce domaine que nous avions depuis fort longtemps été les précurseurs de l'unité dans l'action. Malheureusement jamais réalisée entre les trois pays.

Aujourd'hui, les uns et les autres sont engagés résolument dans cette voie, et nous, relégués à l'arrière, nous subissons le sort de ceux qui sont dépassés. C'est ainsi que notre Mouvement national terrassé par des années d'immobilisme et de routine, mal orienté, privé du soutien indispensable de l'opinion populaire, dépassé par les événements, se désagrège progressivement à la grande satisfaction du colonialisme qui croit avoir remporté la plus grande victoire de sa lutte contre l'avant-garde algérienne. L'heure est grave.

Devant cette situation qui risque de devenir irréparable, une équipe de jeunes responsables et militants conscients, ralliant autour d'elle la majorité des éléments sains et décidés, a jugé le moment venu de sortir le Mouvement national de l'impasse où l'ont acculé les luttes de personnes et d'influence pour le lancer aux côtés des frères marocains et tunisiens dans la véritable lutte révolutionnaire.

Nous tenons à préciser, à cet effet, *que nous sommes indépendants des deux clans* qui se disputent le pouvoir. Plaçant l'intérêt national au-dessus de toutes les considérations mesquines et erronées de personnes et de prestiges, conformément aux principes révolutionnaires, notre action est dirigée uniquement contre le colonialisme, seul ennemi obstiné et aveugle, qui s'est toujours refusé d'accorder la moindre liberté par des moyens pacifiques.

Ce sont là, nous pensons, des raisons suffisantes qui font que notre mouvement de rénovation se présente sous le nom de: FRONT de LIBÉRATION NATIONALE, se dégageant ainsi de toutes les compromissions possibles et offrant la possibilité à tous les patriotes algériens de toutes les couches sociales, de tous les partis et mouvements purement algériens de s'intégrer dans la lutte de libération sans aucune autre considération.

Pour nous préciser, nous retraçons ci-après les grandes lignes de notre programme politique:

*But*: indépendance nationale par:

(1) la restauration de l'État algérien souverain, démocratique et social dans le cadre des principes islamiques;
(2) le respect de toutes les libertés fondamentales sans distinction de race ni de confession.

*Objectifs intérieurs*

(1) assainissement politique par la remise du Mouvement national révolutionnaire dans sa véritable voie et par l'anéantissement de tous les vestiges de corruption et de réformisme, causes de notre régression actuelle;
(2) rassemblement et organisation de toutes les énergies saines du peuple algérien pour la liquidation du système colonial.

*Objectifs extérieurs*

(1) internationalisation du problème algérien;
(2) réalisation de l'unité nord-africaine dans son cadre naturel arabo-islamique;
(3) dans le cadre de la Charte des Nations unies, affirmation de notre sympathie agissante à l'égard de toutes les nations qui appuieraient notre action libératrice.

*Moyens de lutte*

Conformément aux principes révolutionnaires, et compte tenu des situations intérieure et extérieure, la continuation de la lutte par tous les moyens jusqu'à la réalisation de notre but.

Pour atteindre ces objectifs, le Front de libération nationale aura deux tâches essentielles à mener de front et simultanément: une action intérieure tant sur le plan politique que sur le plan de l'action propre, et une action extérieure en vue de faire du problème algérien une réalité pour le monde entier avec l'appui de tous nos alliés naturels.

C'est là une tâche écrasante qui nécessite la mobilisation de toutes les énergies et de toutes les ressources nationales. Il est vrai, la lutte sera longue, mais l'issue est certaine.

En dernier lieu, afin d'éviter les fausses interprétations et faux-fuyants, pour prouver notre désir réel de paix, limiter les pertes en vies humaines et les effusions de sang, nous avançons une plate-forme honorable de discussion aux autorités françaises si ces dernières sont animées de bonne foi et reconnaissent une fois pour toutes aux peuples qu'elles subjuguent le droit de disposer d'eux-mêmes:

(1) L'ouverture de négociations avec les porte-parole autorisés du peuple algérien sur les bases de la reconnaissance de la souveraineté algérienne une et indivisible.
(2) La création d'un climat de confiance par la libération de tous les détenus politiques, la levée de toutes les mesures d'exception et l'arrêt de toutes les poursuites contre les forces combattantes.
(3) La reconnaissance de la nationalité algérienne par une déclaration officielle abrogeant les édits, décrets et lois faisant de l'Algérie une 'terre française' en déni de l'histoire, de la géographie, de la langue, de la religion et des mœurs du peuple algérien.

En contrepartie:

(1) Les intérêts français, culturels et économiques, honnêtement acquis, seront respectés ainsi que les personnes et les familles.
(2) Tous les Français désirant rester en Algérie auront le choix entre leur nationalité d'origine et seront de ce fait considérés comme des étrangers vis-à-vis des lois en vigueur ou opteront pour la nationalité algérienne et dans ce cas seront considérés comme tels en droit et en devoirs.
(3) Les liens entre la France et l'Algérie seront définis et feront l'objet d'un accord entre les deux puissances sur la base de l'égalité et du respect de chacun.

Algérien! Nous t'invitons à méditer la Charte ci-dessus. Ton devoir est de t'y associer pour sauver notre pays et lui rendre sa liberté. Le Front de libération nationale est ton front. Sa victoire est la tienne.

Quant à nous, résolus à poursuivre la lutte, sûrs de tes sentiments anti-impérialistes, forts de ton soutien, nous donnons le meilleur de nous-mêmes à la Patrie.

LE SECRÉTARIAT
(*1er novembre 1954.*)

(P. Éveno et J. Planchais, *La guerre d'Algérie. Dossier et témoignages*, Éditions la Découverte/*Le Monde*, 1989, pp.83–6.)

## Exercices

### *Lexique*

Expliquez les mots et expressions suivants:

un politicailleur véreux (ll.9–10)
le mot d'ordre (l.15)
acculer quelqu'un dans une impasse (l.33)

à cet effet (l.35)
mesquin (l.37)
dans le cadre de (ll.50–51)
l'assainissement (l.55)
mener de front (l.71)
un faux-fuyant (ll.78)
la levée (l.88)
en contrepartie (l.94)

### *Grammaire et stylistique*

(a) Le premier, les seconds (ll.3–4) – ces dernières (l.81): que désignent ces pronoms, très exactement, dans le contexte? Remplacez par 'celui-ci, celle-là' et inventez vous-même quelques phrases qui utilisent ces pronoms.
(b) 'vis-à-vis de' (l.99). Faites deux phrases avec cette expression et deux phrases avec 'à propos de'.
(c) Faites une liste des constructions verbales avec 'à' et 'de' utilisées dans le texte. Exemples: 'notre souci est de . . .' l.4 – 'pousser à', l.5.
(d) Commentez l'utilisation des participes (ll.23–34), en vous souvenant que le participe passé a un sens passif (il décrit souvent un état – voyez les quatre exemples des lignes 25–29), alors que le participe présent a un sens actif (l.32). Quel est l'effet obtenu?
(e) La rhétorique révolutionnaire s'exprime dans des expressions telles que 'la souveraineté algérienne une et indivisible' (ll.85–86). Trouvez-en d'autres du même type.

### *Compréhension*

(a) Expliquez la notion, pour le FLN, de 'libération nationale'.
(b) Ce texte constitue-t-il une déclaration de lutte armée?

### *Questions orales ou écrites*

(a) À votre avis la proclamation du FLN du 1er novembre 1954 signale-t-elle l'ouverture d'une lutte légitime?
(b) Imaginez pourquoi un/e Algérien/ne serait séduit/e par cette proclamation.
(c) Les buts de la proclamation ont-ils été réalisés à long terme?

TEXT 1.16

## L'éclatement du système des partis politiques

Reconnus officiellement pour la première fois par la Constitution de 1958, les partis politiques ont eu de tout temps mauvaise presse en France. Si, en son article 4, le texte constitutionnel reconnaît qu' «ils concourent à l'expression du suffrage», les Français expriment, eux, une méfiance ancestrale et tout à fait étrangère à l'actuelle «crise de la politique». En 1990, 60% des personnes interrogées déclaraient «avoir plutôt pas confiance dans les partis politiques»; mais elles étaient déjà 58% à professer la même opinion en février 1981 ou en janvier 1988.

Ce rejet de principe a eu quelques conséquences importantes. La première est la faiblesse traditionnelle des partis français. Comparés à leurs homologues européens (allemands, anglais, italiens et scandinaves notamment), ils ont toujours été, à gauche comme à droite, de petites organisations sans base militante importante et sont, en ces années quatre-vingt-dix, plus frappés que les premiers par le recul de l'engagement politique. La faiblesse des effectifs détermine évidemment une grande vacuité des organisations partisanes, même lorsque le modèle reste, comme il est de tradition à gauche, celui du «parti de masse». Longtemps, le PCF (Parti communiste français) a été le seul «vrai» parti, organisé grâce à ses cellules locales et rurales sur l'ensemble du territoire, capable d'une activité militante quotidienne, et solidement inséré dans la classe ouvrière grâce à ses cellules d'entreprise et ses liens avec la CGT (Confédération générale du travail). La crise qui affecte le PCF depuis la fin des années soixante-dix, comme l'effondrement plus récent du modèle communiste, a toutefois largement réduit cette originalité.

A ces traits historiques et structurels s'ajoutent ceux liés à la transformation récente de la vie politique. Présidentialisation de toute la vie politique et donc des organisations, extrême médiatisation des leaders et dictature acceptée des sondages ont entraîné la disparition d'une fonction essentielle des partis: la formation des opinions qui passait d'une part par la présence, sinon quotidienne du moins régulière, sur le terrain et, d'autre part, par la fonction progammatique. De plus en plus, les partis français – ceux qui en tout cas concourent pour le pouvoir – sont des partis de notables et d'élus qui s'animent en périodes électorales lorsqu'il s'agit de sélectionner le personnel politique et de convaincre l'électeur sur un catalogue de bonnes intentions.

L'absence de débats politiques menés par les partis «classiques» a pour conséquence la déshérence d'une large fraction de l'opinion à laquelle plus rien n'est désormais véritablement expliqué. Cela facilite l'émergence de nouvelles organisations qui bâtissent leur succès sur la prise en compte *prioritaire* de questions particulières réputées plus proches des individus, questions qu'ils ont réussi à constituer en «enjeux»: immigration pour le Front national; protection de l'environnement pour les Verts, voire l'Europe et les «valeurs» pour Philippe de Villiers.

*Crises et instabilité*

La conséquence en a été l'éclatement du système de partis tel qu'il s'était stabilisé à la fin des années soixante-dix – l'existence de quatre grandes forces politiques liées deux à deux (gauche contre droite) par des accords électoraux et/ou politiques.

Depuis le début des années quatre-vingt-dix, le système de partis peut être caractérisé à la fois par son émiettement et par son instabilité. D'une part, si l'on se réfère aux élections de la période (régionales de 1992 et de 1998, législatives de 1993 et de 1997, européennes de 1994, présidentielle de 1995), neuf forces ont reçu à un moment donné l'appui d'une fraction notable de l'électorat: Lutte ouvrière (LO), Parti communiste (PCF), Parti socialiste (PS), Parti radical de gauche (PRG, ex-Mouvement des radicaux de gauche), Verts et Génération Écologie, Union pour la démocratie française (UDF), Rassemblement pour la République (RPR), Mouvement pour la France (MPF) et Front national (FN). D'autre part, de considérables évolutions ont marqué la fortune électorale des partis et des situations de crise ont touché tour à tour la gauche, la droite et enfin l'extrême droite.

Certaines organisations comme le PRG, les Verts, GE ou le MPF n'ont connu que des succès éphémères mais restent dans le système comme «groupes de pression» avec lesquels les grands partis doivent composer. En 1992 et 1993, la position du PS comme force dominante de la gauche a été contestée par le succès des écologistes qui entendaient n'entrer dans aucune coalition et réduisaient d'autant la vocation majoritaire du PS. Une recomposition s'est toutefois concrétisée lors des élections législatives de 1997 et des régionales de 1998 avec la mise en place d'une coalition «rose, rouge, verte» qui a gagné les élections de 1997 et confirmé son succès lors des régionales de 1998.

En revanche, les effets de la dissolution manquée de 1997 et des régionales de 1998 ont accentué la crise de la droite confrontée non seulement au problème des relations avec le FN, mais aussi à des difficultés internes. Si le RPR a réussi à maintenir son unité, l'UDF a éclaté. D'une part, Charles Millon, élu président de la région Rhône-Alpes avec les voix du FN en mars 1998, puis invalidé et non réélu, a tenté d'organiser une nouvelle formation appelée La Droite. D'autre part et surtout, Alain Madelin, président de Démocratie libérale (DL – ex-Parti républicain), a choisi en mai 1998 de quitter l'UDF et de reprendre son autonomie. Créée le 14 mai 1998, l'Alliance – union de l'UDF, du RPR et de DL – n'est jamais allée au-delà d'une entente électorale qui, de toute manière, existait depuis 1981. En outre, l'UDF a décidé de présenter sa propre liste lors des élections européennes de juin 1999.

Cet éclatement et cette instabilité peuvent, du fait des contraintes institutionnelles, apparaître plus formels que réels. Poussés par le scrutin majoritaire à deux tours lors des élections législatives, les partis sont conduits à conclure des alliances ou à entrer dans des coalitions. Le second tour de l'élection présidentielle, ouvert seulement aux deux candidats arrivés en tête au premier tour, produit forcément un président élu avec une majorité des suffrages. Toutefois, ces mécanismes ne garantissent plus qu'à une majorité présidentielle ou parlementaire corresponde une majorité d'opinion. La «gauche plurielle», en 1997, a obtenu la majorité des sièges à l'Assemblée nationale avec seulement 43% des suffrages exprimés. En 1995, Jacques Chirac a été élu avec 52,7% des suffrages exprimés, mais la droite modérée ne représentait au premier tour que 43,8% des électeurs et le ralliement d'une partie des électeurs du FN, en l'absence d'un accord entre la droite et l'extrême droite, s'est révélé précaire. De toute manière, l'institutionnalisation du FN a privé durablement le RPR, l'UDF et DL de toute possibilité de conquérir une majorité des suffrages. Il n'est pas certain que la scission de l'extrême droite, effective depuis janvier 1999, change rapidement cette situation. Ainsi l'éclatement et l'instabilité du système de partis produisent-ils, à tout le moins, les très rapides changements de majorités gouvernementales connues depuis 1981 et la répétition des périodes de cohabitation.

(Colette Ysmal, *L'État de la France*, Éditions la Découverte, 1999–2000, pp.486–8.)

## Exercices

### *Lexique*

Expliquez les mots et expressions suivants:

un homologue (l.10)
une base militante importante (ll.12–13)
le recul (l.14)
la vacuité (l.15)
la fonction programmatique (l.29)
un parti de notables (l.31)
la gauche plurielle (l.87)

### *Grammaire et stylistique*

(a) Faites des phrases avec 'en revanche' (l.68).
(b) 's'est révélé précaire' (l.92): traduisez cette expression en anglais et écrivez d'autres phrases avec 'se révéler'.

### *Compréhension*

(a) Expliquez la 'dictature acceptée des sondages' (ll.26–27); 'la dissolution manquée de 1997' (l.68).
(b) 'Cet éclatement et cette instabilité peuvent, du fait des contraintes institutionnelles, apparaître plus formels que réels' (ll.80–81): expliquez cette phrase.
(c) Résumez l'argument du texte en vingt mots.

### *Questions orales ou écrites*

(a) Quels sont les principaux problèmes pour les partis de droite d'une part et de gauche d'autre part, depuis quinze ans?
(b) Le système français des partis politiques est-il moins démocratique de nos jours à cause de l'éclatement de ce système? Comparez avec votre pays.

TEXT 1.17

## Les députées de la nouvelle législature en 1997

77% de candidats mais plus de 89% d'élus. Un peu plus de 22% de candidates mais un peu moins de 11% d'élues. Les hommes seraient-ils de meilleurs candidats que les femmes? Les électrices et les électeurs préféreraient-ils être représentés par un homme plutôt que par une femme? . . . Ce que montrent ces chiffres c'est que les militantes sont de 'bons petits soldats' qui acceptent de se faire instrumentaliser par des partis marginaux, dont elles sont les supplétives, et tout autant par les grands partis, dont elles sont la bonne conscience. En acceptant des circonscriptions difficilement gagnables par leur camp, elles leur permettent à celui-ci d'afficher un pourcentage relativement 'honorable' de candidates, sans bénéfice pour elles, ni personnel ni collectif.

Dans les assemblées élues au lendemain de la Seconde guerre mondiale, les députées représentaient un peu plus de 5% des élus. Leur nombre a ensuite décru pour ne retrouver ce seuil qu'en 1981. Il a ensuite stagné. La barre des 10% a été franchie pour la première fois en 1997. L'événement a été salué par la presse. Il ne doit pas faire oublier que 10% ce n'est pas, loin s'en faut, la parité, et que la progression reste modeste si on la compare à celle d'autres pays européens au cours de la dernière décennie. Nombre de députées socialistes, vertes et communistes de 1997 ne figuraient pas, au moment de leur désignation, parmi les candidats considérés par les spécialistes électoraux des états-majors comme pouvant gagner. L'élection de ces candidates est évidement liée au relatif raz-de-marée de la gauche. Il semble aussi que les candidates, de gauche mais aussi de droite, ont bénéficié d'un avantage, parce que femmes. Elles ont, en tout cas, déjoué les pronostics des états-majors. Leurs performances ont été d'autant plus remarquables que, pour ce qui concerne les candidates socialistes, elles étaient dotées d'un 'capital politique' inférieur à celui des candidats. La majorité d'entre elles détenait certes un mandat (et nombre d'entre elles avaient déjà mené, comme suppléantes ou comme candidates, une campagne législative) mais ce mandat était plus souvent d'adjointe que de maire, d'élue communale que d'élue départementale. Et une élection anticipée n'était pas de nature à leur faciliter la tâche. Elles auraient pu espérer, en disposant d'une année de campagne, se faire connaître ou mieux connaître. Les résultats du scrutin montrent que ces handicaps n'ont pas joué mais que ces femmes ont au contraire obtenu, en moyenne, des résultats légèrement supérieurs à ceux des candidats socialistes.

Le nombre d'élues au soir du 1er juin 1997 tous partis confondus était de soixante-trois, contre trente-cinq en 1993. Si l'on examine l'évolution par sexe d'un scrutin à l'autre au sein des groupes politiques on constate que la proportion de femmes – ce que laissait présager l'évolution du nombre des candidates par tendance – est nettement plus forte à gauche qu'à droite. Les élues du PC passent de deux à cinq et représentent 13,5% du groupe parlementaire contre

8% en 1993. Les élues socialistes passent de trois (il y avait quatre sortantes parce que Frédérique Bredin, battue en 1993, avait retrouvé son siège à l'occasion d'une partielle) à quarante-deux, soit 17,1% du groupe contre 4,5% à l'issu du précédent scrutin. Les Verts, à la faveur de l'accord électoral avec le PS, font leur entrée au Palais Bourbon et obtiennent huit élus dont trois femmes (soit 37,5%). L'UDF, qui avait en 1993 onze élus, n'en a plus que sept (6,4% contre 5,3%), et le RPR, cinq contre dix-sept (3,6% contre 7%). Il faut ajouter à ce décompte une élue d'outre-mer, classée centre gauche.

Le gouvernement de Lionel Jospin formé en juin 1997 compte vingt-six ministres dont huit femmes, soit 30,7%.

(Fançoise Gaspard et Claude Servan-Schreiber, 'Elections législatives des 25 mai et 1er juin 1997: les femmes dans la compétition électorale en France', *Parité-Infos*, 1997, pp.3–4.)

## Exercices

### *Lexique*

Expliquez les mots et expressions suivants:

loin s'en faut (l.15)
le raz-de-marée (l.21)
déjouer (l.23)
détenir un mandat (l.26)
une suppléante (l.27)
une adjointe (l.28)
le scrutin (ll.31, 44)
tous partis confondus (l.35)
présager (l.38)
le décompte (l.48)

### *Grammaire et stylistique*

(a) 'laisser présager' (l.38): faites des phrases avec ce verbe.
(b) Donnez des exemples de langage dans le texte qui indiquent le point de vue des auteurs sur les femmes et la politique.

### *Compréhension*

(a) 'Ce que montrent les chiffres c'est que les militantes sont de "bons petits soldats" qui acceptent de se faire instrumentaliser par des partis marginaux, dont elles sont les supplétives . . .' (ll.4–6): exprimez le sens de cette phrase à votre façon.
(b) Que comprenez-vous par 'le capital politique' (l.25), 'une élue communale' (l.28), 'une élue départementale' (l.29)?
(c) Quelles sont les influences les plus importantes sur le nombre de députées dans l'Assemblée nationale?
(d) Décrivez et expliquez l'évolution du nombre de députées après les élections de 1993 et de 1997.

### *Questions orales ou écrites*

(a) Devrait-on imposer la parité en ce qui concerne les députés et les députées?
(b) La progression du nombre de femmes dans l'Assemblée nationale reflète-t-elle davantage d'égalité dans la société française en général?

## TEXT 1.18

# Jacques Chirac: Le président et le fantôme du général

Déjà la cinquième fête nationale de son septennat, et Jacques Chirac tente encore de définir le socle de son mandat. Au fil de ses campagnes électorales ou de ses programmes, le président de la République a toujours revendiqué le gaullisme comme principale source d'inspiration. «Non des tables de la Loi figées pour l'éternité, mais des principes vivants, un comportement qui allie fidélité à son histoire et adaptation à son époque, aux aspirations des femmes et des hommes qui la vivent», définissait-il lors de sa dernière intervention sur le sujet, dans un message envoyé aux cadres du RPR le 24 avril dernier. Lui-même a pris l'habitude de se décrire non comme l'«héritier» de Charles de Gaulle, mais comme l'un de ses «disciples».

Les Français, interrogés par BVA pour L'Express, donnent volontiers acte au chef de l'État qu'il correspond mieux que tous les autres, mieux que Charles Pasqua et Philippe Séguin – les deux rebelles – à l'image qu'ils se font de l'héritage du Général. Ce brevet en gaullisme se révèle néanmoins d'une grande perfidie: Chirac, certes, est gaulliste, mais le thème n'est plus d'actualité, le qualificatif ne signifie plus grand-chose, le socle est creux. Pour les deux tiers des personnes interrogées, le fantôme de Colombey n'indique plus aucun chemin et se contente de renvoyer un écho plein d'exigences. Même les sympathisants de la droite parlementaire restent partagés sur l'intérêt de convoquer l'homme du 18 Juin: 49% d'entre eux considèrent le gaullisme comme d'actualité, 49% le jugent dépassé. Difficile de bâtir sur ce flou idéologique autre chose qu'une rhétorique ou une mythologie; inutile, en tout cas, de vouloir y puiser la méthode pour un mandat présidentiel. La principale qualité gaulliste? L'absence de réponse (23%) tient lieu de première des réponses. L'identité gaulliste? La grandeur de la France (23%) ne devance que de justesse le silence perplexe des sondés qui ne se prononcent pas (22%).

Des cendres du gaullisme, définitivement froides, peut-il renaître une idéologie du rassemblement? Fossoyeur obligé, Chirac a tout intérêt à inventer autre chose. Depuis le discours qu'il tint à Rennes le 4 décembre 1998, il s'emploie à dessiner les contours d'une inspiration originale. L'ambition laisse surtout apparaître les atours d'un candidat à un deuxième mandat, sans qu'un quelconque chiraquisme estompe pour l'heure le gaullisme. «C'est en libérant les nouvelles énergies démocratiques que nous pourrons dessiner le visage de la France de demain», lança Chirac à Rennes. A Bordeaux, au début du mois, il réclama que la «démocratie locale» soit le «moteur d'une démocratie de participation». Le chef de l'État profitera aussi de ce déplacement girondin pour démontrer que l'économie moderne peut se réconcilier avec «tous les territoires et tous les hommes».

Cette quête d'un humanisme dans lequel il soit possible d'être à la fois mondial et petit apparaît comme l'esquisse d'un projet. Celui que la droite s'échine à construire depuis deux décennies, sans succès. Ses trois derniers gouvernements poussèrent leur ultime soupir au bout d'à peine deux années. Le mandat de Jacques Chirac lui-même souffre de ne pas s'inscrire dans la pérennité de l'action, dès lors que la cohabitation dilapide, jour après jour, la consistance et l'influence du pouvoir présidentiel.

*L'occasion d'une clarification*

A l'absence d'un fondement idéologique s'ajoute donc la faiblesse de la construction politique d'un septennat. Il faut l'acrimonie tout en talent d'un Valéry Giscard d'Estaing pour souligner que ce «président de culture gaulliste» ne cesse de déroger à l'«esprit authentique de la V^e République». Plus ou moins constructive, plus ou moins conflictuelle, la cohabitation ne fait qu'accroître la difficulté de sa tâche.

Fidélité à l'âme d'une République, inventivité face à l'équation Europe-nation, le chef de l'État doit trancher ce double nœud ô combien gaulliste avant d'aborder les futures échéances. Si elle n'a pas été souhaitée, loin de là, par l'Élysée, la création du Rassemblement pour la France fournit l'occasion d'une clarification. Malgré leur désarroi, les sondés continuent d'accorder au classique RPR la primauté de la représentation gaulliste. L'électorat de droite se divise sur la question: 56% des personnes interrogées considèrent que le parti de Nicolas Sarkozy représente le mieux les valeurs du gaullisme, 33% penchent en faveur du mouvement de Charles Pasqua et de Philippe de Villiers, dont le score aux élections européennes prouve cependant qu'une certaine idée de l'indépendance nationale n'a pas encore vécu.

Les chiraquiens l'ont bien compris, qui plaident pour que ne soit pas excommunié le RPF. Utilité idéologique, certes, d'une stratégie de vaste balayage. Elle se heurte toutefois à un calendrier problématique: c'est sous la présidence française, en décembre 2000, que l'Union européenne doit réformer ses institutions et procéder à un élargissement du vote à la majorité qualifiée, que combattront le RPF et de nombreux gaullistes. Pragmatisme politique surtout: dans quelques départements du Sud, la formation de Pasqua peut permettre de fixer un électorat, voire de vampiriser le Front national.

Avant même son intervention du 14 Juillet, Chirac a entendu ses fidèles lui suggérer de ne pas en rester là. Ils lui demandent, sur sa lancée, de préparer un «discours de la méthode» qui réinstallerait, à l'automne, le président au cœur de la vie politique. Pour que ne meure pas tout à fait si ce n'est la lettre, du moins l'esprit des institutions voulu par un général deux étoiles.

(Eric Mandonnet, *L'Express*, 15 July 1999.)

## Exercices

### *Lexique*

Expliquez les mots et expressions suivants:

le socle de son mandat (l.2)
au fil des campagnes électorales (l.2)
le cadre (l.8)
la perfidie (l.15)
l'esquisse d'un projet (l.40)
le sondé (l.57)
vampiriser (l.71)

### *Grammaire et stylistique*

(a) Que comprenez-vous par 's'échiner' (l.40), 'trancher' (l.54), 'avoir vécu' (l.63)? Faites des phrases avec ces verbes.

(b) Identifiez des métaphores dans le texte et expliquez comment l'auteur les utilise pour illustrer ses analyses, et dans quel but.

### *Compréhension*

(a) Expliquez la phrase: 'le qualificatif ne signifie plus grand-chose, le socle est creux' (ll.15–16)

(b) Qui est 'le fantôme de Colombey' (l.17)?

(c) Expliquez le sens et le style de la phrase: 'Il faut l'acrimonie tout en talent d'un Valéry Giscard d'Estaing pour souligner que ce "président de culture gaulliste" ne cesse de déroger à l'"esprit authentique de la V^e^ République"' (ll.48–50).

(d) Quel rôle dans la vie politique française les personnages suivants jouent-ils, ou ont-ils joué: Valéry Giscard d'Estaing (ll.48–49), Nicolas Sarkozy (l.60), Charles Pasqua (l.61) et Philippe de Villiers (l.61)? Cherchez des informations sur l'internet, par exemple.

(e) Jacques Chirac essaye-t-il de renouveler le gaullisme, ou de maintenir ses caractéristiques traditionnelles?

### *Questions orales ou écrites*

(a) L'idéologie de de Gaulle est-elle pertinente au monde actuel? Peut-on la moderniser?

(b) Dans quelle mesure la scission du mouvement gaulliste à la fin des années 1990 a-t-elle nui à son avenir?

PART II

# The French economy

François Nectoux

# Introduction

At the dawn of the twenty-first century, the French economy is increasingly integrated into the European Union, which has become an economic giant. Indeed France, along with eleven other countries of the EU, has abandoned its national currency in favour of the Euro. However, some aspects of the French economy remain unique and its characteristics are sometimes difficult to understand. Viewed from abroad, it is easy to give contradictory descriptions of the French economy. On the one hand, France is still seen as a kind of Eden flowing with champagne, cognac and *foie gras*, where markets in small Provençal towns are piled high with bright displays of vegetables and *fruits de mer*. On the other hand, it is also the land of high technology, of the *train à grande vitesse* (TGV), and of the highest concentration of nuclear plants to be found anywhere in the world.

The main French economic indicators also send out signals which, at first sight, seem somewhat contradictory. For instance, France has one of the highest rates of unemployment in Europe, but, at the same time, it achieves a respectable rate of economic growth and a large trade surplus, and its rate of inflation is one of the lowest among the large industrialized nations, at times even lower than in Germany and Japan. Another surprising feature is that, since the mid-1980s, a period when socialist governments have been in power for most of the time, income differentials have increased, thus reversing the trend of the three previous decades towards more social equality. Another baffling characteristic of the French economy is the apparent domination of the public sector (the technological developments mentioned above were developed and marketed by publicly-owned corporations or utilities), which coexists with vibrant capitalism; and, as noted above, despite its renowned independent and often nationalistic approach to economic affairs, France is now abandoning the franc, symbol of its sovereignty, to merge even further into the integrated economy of the European Union.

How can these different facets of the French economy be reconciled, and is it possible to find a common thread uniting the conflicting trends at work in it? Five starting points could be proposed to describe and analyse the development of the economy of France since the Second World War:

- The process of modernizing the economy has been so rapid that a number of deep tensions, contradictions and problems of adaptation have arisen in a society which had previously been remarkably slow to emerge from its rural roots.
- This modernization process was made possible through the emergence of a relative economic and social consensus regulated by the state, which also directly controlled a large part of the economy. However, this model of economic regulation, which was never fully developed, started to show signs of strain in the 1960s and progressively collapsed during the 1970s and 1980s. This was due to a number of factors which included the impact of the

mid-1970s world economic crisis and the inherent tensions it created in capital management and between social groups.

- Modernization was also accompanied by the opening up of the French economy to the rest of the world. After the loss of the colonial empire, France participated in the creation of the European Economic Community, French industries and services had to operate from the early 1960s in a wider and more competitive market environment. Not only did this so-called *'contrainte extérieure'* accelerate the pace of change in the economy at large, but it also radically altered and reduced the ability of the state to intervene and regulate the workings of the economic system.
- Since the mid-1980s, the integration of the French economy within what is now the European Union has accelerated, culminating in the adoption of the Euro, the single currency now shared by 11 of the 15 Union members. As a consequence, the whole economy is going through another accelerated transformation which affects all markets, as well as the role of public institutions.
- The collapse of the post-war development model in the 1980s and 1990s has had devastating social consequences. Mass unemployment and social exclusion have become permanent and costly fixtures of French society and, at the beginning of the new century, these issues had not yet been resolved.

These changes have dramatically affected the daily lives of French people over the last three generations. Today around three-quarters of the population live in urban areas (one-fifth of these in the Paris region) and six out of seven are wage-earners as opposed to self-employed workers. At the end of the 1940s, nearly two-thirds of the working population were employed in agriculture or in industry. Now, seven out of ten people are employed in services and the overwhelming importance of sectors such as education, commerce, transport, finance, health and communications is mirrored by changes in the way people consume, and the way they organize their lives. Income levels have increased considerably: for instance, the minimum wage level, in real terms, increased 3.4 times between 1951 and 1996. Such increases have also brought new patterns of consumption, while the training and education of the work-force has also improved considerably. There have therefore been great improvements in living standards and in the opportunities offered to most of the population.

However, these changes have their darker side. Since the 1950s socio-economic life has been beset by deep tension and conflicts, particularly because the ways in which modernization has been implemented have relentlessly destroyed more traditional sectors as well as the ways of life associated with them, and excluded certain social groups from the new economic framework. Furthermore, this process of social exclusion was exacerbated from the mid-1970s onwards by the recurrent world economic crisis. Since 1982, unemployment in France has never dropped below two million, and has often reached three million – more than 13 per cent of the active population. Long-term unemployment has developed into a form of permanent social exclusion. A heavy toll has been exacted on some parts of society, such as single-parent families, the families of immigrant workers and young unskilled people who are excluded from the mainstream of expansion. This has created the so-called '*société à deux vitesses*' (two-speed society).

There are many ways of describing the further changes which have affected the French economy since the 1970s and the progressive abandonment of the post-war 'French model': as the movement towards an 'advanced' or 'post-industrial' open economy, as the development of activities based on a 'service economy' or on 'information production', or as a shift towards 'post-Fordist' production and regulation systems. But however these changes are described, the roots of many of them are to be found in the evolution of the production system.

Part II therefore begins by focusing on the ways the French system of production has adapted over the last few decades and looks at the changing nature and structure of the work-force. We look at the ways in which the added value obtained from the production system is used, concentrating on the distribution and redistribution of income. We also consider the pricing systems, noting that the French economy had strong inflationary tendencies which were only broken in the mid-1980s, and we look at the financial system whose very specific features changed considerably in the last two decades.

Next we examine one of the peculiarities of the French economy. Although the economy is firmly entrenched in a market-based capitalist system, the role of the state was central both to its reorganization in the post-war period and to providing the necessary tools for its growth in the 1960s. However, since the mid-1970s the role of the state in the organization of the economy has been called into question and has changed rapidly.

Finally, the French economy is now facing new challenges within the European framework, which again call into question the present structures, practices and policies. The consequences of deeper integration within the European Union, France's exposure to the deregulated global exchange networks and the reorganization of 'flexible' markets on the domestic front are therefore examined. Some conclusions will be drawn as to the possible development of the French economy in the future. One of the most crucial challenges in the construction of some form of new, post-crisis consensus is posed by the need to reduce the social cost of economic efficiency, and especially unemployment. A second challenge is to find an equilibrium within the European market. Will the French economy retain some of its specific characteristics or will these disappear in a homogeneous European system? A final matter for reflexion concerns the future role of the public sector and public authorities within the EU and a liberalized world economy.

# Growth and crisis in the production system

The production and exchange of goods and services, which constitutes the basis of economic life, has evolved since the Second World War through periods of growth and recession which in France have broadly followed the same patterns as in other industrialized economies. However, at a more substantive level, the French production system has evolved with a rhythm of its own. Thus we shall first describe the main stages in this evolution, and then go on to analyse the changes in the labour force and in the structure of firms.

## From economic growth to crisis

In France, as in other European countries, economic development in the second half of the twentieth century has taken place in two periods which have radically different characteristics. The first extends from immediately after the Second World War up to 1974. During that time France experienced unprecedented growth, comparable to that of Japan or West Germany. The strength of this trend was due to an accumulation of factors, such as the considerable growth of productive and infrastructural investments, the acceleration of technological developments, as well as the increase in the size and qualifications of the workforce, but also to the organizing, funding and regulating role of the public sector and government [see Text 2.1].

The result was a huge movement of population from rural to urban areas, the creation of millions of jobs and a general improvement in standards of living. But it also provoked social tensions in a society which was not, as yet, adapted to new ways of consuming and producing but which ruthlessly excluded the remnants of previous modes of production. The revolt of May 1968 was an illustration of the underlying social problems affecting the system, which had not yet been properly addressed by the political decision-making process.

When the economic crisis hit France in 1974, new changes in the production system became inevitable, especially because the crisis coincided with the full opening up of the French economy to the rest of the world, and new tensions resulted from the need to improve the competitiveness of France's economy on the European and world markets which were now less regulated and therefore less and less predictable. Since the mid-1970s the impact of economic difficulties (including that of the recurrent world economic crisis which peaked in 1973–5, 1980–82 and 1990–93) on many French households has been considerable. Even though a great majority continue to see their standard of living increase, unemployment has risen rapidly. This division between a better-off majority and a large minority excluded from rising living standards, or threatened by the uncertainty of its economic position and identity, is at the root of many of the socio-political upheavals experienced in France since the late 1970s.

## The 'Trente glorieuses'

At the end of the Second World War, the economic situation in France presented a sorry picture. By the end of the nineteenth century, France had been one of the leading economic powers in the world, drawing on its large population, vast agricultural resources and powerful pockets of industry, as well as on its sizeable colonial empire. However, its economic situation deteriorated considerably between 1920 and 1945, with an ageing population and lack of productive investment. The destructions of the Second World War added their toll. At the Liberation, France seemed an inward-looking, still largely rural economy, with an outdated industrial sector that had been severely damaged, and relatively limited trade with the outside world, except with its colonial empire within which it was living in semi-autarky.

In view of this, the high rates of growth in the national product in the decades following the Second World War are all the more impressive. The thirty years which followed the Liberation have been dubbed the 'Trente glorieuses', and for good reason. The annual growth of the Gross Domestic Product (GDP) was such that it was multiplied by a factor of three between 1950 and 1975 (in real terms).[1] The fastest growth occurred during the 1960s and early 1970s: between 1960 and 1973 it was multiplied by 2.1. As illustrated in Figure 2.1, the rate of growth was far higher than in the United Kingdom over the whole period, and higher than in West Germany during the 1960s and 1970s. Although this growth affected every sector of the economy, it was at its most rapid in industry, where it reached a very high 7.5 per cent average annual rate of growth between 1959 and 1973. Agriculture, by comparison, averaged 2.5 per cent.

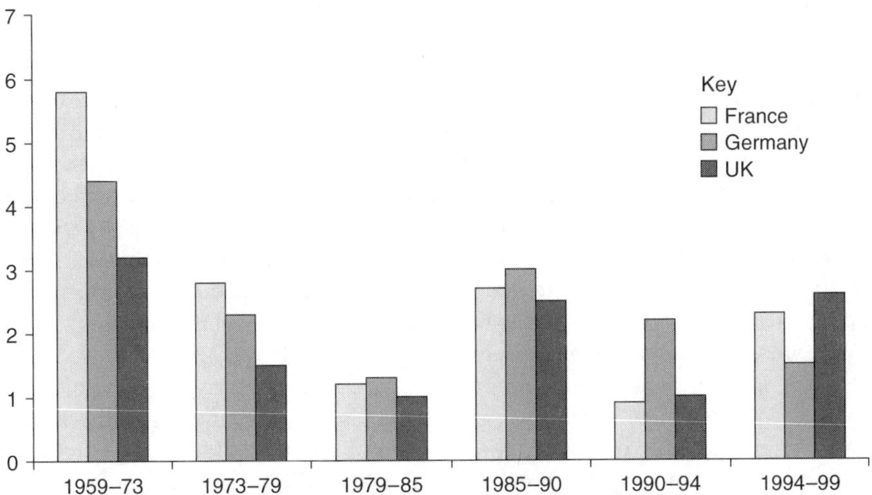


**Figure 2.1 Comparison of annual GDP growth rates between France, Germany and the United Kingdom (per cent, average over each period) 1959–99**
*Source*: OECD, *Economic Perspectives*, various issues.

## The impact of investment

A major reason for the high growth of the *Trente glorieuses* period was the pattern and growth of investment. The rate of investment (as a proportion of GDP) was one of the highest in the world, only bettered by that of Japan. Productive investment, especially in industry, increased considerably in the 1950s and 1960s, speeding up the introduction of modern technology and the more efficient organization of labour (largely in the so-called *'travail à la chaîne'* of the Fordist type, widely attacked by unions for its dehumanizing nature). Investment in construction also played a considerable role in stimulating economic growth. Both housing and urban infrastructure projects, largely in the public sector, were necessary not only because of the requirements of new urban populations, but also because of the very poor state of the existing housing stock after the war. There were considerable infrastructure investments during the 1950s and 1960s in the transport and energy sectors (for instance, a large number of hydroelectric dams were built in these decades).

The proportion of domestic resources devoted to investment during these three decades therefore reached high levels, growing continuously from around 20 per cent of GDP during the 1950s to 23.4 per cent in 1973. A large proportion of this investment was made by the public sector, either by government ministries or by the nationalized industries.

## Labour as a factor of growth

A contributing factor to growth was that considerable reserves of labour were available: new workers came from rural areas, immigration increased, especially in the 1960s, and women again started entering employment in greater numbers. The working population grew from 19.4 million in 1954 to more than 22 million in 1975. Thus, while the number of people newly entering the labour market was stable during the 1950s, it increased by more than 290,000 per year between 1962 and 1973.[2] The new labour force was better educated, better trained, and used better equipment. As a consequence, labour productivity improved continuously over the period, so that between 1951 and 1973 it increased over the whole economy by 5.2 per cent a year, with the rate reaching 5.1 per cent in industry and 6.3 per cent in agriculture.[3] Another contributory factor to growth is also related to the expansion of the new, mostly urban, labour force. Families in this growth economy increased the domestic demand for new household goods (from cars and televisions to bathrooms) which was all the greater because of the low level of provision before the war [see Text 2.2].

There are therefore a whole range of explanations for the new growth economy: high investment rates, the development of new technologies, the larger and better skilled work-force, the growth of demand. However, all these elements would not by themselves have created the conditions for balanced economic growth, and sustained it for nearly three decades. Something more was required and two other factors played a central role: first, the 'Fordist' production system which was instituted in a large part of industry; second, the specific role played by the public sector in coercing, inducing and organizing economic agents and regulating the flows of activity within the market system. These specific elements will be examined later.

## The unfinished crisis: disruptions in the production system

After nearly three decades of solid economic growth and rising incomes, the impact of the two so-called 'oil crises' in 1973–4 and in 1979 was such, in France as elsewhere, that they were seen as the main causes of the economic crises which followed, whereas in fact these had deeper roots than simple increases in oil prices, however great those increases may have been. We will first discuss some of the symptoms of the economic crisis and will then examine some of these deep-rooted problems. Contrary to some other countries, such as Japan or the UK, France weathered the impact of the first oil crisis relatively well. But the second economic crisis in the early 1980s had a greater impact in France than elsewhere, with rates of growth between 1979 and 1985 lower than those of most of France's competitors, and economic recovery occurring later.

As in other industrialized countries, the economic crisis which developed in France during 1973–4 cannot be compared with the Great Depression of the 1930s. It was characterized by a slow-down of activity rather than a full recession (marked by an absolute fall in production), and after 1973 the annual rate of growth was almost always higher than 1 per cent, the exceptions being 1975 and 1993 (see Figure 2.2). The first two periods of crisis, in the mid-1970s and in the early 1980s, were also marked by high inflation (which stood at over 10 per cent a year for six years in the decade between 1973 and 1983, and over 13 per cent in three of those years), hence the term 'stagflation' (stagnation plus inflation) which was used to describe this situation. By stark contrast, in the

**Figure 2.2 Annual GDP growth and rate of inflation, 1970–99 (per cent)**
*Note*: 1999 figures are provisional.
*Source*: OECD, *Economic Perspectives*, various issues.

crisis period of the early 1990s, there was no inflation to speak of, and analysts were then worried by possible deflation (general fall of price levels).

The modest expansion in the second part of the 1990s, with annual rates of growth of between 2 and 4 per cent between 1997 and 1999, accompanied by the quasi-disappearance of inflation, appeared to continue unabated at the beginning of the new century. The question is whether the French economy then entered a 'virtuous circle', or the so-called 'new paradigm', to use the term applied to the structural conditions of accelerated growth in the economy of the United States in the 1990s. Whatever the answer, the preceding crisis deeply modified some of the structural elements of the economy.

The most remarkable change is that the industrial sector in France is no longer the locomotive of economic growth that it was during the 1960s. The growth of industrial output fell to 3 per cent a year between 1973 and 1979 and it was negligible from 1979 to 1985. Between 1985 and 1998 it grew again, but only at an average annual rate of around 2.5 per cent. At the same time, although services were growing at a slightly faster rate, they were not replacing industry as a force pulling the economy forward.

Another trend, which may provide one of the main explanations for the crisis, was the slow-down of investment in the economy. Indeed, whereas gross capital investment (housing, productive investment, collective infrastructure and so on) had been growing constantly during the *Trente glorieuses*, reaching an all-time high of 24.5 per cent of GDP in 1974, it then fell to less than 19 per cent in 1984 before climbing back slightly, reaching 21 per cent in 1990, and falling back again to around 17 per cent in 1998. This is despite the fact that firms had, since the late 1980s, recovered their gross margin.

The crisis in industry contributed to the growth of unemployment from the early 1970s onwards. Many plants closed down and even those industries which managed to survive, such as the car industry, shed large numbers of jobs, either because of reduced demand or because employers concentrated their investment in labour-saving machinery. However, improvements in labour productivity, which had been considerable during the post-war period, slowed down significantly after the mid-1970s. The growth of output per hour worked had reached 5.2 per cent per year between 1951 and 1973; it fell to 2.5 per cent per year between 1981 and 1990, and to 1.5 per cent between 1991 and 1998, in a similar pattern to that found in other industrialized countries.

These factors – the persistence of high unemployment, the slower progress of labour productivity and the low investment levels – indicate that the structural aspects of the economic crisis are still not fully corrected, despite the better performance of the economy as a whole since the late 1990s. However, it is also clear that the two decades of upheaval, from the mid-1970s to the mid-1990s, have completely changed the production system in France, especially in industry. Production methods, the organization of industrial firms, their relation to the market, the forms of competition and the role of the state have all been challenged and have undergone considerable modifications.

In fact, by the late 1960s, structural problems were beginning to unbalance the institutional and market framework of the *Trente glorieuses*. These problems were partly those of the international market, such as the crisis in the international monetary system, the intense competition and over-capacity in a number of heavy industries all over the world and the decline in profitability of industrial assets in a number of countries such as the United States. These factors had a greater and greater impact on a French economy which was increasingly integrated into the world economy.

Other warning signals were specifically related to the evolution of the domestic economy. Since 1964 there had been a slow-down in the growth of the productivity of industrial capital. Among other factors, this was due to the lack of investment flexibility between sectors, inadequate adaptation to technology and markets, and an insufficient increase in productivity in sectors which were important at the international level. These elements were in part inherent to the mode of development of industry (and of the economy as a whole) after the Second World War.

## The emergence of the 'state Fordist' model

The type of development specific to the French economy during the *Trente glorieuses* was largely based on the so-called 'Fordist' model. The foundation of this is the generalization of investment in large manufacturing units producing efficiently for mass-consumption markets. Economies of scale in manufacturing units are accompanied by labour organization techniques which improve labour productivity through an intensification of the use of capital (with shift work, assembly lines and the so-called 'scientific organization of labour'). The result was the production of relatively cheap products requiring mass markets.

Another aspect of this industrial development model was, therefore, that, in order to allow for the mass consumption of newly developed technological products, such as 'white' and 'brown' goods like refrigerators and television sets, it was necessary to obtain increases in purchasing power more or less in line with the growth in output. This in part explains the place of neo-Keynesian models in economic policy at this time, as the management of demand was crucial to the profitability of industrial capital. It also explains the popularity and resilience of political slogans often used at the time, such as 'le partage équitable des fruits de la croissance' (sharing the benefits of economic growth fairly between labour and capital).

The Fordist industrial model as developed in France was not identical to the one that operated, for example, in the United States. For instance, there was less reliance in France on automation and assembly lines, but a far more highly developed system of shift working. Typical of such industrial firms were car manufacturers (dominated by Renault, Citroën and Peugeot), the steel industry (de Wendel, Usinor), other electrical manufacturers (Compagnie Générale d'Électricité), aluminium (Pechiney and Ugine), aircraft manufacturing (Sud-Aviation, soon to become Aérospatiale), mechanical engineering (the Schneider group) and glass and construction materials (Saint-Gobain). Indeed, France saw industrial output and the labour force increasingly concentrated in large units so that plants employing more than 500 people accounted for just over 35 per cent of industrial employment in 1960, but around 45 per cent in 1974.

What is specific to the French Fordist model is the central role played by the state in 'regulating' economic activity. This did not only concern the establishment of the 'rules of the game' in competitive markets. It went further afield, into spheres such as income distribution and monetary/financial flows, investment planning, labour markets and the spatial organization of activities, as well as direct control of part of the industrial and financial sectors. In a system in which equilibrium depends largely on continued growth in production and investment on the one hand, and on a social consensus guaranteeing the sharing out of the *fruits de la croissance* on the other, there was a need for some form of regulation of companies, and of investments and consumption. In France, unlike other market economies, the central role played by the state, as we will see later, was largely rendered necessary by inadequacies in the structure of the economy, and by the legacy of history. But this had little to do with a specific ideology concerning the role of the public sector. Instead, it derived from the traditional pattern of relationships between state power and the market in a country in which the private sector had often relied on the public sector to take the lead in financial or infrastructural terms. Hence the French pattern of a mixed economy often associated with intermingled public and private interests in the production system.

## The demise of the French model

The model for balanced growth developed during the 1950s and 1960s was not only somewhat fragile and rigid, but it was only partly successful in its aims. Management structures were badly prepared for the sort of intense competition that the gradual opening of markets at international level forced upon them from the mid-1960s, and more especially from the mid-1980s onwards. In addition, the model had inherently unstable features, at an international level as well as in the French domestic economy.

It began to show signs of strain in the late 1960s when the colonial empire had been lost and the main foreign markets in Europe, after the complete opening of EC markets in 1968, were highly competitive. At the same time social tensions in France were reaching breaking point. In many firms, 'restructuring' and the continuing use of management methods derived from Taylorism had alienated many employees. The education system, which had not adapted to providing mass education and modern skills, broke down (see Part III). These factors gave rise to the May 1968 movement. Although the *Accords de Grenelle*, ending the 1968 strikes, gave a boost to the economy, it was a sign that everything was not perfect in the affluent consumer society of the 1960s.

As far as manufacturing was concerned, the system no longer provided the required economies of scale and the increase in labour productivity that the accumulation of capital and the scientific organization of labour had promised. On the contrary, from the mid-1960s onwards, the profitability of corporate industrial capital fell, as did the use of productive capacity, while unemployment and inflation began to rise, well before the oil crises. These warning signs only took on their full meaning in the 1980s, when the profit rate of industrial capital became lower than the rate of return on financial investment, and productive investment fell across the economy, especially in industry. In a number of sectors such as steel, shipbuilding, textiles and clothing, the electrical and electronics industries, motor cars and heavy engineering, competition from foreign producers was becoming intense, and these were the sectors which had been the most heavily capitalized during the previous decades, and which employed a large number of people in large plants.

Changes in the structure of both domestic and foreign demand and the relative saturation of many domestic markets called for a complete revolution in the organization and management of industry. The new requirement was for 'flexible' labour and capital in order to respond swiftly to competition, new patterns of demand and technological developments, and also for firms to disengage from unprofitable activities and to shed both over-capacity and excess labour. During the late 1970s and the 1980s French managers used the word '*dégraissage*' (slimming down) when reducing the work-force, and referred to the '*fermeture des canards boiteux*' (closing down lame ducks) for shutting obsolete, unprofitable or unwanted industrial plants [see Text 2.3].

The impact on French industry was dramatic. Not only did industrial employment fall as a percentage of total work-force (see Tables 2.1 and 2.2) but it fell in absolute numbers from 8.3 million persons (including construction) in 1974 to 6.4 million in 1988 and 5.3 million in 1998 – nearly three million jobs lost. This particularly affected large production units. Indeed, the concentration of activities so characteristic of the previous period was completely reversed. Whereas in 1974 plants with 500 employees or more were employing 45 per cent of all wage-earners in industry (including construction), this had fallen in 1997 to around 25 per cent.

**Table 2.1 Evolution of added value by sector as percentage of GDP**

| (% of GDP) | 1959 | 1973 | 1990 | 1998 |
|---|---|---|---|---|
| Agriculture | 9.7 | 6.4 | 3.5 | 3.1 |
| Industry | 35.0 | 41.8 | 28.3 | 26.1 |
| Services | 55.3 | 51.8 | 68.2 | 71.8 |

*Sources*: For 1959 and 1973 data, J.-F. Eck, *Histoire de l'économie française depuis 1945* (A. Colin, 1992); for 1990 and 1998 data, INSEE, *Comptes Nationaux*, www.insee.fr/vf/chifcles/.

**Table 2.2 Evolution of employment by sector, 1949–98 (per cent)**

| | 1949 | 1959 | 1973 | 1980 | 1990 | 1998 |
|---|---|---|---|---|---|---|
| Primary | 29.2 | 22.1 | 10.9 | 8.8 | 5.3 | 4.7 |
| Industry | 35.0 | 35.2 | 37.8 | 33.1 | 25.5 | 23.4 |
| Services | 35.8 | 42.7 | 51.3 | 58.1 | 69.2 | 71.9 |

*Sources*: For 1949 to 1973 data, J.-F. Eck, *Histoire de l'économie française depuis 1945* (A. Colin, 1992); for 1980 to 1998 data, INSEE, *Enquêtes Emplois 1980 to 1998*, www.insee.fr/vf/chifcles/.

Whole industries nearly disappeared (big shipbuilding is now mainly concentrated in one yard) and many giant plants closed. Renault, for instance, employed more than 30,000 people in its Billancourt plant near Paris in the early 1960s, but it closed it down in 1992. In some cases, whole regions suffered a spate of closures (for instance, the Lorraine region lost most of its steel plants in the 1970s). Large firms are still growing in terms of their share of output, but they now organize production in smaller, more flexible units, making more use of external subcontracting, more flexible working conditions, and increasingly relying on short-term contract workers. Similar flexibility can increasingly be found in capital structures: firms now often switch activities, diversifying their activities away from their first area of specialization or, on the contrary, refocusing their activities. Large industry-based or service groups, although still under-capitalized compared with their European or North American competitors, are now behaving more like general holding companies, as centres of industrial and financial power and, since the early 1990s, takeovers and mergers have become increasingly frequent.

The shift from a mass Fordist model of production to the so-called 'post-Fordist' model has also reduced the pre-eminent role of the government and the public sector within the market economy. There are two reasons for this. The first reason is that the opening of the French economy to the European market and to the rest of the world economy in general made the government's intervention tools inoperative (and in some cases, illegal, according to the 'free market' interpretation of EU rules on competition and deregulation). The second reason is that the Fordist model itself had failed to protect the basic equilibrium on which it had built the social consensus in France, and the sustained improvements in living standards could no longer be guaranteed. Another role for the government had to be devised, with a different regulatory system, which will be examined below.

## The labour force and the unemployment crisis

One of the main changes that has affected the French economy (and French society) since the middle of the twentieth century is the socio-demographic evolution of the country. Not only has the population increased significantly, but its structure and dynamics are having a considerable impact on some of the most crucial aspects of the economy, from the characteristics of the labour force to those of household consumption and income distribution.

### A growing labour force

An important aspect of economic growth in the 1960s was its massive labour requirements. These were satisfied by many people leaving agriculture to work in industry in the 1950s, by calling on large numbers of immigrants to work in

France, by the growth of the population, as described above, and by the increased participation of women in the work-force, especially from the end of 1960s onwards. These trends more than compensated for the opposing factors, namely entry into the labour force at a later age (because of the tremendous expansion in education) and the earlier retirement age.

During the 1960s the French economy absorbed some 200,000 new workers per year. Indeed, the return to mainland France of over a million French settlers from Algeria (*les pieds-noirs*) just before independence did not put much strain on the labour market. However, since the beginning of the period of economic crises, the potential for employment creation has been considerably weakened and a large number of jobs have disappeared; but the number of new arrivals on the labour market did not decrease proportionately, despite the nearly total ban on new immigration after 1974. Around 150,000 new persons on average entered the labour market each year between 1973 and 1998, with the flow only slowing in some years, such as 1983 or 1995. An equivalent number of jobs should have been created every year during this period simply to keep unemployment at stable levels, but industrial and agricultural sectors were shedding labour as quickly as possible, as described below. Although the service sector created a large number of jobs (more than 5.1 million additional jobs between 1973 and 1998), this could not compensate for the 2.7 million jobs lost in industry and construction and 1.3 million lost in agriculture during the same period, and at the same time provide new jobs for the new arrivals in the work-force, some 3.7 million people. Hence there was a considerable increase in unemployment, which rose from 0.6 million to some 3.1 million persons from 1973 to 1998. This has been the central problem for the French economy since the end of the *Trente glorieuses.*

## Two decades with more than two million unemployed

During the 1950s and 1960s, France experienced little unemployment other than so-called 'frictional' unemployment. In 1965, for instance, the number of unemployed stood at only 250,000. The 1980s and 1990s were very different (see Figure 2.3). Unemployment began to rise slowly at the end of the 1960s. It then shot up, reaching almost three-quarters of a million by 1974 and rising inexorably towards two million in 1982 and 2.4 million in 1985. The slight recovery of the economy in the late 1980s then allowed for a fall to some 2.3 million in 1990, but this was a brief respite [see Text 2.4]. With a new recession, jobs again disappeared, and unemployment passed the three million mark in 1996.[4] Although the growth experienced in the last years of the 1990s improved the situation, the fall in unemployment was very slow, and it was only in 2000 that unemployment again dipped under three million.

As in other countries, unemployment affects some groups more than others, with the more vulnerable being younger people trying to enter the labour market, women and unskilled workers. In 1999 there were still 24 per cent of active young men under the age of 25 who were unemployed, and nearly 30 per cent of young women, as against 11.8 per cent for the whole of the active

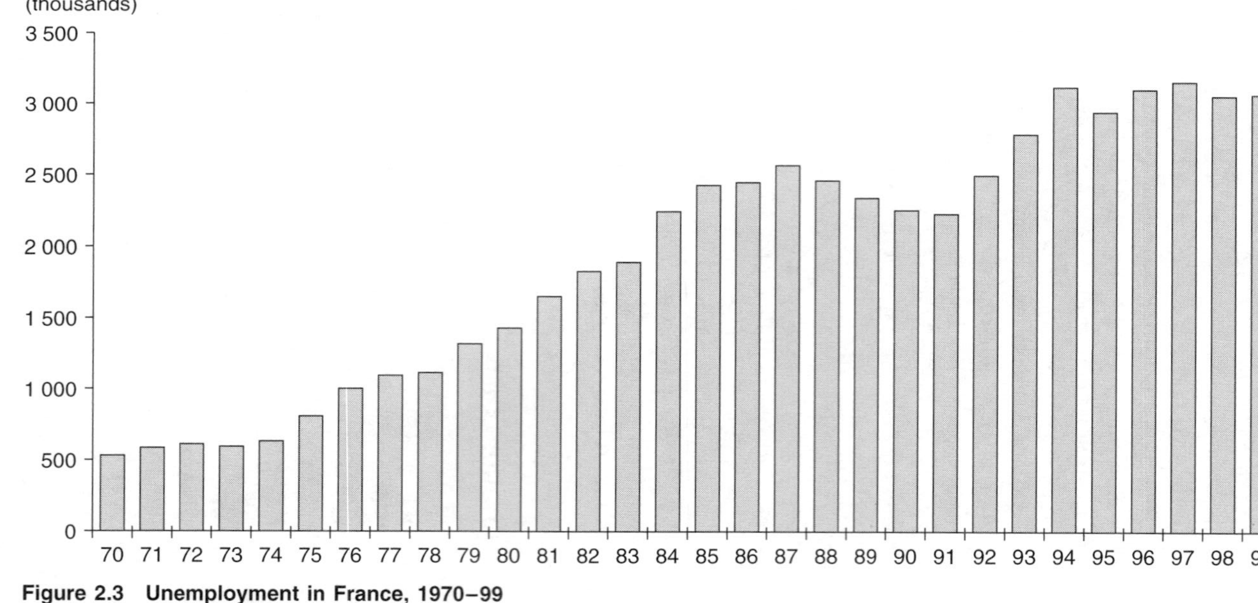


**Figure 2.3 Unemployment in France, 1970–99**

*Source:* Data from the Institut national de la statistique et des études économiques (INSEE), '*Emploi*' surveys conducted in March of every year. The data are not adjusted for seasonal variations, and unemployment is calculated according to the ILO definition.

population. It is not only young women who suffer more than men. Some 13.6 per cent of women in general were unemployed in 1999, as against 10.2 per cent of men. As a consequence, 52.5 per cent of the jobless were women, although they only represented 45.4 per cent of the working population. Immigrants are also particularly affected by unemployment.

In one sense, long-term unemployment, which affected more than one million people, is only the most dramatic symptom of an underlying change in job structures [see Text 2.5]. The traditional employment pattern up to the 1970s was of a large, but shrinking, number of self-employed working people (in agriculture, retail and services, and crafts), while the increasing number of wage-earners were occupying full-time, permanent employment, with relatively little job and geographical mobility. Now the number of self-employed people has fallen dramatically, and the development of unemployment has been accompanied by new trends in the employment conditions of wage-earners. The economic crisis has allowed the development of 'flexibility' in the labour market, with a wide range of differing labour conditions, from a core of employees with secure long-term jobs at one extreme, and long-term unemployment and total exclusion at the other end of the scale. In the middle are people with short-term contracts, part-time employees wanting to work more (although not as many as in some other countries) and a number of people in state-subsidized temporary public work. In 1998 more than 22 per cent of the active population belonged to these last two categories, that is, the unemployed and those in so-called 'precarious' employment.[5] The continued existence of such a segmented labour market, with an increase in labour 'flexibility', was one of the main problems of the 1990s [see Text 2.6].

This situation arose despite government attempts to apply policies and programmes aimed at reducing unemployment. Apart from specific macro-economic policies designed to accelerate economic growth, governments since the 1970s have also developed policies aimed at specific jobless groups, either to exclude them from the working population and therefore from unemployment figures (this is the case for older unemployed people) or to give them temporary training and temporary jobs (as is the case with younger unemployed people). The retirement age for men was lowered from 65 to 60 with effect from 1982. In addition, from the mid-1970s onwards, a number of schemes were put together to eliminate people aged 55 and over from the unemployment figures: *pré-retraites* (early retirement schemes), for example, were introduced in industries like steel that were fast losing jobs. Such schemes guaranteed an income to people up to the time they reached statutory retirement age and could draw a pension. As in other countries, governments also frequently modified the statistical definition of unemployment with a view to reducing jobless numbers.

But the most wide-ranging schemes concerned young people. Various public sector temporary 'work experience' and 'youth training' schemes were organized, such as community work (TUC: 'Travaux d'utilité collective') and work placements (SIVP: 'Stages d'insertion à la vie professionnelle'), which by 1987 had assisted up to a million people aged 16–25. In the 1990s, the scope of these programmes narrowed, with more emphasis being given to skills training, in the 'contrats emploi-formation' for instance. All these schemes and policies providing temporary jobs or training to the unemployed were collectively described as the 'traitement social du chômage' (social remedies for unemployment) and were different from the 'traitement économique' (economic solutions). However, they had no significant impact on people's employability, nor did they help reduce long-term real unemployment; their main effect was to provide temporary relief to the long-term unemployed and to reduce official jobless figures.

The critique of this kind of strategy led to a new type of interventionist labour policy, as part of the programme of the new *gauche plurielle* government of Lionel Jospin formed in 1997 [see Part I]. Alongside new programmes aimed at getting the long-term unemployed back to work (through individually tailored training and work experience), two new schemes were introduced that attempted to have a longer-term impact on the job prospects of the unemployed than the traditional *traitement social*. The 'emplois-jeunes' scheme, introduced in 1998, aimed at providing long-term jobs for people under 25. These were offered mostly in public organizations, utilities and the voluntary sector; they were guaranteed for five years, with wages close to the SMIC (salaire minimum de croissance), and were state-subsidized. The purpose of this operation was to 'insert' young people into the labour market for a long period of time in order for them to get real experience and to prevent them being considered outsiders. The cost of subsidy was considered to be lower than the unemployment and social benefits that would have been drawn from the public purse had the scheme not existed. In 1999 more than 200,000 young people were participating in the programme.

The second new scheme launched in 1998 was concerned with working time. Its premises are that a generalized and compulsory lowering of full-time working hours from 39 to 35 hours per week, with a strict limit imposed on permitted overtime, will bring about some 'redistribution' of labour within the active population: that is, firms will have to take on new workers in order to compensate for the lower number of hours worked by existing employees and this will therefore bring down unemployment. This policy relies on the principle of 'solidarity', although wage-earners are guaranteed the same earnings for working fewer hours and the difference is paid by government subsidies (economic models having shown that the cost of this will be lower than the social cost of unemployment). This system has provoked considerable debate in France and elsewhere. Strong opposition was voiced by the employers' federation (Medef) and by free-market liberals, who claimed that the policy would create extra costs for business and prevent the development of an efficient and flexible labour market. Many unions also rejected and protested against aspects of the scheme. However, its implementation has had unexpected effects. The 'loi des 35 heures', or 'loi Aubry' (so named after Martine Aubry, the Minister for Employment and Solidarity who piloted its adoption by parliament) is in fact made up of two laws, one passed in 1997, which introduced a negotiated and voluntary path to the 35-hour week for firms of more than twenty employees, and another finally passed in 1999 which introduced a compulsory 35-hour week in 2002 for those firms which had not yet introduced it. The negotiations for the implementation of the scheme became in fact an opportunity for employers, unions and employee representatives to organize flexibility of employment such as seasonal variations in working time, and the flexible working week. Thus, in true French tradition, the modernization and flexibility of working practices are being obtained, not so much through deregulated markets, but through state-brokered, negotiated regulation. It is still too early to gauge the real impact of the *lois Aubry*; in early 2000 they were estimated to have preserved or created only a few tens of thousands of jobs, but it appears that they have deeply modified the structure of the labour market.

## Structure of employment: the decline of industry and farming

The economic shifts of the last few decades have dramatically affected the structure of employment. Whereas agriculture employed some six million people in the mid-1950s, this number had fallen to 1.9 million by 1980, and to under one million by 1998. This fall appears unstoppable. The shift away from agricultural employment obviously played an important part in the rural exodus between the 1950s and the 1970s. Thus the rural population fell from 43 per cent in 1946 to around 20 per cent in the mid-1990s.[6] Agriculture in many areas has now been marginalized in terms of employment, and rural areas situated on the periphery of large towns are once again seeing their populations grow as commuters colonize them.

By contrast, the industrial work-force has followed a completely different path. As noted earlier, the growth pattern of the *Trente glorieuses* was largely industry-based and this was reflected in employment figures. Whereas industry (including the building industries) employed some 6.6 million people in 1954, this number had increased to 8.3 million by 1974 (including nearly two million in construction). However, this trend was reversed by the economic crises as manufacturing and other industries started shedding jobs. More than 1.3 million jobs were lost in manufacturing industry, and some 450,000 in the building industry, between 1974 and 1988. After a brief respite, the downward spiral continued, with a total of only 5.6 million people employed in the sector in 1998. The prospects for job growth in this sector are fairly minimal, as the investment occurring in industry is now mainly oriented towards the introduction of new technology and productivity improvements. By contrast, services employed more than 16 million people in 1998, more than two-thirds of the total number of jobs in the economy and more than twice the number in 1954 (7.3 million). Although this massive creation of jobs has been slowed down by the recurrent economic crises, it has never been interrupted by them. However, employment in services is not homogeneous and trends vary from sector to sector.

## Characteristics of work

Perhaps one of the main changes in the work-force has been the growing importance of wage-earning employment. In 1954, 34 per cent of jobs were provided through self-employment, but this proportion had fallen to less than 11 per cent by 1998. This was mostly due to the fall in the number of farmers, but other contributory factors were the reduction in the number of independent shopkeepers and craftsmen. However, the number of self-employed service workers has increased again since the mid-1980s.

Another important characteristic of work is its duration, calculated either as hours per week or weeks per year. Both have shown a marked downward tendency. Although the legal length of the working week was fixed at 40 hours per week in 1936, the real working week for full-time employees in industry and services has often been higher, because of the widespread practice of overtime. In the 1960s blue-collar workers were putting in more than 46 hours a week, but working time was beginning to decrease for white-collar workers. However, it was the economic crisis which had the strongest impact on working hours, with weekly hours falling from around 44.5 in 1973 for blue-collar workers, the longest hours in the EEC, to fewer than 41 hours in 1981. The legal length of the working week was lowered to 39 hours in January 1982, but this was, by then, no more than the recognition of an existing trend. By the end of the 1990s both blue- and white-collar full-time workers were working just under 40 hours a week, including overtime, which is lower than in the UK (some 44 hours per week), but comparable to most other countries of the EU. Part-time working developed considerably during the 1990s, but it still only affected 17 per cent of the work-force in 1998, and these were overwhelmingly women (nearly 32 per cent of female employees, compared with 24 per cent in 1990). Another factor which has contributed to reducing working time is the extension of annual paid leave. This first appeared in 1936, and it slowly expanded, reaching four weeks in the 1960s and five weeks in 1982, with the result that yearly working time in industry in France had fallen to 1763 hours by 1991, far lower than in Japan (2119) but higher than in Germany (1643). In 1998 it was only 1500 hours.

Another important aspect of working life is the lifetime duration of work. The generation in retirement in the early years of the new century is privileged, as it is a small age group which was able to benefit from improved financial conditions and a lowering of the retirement age. However, even before the male retirement age was lowered, a large number of people were taking earlier retirement, either because of their job (teachers and miners, for example, can retire early) or because of early retirement schemes. In the future it is not certain that the retirement age will stay as rigidly fixed as it is now, because of the changes in the demographic structure of the population (an ageing labour force), and also because of the changes in employment conditions. The developing flexibility of working conditions is likely to modify the whole pattern of employment. The development of education and skills training since the 1970s is another indicator of such trends.

Individuals now have a tendency to postpone their entry into the labour market because of two interconnected factors: their difficulty in finding their first 'real' job and the greater number of young people who stay in the education system or in vocational training. Only 28 per cent of this age group is economically active, that is with a job or on the dole (as against 45 per cent in the early 1980s). In addition, it is now more and more common for individuals to undergo periods of training during their working lives and employers are now obliged to finance such training and to provide 'congés de formation' (paid training leave) for employees. Indeed, it was estimated that, in 1996, some 10 million people, two-thirds of them in employment, had training paid for by their employers or by the state.

## Regional revolutions: the geographical distribution of the French economy

Throughout the last century there were considerable population movements as a result of changes in the economy. Alongside the overall population increase (from 36.5 million in 1851 to 60 million in 1999) there has been a population shift from regions with a declining economic base towards other areas with promising development potential. Industrial development in nineteenth-century France took place in the areas of natural resources such as the north and Lorraine, where coal was found, and where the iron and steel industries developed alongside textiles in the north and in the Vosges. Thus a large proportion of manufacturing industry was established on the eastern side of a line drawn between Le Havre, Reims and Lyons, with pockets elsewhere (for instance, a number of relatively isolated industrialized towns around and in the Massif Central, such as Le Creusot, Saint-Étienne and Clermont-Ferrand, or shipbuilding in the main coastal towns). The pre-eminence of Paris as the main French market also helped the development of industry there and made it the core of service activities.

The economic crises since the mid-1970s changed this map to a far greater degree than all the efforts of governments since the 1950s through regional planning policies known as 'l'aménagement du territoire'. The influence of central government was in fact more as a support than as a means of inducing radical change. The traditional industries simply could not withstand the crisis and whole regions, such as the Nord–Pas de Calais (textiles, coal and metallurgy) or Lorraine (steel and metallurgy) saw their century-old industrial base disappear. The lack of investment, the competition of foreign industries with recent investment and lower production costs, coupled with reduced demand and high production costs either brought these industries to their knees or forced thoroughgoing 'restructuring'.

Thus coal mining in the Nord–Pas de Calais employed 220,000 people in the 1950s, but the last pit closed in 1991. In more modern industries (motor cars, chemicals, household goods) the pressure of international competition and the need to increase productivity and efficiency did not always reduce the size of the work-force. For instance, Renault increased its total work-force from 61,000 in 1960 to 147,000 in 1998, but its principal and oldest factory, at Billancourt in the west of Paris, was closed in 1992, after a steady reduction in employment from nearly 30,000 in the mid-1960s. The transfer of activities to another part of the country, or to another country – a phenomenon known as *délocalisation* – has become more and more frequent as firms invest in plant and machinery which have a shorter lifespan than previously and are tied no longer to physical resources but instead to mobile networks such as labour skills, transport, markets and communications. The cost and 'flexibility' of labour also plays an important role. Textiles and electronics have been particularly affected by *délocalisation*.

Regions with more advanced industries and services, especially the Ile-de-France and Rhône–Alpes, and some regional metropolitan centres such as Toulouse and Strasbourg, have benefited from a concentration of the workforce and wealth. The western part of France is still largely under-industrialized (although there are some flourishing industries such as agribusiness in Brittany or aerospace in Toulouse). Predominantly rural regions with a weak and/or traditional agricultural base, and little industry, such as mountainous areas, parts of the west of France and parts of the Massif Central (such as Lozère, Corrèze and Creuse), were badly hit by the rural exodus, following other regions such as the Auvergne, and suffered an absolute decline in population numbers.[7] Hence the expression 'le désert français'.[8]

The main aim of regional planning during the 1960s and 1970s was to combat the effects of this process, with its concomitant loss of local services and ageing of the dwindling local population. Considerable regulatory, planning and financial efforts were made to entice industries and services away from Paris and the Ile-de-France, to rejuvenate old industrial regions like the north and Lorraine, and to open up under-developed regions (such as the Massif Central and Brittany). Considerable investments were made in infrastructure, such as motorways, railways, industrial zones, cultural and education facilities and so on, in areas distant from Paris. Industries wishing to set up in the Paris area were penalized. However, up to the 1980s the policy of decentralization was largely a failure, and even the main transport investments adopted the traditional 'star' shape, with Paris as the focus.

Even now the Ile-de-France region still plays a comparable role to that of the south-east of England in Great Britain. In 1997, with 2.2 per cent of France's total surface area, it had 18.9 per cent of its total population, with 21 per cent of jobs and 29 per cent of national GDP. Such an unbalanced distribution of population, income and resources results in considerable inequalities between regions. A typical example is unemployment, which is especially high in parts of the south (up to 16.5 per cent in Languedoc-Roussillon, 15.1 per cent in Provence-Côte d'Azur) or in the north (15.4 per cent in Nord–Pas-de-Calais), but less than half these levels in other, more privileged, regions (it reached only 7 per cent in Alsace, as against a national average of 11.7 per cent in 1997).

More recently, new factors and policies have altered some of the past trends. The development of regional urban centres such as Grenoble, Toulouse and Montpellier, as well as the movement of population into rural areas close to large cities (the so-called 'rurban' areas), have been accompanied by government policies concerning decentralization of the public sector, such as the 1982 *loi Defferre* and the 1991 decentralization of a number of public services and bodies, which have given new economic powers to the regions and departments alongside their newly found political role. Regional planning was to a degree revitalized by the 1995 *loi Pasqua* (from the name of the minister of interior at the time) and other reforms. Increasingly, regional planning is organized at local level, with pluri-annual programmes being organized between the different actors such as regions, *départements,* towns or *communautés urbaines* (groupings of local concils in a conurbation) and the state, through the so-called 'contrats de plan'. Another illustration of the way local tiers of planning have become more important is the emergence of new entities, *pays* or *bassins,* which are socio-geographical areas cutting through and uniting administrative units because of their social and economic communality. 'Contrats de pays', similarly, are negotiated between different tiers of authorities for common medium-term investment and activity programmes. However, this decentralization is much less thoroughgoing than in other countries such as Italy, Germany or Spain, where much of the public budget is region-based. Even new communications infrastructures (such as the TGV) are controversial in the sense that they help to draw people and activities to Paris as well as away from, it since the cross-country lines have not been developed as fast as the 'star'-shaped network.

A fundamental issue of regional planning today that is not *désenclavement*, or opening up at national level, is integration at European level. For instance, there are now two large areas of development in Europe. One is the 'central arc' going from central and south-east England through the Netherlands, the Rhine valley and Switzerland down to the north of Italy, which encompasses some of the most dynamic regions of France (especially the Rhône-Alpes region). The other is the 'Mediterranean arc' going from Barcelona or even Seville up to Provence-Côte d'Azur and down to the Rome region through the north of Italy. In this very simplified vision of Europe, most of the Atlantic seaboard as well as the Massif Central are once again excluded from the most dynamic areas of Europe. The significance attached by recent French governments to the development of fast transport infrastructures in these areas is an indication of the seriousness with which the issue is treated. Many so-called 'structural' European programmes and budgets now have an impact on regional development. This is especially the case with the structural funds of the Common Agricultural Policy, which provide for the development of infrastructure and social support of rural mountainous areas, but also other funds such as the European Social Fund, which increasingly contributes to rehabilitation programmes in industrial and urban zones hit by recession.

## International competition: the opening of the economy to the rest of the world

One of the most significant structural changes in the the French economy since the 1970s has been its ever-greater integration into the global market, and especially into the European economic space. This concerns not only trade in manufactured goods or in services, but also investment and financial flows, the internationalization of large companies and, increasingly, the very fabric of economic regulation. Economic regulation is increasingly influenced by transnational institutions such as the European Central Bank, and by the loose collections of international corporations, financial institutions and markets.

As regards international trade proper, the change between, say, the 1950s and the late 1990s appears striking. In the 1950s, France was only importing and exporting around 11 to 15 per cent of its GDP, depending on the year (12.8 per cent in 1949, 14.1 per cent in 1950). Furthermore, a third of exports (34 per cent as late as 1958) and a quarter of imports were going or coming into 'tied' and dependent markets which used the franc as currency, namely the colonies, and especially Algeria. In other words, if the economy of France was not self-sufficient, it was not far from being so. Since then, all colonies have gained their independence, while France signed the Treaty of Rome in 1957 which created the Common Market in 1958. These events helped the ever-growing internationalization of the economy.

With 5.6 per cent of world export markets in 1998, France is the fourth largest exporter in the world, after the United States, Japan and Germany, and ahead of the UK and Italy. It is also the third largest exporter of services behind the United States and the UK, with a 6.4 per cent share of world trade in services. France is second only to the United States in terms of exports of agricultural and food products, and is also a major exporter of transport and engineering equipment (aeroplanes, railway equipment and so on), as well as cars and communication equipment. Total imports of goods represented around 26 per cent of GDP in 1998, against around 22 per cent a decade before. France is now completely dependent on imports from other countries to satisfy consumer demand, and it is also dependent on foreign markets, particularly other European countries, for outlets for its own products. In 1998 some 78.6 per cent of French exports were made to Organization for European Cooperation and Development (OECD) countries, 63 per cent to EU markets, and 15.6 per cent to Germany, which is France's main economic partner.

Before the 1990s international trade was often seen as a weakness of the French economy and for a long time it was in deficit, particularly in the 1980s. In 1982 the deficit reached 136.4 billion francs, or 1.9 per cent of GDP, with imports 20 per cent higher than exports.[9] The considerable gap in energy trade after the second oil crisis, and also the sudden surge in household consumption following the government's policy of encouraging growth in demand in 1981/2, were two of the reasons for this. Deficits in the late 1980s were also the result of imbalances in trade in manufacturing goods, as French firms appeared to be too slow in reorienting their activities swiftly enough in geographical terms and in terms of product specialization. However, the situation improved at the start of the 1990s; the deficit in industrial trade was replaced by a surplus in 1992 which became considerable in later years as France joined Germany and Italy as one of the foremost exporting nations in the world. Indeed, whereas exports paid for only 90 per cent of goods imported in 1990, in 1998 the rate had increased to some 103 per cent, and the surplus in export of goods and services represented 2.1 per cent of GDP [see Text 2.7].

Another aspect of the internationalization of the French economy is the growing importance of direct investment flows from and to France. These take the form of direct acquisitions of firms and capital, or financial investments. France is the fifth country in the world in terms of investments abroad, and the third largest destination of investments from abroad (two-thirds of these in France come from other countries of the EU, but the largest individual country is the United States, which owns a fifth of all foreign investments in France). Since the beginning of the 1990s, the flows of international investments to and from France have increased considerably, especially in relation to the European Union. The deepening integration of the internal market and the increasing impact of the Euro accelerated the constitution of large holdings or corporations big enough to compete in the whole of the European market, either by merger, takeover or acquisition. On the French side, this was particularly the case in sectors such as insurance: the merger of two of the largest groups, AXA and UAP, in 1997, and the acquisition of GAN by Groupama in 1998, were accompanied by acquisitions of other insurance companies in Italy, the UK and Germany. Banking was another case in point: the acquisition of Paribas by BNP in 1999 after a hard-fought battle with another bank, Société Générale, made the new group truly international. In services there was the merger of Lyonnaise des Eaux and Suez in 1997, and the merger of Havas and Générale des Eaux in the new company Vivendi in 1998, also accompanied by acquisitions in Europe. In distribution, Carrefour and Promodès, the two largest supermarket distribution groups, merged in 1999 to form the second largest group in order to compete with the American Wal-Mart. In energy there was the takeover of the giant petrol group Elf by Total in 1999 and in industry Aérospatiale and Matra merged in 1999 with the German industrial giant Dafsa to form EADS, third largest defence manufacturing group in the world. Aluminium producer Pechiney merged with Alcan and Algroup the same year. Many of these movements of international capital entail corporate restructuring, helping companies to focus on technologies for the future. An interesting recent example is Rhône-Poulenc, the French chemicals company, which merged its biotechnology activities with those of the German group Hoechst, creating the new company Aventis. Some acquisitions are symbolic rather than important in terms of world market development and this was the case in 1999 with Renault's acquisition of a 38 per cent share of the capital of Nissan, the Japanese car manufacturer.

# Distributing incomes

The ways in which income from economic activity is distributed between agents such as firms, shareholders or households, and redistributed through taxes and social contributions, and the ways in which financial resources are allocated to investment in the economy, largely depended on the focal role of the state during the period from the end of the Second World war to the mid-1980s, primarily because of the inadequacies and limitations of the French private financial sector in establishing itself as a proper financial mechanism for the management of incomes and financial resources. However, the income distribution and financial management system which was developed during the *Trente glorieuses* subsequently changed radically, for reasons explored below.

## Income distribution and redistribution

During the period of uninterrupted growth up to the early 1970s, the average income of French households increased steadily in line with national output, or even faster. This is illustrated by the increase in real terms of the minimum wage (the 'Salaire minimum interprofessionnel garanti' – SMIG – which then became the 'Salaire minimum de croissance' – SMIC); this was multiplied by 3.37 between 1950 and 1991. Furthermore, inequalities in income distribution decreased steadily, especially from the late 1960s to the mid-1980s, particularly benefiting low wage-earners and retired people. In terms of the distribution of gross national income between capital earnings, income from self-employment and wages, the share going to wages increased from 61 per cent to 73 per cent between 1960 and 1980. In terms of the different groups of wage-earners, there was also a narrowing of differentials from 1969 onwards. Between 1970 and 1984, for instance, the proportion of gross wages going to the highest paid tenth in relation to the lowest paid tenth of all wage-earners went from around four to less than three.

However, one should not conclude that France had become a particularly egalitarian society. Indeed, France in the early 1970s was still more unequal in terms of income distribution, either before or after redistribution by taxes or benefits, than most European countries. Even during the 1950s and 1960s, when the share of gross national income represented by wages increased considerably, inequalities among wage-earners also increased enormously. It was the increases in low wages after May 1968 and the introduction of wage indexation in the 1970s which up to the mid-1980s allowed for a narrowing of wage differentials.

Even more important in improving living conditions has been the considerable development and impact of income redistribution through social contributions and benefits, especially old age pensions, family benefits and unemployment benefits. These are very important in society insofar as they guarantee some form of minimum income to households with no other resources. However, their impact on inequality was limited by the fact that national insurance

**Raymond Barre** (b. 1924)

Raymond Barre started public life as a ministerial advisor in the 1960s (especially at the Ministry of Industry). He became a European commissioner and vice-president of the Commission, and was also a well-known university professor of economics (his macroeconomics textbook is a classic). He was Minister of Foreign Trade in 1975 and in 1976 was appointed Prime Minister and Minister of Finance and the Economy by President Giscard d'Estaing. Apart from being publicly hailed as 'the best economist in France' by Giscard, and adopting a sententious tone in his public speeches, his main claim to fame was the implementation of a strict monetarist and neo-liberal economic policy in 1976–9 as a response to the economic crisis. After the right lost the elections in 1981, he continued as a *député* for Lyons, and in 1995 became its elected mayor. Seen after 1981 as an independent voice able to transcend the divisions of the right in opposition, he was an unsuccessful candidate at the presidential elections in 1988.

contributions were not progressive and by the fact that a large proportion of tax revenue is derived from indirect taxation which is not progressive either.

The trend towards an increasing share of national income going towards wage-earners and low-income groups experienced several setbacks after the 1974 crisis. First, the Barre government (1976–81) attempted to reverse the labour–capital relationship in national income distribution by attempting to restore the profit margins of firms through various tax and credit policy measures, without very great effect. Second, the socialist/communist coalition of the first Mauroy government in 1981 attempted to get out of the economic crisis by applying policies aimed at repeating the patterns of the *Trente glorieuses*, in an accelerated fashion. The idea was to 'bring back' economic growth through increases in what was called in the rhetoric of the period 'popular consumption' (that is, the consumption of lower-income groups) and public sector-led productive investments.

This policy temporarily reduced income differentials, through significant increases in the SMIC (which rose by 22 per cent between 1981 and 1982), family allowances, pensions, and so on. However, the result was short-lived. This reflationary *politique de relance* contributed to severe inflation, retail prices increasing by nearly 14 per cent in 1981. Furthermore, it isolated the French economy amongst its trading partners, which at the time were all implementing restrictive, anti-inflationary, monetarist policies. As a consequence, the French trade balance went heavily into the red, the country's external debt surged and there were strong speculative pressures on the French franc. This led to a brutal change in the government's economic policy, which was so radical that it reversed the income distribution trends of the previous decades.

The new incomes policy put together in 1983 by Jacques Delors had ironic results since one of the most lasting achievements of a government committed to reducing income differentials was to widen those differentials. An important consequence of Delors' policy was to set up a new framework for wage negotiations, which broke the yearly pattern of wage increases more or less automatically indexed on the previous year's inflation and growth of productivity, the so-called *échelle mobile des salaires*, whose impact was to reinforce inflation trends, whatever their cause. Thus, between 1982 and 1985, several policy measures and new trends slowed down wage increases and made income differentials greater. Another noticeable effect was the considerable increase in unemployment from 1983 onwards, since the government had abandoned its attempts to protect industrial jobs. This, together with the wage freeze of 1982, the changes in wage negotiations which broke the link between wage increases and past inflation, and the new policy measures aimed at restoring companies' gross earnings and profits (especially after 1984 when the Fabius government took office), as well as measures to restore the finances of the national health and social benefit systems – all these factors caused wage differentials to increase. Between 1984 and 1988, for instance, the highest 10 per cent of wages rose between 2.91 and three times the increase of the lowest 10 per cent of wages. Other types of earnings usually associated with the highest income groups (property and capital earnings) also increased far more than average wages during this period, exacerbating income differentials [see Text 2.8].

The fact that the new incomes policies reversed the distribution of national income in favour of capital and high-income earners signalled the end of the model of resource distribution effective since the Second World War, according to which benefits from economic growth were distributed first to consumers. During the second half of the 1970s, the consequences of the Chirac government's anti-recessionary policies had been to increase the share of wages in firms' added value from 64 per cent to around 68 per cent, because of the attempt to maintain the purchasing power of household income despite the lower growth of output and national income. The expansionist policy of 1981–2 increased this share to nearly 69 per cent in 1982. But the new economic policy started in 1983 (which has been pursued with a great sense of continuity by all governments since) completely reversed these trends [see Text 2.9]. The share of wages in firms' added value effectively decreased to 60 per cent in 1989, and fell to a low of 56 per cent in 1998. Parallel to this decrease, the proportion of firms' gross margins increased from 26 per cent in 1982 to more than 33 per cent in 1988 and to 40 per cent in 1998.

As a consequence of this momentous change, the inequalities between wage-earners widened. The increased number of jobless people also deepened income inequalities in the society at large. New forms of poverty appeared, caused by long-term unemployment and the disintegration of more traditional forms of survival through family support as a result of the increase in the number of households composed of single old people, single parents (mostly women) and so on. Because of the structure of social security in France, which originally was not a universal welfare provision but was basically an insurance linked to the employment of the head of the household, and which was only slowly extended over the years (national unemployment benefits only appeared in 1958), a number of households and individuals slipped through the protective welfare net in a way which was not properly prevented until the late 1990s. However, it is important to note that not all social categories have suffered equally; some groups, especially pensioners with a *retraite complémentaire,* saw their relative position improve.

## Income redistribution

Redistribution of income is organized through national insurance schemes and the taxation system (VAT and income tax). Taxes on income are lower in France than in other countries such as the UK, especially for people with children. On the other hand, the national insurance system, which finances unemployment benefits, basic pensions, accident and illness benefits, child benefit and the reimbursement of medical treatment, is particularly expensive, and the compulsory contributions are amongst the highest in the world.

As the population is ageing, and medical consumption is increasing, and as the number of people receiving unemployment benefits is also growing, the financial burden on the national economy of the *revenus de transfert* (social transfers) and of the health service has increased. The total funding of the social protection system represented 20.6 per cent of GDP by 1998, the highest rate in any industrialized nation, whereas total taxes (on incomes from capital and labour, and on consumption, through VAT and other duties) only represented 24.3 per cent, lower than in many other countries. At 3.3 per cent of GDP, income tax is particularly low in France, even lower than in Japan and the United States, and five times lower than in Sweden. The sums redistributed to households represented 32 per cent of the disposable income of all French households in 1992. Some 43.2 per cent of this is made up of pensions, 33.5 per cent of health benefits, 13.5 per cent of family benefits (maternity, child and housing benefits) and 9.7 per cent of unemployment and 'social exclusion' benefits.

Considerable problems have been encountered by the system since the 1970s, although many reforms have been implemented and have improved it in many ways. It is a complex system. Each benefit is administered by a different mutualist organization (such as a *caisse primaire de sécurité sociale*) in which trade unions, employers' organizations (such as the *Conseil national du patronat français* – CNPF, which has now become the Medef: *Mouvement des entreprises de France*), public administrations and other bodies (for instance family organizations) have representatives on the board. Their job is to balance contributions ('cotisations') against benefits or costs reimbursements. Furthermore, some economic sectors or professions, such as the miners, have their own, specific *caisses*, as opposed to the *régime général* which covers most employees.

Until recently this system of redistribution was not even able to provide insurance for every household. People who, for one reason or another, had fallen through the net and were not insured did not receive benefits at all. In France, there was no universal 'welfare state' comparable to that of the UK. It was only in 1988 that the idea of a minimum guaranteed income was implemented. Ten years later, in 1998, some 3.4 million people received benefits which guarantee them a minimum income level, through various *minimum sociaux* (complementary benefits). The most important, launched in 1988, is the RMI (*Revenu minimum d'insertion*), affecting around 1.1 million households, including a total of more than two million people, who need to undertake some form of retraining or other agreed activities for their 'social reinsertion'.

However, this programme yielded painfully few positive results at this level, largely because unemployment was still rising. Other programmes aimed at mending the hole in the health insurance net since, even though people claiming the RMI were also automatically covered by social insurance, many 'excluded' people were not. It was only in 1999 that health insurance was made available to all through the CMU ('couverture maladie universelle') to which anybody not covered by an existing scheme could belong, whatever their circumstances. The fact that it was estimated that several hundreds of thousands of people were potential beneficiaries of such a measure serves to demonstrate the extent of social exclusion and poverty in present-day France.

Other urgent questions were raised with respect to the social protection system during the 1990s. One concerns the financial problems of social insurance. Not only is the health insurance system enormously costly and in recurrent deficit, but the funding principles (through insurance premiums) are particularly unfair, as high-income groups pay a smaller proportion of their income in premiums and usually make more use of health services than low-income groups. One change has been to replace an increasing share of social insurance premiums with a social income tax, the CSG ('contribution sociale généralisée') which has a higher financial yield and is socially fairer. Another issue related to the health insurance system is the high medical spending of French households, arguably the world's greatest consumers of pills and medical services after those in the United States. The ageing of the population will further increase the proportion of household consumption which is devoted to health, even though governments since the mid-1990s have attempted to institute a stricter control of the prescription and consumption of medicines, against considerable resistance from pharmaceutical companies and most of the medical profession.

Another major problem is the future of the pension system. The main pension scheme (*retraite de base*) as well as the occupational pensions schemes (*retraites complémentaires*) are organized under a 'redistribution' system: that is, at any given time the contributions of people in work are used to finance the pensions of retired people. This is a system based on 'intergenerational solidarity', which can be contrasted with the 'capitalization' system, used for instance in the UK to fund most pensions except the minimal state pension, where the premiums are invested during the working life of the insured person, in order to build up the future value of his or her pension. The problem with the French system is that it requires either a growing number of employed people financing current pensions or at least a stable distribution of the population between contributors and pensioners (the so-called 'dependency ratio'). The latter has been and is still the case; for instance, during the 1980s, retired households benefited from a considerable increase in real income. But the expected ageing of the population and the fall in the birth rate have been interpreted by many analysts as likely to bring about a collapse of the existing system within a few decades. Some analysts now claim that a system based on capitalization would also help to re-establish saving levels and encourage investments. Alternatively, supporters of the current system underline the inherent dangers of alternative systems such as the pension funds of the UK or the United States, which do not seem to increase levels of long-term savings but rely for their efficiency on the short-term speculative efficiency of fund managers, rather than on the good health of the economy.

In order to guarantee the future financial equilibrium of the pension system, the 'Juppé reform' (from the name of the prime minister responsible for it) changed the basis for pension contributions in the mid-1990s, increasing the number of years' contributions needed in order to benefit from a full pension. There are also plans to launch some form of complementary, voluntary form of 'capitalization' pension funds, although there is little interest from ordinary people, and the main pressure for it comes from insurance companies.

These questions will continue to be at the forefront of all the political debates in the near future. The system put together in the 1950s in order to regulate income distribution and provide social protection was significantly reformed during the 1990s, but more needs to be done. The large increase in social spending during the 1980s, because of the growing needs generated by the economic crises (larger numbers of unemployed, social exclusion, increase in the number of pensioners) is not likely to disappear. However, in the context of a deregulated European and international market, the considerable financial burden on firms represented by the *charges sociales* (employers' contributions), which can increase the cost of labour by up to 50 per cent, is seen as a major impediment to the competitiveness of French firms. On the other hand, any attempt to dismantle or significantly reduce the level of social protection would be fiercely resisted, as shown for instance by the 1995 strikes in the public sector, which were directed against possible reductions in social advantages of public sector employees [see Text 2.10].

## Consuming and saving: the end of the old habits of thrift?

Consumption patterns of the French population have changed in ways that are difficult to imagine. At the beginning of the twentieth century, food and clothing represented 70 per cent of all household expenditure, and housing another 19 per cent, so that not a great deal was left for other spending. In 1960 less than half (46 per cent) of average household consumption was devoted solely to food and clothing, but the proportion had fallen to less than a quarter (23.7 per cent) by 1998. On the other hand, other components of household budgets have seen their share and significance grow – especially housing, transport, health and leisure – and these are expected to absorb an even greater share of disposable income in the future. These trends had a major impact on economic growth during the 1960s, when there was a strong and sudden increase in the acquisition of consumer durables such as cars, washing machines and televisions. Although a level of saturation is being reached for a number of goods, and consumption is not growing as fast as, say, in the 1960s, new goods are appearing, especially in communication and entertainment (from computer-based equipment to mobile phones), that create new needs. An increasing proportion of consumption is in services; transport and communications accounted for 16.6 per cent of total consumption in 1998, and other categories such as health, leisure and personal services are also growing in importance.

Saving patterns, which play a considerable role in supplying financial resources to the economy, have also changed considerably. In the 1960s and 1970s, French households were particularly savings-conscious (in 1978, households saved more than 20 per cent of their disposable income). This changed during the 1980s – with a gross savings ratio which nearly halved to 10.8 per cent in 1987 – and despite a recovery since (it was 15.6 per cent in 1998) it has remained below 1970s levels. This change is in part due to increased credit. France was slower than some other countries in developing modern payment methods (cheques only became a widespread means of payment in the mid-1960s), but more recently credit cards have spread with a vengeance and the indebtedness of households during the 1990s has increased a great deal, with the result that net savings ratios have fallen.

This signals a change in economic behaviour which has run in parallel with the revolution in financial circuits and capital markets during the 1980s. Whereas in the 1970s half of national wealth was still in property and 30 per cent in short-term deposit accounts (such as the popular 'Caisses d'épargne'), the rest being held in stock and bonds, by 1997 property only represented 30 per cent of wealth, with short-term deposits down to 25 per cent, but capital stocks rising from 20 per cent to 28 per cent, largely because of the explosion of the SICAV (unit trusts).

Therefore the old, traditional, practices of thrift, which were typical of a France still imbued with rural values, and of a financial system which was also very conservative, which were perpetuated in many ways up to the end of the 1970s, have given way to a far more 'dynamic', short-term and open system of financial resource collection. Households are more and more trading long-term security for maximum short-term financial efficiency, and rely on a wider range of new products offered by institutions which are now more competitive, more open and deregulated. As in other areas, France, slower at first, has enthusiastically adopted aspects of the free market behaviour characteristic of other European countries within the framework of the deregulation of the 1980s.

## From inflation to price stability: the end of the cycle?

Inflation has been a constant concern of economic policy in France since the First World War. After 1945, France suffered from inflation levels higher than those of many other main industrialized nations, with the result that the franc had to be devalued at regular intervals. It is only since the late 1980s that inflation has been contained at levels no higher, and often lower, than in comparable countries [see Text 2.11]. For instance, the inflation differential between France and Germany, which has long been one of the main criteria of French economic policy, reached around 8 per cent in 1980 in favour of Germany. Policies of the *franc fort* and of *désinflation compétitive* reduced it to zero in 1990 and in the following years annual inflation in France was between 1 and 4 per cent lower than in Germany (in 1999, inflation in both countries was less than 0.5 per cent).

During the *Trente glorieuses* some periods were characterized by bouts of high inflation, for instance at the time of the Korean war, in 1952, or during the late 1950s, at the very start of the Fifth Republic, and again in 1963. On each occasion an anti-inflationary plan was put into action, often taking the name of the finance minister at the time: the *Plan Meyer* in 1948 which brought to an end the explosive inflation of the post-war period, the *Plan Pinay* in 1952, the *Plan Armand-Rueff* in 1959, the *Plan Giscard* (the future president) in 1963. The influence of the international markets explains some inflationary crises (such as the overheating of the world economy after the Korean war boom in 1952). But most of these crises, as well as the 'ordinary' level of inflation (which averaged more than 4 per cent in the 1960s), were due to domestic factors. The main factor was that inflationary pressure was created by the conditions of accelerated growth, with a rising demand fuelled by the growth of incomes as well as public expenditure.

In fact France's economy, which was relatively isolated from international markets at least up to the mid-1960s, did not necessarily suffer from a certain level of inflation, and could even be said to have benefited from it. Indeed, in a period during which considerable investments were made, inflation reduced the real cost of borrowing. Real interest rates were very low indeed and represented an inducement to investment.[10] Furthermore, financial resources were subsidized by the public sector through the 'prêts à intérêts bonifiés' of the public *institutions financières spécialisées.*

However, periods of high inflation were another matter. If and when an inflationary spiral threatened to get out of hand, the French government had a vast array of policy tools at its disposal. These ranged from the crudest and most interventionist, such as blocking prices and wages by decree (allowed under an Act of 1945), to budgetary policies (such as increasing taxes in order to reduce household expenditure and demand, and reducing the government's budget deficit) and tools of monetary policy such as credit controls, incomes policies and so on. A number of tools were also used to control flows with the rest of the world. The franc was devalued six times between the end of the Second World War and the end of the 1960s, and exchange controls were frequently imposed.

Despite crises such as that of 1958 which had to be dealt with through a strongly deflationary policy, after which the *nouveau franc* was adopted (worth 100 old francs), inflationary pressure in the French economy was not such, therefore, that it prevented the return to expansionist policies, and individuals adapted their behaviour to this. However, the economic system started to lose its capacity to regulate inflation towards the beginning of the 1970s.

The oil crisis, and the indirect impact it had on production costs, the collapse of the international financial and money regulation systems after 1970, as well as the continued efforts by households and firms to maintain their level of income, took inflation to levels that had been unknown in France since the early 1950s. In 1974 inflation came close to 15 per cent, and in 1980 and 1981 it reached 13 per cent (see Figure 2.2). But this time neither the characteristics of inflation nor the position of France within the world market made it possible to apply the old Keynesian-inspired recipes for stifling inflation, as the inflationary process was not a simple over-heating in domestic demand. France was experiencing 'stagflation', which is the conjunction of inflation with stagnation, or at least a slow growth in GDP. This was occurring in an economy which was now open to the world markets and which was far less regulated and controlled than previously.

Indeed, instead of being the result of increased demand, price increases were very often the result of cost-induced inflation, either through imported goods such as oil, or through the high costs of production in a number of sectors where investment and changes in production methods or technology had not been carried out early enough, so that productivity was increasing slowly. This was particularly the case in traditional industries, with the result that labour costs were high, and they were accused of causing inflation.

However, once the prices–wages–profits spiral has begun it is a cumulative phenomenon and inflation can get very high. This was especially true in France where mechanisms in the framework of social regulation helped to stimulate inflation. These mechanisms included the *échelle mobile des salaires,* the automatic indexation of wages on inflation rates which, as was suggested earlier, was more or less officially accepted in the early 1970s as an intrinsic part of the annual wage round and of incomes policy.

We have already described the failure of the 1981 Mauroy government to beat stagflation through a reflation strategy based on increases in the spending power of low-income households, a strategy which only succeeded in stimulating inflation further. This was accompanied by a high external trade deficit, a loss of confidence in the franc resulting in three devaluations, and a high level of indebtedness in the French economy. After bitter disputes within the governing coalition, an anti-inflation strategy was implemented in several stages, which in the end resulted in a complete reversal of the 1981 strategies. Ultimately, the government adopted the same principles as those applied by the Barre government in 1976–9 in its monetarist anti-inflationary strategy [see Text 2.12].

We can distinguish three stages on this route. First, anti-inflationary policies were implemented between 1982 and 1984. The second period, up to 1988, under both conservative and socialist governments, consolidated these policies within a framework of market deregulation. The third period, from 1988 onwards, reinforced anti-inflation policies by making them the centrepiece of government economic strategy, based on the concepts of *désinflation compétitive* and the *franc fort,* and later buttressed by efforts to reduce public budget deficits in order to prepare for the arrival of the Euro.

The so-called *Plan Delors* of 1983, named after Jacques Delors, at the time finance minister in the Mauroy government, followed efforts in 1982 aimed at reducing demand (particularly through freezing public expenditure, a temporary wage and price freeze, and currency export controls). Its most lasting and significant structural effect was to break the link between inflation rates and annual wage rounds, a goal that conservative governments, especially the Barre government of 1976–81, had unsuccessfully tried to achieve in the 1970s. The *désindexation des salaires* first applied in the public sector but spread across the economy and had a great impact on inflation, as did the monetarist control of credit and public borrowing, and the strengthening of competitiveness across the French economy. Freeing markets and ending price controls, which began during the 1984 Fabius government and was continued after 1986 under the Chirac government, completed the elimination of inflationary culture in France. By 1990 the 'inflation differential' with France's main trading partners had disappeared (that is, the rate of inflation in the 1990s was lower in France than in its partner countries, especially Germany).

It is important to stress the role played by the opening up of the French economy and its integration into the European market in the successful elimination of structural inflationary trends. Of particular relevance was the place of the franc within the ERM. The anchoring of the franc to the Deutschmark (DM) within the ERM in 1982/3, in very difficult and adverse circumstances, including strong opposition from within the ruling coalition (which would have preferred further devaluation and the removal of the franc from the ERM), was a tremendous change, the importance of which is only now being fully perceived. Once it was decided to keep within the European monetary fold, the discipline of policies then being followed by France's major European partner was accepted, at least in its monetary aspects.

The change in strategy therefore had several features: reducing inflation through internal measures such as the reduction of demand by increasing the basic VAT rate and national insurance premiums; freezing wages in 1982 for six months; credit controls; reducing government spending; and other deflationary measures such as draconian price controls. As previously described, incomes policy and wage negotiation structures had undergone a complete change, and this radically altered inflation policies. There were also measures to re-establish currency stability and French credit by reducing external borrowing and the budget and trade deficits. This was achieved in a few years, moving progressively towards what became by the end of the 1980s the 'official' theme of economic policy, the defence of the *franc fort* and *désinflation compétitive.*

The defence of the currency simply means that since 1983 governments have considered that in an open economy such as that of France in Europe, where imports consist not only of consumer goods but also of machine tools and raw materials, devaluation not only disrupts the economic planning of firms but also has an inflationary role. Competitive disinflation means that French governments accept that French firms will be able to survive and develop only if they are able to be competitive on the domestic market as well as on international markets, by reducing their costs, increasing productivity and limiting wage increases. In this context, less efficient firms which competitive devaluation would have allowed to survive, at least in the short term, eventually disappear. Hence the growth in unemployment.

This new policy framework was reinforced by the deregulation of markets started by Pierre Bérégovoy when finance minister between 1984 and 1986. Most price controls were abolished and there was a so-called 'Big Bang' (the deregulation and opening of financial markets). This was intensified in the

**Pierre Bérégovoy** (1925–93)

Born into a working-class family, he was employed as a skilled industrial worker, but soon became a trade union official at Gaz de France, and rose through its hierarchy to become an important figure in the Socialist Party at the end of the 1960s. General Secretary to the Presidency when Mitterrand took power in 1981, he became Minister for Social Affairs in 1982 and, having sorted out the social security deficit, he became Finance Minister in 1984–6, and again in 1988–92, after which he reluctantly served as Prime Minister in 1992–3. He is widely credited with having implemented a strict orthodox anti-inflationary policy consisting of 'competitive disinflation' and 'the strong franc', in order to peg the franc and the French economy to that of West Germany, and to improve France's economic competitiveness in the integrated Europe. He was ultimately successful in this respect, but at a very high social cost (especially that of increasing mass unemployment). He committed suicide after the left lost the legislative elections of 1993.

period of cohabitation (1986–8) when Finance Minister Édouard Balladur implemented a similar policy, speeding up the end of price controls and bringing in more radical deregulation measures (such as the repeal of the 1945 Act allowing price controls by the government).

Thus government economic strategies in the 1980s moved from a domestically oriented strategy, in which it was expected that French firms would recapture the domestic market, assisted by the government's incomes policy and reflation strategy, to a strategy based on the recognition of the interdependence of markets (including financial markets) and the integration of the French economy within the European market. At this stage the 'German model' became the main preoccupation of French governments. The aim was to reduce the 'inflation differential' between the two countries, to reach and surpass the labour productivity of West Germany and to adopt an export strategy. This is the meaning of the strategies of competitive disinflation and the strong franc, anchored to the Deutschmark, which are still the basis of French government economic policies.

It can therefore be said that the 1980s saw a complete revolution in the mode of regulating the French economy as far as pricing mechanisms, labour markets and monetary flows are concerned. The opening up of the economy to external markets (mostly European ones) has wider implications and more far-reaching consequences than simply increasing the volume of trade. The best symbol of this is probably the way the role and perception of currency devaluation has been modified in the last four decades. Whereas it was previously possible to see such devaluations as proactive adjustments helping to improve the competitiveness of French exports within a world economy which was relatively strictly organized around a stable international monetary system based on the US dollar, the situation is now completely different. Because of the importance of imports in industry and services and the inflexibility in consumption patterns of imported goods, a devaluation is now seen as having a marked inflationary effect on the economy. Furthermore, for a country such as France which wanted to stay within the ERM, devaluations are difficult to implement except either to signal, in reaction to the deregulated international money market, that speculative selling has defeated the coordinated efforts of the European central banks to maintain the parity of the franc, or to signal (as in the 1982 and 1983 devaluations of the franc) that the government has recognized the weaknesses of the current economic situation and that policy changes will be implemented. Thus, in the early 1980s, monetarist policies largely replaced reflationary policies, partly under pressure from France's partners within the ERM, and especially Germany.

It can be said that economic policies in the 1990s, whether pursued by the socialist governments of Rocard, Cresson and Bérégovoy or the conservative government of Juppé, or Jospin's 1997 socialist and *gauche plurielle* government, have been consistently similar. However, several additional factors had to be taken into consideration. The first was a new recession in the early 1990s, followed in 1993 by a monetary and financial crisis within the European monetary system, during which the franc was attacked by international speculation on the money markets, testing the government's resolve. The other significant factor was the signature of the Maastricht Treaty, which came into force in 1993, and the consequent prospect of the arrival of the Euro in 1999, finally replacing the franc in 2001. In order for France to be part of the first wave of countries adopting the Euro as their common currency, it had to comply with a number of stiff tests to demonstrate the stability and tight control of monetary and financial flows in the economy. The purpose was to make sure that the Euro would become a stable and strong currency. Therefore successive governments had to reduce public deficits to less than 3 per cent of GDP, reduce public debt to less than 60 per cent of GDP, control inflation to a level comparable to that of the average of the Eurozone, and so on. These tests could only be satisfied by the rigorous application of tight monetary and income policies. Furthermore, the governments had to relinquish the control of monetary policy to a newly independent Banque de France (especially the fixing of the leading interest rates), as a first stage towards relinquishing these powers to the newly formed European Central Bank in 1999. All this occurred when (at least up to 1998) the number of people on the dole was growing again. As a result there was strong opposition to the very tight monetary policies conducted at the time, and demands were made for the launch of reflationary policies. However, every government kept to a tight monetary policy and, in 1998, France was declared to have satisfied the criteria necessary to be part of the Eurozone. At the time, the economic situation eased somewhat: inflation fell to very low levels (less than 1 per cent in 1998, less than 0.5 per cent in 1999), France experienced a wave of expansion with respectable rates of GDP growth and, along with the rest of the EU, managed to avoid the effects of the Far East financial crisis in 1997–98. Unemployment figures finally began to fall as well.

## Financing the development of the economy

From what has been said above, it becomes clear that the financing of the economy is now constrained not only by the behaviour of firms and households in relation to saving or self-financing, but also by international monetary and financial markets. These are now fully open and respond to international trends and constraints.

In the past, as noted earlier, the problem of the French financial system was not a lack of resources, but rather its structural and operational inadequacies. The financial markets were very small, compartmentalized and limited in scope. Strict controls prevented the development of new products more adapted to the investment needs of the economy. As a result, the public sector had to play a central role in securing and distributing financial resources during the *Trente glorieuses*. Institutions such as the *Caisse des dépôts et consignations*, which collected the funds from the popular savings banks like the *Caisses d'épargne*, developed considerably and, from the 1960s onwards, were one of the main sources of financing for local authorities' infrastructure programmes and public housing. Similarly, the network of public *institutions financières spécialisées* concentrated on collecting resources for specific types of investments like motorways, electricity generation, small and medium-sized industrial firms and telecommunications.

Although the limitations of the banking system and financial markets were recognized quite early on, with reforms of the banking system in the mid-1960s and in the 1970s, it was not until the mid-1980s that the financial markets underwent a real change. The deregulation process – the 'Big Bang' – which occurred in France at about the same time as in the UK, allowed an opening of the market to all operators (including foreign ones) and an explosive growth of financial products in newly organized markets, linked with the rest of the world, especially in the Stock Exchange, and in the new money and other futures markets such as the MATIF.

As for the individual investor, a whole array of financial and monetary products created for the individual in the 1960s and the 1970s became very popular in the 1980s, especially the SICAV (unit trusts). The banks for a time lost some ground in their role as intermediaries between the investor and the money markets, both in lending to firms and in collecting savings and selling financial products. This process, dubbed '*désintermédiation*', soon brought a reaction from the banking system which swiftly took control of most of the new financial products (such as unit trusts), bringing about a process of '*réintermédiation*' which was more or less completed by the end of the 1980s, with large international banks and financial companies offering the whole range of financial services and involved in capital restructuring and merger or acquisition across borders in order to increase their size and competitiveness on the European market.

The result of these changes was to involve savings more closely with the financial markets, moving them away from traditional investments such as property or short-term deposit accounts, towards financial investment, as we saw earlier. Similarly, the structure of firms' borrowing was modified so that they borrowed more on the money market and less from banks (indeed, firms reduced their debts and borrowing to practically nothing in the 1990s, financing investments largely through self-financing: that is, using their profits, the level of which had increased considerably). However, savings did not regain their

1960s levels. Even more worrying, the level of investments was still relatively low at the end of the 1990s, especially productive investments.

The whole framework and the operating modes of the market in financial resources have therefore changed from a set of state-regulated markets with strict boundaries, rules and objectives, to an open, largely deregulated, multi-products market, in which the role of the state has been completely modified and has shrunk significantly. The earlier, interventionist, policies were, at least in part, forced upon the state because of the inability of French financial structures and agents to organize an efficient and modern framework for collecting and distributing the financial and monetary resources necessary for the considerable growth of the French economy during the *Trente glorieuses*. Again, although the specific role of the French state in taking over some of the market-regulating functions appears to be one of the characteristics of the French economy in the post-war period, it is also clear that the economic role of the state has been deeply modified since the early 1980s. It is this role, and the recent changes which have affected it, that will be examined in a wider context in the next section.

## The changing role of the state and the public sector

It should now be clear that during the post-war period the role of the state in France has been fundamental in regulating the market economy through the direct participation of the public sector in production activities, income distribution, control of monetary and financial flows, and so on. The typical model of French interventionism, somewhat grandly dubbed *modèle d'économie mixte* during the 1960s, was largely the result of various coalitions of post-war politicians – including right-wing leaders such as de Gaulle – with a considerable input from 'technocrats' and civil servants who had used the war period to define the broad lines of a new economic framework which would avoid a repetition of past crises and problems. However, this model was far from being a consensual one. After all, the various factions in the Resistance movement ranged from the Communists to the nationalist right, but the two years 1945–6 saw coalition governments create a new structure in which the state had a central role.

Not that this was unknown in France. Even in the past, interventionist practices had not stopped at the traditional roles of the public sector as a protector, as a legislator and as a provider of basic public services and infrastructures. Many industries were created in France as royal manufactures in the seventeenth and eighteenth centuries, and although the French Revolution was based on free-market economic principles, the free-market nineteenth century was itself not short of what analysts called 'conservative interventionism',[11] which consisted in regulating markets (especially in protectionist periods) and stimulating and organizing the private sector. The experience of the two world wars in the twentieth century also increased interventionist tendencies in all political circles. However, the system which developed after the Liberation, and which persisted until the mid-1980s, gave a specific role and authority to the public sector and this became a hallmark of the French economy.

The tradition of interventionism and the size and significance of the public sector had little or nothing to do with anti-capitalism or a socio-economic ideology which rejected market forces. On the contrary, these specific characteristics of post-war French capitalism were developed by the generation that grew up in the early part of the twentieth century, both because they sought to avoid problems they identified in economic management in the first half of the century and because the specific weaknesses of the systems of economic and social regulation in the 1940s and 1950s eased the way for public, interventionist solutions. These were even espoused by populist, nationalist politicians such as de Gaulle who, after 1943, publicly insisted that he was ready to substitute state intervention for inefficient market forces and private interests where it was necessary in order to restore France's power and *grandeur* in all aspects of life, including the economy.

## The Interventionist model from the Liberation to the 1980s

In the late 1980s, the public sector employed, either as civil servants or in nationalized industries, around 25 per cent of all wage-earners (a fifth of all working people) and government and local authority receipts amounted to 44.5 per cent of GDP. These two indicators taken together show that France had at that time one of the most 'state–oriented' of all industrialized market economies.

But however large the public sector had become by the early 1980s, it would be misleading to categorize France as having a state-driven economy. Indeed, there are many important utilities or infrastructures which elsewhere are usually assumed to be part of the public sector, and which in France are, at least in part, in the hands of the private sector. For instance, motorways are built and managed by private consortiums and most are toll roads. Local water distribution companies, bus routes and local industrial development agencies are also frequently organized through joint ventures between the public and private sector, called *sociétés d'économie mixte*.

Nevertheless, the *Trente glorieuses* saw the creation and development of a large public sector in the industrial, financial and services sectors; during this period the state developed interventionist tools inspired by Keynesian economic principles of demand management, but also deployed a range of more straightforward controls (such as price controls). Another important aspect of the government's arsenal for the economic management of the economy consists of the regulatory as well as the informal framework for labour markets and competition, and the various agencies and institutions concerned with macroeconomic and regional planning, whose job is to help organize the actions and policies of the public sector and of government, and also to coordinate the behaviour of the various economic agents within the economy.

Therefore there are three ways of approaching the analysis of the specific role of the state (taken here in its wider meaning, to include the public sector as well as local authorities) and the ways it has changed in the last few decades. These concern the extension of the public sector in terms of productive activities as well as resource allocation, the role of the state in regulating the market system, and the role of the state in coordinating the economic agents in the economy.

## The development of the public sector

When de Gaulle's administration reshaped the instruments of the French state in 1944–5, the aim was to give France the means to regain its *grandeur*, as well as rebuilding a country largely destroyed by the war. Administration was already highly centralized, an inheritance of the Napoleonic tradition enshrined in the concept of *service public*. There was also an embryonic public sector of nationalized firms and utilities, dating from the pre-war period.

The thinking of Resistance groups had been that peace could only be established and maintained within France and between France and its neighbouring countries if the worst excesses of the market system were at least tempered, if not eliminated, through state intervention. A strong public sector was therefore needed alongside an efficient system of income redistribution and social welfare. Although an anti-capitalist political economy was powerful in France in the 1950s and the 1960s, the managers, politicians and *technocrates* who were in charge of the economy had little, if any, sympathy with any kind of socialist or communist vision. Civil servants like Jean Monnet, Jean Ullmo and Jean Saint-Geours, or politicians such as Maurice Schumann or Pierre Mendès-France were mainly interested in improving the efficiency of the French economy and preventing the recurrence of crises such as that of 1929 or the worsening European economic relations which characterized the whole period between the two world wars, and which they believed had led to the catastrophe of the Second World War.

The nationalization programme carried out by the de Gaulle administration in 1945–6 included firms nationalized because previous owners had collaborated with the occupying forces (Renault, for instance) together with others for which the rationale was more economic. This was especially the case in the financial sector, where the largest insurance companies, the four largest high street banks and the central bank, the Banque de France, were all nationalized. A number of utilities were also nationalized, such as gas and electricity (GDF – Gaz de France – and EDF – Électricité de France). During the 1950s and the 1960s the size of the public sector increased with the creation of public companies such as Elf-Aquitaine (oil) and SNIAS, better known as Aérospatiale (aircraft). The public sector was also considerably extended in the financial system, mainly by right-wing Gaullist governments. The public *institutions financières spécialisées* were created to cope with the weaknesses of existing financial markets and, at the periphery of the public sector, the mutualist banks developed (such as the Crédit Mutuel and, most important, the local and regional mutual network of the Crédit Agricole, which by the 1980s had become the largest high street bank in France). In the late 1970s the right-wing government took a controlling stake in the main steel companies Usinor and Sacilor, which were both in financial crisis.

But the formation of the coalition of the left following elections in 1981 further extended the scale of the public sector to unprecedented levels in a market economy. The extension of the public sector by the Socialists in 1981 had precise objectives (which were only partly fulfilled or were soon abandoned). Nationalized industries were supposed to become the driving force in each specific sector and help to modernize and increase the efficiency of the rest of their sector. Nationalized financial institutions were expected to participate in the efficient allocation of capital to companies. The 1981 programme (implemented by an Act of 1982) covered some of the most important industrial firms in the country. Five major industrial groups, CGE, Saint-Gobain, Pechiney, Rhône-Poulenc and Thomson-Brandt, were fully nationalized; other firms which were partly publicly owned were taken over (Usinor, Sacilor, CII-Honeywell-Bull); while in others the state took a majority stake (Dassault, Matra). At the end of the process the size of the public sector work-force in industry had increased from 5 per cent in 1980 to 20 per cent in 1985, while the state's share of industrial added value grew from 8 per cent to some 24 per cent, and of industrial investment from 12 per cent to 35 per cent.[12]

In the financial sector nationalizations were taken even further, since two major investment groups, Paribas and Suez, and thirty-six banks were taken over, with only small family firms and foreign banks being left out. In total, the nationalized financial sector controlled some 88 per cent of bank deposits and 78 per cent of credit in the economy. These nationalizations, and the widespread corporate restructuring which followed, show the significance the Socialists accorded in 1981 to the control of monetary and financial structures in order to implement their programme of investment and modernization.

The public sector is greater than the sum of the main nationalized companies or agencies in the banking system, the public services (including transport, energy and telecommunications) and industry. These large companies own or partly control many subsidiaries, which means that in 1991, for example, the 108 nationalized groups controlled 2,505 subsidiaries. In addition, many service or infrastructure activities, especially at local or regional level, are managed by companies whose capital is shared between public bodies (central government bodies or local authorities) and the private sector. These *sociétés d'économie mixte* are frequently found in activities such as the construction and management of public housing and capital goods, and utilities such as waste collection and disposal, water distribution, local public transport and leisure activities. This system has been a major tool for local and regional development and for channelling public finance.

The size of the French public sector up to the mid-1980s only makes sense if it is related to the overall ambition of governmental economic action from the start of the *Trente glorieuses* to the mid-1980s, which was to influence the market and, where necessary, substitute public action and regulation for markets which were considered 'imperfect'. As such it is integrated into the vast array of interventionist policy instruments developed in France during the post-war period, from monetary, tax and incomes policies to long-term macroeconomic planning and regional planning.

## The use of intervention instruments up to the mid-1980s

As we have seen, the so-called *politique conjoncturelle*, ranging from instruments of short-term intervention in monetary and credit matters to price controls and incomes policies, was particularly important in France. Regulation of the money supply was made possible through changes in interest rates as well as through strict control of banks' activities (including the control of levels of lending, known as *l'encadrement du crédit*). These allowed for a fine-tuning of monetary policies, but can be seen, retrospectively, to have stifled the banks' responses to market evolutions. Other important short-term policy instruments were, as in other countries, aimed at regulating economic relations with the rest of the world, such as exchange rates, exchange controls and protectionist policies.

Given the growing importance of the public sector in income redistribution, as well as the ever-increasing size of the budgets of public bodies, it is not surprising that both incomes policies and budgetary policies (including taxation and public expenditure) have played a central role in the range of mechanisms used by French governments to implement austerity (anti-inflationary) policies and expansionary (anti-recessionary) policies. The originality of the French mechanisms is that the policies have been implemented rather abruptly and the scope of the changes has been large. For instance, in May 1968 the *Accords de Grenelle* which brought the strikes to an end increased the SMIG by 35 per cent in one go. Similarly, in 1981, the government increased the SMIC by 18 per cent, alongside large increases in family benefits and state pensions, but the following year froze all wages from June to November!

By the mid-1970s neo-Keynesian short-term demand management policies were clearly in trouble, given the interaction between European economies which prevented any effective autonomous decision making with respect to demand policies which were, at least in part, determined by external factors. Indeed, in 1976, for the first time, elements of a formal monetarist policy were put in place, when the Barre government published the annual growth rate for the monetary aggregate as a supply-side policy objective, in contrast to the earlier period when money control was seen as an emergency crisis management tool, rather than as a central plank of day-to-day economic regulation.

## Rise and fall of the planning system

The French system of economic planning, often called *la planification indicative* or *la planification souple*, found its origin in the coordinating role of the public sector in post-war reconstruction. There was a broad consensus in France at the time that the old pre-war economic framework was inadequate to reconstruct

**Jean Monnet** (1888–1979)

Jean Monnet was one of the original 'fathers of Europe', the small group of politicians and civil servants who took the first steps towards the creation of the Common Market and the European integration process. He was probably the most influential of them, but his role in the French economy is historically as important. Having worked as an international civil servant at the League of Nations, then as an economic consultant and international 'trouble-shooter' before the Second World War, he joined the Free French in London in 1940 with de Gaulle, and was sent by Churchill to work on the economic coordination of the Allies' war effort in New York. At the Liberation, as economic advisor to de Gaulle, he developed the tools of the 'French model' of economic development, based on a strong strategy of state interventionism and public, coordinated investments for the modernization of the country. In particular, he developed the planning system (creating the Commissariat Général au Plan in 1947 and becoming its first director, a post he held until 1952). He was also the driving force behind the launch in 1952 of the European Steel and Coal Community, the first building-block of European integration, and was the first president from 1952 to 1955. He then retired, and devoted himself to tireless campaigning for the development of a political, federal Europe.

and modernize France's infrastructure. There was a deliberate will to associate corporate interests and unions, industrial leaders and government ministries, in order to build a social consensus around economic and social objectives. Launched in 1947 with Jean Monnet (the inventor of French planning) as its first director, the national planning agency, the *Commissariat Général au Plan* was a small body, answerable only to the prime minister and independent from the civil service, which worked with a range of specialized commissions bringing together experts, industrialists and trade unionists. Later, in the 1950s and the 1960s, the aims of the plans became the modernization of the French economy in the context of the considerable social and economic upheaval resulting from the rural exodus and economic growth. From the *Deuxième Plan* (1954–7) to the *Quatrième Plan* (1962–5), the construction of new urban and communications infrastructures and housing, the support for new industries, and the organization of modern public services were areas which were given priority. The planning system was complemented by the system of regional planning, *l'aménagement du territoire*, described above.

Planning in its various forms was an important part of structural economic policy during most of the *Trente glorieuses*. Not only did it provide a framework for state budgets and policies and for economic plans of firms, but it also served as a consensus-building exercise between economic actors such as unions, management, the state and sectoral or industrial lobbies. This was particularly relevant during the period of industry-led growth as the dominant Fordist model, with its rigid organization of social relations, required some kind of forum in order to negotiate and organize the *partage des fruits de la croissance*. With hindsight, the *Quatrième Plan* represented the high point of planning. The *Cinquième Plan* introduced new objectives of industrial competitiveness, which obviously resulted from the changes that had recently occurred in France's international economic environment, such as the loss of the colonial empire, the growing role of intra-European trade and the progressive freeing of markets introduced with entry into the EEC and the Kennedy Round of the GATT negotiations. At the same time, these new objectives introduced elements of weakness into the planning system, since international economic events could not be controlled from within France.

Indeed, planning lost much of its significance during the 1970s. The gradual opening of the French economy made it more difficult to establish its future trends, since the main parameters and variables were now dependent on international financial and monetary markets, on international trade and on the economic policies of the main economic and trading partners. The Socialists in 1981 attempted to re-establish some role for planning, but the pressure of short-term anti-inflation policies, and the changes in the direction of government policies in 1983, soon thwarted this attempt. This painful experience meant that the preparation of the *Dixième Plan* and the *Onzième Plan* was much less ambitious and included no quantified objectives. Now the *Commissariat Général au Plan* is more of a think-tank, preparing well-received prospective studies on the economy and society and helping long-term governmental strategies, but without any significant impact on real decision making.

## Sectoral policies

Parallel to these general policies, French governments often promoted policies for specific sectors such as industry and agriculture. In the 1950s industrial policy mainly concentrated on the need to strengthen 'strategic' or 'basic' sectors such as the steel industry, energy, chemicals and shipbuilding. With the 1960s new parameters entered into the policy-making framework as a result of the opening up of the French economy to world markets.

A major part of industrial policy in the 1960s and 1970s therefore concentrated on two points: first, the promotion of *grands projets* such as the nuclear programme, the 'Plan Calcul' which aimed at building a national computer industry, the Airbus, Concorde, the telephone industry and, later, the TGV; second, considerable resources were devoted to helping develop industrial 'winners', that is large private or nationalized firms in important sectors, which would be able not only to compete on equal terms with foreign multinationals, but also to stimulate modernization and promote greater efficiency in the rest of their sector. In the 1970s industrial policy and most of the financial support to industry (in the shape of investment subsidies, specific tax advantages, and so on) were concentrated on a very small number of large companies, such as CGE, Thomson-Brandt, Aérospatiale and Dassault, operating in modern, high-technology industries.

The socialist government of 1981 attempted to reverse this policy, which they saw as piecemeal and dangerous because it neglected the industrial fabric of each of the sectors. They put forward a strategy based on the concept of *filières industrielles*, according to which, support would take into consideration not only the large, well-known manufacturing firms in each sector, but also all the other 'upstream' and 'downstream' activities which were dependent on it and each other. However, this was soon abandoned as the Mauroy government was forced to concentrate on supporting ailing industries like steel and textiles in order to avoid increasing unemployment [see Text 2.13]. The change of policy in 1983–4 inverted the basic role of sectoral policies, by re-establishing the primacy of 'market forces', limiting the role of industrial policy to 'accompanying support' (mostly for research and development, training and the location of investments) and concentrating the government's action on improving supply conditions for industrial firms through reductions in taxation, market deregulation and so on. These were preoccupations comparable to those of the first Thatcher government in the UK in 1979, but in France they were first expressed by a socialist government before forming the centrepiece of government policies during the 1986–8 *cohabitation* period when the parties of the right were in power.

The most striking example of sectoral policy is obviously the agricultural policy conducted by governments of all shades with remarkable consistency from the post-war period until the early 1980s, when the EC Common Agricultural Policy was reformed. In the years following the Second World War the two main purposes of agricultural policy were to guarantee a secure supply of food for the French population (for most French people, at least in urban areas, the war had been a period of hunger) and to modernize the often backward agricultural sector in order to guarantee a regular income to farmers. The government had the choice between speeding up the reduction in the numbers employed on the land (at the cost of a massive rural exodus and rural depopulation) together with helping to create a system of large, mechanized farming units, and attempting to keep the 'family farm' as the basic unit, but pursuing specific policies which allowed these smaller units to become more efficient, collaborating through a network of cooperative organizations for part of their activities in order to obtain necessary economies of scale for such activities as distribution.

This latter model was adopted, supported by a social consensus in the rural areas from the main farming unions, especially the young farmers' organization, the CNJA. The government organized the restructuring of land ownership, which was very fragmented in France, supported the constitution of numerous cooperative organizations for most products, improved the technical training of farmers, encouraged and subsidized mechanization (the number of tractors in France increased from 140,000 in 1950 to nearly 1.5 million in 1980) and provided finance for investment through the Crédit Agricole network. The policy was highly successful. The number of farms was considerably reduced, so that by the 1980s there were around a million farms, 600,000 of which had only one person working full-time, but France had become the principal agricultural country of Europe, generating some 24 per cent in value of EC agriculture production by the end of the 1980s, and the second largest world exporter of agricultural products behind the United States. Furthermore, this was done by preserving, at least in part, the 'family farm' model.

However, this model and this success came under threat as policies changed in the late 1980s and 1990s. Small farms have increasing difficulty in surviving within the new parameters of EU farm policies: set-aside, indebtedness, the increased costs of inputs and the falling levels of guaranteed EU prices have led to a large number of farmers leaving the industry. In the longer term, it is difficult to see the modern 'family farm' surviving, and large-scale farming industries on the UK model are likely to become as dominant in more and more French rural regions as they have already been for several decades in some areas such as the Beauce or Brie. In the meantime, it is not surprising to see smaller farmers protest against the demise of a model which was as much a social as a strategic economic policy [see Text 2.14].

## Taxation and social security: the financial significance of the public sector

A major issue of economic policy is the size of the sums taken by the state from the taxation and contributions of economic agents such as households and firms. In France, as in all industrialized economies, these have considerably increased as a proportion of the national product since the Second World War, and whether the public sector controls too much of national income is a hotly debated issue.

The share of GDP taken by central and local taxes and all national insurance contributions (the so-called 'prélèvements obligatoires') increased from 35 per cent in 1973 to 44.6 per cent in 1984 and 46.1 per cent in 1998, a level higher than in many industrialized nations except those in northern Europe,[13] but it is nevertheless comparable to what most European countries have experienced in the last few decades. Indeed, the UK is one of the very few European countries in which this percentage remained more or less stable in the 1980s and 1990s.

In the league table of 'taxes' levied by the state, France is seen as having one of the highest levels in Europe and in the world; it tended to decrease marginally in the late 1980s, dropping from a maximum of 45.6 per cent in 1985 to 43.7 per cent in 1991, before increasing again in the mid-1990s.[14] This level is higher than in Germany (37.5 per cent in 1997 as against 46.1 per cent in France the same year), the UK (35.3 per cent), the United States (28.5 per cent) and Japan (28.4 per cent). Only in northern Europe can higher levels be found, such as 53.3 per cent in Sweden.

However, the terms of the debate should be made clearer. Firstly, statistics for international comparison are ambiguous.[15] Furthermore, this money does not go into the pockets of civil servants. Most of it is redistributed to households or is used directly to fund the health service. In fact, in terms of income tax, France is one of the least heavily taxed European countries. Despite the fact that income tax is highly progressive, there are a large number of 'dégrèvements' (tax allowances) and the system of the 'quotient familial' (tax-free allowances for dependent relatives) is so broadly applied that in 1989 personal income tax yielded only 11.8 per cent of all public revenue in France (as against 29.5 per cent in Germany and 26.6 per cent in the UK). Taxes on company profits are also relatively low: at 5.5 per cent of total revenue they are at a comparable level to the German, but less than half the UK level of 12.3 per cent.

By contrast, social insurance contributions are very high, as are indirect taxes on consumption, although the latter decreased considerably during the early 1980s. A large proportion of national insurance contributions is directly paid by employers over and above wages, and a proportion of wages is also deducted for the various *contributions sociales*. Herein lies the problem, as noted earlier. Typically, for every 100 francs a firm pays in wages, it pays at least a further 35 to 40 francs in compulsory insurance contributions. These contributions increase labour costs and therefore reduce the competitivity of French firms compared to those in countries with less extensive social security coverage. Since the mid-1980s, this problem has been recognized and the contributions paid by employers have been to some extent reduced. In particular, considerable efforts were made by the Juppé and the Jospin governments to reduce the employers' social insurance costs for unskilled and low-paid workers, as these were so high that they were a deterrent to the employment of these low-productivity workers.

As noted earlier, attempts have been made to bring the French system closer to the UK system, by funding more of social and health expenditure through the tax system rather than through the national insurance system. Measures were taken to this end with the creation of the *Revenu minimum d'insertion* (RMI) in 1988 and of the *Contribution sociale généralisée* (CSG) in 1991, the latter being a 7.5 per cent tax on personal taxable income to fund the national health service and compensate for an equivalent reduction in national insurance contributions.

However, in the longer term, the question of the purpose, funding and organization of the various insurance and welfare benefits, and pensions, is still at the heart of the political and economic policy agenda. Not only are the recurrent deficits in the health and unemployment insurance systems likely to continue, given the uninterrupted growth in medical consumption, the ageing of the population and high unemployment, but this problem will also be compounded by the question of the continued funding of the pensions system in the twenty-first century. The complexity of the parameters and of the possible policy choices, which affect all economic agents, from households to firms and the state, illustrates the fact that the mechanisms for social regulation established in the aftermath of the Second World War, in a society largely united behind a consensus for 'redistributive growth', are no longer adapted to the recent socio-demographic trends and are too rigid to take into account the current, more complex, and fast-changing environment of an open French economy.

## The state and the 'social partners'

One specific characteristic of the regulation model developed during the *Trente glorieuses* is the way in which social groups, socio-economic interests (such as employers' organizations, professional bodies or specific pressure groups such as family organizations) and the public sector collaborated to manage and build policy consensus in a number of economic and social areas.

Part I of this book shows that, until recently, deeply conflictual socio-political relations were a hallmark of France and that crises often erupted. However, in a number of instances, ideologically antagonistic groups and institutions, often with opposing economic interests, have been able to work together within specific regulating institutions. Three main examples are particularly important: the management of the social welfare and income redistribution system; the organization of various frameworks for labour relations (either at national level, or at branch or firm level); and the consultation of social groups and of the various economic interests in the planning process.

The management of the social insurance and welfare systems is based on a three-tier system ('gestion tripartite', or 'gestion paritaire') on the boards of the various *caisses*: *Caisses d'assurance-maladie* (health insurance) *Caisses d'allocations familiales* (mainly child and housing benefits) and the ASSEDIC (unemployment benefits). These *caisses* have management boards at benefit or insurance level and at local and regional level, with a national body on top, and each management tier includes representatives of the *patronat* (management, organized through the employers' organizations), the unions, the relevant government ministries and sometimes other social interests such as family associations). This management by the so-called 'partenaires sociaux' (social partners) originated in the attempt, after the Second World War, to find a way to retain the mutual insurance system which had already developed in some industrial sectors. The unions, especially, were keen to be able to have a say in the use of their members' contributions. One of the results of this strategy is that a work place-linked system was adopted in preference to the kind of state-controlled national insurance system and the universal welfare state to be found in the UK. This obviously goes a long way towards explaining the complexity of the existing social insurance and welfare system in France, as the gaps in the social protection of the French population have been filled in a piecemeal and ad hoc way over the last four decades. On the other hand, this system has brought the unions together with management representatives to run one of the most important parts of the socio-economic structure of modern France.

A second example of collaboration between the *partenaires sociaux*, or the two sides of industry, is obviously the way in which negotiations of wage settlements or working conditions and the resolution of industrial disputes became progressively codified, very often with the participation of a government ministry in the process. Three-tier negotiations ('négociations collectives') between the *partenaires sociaux* and the state have been a feature of the procedure for resolving important conflicts. Examples would be the negotiations that led to the legendary *Accords de Matignon* in 1936, and the *Accords de Grenelle* in 1968. Even in normal circumstances, contacts and negotiation between the two sides of industry and the government have been a regular feature of the last four decades, partly because of the influence of the public sector as an employer, but also as part of incomes and employment policies. Such *concertation sociale* to some degree compensated for social and ideological conflicts, and was superimposed on the idea of 'class struggle' which coloured industrial relations in France up to the 1980s. At the level of the firm and the economic branch, the difficult reconciliation of these two extremes – antagonism on the one hand and dialogue on the other – brought about the creation of a number of formal institutions to assist in some form of regulation. The system of *conventions collectives* (negotiated agreements on wages and working conditions, which can be applied to a whole branch at regional or national level, and which, once generally applied, are legally binding on the relevant economic sector), the *comités d'entreprise* (works councils composed of employer and worker representatives, with rights to information and consultation and responsibility for a number of welfare functions in the firm) and other comparable institutions saw their role strengthened in the early 1980s by the *lois Auroux* which reiterated the importance of dialogue between both sides of industry in the socio-economic structure.

As described above, the planning system was a further significant example of the way in which public administration in the post-war period attempted to build some form of socio-economic consensus in the midst of social antagonism. Some of the main inputs into economic planning were the reports of the *Commissions de modernisation*, which included representatives of unions and other interest groups. Although ultimately this kind of consensus-building dialogue on economic strategy had little impact on specific economic policies, and only an indirect impact on smoothing out sources of conflicts, it is undoubtedly a good illustration of the numerous attempts in France at the time to find an alternative way between deregulated, free-market capitalism and unfettered socialist interventionism and state control.

This alternative way derived in part from the ideas of the technocratic elites in the government and nationalized industries, but was also part of the socio-economic strategy of many political groupings, such as the Christian Democrats of the MRP during the Fourth Republic. The populist nationalism of de Gaulle himself also hoped to organize an alternative strategy in France in which class collaboration and national consensus would be important ingredients in regulating the economy. Though flexible planning could be seen as one such instrument, others were developed with varying degrees of success. For instance, a pet project of de Gaulle's was the profit-sharing schemes for employees of firms.

The efforts at building social consensus and regulating negotiation, as well as the modes of intervention in the economy (including the participation of the public sector in the system of market production) were important strategies for overcoming rigidities in the socio-economic structure rather than ideological constructions. As such, they helped prevent and/or resolve crises in a divided and fast-changing system which still organized labour and capital relations in an inflexible way inspired by Fordist methods. They were useful during the *Trente glorieuses*, but their impact was much reduced after the economic structure of France was changed by economic crises. The idea of collaboration between social partners is itself in deep crisis, as has been shown by the threat in 1999 and 2000 by the employers' organisation, Medef, to withdraw from the co-management of national insurance institutions.

## The changing face of the public sector

It was assumed, after 1981, that the nationalized companies would play a central role in restructuring and modernizing French industries and services. However, their role within the economy very quickly became ambiguous, and their relations with the government uneasy. This can be seen in the way corporate strategies and support from government were defined and rapidly evolved, as well as in the fact that financing the expansion of these nationalized industries had to be reorganized. In this context, the privatizations of 1986–8 encouraged a questioning of the presence of a public sector in competitive markets, and in the 1990s privatizations were carried out at an accelerated pace by governments of the right and of the left alike [see Text 2.15].

It rapidly became clear in the mid-1980s that a major issue was the financing of capital investment in the public sector. With the new policy of austerity after 1983, it was necessary to find financial resources for nationalized firms on the financial market, as government budget resources were more and more limited. For instance, Jacques Delors, finance minister at the time, introduced 'certificats d'investissement' sold on the Stock Exchange in order to give a 'financial breathing space' to the public sector. Even before 1986, government circles increasingly accepted the need to find resources, on the market if necessary, by selling part of the capital of nationalized companies.

The privatization programme of 1986, which affected not only firms nationalized in 1981 but also companies nationalized by de Gaulle, broke a kind of taboo. The privatization law provided for the sale of 65 companies, groups or banks, although in fact only fifteen in total were sold. The most notable privatizations were those of important banks such as the Société Générale, Paribas and Suez, as well as the largest TV channel (TF1) and large industrial groups (especially CGE, Matra and Saint-Gobain, and part of Elf-Aquitaine). The financial capacity of the French capital market was too small for the successful flotation of a large number of companies and the privatization

**Jacques Delors** (b. 1924)

Jacques Delors is remembered in Europe as the enthusiastic President of the Commission of the European Communities between 1985 and 1995, when he was a driving force for relaunching the process of integration, and especially the adoption of the social chapter, the Single European Act and the Maastricht Treaty. However, his economic role in France was also fundamental. Having been a civil servant in the treasury and planning, and involved in the CFDT trade union, he became an advisor to the Gaullist modernizing Prime Minister Chaban-Delmas in the early 1970s. He then joined the Socialist Party and, when François Mitterrand became President of the Republic in 1981, he was given the post of Finance Minister, implementing the radical economic programme of the socialist government. He also steered economic policy through the U-turn of 1982–3, during which he developed monetarist and more neo-liberal policies, and anchored France to the European economic and monetary system. Throughout his public life he has been strongly inspired by his Christian social ideals, and in 1995–6 he was briefly spoken of as a possible – and potentially very popular – candidate for the Presidency.

programme was halted for a time, but, although the socialist governments of the late 1980s attempted to freeze the privatization programme and stabilize the relationship between public and private sectors, this strategy was soon abandoned. The public sector could not keep rigidly to the same corporate structure as in 1988 if it was to stay competitive on the international and domestic market. The search for capital and expansion opportunities and the need for corporate alliances at the European level, for instance, required a degree of flexibility in the capital structure that such companies' nationalized status did not allow [see Text 2.16].

Furthermore, the free market credo of the EC increasingly prevented the state from providing the public sector with funds for development. Thus in the mid-1980s the EC Commission forced Renault to reimburse government subsidies which were seen as anti-competitive. Partial privatization was therefore increasingly accepted. Renault, for instance, swapped 25 per cent capital with the private Volvo group in 1990 in order to constitute a European-sized group. This attempt failed, but it paved the way for the privatization of Renault which occurred in 1996 in the new privatization programme undertaken by the right-wing Balladur government. Even the privatization of the BNP, the UAP and AGF, jewels in the Gaullist crown of post-war financial institutions, was considered by most people as the continuation of an accepted trend [see Text 2.17]. The Jospin government continued to open the capital of many nationalized corporations, such as France Telecom in 1997, Thomson CST in 1998, Air France and Aérospatiale in 1999. As in the UK, the sale of shares of these companies to the general public was usually very successful, and oversubscribed.

## Deregulation and supply-side economics

These changes in the public sector are only one aspect of a more general reconsideration of the interventionist framework [see Text 2.18]. Since 1983, 'market forces' have increasingly been given a major role and this has led to a general deregulation of the economy, which has not been taken as far as in Britain and America, but which is nevertheless real. This has been true particularly of the financial sector, where since 1985 the financial and money markets have been largely deregulated and open to foreign operators, a complete change from the long period in which state controls and corporatist restrictions on market operators were the norm [see Text 2.19]. The state has also relinquished some of its powers, such as the 1945 Ordonnance authorizing governments to control and freeze prices in the economy.

The context of economic policy making is European construction. The whole policy of *désinflation compétitive*, which has been at the heart of the economic policy followed in France since the mid-1980s, recognizes the need for competitiveness and the fact that, because the economic structure of Europe is now far less rigid, and the production system more diverse and complex, than in the immediate post-war period, the traditional modes of regulation at state level are virtually inoperative [see Text 2.19].

Since the late 1980s, government and other decision-making authorities in France seem to have managed quite well within the monetarist, supply-side economic framework. For instance, in 1991–2, France was one of the few EC countries (and the only large one) which had already managed to satisfy all the 'convergence criteria' laid down in the Maastricht Treaty for entering into the European Monetary System and the single currency system. In 1993 the situation changed dramatically. Public finances deteriorated from 1992 onwards, and the ratio of PSBR (public sector borrowing requirement) to GDP shot up. The crisis in the French economy was accompanied by the collapse of the Exchange Rate Mechanism. In July 1993 France had to accept a change in the ERM currency fluctuation bands from plus or minus 2.25 per cent to plus or minus 15 per cent. This in fact meant a temporary devaluation of the French franc and the quasi-abandonment of rapid movement towards monetary union and a single European currency. However, the defeat of French economic policy did not signal an overturn of the policy of *désinflation compétitive* and the Balladur government continued to pursue the same line as that of the preceding Bérégovoy government, while the franc recovered its parity with the DM by the end of 1993. The following Juppé and Jospin governments followed the same strategies and, by 1998, France had again managed to satisfy all the Maastricht convergence criteria for the entrance into the Euro zone in 1999.

## Conclusion: expectations and problems for the new century

If we compare France's economic position in the late 1940s and early 1950s with its position at the start of the twenty-first century, we perceive striking differences in its economic structure. From the economic point of view, France in 1945 resembled two countries, a kind of 'dual economy', the one industrialized but the other still largely governed by activities closer to traditional rural societies. The country's considerable achievement since then is to have succeeded in modernizing its economy into a system based first on industry and subsequently on a powerful service sector with a highly trained work-force able to compete with countries such as Germany in terms of labour productivity, open to international trade and increasingly integrated into the European economic sphere. This was accomplished by means of a specific French model of economic growth variously described as 'state Fordism' or 'the Colbertist model of an administrated debt economy'.[16]

Despite all the problems which have been described above, this model successfully associated several elements. It gave a central role to the state, associating consensual interventionism and a strong regulatory apparatus with a flexible planning system coordinating the market economy and the public economy. It also relied on the adoption of a Fordist model of production and mass-consumption patterns which required the rapid modernization of production capacity and the development of a significant domestic market. In addition, it depended on the opening up of the French economy at the end of the colonial era, the creation of the EEC, the reduction of trade barriers through the GATT and the convertibility of the franc in 1959. A fourth factor, which is often neglected in the assessment of the modernization process, is the consensus which cemented the various social forces around some aspects of the model despite the strong oppositions between social groups. Whatever political oppositions may have existed, it is nevertheless clear that there was a strong undercurrent in favour of economic modernization and structural change. Within the consensus around the drive for investment and improvements in infrastructure and productivity, debates and conflicts could be extremely heated, but they did not undermine the basic consensus, and only the May 1968 movement challenged some of the assumptions on which consensus was based, with few long-term consequences.

Similarly, the way the French economy rode out the crises of the 1970s onwards demonstrates a remarkable capacity for change, particularly in abandoning the tenet that the state had a central role to play in the market economy, so that by the end of the 1990s France was again one of the most successful of the industrialized economies in terms of growth, monetary stability and trade.

However, it would be misleading to assert that a new 'post-Fordist' model has been established in the France of the new century. Indeed, when, early in 2000, given the renewed growth and excellent results of French firms, an economic magazine was asking on its front page 'Are the *Trente glorieuses* back?',[17] it replied categorically that they were not. The so-called 'new economy' is largely a myth. First, one characteristic of modern production systems is the heterogeneity of patterns of labour and capital organization and the varying degrees of insertion into the world market. Second, there is a series of challenges which must be faced before a new social consensus on the economy can be achieved. For the moment, the only point of agreement is the need for the autonomy of the market in relation to the state, but the rejection of interventionism has not thrown up new ways of managing the interaction between the economic and the social spheres.

The two principal challenges that the French economy must now address are the exclusion of more than one-tenth of the working population from economic life through unemployment, and the long-term question of the financing and organization of social welfare in an advanced economy. These two interrelated issues signal that, for all its successes, the French economy has been scandalously unsuccessful in generating adequate levels of employment. For the whole of the 1990s, unemployment appeared to have stabilized at an official level of at least three million and it was only with the approach of the new century that it started to decrease. As a consequence there has been a marked growth in inequality within an increasingly consumerist society, hence an increase in the tendency for social conflict. Serious long-term difficulties have been identified in financing the redistribution system inherited from the Fordist period of growth, with the public sector having fewer powers to organize and limit the impact of change and conflict. There is a more efficient or directly market-related system of social welfare with means-tested allowances. On the other hand, three million unemployed people represents a huge loss of human resources, while one of the consequences of the internationalization of markets has been the disappearance of entire ways of life and the destruction of local communities. Competitive disinflation has led to the creation of a two-speed society (*société à deux vitesses*) which requires the exclusion of certain categories of the population; unemployment affects both young and older worker disproportionately, and there is clearly a need to change the whole concept of work. A new social consensus will have to be sought, probably at the European level, in order to prevent the further break-up of social structures. Thus, although the model of 'redistribution through growth' which obtained during the *Trente glorieuses* is now dead, it has not been replaced by even the outline of a new model which would be broadly acceptable.

## Notes

1 The GDP is, broadly, the sum of all the added value created by all domestic economic sectors, plus taxes on consumption (VAT, customs duties), in a given year.

2 The working population remained at around 19.4 million between 1955 and 1962 but grew rapidly to 21.75 million by 1973. The economic crisis of the mid-1970s did not halt the rise in the working population, which had reached 23.45 million in 1983 and 24.4 million in 1991, but since 1973 an increasing proportion of the work-force has been unemployed (see INSEE, *Annuaire rétrospectif de la France, 1948–1988*, La Documentation française, 1990).

3 Labour productivity is calculated as the added value per worker. Its growth would be even higher if calculated per hour worked. The fact that agriculture has the fastest growth in productivity but the slowest growth in added value over the period is not surprising. On the one hand, the costs of agricultural inputs (fertilizers, pesticides and so on) have grown faster than the input costs of other sectors, and, on the other hand, the relative market value of agricultural products has fallen, because of its lower income elasticity. At the same time, the reduction of labour time has been enormous, hence the high growth in labour productivity. The relationships between added value, investment, labour productivity and so on have been studied by authors such as Perroux, Malinvaud and Dubois.

4 All figures on unemployment given here are estimates calculated according to the definitions of the UN's International Labour Organization (ILO) in order to facilitate international comparisons.

5 See M. Freyssenet, 'Grandes tendances', and P.-A. Audirac, 'Les métamorphoses de l'emploi', in *L'État de la France 1992* (La Découverte, 1992).

6 In France the rural population is the population living in the countryside and in built-up areas of less than 2,000 inhabitants.

7 For instance, mountain regions such as the department of Ariège in the Pyrénées or the department of Lozère in the Massif Central have both lost more than half of their population since the middle of the nineteenth century. But the Nord–Pas de Calais region doubled its population, from 1.85 million to 4.0 million between 1850 and 1997.

8 J.-F. Gravier, *Paris et le désert français* (Le Portulan, 1947).

9 One has to be cautious with trade statistics, as definitions can vary. Figures presented in the text, from the customs administration, are estimated CIF-FOB (CIF for imports and FOB for exports).

10 At the same time, returns on savings were very low, and outlets for savings very few: hence the major difficulties of the financial system in France in financing the considerable investment requirements of the French economy in a high growth period. The public sector *had* to take a leading role in this context.

11 See P. Rosanvallon, 'État et société, du XIX[e] à nos jours', in A. Burguières and J. Revel, *Histoire de la France: l'État et les pouvoirs* (Éditions du Seuil, 1989).

12 These figures exclude energy, which is mostly in the public sector. If this is included, the share of nationalized industries' added value in 1985 rises to 28 per cent and of investments to 49 per cent.

13 Rosanvallon, 'État et société'.

14 These figures and the following ones are from the OECD and have been only partly standardized. Figures provided by the French statistical office (INSEE) may be slightly different.

15 For instance, the difference in percentage of public money in the national income between France and Germany would be largely eliminated if the French VAT on local authority activities (which does not exist in Germany) was abolished, thereby reducing by a similar amount transfers from central government budgets to local authority finances, and if some national social insurance systems were transformed into assurance systems managed by industrial branches (therefore outside the public finance system, as in Germany), replacing many of the subsidies with tax credits. All these measures can easily be neutral in terms of taxation and public resources. (See D. Clerc, 'Les Prélèvements obligatoires', *Alternatives économiques*, 100, September–October 1992).

16 This expression was used by the economic journalist E. Israelewicz, 'La Modernisation du capitalisme français', in *Le Monde*, 5 May 1993. The term 'Colbertist' refers to the finance minister of Louis XIV, Jean-Baptiste Colbert, who strictly regulated trade and industry and developed a state (or royal) manufacturing sector at the end of the seventeenth century. The expression 'debt economy' (*économie d'endettement*) refers to the financial economy of the 1950s and 1960s in which resources for investment were secured mostly through borrowing from financial intermediaries.

17 *Alternatives économiques*, 178, February 2000.

# Suggestions for further reading

## General literature in English

The characteristics of the French economy continue to change at a very rapid pace, and it is difficult to find up-to-date analyses in English. There are very few recent books in English which specifically provide an overall presentation of the French economy. However, several edited books have been published in recent years that include chapters and essays on the French economy, and a number of studies of specialized areas of interest or of economic history can be found. J. Szarka, *Business in France: An Introduction to the Economic and Social Context* (Pitman, 1992), is already dated but still provides a useful and clear general presentation of the main aspects of the French economy in a matter-of-fact business approach. There is a very short introduction to the French economy in J. Girling, *France: Political and Social Change* (Routledge, 1999), and a more significant chapter in B. Foley's *European Economies since the Second World War* (Macmillan, 1998). Also useful is the short chapter by P. Holmes on France in D. A. Dyker (ed.), *The National Economies of Europe* (Longman, 1992). More substantial analysis, in the context of the integration of the French economy within the European Union, can be found in several chapters of the book edited by A. Guyomarch *et al.*, *France in the European Union* (Macmillan, 1998), especially about industrial, agricultural and economic policies.

Recent information on the French economy can be found in English in the annual publication of the Paris-based international organization the OECD, *France: Economic Survey* (also published in French). The London-based Economist Intelligence Unit also publishes a quarterly, *France: Country Profile* and an annual, *France: Country Report*, which in a few dozen pages present a basic description of the French economy and its current situation, backed up by statistics. Banks such as Barclays also publish economic guides to France. Articles on the French economy are published by academic journals in English such as *Modern and Contemporary France* (Carfax).

## General literature in French

There is obviously a wealth of good textbooks in French, which can profitably be used by English-speaking students studying French and French economics. An example of a simple introduction to the current economy is the short book by P. Bauchet, *Comprendre l'économie française* (Economica, 1998). Similarly, J. Crozet *et al.*, *Les grandes questions de l'économie françaises* (Nathan, 1998) adopts a didactic, question-and-answer approach. There are other relatively more advanced studies, such as those used as textbooks by French students. In this respect, the two-volume textbook by M. Parodi *et al.*, *L'économie et la société française au second XXème siècle* (Armand Colin, 1995 and 1998), is a precious resource, the first volume studying the general structure and characteristics of the French economy, and the second focusing on the analysis of the different sectors of the economy. The textbook by J.-F. Eck, *La France dans la nouvelle économie mondiale* (Presses Universitaires de France, 3rd edn, 1998) presents a solid analysis of the economy within the world system.

D. Clerc, *Déchiffrer l'économie* (Syros, 1997) (frequent re-editions) is a more didactic, general economic textbook, which is useful because it brings out new approaches to some of the main issues affecting the French economy. Another popular French textbook is M. Baleste, *L'économie française* (Masson, 1995) (new editions at regular intervals). This book presents a detailed view of the different sectors of the French economy, within an economic geography approach, but it excludes most of the questions of political economy and is very simplistic on socio-economic topics.

## Specialized and more advanced literature

It would be impossible to present an exhaustive list of the specialized literature on the French economy. We can only present a few of the most interesting of recent books as well as some classics. We begin with books which employ a historical approach, and then look at some of the major areas of analysis.

A major study of the historical evolution of the French economy is the encyclopaedic collection edited by F. Braudel and E. Labrousse, *Histoire économique de la France* (Presses Universitaires de France, 1982). The twentieth century and in particular the most recent period is covered in Part IV, Volume 3: 'Années 1950 à nos jours'. Another, more succinct, history of the nineteenth- and twentieth-century French economy is J.-C. Asselain, *Histoire économique de la France*, 2 vols (Éditions du Seuil, 1984). There are two well-known books on the evolution of the French economy during the *Trente glorieuses*. The first, J. Fourastié, *Les Trente glorieuses ou la révolution invisible* (Fayard, 1979), is quite simple to read and presents a 'modernist' analysis of the period. The second, D. Carré, P. Dubois and E. Malinvaud, *La Croissance française* (Éditions du Seuil, 1972) (published in English as *French Economic Growth*, Oxford University Press, 1975), is a masterpiece of econometric analysis and, as such, quite difficult to understand (a shorter version has been published under the title *Abrégé de la croissance française* (Éditions du Seuil, 1973)).

Another major study, J.-M. Jeanneney (ed.), *L'économie française depuis 1967* (Éditions du Seuil, 1989), presents the transition from post-war growth to the period of economic crisis in the 1970s and early 1980s. This too is a detailed and complex study with an econometric approach. A more descriptive approach is taken in the excellent and exhaustive study in two volumes by A. Gauron, *Histoire économique et sociale de la Ve République* (La Découverte, 1983, 1988). F. Caron, *An Economic History of Modern France*, 2 vols (Methuen, 1979), an English translation of a French book, deals, in Volume 2, with the changes in the French economy during the twentieth century, but stops in the late 1960s. Another sound, historically oriented book, which covers the most important aspects of the current economy and is regularly updated, is J.-F. Eck, *Histoire économique de la France depuis 1945*, 5th edn (Armand Colin, 1996). A short but more advanced book is A. Gueslin, *Nouvelle histoire économique de la France contemporaine – l'économie ouverte 1948–1990* (La Découverte, 1990) whose analysis of the financing of the French economy is especially useful. In English, the collections edited by J. Militz and A. Wyplosz, *The French Economy: Theory and Practice* (Westview, 1985) and by S. S. Cohen and P. A. Gourevitch, *France in a Troubled World Economy* (Butterworth, 1982) are still useful in parts as analysis of the *Trente glorieuses* period and its aftermath. The post-war period is analysed in detail in F. Lynch, *France and the International Economy: from Vichy to the Treaty of Rome* (Routledge, 1997).

A great number of authors have focused on the period of the early 1980s, as it saw a dramatic shift in the economic structures and the political economy of the country. The major assessment of the changes in this crisis-stricken period is A. Fonteneau and P.-A. Muet, *La gauche face à la crise* (Presses de la FNSP, 1985). (This book has been adapted into English as *Reflation and Austerity: Economic Policy under Mitterrand*, Berg, 1990), while a book in English on the same topic is H. Machin and V. Wright (eds), *Economic Policy-Making Under the Mitterrand Presidency* (Pinter, 1985). G. Ross *et al.* (eds), *The Mitterrand Experiment: Continuity and Change in Socialist France* (Polity Press, 1987) covers both economic and political aspects of the early 1980s crisis. At a more advanced, but still general, level, the collection by J. F. Hollifield and G. Ross, *Searching for the New France* (Routledge, 1991) includes several economic chapters written by specialists which illuminate recent structural changes in the French economy, especially A. Lipietz, 'Governing the Economy in the Face of International Challenge', an approach to the changing economic role of the state from a well-known 'Regulation School' analyst, and J. Jenson, 'The French Left: A Tale of Three Beginnings', which links changes in the economic and in the political spheres. A classic article analysing the context and the consequences of the left U-turn in economic policy in the early 1980s is by G. Ross and J. Jenson, 'The Tragedy of the French Left', in *New Left Review*, 171, 1988. A similar theme is explored in some of the chapters of the book edited by M. Maclean, *The Mitterrand Years: Legacy and Evaluation* (Macmillan, 1998) and also in several essays in the collection edited by A. Daley, *The Mitterrand Era: Policy Alternatives and Political Mobilization in France* (Macmillan, 1995).

A comprehensive list of books on specific aspects or sectors of the French economy would be excessively long. The titles that follow are of interest in their own right and complement the more general publications listed above. A short but exhaustive presentation of the labour market in France is D. Gambier and M. Vernières, *L'emploi en France* (La Découverte, 1991), and in R. Castel, *Métamorphoses de la question sociale: une chronique du salariat* (Fayard, 1995), which is fast becoming a classic, if complex, study. J. Freyssinet, *Le chômage* (La Découverte, 8th edn, 2000) focuses on unemployment issues, as does the book by D. Clerc, *Condamnés au chômage?* (Syros, 1999). Employment policies are introduced in DARES, *La politique de l'emploi* (La Découverte, 1997). In English, the issue of mass unemployment in France is analysed in the comparative study by N. Whiteside and R. Salais, *Governance, Industry and Labour Market in Britain and France* (Routledge, 1998). The impact of the economic crisis on French household income during the 1980s is studied in CERC, *Les Français et leurs revenus* (La Découverte, 1990), and contemporary consumption patterns in R. Rochefort, *La société des consommateurs* (Odile Jacob, 1995). Problems of the French welfare system are described in N. Murard, *La protection sociale* (La Découverte, 1996) and in the massive textbook by M. T. Join-Lambert *et al.*, *Politiques sociales* (Dalloz, 1997).

The evolution and economics of French agriculture are analysed in C. Servolin, *L'agriculture moderne* (Editions du Seuil, 1989) while an older study, with more sociological content, by H. Mendras, *La fin des paysans* (Armand Colin, 1970), is still highly relevant. French industry is analysed, for instance, in N. Holcblat and M. Husson, *L'industrie française* (La Découverte, 1990) and in H. Le Tellier and A. Torres, *La France, l'industrie, la crise* (Le Caster Astral, 1993), while the economics of French international trade are presented in F. Milewski, *Le commerce extérieur de la France* (La Découverte, 1992) and in CEPII, *Competitivité des nations* (Economica, 1998). In English, essays by C. Gulvin, G. Cumming and D. Henley in the book edited by T. Chafer and B. Jenkins, *France: from the Cold War to the New World Order* (Macmillan, 1995) present a view of the insertion of the French economy in the new international economic framework. The specific economic relations of France with the developing world, especially Africa, are analysed in detail in J. Adda and M.-C. Smouts, *La France face au Sud: le miroir brisé* (Khartala, 1989) and in M. Vernières, *Nord–Sud, renouveler la coopération* (Economica, 1995).

The development of the financial systems has been crucial for the modernization of the French economy. The revolution of the 1980s is analysed in J.-P. Faugère and C. Voisin, *Le système financier français* (Nathan, 1989). This analysis is extended to include the impact of the changes in the financial system on the structure of French capitalism in O. Pastré, *Les nouveaux piliers de la finance* (La Découverte, 1992). The impact of the recent launch of the Euro is discussed in an issue of *Cahiers français*, 'La monnaie unique' (n° 282, La Documentation Française), and the book edited by J. P. Fitoussi, *Rapport sur l'état de l'Union européenne* (Fayard, 1999). An excellent, if uncritical, presentation of the monetary policies which have been followed by all the French governments since the mid-1980s in view of furthering monetary and economic integration in Europe is by J. C. Trichet (who was implementing them as the director of Banque de France): 'Dix ans de désinflation compétitive' (*Les notes bleues de Bercy*, Ministère des Finances, 16th October 1992).

The role of the state has been for a long time one of the specific characteristics of the French economy. There is a good historical analysis in English of the period up to the late 1970s in R. Kuisel, *Capitalism and the State in Modern France* (Cambridge University Press, 1981) (translated into French as *Le Capitalisme et l'État en France*, Gallimard, 1984). Another, more recent, book analyses the role of the state in the French economy from a free-market point of view: M. Lévy-Leboyer and J.-C. Casanova, *Entre l'État et le marché: l'économie française des années 1880 à nos jours* (Gallimard, 1991). Another interesting book, which uses more of the 'regulation' framework of analysis, is F. Fenton, *L'état et le capitalisme au XXe siècle* (Presses Universitaires de France, 1992). The practice and methods of government economic policies up to the early 1980s are studied in great detail in M. Pebereau, *Les objectifs de la politique économique*, (Armand Colin, 1985) and M. Pebereau, *Les instruments de la politique économique* (Armand Colin, 1988). There are many books on the French experience with economic planning. Two well-known classics are C. Gruson, *Origines et espoirs de la planification française* (Dunod, 1968) and P. Massé, *Le plan ou l'anti-hasard* (NRF, 1965).

Finally, this selective presentation would be incomplete if it did not highlight the considerable work (in weight as well as in scope) of V. A. Schmidt, *From State to Market? The Transformation of French Business and Government* (Cambridge University Press, 1996) which manages to provide a detailed survey and relevant analysis of the profound changes which have intervened in French business, government economic policies and economic behaviour between the mid-1970s and the mid-1990s.

## Yearly publications, journals and papers

It is in the numerous journals, newspaper articles and annual publications that most of the information about and analysis of the French economy can most usefully be found. First, the celebrated daily newspaper *Le Monde* is in itself a precious source of information on all aspects of current economic affairs. The Tuesday issue contains an *Economy* supplement. It is also complemented by the *Dossiers et documents* series which reproduces articles on specific topics, including economic topics. Each year a special issue of the series contains a *Bilan économique et social* which presents a considerable amount of topical information on the world and the French economy. Other national newspapers also cover economics in a useful way: *Libération* often publishes economic articles with a didactic approach, whereas *Le Figaro* contains good business coverage. *Les Échos* is a specialized financial daily.

All weekly news magazines, from *Le Nouvel Observateur* to *L'Événement du Jeudi, L'Express* and *Le Point*, contain economic news, but there are also specialized economic and management magazines which are worth reading. One which is popular with students and teachers in France is the monthly *Alternatives économiques*, which often presents original views in a clear and understandable way. The two most popular management magazines are the fortnightly *L'Expansion* and the weekly *Le Nouvel Économiste* which also have a wealth of economic analysis as well as annual supplements on specific subjects. The monthly *L'Usine nouvelle* specifically deals with industry and industrial management.

In addition to *Le Monde*'s *Bilan économique et social*, a number of yearly publications give a good round-up of recent issues and changes in the French economy. The most useful, however, is undoubtedly *L'état de la France* (La Découverte), which contains a wealth of articles by specialists and numerous statistics, and has become since the late

1980s a precious reference tool. The 1999–2000 edition, for instance, contains a section entitled 'Radioscopie de l'économie' with articles on recent structural and policy trends, as well as detailed and up-to-date analysis of the situation in the main sectors of the economy. It also contains sections on the economy of each region, as well as essays on policy issues.

Most economic information and analysis comes from studies performed and published by research centres such as the CEPREMAP (well known for its links with the 'Regulation School'), the CREDOC (specializing in research on consumers and households), the CERC (*Centre d'étude des revenus et des coûts*), the OFCE (*Observatoire français des conjonctures économiques*, with its excellent monthly journal, *Observations et diagnostics économiques*) and of course the INSEE. Academic journals also are important, for instance *La Revue économique, La Revue d'économie française, La Revue d'économie financière* or *La Revue d'économie industrielle*. The OFCE publishes every year a summary of some of its most important articles about the evolution of the French economy; for instance, in the year 2000: *L'économie française 2000* (La Découverte).

Official economic and social statistics (including the National Accounts and the Census) are produced by the INSEE (Institut national de la statistique et des études économiques). But, as its name indicates, in addition to being a statistical powerhouse it is also a research centre of very high standing. The yearly *Tableaux économiques de la France* published by the INSEE accumulate an enormous quantity of economic and social statistics in a relatively slim yearly volume. The INSEE also publishes long statistical series, for instance the *Annuaire rétrospectif de la France 1948–1988* (La Documentation française, 1990). It also produces the massive yearly *Annuaire statistique de la France*. Another useful INSEE publication is *Données sociales*, a compendium of socio-economic studies and statistical articles by specialists covering topics such as household consumption, employment patterns, income, and so on. It is published every few years at irregular intervals (1984, 1988, 1990, 1993, 1996, 1999). A shorter yearly socio-economic compendium of articles and statistics is INSEE, *France, portrait social* (INSEE, annual). Regional statistics are published in *La France et ses régions*. National accounts are published in a technical series, but a detailed statistical summary can be found every year in *Extraits et tableaux des comptes nationaux*, and these accounts are commented on and analysed in the annual *Rapport sur les comptes de la nation*, which is now published in a shortened yearly version, *L'économie française* (Livre de Poche, annual), and includes a number of topical economic studies.

The INSEE also publishes journals and information bulletins. The most prestigious journal is the monthly *Économie et statistique*, with in-depth analyses of social and economic subjects which are sometimes difficult to follow but always challenging, and the regular bulletin *INSEE Première* is worth following.

The official publications office, La Documentation Française, publishes all sorts of official information. Of particular relevance for the study of the French economy is the bi-monthly *Problèmes économiques*, which is entirely made up of articles culled from various papers in France and across the world. A most useful source of information is the *Cahiers français* series of thematic dossiers; those on economic topics such as economic policy, financial systems, the integration of France into Europe, international trade, industry and planification are invaluable.

These are complemented by the official bulletin of the Ministère des Finances, *Les notes bleues de Bercy*, which provides information and analysis on the latest trends in French foreign trade and balance of payments, financial and monetary statistics, government budgets, fiscal policies, prices, and so on. In the financial sector, most banks also publish research and information bulletins, which are often distributed free.

## Useful websites

The internet has not yet penetrated French society as it has other countries, but it is catching up very fast. Much statistical information and public documentation can be found on a variety of sites. This is particularly true of the various ministries, for instance the Ministry of Finances has a well constructed site on http://www.finances.gouv.fr, which contains considerable statistical resources and innumerable information pages. Other ministerial sites are often more specialized in the economics of their own area of competence (an example is that of the Ministry of Agriculture: http://www.agriculture.gouv.fr). Statistics and studies on the labour market and unemployment issues can be found in the pages of DARES, the research department of the Ministry of Employment and Solidarity, on the site of the ministry: http://www.travail.gouv.fr, and many socio-demographic studies and statistics can be found on the site of the National Institute for Demographic Studies, INED: http://popinfo.ined.fr. Other employment information can be found on the ASSEDIC and ANPE sites (http://www.unedic.fr and http://www.anpe.fr). Monetary and financial information can be found on the Central Bank site, http://www.banque-france.fr.

Most statistics of an economic nature are available on the enormous INSEE site on http://www.insee.fr which contains not only downloadable tables and surveys but also a number of studies and summaries which can be very useful (for instance archives of *INSEE Première*). The sites of the two assemblies of the parliament, http://www.senat.fr and http://www.assemblee-nationale.fr provide a wealth of official documents, public debates and reports and white papers on many economic issues. However, most official reports are available on line (and downloadable through PDF or HTML formats) through the site of the government's official documentation and public information agency, La Documentation Française. This site, on http://www.ladocfrancaise.gouv.fr, also contains many other sources of information and should be a first port of call for documentation.

Some research institutes have developed their own sites; this is the case of the well-known OFCE (Observatoire français des conjonctures économiques): http://www.ofce.sciences-po.fr. It can also be very useful to search the sites of international organizations for statistics and studies concerning the French economy. This is the case of the OECD (Organization for Economic Co-operation and Development): http://www.oecd.org; or the statistical office of the European Union, Eurostat: http://europa.eu.int/eurostat.html; the World Bank: http://www.worldbank.org; the International Labour Organization: http://www.ilo.org, among others.

Many newspapers and magazines are now maintaining good and informative websites, some with extensive archives. A typical example is that of *Le Monde*, the well-known reference evening daily newspaper, on its site http://www.lemonde.fr. Useful economic information and analysis can be found this way, sometimes organized in special dossiers (for instance, in 1999 and 2000, both the sites of the daily newspaper *Libération* and magazine *L'Express* contained an extensive file of pages on the topical issue of 'the 35 hours', the new, controversial policy of legally reducing working hours for all French employees in order to provide new employment for the jobless: http://www.liberation.fr and http://www.lexpress.fr).

TEXT 2.1

## Travail, capital et État pendant la période de croissance de l'après-guerre

*Des facteurs nouveaux sont intervenus*

Les principaux d'entre eux peuvent être groupés autour de trois constatations: les Français ont maintenu à un niveau élevé leur effort de travail, les unités de production se sont équipées et réorganisées, l'administration économique du pays a fait preuve de dynamisme.

*Les Français au travail*

S'il est impossible de mesurer l'intensité de l'effort fourni par la population active, on peut voir à divers indices que les Français ont donné une certaine priorité au travail. Les évolutions des taux d'activité, de la mobilité géographique et de la durée du travail sont assez révélatrices.

Sans doute l'allongement de la scolarité et la forte réduction du nombre des travailleurs indépendants de l'agriculture et du commerce ont-ils eu pour effet d'abaisser les taux d'activité aux âges extrêmes. Mais en proportion croissante les femmes ont recherché un emploi: la chose apparaît de façon particulièrement nette sur les taux d'activité aux âges inférieurs à 40 ans (à l'âge de 25 ans ce taux est passé de 47% en 1954 à 52% en 1962 puis 56% en 1968).

Quoiqu'elle soit encore faible par rapport à des pays comme les États-Unis, la mobilité géographique semble assez remarquable. Elle a été s'accélérant; et surtout elle s'est située à des niveaux qui apparaissent élevés si l'on a présentes à l'esprit les grandes difficultés de logement qui ont prévalu durant tout l'après-guerre dans la plupart des agglomérations urbaines. Beaucoup ont accepté des conditions de vie très inconfortables dans le but d'avoir un meilleur emploi.

Enfin le maintien, jusqu'à une date récente, d'une longue durée du travail semble avoir résulté en grande partie d'une transformation des attitudes de la population adulte. Par exemple, la durée annuelle du travail, qui dans l'industrie avait diminué d'environ 20% entre 1896 et 1929, puis avait été encore fortement réduite par la crise et la législation de 1936, s'établit durant l'après-guerre à un niveau peu inférieur à celui de 1929, l'existence et l'allongement des congés étant compensés par une croissance de la durée hebdomadaire. Les syndicats ouvriers, qui militaient dans l'immédiat après-guerre pour une réduction de cette durée, se rendirent compte par la suite qu'une telle action n'était pas désirée, du moins jusqu'en mai 1968. Quelques enquêtes d'opinion firent aussi apparaître que la plupart des salariés faisaient passer le souci d'une amélioration de leur revenu bien avant celui d'une diminution de leur temps de travail. Ainsi la France se trouvait-elle vers 1965 l'un des pays dans lesquels la durée du travail était la plus élevée.

*Entreprises équipées et modernisées*

La modernisation de l'appareil de production joua un rôle important. C'est sans doute grâce à elle que les gains de productivité ne se ralentirent pas durant les années 1960 et même qu'ils s'accélérèrent quelque peu dans l'industrie. A deux époques, des options essentielles furent prises. Dès les premières années de l'après-guerre, le pouvoir politique et les responsables du secteur public entreprirent une reconstruction optimiste de l'infrastructure et des industries de base. A la fin des années 1950 et au début des années 1960, les chefs d'entreprises prirent conscience des exigences de la production moderne et acceptèrent de s'y soumettre. Ils comprirent l'information qui leur avait été donnée dans le cadre du mouvement en faveur de la productivité. Ils en acceptèrent les conséquences et ne freinèrent pas l'ouverture du Marché commun. Beaucoup surent profiter de l'ouverture des frontières.

Sans doute l'inflation antérieure avait-elle assaini la situation financière des entreprises. Sans doute diverses mesures de caractère fiscal avaient-elles eu pour effet de rendre plus léger le coût effectif de l'utilisation des équipements. Sans doute la concurrence extérieure obligeait-elle, dans beaucoup de cas, à des réorganisations importantes. Mais, si les chefs et dirigeants d'entreprise n'avaient pas eu la volonté de promouvoir l'expansion de leurs firmes, la modernisation aurait été plus lente.

Comme il arrive toujours dans les périodes connaissant des transformations rapides, les succès furent accompagnés d'une certaine proportion d'échecs. Ces derniers ont périodiquement retenu l'attention du public. Mais lorsqu'on prend un certain recul par rapport aux événements, on voit se dégager l'image d'une modernisation douée d'une efficacité d'ensemble indéniable.

*Une politique économique dynamique*

A de multiples endroits nous avons noté le rôle joué par les pouvoirs publics. Ce rôle devait être important puisque existaient à la fin de la guerre un secteur public productif notablement grossi par les nationalisations de 1946, des organismes de contrôle ayant vocation économique, enfin un personnel administratif de haute qualité. Mais de tels atouts étaient contrebalancés par l'inexistence presque totale d'instruments d'observation économique, par la médiocrité de la formation économique des cadres, enfin par l'absence d'une doctrine claire et largement admise.

Que la politique économique suivie apparaisse rétrospectivement comme douée dans l'ensemble de dynamisme et de cohérence, nous pouvons l'attribuer à une transformation de l'action de l'État qui doit beaucoup à la conjonction des efforts de quelques groupes d'hommes et aux progrès de la connaissance économique. En raison soit de ses fonctions, soit de son expérience, chacun de ces groupes était sensibilisé à un des aspects du développement économique et avait la volonté d'en améliorer les conditions. La juxtaposition de tels efforts engendra un système qui doit beaucoup à l'empirisme mais qui semble doué d'une certaine efficacité.

Ainsi fut engendré un système économique mixte, système dans lequel les marchés jouent un grand rôle, la concurrence est maintenue ou rétablie entre les producteurs nationaux comme entre eux et l'extérieur, système dans lequel existe aussi une planification indicative aidant à une prise de conscience des exigences et des caractéristiques du développement, système enfin dans lequel l'État assume certaines responsabilités directes dans la gestion économique.

Par la direction des entreprises publiques, par le financement public de gros investissements, par ses interventions dans l'aménagement du territoire ou dans la réorganisation des grandes entreprises, l'État réalisa en effet un grand nombre d'opérations ponctuelles visant à favoriser la croissance économique. Sans doute ces opérations ne réussirent-elles pas toutes, Néanmoins sans que la doctrine en fût vraiment explicitée, elles s'inscrivent le plus souvent dans une vue assez cohérente de l'action de l'État sur le développement économique.

(J.-J. Carré *et al.*, *Abrégé de la croissance française*, Éditions du Seuil, 1973, pp.259–62.)

## Exercices

### *Lexique*

Expliquez les mots et expressions suivants:

contrebalancer (l.68)
une économie mixte (l.81)
une opération ponctuelle (l.90)

### *Grammaire et stylistique*

(a) 'une certaine priorité' (ll.8–9): appréciez la place de l'adjectif et indiquez la différence avec 'une priorité certaine'. Même chose pour l'expression 'certaines responsabilités' (l.86).
(b) Proposez une construction différente (et moins littéraire) pour les phrases qui commencent par 'sans doute' (ll.51–52).

### *Compréhension*

(a) Que mettez-vous sous l'expression 'des instruments d'observation économique' (l.69), 'une doctrine claire et largement admise' (ll.70–71), 'une planification indicative' (l.84)?
(b) Précisez les responsabilités directes que l'État assume dans la gestion économique (l.86), et dégagez les grandes lignes de 'l'action de l'État sur le développement économique' (l.93).

### *Questions orales ou écrites*

(a) Pourquoi le rôle de l'État durant la période des *Trente glorieuses* peut-il être perçu comme crucial pour favoriser la croissance et amener la modernisation de l'économie française?
(b) La durée hebdomadaire du travail en France est beaucoup plus basse aujourd'hui que durant les années 1960. Est-ce un signe d'inefficacité, ou de plus haute productivité?

TEXT 2.2

## «Consommez», le nouveau mot d'ordre

Durant la première moitié du siècle, les Français ne sont pas encore à proprement parler des consommateurs. Le pouvoir d'achat individuel est faible et il ne progressera que de 80% en cinquante ans, ce qui est peu, très peu, en comparaison de ce qui se passera ensuite, puisque de 1950 à nos jours, ce même pouvoir d'achat sera multiplié par quatre! Nous disposons donc aujourd'hui d'un revenu en termes réels – hors inflation – sept fois plus important qu'il y a cent ans.

Durant toute la première moitié du siècle la société est avant tout rurale. Au début des années 50, trois Français sur cinq vivent encore dans une commune de moins de 10 000 habitants. L'autoproduction familiale est de mise, tant en ce qui concerne l'alimentation que les vêtements. Les produits industriels destinés à la vie privée sont rares bien que leur diffusion s'accroisse peu à peu. Il y a une voiture pour 13 400 habitants au début du siècle et l'on entrera dans la seconde moitié du siècle avec encore «seulement» une automobile pour 20 habitants. En 1900, notre pays dispose d'un poste téléphonique pour 556 habitants, il y en aura un pour 18 personnes au milieu du siècle.

Le progrès technique, l'exode rural sont des facteurs essentiels de développement de la consommation. Mais l'essentiel est ailleurs. C'est l'augmentation massive et régulière du pouvoir d'achat qui nous fera basculer dans la société de consommation, à partir du début des années 50.

*Une société qui aspirait à son ascension collective, qui croyait en son avenir*

Au cours des années 50 et 60, l'extension du salariat et des prestations sociales ont permis un enrichissement généralisé et spectaculaire sur fond d'uniformisation des comportements. Les attentes de cette époque mettaient en avant l'obtention d'un statut pour tous, l'aspiration à une reconnaissance sociale dont les attributs étaient l'automobile, l'équipement de la maison, les arts ménagers, les départs en vacances . . .

L'imaginaire qui soustendait cette époque était celui d'une société certes stratifiée en classes sociales, mais qui aspirait à son ascension collective, qui croyait à son avenir. Les modes de vie et donc de consommation demeuraient familiaux: l'alimentation, la mode vestimentaire étaient les mêmes à l'intérieur de la cellule familiale. Lorsque le premier poste de télévision apparaît dans les foyers, on installe sur le dessus un cadre avec la photo des grand-parents comme pour se convaincre de l'ascension familiale que son acquisition représente.

*Après Mai 1968, la consommation devient résolument individualiste*

Tout cela changea brutalement après Mai 68 pour déboucher sur un mode de consommation résolument individualiste. Finie l'unique chaîne haute fidélité trônant au milieu du salon, celle-ci se multiplia pour le bonheur des fabricants. Il devenait la règle de voir cohabiter une chaîne hi-fi de «qualité» dans la chambre des parents ou dans la pièce principale, avec des chaînes plus compactes, dans la chambre de chaque enfant. Les marchés sont segmentés à l'extrême.

De même les habitudes alimentaires changèrent. La généralisation du travail des femmes permet le développement du marché des plats cuisinés, venant se substituer à celui des ingrédients alimentaires de base. Aujourd'hui, la table du petit déjeuner d'une famille de quatre personnes ressemble à une épicerie en modèle réduit. Chacun a sa propre marque de céréales, de confiture et de boisson chaude. Il y a trente ans, ne pas tous manger la même chose au repas matinal était un signe d'incivilité manifeste!

En cinquante ans, la structure de la consommation s'est profondément transformée. Au début de la seconde moitié du siècle, un franc sur deux du budget familial était consacré à l'alimentation. Nous en sommes aujourd'hui à un franc sur six seulement. En revanche les dépenses de loisirs, de vacances, de transports, mais aussi consacrées au logement et à la santé ont explosé . . . Ces cinq postes représentent aujourd'hui 54% de notre budget de consommateur, contre 32% en 1960.

La consommation a connu une période d'essoufflement provisoire dans le courant de la décennie 90. Cela a démarré juste au lendemain de la guerre du Golfe. Pétris d'inquiétudes sociétales de toutes natures (chômage, sida, insécurité urbaine, avenir des retraites . . .) les consommateurs ont joué la prudence et critiqué le narcissisme hyperindividualiste et les excès de gaspillage. On a assisté au retour de thématiques plus rassurantes: le terroir (dans l'alimentation, la presse magazine, les vacances), la santé (tendance amplifiée par les peurs alimentaires dont la vache folle fut la première de la série), la famille.

Depuis deux ans, la consommation est à nouveau très dynamique grâce à l'arrivée de nouveaux produits: téléphones portables, ordinateurs domestiques, télévision par satellite, équipement pour surfer sur Internet. Ils permettent de s'équiper en «consommateur-entrepreneur» tel que la société le demande désormais: interpénétration croissante du travail et de la vie familiale, apprentissage continu tout au long de la vie, mobilité accrue et capacité de communiquer en toute circonstance. Bien entendu, comme à chaque étape de développement de la société de consommation, s'entremêlent potentialité accrue d'épanouissement et d'autonomie et risque d'asservissement aux objets qui deviennent indispensables. La consommation ne fait pas le bonheur, elle est juste . . . le moteur principal de la croissance économique depuis déjà un demi-siècle.

(Robert Rochefort, '"Consommez",
le nouveau mot d'ordre', *La Croix*, 10 July 1999, p.10.)

## Exercices

### *Lexique*

Expliquez les mots et expressions suivants:

| | |
|---|---|
| un mot d'ordre (titre) | l'autoproduction familiale (l.10) |
| le pouvoir d'achat (l.2) | les foyers (ll.32–33) |

| | |
|---|---|
| déboucher sur (l.36) | une thématique (l.61) |
| les arts ménagers (ll.26–27) | le terroir (l.61) |
| un signe d'incivilité (l.48) | épanouissement (ll.71–72) |
| narcissisme hyperindividualiste (l.60) | asservissement (l.72) |

### *Grammaire et stylistique*

(a) Remarquez l'utilisation fréquente dans ce texte du présent et du futur pour la description d'événements passés. Quel est l'effet de style que recherche l'auteur? Réécrivez le premier paragraphe en conjuguant les verbes à des temps passés tels que passé composé ou imparfait. Quelle en est la conséquence au niveau du style?

(b) Dans l'avant-dernière phrase du texte, remarquez l'inversion du verbe ('s'entremêlent') et des sujets ('potentialité' et 'risque'). Pourquoi cette inversion? Trouvez une autre phrase dans le texte (ou inventez-en une vous-même) dans laquelle vous pouvez faire une inversion similaire.

### *Compréhension*

(a) Le texte distingue différentes périodes dans le vingtième siècle, chacune ayant un mode de consommation spécifique. Dressez une liste de ces périodes, et pour chacune d'entre elles identifiez les principales caractéristiques de la consommation des ménages.

(b) Quels sont, selon le texte, les changements dans les comportements familiaux qui accompagnent les modifications du mode de consommation?

(c) Le texte signale que depuis les années 1960, 'les marchés sont segmentés à l'extrême'. Que cela signifie-t-il, et pourquoi?

### *Questions orales et écrites*

(a) Pourquoi et comment l'augmentation des revenus est-elle un élément explicatif important des changements de mode de consommation?

(b) En utilisant le dernier paragraphe du texte comme point de départ, quels seront selon vous les prochains changements de mode de consommation qui interviendront dans les dix prochaines années?

TEXT 2.3

## La politique industrielle de la sidérurgie: de plan en plan, une gestion désastreuse

Cent milliards de francs au bas mot. Voilà ce qu'aura coûté aux Français le sauvetage de la sidérurgie. Cent mille emplois perdus. Voilà ce qu'aura coûté à l'une des parties les plus fières de la 'classe ouvrière' la crise de l'acier. A supposer, bien entendu, que la 'sortie du rouge' promise pour cette année se vérifie et perdure; et les pronostics restent, à cet égard, prudents.

Un désastre. Le fait a été, toutes ces longues années, assez illustré par tant de rage et de désespoir mêlés qu'il n'est pas besoin d'y revenir. Si ce n'est peut-être pour rappeler qu'on n'a pas fini d'en observer les conséquences. Au niveau local de ces vallées mono-industrielles en ruine, d'abord, au niveau politique, ensuite. L'élection présidentielle a mis en lumière des sidérurgistes qu'on ne s'attendait pas à voir voter pour M. Le Pen. L'effondement du Parti communiste et la montée de l'extrême droite trouvent, parmi d'autres facteurs, leur ferment sous la rouille des laminoirs.

Pouvait-on faire autrement? Telle est bien la question en 1988 qui, en condensé, concerne l'industrie française tout entière face à la crise.

Cette crise sidérurgique, cela a été dit et redit depuis, n'était pas nationale mais mondiale, c'est-à-dire incontournable. Due à l'évolution des techniques d'abord: il faut moins d'acier pour faire une voiture ou un pont. A la division mondiale du travail ensuite: l'acier coulé au Japon puis en Corée et au Brésil n'est pas moins bon et il est moins cher. Toutes les nations développées ont dû fermer des usines. Mais la gestion de la crise a été différente selon les pays, et tout est là.

Premier constat: l'acier restera le symbole de la faillite du grand patronat français et des célèbres familles de Wendel ou Schneider. Organisées en quasi-cartels, elles font preuve d'un aveuglement inouï qui les poussera à construire l'usine de Fos-sur-Mer – la sidérurgie *'au bord de l'eau'* censée représenter l'avenir – en 1971, trois ans avant la chute irrémédiable des marchés. La collusion politique avec l'administration parisienne, à laquelle s'ajoutent l'influence des même corps d'ingénieurs et les intérêts des élus locaux, supprime tout contre-pouvoir. La solution trouvée sera, naturellement, d'en appeler aux crédits publics. Après les profits privés, il fallait 'nationaliser les pertes'. Ce fut fait bien avant 1981, dès 1978.

Deuxième constat: le dirigisme d'État succède au dirigisme privé mais n'élimine pas le gâchis. La crise est née dans les esprits, refusée dans sa gravité pendant exactement dix ans (1974–1984). Le gouvernement de gauche en témoigne, par son plan de 1982, qui voudra *'relancer'*. On mettra ensuite longtemps avant d'admettre que l'analyse industrielle (les avantages des fours électriques, les comparaisons de coût internationales . . .) n'existe pas parce que les outils les plus élémentaires manquent (une comptabilité précise par exemple). Les facteurs de décision sont l'appartenance aux clans – Usinor contre Sacilor, le Nord contre la Lorraine, les produits plats contre les produits longs, etc., et l'arbitrage politique au sommet.

Le troisième constat porte sur l'Europe, l'acier étant la seule industrie où existe une réelle organisation communautaire (la Communauté européenne du charbon et de l'acier ou CECA). '*L'état de crise manifeste*' déclenché en octobre 1980 par Bruxelles conduira à un plan de réduction homothétique des capacités par pays. Coupe globale indispensable, mais, faite ainsi, elle ne favorise aucun rapprochement intra-européen et conserve leur drapeau aux aciéries. La création de groupes européens – amorcée seulement – est urgente, étant données les surcapacités restantes.

Au bout du compte, le dysfonctionnement des 'décideurs' français aura coûté cher. La chute de la production française d'acier depuis 1974 (– 34%) est la plus forte de celles qu'ont connues des pays développés, les États-Unis mis à part. Les meubles ont été mal sauvés. Sans doute a-t-on aussi gâché deux ou trois ans par crainte politique de regarder la vérité et de la dire. Plusieurs milliards de francs d'aides publiques auraient pu être épargnés.

Refus d'admettre la crise des 'cathédrales' industrielles, ignorance de gestion, collusion inefficace de la technostructure privée et publique, obstination coupable des élus locaux, la crise sidérurgique symbolise coûteusement la mauvaise traversée par l'industrie française des années 70 et 80. Elle explique aussi, par tant d'argent mal investi, le retard national dans les technologies de pointe.

Puisse la leçon servir et réhabiliter définitivement la nécessité d'une politique industrielle mieux faite, mieux outillée, voyant large et loin, mais non exempte de prudence et d'humilité.

(Eric Boucher, 'La politique industrielle de la sidérurgie: de plan en plan, une gestion désastreuse', *Le Monde*, 21 May 1988.)

## Exercices

### *Lexique*

Expliquer les mots et expressions suivants:

au bas mot (l.1)
la sortie du rouge (l.4)
trouver son ferment sous la rouille des laminoirs (ll.12–13)
la crise est incontournable (l.17)
un contre-pouvoir (ll.28–29)
le gâchis (l.33)
homothétique (l.45)
le dysfonctionnement des 'décideurs' (l.50)
les meubles ont été mal sauvés (l.53)
une 'cathédrale' industrielle (l.56)

### *Grammaire et stylistique*

(a) 'Plusieurs milliards de francs d'aide auraient pu être épargnés' (ll.54–55) – 'Voilà ce qu'aura coûté le sauvetage de la sidérurgie' (ll.1–2). Révisez le futur antérieur et le conditionnel passé dans une grammaire. Et faites vous-même des phrases en employant ces modes/temps. Prêtez une attention particulière aux phrases avec 'devoir', 'pouvoir' et 'vouloir'.

(b) 'Puisse la leçon servir . . .' (l.61). Justifiez le subjonctif. Écrivez d'autres exemples inventés.

### Compréhension

(a) Expliquez l'expression 'nationaliser les pertes' (l.30).
(b) Résumez les différentes causes de la crise sidérurgique exposées dans l'article, à l'échelle mondiale et à celle de la France. En quoi cette crise symbolise-t-elle 'la mauvaise traversée par les industries françaises des années 70 et 80' (ll.58–59)?

### Questions orales ou écrites

(a) Pourquoi a-t-il été nécessaire d'établir une politique européenne commune de réduction des capacités de production d'acier?
(b) La concurrence des pays du Tiers-Monde: les industries de base comme la sidérurgie ont-elles encore une place dans la structure industrielle de la France?

TEXT 2.4

## Pourquoi la France a-t-elle trois millions de chômeurs en 1992?

Quoi? Demain pire qu'aujourd'hui? Alors qu'avec 2,7 millions de demandeurs d'emploi – dont près de 800 000 inscrits à l'ANPE depuis plus d'un an – la France affiche déjà l'un des plus exécrables taux de chômage des grands pays industrialisés . . . Pendant des années, les gouvernements successifs se sont battus pour assainir notre économie, restaurer nos grands équilibres, rendre compétitives nos entreprises. Résultat? Rien. Le cancer est toujours là. Pourquoi?

*Parce que la croissance est beaucoup trop faible*: 4,5% de croissance en 1989, 2,8% en 1990, quasiment zéro au premier semestre 1991 . . . Le ralentissement mondial, amorcé bien avant la guerre du Golfe, a eu des effets dévastateurs sur la conjoncture française. Logiquement, les offres d'emplois se sont effondrées, et les entreprises, après avoir éliminé les intérimaires et les salariés en contrat à durée déterminée, ont fini par licencier. Sombre perspective: les gros plans de licenciements annoncés dans le textile, l'électronique ou l'automobile n'ont pas encore pris leur effet. Quelque 70 000 chômeurs supplémentaires sont déjà prévus pour la rentrée.

Certes, d'autres font pire que nous, puisqu'ils sont carrément en récession: les États-Unis ont ainsi engrangé 2 millions de chômeurs de plus en un an, et la Grande-Bretagne 600 000, mais leur taux de chômage n'a pas encore rejoint le nôtre.

Ainsi, il aura suffi de quelques mois de déprime conjoncturelle pour détériorer gravement la situation de l'emploi, alors que trois années de belle croissance, entre 1987 et 1990, n'ont pratiquement pas permis de réduire le niveau du chômage.

*Parce que la psychologie n'arrange pas les choses.* Comme toujours, les comportements psychologiques viennent aggraver la situation. Les ménages, dont le pouvoir d'achat a globalement augmenté l'an dernier, restreignent ou diffèrent leur consommation par peur du lendemain. Les chefs d'entreprises, dont les charges n'ont pas progressé, abandonnent par excès de prudence leurs projets d'investissements, stoppent les embauches, ou commencent même à licencier, au risque de rater le train de la reprise. La France vit recroquevillée sur elle-même, et le climat de morosité s'auto-alimente.

*Parce que la formation est inadaptée.* Les listings de l'ANPE s'allongent, mais pendant ce temps-là, des dizaines de milliers d'offres d'emploi ne trouvent pas preneur. L'Agence nationale en recense actuellement 62 000. Le CNPF, lui, les chiffre à au moins 300 000 . . . Qui croire? Dans certains secteurs comme le BTP, la construction électrique ou l'hôtellerie, les besoins en main-d'œuvre qualifiée sont manifestes. Pour y voir plus clair, Martine Aubry s'apprête d'ailleurs à mener une enquête serrée sur le terrain afin de déterminer les besoins réels des entreprises.

Les causes? Il y a d'abord les carences de l'éducation. Beaucoup trop de jeunes arrivent sur le marché du travail sans aucune qualification ou avec une formation qui ne correspond nullement aux besoins des entreprises. Le gouvernement mise aujourd'hui sur le développement de l'apprentissage pour arranger les choses: une grande négociation sur ce thème démarrera à la rentrée entre les partenaires sociaux.

*Parce que la démographie est contre nous.* Entre 1987 et 1990, la France a créé 850 000 emplois. Dans le même temps, le nombre de chômeurs n'a diminué que de 70 000. Douze fois moins! Pourquoi une telle différence? Parce que notre pays doit faire face à une marée de nouveaux arrivants sur son marché du travail. Selon l'INSEE, ils seraient environ 200 000 chaque année à venir grossir le flot des demandeurs d'emploi.

S'agirait-il des immigrés, qui, en rangs serrés, viendraient inonder notre ANPE? Nullement. En dix ans, le nombre de travailleurs étrangers n'a progressé que de 4,4%. Si notre population active augmente rapidement, c'est en premier lieu à cause des jeunes, tout juste sortis du système éducatif, qui viennent s'inscrire chaque automne à l'ANPE. La France, dont la natalité est aujourd'hui insuffisante pour assurer le renouvellement de ses générations, paye ici le prix de sa vigueur démographique du début des années 70. D'autant plus lourd que, pour beaucoup, les gosses nés dans cette période ont été peu ou mal formés, et qu'ils ont le plus grand mal à s'insérer dans la vie active.

A cela s'ajoute l'afflux des femmes sur le marché du travail. Il y a celles qui préfèrent travailler plutôt qu'être mères au foyer. Et celles qui ont impérativement besoin de trouver un emploi. Celles qui cherchent simplement à arrondir les revenus du ménage. Celles enfin qui souhaitent se remettre au travail une fois leurs enfants élevés. Bref, plus aucune femme ne veut désormais rester à la maison: en neuf ans, la population active féminine s'est accrue de 1,5 million. A peu près autant que le chômage.

Bref, la France croule sous les forces vives. Quand ses voisins, à la démographie anémiée, profitent du moindre souffle de croissance pour réduire leur chômage, elle doit créer des milliers d'emplois supplémentaires pour simplement espérer le contenir.

*Parce que le traitement social a montré ses limites.* Les TUC, les PIL, les PLIF, les SRA, les SIVP . . . Même combinées, les 26 lettres de l'alphabet sont à peine suffisantes pour retracer la myriade de formules de 'stages parking' sorties depuis dix ans des tiroirs du ministère du Travail. Pendant les années 80, l'essentiel de la politique de l'emploi n'a guère consisté qu'à les multiplier. Avec, pour principal objectif, de camoufler la montée du chômage en faisant patienter hors de l'ANPE des centaines de milliers de demandeurs d'emploi potentiels.

En 1988, Jean-Pierre Soisson décide de mettre le holà. Il supprime les formules trop 'immorales' comme les SIVP, réforme les TUC, tente de rendre les différents stages plus formateurs. Désormais, on en fait moins, mais on en fait mieux. Ainsi le nombre de jeunes en TUC (rebaptisés contrats emploi solidarité), qui frisait les 300 000 en 1986, n'est plus aujourd'hui que de 160 000. Moyennant quoi le ministère du Travail dépense moins: en 1990, il a pu rendre neuf milliards de francs initialement prévus pour le traitement social et non dépensés.

*Parce que le coût de la main-d'œuvre non qualifiée serait trop élevé.* Bien que tout le monde n'en soit pas convaincu, Pierre Bérégovoy voit là l'une des principales causes du chômage. Aussi prévoit-il d'accentuer la politique de réduction de charges en faveur des PME – il pourrait exonérer de charges sociales les entreprises embauchant un deuxième et un troisième salarié. De son côté, Martine Aubry va donner un coup de pouce aux *'emplois de proximité'* (gardes d'enfants, femmes de ménage, aides ménagères etc.). Reste que ces coups d'épingles ne pourront, à eux seuls, faire fléchir rapidement la courbe des demandeurs d'emploi. Pas plus qu'aucune des mesures de fond planifiées par le gouvernement, qui nécessiteront beaucoup de temps. On n'évitera pas les trois millions de chômeurs.

(Philippe Eliakim and Olivier Drouin, 'Pourquoi la France a-t-elle trois millions de chômeurs en 1992?', *L'Événement du Jeudi*, 4–10 July 1992.)

## Exercices

### *Lexique*

Expliquez les mots et expressions suivants:

exécrable (l.3)
assainir (l.5)
un intérimaire (l.11)
un contrat à durée déterminée (ll.11–12)
engranger (l.17)
la déprime (l.20)
l'ANPE (l.32)
le CNPF (l.34)
le BTP (l.36)
les partenaires sociaux (l.45)
les forces vives (l.68)
camoufler (l.77)
mettre le holà (l.80)
friser (l.84)
exonérer (l.91)
donner un coup de pouce (l.93)
un coup d'épingle (l.94)

### *Grammaire et stylistique*

(a) 'Le nôtre' (l.19). Utilisez vous-même des pronoms possessifs dans des phrases que vous inventerez.
(b) 'S'agirait-il des immigrés, qui, en rangs serrés, viendraient inonder notre ANPE?' (ll.51–53): justifiez le mode/temps des verbes.

### *Compréhension*

(a) Que signifie l'expression 'les gros plans de licenciements' (ll.12–13)?
(b) 'La France croule sous les forces vives' (l.68). Comparez la perspective démographique optimiste exposée dans ce texte et la notion généralement admise selon laquelle la population française est une population vieille.
(c) Résumez les causes du chômage telles qu'elles sont exposées dans le texte et comparez la situation en France et dans votre pays.

### *Questions orales ou écrites*

(a) Dans quelles conditions les mesures de 'partage du travail' (comme par exemple la réduction du temps de travail, le développement du temps partiel) pourraient-elles aider à résoudre la question du chômage en France?

(b) Certains économistes préconisent une réduction des salaires et du SMIC pour les jeunes pour réduire le chômage. Qu'en pensez-vous?

TEXT 2.5

## L'irrésistible ascension du chômage de longue durée

Le chômage de longue durée constitue le noyau dur du chômage d'aujourd'hui. La plupart des pays développés connaissent cet allongement de la durée du chômage au-delà de un an.[1] Mais ce seuil n'a pas toujours été de un an. Dans les années 70, après six mois de chômage, on était considéré comme un chômeur de longue durée.

Aujourd'hui, l'observation et l'analyse du marché du travail a mis en évidence qu'au-delà d'une année de non-emploi la probabilité de sortir du chômage diminuait. Ainsi, parmi les chômeurs qui entrent dans leur treizième mois, plus de 40% sortent du chômage avant 18 mois, ensuite, les sorties diminuent lentement au-delà de cette durée. Il en résulte que sur une cohorte de 1 000 demandeurs d'emploi enregistrés en 1994, 240 sont encore au chômage au bout de un an (1995) et 41 le sont encore à 36 mois (1997). Au bout de trois ans, si 959 demandeurs d'emploi sont sortis, parmi les motifs de sortie, la reprise d'emploi décroît avec l'ancienneté du chômage. De manière symétrique, la part des chômeurs qui se découragent et qui interrompent leur inscription à l'ANPE augmente avec l'ancienneté du chômage.[2]

Les chômeurs de longue durée étaient 60 000 en septembre 1974, ils dépassent les 500 000 en 1983 pour, aujourd'hui, après avoir connu un pic à près de 1 160 000 en 1998, tendre vers le million.

De plus en plus nombreux, leur proportion augmente parmi l'ensemble des demandeurs d'emploi: près de 40% aujourd'hui, contre 12% en 1974. En réalité ces données sont sous-estimées. Le chômage de longue durée ne concerne statistiquement que les chômeurs qui connaissent 12 mois d'interruption continue de travail. Toutes les sorties du chômage, quelles qu'en soient les raisons et la durée (stages, contrats aidés, intérim . . .), interrompent l'inscription à l'ANPE et font perdre au chômeur le «statut» de chômeur de longue durée. Le retour à une situation de chômage ne tient pas compte des périodes précédentes, c'est-à-dire du chômage de récurrence qui se caractérise par une alternance de périodes de chômage et de périodes d'activité. Ce constat est illustré par la montée de l'activité réduite (quelle que soit sa durée) parmi les demandeurs inscrits à l'ANPE. Ainsi, plus de 50% des chômeurs de longue durée, inscrits en 1997, ont exercé une activité réduite au moins une fois au cours de leur période de chômage. En prenant en compte cette récurrence du chômage, la part des chômeurs de longue durée est plus élevée: plus d'un demandeur d'emploi sur deux a eu une période de chômage de 12 mois au cours des 18 derniers mois. Enfin, un nombre non négligeable de demandeurs d'emploi âgés (plus de 55 ans) sont dispensés de recherche d'emploi et sont sortis des

[1] Au sein de l'Union européenne, 50% en moyenne des chômeurs sont des chômeurs de longue durée (48% en 1990).

[2] DARES-ANPE, in *Données sociales*, INSEE, 1999.

fichiers de l'ANPE: en 1997, parmi les chômeurs de longue durée, environ 30% des sortants de 50 ans et plus ont été dispensés de recherche d'emploi.

La perception qu'ont les individus de leur situation est toute différente, comme l'indique l'enquête emploi qui repose sur les déclarations des chômeurs. Alors que l'ancienneté moyenne du chômage, en mars 1998, pour l'ANPE, est de 436 jours (soit l'équivalent de 14 mois), celle qui résulte de l'enquête emploi de l'INSEE est voisine de 16 mois.

Massif, le chômage de longue durée ne peut plus se limiter, aujourd'hui, aux seules populations âgées. Il concerne de plus en plus une population large et apparaît comme une composante rigide du marché du travail. À la fin de la décennie 90, deux grandes catégories dominent. Les premières victimes sont les 50 ans et plus: plus de 55% de cette catégorie est au chômage de longue durée. En dehors de l'âge on retrouve les caractéristiques classiques qui pénalisent plus certains actifs sur le marché du travail: les femmes, les bas niveaux de qualification et les moins bien formés, les demandes d'emploi qui font suite à un licenciement (économique ou non) ou à une reprise d'activité (souvent des femmes). Par ailleurs, les taux suivent, sur le territoire, ceux du chômage en général: ils sont dans les deux cas minimaux en Alsace et maximaux en Haute-Normandie.

La progression du chômage de longue durée conduit, maintenant, à distinguer des catégories de chômeurs de très longue durée (de 2 ans et plus). Loin d'être négligeable, cette population représente près de 530 000 demandeurs d'emploi (avril 1999), soit l'équivalent du total des demandeurs d'emploi du début des années 70.

Cet allongement de l'ancienneté traduit la dimension nouvelle du fonctionnement du marché du travail. Si les reprises économiques ont eu un impact limité sur le nombre de demandeurs d'emploi, ne faisant pas revenir le chômage à son niveau antérieur, les plus éloignés de l'emploi (les moins immédiatement «employables») sont, dans leur grande majorité, menacés d'exclusion. Pour avoir un effet positif sur le chômage de longue durée, les reprises économiques doivent être non seulement plus créatrices d'emploi mais aussi plus durables. En effet, lors de ces périodes les demandeurs d'emploi les plus directement employables ont accédé à un emploi en laissant de côté les chômeurs les plus fragiles. Au cours de la décennie 90, cette situation s'est aggravée. Si, parmi les demandeurs d'emploi inscrits à la fin 1989, 17% l'étaient encore un an après, parmi ceux qui s'inscrivirent fin 1996, 27% étaient encore au chômage un an après.

(Olivier Mazel, *La France des chômages*, Gallimard, 1999, pp.66–70.)

## Exercices

### *Lexique*

Expliquez les mots et expressions suivants:

un noyau dur (l.1)
le seuil (l.3)
un pic (l.18)
le chômage de récurrence (l.28)

dispensés de recherche d'emploi (l.37)
une composante rigide (l.47)
un licenciement (l.52)
loin d'être négligeable (ll.57–58)

### Grammaire et stylistique

(a) 'Ainsi, . . .' (l.8): trouvez d'autres mots ou expressions de sens équivalent qui pourraient remplacer cet adverbe.
(b) Le prénom adverbial 'en' est utilisé deux fois dans le texte (ll.10 et 24). A chaque fois, remplacez 'en' par ce qu'il représente.
(c) Réécrivez la dernière phrase du texte sans utiliser la préposition 'parmi'. Ceci permet de simplifier la construction de la phrase. Pourquoi selon vous l'auteur a-t-il tenu à utiliser 'parmi'?

### Compréhension

(a) Quelles sont les catégories de personnes les plus affectées par le chômage de longue durée?
(b) Quelles sont les causes de la sous-estimation du nombre de chômeurs de longue durée (ll.22–39)?
(c) Pourquoi l'allongement du chômage de longue durée traduit-elle de nouveaux modes de fonctionnement du marché du travail en France?

### Questions orales ou écrites

(a) Le texte explique que la probabilité qu'un chômeur retrouve un emploi diminue au fur et à mesure que la durée de son chômage augmente. Quelles sont selon vous les raisons de ce phénomène?
(b) Quelles sont selon vous les meilleures méthodes pour combattre le chômage de longue durée?

## TEXT 2.6

# La fin du chômage?

Un million d'inscrits à l'ANPE en 1977, 2 millions en 1982, 3 millions en 1993 ... Pour tout Français né après 1960, le chômage et la peur qu'il engendre sont devenus naturels. Une sorte de nature contre nature, un horizon bas et lourd auquel s'est résignée une société entière.

Bien sûr, il reste 2,8 millions de Français qui pointent à l'ANPE. Mais, pour la première fois depuis très longtemps, une lueur perce. Plus qu'une lueur, une véritable éclaircie, qui permet d'envisager une forte diminution du nombre des sanstravail pour les années qui viennent.

Si l'optimisme revient, c'est d'abord que l'économie française n'a jamais engendré autant d'emplois. Le secteur privé a même atteint un pic historique: il occupe désormais 14,5 millions de salariés. Au total, de mi-1997 à mi-1999, ce sont 650 000 nouveaux postes de travail qui ont été créés. Le chômage a donc reculé de plus de 10% en deux ans, pour retrouver grosso modo son niveau de 1992. Certaines régions ont même déjà rétabli une situation de plein-emploi ou presque: treize départements affichent un taux de chômage de moins de 8%. Et certains secteurs souffrent même de pénurie de main-d'œuvre.

*Dix ans de croissance forte à venir*

Mais qu'est-ce que le plein-emploi? Le Zéro chômeur? Cela n'existe pas. L'objectif gouvernemental serait de ramener le taux de chômage entre 4% et 6% de la population active. Pour les experts de Matignon, au rythme actuel de baisse, le chiffre de 4% serait atteint en 2009. Il reste donc du travail . . .

La condition fondamentale de ce retour au plein-emploi, évidemment, c'est d'abord la croissance. Une croissance forte. Aujourd'hui, maints facteurs poussent à croire que les années à 3% ne devraient plus relever de l'exception.

Premièrement, parce que l'économie française s'est débarrassée, après deux décennies d'efforts, des déséquilibres qui lui interdisaient une politique expansionniste, l'inflation et le déficit extérieur. Dans les années 70, les prix augmentaient ainsi de 15% l'an, tandis que la balance commerciale alignait les soldes négatifs. Depuis dix ans, l'inflation a été considérablement réduite, et les excédents du commerce extérieur dépassent 100 milliards de francs. On peut donc pousser les feux sans risque.

L'autre événement majeur, c'est l'arrivée de l'euro. Durant la décennie 90, la mise en place de la monnaie unique a joué comme un frein à la croissance et à l'emploi. La réduction à marche forcée des déficits publics, la succession de crises monétaires malgré l'alignement des taux d'intérêt pratiqués par la Banque de France sur ceux de la Bundesbank allemande, tout cela a plombé la France pour plusieurs années.

Mais, aujourd'hui, la France touche les dividendes de ces sacrifices. L'euro, jugé une monnaie solide, permet à la Banque centrale européenne de pratiquer de faibles taux d'intérêt. Terminées, également, les crises monétaires, les dévaluations italiennes venant saboter les efforts de compétitivité de l'industrie. Et, comme la France n'est pas la seule à bénéficier des bienfaits de la monnaie unique, elle est entraînée par le dynamisme des autres pays européens.

Deuxième raison d'être optimiste: la croissance, si elle est plus forte, devrait également être plus généreuse en postes de travail.

Qu'est-ce qui explique ce «miracle»? Le développement du temps partiel d'abord. Les entreprises, encouragées par un abattement spécifique de charges sociales, ont multiplié les postes à horaires réduits, y gagnant en flexibilité. Ce qui revient à employer plus de personnes pour la même charge de travail. Cela ne s'est pas fait sans abus: près de 40% des 4 millions de salariés à temps partiel souhaitent travailler plus. Les trente-cinq heures, en permettant dans de nombreux cas d'augmenter le volume de travail de ceux qui le souhaitent, devraient corriger en partie ces excès.

*Les socialistes convertis à la baisse des charges*

Les allégements de cotisations sur les bas salaires ont également joué leur rôle. La France a longtemps été pénalisée par un coût du travail trop élevé pour les emplois non qualifiés.

Entamée à partir de 1993, la baisse des cotisations sociales patronales sur les bas salaires (près de 40 milliards par an) a partiellement réglé ce problème. Déjà, 180 000 emplois ont vu le jour grâce à cette politique, et 60 000 autres devraient naître l'an prochain.

*Un fonctionnaire sur deux à la retraite d'ici à 2010*

Troisième et dernier facteur favorable: l'évolution de la population active. Certes, celle-ci est encore orientée à la hausse: les entrants sur le marché du travail étant plus nombreux que ceux qui font valoir leurs droits à la retraite, l'effectif des candidats à l'emploi augmente tous les ans de 150 000 en moyenne. Autant d'emplois qu'il faut créer pour simplement stabiliser le chômage.

A partir de 2005, pourtant, viendra le temps du contre-choc démographique. Des classes d'âge moins fournies entreront sur le marché du travail, alors que la génération des baby-boomers (ceux nés entre 1945 et 1965), s'en ira cultiver son jardin.

*Le boom de l'emploi ne profite pas à tous*

L'économie française semble donc en passe de réunir des conditions optimales pour vaincre le chômage de masse, et en particulier une croissance plus vive. Certes, il restera le «stock» de chômeurs inemployés de longue date, qui peineront à se remettre en selle. Ceux-là nécessiteront des politiques de formation et de réinsertion lourdes: la fin annoncée du chômage pour une moitié du pays ne signifie pas qu'on doive interrompre les efforts en faveur de l'autre.

(Lionel Steinmann, 'La fin du chômage', *L'Expansion*,
21 October–3 November 1999, pp.48–52.)

## Exercices

### *Lexique*

Expliquez les mots et expressions suivants:

une véritable éclaircie (ll.6–7)
grosso modo (l.13)
afficher un taux de chômage (l.15)
les experts de Matignon (l.20)
aligner les soldes négatifs (ll.28–29)
pousser les feux (l.31)
cela a plombé la France (l.36)
les abattements de charges sociales (ll.47–48)
le contre-choc démographique (l.68)
la génération des baby-boomers (l.70)
cultiver son jardin (ll.70–71)
la réinsertion (l.77)

### *Grammaire et stylistique*

(a) Notez le nombre important de phrases et de propositions sans verbe tout au long du texte. Ceci est typique du style 'journalistique'. Sélectionnez toutes les propositions sans verbe dans les deux derniers paragraphes du texte et complétez chacune d'entre elles en ajoutant un verbe qui correspond au sens de la phrase. Qu'en résulte-t-il au niveau du style?

(b) 'La condition fondamentale . . . c'est d'abord la croissance' (ll.22–23). Notez l'emploi du prénom indéfini 'ce', qui permet l'inversion de la phrase. Réécrivez-la en commençant par 'La croissance . . .'.

### *Compréhension*

(a) Quelles sont les trois principales raisons qui sont mises en avant pour prédire une chute du chômage dans les années à venir? Quelle est la plus importante d'entre elles, selon l'auteur?

(b) Comment la préparation, puis la réalisation de l'union monétaire européenne ont-elles influencé l'évolution du chômage en France?

(c) Pourquoi le développement du travail à temps partiel a-t-il des aspects problématiques?

### *Questions orales ou écrites*

(a) Quelles sont selon vous les raisons pour lesquelles une économie comme celle de la France ne peut complètement éliminer le chômage?

(b) Quelles pourraient être les événements, économiques ou autres, qui pourraient empêcher la baisse du chômage en France telle qu'elle est prédite dans ce texte?

TEXT 2.7

## Le commerce extérieur français reste excédentaire

Qu'il est loin le temps des déficits . . . Alors que l'on attendait une baisse de l'excédent, parvenu à un niveau record en 1997, celui-ci s'est maintenu à un point élevé: 160 milliards de francs (24,4 milliards d'euros), selon les Douanes, soit un peu moins qu'en 1997 (166 milliards de francs), mais deux fois plus qu'en 1996 (84 milliards de francs). Le taux de couverture du commerce extérieur est, en outre, resté lui aussi à un niveau élevé: 110%. Le temps des déficits commerciaux semble définitivement révolu.

Cette situation doit néanmoins être nuancée. La stabilité de l'excédent masque d'abord un ralentissement de la croissance des échanges, surtout côté exportations. La progression des importations s'est en effet légèrement tassée (+7,2% en 1998, contre +9,4% en 1997), tandis que la progression des exportations s'est réduite de plus de moitié (+6,1%, contre +14,4%). Le résultat des branches est encore plus contrasté. Certains secteurs s'en sont bien sortis. Le poste automobile et matériel de transport terrestre affiche un excédent qui demeure deux fois plus élevé qu'en 1996 (60 milliards de francs). Le secteur a en effet bénéficié de la bonne tenue du marché européen, qui absorbe 80% des ventes d'automobiles françaises. Deuxième excédent du pays, juste derrière les biens d'équipement professionnel, la branche automobile fait désormais figure de point fort en matière de commerce extérieur.

L'aéronautique n'est pas en reste. Les ventes record d'Airbus (+15%) ont dopé l'excédent de la branche, qui a dépassé 50 milliards de francs de recettes nettes (7,6 milliards d'euros). Un résultat remarquable: malgré la crise, les pays asiatiques ont continué à acheter près de la moitié des appareils. La bonne tenue du secteur est aussi liée aux exportations . . . dans l'espace. Seize fusées et dix-neuf satellites ont été «déclarés en orbite» en 1998, contre respectivement neuf et quatorze l'année précédente. Ce nombre élevé de lancements spatiaux a fait progresser les exportations de 9 à 13 milliards de francs. Enfin, les ventes de matériel militaire se portent bien.

D'autres secteurs ont en revanche davantage souffert de la crise à l'étranger, si bien que l'industrie civile prise dans son ensemble a réduit son excédent commercial de près de 23 milliards de francs, notamment du fait de la faible croissance des exportations dans les produits chimiques de base et dans la sidérurgie.

*In fine*, c'est l'effondrement des cours du pétrole qui, en réduisant la facture énergétique de 25 milliards de francs, a permis de maintenir le niveau de l'excédent. Le poids relatif des échanges avec l'Union européenne, qui absorbe les deux tiers des exportations françaises, a également permis d'amortir l'impact de la crise asiatique. Certes, la progression de ces échanges s'est ralentie de moitié en un an, mais ils ont encore crû de plus de 6%. Cette hausse a largement permis de compenser le plongeon des exportations vers les pays d'Asie en développement rapide (–18%) et vers la Russie (–25%), d'autant que ces pays occupent une faible part dans le total des exportations (respectivement 5% et 0,6%).

Au sein même de l'Union, quatre pays absorbent plus des deux tiers de ces échanges. L'Allemagne est de loin le premier client européen de l'Hexagone: elle lui achète un quart de ses exportations à destination de l'Union, devant le Royaume-Uni (16%), l'Italie (14,5%) et l'Espagne (14%). C'est aussi son premier fournisseur, puisque la France lui achète plus de 27% de ses importations européennes, devant l'Italie, le Royaume-Uni et l'Espagne. A l'inverse, les pays hors Union européenne représentent une faible part des échanges: les États-Unis importent de France à peine plus que la Belgique et le Luxembourg réunis! Les entreprises françaises demeurent peu présentes sur les marchés des pays émergents d'Asie, pourtant en fort développement jusqu'à la crise actuelle: ils ne représentent guère plus de 5% du total des exportations.

Si le degré élevé d'intégration avec l'Union européenne a permis aux entreprises françaises de moins ressentir le choc de la crise asiatique, contrairement à l'Allemagne et à l'Italie, plus engagées sur ces marchés, cette caractéristique constitue aussi un point faible. Car ces pays, à commencer par la Chine, demeurent dotés d'un fort potentiel de développement.

(Sandrine Trouvelot, 'Le commerce extérieur français reste excédentaire', *Alternatives Economiques*, No. 170, May 1999, pp.60–63 © *Alternatives Economiques*.)

## Exercices

### *Lexique*

Expliquez les mots et expressions suivants:

le taux de couverture (l.5)
définitivement révolu (l.7)
afficher un excédent (l.14)
la bonne tenue (l.16)
faire figure de (l.18)
*in fine* (l.34)
amortir l'impact (l.37)
compenser le plongeon (l.40)
l'Hexagone (l.45)

### *Grammaire et stylistique*

(a) Notez la fréquente utilisation de termes et expressions exprimant l'évolution et les tendances de phénomènes économiques (depuis 's'est . . . légèrement tassée' (l.10), 's'est réduite . . .' (l.12), 'ont dopé l'excédent . . .' (ll.20–21), jusqu'à 'la faible croissance . . .' (ll.31–32) ou 'l'effondrement' (l.34)). Dressez-en une liste, et pour chacune de ces expressions, cherchez un synonyme ou une métaphore équivalente.

(b) Remarquez dans les premiers paragraphes du texte l'emploi de nombreux termes et expressions indiquant une incertitude: par exemple, 'selon les Douanes . . .' (l.3), 'semble' (l.7), 'néanmoins être nuancée' (l.8). Pour renforcer ces expressions d'incertitude, mettez les verbes des phrases correspondantes au conditionnel.

### *Compréhension*

(a) Quels sont les secteurs économiques qui sont responsables de la majeure partie de l'augmentation de l'excédent du commerce extérieur français?
(b) Pourquoi le constat de la bonne situation du commerce extérieur doit-il être nuancé?

### *Questions orales ou écrites*

(a) Pourquoi est-il important que l'économie française ait un excédent de son commerce extérieur?
(b) Pourquoi la faible présence de la France sur les marchés des pays émergents d'Asie est-elle une faiblesse du commerce extérieur français?

TEXT 2.8

## Le patrimoine des Français augmente, les inégalités aussi

A quelques jours du débat budgétaire, voilà une étude qui tombe à pic: l'Institut national de la statistique et des études économiques (*Insee*) publie une radiographie détaillée des revenus et des patrimoines des Français. De prime abord, ce document n'est guère embarrassant pour le gouvernement. Ce dernier peut arguer qu'il est conscient des inégalités de la société française et que ses réformes fiscales ont précisément pour but de les résorber. A lire le rapport de l'Insee, cependant, on comprend pourtant que ces arguments n'épuisent pas le débat. Quels que soient les effets redistributifs des mesures envisagées par le gouvernement, les inégalités de patrimoine continuent, envers et contre tout, à augmenter, tandis que les inégalités de revenus ont cessé de diminuer.

*Les inégalités de patrimoine*

A la fin de 1997, le patrimoine brut des ménages (c'est-à-dire hors endettement) était, en moyenne, de 801 000 francs par ménage, mais de seulement 5 000 francs pour les 10% de ménages les plus pauvres (le premier «décile») et de 1 955 000 francs en moyenne pour les 20% les plus riches (les neuvième et dixième «déciles»).

Les disparités sont donc très fortes et ne cessent de se creuser. Certes, l'évolution des revenus du patrimoine ne le laisse pas apparaître car, compte tenu, notamment, de la baisse des taux d'intérêt, ces revenus courants ont baissé: ils s'élevaient à 20 600 francs en moyenne, par ménage, en 1997, contre 22 000 francs en 1991 (en francs constants). Mais cette statistique est trompeuse, car elle ne prend pas en compte d'autres paramètres et en particulier, les fantastiques plus-values engendrées durant la même période par l'envolée de la Bourse.

Pour apprécier les véritables évolutions, l'institut présente donc ce que les économistes appellent la «performance réelle» du patrimoine de rapport, c'est-à-dire son rendement avant impôts, prenant en compte les revenus qu'il procure, les plus-values ou moins-values éventuelles et l'inflation. Cet indicateur fait apparaître que la performance du patrimoine augmente. L'Insee relève ainsi que, de fin 1995 à fin 1998, cette performance a été de «*plus de 10% en moyenne*» par an, contre seulement 4% de fin 1990 à fin 1995. La hausse des actions françaises explique, pour l'essentiel, cette amélioration spectaculaire des rendements du patrimoine.

L'année 1998 a été particulièrement faste pour les détenteurs de patrimoine et donc, au premier chef, pour les ménages les plus fortunés. La performance a, en effet, été, cette année-là, de 13%. L'Insee précise que «*tous les types de placement ont permis de "gagner de l'argent"*», ce qui n'était «*pas arrivé depuis 1989*». Au cours de cette même année 1998, la performance, pour les actions françaises, a approché 30%; pour les obligations, elle a été de 10%; pour les terres et les logements, elle s'est située entre 6% et 7%.

*Les inégalités de revenus*

L'évolution des revenus des ménages est évidemment beaucoup plus faible que celle des revenus du patrimoine. De 1970 à 1996, le revenu disponible des ménages (avant impôts) n'a enregistré une progression moyenne que de 1,4% l'an. De plus, l'Insee observe qu'en début de période les inégalités de revenu fiscal (les revenus déclarés au fisc; hors revenus du patrimoine) ont diminué. De 1970 à 1975, pour le premier «décile» des salariés (les plus défavorisés), les revenus fiscaux ont aūgmenté plus vite (5,1% l'an) que pour le neuvième «décile» (4,1%). Mais, entre 1990 et 1996, les inégalités ont recommencé à se creuser: pour les deux mêmes «déciles», on constate dans le premier cas une baisse de 2,7% l'an et dans le second une hausse de 0,9% par unité de consommation (c'est-à-dire par foyer fiscal).

Il faut aussi prendre en compte les effets redistributifs du système des prélèvements et des prestations. L'Insee remarque ainsi que, pour les salariés, «*l'éventail des revenus disponibles s'est resserré jusqu'en 1990*», même si c'est à «*un rythme plus rapide dans les années 70 que dans les années 80*». Entre 1970 et 1990, le rapport entre le premier et le dernier «décile» est ainsi passé de 3,6 à 3. Ensuite, pour la période 1990–1996, les inégalités ont de nouveau augmenté, même si ce n'est que «*de façon peu significative*». Ou, à tout le moins, précise l'institut, cette période marque la «*fin progressive du mouvement de baisse des inégalités de revenus*».

En guise d'explication, l'Insee relève que les réformes de l'impôt sur le revenu ont pesé sur ces évolutions. Jusqu'en 1884, «*l'impôt a au total contribué de façon accrue à la réduction des inégalités*», mais, depuis, «*un mouvement inverse s'est produit, la progressivité de l'impôt augmentant légèrement, mais sa part dans le revenu disponible diminuant: sur cette période, l'impôt contribue au total de moins en moins à réduire l'inégalité*». Cette formule prend une forte résonance à la veille du débat budgétaire . . .

(Laurent Mauduit, 'Le patrimoine des Français augmente, les inégalités aussi', *Le Monde*, 7 October 1999, p.6.)

## Exercices

### *Lexique*

Expliquez les mots et expressions suivants:

arguer (l.5)
le patrimoine (l.12)
décile (l.14)
le rendement avant impôt (l.26)
les détenteurs (l.33)
au premier chef (l.34)
les prélèvements et prestations (l.53)
l'éventail des revenus (l.54)
relever que . . . (l.61)
prendre une forte résonnance (l.66)

### *Grammaire et stylistique*

(a) 'on constate . . . une baisse de 2.7% . . .' (ll.49–50): réécrivez cette proposition à la voix passive, sans utiliser le pronom 'on'.
(b) Trouvez deux exemples de verbes pronominaux dans les deux derniers paragraphes du texte. Pourquoi les appelle-t-on ainsi?

### *Compréhension*

(a) Quelle a été l'évolution des revenus des ménages durant chacune des trois décennies 1970, 1980 et 1990?
(b) Quelle est la partie du patrimoine qui a le plus augmenté en valeur durant les années 1990?
(c) Selon l'article, les réformes de l'impôt sont-elles efficaces pour réduire les inégalités de revenu?

### *Questions orales ou écrites*

(a) Pourquoi les inégalités de patrimoine sont-elles plus profondes que les inégalités de revenu?
(b) Quelles sont les differentes politiques que les gouvernements peuvent appliquer pour réduire les inégalités de revenu?

TEXT 2.9

## Vivre en France avec un bas salaire: pas la peine de rêver

D'un geste précis, Martine saisit sur la pile un petit drap jaune, le plie suivant les contours du modèle, le fronce en un savant mouvement, fixe son ouvrage d'un coup de fer brûlant, et le place dans une boîte en carton. Voilà. Martine s'essuie le front, une demi-seconde. Puis elle saisit sur la pile un autre petit drap jaune, le plie, le fronce, applique à nouveau son fer brûlant. Encore et encore, jusqu'à ce que la cloche la libère de l'obsession de la cadence. Martine est repasseuse dans un atelier de confection de layette près de Cholet. Elle doit faire ses deux cents draps de bébé par jour.

Comme les cent cinquante ouvrières de son usine, Martine n'est pas bien payée: à peine 4 400 F net. Alors elle met le paquet pour augmenter son rendement, et toucher la 'prime de production' réservée à celles qui dépassent la cadence. Certains mois, elle se fait 100 F de mieux, parfois plus, jusqu'à 400 F. Est-ce que ça vaut le coup de ne pas lever les yeux de l'ouvrage et de repasser à cent à l'heure? '*Je me crève pour une misère*', soupire-t-elle.

Des Martine, il y en a plein l'industrie textile, à suer devant leur fer ou leur machine à coudre pour une fiche de paye minuscule. A ceci près que la nôtre est en quelque sorte privilégiée. D'abord parce que son entreprise, le groupe Salmon-Arc-en-ciel (850 salariés), ne se porte pas si mal que ça: 10 millions de francs de profits prévus en 1990, un chiffre d'affaires de 280 millions en constante augmentation, et chaque année de nouvelles embauches. Surtout parce que, chose rare dans le textile, son patron a la fibre sociale.

Regardons les choses de près. Le patronat de l'habillement acculé à la plus extrême rigueur par la concurrence du Sud-Est asiatique, n'a, dans son ensemble, pas levé le petit doigt depuis dix ans pour gonfler les fiches de paye. Sa grille de rémunérations, obsolète jusqu'au grotesque, fixe ainsi à . . . 3 478,20 F brut le salaire du premier échelon ouvrier, à 3 578,50 du second, et le reste à l'avenant: douze des quatorze classifications ouvrières sont sous le SMIC (5 286,32 F brut). Grille naturellement inapplicable: comme il est interdit de payer moins que le SMIC, tout le monde le perçoit et n'en parlons plus. Les moins qualifiés comme les plus habiles. Aucune progression possible. Aucun espoir de carrière. Ainsi va la confection.

Pas le groupe Salmon. Le salaire de chacun des neuf échelons ouvriers est supérieur au SMIC. Très légèrement pour le plus bas, de plus en plus à mesure que l'on s'élève dans la classification – il est donc possible ici de faire carrière.

Cela, Martine le sait. Et toutes ses collègues avec elle. '*Il faut reconnaître que notre entreprise fait un petit effort*', disent-elles, en précisant, fort logiquement: '*Ça pourrait être pire.*' Et elles sourient, avec une lasse indulgence. Car au fond, toucher 4 400 F au lieu de 4 200 F, quelle différence?

Toutes les ouvrières d'Arc-en-ciel, bien sûr, ne souffrent pas. Celles dont le mari travaille parviennent à peu près à s'en sortir. Beaucoup ont acheté une petite maison dans le bocage (avec, si possible, jardin potager), dont elles payent les traites avec plus ou moins de difficultés. Beaucoup viennent à l'usine en voiture, en se débrouillant pour y amener des collègues et partager ainsi les frais d'essence. Beaucoup réussissent à partir en vacances, souvent en camping sur la côte vendéenne toute proche. Même si les fins de mois sont régulièrement tendues, et la viande rarement quotidienne, ce n'est pas la misère. Ni Zola ni le coron. D'autant qu'ici, entre Cholet et Angers, en pleine campagne, le coût de la vie est bien plus faible que dans les grandes villes, et les sollicitations plus limitées.

N'empêche, c'est dur. Beaucoup d'ouvrières, comme Josiane, avouent connaître des tensions dans leur ménage. *'Chaque jour, chaque instant, on doit faire attention à l'argent qui file, se retenir de dépenser, calculer au plus juste. Est-ce que je peux acheter cette robe? Est-ce qu'il peut s'offrir ce pantalon? Forcément, on finit par s'engueuler, par se renvoyer nos fiches de paye à la figure.'* L'harmonie du couple supporte mal les bas salaires. Les enfants en souffrent doublement.

Se battre pour arracher plus? Lancer une bonne grève et faire plier le patron? Certaines y pensent. Mais sans jamais passer à l'acte. La dernière grève chez Salmon-Arc-en-ciel date du début des années 60. Dans cette vieille terre chouanne, il n'y a guère de tradition de lutte sociale. Et puis ici on ne rêve pas, on serait plutôt du genre terre à terre. Les réalités économiques de l'industrie textile? La fragilité de l'emploi, les Chinois qui cousent des chemises pour 150 F par mois? On connaît cela par cœur. N'importe, toutes les ouvrières, sans exception, considèrent leurs salaires comme scandaleusement bas, et se disent victimes d'une '*injustice*'. Toutes estiment qu'on pourrait raisonnablement les payer 'au moins' 1 000 F de plus.

(Philippe Eliakim, 'Vivre en France avec un bas salaire: pas la peine de rêver', *L'Événement du Jeudi*, 5–12 July 1990.)

## Exercices

### *Lexique*

Expliquez les mots et expressions suivants:

un coup de fer (l.3)
la cadence (l.6)
la layette (l.7)
mettre le paquet (l.10)
à cent à l'heure (l.14)
se crever (l.14)
ne pas lever le petit doigt pour (l.24)
la grille des rémunérations (ll.24–25)
à l'avenant (ll.26–27)
s'en sortir (l.40)
une traite (l.42)
se débrouiller (l.43)
s'engueuler avec quelqu'un (l.53)
passer à l'acte (l.56)
terre à terre (l.59)

### *Grammaire et stylistique*

(a) Relevez les expressions du langage familier. Quelle différence voyez-vous entre 'faire 100F de mieux' et 'se faire 100F de mieux' (l.12)?

(b) Écrivez un paragraphe ou court dialogue en style familier décrivant les difficultés de la vie quotidienne d'un ouvrier sans le sou.

### *Compréhension*

(a) Où est Cholet? Quelles en sont les activités industrielles? Qu'est-ce qu'une terre 'chouanne' (l.58)?
(b) Expliquez l'allusion à Zola et au coron (l.46).

### *Question orale ou écrite*

(a) Quels sont les arguments économiques qui peuvent être présentés contre l'existence d'un salaire minimum tel que le SMIC? Et quels sont les arguments économiques pour le maintien d'un tel minimum?

TEXT 2.10

## Doit-on réorienter la logique du système de protection sociale?

Dans le contexte de crise financière qui caractérise la protection sociale aujourd'hui – taux de prélèvement stabilisés, mais à des niveaux élevés et croissance des dépenses – certains considèrent que la société doit réorienter ses priorités en faveur de la protection des plus pauvres, quitte pour y parvenir à rogner sur les classes moyennes. Le problème est généralement posé en critiquant les intérêts acquis en matière de protection sociale des privilégiés et les solutions apportées consistent à augmenter le nombre de prestations sous conditions de ressources et à renvoyer à l'assurance privée une grande partie des risques jusqu'alors couverts par la protection sociale. Peut-on l'envisager?

*Les prestations d'assurance sociale*

Pour la vieillesse, le chômage et les prestations de maladie/maternité de remplacement, la protection sociale a une fonction d'assurance contre la perte de salaire. La mise sous conditions de ressources est difficilement applicable dans ce cas. Par exemple, ne plus couvrir les salariés dont les salaires dépassent un certain seuil reviendrait à perdre leurs cotisations sans gain pour les autres salariés, car pour maintenir leur niveau de vie après la retraite ces salariés devraient utiliser les économies de cotisations pour financer leur retraite par capitalisation. De même, pour se protéger contre le chômage, ces salariés devraient s'affilier à des mutuelles ou des sociétés d'assurance privées. Les plus démunis de ces salariés ne gagneraient rien, puisque le système actuel assure déjà des taux de remplacement plus favorables pour les bas salaires.

Nous avons vu que l'assurance sociale est la couverture de risques qui relèvent simultanément d'une logique d'assurance privée et d'une logique de solidarité sociale. L'obligation d'adhérer supprime les phénomènes de sélection adverse et assure à la protection sociale une situation de monopole qui lui permet, dans une logique même d'assurance, d'effectuer une redistribution de type verticale. De par leur mode de financement, ces prestations assurent aussi une redistribution horizontale. Mais cette redistribution a une limite: le consentement des contribuables. En effet, la redistribution s'effectuant des riches vers les pauvres est généralement justifiée par le degré d'aversion à l'inégalité de revenu, ou vis-à-vis de la pauvreté, de la société. On peut justifier cette aversion par la parabole du voile d'ignorance, qui suppose que les individus acceptent de contribuer au financement de la protection sociale dès lors qu'ils n'ont aucune certitude quant à leur position future dans la société. On peut justifier de la même façon, le consentement vis-à-vis du système d'assurance sociale. Un individu accepte *ex ante* de payer pour un système, même si *ex post* il n'en bénéficie pas, sur la base de la seule incertitude à laquelle il est soumis. Selon ce même raisonnement, la propension d'un individu à financer ce système décroîtrait avec la quantité d'informations dont il dispose sur sa situation future. Même si la situation d'information parfaite n'existe pas, les individus ont une idée du profil de salaire dont ils pourront disposer, de même qu'une quasi-certitude qu'ils seront un jour retraités. De fait, le système d'assurance vieillesse est relativement peu redistributif, de même que le système d'assurance chômage. En revanche, l'incertitude sur l'état de santé étant plus grande, l'assurance maladie assure une redistribution en fonction des classes de risques relativement importantes. Il est clair que l'individu refusera de participer au financement du système de protection sociale s'il est certain d'être totalement exclu du nombre des bénéficiaires.

La mise sous conditions des ressources des prestations, particulièrement celles d'assurance, impliquant la remise en cause des droits des ménages pourrait gravement perturber l'équilibre consensuel, relativement fragile, aujourd'hui atteint entre la combinaison d'assurance et d'assistance sociale par le système de protection sociale français.

*Les prestations universelles*

Actuellement, le système d'assurance-maladie fonctionne déjà en partie selon un schéma mixte assistance/assurance. En effet, les remboursements d'assurance-maladie ne couvrant pas l'ensemble des dépenses, des mutuelles se sont développées sur une base professionnelle, selon un modèle d'assurance où les cotisations ne dépendent généralement pas du salaire, ni de l'état de santé et du nombre d'enfants à charge. Ne voulant pas accroître le taux de prélèvement obligatoire, l'État n'a pas voulu augmenter les prestations de la CNAM. Le développement des mutuelles témoigne du fait que la protection sociale répond bien à un besoin, qui à la limite n'a pas besoin de l'État pour être satisfait. L'inconvénient est que le système des mutuelles ne permet pas la couverture des plus pauvres. La création de la récente couverture médicale universelle répond à ce besoin en créant une prestation d'assistance pour les plus pauvres, prestation financée par prélèvement sur les mutuelles.

Au total, on aboutit à un système mixte relativement compliqué. Par rapport à un système de prestation universelle, les gagnants sont les plus riches; les perdants sont ceux qui appartiennent aux couches situées juste au-dessus des plus pauvres, qui supportent une cotisation relativement élevée par rapport à celle qu'ils devraient acquitter dans un système entièrement universel.

Pour ce qui est de la santé, il a été proposé de recourir à l'assurance individuelle pour la médecine de ville avec la prise en charge automatique des plus modestes et de conserver le système actuel pour l'hospitalisation. Mais comment établir une frontière entre les différents types de risques (comment traiter une douleur abdominale bénigne qui ne nécessite qu'une visite chez un généraliste mais qui dégénère en appendicite puis en péritonite?). La mise sous conditions de ressources de l'assurance-maladie obligerait ceux dont les salaires dépassent le seuil à s'assurer individuellement. Le coût serait proportionnellement beaucoup plus fort pour ceux qui sont à la limite du seuil que pour les autres et pour les familles nombreuses. Réduire les remboursements de santé pour les salariés les plus aisés en créant un seuil de remboursement dépendant du revenu serait compliqué sur le plan pratique (Comment serait pris en compte le nombre d'enfants? Prendrait-on en compte les revenus non-imposés du capital? Le fait de posséder son logement?) et injuste car ce sont eux qui cotisent le plus (relativement, en particulier, aux titulaires de revenus du capital). Cela les inciterait à s'organiser dans des mutuelles autonomes, qui seraient plus rentables pour eux que les mutuelles actuelles où ils paient volontairement pour les bas revenus, et irait progressivement dans le sens d'une santé à deux vitesses.

Les prestations d'allocations familiales étant perçues comme des prestations de solidarité sont celles qui ont été l'objet des attaques les plus virulentes, les familles aisées avec enfants étant présentées comme les privilégiées du système. Mettre sous conditions de ressources ces prestations ne présente aucune difficulté technique. Mais est-ce pour autant souhaitable? Une réforme de ce type reviendrait à supprimer une partie des objectifs de la politique familiale: à savoir l'organisation des transferts entre les ménages sans enfants et ceux ayant des enfants, au nom de l'enjeu que constituent les enfants pour une société. Les partisans du ciblage des allocations familiales se focalisent sur la redistribution verticale, qui n'est pas l'objectif des allocations familiales. Cet objectif de redistribution est bien sûr louable, mais pourquoi le faire porter sur les seules familles aisées et non pas sur l'ensemble des catégories aisées?

*Conclusion*

Les plus démunis sont mieux protégés dans des systèmes hybrides qui mêlent assurance et solidarité, où ils bénéficient des acquis obtenus par la classe ouvrière et par les classes moyennes, que par des systèmes à deux vitesses. La France a pu développer un système redistributif important et bien accepté socialement (couverture médicale pour tous, RMI, minimum vieillesse, prestations sous conditions de ressources) dans un ensemble qui joue aussi un rôle important d'assurance. Un système financé par les riches qui ne bénéficie qu'aux pauvres est socialement fragile: les classes moyennes, nombreuses, y sont indifférentes et les riches, influents, hostiles. Certes les privilégiés existent dans ce pays, mais faut-il en chercher l'origine dans le système de protection sociale?

(Réjane Hugounenq and Henri Sterdyniak, 'Doit-on réorienter la logique du système de protection sociale?', in 'Emploi et protection sociale', *Cahiers Français*, n°292, July–September 1999, pp.78–79.)

## Exercices

### *Lexique*

Expliquez les mots et expressions suivants:

quitte pour y parvenir (l.4)
rogner (l.5)
sous conditions de ressources (l.13)
couvrir les salariés (l.14)

| | |
|---|---|
| une retraite par capitalisation (ll.17–18) | l'équilibre consensuel (l.51) |
| s'affilier (l.19) | des mutuelles (l.57) |
| relever de (ll.21–22) | un généraliste (l.78) |

### *Grammaire et stylistique*

(a) Relevez dans le deuxième paragraphe toutes les phrases dans lesquelles un verbe est conjugué au conditionnel. Réécrivez ces phrases en mettant ces verbes au conditionnel passé (en faisant attention à l'accord des autres verbes).

(b) '. . . on peut justifier . . . ' (l.31), '. . . on peut justifier . . .' (l.34): mettez à la voix passive les deux phrases dans lesquelles se trouve cette expression.

(c) Dans les deux dernières phrases du texte, notez l'utilisation des pronoms 'y' et 'en'. Quel est leur rôle? Comment pourrait-on réécrire ces phrases sans les utiliser?

### *Compréhension*

(a) Les auteurs cherchent à justifier le système français de protection sociale en utilisant le concept du 'voile d'ignorance', développé par le philosophe social John Rawls. Recherchez, sur l'internet ou dans une bibliothèque, des renseignements sur ce concept.

(b) Pourquoi le système français d'assurances sociales est-il qualifié de système 'mixte'?

(c) Pourquoi les assurances mutuelles ont-elles été développées en France? Quel système a été mis en place afin de procurer le même niveau de protection sociale aux personnes les plus pauvres, qui ne peuvent souscrire à une assurance mutuelle?

### *Questions orales ou écrites*

(a) Quelles sont les principales differences du système français de protection sociale avec, d'une part, le système britannique et, d'autre part, le système des États-Unis?

(b) Les auteurs concluent que le fait que les riches continuent à plus bénéficier du système de protection sociale que les pauvres doit être accepté comme le prix à payer pour que tout le monde continue de financer le système (concept de solidarité). Etes-vous d'accord?

## TEXT 2.11

# 1952–98: le cycle long de l'inflation

Aujourd'hui le rythme de hausse des prix en France est revenu à 0,5% l'an. Il faut remonter quarante-cinq ans en arrière pour retrouver pareille modération. La seule période comparable de l'après-guerre va de 1952–1953 (baisse des prix) à la mi-1957. Du début des années soixante à la fin des années quatre-vingt, on a assisté à quatre phases d'accélération des prix entrecoupées de modérations ou de paliers. Trois peuvent être associées, de prime abord, à des événements français: les rapatriés d'Algérie en 1962–1963, mai 1968, qui provoqua une très importante revalorisation des salaires, et 1979–1982, prolongée par la politique de stimulation des revenus menée en 1981 lors de l'alternance socialiste. Toutefois, la comparaison de l'évolution des prix français et étrangers souligne que les périodes d'inflation ont été largement communes à l'ensemble des pays développés, de même que les ralentissements ultérieurs. Ceci incite donc à relativiser les spécificités nationales qui reflètent plus la diversité des délais de traitement des déséquilibres que de réelles autonomies de gestion.

Les flambées des cours du pétrole de 1973–1974 et 1979–1980 sont souvent mises en avant pour expliquer les poussées d'inflation de ces années-là. Certes, une hausse de coût peut alimenter la hausse des prix, notamment lorsqu'elle touche une ressource peu substituable et provoque une perte d'efficacité productive. Toutefois ces hausses de cours furent précédées par celles d'autres matières premières, qui témoignaient elles-mêmes des pressions de demande accumulées.

La désinflation des années quatre-vingt s'oppose à la période que l'on vient de décrire. Aux États-Unis, après le pic de 1980, la décélération est brutale: en l'espace de trois ans les prix reviennent de 15% à 3–4% l'an et s'installent sur cette tendance jusqu'en 1989. Ailleurs, les dérèglements ont été souvent tels qu'il a fallu adopter des mesures restrictives plus tôt: le Royaume-Uni s'y prend à deux reprises après 1975 puis obtient dès 1983 des performances voisines de celles des États-Unis; l'Allemagne, moins touchée, subit toutefois jusqu'en juin 1982 les séquelles inflationnistes de sa politique de relance de 1978–1980. La France apparaît ici en retard sur ses partenaires, même ceux du Sud de l'Europe. Le «tournant de la rigueur» n'est pris qu'en 1982 avec le «plan Delors». Le contrôle des prix, régi par les ordonnances de 1945, est réactivé: les prix, mais aussi les marges des entreprises, sont bloqués, comme lors du premier plan Barre de 1976. L'innovation consiste à assortir ce contrôle des prix d'un gel des salaires. On échappe ainsi au défaut des blocages traditionnels, qui, ne touchant pas aux rémunérations en période de pénurie de main-d'œuvre, dopaient artificiellement le pouvoir d'achat et la demande des consommateurs. La diminution de la part des salaires dans la valeur ajoutée est amorcée. La désinflation française se poursuit jusqu'en 1986; imposée par le contexte international et la participation au SME qui exclut les dévaluations compétitives, elle suscite un courant de restructuration industrielle assorti d'une montée du chômage, qui tempère durablement les revendications salariales. La désinflation devient alors compétitive dans les dernières années quatre-vingt.

A partir de 1988, la hausse des prix en France devient inférieure à celle de ses partenaires européens; la compétitivité française s'améliore sans recours à la dévaluation. Cette situation dure jusqu'en 1991 et assoit le dogme du franc fort: quand, en 1990, le choc de l'unification allemande fait se poser la question d'un flottement du mark, l'idée est rapidement rejetée par tous ceux qui rêvent de poursuivre ou de s'associer à la désinflation compétitive en s'ancrant à la monnaie allemande.

Mais cet ancrage s'avère moins stabilisant que prévu, car la politique de la Bundesbank reste déterminée par la seule maîtrise de l'inflation allemande. Les capitaux en excès, qui résultent d'une demande interne insuffisante, émigrent vers des cieux plus rémunérateurs, anglo-saxons ou méditerranéens. La livre, la lire, puis la peseta vont ravir la vedette au mark. Respecter les marges de fluctuation du SME n'est alors plus une contrainte mais une drogue douce qui conduit à plus d'inflation. La France fait moins mal que les autres. Financièrement moins attractive, sa reprise se fait sur fond de sous-emploi plus marqué, si bien que la limite des moyens de production disponibles n'est pas aussi nettement franchie qu'au Royaume-Uni en 1988 ou en Allemagne à partir de 1991.

Le reflux des capitaux vers l'Allemagne déclenche le retour de la désinflation européenne. Le maintien des parités fixes impose notamment en France de surenchérir dans la restriction monétaire; celle-ci s'oppose alors aux dérives budgétaires structurelles apparues en moyenne depuis 1989, ainsi qu'aux excès du crédit privé déréglementé. Le franc échappe aux réaménagements de 1992, puis glisse vis-à-vis du mark (de 3,38 F pour 1 DM à 3,44 F, hors périodes spéculatives), mais s'apprécie en taux de change effectif vis-à-vis de l'ensemble des monnaies européennes.

L'objectif de l'euro fait que la Banque de France s'interdit d'utiliser pleinement les marges de fluctuations monétaires, élargies en 1993 à 15%, et fait vivement monter les taux d'intérêt pour enrayer les dépréciations du franc. L'économie s'en trouve maintenue dans un état de sous-emploi permanent qui n'est guère dépassé qu'au Japon. Les fluctuations des prix s'enroulent autour de 2%, de 1993 à 1996, puis de 1% en 1997–1998. Elles résultent de celles du dollar, du pétrole, et de certaines denrées alimentaires, auxquelles se rajoute l'impact du relèvement du taux normal de TVA, passé de 18,6% à 20,6% en août 1995. En fait la désinflation se poursuit régulièrement depuis 1992. L'inflation française se situe un demi-point en retrait de la moyenne européenne; son sous-jacent, mesuré par l'INSEE après élimination des tarifs publics, des produits à prix volatils et correction des mesures fiscales, n'était plus que 1,1%, de septembre 1997 à septembre 1998. La baisse du dollar de la fin de 1998 devrait la réduire encore.

(Philippe Sigogne, 'L'inflation', in OFCE,
*L'économie française 1999*, La Découverte, pp.45–8.)

## Exercices

### *Lexique*

Expliquez les mots et expressions suivants:

entrecouper (l.5)
paliers (l.6)
les flambées des cours (l.15)
amorcer (l.38)
le dogme du franc fort (l.46)
s'ancrer à la monnaie allemande (ll.49–50)
des cieux plus rémunérateurs (l.54)
ravir la vedette (l.55)

### *Grammaire et stylistique*

(a) Notez la fréquente utilisation d'adverbes dans ce texte: par exemple, 'toutefois', 'certes', 'durablement', 'aussi', 'alors' . . . Recherchez ces adverbes, et remplacez-les par des expressions ou d'autres adverbes au sens comparable.
(b) L'expression '. . . plus . . . que . . .' est utilisée dans la dernière phrase du premier paragraphe. Construisez d'autres phrases comparant deux phénomènes, en utilisant les expressions: 'plus..que', 'moins..que' ou 'autant..que', précédées d'un verbe.

### *Compréhension*

(a) Quelles ont été les périodes de l'évolution de l'inflation en France depuis les années 1950?
(b) Quelles ont été les conséquences des politiques monétaires anti-inflationistes menées après 1982?

### *Questions orales ou écrites*

(a) Ce texte analyse l'évolution de l'inflation jusqu'à la fin de l'année 1998. Quelle a été l'évolution des prix en France dans les années qui ont suivi (recherchez l'information sur des sites français d'internet, ou en consultant d'autres documents)?
(b) Pourquoi l''ancrage' du franc au DM?

TEXT 2.12

## Le retournement socialiste de 1982: de la relance à la rigueur

Ce dimanche 13 juin 1982, quand il sort de l'Élysée à midi, Pierre Mauroy se frotte les yeux. Deux heures plus tôt, alors qu'il gravissait les marches du 'château' pour un conseil restreint, il savait que la partie serait presque impossible à jouer. Il voulait obtenir de François Mitterrand le blocage, pour trois mois, des salaires et des prix. Faute de quoi, estime le Premier ministre, *'la gauche serait renvoyée dans l'opposition pour cause de faillite financière. Pour durer, il fallait prendre en main l'économie'*. Un peu plus d'un an après la victoire socialiste, tous les indicateurs sont au rouge. Ce dimanche 13 juin 1982, Pierre Mauroy est tout à fait seul. *'Rocard, Fabius, Chevènement m'étaient tous hostiles. Ils pensaient que tout cela se terminerait mal, que notre électorat et les syndicats ne l'accepteraient pas.'* Jacques Delors, ministre des Finances, est d'accord sur le blocage de ses prix, mais il préfère négocier celui des salaires avec les syndicats. Comment va réagir le président? Mauroy lui a bien fait part de ses angoisses. Mais Mitterrand, occupé à Versailles où festoient tous les grands de la planète pour le premier sommet des pays industrialisés organisé par un président français socialiste, l'aura-t-il entendu? Oui. Mieux même: *'A la fin du conseil, il a demandé quatre mois de blocage, pas trois!'*, rappelle Mauroy.

Le grand tournant de la rigueur est pris. Il sera confirmé le 16 juin en conseil des ministres. Dès lors, Mauroy et Mitterrand rompent avec une année de politique de gauche (augmentation de 10% du SMIC, relèvement substantiel des allocations familiales et du minimum vieillesse, retraite à 60 ans, semaine de 39 heures payées 40). Mais surtout, ils tirent un trait définitif sur dix années d'indexation des salaires sur les prix. Ce que ni Chirac ni Barre n'avaient voulu ou su faire. Le tout avec l'accord des communistes. Pierre Mauroy a rencontré en tête à tête chacun des quatre ministres du PCF. Et il a convaincu Anicet le Pors, ministre de la Fonction publique. *'Si vous refusez,* leur explique-t-il, *nous aurons échoué.'* Ils accepteront. *'Nous avions frappé fort, mais nous n'étions pas certains que c'était suffisant,* raconte François Stasse, à l'époque conseiller économique de Mitterrand. *Et surtout, nous ignorions si le président considérait cela comme une parenthèse ou pas.'* Neuf mois plus tard, le gouvernment de gauche passe de la rigueur à l'austérité. Mitterrand a hésité, poussé dans l'autre sens par Jean Riboud, le PDG de Schlumberger aujourd'hui décédé, Bérégovoy et Fabius. Les trois hommes sont partisans d'une *'autre politique'*: la sortie du SME (système monétaire européen) accompagnée d'un nouveau plan de rigueur. Pour Mauroy, c'est une catastrophe: si le franc flotte, il sombre. Le vendredi 25 mars, Mitterrand donne une nouvelle fois raison à son Premier ministre. Ce jour-là, en conseil des ministres, Jacques Delors présente des *'mesures d'ordre économique, financier et social'*. Un euphémisme pour une ponction de 65 milliards de francs sur les dépenses de l'État et la consommation des ménages! Les communistes avalent. Raymond Barre applaudit. Bilan des courses, neuf ans après le 13 juin 1982? La France a tordu le cou à l'inflation qui passe de 13,5% en 1980 à 3,4% fin 1990. Tous les grands pays industriels constatent que socialisme rime désormais avec vertu économique. Bérégovoy, avocat acharné du franc fort, est devenu le chouchou des chefs d'entreprise. Le commerce extérieur est toujours un peu patraque, mais la France reste le quatrième exportateur mondial.

Revers de la médaille: depuis 1985, les inégalités se sont creusées; selon le CERC (Centre d'étude des revenus et des coûts), les revenus du travail ont été nettement moins favorisés que ceux du capital. Et surtout, malgré quatre années de croissance inespérée et plus de 800 000 créations d'emplois entre 1987 et 1990, les socialistes n'ont pas su endiguer le chômage.

(Martine Gilson, 'Le retournement socialiste de 1982: de la relance à la rigueur', *Le Nouvel Observateur*, 2–9 May 1991, p.8.)

## Exercices

### *Lexique*

Expliquez les mots et expressions suivants:

faute de quoi (l.5)
pour cause de (l.6)
prendre en main (l.7)
tous les indicateurs sont au rouge (l.8)
faire part de (l.13)
bilan des courses (l.40)
tordre le cou à (l.41)
le chouchou (l.44)
patraque (l.45)
revers de la médaille (l.47)

### *Grammaire et stylistique*

(a) Mettre au présent les passages suivants: 'Il savait que la partie serait presque impossible à jouer' (ll.3–4); 'Nous avions frappé fort . . . parenthèse ou pas' (ll.27–30).

### *Compréhension*

(a) Que comprenez-vous par 'blocage des salaires et des prix' (ll.4–5), l'indexation des salaires sur les prix' (l.23)?
(b) Quelle différence faites-vous entre 'rigueur' et 'austérité' (l.31)?
(c) Expliquez la phrase: 'les revenus du travail ont été nettement moins favorisés que ceux du capital' (ll.48–49).

### *Question orale ou écrite*

(a) De la relance socialiste de 1981 au plan d'austérité de Delors de 1983: nouveau réalisme ou trahison des promesses faites aux électeurs?

TEXT 2.13

## Reconversion des vieilles régions industrielles: une usine textile sur les ruines de la mine de la Mure

Aidés par la région, le groupe textile DMC et son partenaire japonais vont créer une usine de soierie artificielle à la Mure, dans l'Isère. A rebrousse-poil de la tendance à la délocalisation dans les pays asiatiques. Dans l'Isère, à la Mure, on prépare la mort de la mine. L'extraction de l'anthracite sera bientôt abandonnée, et, avec elle, supprimée une bonne partie des emplois industriels de la ville. Aussi, la commune a-t-elle dressé un pont d'or pour que s'implante chez elle l'usine de soierie artificielle que veut construire le groupe DMC et son partenaire japonais Unitika. Après dix-huit mois de négociations compliquées à trois, un accord original a été annoncé hier. Une société, Inesota, va être créée, dans laquelle DMC aura 34,5% du capital, le groupe japonais 33,5% et les sociétés de développement régional (SDR) qui dépendent du conseil général de l'Isère, 32%.

Paradoxalement, DMC, qui reconnaît que cette usine représente un investissement relativement lourd – 200 millions de francs pour les seuls équipements industriels de tissage et de teinture – va débourser pour ce projet moins de 25 millions, c'est-à-dire sa part dans le capital. Même engagement minimum pour Unitika. L'essentiel de l'investissement sera couvert par des emprunts bancaires.

Mais, du côté des pouvoirs locaux, on a décidé de mettre le paquet. '*Et encore, nous n'avons pas pu satisfaire l'ensemble des demandes financières des industriels*', remarque le maire de La Mure. Non seulement les SDR vont devenir actionnaires et apporter près de 25 millions, une participation que les groupes privés leur rachèteront d'ici huit ans. Mais les pouvoirs locaux, la municipalité et le conseil général vont financer la formation des futurs salariés (plus de 200), qui coûtera 13 millions. Ils préfinancent le bâtiment industriel sur un terrain vendu 42 francs le mètre carré, ce qui revient à accorder au projet une aide indirecte supplémentaire. Sans oublier les subventions de 50 000 francs par personne embauchée, versées par l'État et le département. '*Ces aides sont incitatives et visent à compenser les pertes d'emplois provoquées par la décision des Charbonnages de France de fermer la mine*', explique le maire.

Du coup, le risque devient moindre pour les industriels privés. '*Nous n'aurions pas pour autant renoncé si les SDR ne nous avaient pas suivis*', se défend le directeur de DMC. '*C'est un développement stratégique pour le groupe, car le marché est en forte croissance.*'

La confection française importe aujourd'hui la quasi-totalité de sa soierie artificielle du Japon, de Taïwan ou de Corée du Sud. Le Japon produit essentiellement des soieries haut de gamme, destinées à la fabrication des chemisiers. Des groupes comme DMC avaient déjà tenté de développer seuls cette activité, en vain. Les groupes textiles japonais sont incontestablement les leaders des soieries synthétiques et ils en détiennent le savoir-faire. Or, *'les délais de livraison sont de plus en plus longs, entre un et trois mois, ce qui ne correspond pas au rythme de la mode'*, remarque un responsable de la société nippone pour justifier son investissement français. *'Nous avons donc intérêt à nous implanter en Europe, plus près de nos clients.'*

(Sylvaine Villeneuve, 'Reconversion des vieilles régions industrielles: une usine textile sur les ruines de la mine de la Mure', *Libération*, 6–7 April 1991, p.10.)

## Exercices

### *Lexique*

Expliquez les mots et expressions suivants:

à rebrousse-poil (l.2)
dresser un pont d'or (l.6)
mettre le paquet (l.19)
préfinancer (l.25)
la soierie (l.35)
haut de gamme (l.37)
une société nippone (l.42)

### *Grammaire et stylistique*

(a) Expressions de mesures. Exprimez en anglais 25 millions de francs, 42 francs le mètre carré.
(b) Précisez le ton des trois premières expressions données dans le lexique.
(c) Quelle différence faites-vous entre 'la confection de chemisiers' et 'les chemisiers de confection'?
(d) 'Aussi la commune a-t-elle dressé un pont d'or . . . ' (l.6). Faites vous-mêmes des phrases commençant par 'aussi'.

### *Compréhension*

(a) Situez l'Isère sur la carte de la France.
(b) Pourquoi 'les délais de livraison (. . .) entre un et trois mois' ne correspondent-ils pas 'au rythme de la mode' (ll.40–42)?

### *Questions orales ou écrites*

(a) Est-ce le rôle des pouvoirs locaux d'aider l'industrialisation de leur région?
(b) Les investissements japonais en France affaiblissent-ils l'indépendance économique du pays?

## TEXT 2.14

# Le tourment agricole de la France: allons-nous vers une agriculture à deux vitesses?

L'Europe communautaire a trop de blé, trop de lait et de beurre, trop de viande bovine, bref, elle a trop de tout, ou peu s'en faut. Mise en place au début des années 60, la politique agricole commune, la fameuse PAC, a réussi au-delà de tous les espoirs. Elle ambitionnait de rendre les pays du Marché commun autosuffisants. Ils sont devenus des exportateurs redoutés. La France arrivant en tête: depuis trois ans, le surplus agro-alimentaire compense grosso modo le déficit de la balance industrielle. Jolie réussite, donc, mais sur fond de crise chronique. Les prix s'effritent et les revenus des agriculteurs restent à la traîne. En 1990, l'exode rural a battu en France tous les records de la décennie. L'heure de vérité approche pour le monde agricole français et, au-delà, pour les 9 millions d'agriculteurs de la CEE. Vont-ils ou non accepter la réforme – radicale – de la PAC concoctée par la Commission de Bruxelles? En deux mots, le projet Ray MacSharry, du nom de son auteur, commissaire européen à l'agriculture, se propose de diminuer très fortement les prix agricoles (–35% pour les céréales) mais de compenser intégralement le manque à gagner pour les agriculteurs petits et moyens, et partiellement pour les gros – en fonction des superficies qu'ils mettront en jachère. Objectifs de la réforme: faire disparaître les excédents communautaires (la CEE produit 20% de plus qu'elle ne consomme); garantir des revenus stables aux petits agriculteurs; stopper la dégradation de l'environnement; fournir aux consommateurs européens des produits agricoles moins chers (et de meilleure qualité); débloquer, enfin, les négociations du Gatt, à Genève. Rude tâche!

Il y a agriculteur et agriculteur. Comparée à la plupart des pays de la CEE, la France agricole se singularise par la disparité des revenus de ses exploitants agricoles. Entre l'éleveur du Limousin et le viticulteur de la région Champagne-Ardenne, l'écart varie de 1 à 7. L'an passé, il s'est encore élargi. Ainsi, le revenu des producteurs de céréales a dégringolé de 13%, après cinq années de baisse ininterrompue. De telles secousses, synonymes de gestion acrobatique, d'ardoises impayées au Crédit agricole ou ailleurs, de faillites, contribuent largement à éclaircir les rangs de la profession. La France compte aujourd'hui 1 million d'exploitations agricoles; à la fin du siècle, 300 000 suffiraient à assurer la même production – exportations comprises. Perdants incontestables du projet MacSharry – s'il est adopté par les Douze –, les gros céréaliers, les barons du Bassin parisien et de l'est de l'Angleterre. Pendant des années, ils ont amplement profité d'un système généreux et pervers qui, financé par le budget communautaire et le portefeuille des consommateurs, incitait à produire à tout va. A l'avenir, les plus gros des céréaliers devront mettre en jachère une partie de leurs terres sans compensation financière. Mais 4% à peine des céréaliers sont concernés. Dans les autres filières (lait, production bovine) également les sacrifices ne concernent qu'une minorité d'agriculteurs. En revanche, tous seront perdants si la réforme PAC n'est pas mise sur les rails. Bruxelles prévoit une baisse des revenus agricoles de 23% d'ici à 1996.

A terme, deux types d'agriculture coexisteront dans l'Hexagone. La première, de type capitalistique, intensive, conduite de manière scientifique, affrontera sur les marchés ses concurrents traditionnels, américains en tête, dans le cadre de règles du Gatt remises à jour. Bénéficiant d'aides financières directes versées par la CEE, l'autre agriculture sera extensive. Et plurielle: une partie non négligeable des revenus des exploitants devrait provenir d'activités annexes, du tourisme vert à des tâches d'intérêt collectif (entretien des routes de montagne, par exemple). Le risque: faire de ces agriculteurs du deuxième type des assistés de la société placés sous perfusion financière. En attendant leur disparition définitive.

(Jean-Pierre Tuquoi, 'Le tourment agricole de la France:
allons-nous vers une agriculture à deux vitesses?',
*L'Expansion*, 3–16 October 1991.)

## Exercices

### *Lexique*

Expliquez les mots et expressions suivants:

peu s'en faut (l.2)
ambitionner (l.4)
rester à la traîne (ll.8–9)
en deux mots (l.12)
le manque à gagner (l.15)
en jachère (l.17)
se singulariser par (l.24)
le viticulteur (l.25)
dégringoler (l.27)
une ardoise impayée (l.29)
le céréalier (l.33)
à tout va (ll.36–37)
la filière (l.39)
un assisté (l.50)
une perfusion financière (l.51)

### *Grammaire et stylistique*

(a) 'Autosuffisant' (l.5). Traduisez ce mot en anglais, et faites vous-même d'autres mots sur ce modèle.
(b) Quelle différence de registre faites-vous entre 'paysan', 'fermier' et 'exploitant agricole'? En quoi ces distinctions sont-elles significatives?

### *Compréhension*

(a) 'Il y a agriculteur et agriculteur' (l.23). A votre avis, que veut dire l'auteur?
(b) 'Entre l'éleveur . . . et le viticulteur . . . l'écart varie de 1 à 7' (ll.25–26). De quoi s'agit-il exactement?
(c) Quelle différence faites-vous entre les termes 'capitaliste' et 'capitalistique'? Qu'est-ce qu'une agriculture capitalistique? Et une agriculture plurielle, intensive, extensive?
(d) Montrez le paradoxe inhérent à la PAC tel qu'il est indiqué dans le texte.

### *Questions orales ou écrites*

(a) Y a-t-il une agriculture française, ou plusieurs? Quelles en sont les conséquences?
(b) Quels sont les dangers sociaux et économiques d'une 'agriculture à deux vitesses'?

TEXT 2.15

## 1982–88: des nationalisations aux privatisations

Les nationalisées de 1982, groupes industriels comme banques, confirment leur redressement alors même que les élections de mars 1986 portent au pouvoir une majorité de droite dont le programme de 'libéralisation' économique fait de la privatisation des entreprises publiques un élément-clé. En défaisant les nationalisations de 1982 réalisées par les socialistes, mais en s'attaquant aussi à celles opérées antérieurement par le général de Gaulle, le gouvernement de Jacques Chirac entend donner une plus grande liberté aux entreprises concernées. En leur permettant de faire appel sans contrainte au marché financier, il veut alléger d'autant les finances de l'État actionnaire soumis à la rigueur budgétaire. Enfin, Edouard Balladur, ministre d'État chargé de l'économie, des finances et de la privatisation, voit également dans la dénationalisation l'occasion de transformer la société française en favorisant l'émergence d'un actionnariat populaire et d'un actionnariat salarié.

*Noyaux durs*

Le programme du gouvernement est ambitieux. Il porte sur soixante-cinq entreprises dans l'industrie, la banque, les assurances et la communication. Un enjeu de 200 à 300 milliards de francs, bien supérieur à ce qu'ont pu réaliser les autres pays occidentaux qui ont lancé le mouvement – RFA, Grande-Bretagne ou Canada.

Le gouvernement avait prévu de privatiser par voie d'ordonnance. Devant l'opposition du président de la République, il devra se résoudre à utiliser la voie parlementaire classique. La mise en œuvre des privatisations porte l'empreinte du ministre d'État. C'est lui qui décide du prix de mise en vente des privatisées, tout comme de la constitution des 'noyaux durs', ces groupes d'actionnaires censés stabiliser, pour un temps, une partie du capital des sociétés rendues au privé, aux côtés des petits porteurs, des salariés et des étrangers (20% du capital au maximum).

Le programme de privatisation lancé à l'automne 1986 avec la mise en vente de Saint-Gobain fait un tabac auprès des Français jusqu'à l'été 1987. Des millions de souscripteurs se disputent les titres de Paribas, du CCF, de la Société générale, d'Havas ou de TF1. Mais le krach boursier du 19 octobre vient mettre un terme à cette euphorie. Suez, mise en vente à la veille du krach, connaîtra une introduction en Bourse catastrophique en dessous même du prix de cession des titres. La privatisation de Matra, prévue pour fin octobre, ne sera effective qu'en janvier. Quant à la suite du programme – notamment les assurances, avec l'UAP et les AGF, – elle est reportée après les élections présidentielles. Au total, en quatorze mois, le gouvernement aura réalisé plus de 40% de son programme de privatisation avec douze opérations de marché et deux ventes de gré à gré.

Volet important des programmes gouvernementaux de la gauche comme de la droite, nationalisations de 1982 et privatisations de 1986 ne constituent pas cependant un simple aller et retour. Certaines des premières n'ont pas encore été rendues au privé. En revanche, les dénationalisations réalisées ont débordé le périmètre de 1982 en au moins une 'vieille' entreprise publique de 1945: la Société générale.

En outre, la physionomie et l'état de santé des privatisées de 1986 n'ont plus grand-chose à voir avec les groupes industriels ou les banques nationalisées en 1982. Redressés, restructurés et modernisés, ce sont eux qui partent aujourd'hui à l'assaut du marché mondial et qui effectuent des acquisitions à l'étranger. Paradoxe ou non, la réussite et le dynamisme des privatisées doivent beaucoup à leur vie passée dans le giron des pouvoirs publics.

(Claire Blandin, 'Des nationalisations aux privatisations', *Bilan du septennat, Dossiers et documents, Le Monde*, 1988.)

## Exercices

### *Lexique*

Expliquez les mots et expressions suivants:

les nationalisées (l.1)
d'autant (l.9)
la rigueur budgétaire (l.9)
un actionnariat (l.12)
un enjeu (ll.16–17)
une ordonnance (l.20)
les privatisées (l.24)
un noyau dur (l.24)
faire un tabac (l.29)
un souscripteur (l.30)
un titre (l.30)
le prix de cession (ll.33–34)
une vente de gré à gré (ll.38–39)
un volet (l.40)
le giron (l.51)

### *Grammaire et stylistique*

(a) Remarquez que 'grand-chose' (l.47) s'utilise toujours dans des phrases négatives. Faites-en quelques-unes de votre cru.
(b) Trouvez les sujets des participes présents des lignes 4 à 9. Quelle est la règle relative à ces sujets? Faites des phrases illustrant ce point de grammaire.

### *Compréhension*

(a) Qu'est-ce à votre avis que 'la voie parlementaire classique' dont il est question ligne 22? En quoi l'ordonnance (l.20) diffère-t-elle?
(b) En quoi les nationalisations de 1982 et privatisations de 1986 ne constituent-elles pas 'un simple aller et retour' (l.42)?

### *Questions orales ou écrites*

(a) Les privatisations de la période de cohabitation de 1986 à 1988 ont-elles été effectuées selon des critères purement marchands, ou bien la vente du capital privatisé a-t-elle été organisée en prenant en compte des paramètres d'ordre politique et stratégique?

(b) Pourquoi un programme de privatisation tel que celui de 1986 ne peut-il pas être effectué d'un coup?

## TEXT 2.16

# Privatisations et transformations des services publics: vers de nouvelles régulations

L'année 1998 a été marquée par une vague de privatisations qui a inscrit, en la matière, l'action du gouvernement de Lionel Jospin dans la continuité de celle de ses prédécesseurs. Le paysage du capitalisme français au début de 1999 confirme que le recul du secteur public aura été l'un des phénomènes majeurs de la décennie.

Le processus de privatisation, gelé depuis 1988, avait repris en 1993 avec le gouvernement d'Édouard Balladur. Sept grandes entreprises ont été privatisées de 1993 à 1995: la BNP (Banque nationale de Paris), Rhône-Poulenc, Elf-Aquitaine, l'UAP (Union des assurances de Paris), la SEITA, Usinor-Sacilor, et Pechiney. Le capital de Bull et de Renault a été ouvert au privé, l'État restant encore majoritaire. Le gouvernement d'Alain Juppé a poursuivi le mouvement. En 1996 ont été réalisées les privatisations des AGF (Assurances générales de France), de Renault (cession de 6% des actions rendant minoritaire la participation de l'État, avec 46% du capital) et de la CGM (Compagnie générale maritime). Le statut de France Telecom a été transformé afin de rendre possible sa privatisation progressive. La part de l'État dans le capital de Bull est descendue en dessous de 50%, en début d'année 1997. Dans le cadre d'une opération visant à réduire l'endettement de la SNCF, un établissement public chargé de la gestion des infrastructures, le Réseau ferré de France (RFF), a été mis en place au printemps 1997; bien que ne préjugeant pas en elle-même d'une éventuelle ouverture à la concurrence ou d'une privatisation du transport ferroviaire, cette évolution, marquant une rupture, s'est inscrite dans la logique des transformations prônées par la Commission européenne. La fin de l'année 1996 avait cependant été dominée par l'interruption des privatisations du CIC (Crédit industriel et commercial) et surtout du groupe Thomson, Thomson-CSF (branche militaire) et Thomson-Multimédia (électronique de loisir).

Contrairement à ce qui s'était passé en 1988, le retour de la gauche au pouvoir en juin 1997 n'a pas remis en cause le processus. Le gouvernement a paru décidé à transférer – totalement ou partiellement – au privé la quasi-totalité du secteur public concurrentiel et à transformer fondamentalement les grands services publics. L'ouverture en octobre 1997 du capital de France Telecom est apparue comme une étape décisive de l'évolution des conceptions des partis de gauche au pouvoir: elle a marqué l'entrée du capital privé dans une entreprise relevant traditionnellement du service public et non pas seulement du secteur public.

*Les nouvelles configurations du capitalisme français*

Les privatisations engagées par la suite ont profondément remodelé les structures de l'économie française. Une deuxième phase de l'ouverture du capital de

France Telecom est intervenue en novembre 1998. La participation de l'État est ainsi tombée à 62%.

Le secteur financier est désormais largement sorti de l'orbite publique. En 1998, le CIC a été vendu au Crédit mutuel, le GAN à Groupama et le capital de la Caisse nationale de prévoyance (CNP) a été restructuré et partiellement mis en Bourse. L'année 1999 devait voir la transformation du statut des caisses d'épargne (transformées en banques coopératives). Surtout, est apparue engagée la privatisation du Crédit Lyonnais.

De même, d'importantes opérations ont touché des groupes industriels. Le capital de Thomson-Multimédia (dont les comptes ont été redressés) a été ouvert, à hauteur de 30%, à quatre partenaires industriels: Alcatel, les américains Direct TV et Microsoft et le japonais NEC. En juillet 1998 a été annoncé le rapprochement d'Aérospatiale et de Matra (groupe Lagardère), Lagardère détenant environ 30% du nouveau groupe. Cette opération (qui signifie une privatisation d'Aérospatiale) a été confirmée à la mi-février.

Très vif au début, le débat sur les méthodes de privatisation est largement retombé. É. Balladur avait privilégié la formule des «noyaux durs» qui consistait à attribuer 15% à 20% du capital à un groupe d'actionnaires stables. Deux grands pôles financiers s'étaient alors constitués autour, d'une part, de la Société générale, de Paribas et des AGF et, d'autre part, de la BNP, de l'UAP et de Suez. Ces relations ont par la suite évolué. Le secteur des assurances a été complètement redistribué: UAP a été achetée par Axa, les AGF par Allianz et le GAN par le Crédit mutuel. La gamme des techniques de cession s'est élargie: introduction en Bourse par étapes successives (France Telecom), vente de gré à gré (GAN, CIC) et nouveaux noyaux (cession prévue du Crédit Lyonnais), tandis que, dans la transformation d'Air France, un rôle important a été dévolu à l'attribution d'actions aux salariés, notamment aux pilotes. Au total, de 1997 à 1999, les recettes de privatisation devaient excéder 100 milliards FF.

*Les services publics en devenir*

Par ailleurs, le gouvernement a poursuivi une action d'adaptation du noyau dur des services au nouveau contexte européen. En juin 1998 a été présentée la «réforme de la réforme ferroviaire»: stabilisation de la dette de RFF avec augmentation des péages versés par la SNCF et mise en place d'un Conseil supérieur du service public ferroviaire. Début décembre 1998, le Conseil des ministres a adopté un projet de loi sur l'ouverture à la concurrence de l'électricité (fin du monopole d'Électricité de France–EDF). La question de l'avenir des grandes entités des services publics de réseau était désormais posée et des réflexions ont commencé à être émises sur l'applicabilité du «modèle France Telecom» (transformation en société anonyme et maintien du statut spécifique du personnel) à EDF, à GDF (Gaz de France), à La Poste et à la SNCF.

Les entreprises de services publics français ont désormais manifesté une stratégie d'expansion à l'international liée aux privatisations dans les autres pays. EDF, GDF et France Telecom sont apparus les plus avancés. EDF-

International, créée en 1992, était en 1998 présente dans une quinzaine de pays et a pris à la fin novembre de cette même année le contrôle de London Electricity qui fournit le courant à deux millions d'abonnés dans la capitale britannique. EDF, qui compte 30 millions d'abonnés en France, en aurait désormais 15 millions à l'étranger. Michel Bon, président de France Telecom, a affirmé sa volonté de bâtir «un véritable opérateur européen . . . solution alternative aux opérateurs historiques partout en Europe».

Ces évolutions, qui peuvent être lues comme une preuve des capacités concurrentielles des services publics français, pourraient rendre de plus en plus difficile la défense des monopoles «à la française» sur le marché intérieur. Elles s'inscrivent dans une problématique où la relation marchande au «client» est destinée à prendre définitivement le pas sur le rapport à l'usager-citoyen.

(Norbert Holcblat, 'Privatisations et transformations des services publics: vers de nouvelles régulations', in *L'état de la France 1999–2000*, La Découverte, pp.450–52.)

## Exercices

### *Lexique*

Expliquez les mots et expressions suivants:

en la matière (ll.1–2)
prôner (l.23)
relever de (l.34)
sortir de l'orbite publique (l.41)
les comptes ont été redressés (l.48)
à hauteur de (l.4)
une problématique (l.93)

### *Grammaire et stylistique*

(a) La plupart des verbes de ce texte sont conjugués au passé composé. Trouvez des exceptions (verbes conjugués au futur, ou à l'imparfait, ou au plus-que-parfait, etc.). Dans chaque cas, expliquez pourquoi ils ne sont pas au passé composé.
(b) 'En 1996 ont été réalisées les privatisations . . . ' (l.12): pourquoi l'ordre habituel du verbe et du sujet a-t-il été inversé dans cette phrase? Réécrivez-la en remettant le sujet et le verbe dans l'ordre habituel. Trouvez d'autres exemples de ce type d'inversion dans le texte.

### *Compréhension*

(a) Répertoriez les différentes phases de privatisations de 1988 à 1998.
(b) Le retour de la gauche au pouvoir en 1997 a-t-il eu les mêmes conséquences sur les politiques de privatisations que son retour au pouvoir une décennie plus tôt, en 1988? Pourquoi?

### *Questions orales ou écrites*

(a) Les changements intervenus dans les statuts et les activités des services publics français depuis le début des années 1990, ainsi que l'application des règles sur la concurrence de l'Union Européenne, forceront-ils la privatisation de ces services dans un avenir proche?

(b) Recherchez le site internet de deux ou trois grandes entreprises françaises qui ont été privatisées dans les années 1980 ou 1990. Pouvez-vous identifier certains changements qui ont pu intervenir depuis leur privatisation?

**TEXT 2.17**

## M. Mitterrand, modernisateur du capitalisme français?

En dix ans, le chef de l'État a rompu à la fois avec le pseudo-libéralisme de la droite et avec le volontarisme de la gauche.

L'économie française n'aura sans doute jamais été, depuis la fin de la seconde guerre mondiale au moins, aussi libérale qu'après dix années de 'socialisme'. Le paradoxe est sans doute l'un des plus inattendus de ceux produits par la décennie Mitterrand. Faut-il, pour autant, en conclure que les socialistes français ont, au cours des dix années écoulées, découvert les vertus de l'économie de marché, mais oublié le socialisme? Les choses ne sont pas aussi simples.

La reconnaissance par les socialistes de la supériorité du marché n'est qu'un aspect d'une révolution plus large: la fin de l'exception française dans le domaine économique. La France n'a pas pu échapper à la vague libérale qui a inondé le monde à partir de la fin des années 70. Elle s'est banalisée. Dans ces conditions, au 'socialisme à la française', M. François Mitterrand a habilement substitué l'ambition européenne. Les multiples reniements auxquels la gauche a dû procéder, avec l'abandon du volontarisme étatique et du dirigisme, ne signifient pourtant pas une conversion totale et aveugle au marché.

Malgré un apparent consensus – sur la politique conjoncturelle, en particulier – entre la gauche et la droite, subsistent des conceptions différentes. La décennie a rendu caduques les controverses entre socialisme et capitalisme pour leur substituer un débat sur le type de capitalisme souhaité. De nouveaux clivages apparaissent à ce sujet; ils ne recouvrent pas nécessairement les frontières actuelles des partis.

Est-il nécessaire de le rappeler? Au cours de la décennie Mitterrand, mars 1983 a été un mois décisif. Après deux années de réformes sociales importantes, les caisses de la France sont vides. A l'issue d'une période tendue d'intenses discussions, le président de la République décide un retour à l'orthodoxie. La France reste dans le système monétaire européen et en accepte toutes les contraintes. La décision est historique.

Pour qualifier ce revirement, chacun, à gauche, y va de sa formule: le *'virage libéral'* (M. Jean-Pierre Chevènement), la prise de conscience de *'l'impossibilité du socialisme dans un seul pays'* (M. Dominique Strauss-Kahn), *'l'abandon de la culture de la dévaluation qui réunissait la gauche et la droite'* (M. Alain Minc), *'la fin de la culture de l'inflation'* (M. Jean Peyrelevade). Avec la fin de l'indexation généralisée des revenus, les gouvernements de M. Mitterrand vont révolutionner la France.

Cette révolution – qui va se traduire notamment par un partage de la valeur ajoutée de plus en plus favorable aux entreprises, cela aux dépens des salariés – est souvent présentée comme une trahison des socialistes. Ceux-ci sont effectivement amenés à abandonner beaucoup de leurs promesses, voire de leurs principes. La lecture comparée des déclarations de 1980 et de 1990 des dirigeants socialistes est à cet égard un exercice cruel.

Il n'est pourtant pas juste de limiter cette révolution à une simple adhésion nouvelle des socialistes à l'économie de marché. Elle a en fait été une double rupture pour le pays: avec le pseudo-libéralisme giscardo-pompidolien d'une part, avec le volontarisme étatique de la gauche d'autre part. *'L'année 1983 ne marque pas seulement*, explique à juste titre l'économiste Elie Cohen, *une rupture avec le socialisme de 1981–1982, mais aussi avec tout le passé de l'après-guerre, une rupture avec l'économie de financement administrée.'*

La France s'engage dans la voie de l'économie de marché, ouverte sur l'extérieur et sans inflation. A l'issue de la décennie, les prix et les changes sont libres – une situation que n'avait pratiquement jamais connue la France. Les conditions de gestion des salariés ont été libéralisées. La politique de désinflation compétitive et du franc fort est encensée par la presse anglo-saxonne. Les capitalistes étrangers sont avides de titres de l'État français. Cette double rupture n'est cependant pas le fruit du hasard. Les socialistes arrivent au pouvoir au moment même où une vague libérale commence à inonder le monde. Elle est ensuite imposée par l'Europe, un choix politique fort du président. L'intelligence de M. Mitterrand a sans doute été d'avoir préféré, au prix d'abandons considérables, surfer sur cette vague plutôt que de la voir noyer le pays.

*'Depuis la fin des années 1960 jusqu'à aujourd'hui*, estime M. Strauss-Kahn, *nous avons vécu l'essouflement des régulations antérieures. Nous ne connaissons pas encore les nouvelles. Aussi, dans l'entre-deux, devons-nous accepter une certaine désorganisation qui prend la forme du marché, du libéralisme.'* M. Mitterrand a en tout cas compris que, les contraintes économiques l'emportant parfois sur la volonté politique, il valait mieux, dans certains cas, leur céder.

Effectivement, il y a toujours, entre la droite et la gauche, des oppositions. D'anciens clivages subsistent, de nouveaux sont apparus. Parmi les anciens thèmes, il y a encore et toujours la place de l'État dans l'économie. Fondamentalement pervers pour la droite, l'État reste profondément indispensable pour la gauche. *'Le marché, cruel, est irremplaçable. Il ne peut fonctionner sans règles, sans un État qui corrige ses excès'*, rappelait M. Bérégovoy, ministre de l'Économie et des Finances. L'État est un correcteur des excès que provoque le fonctionnement du marché, des inégalités qu'il engendre par exemple!

*'Par sa seule présence, même minoritaire, dans le capital des entreprises, le secteur public instille une vue à long terme dans l'économie, par opposition au marché qui soumet les acteurs au reporting trimestriel des dividendes'*, ajoute ce chaud partisan de l'économie mixte.

L'ampleur de la redistribution nécessaire reste aussi une opposition traditionnelle entre les deux camps.

L'attitude plus favorable des socialistes à l'égard du marché ne signifie donc pas la fin des débats économiques. Il y a toujours une droite et une gauche.

(Erik Izraelewicz, 'M. Mitterrand, modernisateur du capitalisme', *Le Monde*, 8 May 1991, pp.1 & 8.)

## Exercices

### *Lexique*

Expliquez les mots et expressions suivants:

| | |
|---|---|
| se banaliser (l.12) | caduque (l.19) |
| le reniement (l.14) | à l'issue de (l.25) |

### *Grammaire et stylistique*

(a) Pourquoi le journaliste écrit-il 'à l'issue de la décennie' (l.50) au lieu de 'à la fin de la décennie'? Commentez ce choix stylistique.
(b) 'Ceux-ci sont effectivement amenés à abandonner beaucoup de leurs promesses, voire de leurs principes' (ll.38–40). Que veut dire 'voire de'? Inventez vous-même des phrases en utilisant cette expression.

### *Compréhension*

(a) Que comprenez-vous par 'volontarisme étatique' (l.15), 'politique conjoncturelle' (l.17), 'l'indexation généralisée des revenus' (ll.33–34)?
(b) A la ligne 20, précisez de quels clivages il s'agit.
(c) Expliquez et commentez les lignes 18–22.

### *Questions orales ou écrites*

(a) Les socialistes ont-ils oublié le socialisme en découvrant les vertus de l'économie de marché?
(b) Que restait-il, en 1991, de la démarche économique de Mitterrand telle qu'elle avait été présentée aux électeurs dix ans plus tôt?

TEXT 2.18

## Les entreprises françaises ont fait le pari de la mondialisation

Au sein d'un mouvement global de concentrations-fusions–restructurations–acquisitions, les firmes hexagonales battent record sur record en termes de volumes et de valeurs des opérations. Selon le groupe d'informations financières Thomson Financial, le montant des fusions-acquisitions annoncées en France dans les neuf premiers mois de 1999 a été multiplié par trois par rapport à la même période de 1998: 150 milliards de dollars, près de 1 000 milliards de francs, soit 18% des transactions européennes. On y trouve toute la gamme des associations possibles: mariages franco-français (TotalFina-Elf, Sanofi-Synthélabo, Carrefour-Promodès . . .), fusions européennes (Seita-Tabacalera avec Altadis, Alstom-ABB dans la production d'énergie . . .), croissances externes majeures transcontinentales (Renault-Nissan, Vivendi-US Filter, Suez-Lyonnaise/Nalco), union multipartite (Pechiney, Alcan et Algroup au sein d'APA . . .).

Il est évident qu'en l'espace de quelques mois des tabous sont tombés. Effet «millénariste», peur panique ou simplement instinct de survie, les grands patrons, rompant avec les usages, achètent, vendent, marient et fusionnent sans ménager les susceptibilités. Et avec des mobilisations capitalistiques exceptionnelles pour le marché français. TotalFina et Elf n'ont pas hésité à monter un dossier et un contre-dossier d'une cinquantaine de milliards de dollars pour lancer leurs offres. L'audace japonaise de Louis Schweitzer a surpris, Renault prévoyant de consacrer près de 33 milliards de dollars à l'acquisition de 36,8% du capital de Nissan.

*L'indépendance, synonyme de «marginalisation»*

Longtemps tenu pour un dogme par certains patrons, le «ni-ni» – ni fusion ni union – est battu en brèche. Face aux alliances dans l'industrie pharmaceutique qui ont donné naissance aux plus grands de la profession (Glaxo-Wellcome, Bristol-Myers Squibb . . .), Jean-René Fourtou, le patron de Rhône-Poulenc, brandissait haut le drapeau de l'indépendance . . . jusqu'à ce qu'il décide de faire convoler au printemps le groupe qu'il préside avec l'allemand Hoechst pour bâtir Aventis. Aujourd'hui, devenu vice-président du nouvel ensemble, il se montre rassurant: «La France et la Bourse de Paris disposeront de la première société du monde dans le domaine des sciences de la vie. C'est un événement qui aurait paru incroyable il y a peu de temps, et, dans les faits, peu de gens y croient encore.» Quel que soit le domaine d'activité, il ne suffit plus d'être gros, il faut être gigantesque. L'exemple de la distribution en France – l'un des secteurs économiques les plus concentrés – est éclatant, où deux parmi les plus grands construisent une alliance superlative. Face à une hypothétique déferlante de l'américain Wal-Mart, Carrefour et Promodès ont décidé de signer la paix pour devenir le premier groupe français (avec près de 30% du marché!) dont le chiffre d'affaires dépassera les 350 milliards de francs.

Prenons un champion tricolore internationalisé de longue date et ancré dans une logique ancienne de partenariats industriels: Pechiney, l'un des leaders mondiaux de l'aluminium. Jean-Pierre Rodier, l'industrieux industriel, s'attache à redresser les comptes, à soulager le poids d'un endettement supérieur à ses fonds propres et à recentrer le portefeuille d'activités. Un travail de fond, long et rigoureux. Le groupe maigrit, avec 64,6 milliards de francs de ventes l'an dernier, mais se muscle. A l'arrivée, un champion français de l'industrie, technologiquement incontesté, actionnaire d'alumineries parmi les plus belles du monde (Bécancour au Québec, Tomago en Australie . . .), qui se retrouve délibérément fondu au sein d'un ensemble multinational (franco-helvético-canadien) APA. Les patrons de ces trois têtes de classe de l'industrie mondiale de l'aluminium ont préféré fusionner volontairement Alcan, Algroup et Pechiney plutôt que de risquer l'OPA hostile à l'absorption. Jean-Pierre Rodier résume ainsi la situation: «Ou nous restions indépendants, au risque de nous retrouver marginalisés, ou nous voulions maîtriser notre destin et entreprenions une fusion nous permettant de créer un leader mondial.» Après avoir assimilé le gouvernement d'entreprise dans sa méthode de management et intégré la création de valeur dans sa logique de gestion, le patron français doit accepter les alliances, quitte à perdre une partie de ses prérogatives.

*Discrétion, silence voire figuration de l'État*

Il est cependant une autre innovation à souligner dans cette évolution du marché français, au crédit de l'État cette fois: le rôle (ou plutôt la figuration) tenu par les autorités françaises dans le déroulement de ces affaires. A moins de secrets très bien gardés, on peut considérer qu'elles sont peu intervenues, même sur des dossiers longtemps considérés comme ultrasensibles. Dans le pétrole, par exemple, avec la neutralité bienveillante exprimée vis-à-vis de TotalFina lors de son offensive sur Elf, quand il s'agissait de reconstituer un grand monopole – privé, il est vrai – par le mariage des troisième et huitième entreprises françaises. Ou, dans le domaine de la défense, avec l'onction discrète apportée au mariage Aérospatiale-Matra d'abord, à la fusion avec Dasa dans EADS ensuite – soit, dans ce secteur on ne peut plus stratégique, une union transfrontalière qui se combine à une fusion privé-public!

La France a besoin de leaders mondiaux, de locomotives économiques, acceptons donc leur constitution, à défaut d'en être les inspirateurs. «Une entreprise doit se composer un portefeuille d'activités où elle détient une position de premier plan», explique Jean-Pierre Tirouflet, le patron de Rhodia, chimiste désormais indépendant qui, passant de la théorie à la pratique, boucle l'acquisition d'Albright et Wilson et devient premier producteur mondial de phosphates pour détergents. De fait, on constate que les opérations annoncées depuis le début de l'année ont fait bondir les entreprises concernées dans les classements mondiaux. L'État qui privatise (environ 150 milliards de francs depuis deux ans) laisse aussi agir et grossir. Avec cependant une crainte: «Toutes ces décisions de fusion-acquisition ont ou auront un impact social ou sur l'aménagement du territoire, note-t-on au secrétariat d'État à l'Industrie. Le fait de ne plus avoir un interlocuteur bien identifié, ou le fait qu'il soit moins proche, peut engendrer des difficultés à conserver une implication citoyenne de l'entreprise.» Déjà, avec le Michelin de Clermont-Ferrand, le courant ne passe pas bien . . . Aventis est une société de droit français, soumise à la fiscalité et aux lois françaises, mais sur 90 000 employés les salariés français seront très minoritaires, une vingtaine de milliers de personnes; le siège d'APA se situera à New York, bien loin des usines alpines de Pechiney. Quant aux actionnaires . . .

Il apparaît clairement que le refrain de la mondialisation se substitue progressivement à l'hymne national des entreprises. «Quelle est la nationalité du groupe que je préside? s'interrogeait récemment un grand patron pas encore pris dans la folie des fusions. Je ne sais pas vraiment. La moitié de mes sites de production se trouvent hors de France; mon chiffre d'affaires est réalisé aux deux tiers en dehors de l'Hexagone, et 40% de mes actionnaires sont des fonds anglo-saxons. Peut-être est-ce l'adresse du siège, mais de nombreux groupes s'installent ici ou là pour des raisons fiscales ou diplomatiques, alors . . . » Alors, pourra-t-on encore établir des classements d'entreprises françaises?

(Christian David, 'Les entreprises françaises ont fait le pari de la mondialisation', *L'Expansion*, 4–17 November 1999, pp.140–42.)

## Exercices

### *Lexique*

Expliquez les mots et expressions suivants:

rompre avec les usages (l.15)
ménager les susceptibilités (l.16)
monter un dossier (ll.17–18)
une déferlante (l.36)
le chiffre d'affaires (ll.38–39)
les fonds propres (l.44)
quitte à . . . (l.58)
une prérogative (l.58)
une onction discrète (l.68)
boucler l'acquisition (ll.76–77)

### *Grammaire et stylistique*

(a) '– soit, dans ce secteur . . .' (ll.69–70): quel est le sens grammatical du mot 'soit' dans cette phrase? Par quels autres mots ou expressions pourriez-vous le remplacer?

(b) 'Il est cependant une autre innovation à souligner . . .' (l.60): remarquez l'utilisation de l'expression 'Il est . . . à souligner'. Par quelle autre expression pourriez-vous la remplacer? Dans cette expression, par quel autre verbe pourriez-vous remplacer 'souligner' sans en altérer significativement le sens?

### *Compréhension*

(a) Quels changements sont intervenus au sein des grandes entreprises françaises durant les dernières années de la décennie 1990? Pourquoi est-ce nouveau?
(b) Quelles sont les principales raisons données aux fusions et acquisitions intervenant dans l'économie française?
(c) Pourquoi est-il important de s'allier à des entreprises étrangères?

### *Questions orales ou écrites*

(a) L'économie française est-elle en retard ou en avance par rapport à l'économie de votre propre pays, dans le mouvement de mondialisation des activités des grandes entreprises?
(b) L'état français devrait-il intervenir plus directement dans le mouvement de concentration des entreprises?

TEXT 2.19

## Le capitalisme français s'émancipe de l'État et obéit à de nouvelles règles du jeu

La fin de la politique économique . . . Pour évoquer cette année 1999 qui s'achève, et le nouveau millénaire qui commence, la formule peut apparaître inappropriée. Car si les tenants du libéralisme pronostiquent depuis longtemps le déclin de l'État et, avec lui, la mise en cause de tous les grands leviers qui lui permettent d'agir sur la vie économique – monnaie, fiscalité, budget, salaires . . . –, il peut sembler incongru de penser qu'ils ont obtenu gain de cause sous un gouvernement de gauche, censé redonner du lustre à l'action publique et contenir les avancées du marché. D'autant que Dominique Strauss-Kahn, avant qu'il ne trébuche sur la ténébreuse affaire de la MNEF, s'est peut-être exposé à de nombreuses critiques, mais sûrement pas à celle d'avoir été un ministre des finances impuissant. C'est même l'inverse: il a pesé sur la vie économique du pays assurément plus que ne l'avaient fait nombre de ses prédécesseurs.

Voilà en tout cas pour les apparences. Mais si l'on s'en tient aux faits, force est de constater que l'État est sorti ébranlé de cette année 1999. Economiquement aussi, c'est une année-charnière. Une année au cours de laquelle tout a basculé. Au détriment de l'État et en faveur du marché.

*Pilotage automatique*

C'est d'abord la fin de la politique monétaire. Avec le lancement de l'euro, le 1er janvier 1999, les partisans de la monnaie unique peuvent, certes, faire valoir qu'il ne s'agit pas d'une perte de souveraineté pour la France, mais d'une nouvelle souveraineté conquise, plus efficace, même si elle est partagée. Il reste que, pour le pays, c'est une page décisive qui se tourne, puisque le gouvernement n'a soudain plus le loisir, pour déterminer sa politique économique, de jouer du ressort monétaire.

Pour le levier budgétaire, le basculement est tout aussi spectaculaire car, dans la foulée, la France se conforme au pacte de stabilité européen et ne peut plus songer – dans la vieille tradition keynésienne chère à la gauche – d'user du budget pour amortir les chocs économiques. Plus question de relancer les dépenses quand la croissance faiblit ou de laisser filer les déficits: avec le programme français, arrêté en janvier, la politique budgétaire est désormais encadrée, pour les années suivantes, dans des rails dont elle ne peut sortir sous peine de lourdes sanctions financières, ce qui la contraint à limiter ses dépenses et à réduire continûment ses déficits. Ce n'est donc peut-être pas la fin de la politique budgétaire – des redistributions de crédits d'un ministère à l'autre, pour marquer des priorités, sont toujours possibles –, mais cela y ressemble fort: on passe, pour les finances publiques, du pilotage manuel, où chaque gouvernement peut décider ce que bon lui semble, au pilotage automatique.

La fiscalité est une autre illustration de cette grande mutation dans laquelle la France est aspirée. Et dont la gauche fait les frais. Dans la tradition socialiste, l'impôt est en effet un autre levier permettant à l'État de jouer son rôle de régulation. Or, dans ce monde économique qui bascule, où les contraintes de la compétitivité prennent le pas sur les impératifs de justice fiscale, les certitudes d'hier sont brutalement ébranlées. Peut-on ainsi encore concevoir que l'impôt sur le revenu puisse avoir un taux «marginal» d'imposition parmi les plus élevés d'Europe, qui culmine à 54%, sans craindre que des cadres de haut niveau ne soient tentés de s'expatrier à Londres ou au Luxembourg, pour travailler dans des pays fiscalement plus accueillants? Peut-on continuer à taxer à 40% les plus-values sur les stock-options sans s'exposer au même danger?

Au risque de froisser ses camarades socialistes qui ne sont pas tous disposés à renoncer à leurs convictions anciennes, M. Strauss-Kahn cherche tout au long de cette année 1999, avec d'infinies précautions, à leur faire comprendre que le début de ce nouveau siècle sera aussi celui des révisions déchirantes. Ce n'est peut-être pas encore la fin de la politique fiscale, mais on en approche.

L'onde de choc n'affecte pas seulement, d'ailleurs, les leviers traditionnels de la politique publique. C'est toute la vie économique du pays qui est bousculée par ce changement de règles du jeu, dont l'arbitre est de moins en moins l'État et de plus en plus le marché. A sa manière, Lionel Jospin en convient quand, invité en septembre sur France 2 à commenter les annonces de Michelin – une nouvelle vague de suppression d'emplois et des profits en hausse –, il doit se résigner à avouer que l'État n'a guère son mot à dire dans la conduite d'une entreprise privée.

*Système d'endogamie*

Autre illustration, plus spectaculaire encore, le ministre des finances – dans le bureau duquel se prenaient jusque-là toutes les grandes décisions concernant la place de Paris – est réduit à un rôle de spectateur quand éclate, quelques mois auparavant, la grande bataille boursière entre la BNP, la Société générale et Paribas. Pour la première fois en France, dans une affaire de ce genre, dont tout l'avenir du secteur bancaire va dépendre, ce sont les actionnaires qui détiennent le pouvoir de décision. L'épilogue est d'ailleurs, à lui seul, révélateur de ce brutal changement d'époque. Comme la France, vieux pays jacobin, n'a toujours connu qu'un capitalisme vivant dans un système d'endogamie avec l'État, elle ne dispose pas d'une législation adaptée au capitalisme de marché qui émerge. La fin de la bataille boursière tourne donc à la confusion, et les arbitrages rendus par les autorités de tutelle (Commission des opérations de Bourse, Comité des établissements de crédit) pour départager les protagonistes n'apparaissent pas incontestables.

Conscient de ces lacunes, le gouvernement annonce donc à l'automne qu'il va dans les premiers mois de 2000 dévoiler un projet de loi déterminant de nouvelles «*régulations économiques*». En clair, il ne s'agit pas de redonner à l'État un pouvoir qu'il a définitivement perdu, mais de définir des «*règles*» pour que le marché fonctionne harmonieusement. Dans ce projet, il y a donc une forme d'aveu: c'est bel et bien le marché qui est devenu le véritable maître du jeu.

(*Laurent Mauduit* 'Le capitalisme français s'émancipe de l'état et obéit à de nouvelles règles du jeu', *Le Monde*, 1 January 2000, p.6.)

## Exercices

### Lexique

Expliquez les mots et expressions suivants:

incongru (l.6)
obtenir gain de cause (l.6)
redonner du lustre (l.7)
jouer du ressort monétaire (ll.23–24)
encadrer dans des rails (l.31)
le pilotage manuel (l.36)
le taux 'marginal' d'imposition (l.45)
un vieux pays jacobin (l.71)
endogamie avec l'État (ll.72–73)

### Grammaire et stylistique

(a) 'C'est toute . . . qui est . . .' (l.56): reconstruisez la phrase sans utiliser cette expression. Pourquoi l'auteur de l'article l'a-t-il utilisée? Introduisez cette expression dans une autre phrase du texte, et analysez le changement de ton qui en résulte.
(b) 'force est de constater . . .' (ll.13–14): trouvez une autre expression qui exprime la même idée.
(c) 'sans craindre que des cadres . . . ne soient tentés . . .' (ll.46–47): construisez des phrases incluant des propositions négatives de ce type, utilisant 'que' avec un verbe au subjonctif.

### Compréhension

(a) Quelles sont les principales raisons pour lesquelles le rôle de l'État français a tendance à décroître?
(b) Qu'est-ce-que 'la vieille tradition keynesienne chère à la gauche' (l.27)? Pourquoi n'est-elle plus applicable?
(c) Quels sont les secteurs de la politique économique dans lesquels le gouvernment français peut encore avoir une influence?

### Questions orales ou écrites

(a) Le texte insiste sur l'introduction de la monnaie unique pour expliquer les changements du rôle de l'État. Dans quels autres domaines le processus d'intégration européenne a-t-il modifié les comportements économiques de l'État?
(b) Ce texte fait référence à une bataille boursière entre grandes banques ayant pris place en 1999. Qu'illustre cette bataille quant au changement du comportement économique des entreprises et banques françaises?

PART III

# Contemporary French society

Jill Forbes

# Introduction

The years since the Second World War have seen deeper and more rapid social changes in France than at any time, perhaps, since the Revolution of 1789. The rural exodus has been completed; most French people now live in towns, and those that remain in the country have had their lives transformed by the provision of public utilities and the modernization of agricultural methods; and town and country have been brought closer together by vast infrastructural improvements in public transport and telecommunications. The nature of work has changed, as has the composition of the work-force; the age structure of the population has altered and, with it, people's aspirations and expectations. The social structure familiar from the pre-war period, with its seemingly rigid divisions between 'ouvriers' and 'bourgeois' and its significant numbers of 'paysans' or people working on the land, has been profoundly altered both by the disappearance of the traditional working class composed of male heavy-industry workers and their families, and by the concomitant growth of tertiary sector employment, together with the emergence of significant new social actors such as young people, old people, immigrants and the poor. Mass secondary education and the mass media have undoubtedly had a homogenizing effect and the cultural specificities which attached to earlier social divisions, with distinguishably different 'bourgeois' and 'working-class' cultures, have been attenuated. At the same time, other forms of cultural diversity have emerged which are based on regional, generational and ethnic differences.

The locomotive of these changes has been economic and political as well as cultural. The French economy experienced unparalleled growth during the *Trente glorieuses*, or the thirty years immediately following the Second World War (see Part II). The consumer society arrived in France with an impact that was rendered all the greater because of the dramatic contrast it created with the relatively low living standards of the pre-war period. But in embracing consumerism and the 'affluent society' France has also lost many of its peculiarities and has become more like other western European countries. Side by side with economic convergence has been a political 'normalization', together with a sustained effort on the part of French leaders to align themselves with Germany and to promote European integration (see Part I). The content of politics has become national and European, where once it was local, because the disappearance of regional specificities and the generalization of television have guaranteed all public figures, however partial or extremist their programmes, a national platform if they wish it. Thus it is unlikely that a figure such as Pierre Poujade who, in the mid-1950s, stood for the defence of local interests against interference from the capital, will ever emerge again, for politics is also conducted on a national and European stage which encourages convergence with the remainder of western Europe [see Text 3.1].

This process of convergence has not proceeded smoothly. The observer of French society notes at least two distinct periods of social change in the post-war period, symbolically separated by the events of May 1968. The changes that took place up to the end of the 1960s, during the Fourth Republic and the presidency of de Gaulle, are usually described in terms of the 'modernization' which accompanied the high economic growth of the *Trente glorieuses*. Living standards improved dramatically and the advent of the consumer society brought with it changes in habits, lifestyles and expectations. Physically, France was transformed by massive programmes of building and renovation. Then came the revolt of students and workers in May 1968. The strikes and demonstrations lasted for over a month, closing down, in the process, industry, business and public services. Banks, broadcasting and transport were all affected alongside the education system and manufacturing industry, and the movement was only brought to an end by the wage increases and other reforms incorporated in the *Accords de Grenelle*. For a short while it seemed as if a political revolution, led by workers and students, might overthrow the government. In the event, no such overthrow took place. However, as a result of May 1968, social and industrial relations changed for good. The old hierarchies and the old paternalism were replaced by the more relaxed, flexible and non-hierarchical forms of institutional and interpersonal relations common today. This was evident in all kinds of ways, from the widespread use of the '*tu*' form of address, to the clothes worn to school and in the street, to eating habits, as well as in the adoption of participatory management in industry and in public institutions such as universities.

With hindsight we can say that May 1968 marked such changes as much as it caused them, since the events now appear to be as much a reaction to what went before as a prefiguration of what was to come. But it would still be difficult to over-state their symbolic significance. Thus, in attempting to make sense of social change in contemporary France, May 1968 continues to present a useful watershed, a point at which the process of change took a different turn [see Text 3.2].

With the start of the 1970s, French society ceased to be bent on unquestioned modernization. For as long as families had been inadequately fed and housed it had seemed obvious that modernization should have as its object the provision of basic amenities and a decent standard of living for all. After May 1968, however, questions began to be posed as to the quality of life created by modernization, and the consumer society was not universally seen as a good thing. Criticism of consumerism is, of course, the luxury of affluence, but it was none the less real.

The election of Valéry Giscard d'Estaing to the presidency in 1974 marked the beginning of a second period of social change. His election coincided with the effects of the first oil crisis which caused the first interruption in rapid growth since the Second World War and led to a less rapid improvement of living standards, if not an actual decline. But Giscard's presidency (1974–81) was a great period of social reform. Virtually all the popular demands of the 1960s and early 1970s were embodied in social legislation, bringing France, often somewhat tardily, into line with other western countries. Contraception and abortion were legalized, equal opportunities legislation was enacted, paternal authority was reduced. In these respects Giscard was a much greater reformer than the Socialists who succeeded him.

But this social modernization also reflected a shift in the debate about social inequalities. Until the end of the 1960s, social policy was implicitly underpinned by a model of a society based on the division into classes. This meant that the process of social change was directed at integration – at incorporating the less privileged workers and peasants into the national community by offering them comparable living standards and social protection to those available to the middle classes. Such an approach was made possible both by economic growth and by central, technocratic control of change which enabled local opposition to be circumvented. It was thus paternalistic in both the positive and negative senses. From the middle of the 1970s onwards, however, other forms of social grouping, based on factors such as race, sex or age, as well as or instead of class, were recognized as significant, and legislation was directed at ensuring equal provision of benefits and amenities for such groups. At the same time, the paternalism of the Gaullist era was dismantled. Individuals of whatever sex or colour had their social rights protected by law, but economically they became more vulnerable since the individual rather than the family became the focus of social and economic change. In this way women achieved equal rights but forfeited the expectation that they would be supported and cared for by father or husband.

From the 1980s onwards, the effects of such policies were to become strongly apparent. They could be seen in the emergence of the 'new poor', a group composed essentially of those whose lack of a family meant they had no entitlement to benefits; in debates over the possibility and desirability of 'integrating' immigrants into French society; and in sporadic outbursts of discontent, particularly among public sector employees, such as nurses and train drivers. As suggested by the film *La Haine* (1995), the impact was also felt among the young people who inhabit housing estates on the edge of the big cities whose violent protests seemed to translate a sense that they had no social influence. In other words the experiences of the 1980s and 1990s, which reaped both the benefits and the disadvantages of the social legislation of the 1970s, suggest that, after a period when living standards and expectations had converged, French society became much less homogeneous. By the turn of the millennium it was obvious that, even though most people in France were materially much better off than in 1945, there were still deep divisions in society but that these could not be explained in terms of the old class model. The pages which follow will explore the major social changes which have taken place in France since the Second World War and will examine some of the factors of convergence and division.

# From country to city

A key element in the post-war modernization of French society was the shift in the balance between the city and the country. People had begun to leave the land in the nineteenth century, during the first period of industrialization, and by the early twentieth century the urban population had become as large as the rural population. However, the post-war 'rural exodus' was different in terms both of the number of people involved, of the speed with which it took place and of the effect on the age structure of the rural population. In the space of twenty years France became a primarily urban society and by the end of the twentieth century 80 per cent of its population was living in towns. Most of the migrants were young people and women and, as a result of these migrations, there was a transformation of life in both the countryside and the towns, as well as of the relationship between the two.

## The agricultural revolution

Great emphasis was placed on the modernization of agriculture, initially assisted by Marshall Aid. The state encouraged the creation of larger and more viable farming units through the rural exodus and *remembrement*, made credit available for mechanization and encouraged the technical education of young farmers. Today the more prosperous French farmers, generally to be found in the north of the country, are the managers or owners of large businesses. But the process of modernization has also created regional disparities and in the southern half of the country and in the hill areas, where farms tend to be smaller and less profitable, modernization has been a mixed blessing, for the rural exodus has also destroyed the village as a local community. Village schools, shops, post offices and churches have all closed and are still closing. The local notables – the teacher, the doctor and the priest – no longer live among the farmers, local bus and rail services have disappeared, and country dwellers are almost entirely dependent on private cars. In short, as one commentator has put it, the village now has to go to the town rather than the town to the village. These changes did not proceed without protest. The movement of small shopkeepers led by Pierre Poujade, which gained 52 parliamentary seats in the 1956 elections, was one important sign that the transformation of the rural economy, particularly in areas such as the small town in the Lot from which Poujade came, was not only causing a whole way of life to disappear but was also depriving some groups of their livelihood.

In the 1970s, however, a reverse movement began to occur. With the experience of two decades of rapid urbanization behind them, many people in France began to rediscover the virtues of country life, though they did so in the knowledge that the utilities (water, electricity, refuse collection, and so on) were now available in the country on much the same basis as in the towns, and that education, the mass media and the communications revolution had improved the level of rural integration into the national community. 'Neo-ruralism', as it was called, brought together critics of the consumer society, defenders of regional cultures, campaigners against nuclear power, ecological organizations and other similar groups. Very few individuals actually left the city to live in the country, but public attitudes towards the country certainly changed, and it was no longer seen as a repository of backwardness.

From 1975 onwards it can also be observed that smaller towns began to grow in population, while the very large cities lost population. Towns such as Nantes, Toulouse, Montpellier, Aix-en-Provence, Orléans, Lyons and La Rochelle all grew, while old industrial centres, such as Douai or Saint-Étienne, declined, as did the ports of Le Havre and Toulon. Paris also saw its population decline. At the same time, vast peri-urban, or 'rurbain', areas developed round many large cities, while migration towards the south coast, especially of elderly and retired people, continued inexorably.

These population movements generally reflect a search for 'quality of life', which was proving elusive in very large cities that had outgrown their capacity to provide such things as good, reasonably priced housing or good schools, together with the realization that the amenities offered by smaller centres of population and their transport links had improved out of all recognition. Small towns began to grow outwards into the countryside and the countryside itself, thanks to increased acquisition of second homes, ceased, at least in some areas, to be as deserted as it had been.

## Modernizing the cities

However, even if they own a second home in the country, or have elderly relatives still living there, most French people today live in towns, and much of the modernization effort of the post-war period has concerned the urban environment. Immediately after the Second World War, housing presented a huge problem. The influx of migrants from the country, the rising population and the dilapidation of the housing stock, partly the result of the War, all combined to create a crisis. Working-class families, in particular, were often extremely badly housed, and one study carried out in Paris in the early 1950s noted that the dwelling of a typical working-class family would have an average of only seven square metres per person. In addition, the existing housing stock was not well equipped, with only 10 per cent of dwellings having inside lavatories and only 60 per cent with running water. Private sector rents were controlled in an attempt to regulate the market and prevent speculation, but although this kept prices down its effect was to discourage private investment in housing. Poor conditions and shortages led to a series of protest movements in the years between 1947 and 1951, and these included squatting and social housing campaigns.

There was therefore an urgent need for the massive housing programme which was duly embarked upon in the 1950s. Writers on the topic tend to divide post-war urbanization programmes into three phases. First, from the mid-1950s, a huge, mainly state-financed, housing construction programme was launched, providing public housing for rent under the management of the

HLM organizations. The main planning instrument for new urban development was the ZUP (*zone à urbaniser en priorité*) which enabled the purchase of land for development, usually at agricultural use price. The ZUPs, which were generally on the outskirts of towns, were invariably developed into large housing estates, known as 'grands ensembles', which were frequently high-rise and system-built. Because of the nature of their architecture and design, and because the local authorities were often unable to finance the provision of adequate services such as transport and lighting, the *grands ensembles* were not well provided with amenities and were never desirable places to live. Intended for families with modest incomes, from the 1970s onwards they became the preserve of immigrants and the poor, so-called 'quartiers chauds' which were often the focus of considerable social unrest.

The second phase, which began in 1963, involved private capital much more widely in housing programmes, so that construction tended to be more closely linked with non-residential developments. The third phase began after the collapse of the property market in 1974, and it saw the end of large-scale projects, whether publicly or privately financed, but greater emphasis on the quality of life, the creation of open spaces and the development of medium-sized and smaller towns.

Taken together, the achievements of these three phases of development were spectacular: between 1945 and 1952 fewer than 100,000 houses were built every year, but by 1974 this had swelled to 500,000 annual completions. As a result of these massive building programmes, the improvement in amenities has been dramatic. Dwellings have become larger, with an average of four rooms by the mid-1990s, and virtually all are now provided with running water, inside lavatories, a bath or shower and heating. This huge, long-term investment means that more than one French family in two now lives in a new dwelling and, by the mid-1980s, more than 50 per cent of households were owner-occupiers or in the process of buying their house or flat. However, the rented sector in France, as in most of continental Europe, still accounts for nearly half of all housing and it is fairly evenly divided between public qnd privately owned property.

At the same time as the towns expanded into the countryside, the city centres changed in both appearance and function. Economic activity in cities shifted from manufacturing industry to services, necessitating the construction of large numbers of office blocks. Most of the city redevelopment projects undertaken in the 1960s and 1970s, such as La Part-Dieu in Lyons and La Défense in Paris, were made viable by office building, while other city centre projects included the creation of commercial centres and shopping malls. Perhaps the most symbolic illustration of the transformation of the city centres was the redevelopment of Les Halles, the old food market in central Paris that Zola had called 'le ventre de Paris', which was turned into a pedestrianized shopping centre and tourist attraction. But virtually all the old markets were moved out of the centres of towns, since changes in storage and transportation rendered city centre locations both impracticable and unnecessary.

From the late 1950s onwards, considerable sums were also invested in the renovation of old and historic areas in cities and in the cleaning and restoration of public buildings, the preservation of the historical environment and the development of tourist attractions. This is especially visible in Paris, where almost all public buildings have been cleaned and central districts like the Marais entirely restored, where a large number of new museums have been created, including the Musée d'Orsay in what was once a railway station, and where, since the mid-1970s, there has been a ban on the construction of high-rise buildings. Such projects have been accompanied by ambitious public building programmes such as the Arche de la Défense, the Opéra de la Bastille, the Centre Georges Pompidou, the transformation of La Villette, the construction of the Bibliothèque Nationale de France and the rehabilitation of the Bercy area containing the Ministry of Finances, so that these *grands travaux* amount to the largest scheme of urban transformation since Haussmann's in the mid-nineteenth century. But many other cities and towns have also restored old central districts, created pedestrian zones and routed traffic round their periphery in an attempt to preserve the quality of life and stimulate the local economy through tourism and other forms of business creation.

Alongside the renovation of city centres there has been significant investment in the improvement and extension of public transport. Many cities have built ring roads and rapid transit systems (*métro* networks in Lyons and Lille, trams in Grenoble) or improved existing systems (RER network and new *métro* lines in Paris), thus drawing into their employment sphere outlying towns whose inhabitants rely on good rail and road networks to get to work. In this way, towns like Orléans and Amiens, respectively 130 and 150 kilometres distant from Paris, have become commuter suburbs.

However, such developments, like Haussmann's before them, also exacerbate social divisions. The building of office blocks and the renovation of central districts as expensive residential areas are a form of zoning. The poor who, in the days before rapid public transport, needed to live near their place of work, have been all but expelled from the centre of large cities. In Paris, as the film *Chacun cherche son chat* suggests, gentrification has reached former working-class and immigrant districts like Belleville or La Goutte d'or, and even inner suburbs like Saint-Denis. Districts which once housed small factories are becoming residential, food shops have been transformed into fashion boutiques, while the former inhabitants of such districts have been relegated to the *grands ensembles*. The social stratification of the city thus appears to be an inevitable concomitant of its economic transformation and the rise of tourism.

## Regional development

Similar modernization was pursued at regional level. France essentially had a system of territorial administration inherited from the revolutionary and agrarian age.[1] In 1947, Jean-Claude Gravier published his influential study, *Paris et le désert français*, in which he criticized, among other things, the concentration of resources and amenities in the capital. As a result of his thinking and that of like-minded economists, attempts were made, from the mid-1960s onwards, to develop the regions through the creation of the *Délégation à l'aménagement du territoire et à l'action régionale* (DATAR). This was a body of technocrats which was designed to bypass local elites that were thought to be resistant to change and to encourage planned regional modernization through collaboration between the state (represented by the *préfet*) and private investors. They adopted a strategy of designating *métropoles d'équilibre*, regional cities which were to be developed as counter-weights to Paris: Strasbourg, Nancy–Metz, Lille–Roubaix–Tourcoing, Nantes–Saint Nazaire, Bordeaux, Toulouse, Lyons–Saint-Étienne, Marseilles–Aix, served by vastly improved transport links. In the same way as with town planning, little faith was placed in local participation in regional development, although several big cities like Marseilles, Bordeaux and, more recently, Lille, have had mayors, like Gaston Defferre, Jacques Chaban-Delmas or Pierre Mauroy, who have been extremely influential nationally as well as locally and who have been able to influence planning decisions in the way they wished. Thanks to Mauroy's influence, the Channel Tunnel rail link, for example, was routed through Lille, even though this diverged from existing railway routes, and it has played an important part in attracting new investment and new jobs to a region which had been badly hit by the decline of heavy industry.

The inadequacies of the technocratic system were recognized in the report *Vivre ensemble*, published by the Commission Guichard in 1975, which proposed grouping the *communes* into larger units, reducing the power of the *préfets* and enacting a degree of fiscal reform so as to give local authorities an adequate tax base. The *commune*, as an administrative unit with its elected *maire*, has resisted all proposals for reform and, indeed, experienced something of a revival in the countryside from the 1970s onwards. As a focus for community-based activities, the *communes* have been well placed to benefit from the rediscovery of country life, and their continued existence in large numbers (36,000 of them) remains a peculiarity of French local administration. However, the socialist government elected in 1981, influenced both by Gaston Defferre, who became the minister of the interior, and by Michel Rocard, who had argued in *Décoloniser la province* (1967) for devolution to the regions, undertook a far-reaching reform of regional government that reduced the power of the *préfet* and gave budgetary and planning power to elected regional assemblies. The impact of these planning authorities on land use and infrastructural developments has been a vital element stimulating regional economies and the developing of European links.

## Communications

France has the largest surface area of all western European and European Union countries, but it is one of the least densely populated and its population, unlike that of the UK or Germany, is not highly concentrated in large cities. The development and improvement of communications has therefore been even more vital in France than elsewhere, not just in stimulating economic growth but also in bringing about cultural change.

Of course, communications improved dramatically in the nineteenth century, with the advent of the railways and the construction of roads to serve them. Even so, as Eugen Weber reminds us,[2] many country areas remained virtually inaccessible right up to the beginning of the twentieth century, and it was not until the First World War that many men travelled more than a few kilometres beyond their native village. On the other hand, the inter-war years saw huge improvements in the roads and the rise of public and private motor transport as well as the beginnings of tourism based on the private motor car or bicycle, which was stimulated by the publication of road maps and the creation of the *Guide Michelin*. The Second World War, and particularly the arrival of the Allied armies and the retreat of the German forces, caused considerable damage to the communications infrastructure, which consequently underwent reconstruction and modernization in the 1950s and 1960s. Private car ownership also grew significantly, with manufacturers like Citroën and Renault developing popular models like the 2CV and the Dauphine, which had existed in prototype on the eve of the war and which were produced in large numbers for the expanding market. In fact, the rise in car ownership appears unstoppable since, by the end of the 1990s, three-quarters of households owned a car and a third owned more than one. After a very slow start in the 1950s, television also became a feature of most French homes during the 1960s. By the 1970s nearly 80 per cent of households owned at least a black and white television and by the 1990s total coverage was achieved. In this way, individuals were able both to travel more easily and to receive in their homes immediate news of national and international events in a way that would have been inconceivable in 1945.

The decades of the 1970s, 1980s and 1990s, however, witnessed a qualitative transformation of communications in France, initially based on the application of new technologies to existing systems and, more recently, on the electronic revolution. Today, as might be expected, 95 per cent of French households are equipped with the telephone. In 1970 the figure was a mere 11 per cent. Under President Giscard, telecommunications underwent a crash programme of expansion and modernization which not only eliminated lengthy waiting lists for telephones and created a network of public call boxes, but also introduced fully automated processes for national and international calls. Other western countries similarly modernized their telecommunications systems in the 1970s and 1980s, but in France the process was both exceptionally rapid and extremely thoroughgoing. In 1970 France was very like East Germany in 1989, and its backwardness created a similar hindrance to economic expansion. By the end of the decade, however, it had acquired one of the most advanced telecommunications systems in the world. At the same time as upgrading its network, France also introduced the *Minitel*, a home computer which offers access to a large range of interactive services, through the telecommunications system, to all telephone subscribers. Paradoxically, the success of this service, which was revolutionary in its time, initially helped to delay widespread use of the internet in France [see Text 3.3].

The rail network has undergone a similar qualitative transformation with the TGV. The development of this high-speed train dates back to the 1960s, but it was given impetus by the oil crisis of 1973, which made the attempt to attract passengers from air to rail both urgent and more economically attractive. The first route, Paris–Lyons, was introduced in 1981 and was served by a new, purpose-built line as well as new locomotives, whereas many subsequently opened routes simply run high-speed trains on existing track. The TGV network now serves all the major cities in France and is gradually being extended to smaller cities as well, a development which will be helped by the introduction of tilting trains which allow higher speeds to be reached on conventional track; it has, in most cases, halved travelling times between Paris and other centres (Paris–Lyons was reduced from over four hours to two hours), making day trips by rail possible to most major destinations. Yet, far from encouraging decentralization, the effect has often been to reinforce the dominance of Paris in terms both of business transactions and of residence. The introduction of the TGV Atlantique, for example, means that Nantes is only two hours away from Paris, while Le Mans has become a suburb of the capital. Indeed, most of the first two decades of the TGV programme facilitated travel up and down France rather than across it and it was only in the late 1990s that investment in cross-country links became a priority.

The TGV also acquired a European dimension, even though this did not occur without opposition, in linking France into the two major European poles of economic development, the London–Milan axis which passes through Lille (but bypasses Paris) and the Mediterranean axis stretching from Barcelona to Genoa through Perpignan and Montpellier. In both cases, new TGV tracks have been constructed providing communication routes which to some extent form a counter-weight to the centripetal pull of the capital city, while at the same time, or so the argument runs, fostering European integration. Further European connexions, along the Rhône–Rhine corridor and between Lyons and Turin, are also planned [see Text 3.4].

Thus, in the space of a mere two decades, the individual's relationship to, and perception of, space has been profoundly transformed in France through greater possibilities for rapid transit combined with highly developed *in situ* communications, enabling information sources from throughout the world to be much more easily accessed. The accompanying cultural revolution is at least as great as that brought about by the railways in the nineteenth century. The integrated high-speed transport system points to the extent to which the concerns of the 1960s now seem irrelevant. It is now extremely easy to travel the length if not the breadth of the country, while new road and rail links facilitate communication between France and its geographical neighbours, and other communications systems have been massively modernized and improved. The psychological impact of such changes is hard to over-state.

# Social structure of post-war France

## Changes in social structure

The rural exodus is only one aspect of the profound modification in the social structure of France which has taken place in the last hundred years. Until the First World War, French society divided broadly into three main groups, *bourgeois, ouvriers* and *paysans*. These were not simply groups based on occupation and income, which could sometimes vary widely within each category, but groups which experienced radically different ways of life.

Of these groups the *paysans* were numerically the most significant, accounting for half the work-force. As has been recalled above, at least until the last quarter of the nineteenth century much of the countryside was inaccessible, communications were extremely poor, and the agents of the state sometimes found difficulties in administering the law. Country people sometimes did not understand the French language, let alone speak it. Although the advent of the railways, universal primary education and conscription all helped to open up the countryside to outside influences and to encourage the spread of a more national culture, it remains the case that many *paysans* lived in a world apart at least until 1914. The second significant grouping was the *ouvriers* or industrial workers, whose ranks swelled from about 31 per cent of the work-force in 1901 to about 38 per cent in 1936, an increase which reflected the progress of industrialization. Although they almost invariably lived in towns, *ouvriers* had a way of life and a culture almost as completely separate as that of the *paysans*; a way of life which was maintained through social, political and recreational institutions such as the trade unions and the Communist Party. The *bourgeoisie*, on the other hand, covered a range of socio-professional groups from office workers (*employés*) to members of the professions (*professions libérales*), some of whom were highly educated and some of whom were not, some of whom owned businesses or were self-employed and some of whom were wage-earners, some of whom were wealthy and some of whom were not.

The changes wrought to this very roughly drawn picture in the post-war period have been of two kinds. First, the number of *paysans* has declined progressively so that by the late 1990s they represented under 3 per cent of the work-force. Where have they all gone? Many joined the ranks of the *ouvriers*, whose numbers stood at about 35 per cent of the work-force in 1946 and rose to about 38 per cent in the mid-1970s, before falling to about 26 per cent by the end of the 1990s. But this does not tell the whole story. In the post-war period the *nature* of work has also altered. The second dramatic change has been the massive expansion in wage-earners in all social categories, accompanied by a decline in the number of self-employed artisans and small shopkeepers, so that now about four-fifths of the work-force is composed of *salariés*, that is people employed by some other person or organization. The changes in the social structure of France since the war are comparable to those observed in other countries where there has been a similar decline in the peasantry, followed by a decline in the traditional working class and an expansion in white-collar jobs. Where France differs, however, is in the spectacular rapidity of the decline in the numbers of people working on the land in the post-war period.

All social categorization, as Pierre Rosanvallon reminds us, is to some extent arbitrary,[3] and despite the increasing sophistication of statistical data it is often contentious and subjective. All those who write on French social structure are at pains to emphasize that the terms commonly employed in social classification no longer mean what they meant 50 years ago. Much discussion has attached, for example, to the definition of an *ouvrier*. In addition, individuals now refer to themselves and others using the language of statistics rather than the older terms. This is clearest in the case of the *paysan* who, these days, is called an *agriculteur* and who is 'un producteur urbanisé qui vit à la campagne, regarde la télévision, et fait ses comptes, comme un cadre ou un commerçant des villes'.[4] But it is also true of the category of *employé* which includes a range of white-collar jobs, and especially that of *cadre*, which covers a wide range of managerial jobs and has no real equivalent in Anglo-American terminology.

Another difficulty encountered in describing the social structure of France is that many commentators are consciously or unconsciously nostalgic about the disappearance of ways of life which attached to particular social categories. This is to some extent true of the *paysans* – a throwback, perhaps, to the days when the country relied for its defence on a peasant army – and the view is sometimes expressed that the country way of life is somehow more authentic and worthwhile than that of the city. But it is even more true of the traditional working class, that is, manual workers in manufacturing industry. Because Marx designated the proletariat as the actor of the revolution, some social scientists have been reluctant to come to terms with the transformations in, and indeed the disappearance of, the traditional working class, despite obvious economic changes: 'Toucher au concept de classe ouvrière,' writes Rosanvallon, 'c'est en fait toucher à la notion traditionnelle de révolution . . . En évitant de s'interroger sur les mutations du monde ouvrier, on pense ainsi faire l'économie d'une réévaluation de l'idée même de révolution.'[5]

The decline of the traditional working class is indisputable. Until the 1960s the working class was identifiable as a distinct group within French society which was both numerically large and conscious of its own politics and culture which were different and separate from those of other classes or social strata. From the mid-1930s to the mid-1950s, working-class consciousness and solidarity were reinforced by the stability of employment in heavy industry, the transmission of jobs from father to son, and by the cohesion created by political and social struggles such as those in 1936 and 1947–8, and were supported by much higher trade union membership than exists today. Thus when, in the early 1950s, Chombart de Lauwe began his study of working-class families in Paris, he found 'un mode de pensée différent de celui auquel sont habitués les intellectuels et une forme d'intelligence qui faisait mon admiration, et que ne soupçonnaient même pas les milieux bourgeois'.[6] But from the 1960s onwards the working population underwent massive restructuring. The growth of the tertiary sector and the service industries, which required a work-force with less physical strength and new skills, a work-force which was indeed often female, created what Serge Mallet called a 'nouvelle classe ouvrière'.

The question, for many, was whether this new working class would behave, politically, as the traditional working class had done. Would it, in other words, be a 'real' working class or would these workers in new industries simply be assimilated into the great mass of the middle classes and lose or abandon their working-class characteristics? The changes in the composition of the work-force have given rise to a fascinating debate about values and about 'moyennisation', or the incorporation of the working class into the middle classes, based on research which probes behind the analysis of social structure in terms of socio-professional groups to look at such things as taste, lifestyle and cultural values, and which has suggested, for example, that income is by no means the only determinant of status and that groups of widely varying income may have the same 'cultural capital' and hence the same cultural values, and vice versa [see Text 3.5].

One of the questions that such studies are designed to answer is whether mobility has increased in post-war French society and whether society has become more or less equal. In other words, have the profound social changes we have referred to been matched by a transformation in individual expectations and opportunities? Raymond Boudon has pointed out that modern industrial societies have, for the most part, ironed out political and legal inequalities, but that inequalities of opportunity have been very resistant to change:

> L'inégalité des chances, chances scolaires et chances socio-professionnelles, est donc, avec les inégalités économiques, la seule forme d'inégalité qui ne paraisse pas affectée de façon sensible par le développement des sociétés industrielles. Un fils d'ouvrier aura certainement un niveau de vie supérieur à celui de son père. Mais ses chances d'accéder à l'enseignement supérieur, comparées à celles du fils de cadre supérieur, ne seront guère plus élevées qu'à la génération de son père. Et ses chances d'accéder à une catégorie sociale supérieure à celui de son père seront du même ordre de grandeur que celles qu'avait son père lui-même.[7]

Although these lines were written over a quarter of a century ago, there is little evidence that the situation they describe has altered, except that disparities in income have widened. This means that, while virtually everyone in France has become richer and the general standard of living has risen, and while it is clear that society has become much less obviously hierarchical and rigid, social mobility is not as great as might have been hoped or expected. Only in one respect has there been significant social mobility in France when compared with, say, Great Britain or Sweden, and it is to be attributed to the rural exodus. Many sons and daughters of farmers did not become farmers in their turn but became *ouvriers* or *employés*, but with the completion of the rural exodus even this form of mobility has disappeared.

Boudon's remarks help to explain the enormous political and ideological investment modern industrial societies place in their education systems which are supposed to function as the agents of equal opportunities. This is why the pages which follow devote considerable attention to the education system in

France. But in asking whether sons will follow fathers' occupations and, if not, whether the sons' occupations will reflect a rise or fall in social status, mobility studies can seem extremely outdated. Are there not other determinants of status, such as race, sex and age, which are perhaps as important, or more important than education and class? As Yannick Lemel emphasizes, many of the features that anthropologists consider central to the study of non-industrial societies have, at least until very recently, been ignored or minimized by social scientists studying industrial societies: 'Les sociologues n'échappent pas aux mouvements généraux de l'opinion qui, d'une différence jusqu'alors "naturelle" font à un moment donné une inégalité intolérable.'[8] We shall therefore proceed to take a closer look at some of the social groups as defined by sex, race and age, which have been the focus of social change in the post-war period, and at the attempts to identify and eliminate the inequalities from which they suffer.

## Women

Since 1945 there has been a revolution in the status of women in France which is closely related to their new economic freedom and their ability to control their own fertility. It is a revolution which has been assisted by and is reflected in the reform of electoral, family and property law and in the changing nature of women's work, and it may be summed up in the different reactions to two events of significance: in 1949, when Simone de Beauvoir published her now celebrated study of women, *Le deuxième sexe*, she was condemned as an existentialist pornographer; but in 1974, when the newly elected President Giscard d'Estaing created the first *Secrétariat à la condition féminine*, he was hailed as an enlightened progressive.

In order to understand the changes it is important to realize that the position of women before 1945 was better than is sometimes suggested.[9] Although the *Code civil* of 1804 did not recognize women as having civil status or legal capacity, the Third Republic brought about progressive improvements, particularly as far as single women and widows were concerned. French women gained the right to education alongside men, they were admitted to the *baccalauréat* and to university degrees, including those of the medical schools, and a number of women's educational institutions were created. The combined effect of increased educational opportunities and a shortage of male labour after the First World War meant that women were able to gain employment in the public sector as doctors, teachers, civil servants and the like. In addition, in a society still composed of large numbers of farmers and small family businesses, there was a strong tradition of wives working alongside husbands. Indeed, not only were women well represented in the labour force but, contrary to popular belief, there were actually more women at work in 1921 than in 1975.[10] Moreover, French legislation was particularly generous in protecting the rights of working women through measures such as maternity leave, which was first introduced as early as 1909. In some respects, therefore, French women were socially and economically better served than their Anglo-American counterparts, who suffered grievously from the economic conditions of the 1930s and from legislation discriminating against married women. French women were needed in the labour force and were accordingly better treated.

However, it was not until after the Second World War that French women gained full citizenship. Although there had been (unelected) women ministers in Léon Blum's Popular Front government in 1936, women voted and stood for election to the National Assembly for the first time in 1945, while the constitution of 1946 stated the principle of equality between men and women. The earlier resistance to giving women the vote in France is usually attributed to the fact that women were held to be more conservative than men, and more likely to support the Catholic church and the anti-republican parties. They would, it was often said, 'voter curé'. This belief was held simultaneously with another, which contradicted it, namely that women would not vote independently but would always follow their husbands in their choice of whom to vote for. These theses were not confirmed by the elections to the Constituant Assembly of 1945, but thereafter until 1974 they would appear to have been borne out in practice.

However, as Janine Mossuz-Lavau and Mariette Sineau have shown, there is a clear correlation between education and work on the one hand, and voting behaviour on the other.[11] As women massively entered higher education in the 1960s, and proceeded from there into the paid labour force, so they moved progressively away from non-participation to electoral involvement: the link between women and conservatism was broken, with the Socialist Party as the ultimate beneficiary. This trend was not lost on politicians and, since Giscard d'Estaing's election in 1974, successive presidents and prime ministers have demonstrated their appreciation of the link between gender and politics by placing 'women's issues' high on their list of priorities. However, although women obtained the vote in 1945 they were not very active in politics. Despite the proportional representation regimes of the Fourth Republic, which might have been expected to assist women candidates, the percentage of women elected to the National Assembly declined from 5.4 per cent in 1951 to only 1.6 per cent in 1973, and did not climb back to the 1951 level until 1981. Even at the 1997 general election only 10 per cent of the *députés* returned to the National Assembly were women, making France one of the most backward countries in the EU in this regard. It was not until Mitterrand appointed Édith Cresson Minister of Agriculture in 1981 that women politicians succeeded in breaking out of the traditional areas of social affairs where they tended to be congregated if they were at all active in politics.

The status of women has also been changed by a series of legal measures affecting the rights of married women to hold property and to have responsibility for their children. The provisions of the Napoleonic Code were gradually abandoned so as to create legal equality for women within marriage. Single women and widows had already been emancipated from the Napoleonic Code which had treated them as minors for the purposes of property owning, but married women, who were the vast majority of women, were not able, until 1965, to manage their own property or, until 1970, to exercise legal authority over their children. Their legal status could lead to considerable difficulties.

For example, a woman could not enrol her child in a school without the father's consent, could not obtain a passport for her child, could not have a bank account without her husband's consent, or run a household without her husband agreeing to how money was spent.

It is easy to imagine the difficulties this caused at times of social upheaval or in the case of disputes between parents. In addition, it had the unfortunate effect of distinguishing between legitimate children, over whom paternal authority was exercised, and illegitimate children, for whom the mother was responsible. From 1965 onwards, the commonest form of marital regime, that is, the one applicable to couples who married without a contract, became one in which each partner managed his or her own property, and in which this property is distinguished from that acquired after marriage (known as the *régime de communauté réduite aux acquêts*). Even so, it was not until 1985 that married women gained the equal right to manage the marital estate. As far as children are concerned, an Act of 1970 substituted the notion of 'autorité parentale' for 'autorité paternelle', thus making the parents equally responsible for their children. In this way married women gained most of the legal and financial freedoms already accorded to those who were not married and saw their status within the family enhanced.

These legislative measures form the backdrop against which the radical changes of the last three decades have taken place. Not all the changes are material (many are purely symbolic) but taken together they have profoundly affected the lives of women throughout France. From the middle of the 1960s onwards large numbers of women began to enter higher education, while prestigious educational institutions, such as the École Polytechnique and the École Normale Supérieure, became coeducational in the 1970s. Women were able to control their own fertility as a result of the legalization of contraception in 1967 and abortion in 1975. Above all, women entered the work-force in ever larger numbers, filling many of the new jobs created by the rapidly expanding tertiary sector. To some extent women competed directly with men for jobs – this was undoubtedly the case for the best qualified. But the overall trend suggests that the rise in women's employment was a response to shifts in the labour market and, while the active population has continued to rise, the relative proportion of men and women who work has altered. Thus among French people aged over 55, for example, about 47 per cent of women are working but only 33 per cent of men. In other words, the change in women's social status is closely linked with deindustrialization, the rise of the service sector and the information society. Today over 80 per cent of women between the ages of 25 and 50 work, 75 per cent of married women with one child work, as do 68 per cent of those with two children. Indeed, it is only among women who have three or more children that the rate of employment drops below 40 per cent.

Nor is part-time working, which concerns some 24 per cent of working women, as highly developed among women in France as it is among those in Germany or the UK (respectively 30 and 45 per cent). Although women working is no novelty in France, what is new is the huge presence of middle and lower middle-class women in the salaried labour force, working essentially in offices rather than on farms or in small family businesses. The perception of women has changed accordingly and, increasingly, a woman's status is determined not by whom she marries, as in the past, but by her job. Thus, for the last three decades, women in France have benefited from considerably increased education and employment opportunities and from the ability to control their own fertility, and these are changes which have undoubtedly led to much greater social and economic freedom.

Have these changes also created different forms of social organization and a radically different perception of women in society? Since the 1970s women's issues have been in the forefront of both official politics and extra-parliamentary groups. The contemporary women's movement was born out of the events of May 1968 and took shape as the *Mouvement de libération des femmes* (MLF). At the same time, a powerful single-issue campaign was mounted through a group known as the *Mouvement pour la libération de l'avortement et de la contraception* (MLAC), supported by the *Association Choisir*. The campaign reached its zenith at the *Procès de Bobigny*, the trial and subsequent acquittal of the mother of a fifteen-year-old girl who had procured an illegal abortion for her daughter who had been raped. Once abortion had been legalized in 1975, the cement which held the various women's groups together disintegrated. The MLF did not survive as an umbrella organization but rapidly splintered into a number of warring groups, each of which had a particular emphasis and political position. However, the intellectual excitement generated by the women's movement has continued unabated, with the publication of numerous essays and scholarly works debating the issues of femininity and difference and with 'women's issues' regularly forming topics of public debate.

As far as official politics is concerned, 1974 saw the creation of the first government department devoted entirely to women's questions, the *Secrétariat à la condition féminine*, headed by the journalist Françoise Giroud. The department had no budget, so that its proposals, published as *Cent mesures pour les femmes*, were frequently symbolic. Even so, they were often very important. For example, a woman's right not to call herself by her husband's name together with a husband's right to call himself by his wife's name are obvious symbols in any challenge to patriarchy. The tradition of a government department devoted to women's affairs was continued with the election of a socialist government in 1981, when Yvette Roudy became *Ministre aux droits de la femme*. Several important measures were enacted under this administration, including the provision for abortion to be reimbursed under the social security system (making it free), together with legislation guaranteeing equal pay for work of equal value. There were also less successful campaigns which attempted to outlaw sexism in the media and to encourage the use of contraception.

In addition, President Mitterrand was always conscious of the importance of the women's vote to the electoral success of the Socialist Party and promoted women outside the normal spheres of social policy and women's affairs. In the 1981 government Édith Cresson was appointed Minister of Agriculture, which did not go down well with the farming community who believed that the appointment of a woman demonstrated the Socialists' contempt for their sector. She subsequently served as Minister of Trade (1983) and Minister of European Affairs (1988) and, briefly, as prime minister (1991), before being nominated, by Mitterrand, to the European Commission. Likewise, Élisabeth Guigou served under Mitterrand as Minister of European Affairs. The first Juppé government of 1995 had a large number of women in junior positions, while the 1997 Jospin government not only had a woman, Martine Aubry, as its second in command, but appointed two further women, Guigou and the Green Party's Dominique Voynet, to Justice and Environment, respectively, as well as many women to junior ministerial posts. Meanwhile, in December 1999 Michèle Alliot-Marie was elected as the first woman to head the RPR, strongly increasing the likelihood that she will, at some later date, become prime minister.

The number of women elected to local and regional authorities and to the European Parliament also increased significantly during the 1990s, but from a very low base. Thus by the end of that decade nearly 20 per cent of *conseillers municipaux*, 12 per cent of *conseillers régionaux* and 5 per cent of members of *conseils généraux* were women, but 30 per cent of French deputies to the European Parliament were women, a figure which suggests that election by proportional representation now favours them. Indeed, after the 1999 European elections, French MEP Nicole Fontane was elected President of the European Parliament. None of the branches of the civil service, except education and the legal services, contained more than 15 per cent of women in senior positions at the end of the 1990s, a figure which nevertheless represented a doubling of the numbers in such posts since the beginning of the 1980s [see Text 3.6].

Three decades of the women's movement, combined with three decades when official politics has devoted considerable attention to the promotion of women, have thus yielded only mixed results. Newspapers and magazines frequently talk of 'post-feminism', as though women had achieved equality with men and as though that chapter of social history was closed. Yet if one considers the purely material gains, the achievements have been patchy, often despite the existence of legislation. Although it was in 1972 that the principle of 'à travail égal, salaire égal' was embodied in legislation, women still earn considerably less than men and this is true at both ends of the salary spectrum. With equivalent qualifications a male manager is likely to earn up to 25 per cent more than a female manager, while an extraordinary 75 per cent of those who earn only the SMIC are women. Women are more highly represented than men in the part-time and temporary jobs that burgeoned in the 1980s and 1990s, and this is not necessarily by choice. In addition, despite the *loi Roudy* mentioned above, there is considerable evidence that two distinct labour markets have developed, each based on gender, and this in turn has had the effect of depressing women's wages and status.

Although much media space has been devoted to the sensitive, caring 'new man', and although there have undoubtedly been some changes in attitude among the generations of men who grew up in the late 1960s and after, nevertheless most surveys show that men have far more time to devote to hobbies and leisure interests than do women, and that most working women – that is, over 80 per cent of the female population – perform 'la double journée', taking responsibility for the house and children as well as for their jobs. Élisabeth Badinter has suggested that differentiation on the basis of gender is disappearing, and this is certainly apparent in the domains of fashion and taste. But surveys do not, or not yet, show that such a change has significantly affected the domestic or professional lives of ordinary men and women in France.[12]

There are also deep ideological divisions among influential women about the meaning of 'equality' which is not recognized as an objective by many French feminists, such as Luce Irigaray or Hélène Cixous, who stress the importance of 'différence'. Such disagreements were publicly aired early in 1999 when the Jospin government, in an attempt to ensure that a greater proportion of women would be selected as candidates for election to the National Assembly and other elective offices, proposed an amendment to the constitution in order to enshrine 'l'égal accès des hommes et des femmes aux mandats électoraux et aux fonctions électives', otherwise known as 'la parité'. Some feminists like Élisabeth Badinter attacked the proposal both as a form of essentialism, based on a belief in 'natural' differences between men and women against which feminists had been battling for decades, and as a breach of the principles of the constitution which is designed to ensure equality irrespective of sex [see Text 3.7].

Conversely, the women members of the Jospin government, as well as philosophers such as Sylviane Agacinski (who is Jospin's wife), argued that it was legitimate to refer to sexual difference within the constitution since, unlike others, it is a 'universal difference', and they turned the universalist argument round by suggesting that, in the past, the universalist principle had been used specifically to exclude women from political life. This fascinating debate illustrated the extent to which sexual equality had become a mainstream concern, since all the participants, with the exception of a few right-wing members of the Senate, agreed on the ends to be achieved, namely greater numbers of women holding elective office. However, it also revealed deep philosphical and ideological differences among women, and many who might be considered feminists (even though some, like Badinter, would challenge the term), opposed the measure precisely in the name of equality. In doing so they clarified the ways in which the women's movement in France, or some parts of it, were often more interested in principles than in practice and how it had, sometimes deliberately, diverged from women's movements in other western countries and especially in the United States.

## Immigrants

During the 1980s and 1990s immigration became a more significant social, cultural and political issue in France. Expressions of racism and xenophobia became frequent; one political party, the *Front national*, based its electoral appeal almost exclusively on an anti-immigrant platform; another, the RPR, adopted a repressive stance towards immigration. Whereas the previous assumption had always been that immigrants would integrate into French society, now, even among those who were sympathetic to immigrants, concern was expressed at their apparent cultural differences and their ability or otherwise to fit into French society.

For more than a century and a half, France has attracted large numbers of immigrants. Historically, this was for both political and economic reasons. The religious tolerance introduced after the 1789 Revolution, which was particularly welcome to Jews and Protestants, undoubtedly helped to establish France as a country which traditionally offered asylum to victims of persecution elsewhere. From the economic point of view, France has needed to increase its labour force at various points in its history to make good the shortfall created by a comparatively low birthrate or the losses caused by war. The territorial acquisitions of the nineteenth and twentieth centuries – Alsace, Lorraine, Nice and its surrounding area, Algeria – combined with the active encouragement of immigration, have all contributed to the mixed origin of the French population. Indeed, it has been estimated that one French person in four has at least one grandparent born outside France. In this respect, therefore, France is comparable to the United States, and French commentators have not hesitated to refer to 'le creuset français' by analogy with the American example, but is very different in experiences and practices from other European countries, such as the UK, Ireland, Italy, Greece or Portugal, with their strong traditions of emigration [see Text 3.8].

Economic immigration occurred in three main waves. The first, at the end of the nineteenth century, coincided with the industrialization of France. Most of the immigrants were Belgian or Italian and they made up something over 3 per cent of the population. A second, much larger, wave occurred throughout the 1920s, reaching a peak in 1931. It was made necessary by the acute labour shortage created by the losses of the First World War and was encouraged and organized by both the state and the employers. Russians, Poles and North Africans joined the Belgians and Italians, to form about 6 per cent of the population, while towards the end of the 1930s there were an increasing number of political refugees, especially from Spain and Germany.

The situation in 1945 was similar to that in the 1920s. Reconstruction and economic growth meant that France, like other European countries, was short of labour and welcomed immigrants, and that the government adopted a policy of deliberately encouraging immigration through the *Office national de l'immigration* (ONI). Initially, the post-war immigrants came mainly from Europe, especially from Italy and Portugal, but increasingly Africa replaced Europe as their major source and Algerians, especially, became much more numerous. By the end of the 1980s non-European immigration, including substantial numbers of refugees from South-East Asia and from sub-Saharan Africa, was much more significant than European immigration, even though the total number of immigrants of European origin remained larger than the total number of immigrants of African and Asian origin. Today there are thought to be something over four million immigrants in France, representing approximately 7.4 per cent of the population. However, the term 'immigrés', in its popular usage, covers groups of people who are very diverse both in their country of origin, as we have seen, but also in their socio-professional and civil status. In particular, it is often used to refer to the children of immigrants who are born in France, hold French nationality and have not migrated from any other country. Conversely, the term is frequently not used of citizens of other European countries who have settled in France to whom it should, strictly speaking, also refer.

Immigration became a significant socio-political issue in 1974. The reasons include the recession created by the oil crisis of 1973 which caused unemployment to rise sharply, changing patterns of urbanization created by the boom of the 1960s, and the information technology revolution which decreased the need for unskilled workers. But it was also the result of changes in the pattern of immigration. Between 1965 and 1973 there were far more immigrants of non-European than of European origin, and the sudden and obvious presence of large numbers of Africans and Asians in French cities provoked outbursts of racism. At the same time, it became clear that, whereas many of the immigrants of the 1950s and 1960s were 'guest-workers', staying in France only as long as it took to save enough money to establish themselves and their families comfortably 'at home', the immigrants of the 1970s and after came to France to settle, bringing their families with them, and having children in France. Thus, from the 1970s onwards, what continued to be referred to as the 'immigrant' problem in fact became a problem of integrating into French society disparate groups of people who had little or no intention of going anywhere else and who, though they might not technically hold French nationality, were at least in some sense French.

## The politics of immigration

President Giscard d'Estaing took steps to reverse the French tradition of welcoming immigrants with the introduction of immigration controls in 1974 and the provision of an *aide au retour* in 1977. These were short-term measures which succeeded in slowing down new arrivals (although the economic crisis and consequent lack of jobs might have stemmed the flow in any case), but not in encouraging many people to leave France. Indeed, by the time it was abolished in 1981, just short of 100,000 people had taken advantage of the *aide au retour* and it is not known how many of those would have left France in any case. In 1981 the socialist government took a different approach. It gave legal status to illegal immigrants who were in employment, a measure which affected some 130,000 people, and at the same time abolished the *aide au retour*. But it also took a series of steps aimed at assisting immigrants to integrate into French society better than they had done previously.

However, the electoral successes of the *Front national* in 1983 changed the approach of all the political parties towards immigration and ensured that for nearly two decades social problems would be seen through what one commentator called 'le prisme déformant de l'immigration' [see Text 3.9].[13] The moral panic caused by the rise of the *Front national*, increasing unemployment and its associated social ills, and François Mitterrand's cynical use of the immigration question to divide his opponents, led to the enactment of a series of repressive laws designed to limit immigration, restrict immigrants' right to acquire French nationality, encourage immigrants to return home and allow the rapid expulsion of illegal immigrants and bogus asylum seekers. The Chirac government presented a bill to parliament in October 1986 proposing to reform the Code of Nationality. Among other things, the bill proposed the abolition of the so-called *jus soli*, the right of all children of foreign parents born in France and having resided in France for five years to acquire French nationality. Instead, the proposal was to require such people to request nationality, a request which could be refused if, for example, the applicant had served a prison sentence.

The bill caused an outcry which led to its withdrawal and the establishment of a *Commission de la nationalité* under the chairmanship of Marceau Long, the recommendations of which, published in 1988, were intended to form the basis for future policy and legislation. The 1986 *loi Pasqua* also modified, in the restrictive sense, the conditions under which foreigners could enter and reside in France and introduced a visa requirement for all those who were not citizens of what was then the European Community. When the Socialists again returned to office in 1988, they did so on a platform promising measures to clamp down on illegal immigration as well as to encourage the better integration of existing immigrants, but once again the right-wing government elected in March 1993 promised to 'maîtriser l'immigration' and, with the second *loi Pasqua* enacted that year, made the acquisition of residence permits much more difficult; it also returned to the restrictions on nationality first proposed in the mid-1980s. The 1993 *loi Pasqua* also created a category of 'sans papiers' composed of people who could neither be legally expelled nor legally given permission to reside in France. In the summer of 1996 some of these people began a hunger strike and occupied the Église Saint-Bernard in Paris. Their case received wide media coverage as well as expressions of support from prominent individuals, and when they were eventually evicted in August, public opinion was shocked by the pictures of the police breaking down the church door with axes and women with children being dragged out.

However, the culmination of the right-wing attack on immigration was embodied in the *loi Debré* enacted in 1996 in the dying days of the Juppé government. Among other measures, this law required French people who had 'foreigners' staying with them to notify the police when such foreigners departed, and it naturally provoked widespread protests. The *loi Debré* was drafted in order to give the government the power to carry out the expulsion of such people legally, but its provisions became a battleground in the general election campaign which followed in the Spring of 1997.

Once in office, the Jospin government attempted to achieve a left–right consensus on immigration questions. It set up commissions on nationality and immigration under the chairmanship of Patrick Weil, the recommendations of which were embodied in the revised *Code de la nationalité* and the *loi Chevènement* concerning immigration. It broke new ground not just in repudiating Pasqua's 'immigration zéro' slogan but in stating publicly that such an aim was neither possible nor desirable, while at the same time declaring that the French nation was 'un alliage d'autant plus fort que ses composants [sont] divers et nombreux'.[14] The 1998 *loi Chevènement* combined tolerance with repression by extending the right to asylum, simplifying immigration formalities and recognizing the need for families to come together, at the same time as reinforcing

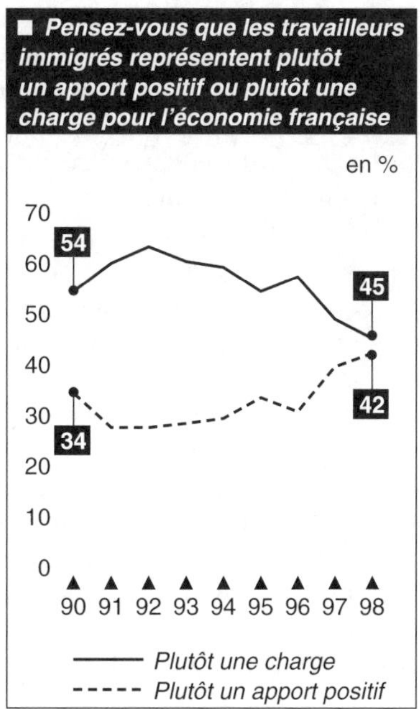


**Figure 3.1 Growing tolerance of immigration**
*Source*: *Le Monde*, 25 March 1999.

provisions for the expulsion of illegal immigrants. The new *Code de la nationalité* reinstated the *jus soli*, so that all children born in France to foreign parents would automatically acquire French nationality at the age of 18, and took measures to deal with the problem of the *sans papiers*.

As can be seen, therefore, since 1983 when the question of immigration first became politically controversial, policy has oscillated between the social concerns of the left and the need for the parties of the right to appeal to the *Front national* electorate, while avoiding overt racism. All parties, however, remain committed to a policy which places strict limits on the number of immigrants entering France. Their commitment has been further reinforced by recent history. The unification of Germany, the opening up of the Eastern bloc countries and the disintegration of the Soviet Union have all given western politicians cause to expect large waves of migration from the east to the west of Europe. Although Germany would be a first destination for most migrants, France, with its traditions of immigration, its relatively buoyant economy and its tradition of cultural and political links with the former Warsaw Pact countries, is also likely to be a preferred destination. In addition, France, like Italy, fears mass immigration from North Africa where it is clear that job creation cannot keep pace with population growth, and where the pressure for young people to emigrate will grow. In this context Islamic fundamentalism, particularly in countries like Algeria where it flourished in the early 1990s, is felt to pose a particular threat.

A widely remarked expression of such fears came from the former President Giscard d'Estaing who, in a controversial interview in the *Figaro Magazine* in 1991, claimed to be voicing commonly held views when he said: 'Le type de problème auquel nous aurons à faire face se déplace de celui de *l'immigration* ("arrivée d'étrangers désireux de s'installer dans un pays") vers celui de *l'invasion* ("action d'entrer, de se répandre soudainement").'[15] The statement caused considerable protest, especially since the positions expressed in it were apparently more extreme than those revealed by the accompanying poll, which certainly showed the French to be very concerned by immigration but also keen to treat legal immigrants no differently from French people; but it was probably typical not just of the views of most right-wing politicians but also of what they considered the views of their electorate to be. However, by the end of the decade there was a perceptible change in official and in public opinion. There were considerable movements of sympathy for refugees and asylum seekers from Kosovo; the Palme d'or at the 1999 Cannes film festival was awarded to *La Promesse*, a Belgian film which revealed the misery of illegal immigrants and their ruthless exploitation by organized gangs; and, following the prime minister's lead, Minister of the Interior Jean-Pierre Chevènement described his department's priorities as the effective integration of immigrants rather than the policing of the frontiers.

## Immigrant communities in French society

There is, as we have seen, no single immigrant community in France, but a variety of communities of more or less recent origin more or less well integrated into French society. However, post-war immigration is an urban phenomenon. Most immigrants are to be found concentrated in three regions – the Ile-de-France, Rhône-Alpes and the Bouches-du-Rhône, around the major cities of Paris, Marseilles and Lyons – and in these areas the concentration of immigrants is much higher than the 7.4 per cent to be found overall in France. About 15 per cent of the population of the Paris region, for example, is made up of immigrants, but only about 3 per cent of the rural population. Some of the immigrant communities have other characteristics which serve to differentiate them from the French population. In the period between 1945 and 1974, the typical immigrant was a young man, often from a rural background, who came to France to work for relatively short periods of time, but who was not accompanied by a family. After restrictive measures were introduced in 1974, the nature of immigration changed. Now it was essentially composed of members of families of existing immigrants, students and refugees especially from Asia and Africa, and of individuals who were likely to come from cities rather than the countryside and who were better educated than earlier generations of immigrants. There are noticeable differences in family size between non-European immigrants and European immigrants, the structure of the age pyramid is different among immigrant groups, and the birth rate is higher than among people born in France.

North African immigrants score noticeably worse than other immigrant groups and than French people across a range of socio-economic indicators: they do less well at school, they are less well trained and they are more likely to be unemployed.[16] Such features, along with lifestyle differences, ignorance of the French language and maintenance of traditional customs, have certainly made some of the immigrant communities more visible and are probably behind the sporadic outbursts of racism which have occurred in French towns in such episodes as protests against the construction of mosques. In addition, public policy has sometimes had the perverse effect of reinforcing cultural differences which might otherwise disappear rapidly. Thus Michèle Tribalat points out that immigration retrictions have created a 'marriage market' among certain immigrant groups whereby the French daughter of immigrant parents is 'sold' for a dowry to a man 'back home' who wishes to settle in France. Restrictive policies thus 'joue[nt] contre l'assimilation des jeunes femmes en France en les rendant captives du marché matrimonial ethnique'.[17]

Even the study of immigration has proved fraught with difficulties. Tribalat's work was criticized by some of her colleagues as being likely to serve the *Front national* cause because it attempted to describe the diversity of French immigrant communities in a more detailed fashion than had previously been possible by seeking to discover their ethnic origins, and the ensuing argument became so heated that it ended in a libel action. Similarly, in the run-up to the census in 1999, an impassioned debate took place about whether it would be racist to include a question about ethnic origins in the census returns.

On the other hand, some immigrant groups have developed a distinctive culture which draws on both that of France and that of their own or their parents' country of origin, and in so doing have demonstrated a capacity for a degree of integration. This is the case with the 'beurs', as the children of North African immigrants are known.[18] One token of such integration is the new enthusiasm for the culture of Marseilles and its immigrants as exemplified in the immense success of the rap group IAM whose single 'Je danse le Mia' was a remarkable hit in 1994 and of the nostalgic, consensual films of Robert Guédiguian. But it was France's World Cup victory in 1998, the lionization of the 'immigrant' Zinedine Zidane who scored the winning goal, and the celebration of the 'black, blanc, beur' team, which brought public acknowledgement of the contribution of immigrant communities to French life and, perhaps, marked the beginning of a new era in community relations [see Texts 3.10 and 3.11].

**Zinedine Zidane** (b. 1972)

The youngest child of Berber immigrants from the Kabylia region of Algeria, Zidane, nicknamed 'Zizou' or 'Yazid', was born in the Castellane district of Marseilles and was signed up for the Cannes youth soccer team at the age of thirteen. He joined the Cannes first division team in 1989, transferred to Bordeaux in 1992, and secured his first cap for France in 1994, when he scored twice against the Czech Republic. By 1996 he was playing for Juventus of Turin and in 1998 he was a member of France's winning World Cup team, scoring two goals in the final against Brazil. Author, with Christophe Dugarry, of *Mes copains d'abord* (Editions Mango Sport, 1999), his contribution to the French World Cup victory turned him into a national hero and symbol of racial harmony and integration.

## Young people and old people

One novel demographic feature of post-war France is the significant increase in the proportion of both young people and old people within the population by comparison with the pre-war years and the nineteenth century. The rise in the number of young people was a phenomenon of the 1950s and 1960s – the post-war baby boom – and as a result of effective birth control it does not seem about to be repeated. By contrast, the increase in the numbers of people over 60 results from improvements in public health which have prolonged life expectancy, and it therefore seems certain to remain a characteristic of French social structure. The rise in the number of young people was welcomed when it occurred, whereas the increase in senior citizens or 'troisième âge', as they are sometimes known, gives cause for concern, but both groups have been singled out as significantly different from the remainder of the population as regards their habits of consumption, and also in their beliefs and political behaviour. In this respect they may be compared to social categories defined by sex or race, as opposed to the more usual class or socio-professional categories which are based on income and occupation, even though the assumption that members of a 'generation' have more in common with each other than they do with people of the same race, sex or class is frequently, and successfully, challenged.[19]

France first became aware that young people formed an important, and to some degree distinct, social group in the late 1950s, when journalists like Françoise Giroud began to publish articles on what they termed the *nouvelle vague* or youth culture. In due course, distinctive leisure activities and patterns of consumption developed among teenagers and students in France, much as they did elsewhere, typified by the magazine and radio show *Salut les copains* and the rise of pop stars such as Johnny Halliday and Sylvie Vartan, as well as the immense popularity of British and American pop and rock musicians. The entertainment, clothing and transport industries all began to cater specifically for young people whose tastes appeared to be less influenced by those of their parents or their own upbringing and social class than by the generation they belonged to. French people who reached adolescence in the 1950s and 1960s also saw their sense of generational solidarity reinforced by external events such as the Algerian war and, later, the war in Vietnam, both of which occasioned massive protests and began the process of challenging paternalism which culminated in the events of May 1968.[20] This cultural revolution seemed to confirm both the existence and rights of young people as a generational group. In May 1968, the conventional wisdom of all the elders was challenged and, at the same time, young people claimed the right to decide their future for themselves. Their success was recognized, politically, by the lowering of the age of majority to 18 in 1974, while in the matter of intergenerational relations in particular, and social relations in general, all commentators concur that May 1968 changed everything, and that authority would never again be exercised in quite the paternalistic fashion that had been the norm before the events.

However, although May 1968 was a watershed in social relations, it also marked the beginning of the decline of the youth generation and of 'youth culture' as a phenomenon. The birth rate began to fall in the 1960s and unemployment began to rise. Often those who were hardest hit were young people who began to find it much more difficult to secure permanent employment commensurate with their qualifications. From the 1970s onwards, therefore, with the exception of the much sought-after graduates of the *grandes écoles*, young people typically began to defer their departure from the family home and to experience longer periods of economic insecurity before settling into permanent employment. The notion of the 'conflict of generations' disappears from sight at this point, a process which is reinforced, in the eyes of some observers, by a greater degree of uncertainty within families as to what constitutes a 'generation', as a result of the creation of new family groups through divorce and remarriage.

Though the constitution of a large generation of retired people has been less immediately visible than that of young people it is no less significant. Life expectancy has increased markedly since the Second World War, so that French women, for example, can now expect to live well into their eighties. Indeed, the *troisième âge* has been joined by the so-called 'quatrième âge' made up of sigificant numbers of old people over the age of 85.

The 1981 socialist government lowered the statutory retirement age for men and harmonized it with that of women at 60, partly as a progressive social measure, partly as a way of creating jobs at a time of unemployment. In fact, however, many people do not retire at 60; instead, retirement can take place at any time between the ages of 55 and 70, depending on the nature of employment, with men in manual jobs often being encouraged to take early retirement. The effect was that the number of retired people in the population rose by 50 per cent between 1981 and 1997, while the proportion of retirees in the population as a whole is set to rise from about 16 per cent in 1995 to 23 per cent in 2020. Poverty used to be common among elderly people but, thanks to the generalization of pensions, and especially to the fact that many women, who after all tend to live longer than men, now have their own pensions, old age has ceased to be a primary cause of poverty. Some old people are still poor, of course, but many more of the elderly actually find they have more disposable income than when they were in employment because their family responsibilities have diminished. In 1995 there were three people of working age (between 20 and 59) for every one over 60; by 2020 it is expected that there will only be two people of working age for every one of retirement age. This means that the elderly and the retired will continue to form a significant consumer group who have the leisure, and often the income, to pursue a range of new activities, from sport to tourism.

# Population, family and social policy

## From pyramid to haystack

At the most recent census (March 1999) France had just over 60 million inhabitants, making it one of the most populous countries of the European Union alongside Germany, Italy and the United Kingdom. Despite a decline in the birth rate and immigration restrictions, the population is projected to continue rising slightly and to reach between 61 and 66 million by the year 2020.

It is not only in absolute numbers but in structure of population that France today closely resembles its major European partners. Life expectancy has increased, standing at present at over 82 years for women and 74 years for men. Infant mortality has declined, but so has the number of live births. This means that the graphic representation of the population structure, which used to resemble a pyramid, now looks much more like a haystack, since there are fewer people under 20 years of age than there are between the ages of 20 and 50, and there are proportionally more people, and especially women, over the age of 60 than there were thirty, forty or fifty years ago (see Figure 3.2). Such trends are to be found throughout western Europe. France is also closely comparable to its European neighbours with respect to demographic indicators such as rate of marriage, rate of divorce, infant mortality and so on. There are variations however: France shares with Denmark, Finland and Sweden the record for the lowest infant mortality in Europe, and, while the divorce rate is relatively lower than that of the UK, for example, so is the rate of marriage. It is only since the 1940s that France has conformed to European demographic trends. In 1942, the birthrate began to rise, as it did in neighbouring countries, creating the so-called 'baby boom'. The population grew as women had more children and infant mortality declined dramatically. After 1964, on the other hand, the birthrate began to decline slowly, and it dropped more sharply after 1975. In other words, the women born after the war chose to have fewer children themselves or, in some cases, to delay childbearing until they reached their thirties but, in the first instance at least, the impact of this trend was mitigated by the fact that the baby boom had created a greater number of women of childbearing age.

The number of children born to each woman is, of course, not the only feature of family structure which has changed. The rural exodus in the late 1940s and 1950s broke up the traditional, extended family in which several generations lived and worked together or in close proximity. Today, many French children, like their counterparts elsewhere in Europe, see their grandparents only during the holidays, if at all. The number of single-parent families has also increased massively. But these families are of two kinds: those in which the children are genuinely brought up by one or the other of their parents, generally, but not always, as the result of divorce, and those born to parents who are not married but who nevertheless live together as a stable, marital couple. The latter phenomenon became statistically significant

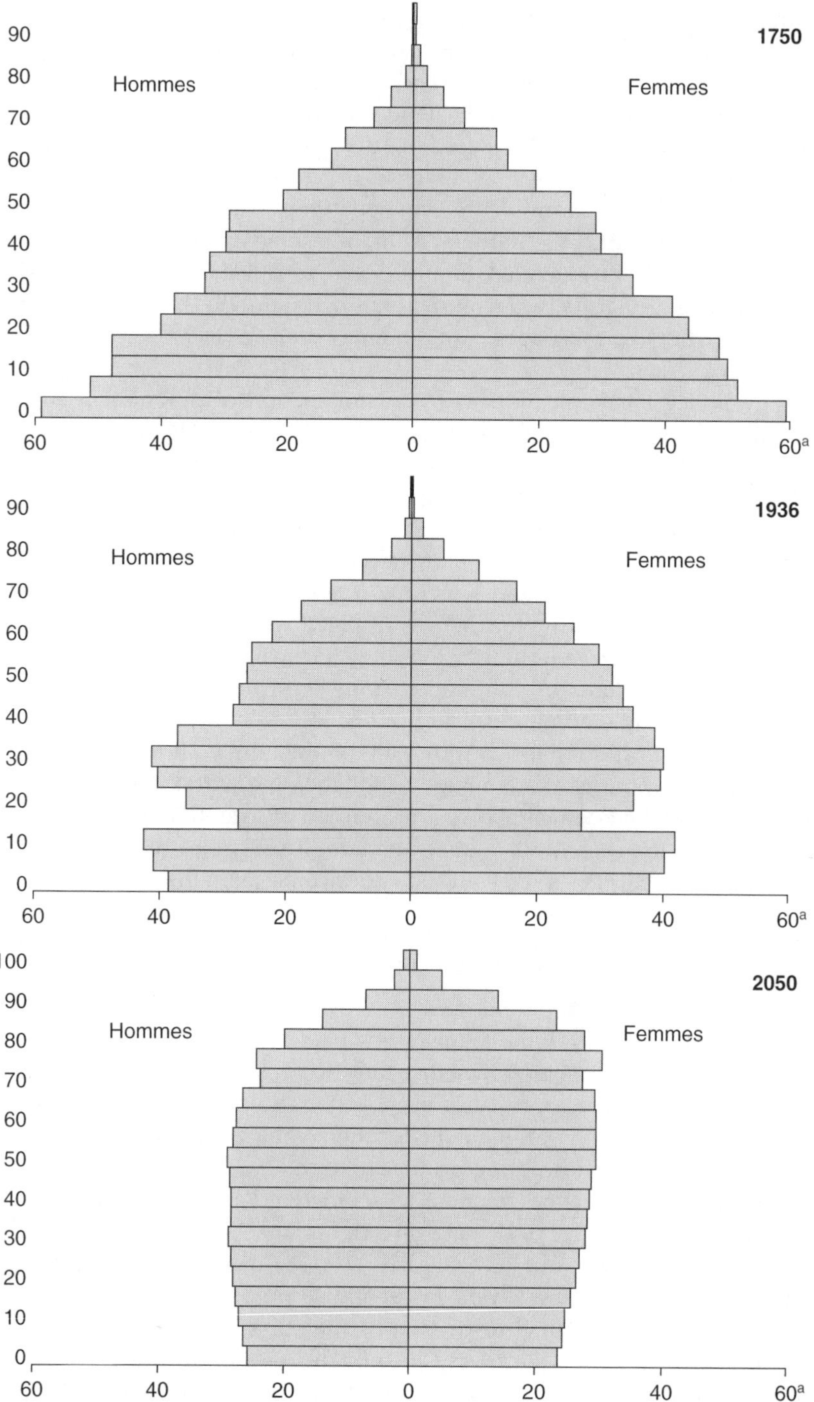


**Figure 3.2 The age pyramid: ages of the French population in 1750, 1936 and 2050 (hypothetical average)**

*Source*: *Le Monde*, 13 April 1989.

towards the end of the 1970s, creating considerable sociological and media interest, and by the mid-1990s France was second only to Denmark among EU countries for the number of couples living together without marrying. More recently, different forms of extended family have been created. Young people marry later than they used to do: the average age of women at marriage is now 27 and men 29, as against 22 and 24, respectively in 1970. Many adult children continue to live with their parents, sometimes introducing a cohabitee into the parental home for some or all of the time, while another new form of extended family is the so-called 'famille recomposée' formed by a marriage between individuals who already have children by a previous marriage or marriages, and who may themselves have a further child or children.

Family policy has been marked by a combination of pragmatism and the belief that social policy can influence behaviour, at least at the margins. Family allowances ('allocations familiales') were created in 1939 and have survived in one form or another ever since. Though often described as generous, they were traditionally graduated to encourage women to have more than one child, and preferably more than two. Thus allowances are negligible for the first child, significant for the second, and generous for third and subsequent children. They have a symbolic value too, as was revealed when the Jospin government was forced to withdraw its initial proposal to means-test the allowances for higher-income families. In addition, a family with three or more children is classified as a 'famille nombreuse' and can benefit from other advantages such as cheaper transport. Perhaps as important as the family allowance, however, was the creation of a fiscal advantage to childbearing with the introduction of the 'quotient familial' which allows a proportion of income to be exempt from direct taxation for each child and dependant. This is one reason why large numbers of French people pay little or no income tax, although in 1998 this benefit was reduced for higher earners.

Other benefits to assist parents with children include the 'allocation monoparentale' and the 'allocation parentale d'éducation'. The former is designed to help those who are single parents and, on the principle that the benefits system should be morally neutral, the allowance is paid to all single parents whether or not they have ever married, whether they are divorced, and whether or not they cohabit. For this reason it has been criticized as discouraging marriage. Similarly, the 'allocation parentale d'éducation' compensates couples in which one partner ceases work to bring up the children.

These measures are complemented by a range of benefits relating to maternity care, maternity leave and maternity rights which are not only generous by European standards but have clearly been influential in reducing infant mortality to historically low levels. Fiscal and social policy is thus designed to assist those with children, irrespective of their marital status. But none of these measures has been successful in influencing the birthrate. This means that, unless the behaviour of couples changes or unless immigration policy is relaxed, the population of France will increase only slightly, and this will primarily be thanks to better health care.

## Marriage and divorce

One of the most interesting features of contemporary social behaviour in France is the decline in the popularity of marriage. Once again, this is a western phenomenon which, though it is ill-understood, is convincingly linked to affluence by Evelyne Sullerot. Pointing to the example of Sweden, where approximately half the population is unmarried, she reminds us that in most western European countries 'l'échange intime de services qui liait le couple des années 40 et 50'[21] (by which she means food, shelter and clothing as well as sex) is no longer necessary. Sullerot suggests that greater affluence, as well as greater social, sexual and economic freedom for women, have led to a decline in the popularity of marriage.

It is certainly true that in the past those members of the community who did not marry were pitied, if not stigmatized, and this was particularly true of women who did not marry, for whom the lack of a spouse also meant that they lacked a social and economic role. For even when women worked, as they frequently did on farms or in small shops, this did not give them the independence they would have needed to have survived without a husband, since their involvement was part of a family enterprise, they were not salaried and their departure from the business would have been inconceivable. However, since the Second World War, failure to marry for lack of an appropriate spouse has been common only among men in poor rural communities, especially in the south-west. Elsewhere it does not mean enforced solitude or social inferiority. The present-day decline in the popularity of marriage is matched by an estimated 13.5 per cent of couples who live together without marrying, but theirs is a positive refusal of wedlock rather than a failure to find a suitable partner. There is also a close relation between education and marriage chances. The more highly educated a woman is, the less likely she is to marry, while the reverse is true for a man, so that the influx of women into higher education may have had some impact on the rate of marriage.

It is sometimes suggested that easier divorce is to blame for the failure of marriages, but this is not borne out by the statistics, which show that within the EU France has neither the high divorce rate of Denmark and the UK, nor the low divorce rate of Italy and Greece. After an initial jump in the divorce rate when no-fault divorce and divorce by mutual consent were introduced in 1975, the rate appears to have stabilized, having in any case risen throughout the 1970s, even before the new legislation. Divorce is much commoner during the early years of marriage and becomes infrequent after a marriage has lasted more than six years. There are also interesting regional and social differences in divorce rates. Divorce is more common among the middle classes – *salariés* and *cadres moyens* – than in the upper- and lower-income groups, and this fact underscores the intimate and persisting relationship between marriage, property and economic survival. In a lower-income family both spouses need each other to survive, while in a high-income family both spouses would have too much to lose from separation. Higher divorce rates are also to be found in the city than in the country, with a particularly high incidence in Paris, and there are lower rates of divorce in those parts of the country, such as the west, where the Catholic Church has traditionally been strong.

Do the decline in marriage and the rise in divorce point to new living patterns? The answer must be yes. First, it is clear that many couples choose to live together without marrying. Whereas previously such couples would probably have married if they decided to have children, today sociologists conclude from an examination of registrations of births in which both parents recognize the child as their own that many couples are also choosing to have children out of wedlock. There are also far greater numbers of people living alone, either by choice or from necessity, than there were 50 years ago. This includes all the elderly, widowed people, predominantly women, but it is increasingly characteristic of large cities and poor rural areas. As early as 1982, for example, nearly one household in two in Paris consisted of a single individual.

## The politics of sexuality

At the end of the eighteenth century France was the most populous country in western Europe and, partly because of this, the most powerful. However, during the nineteenth century the size of the French population declined in relation to that of Germany and Britain, which expanded under the combined effects of empire and the industrial revolution and, as if to confirm the political importance of demography, France was invaded three times by Germany in the space of a century (1870, 1914, 1940). The belief in the intimate relationship between demography and power has not only given rise to a fascinating academic literature, but has coloured the terms in which social policies on sexuality and the family are discussed and enacted. For, in the words of Hervé Le Bras, in France demography is 'une science politique'.[22]

Contraception and abortion were legalized in France in 1967 and 1975, respectively, after lengthy campaigns in both cases. The widespread use of forms of contraception is attested in France as far back as the beginning of the eighteenth century, and comparatively slow population growth in the nineteenth century suggests that it was often effective. Strong fears of depopulation after the First World War led, in 1920, to both contraception and information about contraception being made illegal, and this legislation remained in force until the 1960s. Concern with population growth did not abate after the Second World War, despite the 'baby boom'. The period saw the establishment of the *Institut national des études démographiques* (INED) whose twin function is to study historical demography with a view to interpreting present behaviour in the light of the past, and to make recommendations on present conditions and policy, in particular an annual report to parliament on the state of the French population. There has thus been acute public interest in demographic questions and population structure, which can on occasions strike the outsider as comic. The Gaullist politician Alain Peyrefitte, for example, described the comparative study of the British and French populations as 'le match France–Angleterre'. However, since unification, Germany has once again replaced Britain as the demographic spectre which, at least from the French point of view, is haunting

**Simone Veil** (b. 1927)

One of the best known and most widely respected women politicians of the Fifth Republic, sometimes spoken of as a potential presidential candidate, Veil was deported during the Occupation and survived Auschwitz, where her mother died. She trained as a lawyer and became secrétaire générale de la magistrature in 1970. She was appointed ministre de la santé under Giscard d'Estaing, a post she held from 1974 to 1979, and she piloted the bill legalizing abortion through parliament (*loi Veil*, 1975). In 1979 she was elected to the European Parliament and to its presidency, a post she held until 1982, while from 1993 to 1995 she was ministre de la santé et de la ville in the Balladur government. Although she was consistently given ministerial posts in stereotypically 'feminine' areas, Veil was nevertheless an inspired choice to push through reform of the abortion law, since her personal history allowed her to rebut the charges of 'murder' and 'genocide' levelled by the right-wing opposition at the time.

Europe. It is therefore hardly surprising that, since the Liberation, it has been politically axiomatic to encourage population growth and an increase in the proportion of young people in the population. De Gaulle looked forward to a time when the population of France would virtually double to 100 million and, in a famous phrase, called for the birth of 'douze millions de beaux bébés'. But he was not alone. In general in France, the encouragement of a high birth rate is interpreted as support for national unity and the future of France.

The campaign to legalize contraception and abortion therefore advanced very slowly in the 1960s when the development and popularization of the contraceptive pill gave added weight to demands for repeal. During the 1960s, close analysis of demographic data revealed that a large number of brides were pregnant on marriage, while surveys showed that third and subsequent children were often unplanned or unwanted. Thus the case for legalizing contraception was made on the basis of family planning, which would allow couples to choose when to have their children and how many to have. It was not made on the basis of any principle of sexual freedom, and it was not until the mid-1970s that contraception became widely used among young people (see Table 3.1).

The legalization of abortion was rather different. The campaign was conducted under the slogan 'un enfant si je veux, quand je veux'. By this time the social upheaval of May 1968 had taken place and the women's movement had been formed, so that the pro-abortionists felt much more strongly that the new legislation should embody a woman's right to do what she wished with her own body. The case for legal abortion rested on two premises. The first was that illegal abortions, of which it was estimated there were a large number, were dangerous and sometimes fatal; the second was that there was a social difference in existing access to safe abortion since middle-class women, who were likely to be better informed as well as better off, tended to travel to Britain or Switzerland to secure legal abortions in safe conditions, while poorer women had to rely on back-street abortionists. A further element was that the law was often not enforced. This became particularly apparent after the *Manifeste des 343* (343 well-known women who owned up to having had abortions) was published in *Le Nouvel Observateur* in 1971 but was not followed by prosecution.

**Table 3.1 What has changed women's lives**

*Au cours des vingt dernières années, qu'est-ce qui a le plus contribué, selon vous, à changer la vie des femmes?*

| | Ensemble des femmes | Génération | | | |
|---|---|---|---|---|---|
| | | 15–24 ans | 25–34 ans | 35–54 ans | 55 ans et plus |
| La contraception (la pilule) | 59 | 50 | 59 | 65 | 59 |
| L'accès des femmes aux responsabilités | 43 | 38 | 45 | 44 | 44 |
| Les progrès dans les équipements ménagers | 39 | 21 | 31 | 40 | 53 |
| La possibilité d'accéder à des nouveaux métiers réservés aux hommes | 37 | 53 | 37 | 33 | 31 |
| La légalisation de l'avortement | 31 | 28 | 34 | 36 | 26 |
| Le développement de l'union libre | 21 | 24 | 23 | 22 | 16 |
| Les changements de mentalité des hommes | 17 | 21 | 20 | 15 | 15 |
| La simplification du divorce | 13 | 13 | 10 | 13 | 14 |
| Les mouvements féministes (MLF, etc.) | 9 | 11 | 8 | 11 | 8 |
| Les nouvelles techniques de procréation | 7 | 6 | 7 | 6 | 7 |
| Sans opinion | 2 | 0 | 2 | 0 | 5 |

Le total des pourcentages est supérieur à 100, les personnes interrogées ayant pu donner plusieurs réponses.
*Source*: *Le Nouvel Observateur*, 6–12 December 1990, p.24.

But it was the *Procès de Bobigny* which brought matters to a head. This was the much-publicized trial of the mother of an under-age girl who procured an illegal abortion for her daughter who had been raped. The trial became a *cause célèbre*. The defence lawyer, Gisèle Halimi, was well known for her defence of human rights and a version of the trial was made into a campaigning film, *Histoires d'A*. However, although abortion was decriminalized in 1975, it was not until the socialist government was elected in 1981, and even then only after a fiercely fought campaign, that the operation was recognized for reimbursement under the social security system. In other words, free abortion did not become available until the mid-1980s.

Although there was considerable piecemeal adaptation of policies to take account of changes in social behaviour, it was not until the 1990s that a government felt able to tackle the axiom that social policy should encourage population growth. The socialist administrations of the 1980s began to focus on parents rather than exclusively on mothers, for example by extending the right to take time off work for child care to either parent. But it was the 1994 *loi sur la famille*, extending the *allocation parentale d'éducation* to parents of families of two rather than three or more children, which marked a significant break with earlier thinking. Indeed, the initial, controversial proposal had been for an 'allocation libre choix' which parents would have been able to claim on the birth of the first child.

Legislation on sexual matters, as on matters concerning the family, has to some extent been brought into line with advances in medicine and with common practice, and it has also been influenced by the critique of power, specifically regulatory medical power, undertaken by Michel Foucault and his disciples. Thus the pro-abortion campaign brought together demographic pragmatists, those campaigning for greater social justice and those who believed in the freedom of the individual and refused the right of the state to regulate in this private domain.

At the same time as such campaigns were being organized by women to defend and promote what were essentially seen as women's rights, campaigns were launched to secure equal legislative treatment for homosexuals, with the creation of groups such as the *Front homosexuel d'action révolutionnaire* (FHAR). Following a tradition which dates back to 1791 when the crime of 'sodomy' was abolished, but which the Vichy government suspended in 1942, homosexual acts between consenting males again became legal after the Second World War, but with 21 fixed as the age of consent, rather than 15 which was the age of consent for heterosexual acts. When the voting age was lowered from 21 to 18 in 1974, so was the age of consent for homosexual acts, but the full harmonization sought by the FHAR and others was not achieved until 1982, and then only with some difficulty.

France has a reputation for sexual tolerance, which is founded in part on its toleration of prostitution and homosexuality, but its traditional tolerance has been brought into sharp focus by the AIDS epidemic. The country has the largest number of AIDS cases in Europe. Although the greatest incidence of HIV infection has been among the male homosexual population, particularly those between the ages of 20 and 45 who are middle-class and who live in Paris, the epidemic in France, as elsewhere, is now spreading more rapidly among the heterosexual population, both male and female, and especially among drug users. In addition, a significant number of haemophiliacs were infected with HIV as a result of receiving contaminated blood, for which they collectively sued the directors of the blood transfusion and public health services and responsible members of the government, including Laurent Fabius, who was prime minister at the time.

The relatively large number of cases may reflect more efficient notification, especially in the early years of the epidemic, a larger or more sexually active population of homosexual males, or better facilities for treatment. But it may also reflect a reluctance to pursue active public health campaigns affecting sexual behaviour which is often held to be a matter of individual rather than public concern. Certainly, in the absence of a vaccination against HIV or a cure for AIDS, there has been considerable resistance to proposals for mass testing, together with a reinforcement of measures to ensure that those infected with HIV do not encounter discrimination.

The question of discrimination was brought into sharp focus by the premature deaths resulting from AIDS which revealed lacunae in French legislation relating to a range of social benefits and family law. Since homosexual couples had no legal status they could not, for example, sign a joint lease or request a public sector job transfer under the rules for 'rapprochement de conjoints'. Furthermore, a surviving partner would not be treated as a family member for tax purposes so that, even if he or she inherited the estate of the deceased, a higher rate of tax would be payable on it than if the legatee qualified as a family member, *a fortiori* a spouse. To tackle these inequities the Jospin government proposed sweeping reforms to extend the rights already accorded to 'stable' heterosexual unmarried couples to similar homosexual couples under the *Pacte civil de solidarité* (PACS). The initial bill did not get through parliament as a result of an impressive filibuster, lasting over five hours, by the right-wing députée Christine Bottin, but also because many socialist députés, especially those from rural areas, were uneasy that the government should give priority to legislation which appeared to open the way to 'homosexual marriage' and did not turn up to vote. In the autumn of 1999, however, the Senate finally approved a bill which was not as liberal as the one initially proposed but did at least mark a significant step towards bringing the rights of homosexual couples into line with those of unmarried heterosexual couples [see Text 3.12].

## The welfare state

Like most other western European countries, France instituted a social security system immediately after the Second World War which was gradually extended to cover the whole population and which, in addition to the family and maternity allowances mentioned above, provides benefits during old age, sickness and unemployment. As in other European countries, social security has gradually absorbed a greater and greater proportion of all public expenditure: in 1949 it represented just 12 per cent of GDP, but this had risen by the end of the 1990s to over 20 per cent (see Part II). As we have seen, maternity and family allowances have been particularly successful in reducing infant mortality. Similarly, a series of measures have all but eliminated extreme poverty among old people: the *vignette automobile* (road fund licence) was created in 1956 to finance assistance to the elderly and today the *minimum vieillesse* is a benefit available to all old people who need it, while contributions both to the state pension scheme, *retraite d'état*, and to an occupational pension scheme, *retraite complémentaire*, are obligatory. The proportion of national income spent on each of the sets of benefits has varied with changing social circumstances, but by the mid-1990s old age benefits accounted for over 40 per cent of social security spending, followed by health, which accounted for over 30 per cent. Spending on family and maternity benefits, however, has declined with the declining birthrate, while spending on unemployment benefits fluctuates with the economic cycle.

Perhaps the most interesting phenomenon is the massive growth in health spending in the post-war period, a feature which reflects both increased affluence and some of its less desirable effects. Thus in the period 1980–93 health spending rose by 9.5 per cent, while by the mid-1990s there were almost three times as many doctors as there had been in the 1960s. The nature of health spending has changed too. To the French family, spending on health represented nearly 9 per cent of their budget by the mid-1980s (compared with 14 per cent in Germany and only 1.3 per cent in the UK). Most of this was accounted for within statutory social security contributions but also, and increasingly, by complementary health insurance and by personal expenditure not covered by insurance. This reflects both the increasing importance attached to good health, the greater variety of treatments available and the desire of the state, from the middle of the 1980s onwards, to control spending on health.

Health care in France is not free at the point of delivery except in the public hospitals and clinics. Instead, it is paid for by the patients, who are then reimbursed by their local social security office up to 75 per cent of an agreed cost, except for certain chronic conditions and mortal illness which are 100 per cent reimbursed. Private health insurance schemes, which are optional and which are often occupation-related mutualist associations, reimburse the difference in cost thereafter, also up to a fixed ceiling, and any further expenditure is borne by the patient. The number of individuals covered by complementary insurance rose from 30 per cent in the 1960s to over 75 per cent in the 1990s, suggesting a widespread willingness to spend money on health care.

Does this mean that the population is healthier? Two classic measures of public health, infant mortality and life expectancy, have shown dramatic improvements since 1945, as we have seen. On the other hand, new public health problems, such as those created by HIV and AIDS, or indeed CJD, pose still unquantifiable risks. However, there still remain inequalities in health which tend to reflect inequalities in occupation and income. The class inequalities in infant mortality have virtually disappeared thanks to an active public health policy. In 1954 a manual worker's child was three times more likely to die before reaching twelve months of age than was the child of a member of the professions, but by 1976 this difference had virtually disappeared.

By the same token, regional differences and variations between the city and the country have also been almost completely wiped out thanks to the improvement of living standards in the country areas as well as the decline of dietary and other habits (such as alcohol consumption) which increased infant mortality. Today, the north and Brittany still have slightly higher infant mortality rates than the remainder of the country, but the gap has narrowed considerably. By contrast, inequalities in life expectancy still remain high, as do variable susceptibilities to accidents at work and a variety of occupation-linked illnesses. Thus, while alcohol-related deaths are declining, road accidents (many of which are in fact alcohol-related) are a major cause of fatalities. Women continue to live longer than men and the gap has widened, so that the longevity of French women is one of the highest in Europe. Similarly, occupation still plays a significant part in life expectancy. In the period 1975–90, for example, a teacher could expect to live nine years longer than a manual worker and there is evidence that the gap is widening rather than narrowing, even if the differences are linked more to lifestyle factors such as diet and alcohol consumption than to the different nature of the work.

## The poor

The economic austerity programmes introduced from 1978 onwards not only marked a certain withdrawal from spending on welfare provision on the part of the state, but also the abandonment of any attempt to eliminate poverty. This statement must immediately be qualified by the reminder that there is little agreement in France, as elsewhere, on the definition of poverty, except that in industrialized countries it has a very different meaning, and corresponds to a very different experience, from poverty in under-developed countries. In the mid-1970s, estimates of the numbers of people living in poverty in France ranged from five million to fifteen million, depending on the measure adopted.[23] However, there seems little dispute that poverty began to rise after 1979 as a result of the relative decline in the value of welfare benefits and the rise in unemployment. In addition to rising, poverty began to affect groups different from the traditional clients of the social services. These 'nouveaux pauvres', as they are called, comprise essentially the long-term unemployed 'en fin de droits', that is, who have exhausted their entitlement to unemployment benefits, and they may be either young single people, with no family, and therefore with no claim to the social and welfare protection offered by family benefits, or middle-aged people, especially men, with financial commitments entered into in more prosperous times, with no previous experience of poverty or of the claimant culture, who find it difficult to come to terms with their situation.

The *nouveaux pauvres*, especially the young, became the principal clients of the social services and charity agencies after the mid-1980s. They were also more visible than the traditional poor had been on the streets of the cities, and the phenomenon captured the public imagination, with articles devoted to the 'quart monde' and with the launch of a soup kitchen movement known as the 'restaurants du coeur'. The Socialists' electoral campaign of 1988 recognized that a welfare system which focused primarily on families with children was inadequate to deal with the victims of economic change, and their proposal to create the *Revenu minimum d'insertion* (RMI), which is a benefit designed to assist precisely those for whom no other benefit was available, commanded general consensus. By the middle of 1989 the RMI, which had been introduced in December 1988, had been paid to over a quarter of a million claimants, a figure which suggests that it was meeting a very real need, with most of the beneficiaries receiving about 2000 francs per month, and with a close correlation between the regional distribution of payments of the RMI and the areas where unemployment was the highest (the north and the extreme south-east). By the late 1990s about two million people, including dependants, were claiming the RMI. As has already been suggested, France differs from many other European countries in having tackled the problem of poverty among old people by the introduction of a *minimum vieillesse*. Studies of the operation of the RMI since 1988 confirm this by revealing relatively few old people among its beneficiaries. Instead they point to a claimant population composed of single adults who do not fit in with any of the other categories eligible for benefits, together with those who often have a history of mental illness or of homelessness.

# Work, leisure and lifestyles

Urbanization and economic change have brought new patterns of work, leisure and consumption. Working conditions improved progressively throughout the twentieth century thanks to legislation limiting hours of work and to the provision of statutory paid holidays. Thus the eight-hour day was introduced in 1918, the 40-hour week in 1936, and the 39-hour week in 1982. Statutory holiday entitlement has gradually risen and in 1982 stood at five weeks in addition to public holidays, while the introduction of the 35-hour week may well translate into anything up to twelve days' additional holiday for some managers. Conditions have been further improved both by the national minimum wage and by 'mensualisation', the process by which workers are paid monthly and make national insurance contributions, bringing them in under the net of social protection and giving them the right to sickness and unemployment benefits as well as to a pension. Both the 1982 *lois Auroux* and the 1998 and 1999 *lois Aubry* (discussed in Parts I and II) were efforts to stimulate employment, but they were also attempts to improve the lot of the workers, and have brought about improvements in working conditions.

## Government policy and the labour market

The economic crises of the 1970s brought about a profound restructuring of the work-force. The collapse of the Lorraine steel industry in the early 1970s devastated the whole region and it also marked the start of two decades of decline in heavy industry, culminating in the symbolic closure in 1992 of the Renault car factory at Boulogne-Billancourt. The perception of work and working conditions modified accordingly. In the 1950s and 1960s trade union demands centred round pay increases, union recognition and safety, all features of the 1968 *Accords de Grenelle*. From the 1970s onwards these were partially replaced by the 'thèmes qualitatifs' concerning such things as the organization of work, employee participation and self-management. But economic and technological change brought its own disadvantages such as the loss of autonomy and human contact. Previously men may have worked hard at physically demanding and dangerous jobs, but at least, so the argument ran, they could communicate with one another on the job and draw strength from solidarity, whereas the new technologies, especially information technologies, dehumanized the working environment and created problems of isolation. Thus the criticism of the *cadences infernales* of the production lines in the factories was superseded by attacks on new technologies, which were often viewed with great suspicion.

Gradually, however, such criticisms were themselves made obsolete by new divisions which appeared among the working population. As unemployment rose, the great social distinction came to be between those who had a permanent, full-time job and those who did not, between the official and the unofficial economy. Those in full-time employment benefited from health insurance, paid holidays, security and a high standard of living, whilst those not in full-time paid employment became increasingly marginal. Many of the latter were young people newly arrived on the labour market. For these the government enacted a series of measures, such as the creation of work experience schemes, the *travaux d'utilité collective*, in 1984, and from 1988 onwards introduced fiscal measures to encourage companies to recruit young people, while the 1997 Jospin government made job creation for young people a central plank of its election commitments. Nevertheless, the social effects of the shake-out in the labour market were devastating, and it is no accident, as we have seen, that many of those claiming the RMI were young, single people.

By the end of the 1980s, therefore, changes in the structure of the labour market had had a significant impact on cultural attitudes. First, there was a marked difference between those employed in the private sector, who saw their incomes rise, especially in the boom of the 1980s, and those employed in the public sector, which in the mid-1990s still accounted for one-fifth of the workforce, whose wages remained depressed. Second, despite legislation guaranteeing equal pay for work of equal value, the labour market has, increasingly, become structured on gender lines. Not only do women with similar qualifications systematically earn less than men, but some jobs are performed principally or almost exclusively by women, especially certain public sector jobs such as teaching and nursing. This has also had the effect of depressing public sector pay. Third, there has been a shift in the market value of qualifications documented by statisticians who note a *déclassement* comparable to that of the 1960s: 'Une coupure nouvelle semble s'installer entre les très hauts diplômes et les autres diplômes de l'enseignement supérieur, en particulier ceux que délivrent les universités'.[24] In other words, although the working population may be better qualified, this does not necessarily correspond to an improvement in socio-occupational status.

## Consumption and leisure

Alongside changed attitudes to work have come changed patterns of consumption and leisure. Many of these are, of course, the result of generally rising living standards, for in the post-war period, unlike the 1920s, all social categories shared in the general rise in prosperity. In France, as in other western countries, many consumer durables such as cars, which were luxury items owned by the privileged few before the war, became generalized to the mass of the population. Television sets and, more recently, freezers, dishwashers, video-recorders, personal computers and mobile phones are all items which began as expensive luxuries and are now widely owned [see Text 3.13].

From this point on, sociologists have tended to focus attention not so much on what people buy, since most consumer goods are now widely considered essential, but on different patterns of spending. Considerable differences have emerged over the past 50 years. Most striking is the fall in the percentage of income spent on food and on clothes. Conversely, the amount spent on transport (which includes car purchase), on housing and on health have all risen significantly. Obviously, this does not mean that French people are eating less well or are less well dressed, although it may mean that they travel more and, possibly, that they are less healthy or better covered by health insurance. What it certainly indicates, however, is that they have surplus income to devote to new kinds of spending.

However, such statements are not very informative about the way people live or the different lifestyles adopted. Initially, economists believed that greater affluence would 'trickle down' through all social classes, leading to greater convergence of behaviour and lifestyles, an idea which would seem to be supported by the gradual closing of the gap between income differentials in the 1960s and 1970s. Indeed, one of the criticisms levelled at the consumer society was that it encouraged a stultifying conformity, often to a way of life that was not 'French' but 'American'. This is far from being borne out in practice. A considerable body of work has been undertaken in the sociology of taste, the findings of which suggest that one of the effects of the consumer society, with its large array of choices, is that individuals spend their money very differently, and that what determines their choices are a number of variables among which class is a very important factor but by no means the only one.

As we have seen, the traditional socio-economic categories are crossed by other forms of stratification such as age and gender, so that groups like old people, young people and women have consumption habits which have become significantly different over the last ten or twenty years. Although many old people today are quite affluent, they tend not to be owner-occupiers, not to own cars, to spend less than other social categories on clothes but more on their domestic interior. The entry of women into the work-force has led to a marked increase on spending on restaurant meals in families where women work, while women now spend an astonishing 30 per cent more on clothes than men in a context where overall spending on clothes has declined as a proportion of income. Young people are also a distinct consumer category. Young males, for example, spend up to 37 per cent of their income on transport – essentially car purchase – and, as they are for the most part single, a great deal on eating out but relatively little on housing. Similarly, children have been identified both as significant consumers in their own right and as having a decisive influence on the choice of car, house, television and so on.[25] Other noticeable differences in consumption and lifestyle are regional. In Paris, for example, fewer people, especially single people, own cars, while a greater number live in flats than in houses and so do not purchase a range of household and gardening equipment, but they are much more likely than the rest of the population to eat out.

Food, indeed, is a very good illustration of the differential analyses of consumption as well as being an area where France still remains somewhat different from other developed countries. Despite the generalization of the *journée continue*, that is continuous working through the day, the French still spend more time on meals than other nations.[26] However, they by no means all eat the same thing. France may have a cheese for every day of the year but the likelihood that an individual will eat one kind of cheese rather than another depends on social background as well as age and where he or she lives. In addition, dietary habits are still much influenced by the regional availability of foodstuffs. More oil is consumed in the south, more butter in the north, more fish in Brittany, more poultry in the south-west, reflecting a combination of availability and tradition. But the major opposition would appear to be between the *produits traditionnels* and the *produits modernes*, and this has a great deal to do with historical patterns of availability and distribution. Thus not only do rural families produce for themselves up to 30 per cent of the foodstuffs they consume, but they also consume greater quantities of foodstuffs that can easily be stored: preserves, ham and pasta. Conversely, city dwellers, particularly the new middle classes, have greater access to fresh fruit and vegetables, especially out of season, and to convenience foods, and they are more likely to be influenced by health considerations. They consume, for example, large quantities of mineral water. This does not reflect necessity – many families have freezers – but preferences built up over the years. Similarly, some social categories are more susceptible to pretension and/or to inverted snobbery than others. Many writers condemn fast food, more for its supposed American origins than because it is deleterious to health, while purists complain about the popularization of inauthentic regional recipes 'aux herbes de Provence' [see Text 3.14].

Perhaps the greatest change in the way people live is in the expansion of leisure and the growth of the leisure industries, especially the domestic leisure industries. At the turn of the millennium French people have, at least in theory, more free time than their compatriots had at the beginning of the twentieth century. This is partly due to the enactment of legislation limiting hours of work and providing statutory paid holidays referred to above. In 1967 the average week worked was 45 hours but this dropped after 1982 to 39.5 hours and is due to drop to 35 hours by 2002. However, both figures cover wide differences in practice. Some people, like farmers and senior managers, work long hours because of the nature of their jobs; others, like those in industries in crisis, work short time because they are obliged to do so or, perhaps, take early retirement. Many differences relate to class or income. As recalled in the May 1968 slogan 'métro, boulot, dodo', the poorer inhabitants of the outer suburbs spend more time travelling to work than their more affluent colleagues who can afford to live in the city centre. They are also more likely to work shifts and unsocial hours. Other differences relate to gender, since most surveys reveal, as we have seen, that women report considerably less free time than men. Even so, increased life expectancy, the length of time people now spend in full-time education, together with the possibility of retirement at the age of 60 or earlier in some cases, have all meant that the average working life has become shorter and people have more free time, especially in retirement, than ever before.

What do people do with their free time? If they can afford to do so they take holidays. Theoretically, every worker benefits from a paid holiday and has done since 1936, when the first legislation creating two weeks' statutory paid holidays was translated as 'Front Populaire, la France part en vacances!' Since the introduction of 'la cinquième semaine' in 1982, paid holiday entitlement stands at one of the highest levels in Europe. Yet, although the number of holiday-makers has risen, by no means everyone goes away. In 1964 less than half the population, 43.6 per cent, managed a break away, and by 1996 this had risen to nearly three-quarters – 69 per cent. Of those who do take a holiday approximately one-third went abroad in 1996 [see Text 3.15]. There has also been a growth in so-called *'vacances à thème'*, or activity holidays, while the introduction of *la cinquième semaine* has led to a growth in second, winter holidays. Many of these breaks involve winter sports, and have given rise to a great expansion of resort provision and complex timetabling of school mid-term breaks to enable hoteliers and tour operators to maximize utilization of their plant. People in general move around much more than in the past, assisted in this by the growth of car ownership since the war. Going away for the weekend has become a favourite leisure pursuit, but so has visiting monuments and sites of historical interest or natural beauty.

Two further forms of leisure activity are of some note, the first for its continuing social stratification, the second for its 'democratization'. Most observers have recorded an upsurge of interest in sport in the last twenty or thirty years on the part of both practitioners and spectators, and those who do practise a sport are doing so more regularly. However, despite the general interest in football at the time of the 1998 World Cup, sporting interests are highly socially stratified. Although about half the population now claims to be involved in some sporting activity, sport still remains the province of the young male. Women, in general, are far less involved in sports than are men, although their participation is increasing, especially through activities such as dance, gymnastics and swimming, but for both men and women participation in a sport is closely related to the level of education, so that over 60 per cent of university graduates participate in some sport but only 18 per cent of those who have no academic qualifications at all. In the same way, the sports which have gained in popularity over recent years are those which appeal to the middle classes – tennis, swimming, gymnastics, skiing, not to mention squash and golf – although football and cycling still retain their general appeal.

By contrast, the expansion of the domestic leisure industries has affected virtually all French households. As one writer put it, 'la maison est devenue la première salle de spectacle', absorbing three-quarters of all spending on culture.[27] By the end of the 1970s virtually every French household (94 per cent) had at least one television set. Although the number of hours actually spent in front of the television naturally varies from social group to social group, by the end of the 1990s the average time spent watching television was three hours a day. Many households now also own video-recorders which they use both to record off air and to watch hired tapes, and the same is true of music centres or other means of listening to and recording music. Spending on books and newspapers has increased, as has the frequentation of museums, whose visitors nearly doubled in number between 1980 and the end of the century. As a result, even though 70 per cent of French people have never attended a concert and 50 per cent have never been to the theatre, it is no longer entirely possible to speak of the cultural divisions along the strict class lines which certainly existed in the 1950s, because the mass media and the domestic leisure industries have created a degree of homogenization and different forms of stratification which have as much to do with age as with class. However, the category *cadres supérieurs et professions libérales* is noteworthy for the amount it spends on culture and the fact that it watches very little television, while the converse is true of poorer groups who, it is thought, will spend most of the additional free time created by the 35-hour working week in home-based leisure activities, and particularly in watching television.

The state supports culture and leisure activities in inverse proportion to their popularity, giving most money to opera, which is seen by very few people, and no money to television, which virtually everyone watches. Indeed, although 'culture' has traditionally been an important plank of government policy, intimately associated in the minds of legislators with both education and the quality of life as well as the position of France in the world, and although in 1981 state spending on culture was virtually doubled, the traditional forms of spending have scarcely altered over the years. Some attempt was made between 1981 and 1986 to 'decentralize' cultural spending both by supporting and creating museums in smaller towns and by encouraging local initiatives and work place efforts. But the Ministry of Culture kept a firm grip on all projects and constituted itself rather than the local people the definitive arbiter of quality. Although what the state considered culture was expanded to include *bandes dessinées*, circus and song, the spectrum of activities obtaining financial support has remained firmly rooted in the traditional notion of 'bourgeois culture'. It is also true to say that, since the war, and more especially since the massive expansion of television, support for culture as traditionally conceived has been associated in the minds of some influential intellectuals, like Régis Debray and Alain Finkielkraut, with a reinforcement of French identity against successive assaults from America and Japan [see Texts 3.16 and 3.17].

## Social institutions: the army, the church, the mass media and the education system

The traditional structuring institutions of French society were the army, the church and the education system. Of these, the army and the church have greatly declined in influence, although some notion of their past significance is important for understanding the present day. The education system, however, remains a crucial force in French society and it has been joined in this respect by the mass media. This section will examine all four institutions and attempt to elucidate their role in modern French society.

### The army

France required national service from all its young men from the eighteenth century until the end of the twentieth century, and for most, though not all, this meant a period spent in the army. National service was disliked so much that wealthy families often paid a substitute; the sons of poorer families, on the other hand, protested by deserting. During the 1950s and 1960s, at the height of the colonial wars, many young men felt objections of principle to service in an army whose role they saw as politically repressive. However, France's last major military engagement was the Algerian war, while the end of the cold war and the changed relationship between the west and the former Soviet block have meant that the rôle of the army is perceived less as that of the defence of the Republic and more as that of international peace-keeper. The rôle of military service evolved in keeping with these changes. Under de Gaulle the possibility of conscientious objection was acknowledged; subsequently, the regime of 'coopération' – that is, community rather than military service – was widely extended, with the result that national service was treated by many *coopérants,* especially the highly educated, as a means of broadening their professional experience.

When elected in 1981, the Socialists promised to reduce military service from one year to six months. This measure was not enacted, either because unemployment was rising and the government viewed national service as a means of massaging the statistics, or because the costs of replacing a conscript army with a professional army were too great, and it was not until 1991 that the length of service was reduced to ten months and new forms of *coopération* were introduced. Yet the failure to keep this election promise occasioned no protest and it must therefore be concluded that French people still believed that national service performed an important social function, even if its military utility was no longer self-evident. However, by the end of the 1990s the costs of a conscript army had clearly come to outweigh the benefits. After his election in 1995, President Chirac announced the creation of an entirely professional army and the 'suspension' of national service, which was to be progressively replaced by 'une journée APD' (appel de préparation à la défense), a day during which young people in France of call-up age, girls as well as boys, would receive lectures on defence organization in France and in Europe. Thus by the year 2002 national service will be entirely phased out.

The theory behind military service was that the people would defend the nation from attack and that this was not only a duty but in some sense constitutive of citizenship, that national service would be 'un creuset unificateur'. Historically, of course, this was true. The Napoleonic wars and, even more, the First World War allowed farm boys to leave their villages for the first and perhaps only time in their lives, taught them to read, write and, in some cases, speak French, and then sent them to die for their country, which they did in millions. The army was, in the words of Henri Mendras, 'l'école de la nation'.[28] But the army was overtaken by events, and the invasion of France at the beginning of the Second World War showed that a large infantry (into which the conscripts went) was no protection against tanks, and that an air force was essential to the defence of the nation. Subsequently, nuclear capacity distanced the conscript army even further from an effective defence role.

Since conscripts could play little role in defence and were probably expensive to manage, it must be concluded that it was its ideological function that kept conscription in existence. One view was that a people's army would not turn against the people, that a military dictatorship was impossible for as long as conscription was maintained. Traditionally, this was an important reason why many left-wing French people, particularly members of the Communist Party, supported military service. But it is also true that the links between the army and politics have been closer in France than in Britain, Germany or the United States, and de Gaulle was only the latest of a series of French leaders who had come to politics via the army. The abolition of conscription therefore marks not just the modernization of the armed forces but also, perhaps, a significant ideological mutation in French society.

## The church

It used to be said that France was a 'Catholic' country. Such a statement is based on history: France was 'la fille aînée de l'Église', Catholicism was the official religion much as Anglicanism is in England, and other religious groups such as Protestants were persecuted. More than that, the church had pretensions to embrace in its fold everyone in France. However, one of the effects of the 1789 Revolution was to break the relationship between church and state, a break which received formal status with the Concordat of 1905. Civil rights were extended to non-Catholic and non-Christian groups much earlier than elsewhere and the Catholic Church retreated from a position of universality, where it could claim to speak for everyone, to a position where it represented one group within society. The republican and anti-clerical movement of the latter part of the nineteenth century forced the Catholic Church into what has been called a counter-cultural position, often associated with monarchism and right-wing, anti-democratic politics.

Nevertheless, until the First World War the church remained a powerful influence in what was still a largely rural society. The priest was a local notable, along with the doctor and the teacher, and he was expected to direct the thoughts and actions of the peasants. The republican party aimed to destroy this power through a secular education system, but it was the urban working class, organized through the trade unions and later the Communist Party, which was in fact most effective at limiting the power of the church.

As social statisticians point out, it is not possible to measure beliefs, only practices, but even this is difficult in France where, since the census of 1872, questions about religion have not been posed as this is considered a 'private matter'.[29] Figures given for different religious groups within France are therefore based partly on extrapolations from social surveys and partly on the numbers of births, marriages and deaths celebrated according to religious rites.

If the majority of French people still declare themselves Catholics, this for the most part amounts to little more than recourse to the church for the rites of birth, marriage and death. In 1997 some 16 per cent of the population declared regular religious observance, a figure which had nevertheless risen slightly since the 1980s, while a quarter of the population said that they had no religious belief nor any feeling that they belonged to a religious grouping. Older people and people in the country seem more attached to religion than younger people and people in the towns, while farmers and retired people are more likely than other social categories to practise a religion (the increase in the latter may explain the increase in religious observance). The above figures might be compared with the 24 per cent attendance at mass recorded in 1955 and the 20 per cent in 1970. Similarly, although about 60 per cent of children continued to be baptized in the 1980s, this compares unfavourably with over 90 per cent in the 1950s.[30] Few people go to confession any longer, nor do they, despite their religious obligation, take communion at Easter.

The figures may be imprecise, but the conclusion is inescapable: Catholicism is declining and, with the exception of fractions of the managerial stratum, those who do practise a religion tend not to be among the most dynamic and youthful sections of the nation. Not surprisingly, the priesthood mirrors the habits of secular society. The number of ordinations has declined dramatically over the last forty years, with the result that not only are there fewer priests, but those there are tend to be elderly. Many *communes* now do not have their own priest but share the services of a clergyman who rotates around a number of districts. Churches have closed and their closure, like that of post offices and schools, has removed both a social centre and a source of influence from village life.

In the period since the Second World War, therefore, the Catholic Church has to a degree retained its cultural pre-eminence but the spread of secularism has meant that many people in France do not look to religion at all for spiritual or moral, still less for political, guidance. In the 1930s and the early 1950s, the church reacted strongly to its loss of influence. Catholic action movements such as the *Jeunesse ouvrière chrétienne* (JOC), the *Jeunesse agricole chrétienne* (JAC) and the *Jeunesse étudiante chrétienne* (JEC) were extremely active, and many members of Catholic social movements were influential in the Resistance. After the war, similarly, following the publication in 1943 of the Abbé Godin's book, *France pays de mission*, which revealed the extent of dechristianization, the church encouraged a new interpretation of the priest's role as an 'urban missionary', and many clerics abandoned the pomp, circumstance and ritual of the church to become worker priests, proselytizing among the most dechristianized urban populations.

It would appear, however, that the French Church was out of step with the Vatican on the conception of its new social role and Rome quickly put a stop to worker priests. More recently, the attitude of John Paul II to such matters as contraception and abortion, an attitude which appears to go against the modernizing thinking embodied in the Second Vatican Council (1962–5), has led many Catholics to ignore the church's teaching on questions concerning private life. AIDS, similarly, has led many Catholics to ignore the recommendations of the Vatican. At the same time, a body of opinion within the church felt that modernization, and attempts to reach out towards the people, had gone too far: the 'intégristes', grouped round the late Cardinal Lefebvre, remained attached to all the old rituals of Catholicism, including the mass sung in Latin. The *intégristes* have attracted attention primarily because many of them espouse right-wing political views and openly support the *Front national*. However, they are also significant because they do point to a revival of interest in religion. At the same time, therefore, as Catholicism has lost both its universality and its cultural appeal for the large majority of people in France, smaller groups of people have become militant Catholics, some of them of a politically reprehensible persuasion.

## Other religions

To the extent that this can be judged – and the statistics are imperfect – Moslems have come to be the second largest religious grouping in France after Catholics (see Figure 3.3). Thus it is estimated that there are about one million Protestants in France, about 600,000 Jews (about half of whom came to France from North Africa at the time of Algerian independence), 500,000 Buddhists but anything up to four million Moslems. Part of the difficulty in obtaining figures has to do with the assumption sometimes made that immigrants from North Africa, Turkey and other Moslem countries will automatically be practising Moslems themselves. As specialists point out, this is as inaccurate as the statement that all French people are Catholics. What is noticeable, however, is the greater Moslem presence in many large cities, as indicated by the existence

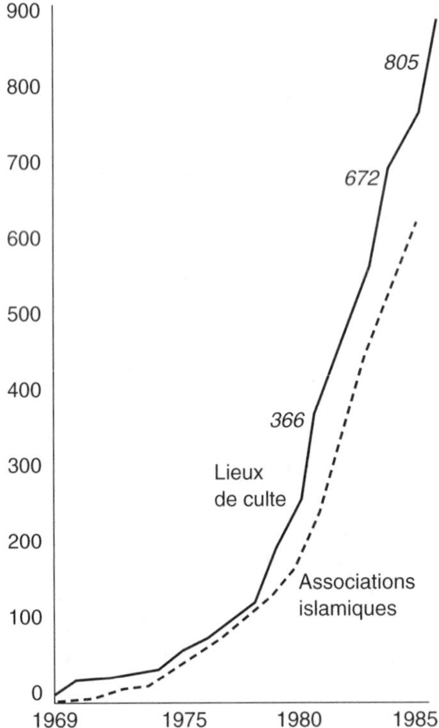


**Figure 3.3 Moslems in France, 1969–85**
*Source*: INSEE, *Données Sociales*, 1990, p.382.

of a mosque, the location and construction of which frequently causes local protests. Though these new mosques may simply indicate that Moslems are settling in one place rather than moving round to find work, they also point to a greater degree of Moslem 'visibility'.

It would seem, therefore, that with the exception of Islam, which despite its dynamism remains a minority faith, religion has lost much of its former influence in French society. There is one respect, however, in which it apparently retains much of its significance and this is in the realm of political geography. All commentators look to traditional religious beliefs to explain political behaviour since 'la religion demeure le facteur le plus explicatif des grands clivages idéologiques et politiques de la société française'.[31] France has a very characteristic religious geography, with the areas most distant from Paris, which were often but not always the most rural areas, remaining Catholic for longer than all other areas, but with Protestant enclaves in the south-west and east and in Paris. Historically, the cities of Strasbourg, Nîmes, Montpellier, Mulhouse and La Rochelle have also had large Protestant communities. Both Judaism and Islam remain essentially urban phenomena, most Jews and Moslems being found in the cities of the south (Marseilles and Nice) and in Paris and its region. Rural communism, especially in a region such as the Limousin, is closely linked with a weak church; conversely, right-wing politics is traditionally associated with Catholicism.

Traditionally, presidents of the Republic were careful to be seen coming out of mass and, in the elections of 1981, the Socialists were considered to have made a breakthrough when the traditionally Catholic towns of the west returned socialist *députés* for the first time. However, belonging to a minority religious grouping is no impediment to personal political success, as is shown by the careers of recent socialist prime ministers: Laurent Fabius, for example, is Jewish, Michel Rocard and Lionel Jospin are both Protestants, while Catherine Trautmann, former mayor of Strasbourg and minister of culture and communication in the 1997 Jospin government, is a Protestant theologian. Traditions developed through two centuries have clearly not disappeared overnight, but the secular decline of Catholicism in France is certainly reflected in the political success of such individuals.

## The mass media

As in all developed countries, the mass media in France have played an important rôle in modernization and social change. In the middle of the nineteenth century France became a leader in the development of communications technologies such as telegraphy, photography and cinema and of mass circulation newspapers, one of which, *Le petit parisien*, was the most widely distributed newspaper in the world before the First World War. However, in France the press reflected the strong provincial political and cultural specificities of the country and did not, as it did in Britain, contribute to forging a 'national' culture in the inter-war years.

The restoration of a free press was a major concern at the Liberation. The provisional government issued a series of *Ordonnances* in 1944 which provided the legislative framework for the press until the 1980s, and were designed to protect newspapers from foreign ownership and concentration and to ensure that readers knew who owned them. However, a framework which was designed for conditions in the late 1940s, when the government allocated paper, set advertising rates and fixed the cover price of titles, became increasingly inappropriate as time went by. The legislation made it impossible for newspapers to merge, or for different titles to enter into association, or to engage in cognate activities or to achieve vertical integration; nor could outside commercial or industrial capital be injected into newspaper companies. What is more, the law made a distinction between national and regional newspapers in prohibiting individuals from being proprietors of both.

The medium-term effect of these measures which were designed to ensure diversity was to reduce dramatically the number of daily newspapers in circulation by the middle of the 1950s, and by the 1970s, with the loss of advertising revenue and readers to television, many well-known titles such as *Le Figaro*, *France soir* and *L'Aurore* were in severe financial trouble. All three were taken over by the Groupe Hersant, disregarding the 1944 *Ordonnances* since Hersant already owned a large number of provincial titles, in a move which was tolerated by the right-wing government in power at the time. However, it was not until 1986 that the *Ordonnances* were finally replaced by a statute which, by setting a ceiling of 30 per cent of total daily newspaper circulation to be owned by any one group, recognized that the distinction between provincial and daily newspapers had become irrelevant. This statute also recognized that it might be desirable, in the national interest, to encourage the creation of large media groups as, indeed, happened in the following decade with the Havas and Groupe Lagardère mergers and acquisitions.

The impact of this history can still be seen in the current structure of the French press. Although France has a range of national daily newspapers published in Paris, among which are *Le Monde*, *Le Figaro* and *Libération*, their combined circulations are much lower than those of the provincial dailies, and they are, arguably, not as politically and culturally influential as daily newspapers elsewhere, and certainly in Britain. On the other hand, the weekly news magazines, such as *L'Express*, *Le Point* and *Le Nouvel Observateur* fulfil an important opinion-forming rôle which elsewhere is occupied by newspapers.

### Le paysage audiovisuel français

Television, by contrast, has had an immense political and cultural influence in post-war France and it has also been the focus of political protest and anxiety. Television was a vital component of post-war reconstruction. Throughout the 1950s, when the medium was in its infancy and very few households owned sets, it was considered an instrument of potential republican inclusiveness and a superb means of bringing art and education to the people, and it was described, by one producer, as providing him with a class of several million pupils. At the same time it was also a means for discovering France and looking at French people, as another producer patronizingly put it, 'in the same way as film-makers went to look at Negroes [*sic*]'.[32] This conception of television as a unifying force was reinforced by the fact that there was, until 1963, only one channel whose schedules were organized on a 'one genre a night' basis.

However, as soon as significant numbers of households acquired television, the medium ceased to be as highly valued for its educational possibilities or its ability to broaden the viewers' horizons and instead came to be seen primarily as a means of political communication. This was partly because de Gaulle was an inspired television performer and manipulator of the medium, calling it 'un moyen sans égal (. . .) pour être présent partout'.[33] But it was also because until 1974 television remained under the control of a Ministry of Information with all its senior managers appointed by the government and frequently chosen for their political sympathies. Until the 1980s it also remained an exclusively public service. This was presented as a means of ensuring programme quality but it also provided channels for political influence. De Gaulle believed he needed to control television precisely because the provincial press was opposed to him. But the clearest expression of the national rôle of television was offered by President Pompidou who, in a celebrated press conference in 1972, described the medium as 'la voix de la France'.

Not surprisingly, the absence of alternative points of view on television ultimately discredited the medium as a purveyor of information, with the nadir in public confidence being reached at the time of the May 1968 events. And it also encouraged the growth of alternative sources of political comment, notably 'peripheral' radio stations like RTL and Europe 1, whose headquarters were sited outside the borders of France in Monaco or Luxembourg. The idea that television should speak for France was not simply a crude expression of a belief in the necessity of censorship; it also translated the idea of an autarkic 'national space', bounded and as far as possible protected from external influences. Censorship was only one, rather blunt, instrument for achieving this end. Another very important and very effective method pursued was that of ensuring that France adopted technological norms which were incompatible with those used in neighbouring countries. This had the simultaneous advantage of censoring content by preventing the importing or viewing of foreign broadcast material and of promoting French manufacturing by creating a closed market for its electronics industries. Thus, as far back as 1922, the Société française électrique opted for long-wave broadcasting so as to prevent the importation of American wireless sets; in 1948 France adopted 819 lines as the black and white TV standard in order to protect domestic TV manufacturers; and in 1967 it chose the SECAM colour process rather than the PAL used elsewhere in western Europe. It was not until the 1980s that this kind of protectionism was rendered obsolete by the diversification of the means of transmitting and delivering audiovisual material through pre-recorded video cassettes, cable and satellite.

The 1981 socialist government promised to take television out of politics by the creation of a tutelary body which would institute an arm's-length relationship between the government and television. The body went through various avatars: the *Haute Autorité* (1982–6), the *Commission nationale de la communication et des libertés* (CNCL) (1986–9) and finally the *Conseil supérieur de l'audiovisuel*

**Table 3.2 French cultural practices**

| PROPORTION DE FRANÇAIS ÂGÉS DE 15 ANS ET PLUS QUI . . . | 1973 | 1981 | 1989 | 1997 |
|---|---|---|---|---|
| Équipement audiovisuel et fréquence d'usage | | | | |
| . . . possèdent dans leur foyer: | | | | |
| au moins un téléviseur | 86 | 93 | 96 | 96 |
| plusieurs | [a] | 10 | 24 | 45 |
| un magnétoscope | [a] | 2 | 25 | 72 |
| une chaîne hi-fi | 8 | 29 | 56 | 74 |
| un appareil non hi-fi | 53 | 53 | 31 | 33 |
| un lecteur de CD | [a] | [a] | 11 | 67 |
| un baladeur («walkman») | [a] | [a] | 32 | 45 |
| . . . regardent la télévision: | | | | |
| tous les jours | 65 | 69 | 73 | 77 |
| plus irrégulièrement | 22 | 21 | 17 | 14 |
| jamais | 12 | 9 | 10 | 9 |
| (durée moyenne d'écoute TV)[b] | 16 h | 16 h | 20 h | 22 h |
| . . . écoutent disques ou cassettes: | | | | |
| au moins un jour sur deux | 15 | 31 | 32 | 40 |
| plus irrégulièrement | 51 | 44 | 41 | 36 |
| jamais | 4 | 25 | 27 | 24 |
| Les rapports au livre | | | | |
| . . . possèdent des livres dans leur foyer | 73 | 80 | 87 | 91 |
| . . . sont inscrits dans une bibliothèque | 13 | 14 | 17 | 21 |
| (dont bibliothèque principale) | 7 | 8 | 13 | 15 |
| . . . ont, dans les 12 derniers mois: | | | | |
| acheté au moins 1 livre | 51 | 56 | 62 | 63 |
| lu au moins 1 livre | 70 | 74 | 75 | 74 |
| lu de 1 à 9 livres | 24 | 28 | 32 | 34 |
| lu de 10 à 24 livres | 23 | 26 | 25 | 23 |
| lu 25 livres et plus | 22 | 19 | 17 | 14 |
| ne sait pas | 1 | 2 | 1 | 3 |
| Les sorties et les visites culturelles | | | | |
| . . . sont allés, dans les 12 derniers mois aux spectacles suivants au moins 1 fois | | | | |
| Danses folkloriques | 12 | 11 | 12 | 13 |
| Danse classique, moderne ou contemporaine[b] | 6 | 5 | 6 | 8 |
| Cirque | 11 | 10 | 9 | 13 |
| Music hall, variétés | 11 | 10 | 10 | 10 |
| Opérette | 4 | 2 | 3 | 2 |
| Opéra | 3 | 2 | 3 | 3 |
| Concert de rock ou jazz[b] | 6 | 10 | 13 | 13 |
| Concert de musique classique | 7 | 7 | 9 | 9 |
| Théâtre joué par des professionnels | 12 | 10 | 14 | 16 |
| . . . ont visité au moins une fois, dans les 12 derniers mois, un ou une: | | | | |
| Exposition temporaire (peinture ou sculpture) | 19 | 21 | 23 | 25 |
| Musée | 27 | 30 | 30 | 33 |
| Monument historique | 32 | 32 | 28 | 30 |

a. La question n'était pas posée; b. La formulation de la question n'était pas strictement identique dans les quatre enquêtes. *Data*: DEP (Ministère de la Culture), enquêtes «Pratiques culturelles», 1973, 1981, 1989, 1997.

*Source*: *L'État de la France* © Éditions La Découverte.

(CSA). But it was only successful because during the 1980s government preoccupation shifted from politics to technology and business, a shift which led to a radical revision of policy. Whereas previously the defence of public sector broadcasting had been seen as axiomatic, now governments of both the left and the right hurried to create new television channels which could take account of viewers' changing tastes and the greater accessibility of programmes from outside France. *Canal Plus*, launched in 1984, and *M6*, launched in 1986, were both designed for more specialist or narrowly targeted audiences, of the kind satellite and cable channels were catering to, and both became very successful, while *La Cinq*, the one attempt to start a new 'general interest' commercial channel, ended in bankruptcy. In the 1980s, therefore, government policy envisaged television less as a means to influence public opinion or to place a particular interpretation on national or world events, and more as a means to encourage consumption and stimulate the advertising, consumer and electronics industries.

It is interesting, in this context, that the major shareholders in *Canal Plus* were consortia like L'Oréal and Perrier, and that when TF1 was sold to the private sector in 1987 the purchaser was the construction company Bouygues. Increasingly, television had become a small component in the construction of international conglomerates which could, in the case of Matra (Bouygues' rival for the acquisition of TF1), range over fields as various as missiles, books, newspapers, public transport and cars. By the 1990s, therefore, the French government's efforts were almost exclusively directed at trying to ensure a strong national presence in such conglomerates by means of its privatizations of electronics and telecommunications firms.

There is little doubt that television made an important contribution to the creation of a unified national culture in France in the 1950s and 1960s, but that it progressively lost this rôle from the 1970s onwards. But although this is recognized in government policies, public discussion still treats television as though it were a national or a European question, referring to the 'paysage audiovisuel français' (PAF) and calling for the protection of the national or European media space from foreign – that is, American or Japanese – penetration.

In 1960 the French government successfully argued that newspapers should be exempted from the free market provisions of the Treaty of Rome on the grounds that cultural products were exceptional. In 1982, shortly after he became minister of culture, Jack Lang made a speech in Mexico City setting out the ideological position of the socialist government, in which he denounced American cultural imperialism and defended the right to 'cultural self-determination'. In 1993 the European Union, led in this instance by France, made an argument based on 'l'exception culturelle' that audiovisual products should be exempted from the General Agreement on Tariffs and Trade (GATT), then in the course of renegotiation. Although 'Europe' had now replaced 'France' as the territory to be defended, the policies, based on screening quotas and import tariffs, had not evolved much since the 1950s. French television was defended in the name of quality and diversity even though its programme output was not necessarily of high quality. Thus television has remained as much a focus of passionate concern as it was in the 1960s, but the object of this concern has shifted from

**Jack Lang** (b.1939)

Lawyer and professor of public law, Lang became director of the Théâtre universitaire de Nancy and of the Festival de Nancy. With the election of the Socialists in 1981 he was appointed ministre de la culture, a post which he held from 1981 to 1986 and again from 1988 to 1992, briefly adding, in 1992 to 1993, the portfolio of education. A charismatic individual, famous for his clothes, his liking for celebrities and his robust defence of the rôle of the state in the support of culture, Lang was the media-friendly 'pageant-master' of the Mitterrand presidency. His most spectacularly stage-managed events were Mitterrand's inauguration ceremony, held at the Panthéon, and the celebration of the bicentenary of the Revolution in 1989. Under Lang, state spending on culture virtually doubled, a series of *grands travaux* were initiated and/or completed, and massive investment was channelled into the creation of new museums, festivals and cultural facilities, as much in the provinces as in Paris. Following the example of de Gaulle's minister of culture, André Malraux, his tenure of office was marked by the explicit recognition of the significance of culture both in the domestic economy and in the promotion of tourism and the image of France abroad.

political interference and censorship to the preservation and promotion of national and European identity [see Text 3.17].

## The education system

The post-war period has been characterized by a massive increase in the demand for education, continuing a trend which had first become apparent in the 1930s. The changed nature of work and the growth of the tertiary sector meant that new skills were required, necessitating longer periods of schooling. At the same time, the general rise in living standards meant that many parents could aspire to a more extended period of education for their children.

This was achieved by a series of measures. In 1959 the period of compulsory schooling was extended to ten years by raising the school-leaving age from fifteen to sixteen, while the education system was also extended on either side of the period of compulsory schooling. By 1996–7 36 per cent of two-year-olds and 99.3 per cent of three-year-olds were in school, compared with less than 50 per cent of three-year-olds in Great Britain, a level of take-up which must be linked to changing patterns of child care and to the massive increase in the number of women with children in the work-force, as well as to the desire to improve performance through early schooling.

At the other end of the spectrum there has been a huge increase in the number of children staying at school after the age of sixteen, so that by the end of the 1990s the number of pupils in the *deuxième cycle* of the *lycée* stood at nearly 90 per cent of the age cohort, as against 36 per cent at the end of the 1960s. In this way, extended secondary education has ceased to be reserved for a small elite and has become accessible to the vast majority of young people in France, while the stated objective for the year 2000 was that 80 per cent of each cohort should have achieved the 'niveau baccalauréat'.[34] Higher education has also experienced continuous expansion in France since the 1960s and the total number of students rose from half a million in 1960 to over two million in the 1990s, with most of the additional students to be found in the universities. This currently represents about 48 per cent of the age cohort and it has transformed the French universities into mass-education establishments (see Table 3.3).

### Secondary education

The content and organization of the secondary school curriculum have undergone a series of modifications since the beginning of the Fifth Republic. The main changes have involved the abolition of the unified *baccalauréat* and its replacement by specific *baccalauréats* in specific disciplines, based on 'filières', or groupings of homologous subjects such as mathematics and physics (1963); the creation of the *Collèges d'enseignement secondaire* (CES), the 'collèges uniques' which provide a single, comprehensive establishment attended by all children in the *premier cycle* (1964); and the abolition of streaming in the *premier cycle* (a measure which was introduced from 1977 onwards).

As far as concerns the content of the curriculum, the French system has two features of note: the strong development of technical education and the value accorded to excellence in mathematics. At the end of the *premier cycle*, at the age of fourteen or thereabouts, young people must choose how they are going to complete the remainder of their education. About 100,000 leave school every year with no qualification. The remainder either follow the academic route to one of the various *baccalauréats* or take up some form of manual or technical training. The latter takes place, for the most part, in institutions known as *lycées professionnels* after the age of fifteen, although some pupils may already find themselves in 'technological' classes when they enter 'quatrième' at the age of about thirteen. The qualifications available are the *Certificat d'aptitude professionnelle* (CAP) and the *Brevet d'études professionnelles* (BEP), the latter being less craft-specific and containing more general education. In 1987 a *baccalauréat professionnel* was created in order to meet industry's demands for skilled labour and, together with the *baccalauréat technique*, accounted for almost half of all *baccalauréat* qualifications achieved in 1997.

Thus a system has been devised which encourages large numbers of young people to stay on at school to receive education and training and which attempts to be sensitive to the labour market. As for those in the academic sections, the abolition of selection by ability has led to a form of streaming by subject. Virtually all the *grandes écoles* and the selective disciplines of the university base entry either on a mathematical *baccalauréat*, especially the *Bac C*, or on a highly mathematical entrance examination, and this has meant that large numbers of pupils study mathematics, with intense competition to do well in the subject. Those who do not wish, or are unable, to do so find themselves in one of the other *baccalauréat* groupings based on arts or social sciences.

### Higher education

The French school-leaver with a *baccalauréat* essentially has three higher education options: admission to a university, admission to an *Institut universitaire de technologie* (IUT) or admission to a *classe préparatoire* leading to a *grande école*. The prestige attached to each of these possible routes is directly linked to the

**Table 3.3 The democratisation of the education system**

| INDICATEUR | UNITÉ | 1970 | 1980 | 1995 | 1997 |
|---|---|---|---|---|---|
| Effectifs d'élèves, d'étudiants et d'apprentis | | | | | |
| Élèves (public + privé) | *milliers* | 11 896 | 12 502 | 12 706 | 11 886 |
| Maternelle | *milliers* | 2 213 | 2 383 | 2 635 | 2 403 |
| Primaire | *milliers* | 4 799 | 4 610 | 4 183 | 3 979,5[b] |
| Collège | *milliers* | 2 920 | 3 137 | 3 430 | 3 305[c] |
| Lycée professionnel | *milliers* | 650 | 773 | 729 | 708,4[e] |
| Lycée général et technologique | *milliers* | 848 | 1 102 | 1 537 | 1 490 |
| Apprentis | *milliers* | 232 | 241 | 306 | 340 |
| Étudiants | *milliers* | 854 | 1 176 | 2 170 | 2 102,5 |
| Préparation aux grandes écoles | *milliers* | 32 | 39 | 76 | 81,2[f] |
| Sections TS (techniciens sup.) | *milliers* | 30 | 67 | 230 | 233 |
| IUT (instituts univers. de technologie) | *milliers* | 24 | 54 | 103 | 109,4 |
| Universités (sans IUT) | *milliers* | 637 | 793 | 1 469 | 1 285,2 |
| Écoles d'ingénieurs | *milliers* | 30 | 37 | 51 | 79,1 |
| Écoles de commerce | *milliers* | 9 | 18 | 53[d] | 46,8 |
| Autres (paramédical, etc.) | *milliers* | 92 | 168 | 287[d] | 267,8[m] |
| Niveaux et diplômes | | | | | |
| Génération au niveau bac | % | 17 | 34 | 63,7[s] | 67,9 |
| Nombre de bacheliers | *milliers* | 167 | 222 | 459[h] | 469[o] |
| Pourcentage d'une génération | % | 21 | 29 | 61[h] | 63 |
| Nombre de licenciés | *milliers* | 40 | 42 | 117,5 | 131[p] |
| Nombre de doctorats | *milliers* | 1,1 | 1,5 | 9,2 | 9,4[p] |
| Nombre de diplômes d'ingénieurs | *milliers* | 8,8 | 11,7 | 21,8 | 22,8 |
| Établissements (public + privé) | | | | | |
| Nombre d'écoles | *milliers* | 74,5 | 67,6 | 61,8 | 58,9 |
| Nombre de collèges | *milliers* | 5,2 | 6,4 | 6,9 | 6,7 |
| Nombre de lycées | *milliers* | 5,6 | 4,6 | 2,7[i] | 4,3 |
| Personnels de l'Éducation nationale | | | | | |
| Total | *milliers* | 650 | 735 | 1 212,2 | 1 076,7[q] |
| Non enseignants | *milliers* | 179 | 222 | 315 | 288,3[q] |
| Enseignants | *milliers* | 471 | 513 | 896,8 | 788,4[q] |
| dont instituteurs et professeurs des écoles | *milliers* | 241 | 292 | 755,2[g] | 302[q] |
| professeurs second degré | *milliers* | 201 | 280 | | 347[q] |
| universitaires | *milliers* | 28 | 41 | 72,8 | 73,6[q] |
| Dépense intérieure d'éducation[k] | | | | | |
| Dépense totale | *milliards FF* | 322[a] | 378[a] | 563[a] | 592[r] |
| Tous ministères | % | 70,0 | 69,1 | 65,4 | 64,6 |
| Collectivités territoriales | % | 14,1 | 14,3 | 20,0 | 20,4 |
| Autres administrations publiques | % | 0,3 | 0,4 | 2,3 | 2,3 |
| Entreprises | % | 4,9 | 5,5 | 5,4 | 5,8 |
| Ménages | % | 10,7 | 10,7 | 6,9 | 6,9 |
| Dépense intér. d'éduc. par hab. | *FF* | 6 100[a] | 6 900[a] | 9 700[a] | 10 100[r] |
| Dépense intér. par élève ou étudiant | *FF* | 21 000[a] | 23 700[a] | 33 800[a] | 35 700[r] |

a. Aux prix de 1995; b. Dont classes d'adaptation, d'initiation, classes spéciales 1er degré (60,6); c. Dont enseignements «adaptés» du 2e degré (118,7); d. 1993; e. Non compris 2e degré agriculture (152,7); f. Dont préparations «intégrées» à certaines écoles d'ingénieurs (2,4); g. Dont 121,4 (milliers) sous contrat dans le privé; h. Données 1996; i. N'incluant pas les lycées professionnels (1,9 millier); k. La dépense intérieure d'éducation représentait 6,5% du PIB en 1975, 6,4% en 1980, 7,3% en 1997; m. Dont IUFM (81,3); o. Session 1997, bac général, technologique et professionnel; p. En 1996; q. Public seulement (1996–97); r. Aux prix de 1997; s. Education nationale seulement (67,9 en comptant toutes les formations).

*Data*: Ministère de l'Éducation nationale, Comptes de l'éducation.

*Source*: *L'État de la France* © Éditions La Découverte.

level of qualification required for entry, the degree of selection practised by the establishment to which entry is sought, and the length of study offered.

Undergraduate studies at university are organized into a *premier* and a *deuxième cycle*, with the *troisième cycle* being the postgraduate level. Thus at the end of two years (*premier cycle*) students are awarded a DEUG (*Diplôme d'études universitaires générales*), at the end of three years a *Licence* and at the end of four years (*deuxième cycle*) a *Maîtrise*. Although in theory the two-year diploma is a nationally recognized qualification, it has little or no value on the labour market and, these days, even the *Licence* is not well looked on by employers, so that most students, if they can, complete the *Maîtrise* which takes a minimum of four years. Hence this level of qualification is sometimes referred to as '*Bac* + 4'.

Access to university is via the *baccalauréat* and every *bachelier* has a right to a university place. However, within this general principle of 'non-selection', forms of selection do occur. Some disciplines, such as economics, require applicants to hold a particular *baccalauréat*, whilst others like medicine, dentistry and veterinary science apply a *numerus clausus* at the end of the first year of study, in this way providing only a limited number of places. Those *bacheliers* who fail to secure a reserved place or who have obtained the 'wrong' kind of *baccalauréat* are therefore obliged to study arts, law or some sciences, subjects in which no limit is placed on the numbers of students admitted.

Two other factors affect choice of university and so act as a form of selection at the point of entry and during the course of university study. The first is the 'carte universitaire' which normally obliges students to attend the local university for at least the *premier cycle*. It is designed to keep first- and second-year students out of Paris, though the requirement is widely flouted. The second form of selection is more insidious. Known as 'la sélection par l'échec', it is particularly apparent in arts faculties where there is a high wastage rate and a high proportion of students who have to repeat one or more years of study to obtain a degree. *La sélection par l'échec* is perhaps the inevitable counterpart of the failure to introduce selection on entry, which has frequently proved to be politically unacceptable in France. But it is equally the result of the inability of a system designed to be much smaller to cope with large and increasing numbers of students, and of inadequate counselling and guidance.

The *Instituts universitaires de technologie* were created in 1966 to fill a gap in the training of technicians. They offer a qualification obtained in two years, the *Diplôme universitaire de technologie* (DUT) which is based on vocationally and professionally oriented courses that are strongly influenced by employers' demands. Entry to the IUT is selective and their 'diplomates' are highly successful in securing employment, with the result that these institutions have become extremely popular. By 1996–7 over 100,000 students were in the IUT.

The *grandes écoles* are unique to France. They are highly selective, socially prestigious and offer high-level vocational training primarily in engineering, administration or business subjects. Some, such as the *École polytechnique* (known as X) or the *École normale supérieure* (ENS), trace their origin back to the late eighteenth century when the state recognized the need to train managers with scientific expertise and teachers with higher education. But many, such as the *École nationale d'administration* (ENA), have been founded since the Second World War. Some *grandes écoles* are financed by the state and are dependent on particular ministries for whose sphere of activity they are intended to provide specialized personnel. In these cases, candidates who are successful in gaining admission to a *grande école* become civil servants and receive a salary while undertaking their studies. Others, particularly the business schools, are run by private organizations such as chambers of commerce and charge fees, although scholarships are available for many students. Entrance to a *grande école* usually takes place one or two years after the *baccalauréat* on the basis of a competitive entrance examination known as a *concours d'entrée*. Prospective entrants first attend *classes préparatoires* held in a small number of *lycées* in large towns in order to prepare for these examinations, and do not usually enter a *grande école* until the age of twenty or twenty-one, while some *grandes écoles*, such as ENA, take students when they are even older, and only after they have first completed a course of study at another *grande école* such as the *École polytechnique*.

The *grandes écoles* train the French business, managerial and, increasingly these days, political elite. Three post-war presidents of the Republic – Georges Pompidou, Valéry Giscard d'Estaing and Jacques Chirac – have been graduates of a *grande école*, as have many other senior politicians, including Prime Ministers Fabius, Rocard, Juppé and Jospin who all trained at ENA. The intimate link between politics, management and the civil service is underpinned by the 'old boy' network of the *grandes écoles* and has been much criticized in recent years. The *grandes écoles* have responded by diversifying and increasing their recruitment, although to nothing like the same extent as the university sector. Thus all the *grandes écoles* now admit both men and women (in some cases, such as those of the *Hautes études commerciales* and the ENS, this has meant the amalgamation of separate establishments) while ENA has made a particular effort to broaden its social base by opening its recruitment to mature students already in employment in the public sector. Recruitment to the *grandes écoles* rose in the 1980s and 1990s, but even so these establishments still represent a minute proportion of the total higher education sector. Moreover, there is little evidence that expansion has greatly altered the social composition of recruitment, and the pupils of the *grandes écoles* are still drawn overwhelmingly from business, managerial or professional backgrounds. The most famous, such as X or ENA, also show a strong geographical bias in their recruitment, with the majority of successful applicants coming from the Paris region.

### Education and the promotion of equality

As Raymond Boudon has reminded us, education has acquired immense significance in post-war industrial societies, since it is seen as the means to iron out social inequalities and promote social mobility. In order to discover how successful the French system has been in these respects we can consider the ways in which class, sex, ethnic or national origin, and geography affect a child's prospects at school and in higher education. As far as class is concerned, research suggests that children's success at school depends more than anything else on what Pierre Bourdieu has called their parents' 'cultural capital', their own level of education and ability to deploy the 'symbolic capital' with which it endows them. Viewed in this way, the education system remains profoundly conservative, reinforcing existing social categories rather than promoting mobility.

As far as sex is concerned, there has, on the face of it, been a dramatic change. Thus in the mid-1980s the number of female students exceeded the number of male students for the first time, although women had been catching up rapidly from the 1960s onwards and numbers had equalized around 1975. However, the academic curriculum remains sexually segregated. Women are far less well represented in science and engineering than in the arts and social sciences, although they are well represented in medicine, economics and business studies, while as far as vocational training is concerned, there is almost total sexual segregation: the boys train to be metalworkers, mechanics, builders, electricians and so on, while the girls train to be secretaries, hairdressers and the like.

Where ethnic or national origin is concerned, it is estimated that in French schools there are over one million children of immigrants, many of whom are not European in origin and many of whom do not have French as their first language. Since 1970 specific measures have been taken to assist their progress through school. However, children of immigrants remain disproportionately highly represented among those children who have to repeat a year of schooling and among those who leave school with no qualifications or with poor qualifications.

Finally, geography can play a part in the creation of inequalities. For example, there is wide variation in the provision and take-up of pre-school education and care, so that, although the national percentage of two-year-olds in school is high, this figure disguises the fact that provision is much better in Paris, Brittany and the south than it is in the north. The same pattern emerges with the percentage of pupils repeating classes, where the industrial north and Basse Normandie score particularly badly, and with the percentage of pupils obtaining the *baccalauréat* which, with the exception of Paris, is much higher in the south than in the north. Since the regions acquired responsibility for the maintenance of secondary schools and their equipment under the decentralization law of 1983, it seems likely that even greater regional disparities will arise in future. In sum, the French education system in the post-war period has not been very effective in promoting social equality or mobility, despite the very large increase in the numbers of young people benefiting from higher education.

## Convergences and differences in French society

The education system is a good weather vane of society since its multiple rôles make it the focus of social change and discontent. A number of protest movements have originated within the education system in recent years which, in addition to drawing attention to aspects of the system that have failed to function properly, have all exposed other problems of a more broadly social nature.

The first and most radical of these was May 1968 which, as has been said, altered the whole spectrum of social relations. Within the university, May 1968 was a protest against the hierarchical structure of the institution as reflected in the content and organization of disciplines, in the lack of personal contact between students and teachers, and in the inability of a university which had expanded very rapidly to deal administratively with large numbers of students. But behind these protests lay a considerable anxiety about life chances. Thus Daniel Cohn-Bendit, perhaps the best known of the student leaders, remarked in an interview:

> L'économie ayant atteint un certain niveau de modernisation, il fallait moderniser l'école . . . A un certain moment la petite et moyenne bourgeoisie en ont fait les frais. L'enseignement a été rationalisé en vue de former les technocrates . . . Les étudiants qui se révoltent le font aussi pour conserver les privilèges de la bourgeoisie, qu'ils perdent momentanément dans une transformation de la société dans le passage du capitalisme concurrentiel au capitalisme monopolistique.[35]

The reform of the university structures and curriculum embodied in the 1968 *loi Faure* did not resolve the debate over the purpose of the university. If the university was not – or only in part – for the disinterested pursuit of knowledge and the training of future scholars, then its function must be to train the work-force. However, from the students' point of view it no longer performed that function as effectively as it had done in the past, since the privilege conferred by a university degree was losing its value; while from the point of view of the government there might well be an increasing number of students and therefore, theoretically, a better trained work-force, but many of these students were not trained to do the right things. The sociologist Alain Touraine described the legacy of May 1968 very pessimistically: 'Lettres, sciences et droit, domaines sans sélection, s'enfoncent dans l'abandon, tandis que la médecine, l'économie et les sciences politiques prospèrent grâce à la sélection et que le pouvoir des grandes écoles, hypersélectives, ne cesse de se renforcer.'[36]

In the decades since 1968 politicians have continued to condemn the non-selective disciplines as 'voies de garage' and several proposals to introduce selective university entry have been made but have failed. Universities have made attempts to devise more vocationally oriented courses and to develop links

**Daniel Cohn-Bendit** (b.1945)

Nicknamed 'Dany-le-rouge' because of his politics and his red hair, Cohn-Bendit was a student of sociology at Nanterre in 1968 and quickly became one of the leaders of 'le mouvement de mai', a self-appointed spokesperson for students' rights and a highly personable television performer. He was expelled from France after the events – an action which was possible because he had, in fact, been born in Germany – and was not allowed to return for ten years. Meanwhile, he converted to Green politics and was elected as a Green to the Frankfurt City Council in 1989. Back in France, he headed the Green list for the 1999 European elections and was elected to the European Parliament. He is the author of several books, including *Le Gauchisme, remède à la maladie sénile du communisme* (1968) and *Nous l'avons tant aimée, la révolution* (1996), and was the inspiration for the ironic 1968 chant, 'nous sommes tous des Juifs allemands'.

with employers. Despite this, however, the issues raised in May 1968 remain posed, and now that the university has become part of a mass-education system, the question of its purpose and efficiency will be asked with renewed urgency in the years beyond 2000.

The second protest movement concerned a proposal to reform private schools. Traditionally, French parents sent their children to private schools for religious rather than social or academic reasons: 90 per cent of private schools (*écoles libres*) are Catholic and many are to be found in traditionally Catholic regions of the country such as the west. Their continuing existence is the counterpart of the prohibition of religious instruction in state schools which are required by law to be 'laïques'. But from 1959 onwards, many private schools began to receive subsidies from the public purse and had therefore become partially integrated into the state system. In his 1981 election manifesto, *110 Propositions*, François Mitterrand called for 'un grand service public unifié et laïque de l'Éducation nationale', but by the time his education minister Alain Savary introduced a bill, it gave rise to massive protests. The summer of 1984 witnessed the extraordinary spectacle of more than one million people demonstrating in the streets of Paris in support of private education, as a result of which Savary was removed from office, his bill was withdrawn and Prime Minister Pierre Mauroy was replaced by Laurent Fabius.

If the freedom to give a child a religious education had been all that was at stake, it is unlikely that it would have aroused so much opposition. After all, little more than 10 per cent of the population are practising Catholics and a series of opinion polls taken in the early 1980s showed that religion only came sixth in a list of reasons why parents opted for private education.[37] Nor, if the issue were purely religious, would it have aroused equal opposition from the left as well as the right. The demonstration revealed the extent to which parents felt disempowered by the state education system. Faced with a decision that a child should repeat a year or that she or he should pursue a course of study different from the one desired, parents wished to retain the option of private education as a 'second chance' where the rules and regulations of the state system do not apply. The demonstration pointed to another trend as well: the developing impatience with the extension of the powers of the state in the policies pursued by the socialist government between 1981 and 1984, an impatience which was to find further political expression in 1986 when the left lost the legislative elections to a right bent on 'moins d'État'. Thus the 1984 demonstrations, in addition to suggesting public loss of confidence in the state education system, also pointed to doubts as to the state's role in the provision of public services in general.

In 1989 a dispute of a different kind broke out in Creil, north of Paris, which challenged the principle of the 'école laïque'. The dispute, which came to be known as the 'affaire des foulards islamiques', concerned three teenage girls who attended school wearing headscarves and refused to take them off when asked to do so by the head teacher, allegedly because wearing headscarves was an essential part of their religious observance.[38] The girls were excluded from school for a period, the matter preoccupied the media for several months and it gave rise to a series of public demonstrations [see Texts 3.18 and 3.19]. This affair brought out into the open a variety of attitudes towards the role of school in society and also revealed strong divisions within the ranks of the government. Above all, in posing the question as to the meaning and purpose of *l'école laïque* in contemporary France, it asked whether the school system had been able to adapt to changing social realities.

For some on the left *laïcité* meant the exercise of equal treatment for all pupils within the school, whatever their social, cultural, political, religious or regional differences outside school. Many socialist teachers subscribed to this view of *laïcité* as a guarantee of equality of treatment, as did women's groups, who saw in the Islamic headscarves the symbol of the oppression of women under Islam. Other groups on the left, however, interpreted the principle of *laïcité* as meaning ideological neutrality, that is the school's obligation not to favour any religion or belief system but to tolerate them all and to respect differences of opinion. On the political right, in general, support was expressed for the old-fashioned concept of *laïcité* which would have required the Creil girls to conform to the sartorial demands of their head teacher.

Like the *projet de loi Savary*, therefore, this affair revealed an education system whose institutional principles were unable to cope with the pressures of contemporary urban society or to adapt to the social circumstances of many of the children it purported to educate. Furthermore, an important element of this debate, which on one level was undoubtedly inflated out of all proportion to its significance, was that the girls in question were *beurs*. In insisting on wearing headscarves in school, they appeared to be wishing to affirm, symbolically at least, a different identity from the one promoted by the French school system, an identity that many people in France, not just those on the right, considered to be 'not French'. In this way, the *affaire des foulards* became entangled with a much wider debate which raged towards the end of the 1980s, not just about immigration and the integration of immigrants and their children into French society, but also about whether France would become an overtly multicultural society by giving more offical recognition to different ethnic or religious communities within a Republic traditionally conceived of as 'one and indivisible'.

If these protest movements reveal a common concern it is that the aspirations of the 1950s and 1960s have not been achieved and, indeed, are now being called into question, and in this the education system is often just the catalyst, the focal point of inequalities and differences which have other and deeper causes.

## Conclusion

French society at the start of the twenty-first century offers the student a fascinating set of paradoxes. It is an urban society with a tremendous nostalgia for rural life, a society which simultaneously asserts its desire for European integration and for cultural independence, an extremely wealthy society which contains pockets of considerable poverty, and a society in which egalitarianism is a guiding principle but in which the search for equality has been all but abandoned.

Since 1945 French society has undoubtedly been modernized. General living standards have risen, the population is better housed, better fed, better clothed, more long-lived and better educated than it was in 1945. Legislation of a progressive kind has been enacted in the domain of private and public life, giving legal force to equality of opportunity, recognizing the rights of women and children, bringing social legislation in line with common practices and new family structures. At the same time, modernization has lost the wholly positive connotations it had in the immediate post-war period. The critique of affluence, consumerism and mass culture, which are seen as the fruits of modernization, is often made in the name of what is authentically French, of a different set of values which some commentators feel have slipped or are slipping away. The periodic demonstrations by farmers against proposals to reform the Common Agricultural Policy regularly unleash waves of support for a way of life which is not only seen as threatened by big European business but which somehow is felt to embody the essence of France. In the same way, the media campaign to defend French culture at the time of the GATT negotiations was conducted in terms of the defence of French and European specificity and identity.

The 1992 Referendum on the Maastricht Treaty was extremely interesting in this context. Whilst most politicians recognized the need for France to compete with its major EU partner, Germany, and probably accepted the economic policy which, as Part II shows, was followed throughout the 1980s and 1990s in an attempt to position France as a viable competitor to Germany, the Maastricht Referendum acquired a cultural dimension which undoubtedly took President Mitterrand and his advisors by surprise. The debate revealed considerable misgivings about European integration, not just from the xenophobic right or the protectionist left, but among pro-Europeans. The fear was expressed that Maastricht would exact too high a social price, particularly in the area of employment.

A parallel issue, which also had a European dimension, was the question of immigration and the treatment of immigrants and asylum seekers which continually resurfaced in the 1980s and 1990s, often causing embarrassment to governments in office. This issue was a constant reminder, if one were needed, that the search for social consensus which post-war prosperity had promised, and which before May 1968 had apparently been achieved, had been abandoned as a policy objective because the economic crisis had caused agreement about social objectives to evaporate.

At the turn of the twenty-first century, therefore, France has to resolve a number of urgent questions, of which some of the most urgent are employment and unemployment, the continuation of the welfare state and the treatment of immigrants in the community. But, beyond these, France will continue to confront the challenges posed to its social and cultural identity both by convergence within Europe, which is reasonably well accepted, and by globalization, which continues to cause profound disquiet in many sections of French society.

# Notes

1 See C. Flockton, 'French Local Government Reform and Urban Planning', in *Local Government Studies*, September–October 1983, pp.65–77.
2 See E. Weber, *Peasants into Frenchmen* (Chatto & Windus, 1979) p.206.
3 P. Rosanvallon, *Crise et avenir de la classe ouvrière* (Seuil, 1979) p.116.
4 H. Mendras, *La seconde révolution française* (Gallimard, 1988) p.34.
5 P. Rosanvallon, *Crise*, p.6.
6 See P. Chombart de Lauwe, *La vie quotidienne des familles ouvrières*, 3rd edn (Éditions du CNRS, 1977) pp.10–11.
7 R. Boudon, *L'inégalité des chances: la mobilité sociale dans les sociétés industrielles* (Armand Colin, 1973) p.12.
8 Y. Lemel, *La mobilité sociale* (Armand Colin, 1991) p.12.
9 For example, by J. Ardagh in *France Today* (Penguin, 1988) pp.330ff. Time has done little to mitigate the essential fatuousness, not to speak of the inaccuracy, of Ardagh's remarks.
10 See *Cahiers français*, 171, May–August 1975, p.20.
11 J. Mossuz-Lavau and M. Sineau, *Enquête sur les femmes et la politique* (PUF, 1983) pp.154ff.
12 See É. Badinter, *L'un est l'autre* (Odile Jacob, 1986).
13 B. Philippe, 'La République et ses immigrés', *Le Monde*, 28 June 1997, p.1.
14 Ibid.
15 *Le Figaro Magazine*, 21 September 1991, p.50.
16 L. Dirn, *La société française en tendances* (PUF, 1990) p.350.
17 M. Tribalat, *Faire France* (La Découverte, 1995) p.33.
18 See A. Hargreaves, *Voices from the North African Community* (Berg, 1992) pp.29–31, for an explanation of the term 'beur'.
19 See *L'état de la France 1989* (La Découverte, 1989) pp.32–4.
20 See, for example, M. Winock, *La République se meurt* (Seuil, 1980); Hervé Hamon and Patrick Rotman, *Génération*, 2 vols (Seuil, 1987–8).
21 See E. Sullerot, *Pour le meilleur et sans le pire* (Fayard, 1984) p.69.
22 H. Le Bras (ed.), *Population* (Hachette, 1985) p.25.
23 L. Dirn, *La société française*, p.361.
24 See *Données sociales 1990*, p.105.
25 See *L'état de la France 1989*, p.133.
26 *Données sociales 1990*, p.188.
27 B. Préel, in *L'état de la France 1989*, p.104.
28 H. Mendras, *La seconde révolution française* (Gallimard, 1988) p.70.
29 See *Données sociales 1990*, p.384.
30 See H. Mendras, *La seconde révolution*, p.82.
31 Ibid., p.83.
32 Jean Krier, quoted in J. Beaulieu, *La télévision des réalisateurs* (INA/La Documentation française, 1984) p.45.
33 C. de Gaulle, *Mémoires d'espoir* (Plon, 1994) pp.223–4.
34 This does not mean that 80 per cent of pupils will actually obtain the *baccalauréat* qualification, but that 80 per cent will take a course of study leading to it.
35 D. Cohn-Bendit, *La révolte étudiante* (Seuil, 1968) p.61.
36 A. Touraine, *Mort d'une gauche* (Galilée, 1979) p.205.
37 See A. Prost, *Éducation, société et politiques* (Seuil, 1992) p.174.
38 See R. Solé, *Le Monde*, 21 October 1989, p.1: 'On ne sait trop comment nommer l'objet du scandale: voile? foulard? tchador? *hidjeb*? Aucun de ces mots n'est satisfaisant, aucun n'est innocent.'

# Suggestions for further reading

## General literature in English

There are few overviews of contemporary French society in English. Of most use, though first published in 1982, is L. Hantrais, *Contemporary French Society* (Macmillan, 1989). A companion to volumes on French politics and the French economy, this contains chapters on demographic features, the family, social welfare, education and leisure, and contains a selection of supporting texts in French as well as a limited number of language exercises. More recent, and with a more socio-economic perspective, is C. Flockton and E. Kofman, *France* (Paul Chapman, 1989) which is particularly strong on spatial questions and the discussion of social inequalities. D. Hanley *et al.*, *Contemporary France: Politics and Society since 1945*, 2nd edn (Routledge & Kegan Paul, 1984) contains much of interest and use, although the contents need updating, and it is particularly strong on the politics of education. It may, however, be too detailed for the average undergraduate. G. Ross (ed.), *The Mitterrand Experiment: Continuity and Change in Modern France* (Polity, 1987), though it is mainly devoted to questions of political economy, nevertheless contains essays of interest on cultural and educational policy, while J. Hollifield and G. Ross (eds), *Searching for the New France* (Routledge, 1991) includes surveys of the welfare state, education, immigration, trade unions and the role of intellectuals in public life. It also contains an excellent bibliography. H. Mendras and A. Cole, *Social Change in Modern France* (Cambridge University Press, 1991) is an excellent, fairly recent essay on social trends based on Mendras's French work, while some of the chapters in M. Maclean, *The Mitterrand Years: Legacy and Evaluation* (Macmillan, 1998) may be usefully consulted. Similarly, J. Howorth and G. Ross (eds), *Contemporary France: A Review of Interdisciplinary Studies* (Frances Pinter, 1987) was an annual publication which may usefully be consulted for essays of topical interest. There are also a number of now classic socio-historical and socio-anthropological studies of France which provide fascinating background reading. Among these must be mentioned L. Wylie, *Village in the Vaucluse* (Harvard University Press, 1957), S. Hoffman *et al.*, *In Search of France* (Harvard University Press, 1963), T. Zeldin, *France 1848–1945*, 2 vols (Clarendon Press, 1973–6), T. Zeldin, *The French* (Collins, 1983) and E. Weber, *Peasants into Frenchmen* (Chatto & Windus, 1979).

## General literature in French

There are comparatively few accounts of contemporary French society which will provide an appropriate and adequate overview. Undoubtedly the most accessible is D. Borne, *Histoire de la société française depuis 1945* (A. Colin, 1990) which is written in an agreeable prose and is intended for students in the *classes préparatoires*. Similar, though by now dated, works are G. Dupeux, *La société française 1945–69* (A. Colin, 1969) and *La société française 1789–1970* (A. Colin, 1972). Though the first only covers half the post-war period, and most discussion centres on the 'modernization' of French society, it is intended as a textbook for university students and is helpful in taking little for granted, while the second volume has the advantage of placing contemporary developments within a broader historical context. More ambitious and perhaps less obviously geared towards the undergraduate market is P. Sorlin, *La société française contemporaine 1914–1968*, vol. 2 (Arthaud, 1971). Although less than half the book is devoted to the post-war period, it is particularly strong on the decline of the working class and contains a useful bibliography and chronology. Also to be recommended in terms of length and price as well as content are the relevant volumes in the Éditions du Seuil series, *Nouvelle histoire de la France contemporaine*: J.-P. Rioux, *La France de la Quatrième République*, 2 vols (Seuil, 1980), S. Bernstein, *La République gaullienne* (1989), S. Bernstein and J.-P. Rioux, *L'apogée Pompidou* (1995) and J.-J. Becker, *Crises et alternances* (1998). All are clearly and accessibly written, with chronology, index and suggestions for further reading.

General studies of the post-1968 period tend to be more polemical or more specialist. In the former category L. Dirn's *La société française en tendances* (PUF, 1990) is a pseudonymous work written by a group of sociologists who do not disguise their socialist sympathies. It does, however, attempt to look to the future and provides a useful summary of social trends and changes in such areas as consumption, leisure, family life, women's issues, community activities and so on. Similarly, H. Mendras, *La seconde révolution française 1965–84* (Gallimard, 1988) considers social change in terms of the break-up of the traditional class system, the decline of institutions such as the church, the army and the trade unions, the changing notions of age group and generation with their impact on work and education and changes in lifestyle. This is probably the best general essay on social change currently available in French. Three further indispensable sources of information on contemporary French society must be mentioned. *Données sociales* (INSEE/La Documentation française) is a volume published every few years (1984, 1988, 1990, 1993, 1996, 1999) by the French statistical office INSEE and is comparable to the British volume, *Social Trends*, though it is much larger and more comprehensive. In addition to essential statistical information on a variety of topics from population to education and income, it frequently contains comparative tables permitting French statistics to be looked at in relation to European trends. It also contains short essays on topics which appear to be of socio-political interest at the time of publication. *Cahiers français* is a periodical published five times a year by La Documentation française which, similarly, attempts a synthesis of information relating to a particular area of social, political or economic concern. Of particular use here has been 'Le Système éducatif', *Cahiers français*, 249, January–February 1991. Finally, the alternative view is given in the now annual *L'état de la France* (La Découverte), latest edition 1999. This contains a large number of very short summaries by experts on issues or problems of social interest ranging from rock music to adults who live alone, accompanied by a wealth of statistical information and suggestions for further reading. It is particularly strong on the analysis of lifestyles and has a section devoted to regional developments containing a *Tour de France*, or handy socio-economic portrait of each of the French regions. New editions are regularly produced.

## Specialist monographs

The changes in infrastructure, land use and communications are often best treated in the general works mentioned above. However, F. Bloch-Lainé, *La France en mai 1981 – forces et faiblesses* (La Documentation française, 1981), commissioned by the incoming socialist government, sets out briefly the policies to be adopted. M. Castells, *City, Class and Power* (Macmillan, 1978) is a classic left-wing essay on urban policy, much of which relates to France, while L. Chevalier, *Les Parisiens* (Hachette, 1967) is a now classic socio-anthropological essay devoted to one city in particular. J. F. Gravier, *Paris et le désert français* (Le Portulan, 1947) is an early, and by now classic, denunciation of the over-development of the Paris region and the under-development of the remainder of France, and it contains an extended statement of the view that France is under-populated, while M. Debatisse, *La révolution silencieuse* (Calmann-Lévy, 1964) is an account of the modernization of agriculture by one of the leaders of the trade union concerned. Hervé

Le Bras, *Les trois France* (Odile Jacob, 1987) attempts to relate urban and regional development to demographic factors, while H. Mendras, *Le changement social* (A. Colin, 1983) attempts the same thing from a sociological perspective. Useful works in English are M. Wynn, *Housing in Europe* (Croom Helm, 1983) and, for regional policy in particular, S. Mazey and M. Newman (eds), *Mitterrand's France* (Croom Helm, 1987).

There is a wealth of specialist literature on French social structure, only a very small fraction of which can be mentioned here. Y. Lemel, *Stratification et mobilité sociale* (A. Colin, 1989) provides a handy summary and analysis of debates over questions such as mobility, stratification and class structure, with useful and extensive bibliographical references as well as comparisons with Anglo-American literature on the subject. Classic studies referred to include S. Mallet, *La nouvelle classe ouvrière* (Seuil, 1963), E. Goblot, *La barrière et le niveau* (PUF, 1967), C. Thélot, *Tel père, tel fils?* (Dunod, 1982) and P. Chombart de Lauwe, *La vie quotidienne des familles ouvrières* (Éditions du CNRS, 1977). The decline of the working class is also addressed in P. Rosanvallon, *Crise et avenir de la classe ouvrière* (Seuil, 1979) and A. Touraine *et al.*, *Le mouvement ouvrier* (Fayard, 1984).

The literature on women is, by now, fairly extensive. M. Albistur and D. Armogathe, *Histoire du féminisme français* (Des Femmes, 1977) provides a useful account of the historical position of women in France, and E. Sullerot (ed.), *Le fait féminin* (Fayard, 1978) brings together a collection of essays on women from a variety of perspectives and translated from several languages. J. Mossuz-Lavau and M. Sineau, *Enquête sur les femmes et la politique* (PUF, 1983) offer a comprehensive study of women's political behaviour and this is usefully complemented by Y. Roudy's polemic, *La femme en marge* (Flammarion, 1975), written before she became the minister responsible for women's rights. In addition, F. Giroud (ed.), *Cent mesures pour les femmes* (La Documentation française, 1976) contains the proposals she introduced as the first secretary of state for women. Further suggestions are to found in the *États généraux des femmes 1989* (Des Femmes, 1990). By contrast, É. Badinter, *L'un est l'autre* (Odile Jacob, 1986) attempts to view the relations between men and women from a more philosophical point of view.

These works can be complemented by several useful anthologies in English: C. Laubier (ed.), *The Condition of Women in France, 1945 to the Present* (Routledge, 1990) is a collection of extracts from original French material relating to such matters as the French women's movement, home life and women and work, linked together with short introductory essays in English; C. Duchen, *Feminism in France: From May '68 to Mitterrand* (Routledge & Kegan Paul, 1986) particularly deals with questions relating to women and the social sphere; while T. Moi, *French Feminist Thought* (Blackwell, 1987) does the same for philosophical and literary writing.

There is now an equally abundant literature on questions of immigration. In English, M. Silverman, *Deconstructing the Nation: Immigration, Racism and Citizenship in Modern France* (Routledge, 1992) provides an excellent and up-to-date summary and analysis of legislation since the war. In French, M. Long (ed.), *Etre français aujourd'hui et demain*, 2 vols (UGE, 1988) contains the transcript of the hearings of the *Commission de la nationalité* in 1987, together with a summary of changes in French legislation on nationality since the Revolution and statistical material relating to the evolving size of the foreign population in France. G. Noiriel, *Le Creuset français* (Seuil, 1988) is an excellent history of immigration since the nineteenth century, with particularly useful comparisons with the American experience; H. Le Bras, *Marianne et les lapins* (Olivier Orban, 1991) is a witty and extremely spirited attack on the implicit racism of French 'natalist' policies and their effects on the immigrant community; while D. Schnapper, *La France de l'intégration* (Gallimard, 1991) states the case for the traditional French 'integrationist' approach to immigration, with interesting reflections on the philosophical and historical foundations for present policies. Michèle Tribalat's controversial *Faire France* (La Découverte, 1995) similarly considers the contribution of immigrants to French society and culture.

On generational conflict, H. Hamon and P. Rotman, *Génération*, 2 vols (Seuil, 1987–8) is a massive documentary account of May 1968. Otherwise the various editions of *L'état de la France* offer much of interest on old people and young people, especially children.

The literature in French on demographic questions is vast and we can do no more than offer a few bibliographical indications. An indispensable classic work is P. Ariès, *Histoire des populations françaises* (Seuil, 1971). For an up-to-date account, one need look no further than J. Valin, *La population française* (La Découverte, 1999) or the successive volumes of *Données sociales*, while the introduction written by H. Le Bras in *Population* (Hachette, 1985) sets in context the French preoccupation with demographic matters. On marriage, divorce and the welfare state, E. Sullerot, *Pour le meilleur et sans le pire* (Fayard, 1984) offers a polemical overview from a distinctly natalist perspective, while J. Mossuz-Lavau, *Les lois de l'amour* (Payot, 1991) looks at questions of sexuality in relation to matters of contraception, abortion, rape, harassment, homosexuality and so on. Much of the literature relating to women also deals with questions of contraception, abortion, marriage and divorce, while M. Foucault, *Histoire de la sexualité*, 3 vols (Gallimard, 1976–84) is the now classic philosophical study of questions of sexuality.

On the French welfare state, F. Ewald, *L'état providence* (Grasset, 1986) and D. Lamiot and P.-J. Lancry, *La protection sociale: les enjeux de la solidarité* (Nathan, 1989) both describe the French welfare system, while N. Murard, *La protection sociale* (La Découverte, 1996) and M.-T Join-Lambert *et al.*, *Politiques sociales* (Dalloz, 1997) both discuss its problems. H. Mendras, *La fin des paysans* (A. Colin, 1970) looks at the decline of agricultural labour. R. Linhart, *L'établi* (Minuit, 1978) offers a graphic description of life on the Renault production line.

P. Bourdieu, *La Distinction* (Minuit, 1979) provides fascinating portraits of the tastes and lifestyles of members of different social classes, and this can be complemented by O. Donnat, *Les pratiques culturelles des Français* (La Documentation française, 1998) as well as by essays in Dirn's *La Société française en tendances* and in *L'état de la France*. P. Ory, *L'aventure culturelle française* (Flammarion, 1989) offers a history of cultural policy since the war, while M. Fumaroli, *L'état culturel* (Éditions de Fallois, 1991) provides a virulent criticism of socialist cultural policies in the post-1981 administration. In English, D. Looseley's *The Politics of Fun* (Berg, 1995) is an unbeatable account of government cultural policies since the war.

A recent essay in English on the place of religion in French society is G. Salemohamed, 'The State and Religion: Rethinking *laïcité*', in G. Raymond (ed.), *Structures of Power in Modern France* (Macmillan, 1999). In French, the best account of the decline of the army and the church as significant social institutions is to be found in H. Mendras, *La seconde révolution française*. On the education system, the most authoritative writer is A. Prost in a series of books: the now dated *L'enseignement en France* (A. Colin, 1968), updated by *L'enseignement s'est-il démocratisé?* (PUF, 1986) and *Éducation, société et politiques* (Seuil, 1992). These can usefully be complemented by *Examen des politiques nationales d'éducation: France* (OECD, 1996). On May 1968, J. Sauvageot *et al.*, *La révolte étudiante* (Seuil, 1968) is a contemporary account, while Hamon and Rotman's *Génération* interviews many of the May 1968 leaders twenty years after the events. M. Atack, *May '68 in French Fiction and Film* (Oxford University Press, 1999) is a fascinating study of the cultural impact of the events. P. Bourdieu and J.-C. Passeron, *Les héritiers* (Minuit, 1964) and *La Reproduction* (Minuit, 1970) offer a thoroughgoing critique of the education system as an agent of equal opportunity, as does R. Boudon, from a more mathematical perspective, in *L'inégalité des chances* (A. Colin, 1973). By contrast, J. Lesourne, *Éducation et société: les défis de l'an*

*2000* (La Découverte, 1988), in a report commissioned by the French government, looks at the relationship between the needs of the economy and demand for education at the end of the century. On the media, the best account in English is R. Kuhn, *The Media in France* (Routledge, 1995) which can be updated with J. Forbes, 'The Press, the PAF and the Decline of Tutelage', in G. Raymond (ed.), *Structures of Power in Modern France* (Macmillan, 1999). In French, J. Charon, *La presse en France de 1945 à nos jours* (Editions du Seuil, 1991) and Jérome Boudon, *Haute fidélité: pouvoir et télévision 1935–1994* (Editions du Seuil, 1994) are both authoritative.

## Useful websites

The following websites are of particular relevance to matters discussed in Part III.

La Documentation française, publisher of official documents and reports: http://www.ladocfrancaise.gouv.fr

INSEE, the French official statistics office: http://www.insee.fr

INED, the French institute for the study of population and demography: http://popinfo.ined.fr

Ministère de la Culture et de la Communication: http://www.culture.fr

Ministère de l'Éducation nationale, de la Recherche, et de la Technologie: http://www.education.gouv.fr

Ministère de la Fonction publique, de la Réforme de l'État, et de la Décentralisation: http://www.fonction-publique.gouv.fr

In addition, *L'état de la France* (La Découverte, 1999) provides useful websites at the end of all its chapters.

TEXT 3.1

## La France poujadiste

La France de ces années-là, quand j'y pense, ce doit être pour les jeunes gens d'aujourd'hui un peu comme cet 'avant-guerre' dont mes parents me rebattaient les oreilles: avant la guerre par-ci, avant la guerre par-là, un de ces temps merveilleux et perdus où l'on avait connu les dernières voluptés de la douceur de vivre. Mais, au fond, toute illusion mise à part, je crois bien que la France de notre enfance ressemblait encore bougrement à celle d'avant la guerre. C'est précisément au cours des années cinquante qu'on sentit se préparer la grande mutation qui allait retourner la société française comme une crêpe, vider les campagnes et faire pousser à côté des banlieues-champignons les primeurs appétissantes de la société de consommation.

La France fut alors déchirée, non point entre la droite et la gauche, mais entre les adeptes de la modernité et les défenseurs de la société précapitaliste et malthusienne. Dans le premier camp, où nous nous placions résolument, nous, étudiants, citadins sans racine et sans héritage, on comptait tous les sectateurs du progrès, les ingénieurs saint-simoniens, les polytechniciens, les amis du genre humain, les curés progressistes, les femmes savantes, les élèves de l'ENA, les constructeurs d'automobiles, les syndicalistes, les lecteurs de Fourastié (lequel décrivait en des 'Que sais-je?' sans cesse réédités les délices de la civilisation 'de 1975'), les économistes de la croissance, les chanteurs marxistes, les professeurs keynésiens, les sidérurgistes, les fonctionnaires de l'INSEE, les journalistes du *Monde* (à part quelques vieux *réacs* hérités du *Temps* de jadis), les voyageurs d'Air-France, la jeunesse étudiante chrétienne, les gymnastes, les sociétés d'import-export, les Éditions du Seuil, les marchands de téléviseurs, les chercheurs de Saclay, les hygiénistes, les chimistes, les militants du *birth-control*, les révérends pères dominicains, tout un monde qui grondait contre les scléroses d'un pays poussif. C'est un État moderne qu'il nous fallait! dynamique! électrique (sinon soviétique)! propre! organisé! efficace! juste! Nous avions honte de notre fumier natal, de nos vieux autobus brinquebalants et nous détestions les sépulcres blanchis qui glorifiaient le passé avec des rimes mais sans raison. Dans l'autre camp s'épanouissaient les chantres de la France villageoise, les propriétaires de leur carré de choux, l'Apollon de Bellac, les petits commerçants, les bistrots qui faisaient la fortune de M. Paul Ricard, la France du XIX$^{e}$ siècle, radicale, protectionniste, pavillonnaire, avec sa traînée de notaires, d'avoués, d'huissiers, d'inspecteurs des poids et mesures, de curés traditionalistes, de boulistes à béret basque, de chiens méchants, de murs sertis de tessons de bouteille, de membres actifs de l'association Guillaume-Budé, de bouilleurs de cru, d'administrateurs coloniaux, d'anciens tenanciers de bordel, à quoi s'ajoutaient les fidèles du maréchal Pétain, les sacristains, les bénédictins, les bouchers chevalins, les officiers de cavalerie, tout un peuple mélancolique qui se sentait menacé par l'invasion du plastique, du Coca-Cola et du cheval-vapeur.

Soudain, en 1955, comme si elle avait senti sa mort prochaine, la vieille France se regroupa derrière l'étendard de la révolte que brandit Pierre Poujade, un de ces fiers-à-bras de gloire éphémère dont notre histoire nationale est pleine à craquer.

'Poujadolf!' Une trouvaille que ce mot-là! reprise dans une caricature de *l'Express* qui adornait le matamore de Saint-Céré d'une mèche et d'une petite moustache sans équivoque. Le champion des boutiquiers renchérit involontairement en intitulant sa profession de foi *J'ai choisi le combat*, qui faisait penser irrésistiblement à *Mein Kampf*. Sacré Poujade! Jusqu'aux élections du 2 janvier 1956, il faisait rire les beaux esprits que nous étions: un fasciste, d'accord! mais un fasciste du Lot! rien à voir avec les brasseries légendaires de Munich et les revolvers des soldats perdus d'Ernst von Salomon . . . Oui mais, le 2 janvier, les Maillotins de Poujade obtenaient près de 2 500 000 voix et 52 sièges à la Chambre; il fallait prendre désormais le poujadisme au sérieux.

(Michel Winock, *La République se meurt*, Éditions du Seuil, 1978, pp.17–19.)

## Exercices

### *Lexique*

Expliquez les mots et expressions suivants:

bougrement (l.6)
retourner quelque chose comme une crêpe (l.8)
un vieux réac (l.21)
brinquebalant (l.28)
un chantre (l.30)
la France pavillonnaire (l.33)
un bouliste (l.35)
un bouilleur de cru (ll.36–37)
un fier-à-bras (l.43)

### *Grammaire et stylistique*

(a) Qualifiez le style des lignes 6 à 10: est-il homogène? Quel effet obtient-il? Étudiez le procédé.
(b) Comment l'humour s'exprime-t-il stylistiquement dans ce texte?

### *Compréhension*

(a) Que comprenez-vous par 'rebattre les oreilles' (ll.2–3)? Expliquez l'expression 'avec des rimes mais sans raison' (ll.29–30). Que comprenez-vous par 'société précapitaliste et malthusienne' (ll.12–13)?
(b) 'Les ingénieurs saint-simoniens' (l.15), 'les femmes savantes' (l.16), 'des "Que sais-je?"' (l.18), 'Saclay' (l.24), 'l'Apollon de Bellac' (l.31), 'M. Paul Ricard' (l.32), 'l'association Guillaume Budé' (l.36): précisez toutes ces allusions. Pourquoi l'auteur choisit-il de citer les Éditions du Seuil (l.23)?
(c) Montrez les traces d'humour. Comment le mot 'Poujadolf' (l.45) est-il fabriqué? En quoi est-ce 'une trouvaille'?

### *Questions orales ou écrites*

(a) En donnant d'autres exemples de ces 'fiers-à-bras . . . dont notre histoire nationale est pleine à craquer' (ll.43–44), dressez une brève histoire de l'extrême droite en France.

(b) En vous inspirant de ce passage, écrivez une page comparant une même société à deux époques différentes, ou bien deux sociétés différentes géographiquement.

TEXT 3.2

## Quand la France s'ennuie

Ce qui caractérise actuellement notre vie publique, c'est l'ennui. Les Français s'ennuient. Ils ne participent ni de près ni de loin aux grandes convulsions qui secouent le monde. La guerre du Vietnam les émeut, certes, mais elle ne les touche pas vraiment. Invités à réunir 'un milliard pour le Vietnam', 20 F par tête, 33 F par adulte, ils sont, après plus d'un an de collectes, bien loin du compte. D'ailleurs, à l'exception de quelques engagés d'un côté ou de l'autre, tous, du premier d'entre eux au dernier, voient cette guerre avec les mêmes yeux, ou à peu près. Le conflit du Moyen-Orient a provoqué une petite fièvre au début de l'été dernier: la chevauchée héroïque remuait des réactions viscérales, des sentiments et des opinions; en six jours, l'accès était terminé. Les guérillas d'Amérique latine et l'effervescence cubaine ont été, un temps, à la mode; elles ne sont plus guère qu'un sujet de travaux pratiques pour sociologues de gauche et l'objet de motions pour intellectuels. Cinq cent mille morts peut-être en Indonésie, cinquante mille tués au Biafra, un coup d'État en Grèce, les expulsions du Kenya, l'apartheid sud-africain, les tensions en Inde: ce n'est guère que la monnaie quotidienne de l'information. La crise des partis communistes et la révolution culturelle chinoise semblent équilibrer le malaise noir aux États-Unis et les difficultés anglaises.

De toute façon, ce sont leurs affaires, pas les nôtres. Rien de tout cela ne nous atteint directement: d'ailleurs la télévision nous répète au moins trois fois chaque soir que la France est en paix pour la première fois depuis bientôt trente ans et qu'elle n'est ni impliquée ni concernée où que ce soit dans le monde.

La jeunesse s'ennuie. Les étudiants manifestent, bougent, se battent en Espagne, en Italie, en Belgique, en Algérie, au Japon, en Amérique, en Égypte, en Allemagne, en Pologne même. Ils ont l'impression qu'ils ont des conquêtes à entreprendre, une protestation à faire entendre, au moins un sentiment de l'absurde à opposer à l'absurdité. Les étudiants français se préoccupent de savoir si les filles de Nanterre et d'Antony pourront accéder librement aux chambres des garçons, conception malgré tout limitée des droits de l'homme. Quant aux jeunes ouvriers, ils cherchent du travail et n'en trouvent pas. Les empoignades, les homélies et les apostrophes des hommes politiques de tout bord paraissent à tous ces jeunes, au mieux plutôt comiques, au pis tout à fait inutiles, presque toujours incompréhensibles. (. . .)

Le général de Gaulle s'ennuie. Il s'était bien juré de ne plus inaugurer les chrysanthèmes, et il continue d'aller, officiel et bonhomme, du Salon de l'agriculture à la Foire de Lyon. Que faire d'autre? (. . .)

Seuls quelques centaines de milliers de Français ne s'ennuient pas: chômeurs, jeunes sans emploi, petits paysans écrasés par le progrès, victimes de la nécessaire concentration et de la concurrence de plus en plus rude, vieillards plus ou moins abandonnés de tous. Ceux-là sont si absorbés par leurs soucis qu'ils n'ont pas le temps de s'ennuyer, ni d'ailleurs le cœur à manifester et à s'agiter. Et ils ennuient tout le monde. La télévision, qui est faite pour distraire, ne parle pas assez d'eux. Aussi le calme règne-t-il. (. . .)

Dans une petite France presque réduite à l'hexagone, qui n'est pas vraiment malheureuse ni vraiment prospère, en paix avec tout le monde, sans grande prise sur les événements mondiaux, l'ardeur et l'imagination sont aussi nécessaires que le bien-être et l'expansion. Ce n'est certes pas facile. L'impératif vaut d'ailleurs pour l'opposition autant que pour le pouvoir. S'il n'est pas satisfait, l'anesthésie risque de provoquer la consomption. Et à la limite, cela s'est vu, un pays peut aussi périr d'ennui.

(Pierre Viansson-Ponté, 'Quand la France s'ennuie', *Le Monde*, 15 March 1968.)

## Exercices

### *Lexique*

Expliquez les mots et expressions suivants:

ennuyer/s'ennuyer (ll.2, 41)
la chevauchée héroïque (l.9)
une réaction viscérale (l.9)
des travaux pratiques (l.12)
une empoignade (l.31)
une homélie (l.31)
de tout bord (ll.31–32)
inaugurer les chrysanthèmes (ll.34–35)
sans grande prise sur (ll.45–46)

### *Grammaire et stylistique*

(a) 'Ils ne participent ni de près ni de loin' (l.2); 'elle n'est ni impliquée ni concernée' (l.22). Étudiez les négatives et faites des phrases en les utilisant.
(b) Le mot 'fièvre' (l.8) commence une métaphore. Quel mot la poursuit?

### *Compréhension*

(a) Quelle différence faites-vous entre 'émouvoir' et 'toucher' (ll.3–4)?
(b) 'Un sentiment de l'absurde à opposer à l'absurdité' (ll.26–27): que comprenez-vous par cette expression?

### *Question orale ou écrite*

(a) Dans quelle mesure le sentiment d'ennui décrit par l'auteur de ce texte peut-il expliquer les événements de mai 1968?

TEXT 3.3

## Internet, ou la fin de la vie privée?

Quand la plupart des informations concernant une personne étaient encore conservées à son domicile, chacun était maître de ses données personnelles, et seule une surveillance physique pouvait menacer la vie privée et porter atteinte au droit à être *«laissé en paix, à l'abri du regard d'autrui»*, comme l'affirme la Déclaration universelle des droits de l'homme. Cependant le développement de l'informatique a permis l'intégration et la centralisation d'informations confidentielles privées. Un renseignement inséré dans une banque de données, puis dévoilé, ne peut être considéré comme un bien exclusif car, une fois qu'il est divulgué, nul ne peut contraindre ceux qui en ont pris connaissance à l'oublier.

Le droit d'être physiquement laissé en paix fait donc place à la protection contre les intrusions informationnelles. De maître autonome et absolu de toutes les informations confidentielles le concernant, l'individu devient régulateur des flux de diffusion de ces informations. Cela oblige à redéfinir la notion même de vie privée, qui devient, dans bien des cas, la *«diffusion plus ou moins restreinte que l'on donne à des faits publics»* – comme, par exemple, une succession d'achats dans différents magasins. De plus, l'origine même des informations peut prêter à confusion: lorsqu'un médecin examine un patient et consigne les résultats de l'analyse sur l'ordinateur de l'hôpital, qui «possède» réellement l'information? Le médecin qui l'a créée? L'hôpital, détenteur de l'ordinateur? Ou bien le patient, source de l'information?

Jusqu'à la popularisation d'Internet, le problème majeur, issu du regroupement des informations sur banques de données à la fin des années 70, tenait à la distance entre le contrôleur et le sujet de l'information: plus cette distance était grande, plus grand était le risque que l'information soit dévoilée ou incorrecte. On connaît les conséquences de ces abus: déni injuste de crédit, tracas fiscal, évaluation médicale ou professionnelle indiscrète . . . La liste est longue, et les cas individuels sont parfois tragiques. Pourtant, si une institution financière ou commerciale vous accorde un crédit, n'a-t-elle pas le droit de s'informer à propos de vos antécédents financiers? De même, pourquoi un propriétaire ne pourrait-il se renseigner sur le passé judiciaire d'un futur locataire?

Que l'on soit ou non d'accord, un point semble acquis: les questions concernant l'exactitude des données et l'identité de ceux pouvant y accéder prennent un tour nouveau avec le développement des réseaux. Les fichiers ont d'abord été regroupés et intégrés sur banques de données, supprimant d'un coup l'éparpillement géographique comme les démarches administratives qui en limitaient l'accès à une élite de contrôleurs d'informations. Avec Internet, l'accès se généralise brutalement. Plus de cloisonnement: tout est instantanément disponible, depuis n'importe où. La question de la protection de la vie privée passe de l'échelle locale et nationale à l'échelle internationale.

C'est ainsi qu'une mosaïque composée des caractéristiques intimes d'une personne se transforme en portrait très précis. Dans son rapport d'activité présenté en juillet 1998, la Commission nationale de l'informatique et des libertés (CNIL) s'inquiète des «*gisements de données*» qui «*peuvent être utilisés à l'insu des personnes pour constituer des profils individuels de consommation ou surveiller la navigation d'un internaute*».

L'approche européenne est aux antipodes de l'autorégulation: inspirée par les exemples suédois, allemands ou français, une directive communautaire sur la protection des données a été adoptée en 1995. Mais le transit de données ne s'arrête pas aux frontières de l'Europe. Les juristes se heurtent à la difficulté d'appliquer aux réseaux la conception traditionnelle du droit, qui se fonde sur le lieu où se déroule un échange ou une infraction et sur la domiciliation des intéressés.

Le désir naturel d'être laissé en paix doit bien pouvoir rapporter beaucoup plus d'argent: puisque tout est à vendre, pourquoi pas la vie privée? On verra sans doute l'avènement d'un marché de la vie privée, où les internautes en mal de discrétion paieront au prix fort la sécurité de leurs données (leur fournisseur de services ne révélera rien), tandis que les autres verront leur intimité offerte au tout-venant.

Notre époque semble parfois croire en un surprenant paradoxe: ceux auxquels la fortune a souri d'éclatante manière seraient, en réalité, les plus malheureux des humains, car privés d'intimité, harcelés qu'ils sont par les paparazzi. Mais, dorénavant, chacun voit se transformer un droit élémentaire en un bien commercial. On peut tout de même s'interroger: s'il est toujours, pour l'instant, interdit de vendre son vote, ou soi-même en esclavage, pourquoi la vie privée serait-elle dispensée de cette règle d'autonomie civique?

(Mathieu O'Neil, *Le Monde diplomatique*, September 1998.)

## Exercices

### *Lexique*

Expliquez les mots et expressions suivants:

autrui (l.4)
divulgué (l.9)
détenteur (l.20)
le passé judiciaire (l.31)
un tour nouveau (l.34)
l'éparpillement géographique (l.36)
le cloisonnement (l.38)
les gisements de données (l.44)
à l'insu de (l.44)
un internaute (l.46)
aux antipodes (l.47)

### *Grammaire et stylistique*

(a) 'nul ne peut contraindre . . .' (l.9). Réécrivez cette phrase au mode affirmatif et inventez-en quelques unes en utilisant la même construction.

(b) 'De maître autonome (. . .) l'individu devient régulateur des flux de diffusion de ces informations' (ll.12–14). Traduisez cette phrase et commentez l'usage de la préposition 'de'.

(c) 'plus cette distance était grande, plus grand était le risque . . .' (ll.24–25). Réécrivez cette phrase au mode négatif.

### *Compréhension*

(a) Quelles sont les principales modifications apportées par l'internet au droit à être laissé en paix?
(b) Le regroupement des informations sur des banques de données pose un problème majeur. Lequel?
(c) Définissez l'approche européenne à la protection de la vie privée.

### *Questions orales ou écrites*

(a) A votre avis, qui doit être le 'propriétaire' de l'information: le créateur, le détenteur ou la source?
(b) Croyez-vous, avec l'auteur de ce texte, que l'internet détruira l'idée traditionnelle de la vie privée?

TEXT 3.4

## TGV: une décennie qui a changé la France

On se bat pour l'avoir ou pour qu'il passe au large. Lui, il roule. Depuis juste dix ans, le TGV est devenu le symbole d'une nouvelle SNCF. Le 27 septembre 1981, les premiers passagers du Train à grande vitesse découvraient un nouveau paysage entre Paris et Lyon, celui que l'on traverse à 270 km/h. Cinq jours avant, François Mitterrand avait inauguré la ligne nouvelle. Ironie du sort: c'est une technologie développée à l'initiative d'un président de droite, Georges Pompidou (à l'occasion du dernier Conseil des ministres qu'il présida), qui allait offrir à un président de gauche, quelques mois après son élection, une scène fabuleuse pour présenter une image de modernité, et celle d'un pouvoir prêt à dépoussiérer ses plus vénérables institutions.

Parmi elles, la SNCF, sauvée par la grande vitesse. Pour mettre en ligne ses TGV entre Paris et Lyon, elle a consacré plus de 14 milliards de francs. Mais elle ne cassait pas seulement sa tirelire. Elle inventait un nouveau produit qui devait lui rapporter de l'argent. Nouveau, dans sa culture. Certes, la société mangeait son pain blanc. Elle lançait son train orange sur la liaison la mieux appropriée pour concurrencer l'avion. La direction tablait sur un taux de rentabilité de 10%. Aujourd'hui, elle l'évalue à 15%. Les investissements sont sur le point d'être amortis, en avance sur le calendrier. Nulle autre liaison, en service sur l'Atlantique ou en projet dans le Nord, le Sud ou l'Est, n'est aussi porteuse.

Au départ, le train orange eut ses détracteurs. Très vite, ils furent soumis. Dès la première année pleine d'exploitation, en 1982, les TGV transportent 6,4 millions de passagers sur le réseau sud-est. Ils ne prennent pas encore le pas sur les trains traditionnels, qui y assuraient un trafic de 12 millions de voyageurs par an. Mais la montée en puissance est au rendez-vous. Elle couche Air Inter sur l'aile, qui perd la moitié de ses passagers sur Paris-Lyon. La compagnie aérienne avait sous-estimé l'impact. Avant le TGV, la vitesse était l'apanage de l'avion. Avec le TGV, elle change de camp, et le rail la symbolise, comme au premier temps du chemin de fer. Le public accroche et multiplie ses déplacements au fur et à mesure de l'arrivée de nouvelles rames. L'an dernier, 20,6 millions de passagers ont pris un TGV sur le Sud-Est: une fréquentation qui a plus que triplé en dix ans. Et, sur l'Atlantique, on a approché les 13 millions de passagers. Le tout grâce à 208 rames qui desservent 86 villes.

Le TGV a tiré la croissance du trafic ferroviaire en même temps qu'il devenait la coqueluche du pays et de son industrie. La SNCF en a profité pour changer de mode d'exploitation. Subrepticement, elle introduit dans son langage des termes comme profit, comme rentabilité. Et, pour les liaisons à grande distance, elle gomme de son registre la notion de service public. Le commercial sur les grandes lignes, avec le TGV, balaie les vieux comportements. La culture cheminot est ébranlée lorsque les derniers présidents de la SNCF – d'André Chadeau à

Jacques Fournier en passant par Philippe Essig et Philippe Rouvillois – ont l'œil rivé sur les comptes d'exploitation. Aujourd'hui, la SNCF est déficitaire dans le fret. Et, dans les transports régionaux et de banlieue, elle équilibre ses comptes grâce aux compensations tarifaires de l'État ou des régions. Seules les grandes lignes rapportent de l'argent, et couvrent les divers autres déficits d'exploitation.

Certes, il y a les autres trains qui sillonnent l'Hexagone. Mais ils appartiennent déjà au passé. L'an dernier, le TGV a transporté un passager sur quatre de grandes lignes. La SNCF lui consacre la moitié de l'ensemble de ses investissements, commandant de nouvelles rames plutôt que de moderniser ses vieux wagons couchettes indignes, et programmant 3 400 km de nouvelles lignes (contre 417 km actuellement sur Paris-Lyon et 287 sur l'Atlantique) selon un schéma directeur conçu pour irriguer tout le territoire.

Le TGV a également gagné son ticket d'entrée dans le monde politique. Pas un maire qui ne souhaiterait avoir une gare TGV à sa porte. Car la grande vitesse ferroviaire a changé la géographie de l'Hexagone. Il faut l'avoir pour se rapprocher de Paris, pour attirer les hommes d'affaires qui courent après le temps, et les touristes pressés d'arriver à destination. Le TGV est un outil d'excellence dans le marketing territorial. Pierre Mauroy s'est battu bec et ongles pour qu'il passe par Lille alors que les élus d'Amiens défendaient leur cause sur le futur trajet Paris-Londres. Strasbourg veut l'imposer à cor et à cri pour conserver le Parlement européen. Même pour Rouen, Laurent Fabius le réclame. Mais, si on veut les gares, on refuse les lignes, qui créent des cicatrices dans le paysage. L'exemple le plus flagrant est aujourd'hui celui de la Provence, où des associations locales refusent les lignes nouvelles. Le cœur des élus balance: pas question de se priver du TGV, impossible de se mettre l'opinion publique à dos. Alors, ils tentent de rejeter la ligne sur d'autres circonscriptions et de garder la gare. C'est une lutte d'influences qui remonte jusqu'à l'Élysée. Pour le gouvernement, le terrain est miné. S'il est hors de question de revenir sur l'extension du réseau grande vitesse, ils hésitent à le figer. En charge du ministère des Transports, Michel Delebarre prit du retard pour présenter le projet de schéma directeur, face aux réactions passionnelles déclenchées par les choix de tracés. Et sur les plus délicats, son successeur, Louis Besson, n'a pas tranché non plus. Mais le temps fait son office. La machine ferroviaire a mis son TGV en marche, avec comme objectif de mettre à trois heures au plus de Paris toutes les métropoles françaises. Pour prendre l'avion de vitesse.

('TGV: une décennie qui a changé la France', *Libération*, 22 September 1991, p.14.)

## Exercices

### *Lexique*

Expliquez les mots et expressions suivants:

au large (l.1)
le Conseil des ministres (l.7)
dépoussiérer (l.10)
la tirelire (l.13)
manger son pain blanc (l.15)
tabler sur (l.16)

amortir un investissement (ll.17–18)
un projet porteur (ll.19–20)
prendre le pas sur (ll.23–24)
l'apanage de (l.27)
une rame de train (l.30)
la coqueluche (l.35)
gommer une notion (l.38)
cheminot (l.39)
l'Hexagone (l.55)
se battre bec et ongles (l.58)
à cor et à cri (l.60)
se mettre quelqu'un à dos (ll.65–66)
le temps fait son office (l.73)

### *Grammaire et stylistique*

(a) 'Lui, il roule' (l.1). Conjuguez cette phrase à toutes les personnes.
(b) Quel est l'effet du passé simple à la ligne 7? Utilisez-le vous-même dans un court paragraphe décrivant une réalisation technologique de votre choix.

### *Compréhension*

(a) Expliquez ce qu'est la 'notion de service public' (l.38) et comment 'le commercial sur les grandes lignes, avec le TGV, balaie les vieux comportements' (ll.38–39). Quels sont les avantages et les inconvénients du 'commercial' dans un service public?

### *Question orale ou écrite*

(a) En quoi la modification de la géographie de la France, grâce au TGV, vous semble-t-elle souhaitable?

## TEXT 3.5

# L'extension du prolétariat

Certains le découvriront avec terreur, mais le prolétariat représente désormais probablement plus de 75% de la population française. 75% de prolétaires, dites-vous? Vous exagérez? Mais non. Certes, dans le langage courant la notion de «prolétaire» a souvent été liée à tort à celle de «pauvre»: cela ne saurait exprimer la place grosso modo identique de vastes secteurs de la population dans le procès de production. Le prolétaire est souvent pauvre, cependant il n'est pas le seul dans ce cas. Parfois, il gagne dignement sa vie. Mais il est celui qui, fondamentalement, vit de la vente de sa force de travail.

La première révolution industrielle (charbon, acier, textile) a produit la «classe ouvrière» de notre vocabulaire classique. Mais déjà Marx, avec des exemples qu'il pouvait trouver à son époque, avait affirmé que ceux qui étaient producteurs de services marchands étaient aussi des prolétaires: les conducteurs de locomotive ne vendaient pas un objet-marchandise, mais un service-marchandise.

La deuxième révolution industrielle (électricité, fordisme) a provoqué le phénomène des cols blancs. Certains conclurent des quelques différences sociologiques entre cols bleus et cols blancs une différence de classes et non point une différenciation au sein de la classe prolétaire, et, déjà, à la minoration de la classe ouvrière. La troisième révolution industrielle (atome, automatisme, informatisation) entraîna le développement massif des milieux des employés. Désormais, la classe ouvrière fut en *«état de disparition progressive»*.

C'est oublier que le vocable «classe ouvrière» est, conceptuellement, tout à fait impropre à désigner ce qu'il représente. Le prolétariat ouvrier n'est pas une classe sociale, il est l'un des milieux sociaux de la classe prolétarienne, aux côtés d'autres milieux sociaux prolétariens comme les employés, les infirmières, les instituteurs, etc. A n'en pas douter, la quatrième révolution industrielle (multimédia, autoroutes de l'information, télétravail) entraînera une nouvelle différenciation sociale au sein du prolétariat. A n'en pas douter, il y aura, comme lors des précédentes révolutions industrielles, une nouvelle mode de la *«disparition de la classe ouvrière»*. Mais, pour prendre le cas qui paraît fort charmant à certains analystes du télétravail, entre la jeune femme rivée chez elle à son écran d'ordinateur, «annualisée» dans la durée et la productivité de son travail par une direction qui la contrôlera dans tous ses mouvements quotidiens, quelle différence de classe avec l'ouvrière d'usine?

Chaque révolution scientifique et industrielle a amené des modifications sociales au sein du prolétariat. Mais chacune de ces révolutions eut une conséquence similaire au moins sur un point: l'augmentation absolue et relative du nombre de prolétaires, la prolétarisation croissante (à ne pas confondre avec l'appauvrissement) de milieux issus de l'artisanat, du petit commerce, du paysannat, de la petite bourgeoisie. Au point de créer dans les pays développés une situation où existe une large majorité sociale prolétarienne. Le seul moyen trouvé par le capitalisme pour freiner cette tendance structurelle est le chômage de masse qui, partiellement, détruit physiquement le prolétariat.

Cette majorité prolétarienne modifiera considérablement à l'avenir les conditions du combat politique. Anciennement, même nos plus grands mouvements sociaux prolétariens étaient minoritaires dans le pays. La Commune de Paris fut largement la dernière révolution du tiers-état. Le Front populaire acquit brièvement la sympathie d'une majorité de citoyens, mais le nombre de grévistes tourna autour du million. En mai 68 ce fut bien plus. Désormais les conditions objectives permettent que des catégories encore plus massives de gens se mettent en mouvement. Or cela est potentiellement porteur d'une force gigantesque pour la démocratie.

On aura l'irruption de secteurs entiers, prolétaires et majoritaires, de la population, eux-mêmes directement et physiquement dans la lutte, déterminant leurs propres objectifs en raison de leurs intérêts de classe! Voilà l'avenir proche.

(Michel Cahen, *Le Monde*, 7 October 1995.)

## Exercices

### *Lexique*

Expliquez les mots et expressions suivants:

grosso modo (l.5)
le fordisme (l.15)
la minoration (l.18)
l'informatisation (l.20)
désormais (l.21)
le vocable (l.22)
impropre (l.23)
le télétravail (l.27)
à n'en pas douter (l.28)
lors des (l.29)
freiner (l.42)
le tiers-état (l.47)

### *Grammaire et stylistique*

(a) 'cela ne saurait exprimer la place grosso modo identique de vastes secteurs de la population dans le procès de production' (ll.4–6). Traduisez cette phrase; identifiez et commentez le temps/mode du verbe.

(b) 'Désormais la classe ouvrière fut en "*état de disparition progressive*" (l.21). Trouvez d'autres adverbes de temps dans le texte et expliquez leur fonction dans sa structure.

(c) 'Voilà l'avenir proche' (l.55). Identifiez les verbes avec lesquels l'auteur désigne cet avenir.

### *Compréhension*

(a) La Commune de Paris; le Front populaire; mai 68. Quel lien voyez-vous entre ces trois moments de l'histoire française?

(b) Identifiez et datez les quatre révolutions industrielles évoquées par l'auteur.
(c) Quelle est la signification donnée ici au terme 'prolétariat'?

### *Questions orales ou écrites*

(a) L'évolution des sociétés modernes a rendu caduc le concept de 'classe sociale'. Partagez-vous ce point de vue?
(b) Vous considerez-vous comme faisant partie du prolétariat?

## TEXT 3.6

# Les mots vieux garçons

*Faut-il dire «M^me le ministre» ou «M^me la ministre»?*

Où est la spécificité du français parmi les langues indo-européennes? C'est qu'il a progressivement perdu la capacité de féminiser librement des noms de personnes à l'aide de suffixes appropriés. L'italien dit sans hésiter *professoressa*, le tchèque *profesorka*, l'allemand forme indéfiniment des féminins en «in». Chez nous, le suffixe «esse» ne reste bien implanté que dans «maîtresse» et «hôtesse» et dans les titres nobiliaires: «princesse, duchesse, comtesse». Pour le reste, le français d'aujourd'hui relègue l'«abbesse», la «chanoinesse», la «prêtresse» et la «papesse» dans leur niche historique, la «demanderesse» dans le jargon du palais, la mot «négresse» dans son ghetto raciste, et s'il reste attiré par les «pécheresses», il fuit tant qu'il peut les «diablesses», «ogresses», «drôlesses» et autres «tigresses».

Or, en même temps qu'elle perdait la féminisation par suffixe, jadis propre au nom, notre langue développait à l'extrême un autre procédé plus simple, lui aussi hérité d'un passé lointain, et semblable à celui des adjectifs: le féminin ne diffère du masculin que par l'addition d'un «e» ou lui est semblable («un» ou «une secouriste», comme «il est» ou «elle est jeune»). Ce procédé concerne des milliers de noms de personnes et est applicable potentiellement à presque tous.

Se sont aussi développés deux petits groupes de mots, ceux en «eur», «euse» et en «teur», «trice», qui servent à former à la fois des noms et des adjectifs («directeur, directrice» comme «plan directeur, idée directrice»), mais qui ne fonctionnent librement que s'ils sont en rapport direct avec un verbe existant dans la langue: est «directeur/trice» celui ou celle qui dirige. Si ce rapport n'existe pas, le suffixe n'est plus senti comme vivant. «Acteur/actrice» ou «instituteur/institutrice» sont des mots très courants, mais qui ne peuvent plus servir de modèles pour de nouvelles formations.

D'où un premier blocage, purement linguistique, concernant un petit groupe de mots en «eur» ou «teur» que leur sens ne lie pas de façon évidente à des verbes: «docteur», «professeur», «recteur», «censeur», «procureur», «sénateur», «facteur» et quelques autres. Ces mots, désignant des fonctions qui jusqu'au siècle dernier n'étaient jamais exercées par des femmes, n'ont pas alors (contrairement à «acteur» ou «instituteur») développé de féminin en «euse» ou «trice», lorsque la langue le rendait encore possible. Plus tard, cette possibilité avait disparu. Ces mots sont pour ainsi dire restés vieux garçons.

Mais à l'obstacle linguistique s'est superposé un blocage social. Il se trouve que toutes ces fonctions (sauf la dernière nommée) ont un certain prestige. Au début du XX^e siècle, quand les femmes ont commencé à y aspirer, elles se sont inconsciemment persuadées que l'impossibilité de former un féminin grammatical était inhérente à l'autorité de la fonction. Le tabou s'est alors étendu à des mots pour lesquels la féminisation ne se serait heurtée à aucun obstacle formel. On n'a pas voulu dire la «juge», la «ministre», la «députée», etc. On a même refusé la «générale», la «colonelle», la «préfète», l'«ambassadrice» (mot aussi bien implanté qu'«institutrice»). Le prétexte en était que ces mots, dans l'usage d'alors, désignaient couramment les épouses des officiers ou fonctionnaires correspondants, auxquelles la République, dans sa générosité, impose une participation non rétribuée aux fonctions représentatives de leurs conjoints.

Cependant, même de nos jours, en dépit des blocages, la puissante dynamique de la féminisation linguistique a continué son œuvre. On dit couramment la «chef» dans les bureaux, la «prof» dans les lycées (on y entend même, malgré le jeu de mots, la «censeur»), la «capitaine» dans l'Armée du salut (pourquoi pas dans l'armée française?), on disait dans les universités une «maître-assistante» tant que cette fonction existait, et, dans la série télévisée qui s'intitule «M$^{me}$ le juge», plus d'un personnage appelle Simone Signoret «la juge».

L'administration continuera peut-être à écrire: M$^{me}$ X est nommée intendant, on appellera quand même cette personne l'«intendante». La SNCF imprime bien parfois «gare de: Le Havre», mais tout le monde dit la «gare du Havre». La norme bureaucratique n'est pas la grammaire de la langue. Au temps de Murger, on appelait «étudiantes», les «grisettes» qui «faisaient la vie» avec des étudiants. Qui s'en souvient aujourd'hui? Dès l'admission des filles dans les facultés, le mot a changé de sens sans demander la permission à personne. De même, quand il y aura assez de femmes dans le corps préfectoral, tout le monde oubliera qu'hier la «préfète» était la femme du préfet.

Bref, le français est vivant, et après une très courte période d'hésitation (un siècle à peine) il ne peut manquer de revenir à sa créativité millénaire. Un peu de féminisme crispé en a barré un instant le cours, beaucoup de féminisme banalisé rompt à nouveau la digue. Ne préjugeons pas ici de la solution que le génie de notre langue apportera à chaque cas litigieux, mais il est certain qu'on n'enseignera pas indéfiniment aux élèves qu'il faut écrire la «déléguée», mais pas la «députée». Les suffixes morts ne ressusciteront pas, et, dans la plupart des cas, le féminin ne différera du masculin que par l'article. On finira (un peu plus tôt, un peu plus tard) par dire «la docteur», même si cette forme nous choque aujourd'hui.

Nous assistons à un débat à fronts renversés. Les prétendus féministes pourraient se réclamer d'une tradition immémoriale, les traditionnalistes supposés défendent en fait le féminisme de grand-mère.

(Paul Garde, *Le Monde*, 11 August 1998.)

## Exercices

### *Lexique*

Expliquez les mots et expressions suivants:

la drôlesse (l.11)
un(e) secouriste (l.17)
le censeur (l.29)
le tabou (l.39)

un conjoint (l.47)
une grisette (l.59)
faire la vie avec (l.59)
la préfète (l.63)
millénaire (l.65)
crispé (l.66)
litigieux (l.68)
à fronts renversés (l.74)
prétendus (l.74)

### *Grammaire et stylistique*

(a) 'deux petits groupes de mots qui servent à former à la fois des noms et des adjectifs' (ll.19–20). Ajoutez vos propres exemples à ceux donnés dans le texte.
(b) Pourquoi préférer 'la gare de Le Havre' à 'la gare du Havre'?
(c) 'le féminisme de grand-mère' (l.76). Traduisez cette expression et inventez-en d'autres sur le même modèle.

### *Compréhension*

(a) Pourquoi qualifier certains mots de 'vieux garçons'?
(b) Expliquez pourquoi les féministes refusent de dire 'la générale', 'l'ambassadrice', ou 'la préfète'.
(c) 'on y entend même, malgré le jeu de mots, la "censeur"' (ll.50–51). De quel jeux de mots s'agit-t-il?
(d) 'au temps de Murger' (ll.58–59). Datez cette référence et expliquez ce qui a changé depuis dans les facultés.

### *Questions orales ou écrites*

(a) Partagez-vous le point de vue de certaines féministes selon lequel autorité et titre vont de pair?
(b) Quelle est l'influence des mœurs sur l'évolution de la langue?

## TEXT 3.7

# Un remède pire que le mal

La loi sur la parité a été adoptée en première lecture le 15 décembre 1998 à l'unanimité des présents. La République universelle se meurt dans l'indifférence. Vive la République des sexes et bientôt des communautés! L'obstruction masculine au partage du pouvoir politique est un mal en voie de guérison. Mais à quel prix! En 1793, les femmes avaient été exclues de la citoyenneté à cause de leur différence naturelle. Deux cents ans plus tard, elles s'imposent en politique au nom de ce même critère. Le biologique fonde le droit grâce à une manipulation des concepts fort dangereuse pour l'égalité des sexes.

Plutôt que d'accuser l'universel d'être masculin pour mieux le jeter aux poubelles de l'histoire, il eût été plus juste de mettre en accusation les hommes qui bafouent le principe de l'universalité. Plutôt que de sexuer le concept d'humanité au risque de l'altérer radicalement, il eût mieux valu se battre pour faire respecter les principes républicains. L'universalisme a explosé devant les revendications biologiques. L'humanité n'est plus ce qui unit tous les êtres humains par-delà leur différence de genre et de race . . . Mais la conjonction de deux groupes d'humains: les hommes et les femmes.

Bien que les paritaires évitent soigneusement d'évoquer leurs différences biologiques pour se référer à leurs différences psychologiques (moins guerrières, moins vaniteuses, plus concrètes, plus préoccupées du quotidien et des autres, plus dévouées au combat pour la vie et la liberté), l'idéal maternel refait subrepticement son apparition, justifiant à la fois la supériorité morale des femmes sur les hommes et leurs prérogatives. Si les femmes sont plus pacifiques et altruistes, on conclut d'emblée qu'elles sont l'avenir radieux de l'humanité. La progestérone, mère de toutes les vertus . . . De là, on induit qu'il y a deux points de vue sur le monde: un point de vue féminin et un point de vue masculin. Le premier étant nettement plus sympathique que le second. Mais chacun sait qu'il n'y a pas un mais de multiples points de vue féminins, notamment sur les sujets qui les concernent au premier chef: l'avortement, le salaire maternel, le travail à temps partiel ou la parité.

Aujourd'hui, les paritaires font semblant de croire que rien n'a changé depuis cinquante ans et que Simone de Beauvoir les a fourvoyées en tenant le discours de la ressemblance des sexes. C'est faire preuve d'une méconnaissance de l'histoire des idées et des mœurs déconcertante. Car c'est justement en faisant la critique systématique des «rôles» imposés aux femmes au nom de leur différence sexuelle que Beauvoir a largement contribué à montrer la voie vers l'égalité des sexes. Elle l'a fait en dénonçant le piège des différences érigées en principe. C'est grâce à cette philosophie qui laissait les différences dans la sphère du privé que les femmes ont fait leurs plus grandes conquêtes: la même liberté sexuelle que les hommes, l'accès à tous les métiers, l'égalité intellectuelle. Si la philosophie différentialiste l'avait emporté, au nom de quoi les hommes auraient-ils voté en 1975 le droit à l'avortement; au nom de quoi l'égalité intellectuelle puisque notre sexe nous prédispose au «concret» et que l'abstraction appartient aux hommes?

Les paritaires n'ont pas vu le temps passer depuis un demi-siècle, et le bouleversement du rapport entre les sexes qui s'opère devant nos yeux. Elles décrivent les femmes contraintes d'adopter une attitude virile, donc de s'aliéner, pour se faire une place dans un monde masculin, et font mine d'ignorer qu'aucune des vertus prétendues masculines (maîtrise de soi, volonté de se surpasser, goût du risque, du défi et de la conquête) ne leur est étrangère. Ce sont ces femmes-là qui ont amené les hommes à découvrir leur féminité, soigneusement refoulée depuis des siècles, et à commencer de se libérer d'un modèle masculin aussi oppressif que destructeur. C'est en reconnaissant que les vertus masculines et féminines appartiennent aux deux sexes que l'on progresse vers l'égalité. L'humanité n'est pas double. Chaque homme et chaque femme est dépositaire de l'humanité tout entière.

En reprenant le discours de la dualité, les paritaires renferment hommes et femmes dans les schémas stéréotypés dont on a tant de mal à sortir. Le vrai progrès vers l'égalité des sexes passe par le partage des tâches quotidiennes, ménagères et parentales, avec les hommes, et l'autonomie financière des femmes. Tant que ces deux exigences ne sont pas remplies, l'égalité est un leurre. Il y aura peut-être demain autant de femmes que d'hommes dans les instances politiques, mais tant que pèseront sur elles la double journée de travail et l'entière responsabilité de la maison et des enfants, seules les célibataires ou celles qui ont les moyens d'être secondées à la maison pourront y accéder. Pour que les femmes trouvent enfin la place légitime que la République leur doit, il suffit que tous les partis politiques décident de se soumettre au principe d'égalité. Ce serait la meilleure façon pour eux de prouver qu'ils servent la République universelle.

(Élisabeth Badinter, *Le Nouvel Observateur* 14–20 January 1999, p.43.)

## Exercices

### *Lexique*

Expliquez les mots et expressions suivants:

la parité/les paritaires (l.1)
le biologique fonde le droit (l.7)
bafouent (l.11)
sexuer (l.11)
subrepticement (ll.20–21)
l'avenir radieux (l.23)
on induit (l.24)
au premier chef (l.28)
les a fourvoyées (l.31)
la philosophie différentialiste (l.40)
s'aliéner (l.46)

### *Grammaire et stylistique*

(a) 'il eût été plus juste de mettre en accusation les hommes qui bafouent le principe de l'universalité' (ll.10–11). Expliquez le temps/mode du verbe.

(b) 'Plutôt que d'accuser l'universel d'être masculin.' 'Plutôt que de sexuer le concept d'humanité' (ll.9 et 11–12). Trouvez d'autres formules répétées dans le texte et décrivez leur impact stylistique.
(c) 'En 1793 les femmes avaient été exclues de la citoyenneté' (l.5). Identifiez et commentez le temps du verbe.

### *Compréhension*

(a) 'Vive la République des sexes et bientôt des communautés!' (l.3). Selon vous, cette phrase exprime-t-elle l'approbation ou la désapprobation de l'auteur?
(b) Où et comment Simone de Beauvoir a-t-elle tenu 'le discours de la ressemblance des sexes' (ll.31–32)?
(c) 'Le vrai progrès vers l'égalité des sexes passe par le partage des tâches quotidiennes' (ll.57–58). Traduisez cette phrase et inventez-en d'autres sur le même modèle.

### *Questions orales ou écrites*

(a) Suffit-il du 'partage des tâches quotidiennes' pour réaliser la vraie égalité des sexes?
(b) Pour ou contre l'universalisme tel qu'il est défendu par É. Badinter: quelle est votre position?

TEXT 3.8

## Plus français que moi, tu rentres chez toi

Au début de l'été, mon père m'inscrivait au tennis de La Baule. Matin et soir, j'étais condamné aux travaux forcés. En socquettes et short blancs, en polo Lacoste, je devais taper à coups de raquette sur des balles Slazenger ou Dunlop. Pour ce père breton dont le tennis du fils signait l'ascension sociale, dénicher les oiseaux, courir les bois avec des paysans du même âge, plaisanter avec des jeunes filles, eût été déchoir. Bon fils, j'allais donc chaque jour cogner sur les balles de caoutchouc laineux. Je me prenais au jeu. Et, puisqu'on comptait les points, je gagnais. Je tapais n'importe comment, mais je l'emportais sur ces jeunes Nantais, Angevins et Parisiens sûrs d'eux, de leur monde et plus encore de leur style. Victoires qu'ils contestaient aussitôt. Certes, j'avais gagné, mais sans style. Je n'aurais pas dû gagner puisque eux possédaient le style. Si j'avais plus de points et eux plus de style, c'est que la règle était mauvaise: on ne devait plus compter les points, mais juger le style.

On n'entre pas dans la bourgeoisie par le mérite. La même remarque vaut pour les immigrés. Contrairement à ce qui était écrit sur les pancartes brandies par les gros bras du Front national ou par les dames patronnesses RPR, être français ne se mérite pas. C'est même dangereux pour un immigré. Un Breton de la deuxième génération peut jouer au tennis, on le lui recommande même comme preuve d'intégration, mais c'est aux vrais bourgeois français de gagner. Un immigré peut consciencieusement s'assimiler, il peut devenir français, mais un cran en dessous. Bretons et immigrés menacent ici les mêmes structures sociales. Ils sont rejetés par un même changement des règles. Ils ont beau avoir suivi l'école française, avoir adopté le mode de vie familial des Français, avoir oublié leur langue, négligé leur religion, ils concurrencent les Français en place, d'autant plus qu'ils leur ressemblent davantage. Alors, on tente de les repousser, sous prétexte qu'ils n'ont pas le style. Inutile de compter les points.

Ainsi, la question des immigrés, qui a beaucoup occupé les Français depuis trois ans, s'est peut-être posée non pas en raison des difficultés de l'intégration, mais à cause de son succès. Les immigrés représentent un danger pour être devenus trop français, comme les juifs 'cosmopolites' de l'avant-guerre à qui il était reproché une trop grande facilité à se couler dans n'importe quelle culture.

Maintenant que la boutique du Code de la nationalité a fermé, il est temps de s'interroger sérieusement sur cette curieuse folie, sur cette affaire Dreyfus sans capitaine qui se termine sans révision de procès. Il est temps de se demander si la 'commission des sages' était vraiment sage et vraiment composée de sages. Temps de savoir si le traitement purement politique de la question ne dissimulait pas une manœuvre sociale destinée à remettre les immigrés à leur place, la plus basse, qu'ils avaient tendance à quitter, tandis que de bons Français de souche dégringolaient de l'échelle sociale. Un grand nombre d'arguments militent pour cette interprétation.

(Hervé Le Bras, 'Plus français que moi, tu rentres chez toi', *Le genre humain*, February 1989, pp.9–10.)

## Exercices

### *Lexique*

Expliquez les mots et expressions suivants:

les travaux forcés (l.2)
Je me prenais au jeu (l.7)
brandir une pancarte (l.15)
les gros bras du Front national (l.16)
une dame patronnesse (l.16)
un cran en dessous (l.21)
la commission des sages (l.36)

### *Grammaire et stylistique*

(a) 'Au début de l'été, mon père m'inscrivait . . .' (l.1). Quel est l'effet de l'imparfait?
(b) 'Dénicher les oiseaux, courir les bois . . . , plaisanter avec des jeunes filles, eût été déchoir' (ll.4–6). Expliquez le subjonctif. Récrivez la phrase en utilisant un autre mode. Pourquoi à votre avis l'auteur opte-t-il pour le subjonctif?
(c) Commentez le style de l'auteur (car, quoiqu'il en dise, il en a un . . . ), et en particulier son sens de la formule. En vous appuyant sur vos commentaires stylistiques ainsi que sur le contenu du texte, précisez votre perception du narrateur.

### *Compréhension*

(a) Expliquez le titre. Faites d'autres expressions sur ce modèle.
(b) 'La boutique du Code de la nationalité a fermé' (l.33): expliquez l'allusion et dites aussi comment la question des immigrés 'a beaucoup occupé les Français depuis trois ans' (ll.27–28), c'est-à-dire depuis 1986.
(c) Expliquez 'cette affaire Dreyfus sans capitaine' (ll.34–35). Montrez son impact.
(d) 'Un grand nombre d'arguments militent pour cette interprétation' (ll.40–41). Précisez lesquels.

### *Question orale ou écrite*

(a) Que pensez-vous de la comparaison entre les immigrés devenus trop français et les juifs cosmopolites de l'avant-guerre (l.30)? Comparez avec la position de François Léotard dans le Texte 3.9.

## TEXT 3.9

# Lâchetés

Comment a-t-on pu en arriver là? Par quelles séries de démissions, de lâchetés, de compromis, de flatteries les plus grands dirigeants de ce pays en arrivent-ils à faire de M. Le Pen l'astre noir autour duquel gravitent ces petites pensées affolées et jalouses? Quelle est la succession de désarrois, quel est l'emporium des ambitions et des calculs qui ont engendré cette poursuite triviale, et passablement déshonorante, de l'un derrière l'autre et de tous vers le pire? Que depuis dix années on ait pu voir une grande force politique, le PS, un chef d'État, François Mitterrand, et le désordre des esprits qui accompagne l'un et l'autre, utiliser le Front national après lui avoir donné naissance, est malheureusement incontestable. Que le parti d'extrême droite ait prospéré sur l'humus délétère des calculs électoraux, des manipulations en tout genre, des mensonges et des impuissances, cela est hélas! vrai.

Qu'il y ait donc un lien étroit entre le Front national et le PS, l'un se nourrissant de l'autre et chacun ne devant sa survie qu'à la menace de l'autre, l'Histoire le montrera, comme elle l'a montré ailleurs en d'autres temps. Mais qu'aujourd'hui, dans cette course aux voix qui est un véritable épuisement de la pensée, il faille se donner comme ligne de conduite '*ils le pensent, donc je le dis*', voilà qui est de nature à décourager tout civisme et, pour tout dire, tout débat. On ne peut pas porter de jugements régulièrement affligeants sur le discrédit qui entoure la chose publique si l'on oublie soi-même que la République suppose, comme premier ressort et premier principe, la vertu, c'est-à-dire, selon Montesquieu, le courage.

Pourquoi ne pas accepter cette idée qu'aujourd'hui le courage se trouve rarement du côté du plus grand nombre? Pourquoi ne pas penser que la dignité de la vie publique tient davantage dans le refus que dans la soumission, dans un jugement libre – fût-il solitaire – que dans une expression convenue, fût-elle populaire?

Or, dans ce dossier carbonisé qui empoisonne la vie politique, et qui s'appelle l'immigration, le courage n'est pas d'en parler, de manière à glisser ensuite, avec d'autres, dans le sens de la plus grande pente.

Ce pourrait être autre chose: retrouver par exemple le chemin de Renan. Lorsque, après la défaite de Sedan, l'imputant en grande partie, face à la Prusse victorieuse, aux carences de l'école, l'historien appela à une réforme intellectuelle et morale, sur quoi la fonda-t-il? Sur la nation, elle-même issue d'un plébiscite quotidien, des adhésions volontaires à un projet. A aucun moment sur la fatalité du sang. Le sang de nos veines n'est pas, à lui seul, le garant d'une identité, qui fut rayonnante tant qu'elle était le partage d'un idéal et d'une espérance. Il n'est pas plus la certitude d'un patriotisme que l'indifférence ou la malveillance ne le serait d'un sang étranger.

Des centaines de milliers d'étrangers, '*mais nos frères pourtant*' ont donné à la France – au-delà de leur vie – une dimension que jamais nos concitoyens par le sang n'ont pu – à eux seuls – lui donner. Sans cette dimension, à la fois immatérielle et charnelle, notre pays serait ramené à des frontières invisibles qui le feraient étouffer, mourir avec lui-même.

Ce n'est pas parce que le contenu du mot 'France' est aujourd'hui, au moment où nous sommes, vulgaire, de notre propre faute, qu'il faut s'enfermer avec lui pour en faire un postulat d'identité, se suffisant à lui-même dans le confort du sang reçu.

Que l'on aménage avec la plus grande rigueur le droit du sol, qu'on le subordonne à des conditions drastiques d'adhésion à une communauté de valeurs (serment solennel, langue pratiquée, service militaire, période probatoire, etc.), que l'on définisse des quotas qui correspondent d'abord à nos intérêts, cela n'est pas contestable et serait fort bien compris de nos compatriotes, comme des pays concernés. C'est d'ailleurs l'esprit (et souvent la lettre) de toutes les propositions faites jusqu'alors par l'opposition.

Mais que – de grâce! – dans un débat où se mêlent l'histoire la plus ancienne, la culture et l'image d'un peuple, le patrimoine de valeurs qu'il incarne, le regard que l'on peut avoir sur lui, on ne change pas le droit pour un avantage de pacotille qui ressemble un peu trop à un espoir électoral.

Penser serait-il interdit, expliquer désuet, convaincre inutile? En 1940, la France connut la douleur de l'invasion. Ce fut à l'honneur de quelques-uns d'y résister. Le mot n'a pas changé. Il fallait de la violence, des armes, des bombes et des meurtres pour y faire face. Ceux qui appelèrent à cet usage, à cette dignité, à ce courage, eurent raison. Je ne suis pas sûr qu'aujourd'hui on mesure la portée du précédent inconsciemment invoqué. Y convoquer l'esprit français légitimement tourmenté par le désordre et l'impatience ajoute à l'amertume: à l'invasion, on résiste par la violence! Et à la violence, par quoi résiste-t-on? Si l'on consulte un jour les Français sur ce sujet, qu'auparavant au moins on montre de leur passé les plus belles images: celles d'un grand peuple qui ne fut jamais une race.

Depuis les gardes suisses tombant devant les Tuileries jusqu'aux légionnaires de toutes races montant au corps à corps les talus de Dien Bien Phu en passant par le groupe Manoukian, combien sont ceux pour qui les 'morts pour la France' ont donné à notre peuple, par le sang versé, beaucoup plus qu'ils n'ont reçu?

(François Léotard, 'Lâchetés', *Le Monde*, 24 September 1991.)

## Exercices

### *Lexique*

Expliquez les mots et expressions suivants:

le désordre des esprits (l.8)
l'humus délétère (ll.10–11)
la chose publique (l.20)
ce dossier carbonisé qui empoisonne la vie politique (l.28)
imputer la défaite aux carences de l'école (ll.32–33)
une dimension immatérielle et charnelle (ll.42–43)
un avantage de pacotille (ll.58–59)

### *Grammaire et stylistique*

(a) Récrivez la phrase des lignes 16–17 en commençant par 'L'Histoire montrera que . . .'. De même, récrivez les lignes 17–21 en commençant par 'On peut être découragé devant le fait qu'aujourd'hui . . .'. Faites vous-mêmes des phrases commençant par 'que'.

(b) 'Un jugement libre – fût-il solitaire', 'une expression convenue, fût-elle populaire' (ll.26–27). Expliquez les subjonctifs. Trouvez vous-même une expression de ce type.

(c) 'Qu'auparavant au moins on montre de leur passé les plus belles images' (ll.68–69). Expliquez l'emploi du subjonctif. Faites une phrase sur le même modèle.

(d) En vous appuyant sur le titre, sur des mots, expressions et paragraphes précis du texte, dites quelle image François Léotard veut donner de lui-même et précisez son ton.

### *Comprehénsion*

(a) 'Ces petites pensées affolées et jalouses' (ll.3–4). Précisez le ton.

(b) Qui sont Montesquieu (l.21) et Renan (l.31)? Expliquez l'allusion des lignes 32–35, Dien Bien Phu (ll.72–73) et le groupe Manoukian (l.73).

(c) Expliquez et discutez la référence à 1940 et à la Résistance (ll.60–61). Expliquez en particulier ce que recouvre l'expression 'Je ne suis pas sûr qu'aujourd'hui on mesure la portée du précédent inconsciemment invoqué' (ll.64–65).

### *Question orale ou écrite*

(a) Montrez comment François Léotard retourne la controverse sur le 'sang' (ll.38–42). Donnez votre avis sur le rapport entre 'sang' et 'race'.

## TEXT 3.10

# La tchatche des rappeurs marseillais

Vedette incontestée de ce milieu hip-hop, IAM est le groupe symbole d'une ville mosaïque. Si les premières étincelles du renouveau ont sans doute jailli des gradins du Stade-Vélodrome, à la fin des années 80, ces musiciens ont ravivé la flamme de la fierté phocéenne. Une de leurs chansons, surtout, a provoqué le premier emballement national pour la nouvelle culture populaire marseillaise. Évocation drôle et nostalgique des années funk de leur adolescence, *Je danse le Mia* s'arrachera en 1994 à six cent mille exemplaires; le plus gros succès d'un rap français prêt à révolutionner la chanson d'ici.

Un tube en forme de flash-back. *Au début des années 80 . . .* Marseille se noie dans la crise. A la fin du règne de Gaston Defferre, la ville part en quenouille. Déjà privée de son statut de port colonial au début des années 60, marquée plus qu'ailleurs par les deux chocs pétroliers de 1973 et 1979, La «*grande machine à gérer les immigrés*», dont parle le sociologue Jean Viard, connaît des ratés. Chômage et drogue rongent les quartiers nord, le centre se paupérise, le port est en faillite. L'image est désastreuse: une ville sale, laide, à la «une» des faits divers. Sur ce terreau fleuriront des haines. En 1984, lors des élections européennes, Jean-Marie Le Pen arrive ici en tête.

La cité compte alors trois vitrines culturelles de prestige: le Théâtre national de la Criée de Marcel Maréchal, le Ballet national de Roland Petit et l'Opéra. Mais on ne retrouve pas l'effervescence des créations «jeunes et populaires» agitée par le ministère Lang. Dans le reste de la France, on parle d'«années rock». «*La porte cruelle de l'Orient*» décrite par Edmonde Charles-Roux semble préférer les déhanchements plus chauds du funk et du reggae. Les idoles ne sont pas Elvis ou Johnny mais James Brown et Bob Marley. Les rythmes noirs ont des vertus fédératrices. Celles de la danse et de la drague, de la flambe et de la «fièvre du samedi soir».

IAM allait, longtemps après, se souvenir de ces moments-clefs où la sensualité afro-américaine rencontrait la culture des minets marseillais. A l'époque, beaucoup se méfient de ces «musiques d'Arabes». «*Les boîtes de nuit refusaient leur entrée à la clientèle des quartiers*», explique Chill, l'un des chanteurs d'IAM et auteur du *Mia*.

Ces gamins exclus de la culture officielle et des fêtes en ville, on n'entendra pas leur voix jusqu'à l'éclosion du rap. A ses balbutiements, au milieu des années 80, le rap français a retranscrit sans finesse les codes vestimentaires, les tics musicaux et linguistiques des pionniers d'Amérique. Mais la faculté d'adaptation d'une musique communautaire aux réalités locales étayera les spécificités. Les enfants des banlieues sinistrées allaient s'identifier à la détresse des Noirs Américains. Jusqu'à imposer à leur tour cette «fureur de dire». Dans le Midi aussi, on allait s'approprier l'efficacité de ce vecteur de paroles.

Dans *Total Khéops*, son premier roman (au titre emprunté à l'un des morceaux d'IAM), Jean-Claude Izzo écrit: «*A Marseille, on tchatche. Le rap n'est rien d'autre. De la tchatche, tant et plus.*»

«*Fiers d'être Marseillais!*» Ce slogan qui, souvent, partira du Stade-Vélodrome à partir de 1986 sera au cœur de l'inspiration des tchatcheurs de la Canebière. C'est à Vitrolles, dans le studio d'enregistrement de Massilia, qu'IAM produira sa première cassette (*Concept*). IAM pour Invasion Arrivant de Mars, Indépendantistes Autonomes Marseillais ou simplement, en anglais, «Je suis», «J'existe». Philippe Fragione, Geoffroy Mussard, Eric Mazel, Pascal Pérez, Malek Brahimi et François Mendy ont longtemps subi la routine d'une ville en décrépitude. Seul remède à l'ennui et aux poches vides, leur passion commune du hip-hop et une imagination qui met en scène le quotidien. Chaque membre de la bande s'invente des personnages au gré de sa fascination pour l'égyptologie, l'Afrique ou l'Extrême-Orient. Philippe, connu aussi sous le nom de Chill, se rebaptise Akhenaton (le nom du premier pharaon à avoir imposé une religion monothéiste); Eric sera Khéops; Geoffroy – ou Jo –, passionné de kung-fu et de taoïsme, devient Shurik'N; Pascal mue en Imhotep, Malek en Sultan et François en Kephren.

Sorti en mars 1991, leur premier album, *De la planète Mars*, rappelle que le Sud a enfanté les civilisations fondatrices. Il évoque le passé glorieux de la cité antique, sa tradition de métissage, vécue au sein même d'un groupe qui rassemble en son sein des gens d'origine italienne (Philippe), malgache (Jo), pied-noir (Pascal), algérienne (Malek), sénégalaise (François) et espagnole (Eric). Insolents, gouailleurs, parfois graves, ces textes scandés avec l'accent témoignent d'une délectable ingéniosité. Entre l'invention lexicale de MC Solaar et l'énergie revendicatrice de NTM, IAM trouve sa voie. Cela ne plaît pas à tout le monde. Le 17 juillet de la même année, l'hebdomadaire d'extrême droite *Minute* stigmatise ces «*purs produits des ghettos maghrébins*» et les paroles «*haineuses, approximatives et si peu artistiques de leur album*», que le journal rebaptise «De la planète meurtre».

Quel single pourrait fournir la clef de cette forteresse effrayée par les rythmes et les discours du hip-hop? IAM a rapidement eu sa petite idée. «*Nous avions écrit le* Mia *à l'époque du premier album,* explique Chill. *En tournée, nous nous sommes aperçus que le morceau recevait toujours un bon accueil, alors que les gens ne le connaissaient pas.*» Le single devait mettre tous les atouts de son côté. Malgré la qualité du texte, la version de la chanson figurant sur l'album manque de l'accroche décisive qui fait les grands tubes. Après *brainstorming*, le groupe décide d'inclure dans le morceau un *sample* – ou échantillon – du *Give Me The Night* de George Benson. Bingo! Cette petite boucle, parfaitement évocatrice des soirées décrites dans le *Mia*, touchera la mémoire affective du plus grand nombre. Autre détonateur, un clip réalisé par Michel Gondry. Une vidéo hilarante, pendant visuel des paroles, à laquelle IAM s'est totalement prêté. Paradoxalement, ce sont les images qui convaincront les radios. «*Et puis,* souligne Laurence Touitou, *il y avait le* gimmick: *le mia, qu'est-ce que c'est? Ça nous a offert un axe promotionnel: mettre en avant cette culture de Marseille.*»

Du projet Euroméditerranée, la ville nouvelle restructurant le port, aux exploits de Gemplus, le roi mondial de la puce électronique, Marseille espère un renouveau. IAM montre l'exemple. En réinvestissant une partie des bénéfices de ses succès dans la scène marseillaise, il a créé une structure de production, Côté obscur, et embauché une douzaine de personnes. Hyperactif comme tous les membres du groupe, Chill prépare cet été le tournage de son premier long-métrage, *Comme un aimant*, écrit avec son camarade Kamel Saleh. «*S'il y a un retour à la prospérité*, confie-t-il, *il faut que tout le monde en profite et que la ville garde son cachet populaire. Je n'ai vu aucun signe qui allait dans ce sens. Les jeunes ont fait beaucoup d'efforts à Marseille. Au pouvoir de faire des gestes, sinon ça pétera.*» Comme souvent, le foot apporte un peu de baume au cœur. «*Même si cela m'a moins ému que la victoire de l'OM en Coupe d'Europe en 1993, celle de l'équipe de France en Coupe du monde a célébré l'image de la société qu'on défend. Son effet vaut 2 000 chansons d'IAM et 10 000 discours politiques.*»

(Stephane Davet, *Le Monde*, 9–10 August 1998, p.7.)

## Exercices

### *Lexique*

Expliquez les mots et expressions suivants:

l'emballement (m) (l.5)
partir en quenouille (l.10)
se paupériser (l.14)
les déhanchements (l.23)
les balbutiements (l.33)
étayer (l.36)
des banlieues sinistrées (l.37)
la tchatche (l.41)
gouailleur (l.62)
ça pétera (l.93)

### *Grammaire et stylistique*

(a) 'Au début des années 80 . . . Marseille se noie dans la crise' (ll.9–10). Commentez le temps des verbes dans ce paragraphe.
(b) Relevez les anglicismes dans le texte et expliquez leur présence.
(c) Identifiez le pays d'origine de chacun des membres du groupe IAM.

### *Compréhension*

(a) En quoi Marseille est-elle 'une ville mosaïque' (l.2)?
(b) Expliquez la disparition du 'statut de port colonial' (l.11) de Marseille.
(c) Quelles sont les différentes significations du sigle IAM?
(d) A quoi pense l'auteur lorsqu'il affirme: 'le sud a inventé les civilisations fondatrices' (ll.57–58)?

### *Questions orales ou écrites*

(a) La musique populaire peut-elle 'apporter un peu de baume au coeur' de la même manière que le foot?
(b) Quelles traditions culturelles ont nourri le rap français?

TEXT 3.11

## La France en avait besoin

Nous aurons donc, aussi, vécu cela. Nous aurons vu à nouveau le beau, le noble visage de la fraternité française. Histoire racontée à nos petits-enfants. Un beau jour, les Français et même, oui, les Parisiens en ont eu assez. Assez, ce n'est pas nouveau? Ce sont depuis toujours des francs-tireurs, des rebelles, des émeutiers? Les révoltes, les révolutions, ils connaissent? Sans doute. Mais cette fois, ce dont ils ont eu assez, c'est d'être moroses, d'avoir peur, de se sentir humiliés et en somme de ne plus s'aimer eux-mêmes, et de ne plus savoir qui aimer. Ils en ont eu assez d'entendre dire qu'ils étaient les plus aigris, les plus grincheux, les moins hospitaliers, les plus désagréables de toute l'Europe et de toute la Méditerranée, tandis que leur jeunesse fuyait vers Barcelone, Lisbonne, Londres, Tunis ou New York, pour y chercher les lumières de l'accueil et de la joie.

Alors ils se sont jetés d'un seul coup, tous ensemble, sur une occasion bien étrange en vérité, bien réelle et même explosive de se réconcilier avec eux-mêmes, avec les autres, et de défouler sans retenue leur besoin de vivre dans l'allégresse et le don. Ils sont sortis dans les rues, ils se sont parlés, ils se sont aimés. Et dans cette fête des retrouvailles, ils ont découvert quoi? Qu'ils étaient bien une nation, une nation unique, vivante et chaude, et qu'ils ne le savaient plus.

Parce que cette nation – un mot associé par les brigands frontistes et autres à la haine et au ressentiment –, ils ont été tout surpris, émerveillés souvent, de lui appartenir dans la fraternité et la joie. Et cela leur a fait beaucoup de bien. Bien plus qu'ils n'auraient pu l'imaginer. Ils avaient déjà connu cela, bien sûr, en 1944 pour la libération de Paris, et en Mai 68, et pendant de récentes grèves? Certes. Mais en ces journées de liesse ils avaient voulu se libérer des autres. Cette fois ils se libéraient d'eux-mêmes.

Alors maintenant, cette «occasion étrange». La Coupe du Monde, qu'est-ce que cela peut représenter d'essentiel, de fondamental pour un peuple non brésilien, non instinctif, non soumis aux mythes originels? Disons-le cette compétition a représenté, pour beaucoup, l'apothéose d'une certaine vulgarité primitive. D'abord parce que son succès dépendait de la télévision, c'est-à-dire de l'instrument impur par excellence, empoisonné par la pub et le fric, destiné à abrutir des veaux pétrifiés. Ensuite, cette Coupe était le couronnement d'un sport dans lequel des mercenaires apatrides, en général bronzés, renouaient avec la tradition des soldats suisses et se vendaient au plus offrant pour des compétitions truquées.

Enfin, ce qui pouvait subsister d'intense et de propre dans ces messes collectives suscitait l'hystérie chauvine, le déchaînement des hordes de casseurs, le culte pagano-fasciste de l'irrationnel sexiste. Le tout accompagné de rites régressifs: on se grime, on s'affuble de masques, on hurle des slogans pour voir les protagonistes se signer, implorer le ciel, s'agenouiller, baiser un crâne porte-bonheur, et après le moindre but se déchaîner dans des vagues d'étreintes, de caresses, de larmes . . .

Ce qui précède, j'en témoigne, traduit le sentiment de beaucoup de nos contemporains, de nos voisins. Et des femmes de presque toutes les classes, de tous les milieux. Partis de là, cependant, voyons où nous sommes arrivés. Avant toute chose, à ce constat énorme: nous assistons au règne effectif et incontesté du premier gouvernement mondial que les hommes se soient jamais donnés. Les décisions de la Fédération internationale sont sans appel: tout le monde s'incline. Sur le terrain, une délégation sans précédent est donnée à un homme seul, l'arbitre, plus puissant qu'un juge d'instruction puisqu'il peut sur l'instant, à chaud, avertir, sanctionner, bannir et, au nom de sa seule interprétation du règlement, léser les intérêts financiers de clubs qui se sont offerts, parfois à prix d'or, des joueurs surdoués.

Enfin, qu'avons-nous vu sur le terrain? Une guerre? Non. Un affrontement contenu par l'arbitre dans les limites de la chevalerie, et des supporters qui rejettent les images du hooliganisme et du néonazisme. On a surtout vu, en France, des ethnies, des couleurs et des différences devenir complémentaires, donner la preuve qu'elles n'attendaient qu'une occasion de vivre et de travailler ensemble, qu'elles pouvaient fuir la juxtaposition entre communautés séparées, qu'elles se sentaient heureuses de triompher ensemble.

«*Merci Zidane, vive la France!*»: nous avons tous entendu ce cri d'un beur. Facile à traduire: merci, Zidane, de vaincre pour nous, merci de nous assurer, toi, la possibilité de crier «vive la France!» grâce à ce que tu as fait avec Thuram et Karembeu. Merci de faciliter une intégration dans ce pays où, même Français de passeport, nous n'étions pas encore à l'aise, pas vraiment chez nous. Jamais on n'aurait rêvé qu'un jour le pouvoir intégrateur de l'armée, de l'Eglise et même de l'école pourrait être remplacé par celui d'une compétition sportive, il est vrai planétaire.

J'ai écrit ici même que le seul véritable adversaire de Le Pen, c'était Zidane. Pauvre Le Pen. Il n'est pas vaincu aux points mais par KO. Pas plus qu'Aimé Jacquet n'a consenti à pardonner à ses détracteurs, nous ne ferons cette charité à ceux qui se sont exclus de la grande fête de la France.

(Jean Daniel, *Le Nouvel Observateur*, 16–22 July 1998, p.25.)

## Exercices

### *Lexique*

Expliquez les mots et expressions suivants:

| | |
|---|---|
| des francs-tireurs (l.4) | les brigands frontistes (l.19) |
| des émeutiers (l.4) | ces journées de liesse (l.24) |
| grincheux (l.8) | l'apothéose (l.29) |
| défouler (l.14) | la pub et le fric (l.31) |
| l'allégresse (l.15) | apatrides (l.33) |
| des retrouvailles (l.16) | léser (l.53) |

### *Grammaire et stylistique*

(a) 'Nous aurons (. . .) vécu', 'Nous aurons vu' (l.1). Identifiez le temps/mode du verbe et expliquez pourquoi l'auteur en fait usage.
(b) 'se signer, implorer (. . .), s'agenouiller, baiser (. . .), se déchaîner.' Traduisez les lignes (ll.40–41) en anglais et expliquez l'effet stylistique recherché. Recherchez un autre passage dans le texte où un effet similaire est créé.

### *Compréhension*

(a) 'les Français (. . .), les Parisiens (. . .) sont depuis toujours des francs-tireurs, des rebelles' (ll.3–4). Identifiez l'origine de cette réputation française et parisienne.
(b) Cherchez dans le texte les images positives et négatives de la Coupe du Monde et identifiez celles qui traduisent le mieux l'attitude de l'auteur.
(c) 'même Français de passeport, nous n'étions pas encore à l'aise' (ll.65–66). Qui parle dans cette phrase et pourquoi n'étaient-ils pas encore 'à l'aise'?

### *Questions orales ou écrites*

(a) Faut-il considérer la Coupe du Monde (de football) comme 'l'apothéose d'une certaine vulgarité primitive'?
(b) Le rôle des sports comme force d'intégration des immigrés.

## TEXT 3.12

# Lettre ouverte à Bernadette Chirac

Madame,

Vous avez porté sur le Pacs une condamnation claire et nette. Permettez-moi de répondre à vos interrogations et de discuter vos arguments, car, si votre bonne foi ne peut être mise en doute, il me semble que vous êtes singulièrement mal informée.

Pourquoi les affections privées devraient-elles jouir de la reconnaissance publique? demandez-vous. Pourquoi, ai-je envie de vous rétorquer, la reconnaissance publique devrait-elle être réservée à une seule catégorie d'affection, et déniée à une autre? Qu'est-ce que le mariage, dont vous vous faites une si ardente apologiste, sinon la reconnaissance publique d'un amour privé? Pourquoi les homosexuels devraient-ils toujours être traités en sous-citoyens et leurs affections ignorées, pourquoi devraient-ils être pénalisés parce qu'ils aiment à leur façon, qui vaut bien celle des couples mariés? Vous introduisez dans le corps social une discrimination qui n'est pas seulement injuste mais humiliante. Le pouvoir du peuple ne consiste pas à favoriser exclusivement l'opinion ou les pratiques les plus répandues dans la nation. Une démocratie moderne est tenue d'accorder aux minorités les mêmes droits qu'à la majorité. Les 4 ou 5 millions d'homosexuels en France ne constituent qu'une petite minorité, je vous l'accorde: pas même 1 sur 10 citoyens. Admettez-vous que, parce qu'ils sont minoritaires, ils doivent être éternellement exclus des avantages dont jouit la majorité?

Fallait-il faire une loi? Il était sans doute possible, comme vous le suggérez, qu'en étendant les droits des concubins hétérosexuels aux concubins du même sexe, on arrivât à régler certains problèmes pratiques, en matière de droit au bail, de droit successoral, de droit à l'imposition commune, etc. Comment se fait-il que le pouvoir hétérosexuel n'ait jamais proposé, de lui-même, cette solution? Comment se fait-il que, sans la pression des associations gays, à l'époque où l'épidémie de sida rendait intolérable le vide juridique au sujet de la minorité homosexuelle, il n'y avait aucune chance qu'un pacte de solidarité civile fût jamais élaboré?

Mais le principal n'est pas là. Le Pacs, pour les homosexuels que la tradition judéo-chrétienne persécute ou marginalise depuis deux mille ans, est bien plus que la conquête de quelques aménagements juridiques et fiscaux. Ils ne se contenteraient pas de recevoir, comme une aumône glissée à la sauvette, un allègement en matière d'impôts ou de droits de mutation. Ce qu'ils veulent, c'est un acte symbolique, qui reconnaisse enfin, après vingt siècles de mise au ban, leur identité, leur qualité, leur dignité d'homme ou de femme à part entière. La question matérielle est bien secondaire à leurs yeux. La commisération bienveillante que vous leur témoignez leur paraît une insulte presque aussi grave que les maltraitances et les quolibets de jadis. Ce qu'ils exigent en réclamant le

Pacs, c'est une réparation morale, analogue à celle que les juifs ont réclamée et obtenue après l'Holocauste, c'est le rachat d'une injustice millénaire. Et cet acte symbolique, cette réparation, ce rachat, seule une loi, votée solennellement par l'Assemblée nationale, pouvait les leur offrir.

J'exagère en parlant de maltraitances, de persécution? Il y a trente ans encore, je puis vous apporter là-dessus mon témoignage personnel, l'homosexuel était traité en paria. Et vous, Madame, qui montrez tant de goût pour la France profonde, demandez-vous si les choses ont tellement changé pour lui dans les campagnes, même au fond de votre bien-aimée Corrèze.

Réduire l'homosexualité au spectacle qu'en donne la Gay Pride est une simplification abusive, qui ne prouve que votre ignorance du problème. D'abord vous confondez l'effet et la cause: la Gay Pride n'est qu'une réaction, farfelue, baroque, outrancière, à la longue obligation de clandestinité. L'immense majorité des homosexuels ne la considère pas d'un meilleur œil que vous. Ils ne demandent nullement, après avoir rasé les murs si longtemps, à s'exhiber en tenue de carnaval. La plupart de ceux qui vous ont choquée en défilant dans les rues avec des plumes sur la tête désavouent le Pacs, comme étant une formule timorée, trop prudente, trop sage, prélude à l'embourgeoisement.

Pour autant, le Pacs n'a rien à voir avec le mariage, et voilà le dernier point sur lequel je voudrais attirer votre attention. C'est un amalgame mensonger que de soutenir que le Pacs représente une menace pour la famille. Le projet discuté à l'Assemblée nationale ne prévoit pour les couples homosexuels ni mariage, ni adoption d'enfants, ni procréation médicale assistée. Peut-être le jour viendra où il faudra discuter de ces possibilités, posément, en abandonnant les idées toutes faites, les clichés. Les homosexuels seraient-ils forcément de mauvais parents? En quoi un père brutal, une mère hystérique seraient-ils des modèles insurpassables? Le sort d'un enfant martyrisé par des parents alcooliques vous paraît-il plus enviable que celui d'un enfant élevé par un couple gay où règnent l'harmonie, la bonne entente, l'affection réciproque? Encore une fois, remettons cet examen à plus tard, dans le cas où un nouveau projet serait avancé. Pour le moment, constatez, Madame, l'extrême modération du Pacs qui, loin de s'attaquer aux «*structures de base de notre société*», les renforce plutôt, en permettant à des êtres condamnés autrefois à la solitude et à l'anxiété de se sentir citoyens de plein droit.

(Dominique Fernandez, *Le Nouvel Observateur*, 12–18 November 1998, p.29.)

## Exercices

### *Lexique*

Expliquez les mots et expressions suivants:

rétorquer (l.7)
un(e) apologiste (l.10)
des concubins (l.23)
le bail (ll.24–25)
l'imposition (l.25)
une aumône (l.34)
à la sauvette (l.34)
la mise au ban (ll.36–37)

les quolibets (l.40)
millénaire (l.42)
le rachat (l.42)
en paria (l.47)
de plein droit (l.74)

### Grammaire et stylistique

(a) Examinez la structure des 'interrogations' dans le texte. Pourquoi l'auteur en fait-il un tel usage?
(b) 'Ce qu'ils veulent, c'est un acte symbolique' (ll.35–36), 'Ce qu'ils exigent (. . .), c'est une réparation morale' (ll.40–41). Traduisez ces phrases en anglais et inventez-en sur le même modèle.
(c) 'dans le cas où un nouveau projet serait avancé' (ll.70–71). Expliquez et commentez le temps/mode du verbe.

### Compréhension

(a) '[le] droit au bail', '[le] droit successoral', '[le] droit à l'imposition' (ll.24–25). De quels 'droits' s'agit-il et pourquoi fallait-il le Pacs pour étendre aux homosexuels 'des avantages dont jouit la majorité'?
(b) Quelle est cette 'tradition judéo-chrétienne' mise en cause dans le texte (ll.31–32)?

### Questions orales ou écrites

(a) Une démocratie moderne est-elle 'tenue d'accorder aux minorités les mêmes droits qu'à la majorité'?
(b) Faudrait-il accorder aux couples homosexuels le droit d'adoption d'enfants?

TEXT 3.13

## Cherche consommateur unique et unifié

Les Américains ont deux marottes: Dieu et le dollar, qui, tous deux, communient d'ailleurs sur chaque billet vert. A partir du 4 janvier 1999, les Européens, avec l'euro, graphiquement représenté par l'epsilon grec, symbole des débuts de la civilisation européenne, traversé de deux traits parallèles préfigurant la stabilité escomptée de la monnaie unique, s'efforceront eux aussi de concilier spiritualité et mercantilisme.

Jusqu'à présent, l'Amérique était seule à pouvoir compter sur des acheteurs en nombre et à domicile: ses 268 millions d'habitants rodés à la production en masse des articles qui leur sont vendus dans des magasins reproduits à l'identique sur son vaste territoire. Dorénavant, l'Europe alignera davantage de divisions que les États-Unis aux avant-postes de son marché unique: 290 millions de consommateurs à Onze, 380 millions à Quinze lorsque Britanniques, Suédois, Danois et Grecs, encore à l'écart de la monnaie unique, auront rejoint leurs euro-compagnons.

Pour tous ceux que le commerce et le marketing intéressent – et ils sont nombreux –, la cible est gigantesque: unique et unifiée par la grâce de l'euro et par la transparence des prix qui en résulte. Faut-il en conclure à la génération spontanée d'un nouveau modèle d'euro-consommateur, résigné à l'uniformité marchande de l'emballage comme du contenu et décidé à renier ses racines, locales ou culturelles? Rien n'est moins sûr. Car si on n'a jamais autant parlé de l'euro, de l'Europe élargie, de l'abolition des frontières de toute nature, jamais, dans le même temps, les rayons de «produits du terroir» n'auront occupé autant de place sur les gondoles des supermarchés, et jamais les ouvrages vantant les mérites méconnus des Cévennes ou de la Forêt Noire n'auront connu autant de succès en librairie.

Les spécialistes de la grande distribution, en contact direct avec le grand public, ont bien compris qu'il leur faudra pratiquer longtemps sans doute le grand écart entre ces deux signaux apparemment contradictoires que leur adressent leurs clients: l'aspiration à un espace européen global et le maintien d'un ancrage de proximité. Ils savent aussi que c'est sur eux – et sur les épaules des consommateurs – que repose une partie du succès de l'euro, en tout cas sa popularité.

A en croire le dernier baromètre Promodès-Louis Harris, celle-ci est en bonne voie, mais il existe une série d'incertitudes que les professionnels sont tenus d'intégrer dans leurs stratégies commerciales. «L'Europe ne rendra pas le consommateur plus homogène; c'est même l'inverse qui devrait se produire», reconnaît Franck Riboud, PDG de Danone, le numéro un français de l'agroalimentaire. «L'uniformisation des produits n'existe pas. Le goût d'un yaourt est différent d'un pays à l'autre. En Allemagne, par exemple, la cuillère doit tenir verticalement dans le yaourt car les Allemands préfèrent les produits crémeux et riches. Dans le sud de l'Europe, la demande est inverse: le yaourt doit être fluide et léger», indique-t-il.

«En Europe, nous sommes déjà dans l'ère du micro-marketing. Nous devons faire preuve d'une compréhension de plus en plus fine, pertinente et locale des consommateurs. La montée en puissance des marques et des produits régionaux illustre parfaitement l'importance du respect de la tradition pour les consommateurs. L'Europe va renforcer cet aspect régionaliste, tout au moins dans nos industries de grande consommation», ajoute-t-il, expliquant comment, lors du lancement d'un nouveau produit à l'échelle européenne, tout l'effort de commercialisation doit être orienté en fonction des critères propres à chaque pays en ce qui concerne le goût, le prix, la stratégie commerciale et la campagne publicitaire.

Maurice Lévy, président de Publicis, confirme ce dernier point. «Nous commençons à bien comprendre les mentalités et les particularités de chacun des pays avec lesquels nous sommes en relation. Il n'y a pas, à l'heure actuelle, d'émergence nette de la notion de consommateur européen qui aurait exactement le même mode de vie, le même comportement d'achat, le même rythme de travail que son voisin, affirme-t-il. Nous sommes donc encore très loin d'une forme de communication standardisée. En revanche, ce qui fonctionne assez bien en termes de communication européenne ou même internationale, ce sont les campagnes qui portent sur des produits ou des objets constituant une cible homogène. C'est le cas des cosmétiques ou des produits de luxe dont la marque est l'instrument essentiel de la communication.» Comment la grande distribution entend-elle s'adapter à cette nouvelle donne commerciale post-euro? «Nos magasins sont différents en fonction de chaque pays. Les produits frais qui y sont vendus sont très 'couleur locale' et ils le resteront. Seuls les produits de marque Carrefour seront identiques, fait valoir Daniel Bernard, PDG de ce géant des hypermarchés. A mon avis, l'euro ne fera pas disparaître la culture locale. Au contraire, ce sentiment restera très vivace et tous nos objectifs commerciaux tendent à développer nos gammes de produits du terroir, de produits authentiques, de qualités et de variétés traditionnelles.» Toutefois, ajoute-t-il, «les différences persistent essentiellement dans l'alimentation. Dans d'autres domaines, on assistera peu à peu à un échange d'expériences, à une évolution des comportements».

(Serge Marti, *Le Monde*, 31 December 1998, p.11.)

## Exercices

### *Lexique*

Expliquez les mots et expressions suivants:

| | |
|---|---|
| une marotte (l.1) | renier (l.19) |
| le mercantilisme (l.6) | les gondoles (l.23) |
| rodés (l.8) | l'agroalimentaire (ll.36–37) |
| dorénavant (l.10) | une cible (l.60) |
| davantage de (l.10) | vivace (l.68) |

### *Grammaire et stylistique*

(a) 'aux avant-postes' (l.11). Formez cinq autres expressions sur le même modèle et écrivez-les au singulier et au pluriel.
(b) 'unifiée par la grâce de l'euro et par la transparence des prix' (ll.16–17). Identifiez la figure de style employée ici. Quel en est l'effet?
(c) 'les rayons de "produits du terroir" n'auront occupé autant de place (. . .) jamais les ouvrages (. . .) n'auront connu . . .' (ll.22–24). Identifiez et commentez les temps des verbes employés dans cette phrase.
(d) 'grande consommation' (l.47); 'grande distribution' (l.26). Recherchez dans votre dictionnaire d'autres expressions dans lesquelles l'adjectif 'grand(e)' est utilisé de la même manière.

### *Compréhension*

(a) Que signifie l'expression les 'produits du terroir' (l.22)? Donnez-en des exemples.
(b) Quels mérites faut-il accorder au symbole de l'euro selon l'auteur de ce texte?
(c) En quoi consiste le 'micro-marketing' (l.42)? Cette approche va-t-elle s'intensifier dans les années à venir?
(d) Expliquez la 'nouvelle donne commerciale post-euro' (l.63).

### *Questions orales ou écrites*

(a) Etes-vous pour ou contre la création d'un 'espace européen global'?
(b) Homogénéité ou diversité – quel sera, à votre avis, l'impact de la création de l'euro sur les habitudes des consommateurs?

TEXT 3.14

## Décadence du repas bourgeois

L'arrivée du barbecue dans la société française il y a plus d'une vingtaine d'années et sa diffusion fulgurante témoignent de presque toutes les grandes transformations de notre pays: on peut y lire toute notre histoire sociale récente. Le mot même révèle l'américanisation de la France. Le cow-boy faisait griller une pièce de viande pour la dévorer à pleines dents.

Que cette pratique alimentaire de sauvage ait pénétré la gastronomie la plus civilisée du monde mérite une explication. Ni un paysan ni un ouvrier et encore moins un bourgeois du début du siècle n'auraient imaginé qu'on puisse manger dehors de la viande presque crue. Les premiers ne mangeaient pratiquement pas de viande, les seconds la mangeaient rôtie, et tous la mangeaient dedans, à la cuisine ou à la salle à manger. Manger dehors? quelle incongruité! Certes les ouvriers et les paysans emportaient le casse-croûte dans les champs ou sur les chantiers et les bourgeois organisaient des pique-niques mais le repas était froid et frugal pour le travailleur (qui, à l'atelier, faisait parfois réchauffer la gamelle), opulent et raffiné pour la partie de campagne. Mais dans tous les cas c'était le contraire d'un vrai repas pris à la maison.

Or aujourd'hui un Français sur trois a son barbecue, pour moitié acheté dans les quatre dernières années. En 1980, s'il s'en est vendu près de quatre cent mille, 80% viennent de Taïwan, 15% seulement ont été fabriqués en France et le reste ailleurs. Bien sûr on ne peut compter ceux fabriqués sur place, en pierre et somptueux dans les résidences secondaires luxueuses, ou de fortune, faits d'une jante d'automobile montée sur trois pieds par exemple. Innovation récente qui a suivi la courbe logistique classique en S, le barbecue est 'transclassiste', comme on dit, les plus beaux ne sont pas nécessairement en haut de l'échelle sociale. C'est un gadget de grande consommation très diversifié: un beau, français, solide, sans danger vaut 1500 francs tandis qu'un léger et dangereux venu de Taïwan vaut 150 francs.

Le rôti, le bouilli et le mijoté étaient les trois grands modes de cuisson de la cuisine bourgeoise et paysanne. Le feu dans l'âtre servait à bouillir la soupe paysanne et à rôtir le gigot bourgeois. Sur la braise, dans le potager (qui pourrait paraître l'ancêtre du barbecue mais ne l'est pas) le lait chauffait pour faire monter la crème, les ragoûts mijotaient lentement. Mais de grillade point. Le beefsteak, nouveauté anglaise, nous est venu à la fin du siècle dernier avec le sport et le *five o'clock tea.*

J'incline à penser que le scoutisme, autre innovation anglaise, a été le grand éclaireur du barbecue en habituant les jeunes bourgeois à la cuisine grillée dans la nature. Mais ce n'était là encore que jeux de petits sauvages, le contraire de la cuisine et du repas bien ordonnés. Les chantiers de jeunesse enfin eurent aussi leur rôle et je subodore un relent de vichysme dans le fumet du barbecue.

Les ouvriers jardiniers qui faisaient la cuisine en plein air pendant qu'ils bêchaient leur jardin se flattent d'être les inventeurs et les promoteurs du barbecue mais c'est une prétention visiblement usurpée: comment une pratique d'hommes, hors de leur maison, se serait-elle transmise? La guerre d'Algérie et le retour des pieds-noirs paraît une influence beaucoup plus plausible: le petit fourneau méditerranéen qu'on tient devant la porte est évidemment une sorte de barbecue. Le méchoui surtout, sans lequel il n'y a plus de belle fête de village, est une exaltation somptueuse du barbecue.

Tous ces précédents historiques n'auraient été que de faible poids sans un phénomène social massif: la décadence de la bourgeoisie. Il suffit de comparer le repas de la famille bourgeoise et le déjeuner autour du barbecue pour comprendre que celui-ci est la négation de la bourgeoisie. La mise en scène du repas reproduisait dans la salle à manger les clivages fondamentaux de la société: les parents au centre avec leurs invités, en bout de table les enfants et les familiers (parents pauvres, gouvernantes . . .), debout, les serviteurs servant et regardant le spectacle que se donnait (et leur donnait) la famille, sous la houlette active de la maîtresse de maison dont c'est le triomphe. Bourgeoisie, classes moyennes et prolétariat étaient rituellement situés dans la salle à manger comme dans l'ensemble de la société. Ce rite ne peut se perpétuer si les domestiques disparaissent et si l'on renonce à saisir toutes les occasions de hiérarchiser les individus. Comment vivre bourgeoisement si l'on n'a plus de domestiques pour vous servir et vous observer?

Le rassemblement familial et amical autour du barbecue est un rite en tous points opposé au repas bourgeois. Ni hiérarchie affirmée ni répartition ritualisée des rôles. Hommes et femmes, jeunes et vieux, les invités et leurs hôtes, en tenue également débraillée (de bon ton, discrète ou vulgaire), se font cuire chacun sa brochette. L'homme qui a allumé le feu préside à l'ensemble, distribue les brochettes, se glorifie dans un nouveau rôle masculin et rabaisse d'autant la femme cantonnée à la salade et aux légumes. Rite de classe moyenne où le spectacle ne sert plus à confirmer les positions sociales de chacun mais plutôt à classer et à reclasser les familles sur une échelle discrète où chacun s'efforce de gravir un nouvel échelon.

Tout est inversé: le grillé remplace le rôti, le dehors le dedans (sans pour autant être dans la nature), l'égalité la hiérarchie, et l'ascension la stabilité car il y a des barbecues riches et élégants ('classes' comme on dit) et d'autres simples et populaires. En un mot les sauvages américains ont détruit tout l'ordre immuable de la bourgeoisie française grâce à un misérable petit outil qu'ils ont fait fabriquer par les Chinois . . .

(Henri Mendras, 'Décadence du repas bourgeois', in Pascal Ory' (ed.), *Mots de passe 1945–85*, Éditions Autrement, 1985.)

## Exercices

### *Lexique*

Expliquez les mots et expressions suivants:

le casse-croûte (l.12)
la gamelle (l.15)
une partie de campagne (l.15)
le rôti, le bouilli, le mijoté (l.28)
un âtre (l.29)
le gigot (l.30)
le pied-noir (l.44)
le méchoui (l.46)
sous la houlette de (ll.55–56)
débraillé (l.65)
de bon ton (l.65)

### *Grammaire et stylistique*

(a) Justifiez le subjonctif de la ligne 9. Quel autre mode eût-on pu utiliser?
(b) 'Je subodore un relent de vichysme dans le fumet du barbecue' (l.39). Examinez la formule: quels mots 'filent' la métaphore? Essayez d'appliquer ce procédé dans des phrases de votre cru.
(c) 'pique-nique', 'sport', 'five o'clock tea' – nombreux sont les mots du texte empruntés à l'anglais. Trouvez-en d'autres ici.

### *Compréhension*

(a) Que comprenez-vous par l'expression 'transclassiste' (l.23)? Quelle est la racine de ce néologisme?
(b) Qu'est-ce que le 'vichysme' (l.39)?

### *Question orale ou écrite*

(a) Écrivez un article d'imitation sur la sociologie du fast-food.

TEXT 3.15

## La transhumance des aoûtiens, bête noire des entreprises

Tous les Français n'ont pas, en août, les pieds dans l'eau et la tête au soleil. Air France, Air Inter, la SNCF ou la RATP, on s'en doute, ne peuvent pas convoyer des millions de vacanciers sans gérer au compte-gouttes l'octroi de congés payés durant l'été. On imagine mal les hôpitaux sans infirmières, les prisons sans gardiens, les commissariats désertés. Dans le secteur privé, si quatre entreprises sur dix ferment leurs portes en août, beaucoup doivent ruser pour pousser leurs salariés à partir à l'automne, en hiver ou au printemps.

Dans les travaux publics, quand les directions départementales profitent de la grande migration pour refaire les routes, on emploie parfois de drôles de méthodes: '*Certaines boîtes fixent arbitrairement la durée maximum des congés qu'il est possible de prendre en été. Parfois, elles tolèrent même des arrangements du type: officiellement, l'ouvrier est en vacances et touche ses congés payés; en réalité, il travaille. Au noir ou pas*', explique Jean-Jacques Peyre, à la fédération CFDT du BTP.

Certaines entreprises ouvrent leur chéquier pour inciter leurs salariés à déserter les plages. Cobra (bracelets montre) a un besoin impératif de 80% de son personnel tout au long de l'année: la direction propose une prime de 3000 francs aux salariés qui acceptent de ne partir que quinze jours en été. Le découpage des trois autres semaines de congés payés donne encore droit à une prime de 1000 francs. Un système plutôt efficace puisque 90% des 150 salariés était au travail cette semaine. Dans le commerce et la restauration, le recours systématique aux contrats à durée déterminée ou aux intérimaires permet, le plus souvent, de passer l'été sans encombre.

Dans le public, autres méthodes, autres mœurs, mais problématique similaire. On ne remplace pas au pied levé un gardien de prison, un conducteur de train ou un pilote d'avion. Là, on parle de '*réquisition*'. En été, certaines prisons font figure de bataillons disciplinaires. '*Les gardiens prennent leur mois de vacances entre avril et octobre. A tour de rôle. Ceux qui sont partis en avril cette année partiront en mai l'an prochain, puis en juin et, dans quatre ans, en août*', détaille Jean-Paul Roman, délégué FO, à Fleury-Mérogis. Pas vraiment la panacée. Pour des raisons familiales, certains bouleversent parfois les rotations en prenant, en juillet ou en août, la place de collègues jugés moins prioritaires. Pour ces derniers, la potion est amère. '*Lorsque notre tour saute, il n'y a pas de repêchage l'année suivante. Et, comble de galère, on est rarement prévenus à temps. Nos réservations vacances sont déjà faites*', explique un gardien à Fleury-Mérogis.

Moins tendue mais aussi difficile la situation des agents SNCF, RATP ou du personnel d'Air France et d'Air Inter, dont l'attribution des vacances est soumise à un savant calcul. '*Chacun est crédité d'un nombre de points en fonction de son ancienneté, de sa situation de famille et de la période de congés qu'il a prise l'année précédente*', explique Jean-Claude Raoul, à la direction du personnel de la SNCF. Le total obtenu détermine le mois accordé. '*Une année d'ancienneté rapporte environ 1 point, le fait d'être marié 10, un enfant en âge scolaire 12 et ainsi de suite. Dans ma situation, je dois cumuler pas mal de mois de vacances en dehors de la période protocolaire* (de mai à octobre) *pour avoir une chance de décrocher un jour le mois d'août*', précise un contrôleur grandes lignes, célibataire, abonné aux mois de pluie.

Si bien que certaines corporations, au sein même de la SNCF, ont contourné la règle nationale en signant des accords plus souples. Résultat: de peur de voir une mosaïque d'accords particuliers se substituer à la règle générale, la SNCF, a retravaillé sa copie. Désormais, elle accorde une prime sonnante et trébuchante aux agents qui posent leurs vacances en dehors de la période rouge. Pour faire voler ses avions, Air France préfère offrir des jours de congé supplémentaires aux amateurs de sports d'hiver tandis que la RATP, qui vient de décentraliser la gestion des vacances en élargissant l'autonomie des divers chefs de dépôts, autorise cette année ses ouailles à prendre leurs congés à la carte.

Même l'administration pénitentiaire semble se réveiller. Elle compte assouplir son système en incitant les gardiens à ne prendre que quinze jours l'été, plutôt qu'un mois plein. Objectif: alléger la grille pour y faire figurer plus de monde. Une chance, ce souci des entreprises ou des administrations va de pair avec l'évolution des mœurs du vacancier qui préfère maintenant partir moins longtemps mais plus souvent.

('La transhumance des aoûtiens, bête noire des entreprises', *Libération*, 15–16 August 1992.)

## Exercices

### *Lexique*

Expliquez les mots et expressions suivants:

gérer au compte-gouttes (l.3)
le contrat à durée déterminée (l.21)
intérimaire (l.21)
sans encombre (l.22)
au pied levé (l.24)
à tour de rôle (l.27)
notre tour saute (l.32)
comble de galère (l.33)
le repêchage (l.33)
et ainsi de suite (ll.41–42)
une prime sonnante et trébuchante (l.49)
les ouailles (l.54)
aller de pair avec (l.58)

### *Grammaire et stylistique*

(a) 'au compte-gouttes' (l.3). Cherchez le pluriel de ce mot et commentez, à l'aide d'exemples de votre cru, le pluriel des mots composés.
(b) 'drôles de méthodes' (ll.9–10). Quel est le ton de cette expression? Faites-en d'autres sur le même modèle.
(c) 'Pas vraiment la panacée' (l.29). Analyser les phrases commençant par une négative. Faites-en vous-même en utilisant d'autres négatives.

### *Compréhension*

(a) Qu'est-ce que la CFDT (l.13), le BTP (l.13), FO (l.29), la SNCF (l.40) et la RATP (l.52)?

(b) Comment comprenez-vous l'expression: 'la SNCF a retravaillé sa copie' (ll.48–49)?

(c) Expliquez le titre et commentez le choix des mots: précisez-en le registre.

### *Question orale ou écrite*

(a) Comment les grandes entreprises répondent-elles aux problèmes que posent les 'aoûtiens' ou personnes qui prennent leurs vacances en août? Quelles solutions proposez-vous vous-même?

## TEXT 3.16

# La France et ses langues

Le débat qui s'est engagé depuis que le premier ministre a proposé une révision constitutionnelle, autorisant la République à ratifier la Charte européenne des langues régionales et minoritaires qu'elle a signée le 7 mai, a donné lieu à l'expression d'oppositions si farouches qu'elles suscitent un sentiment d'irréalité. Sommes-nous donc revenus deux siècles en arrière quand, sous le régime de la Terreur, l'abbé Grégoire persuadait la Convention, présidée par Robespierre, le 4 juin 1794, six semaines avant le 9 Thermidor, de «*la nécessité d'anéantir les patois et d'universaliser la langue française*»? A nouveau les langues autres que le français sont présentées comme menaçant, si peu qu'on les reconnaisse, de détruire l'unité nationale, quand ce n'est pas d'affaiblir le français . . . On croit rêver!

Il serait temps que chacun soit informé de la réalité, qui est exactement à l'opposé: l'unité nationale réclame, en effet, qu'on protège l'exceptionnel patrimoine linguistique de la France au moment où le règne sans partage du français préside au dépérissement des langues historiques de la métropole. Lorsque l'abbé Grégoire déclarait la guerre aux langues des provinces, la moitié des citoyens de la République ne parlait ni ne comprenait le français. En dehors des villes et des départements centraux, la population était monolingue dans les langues régionales, et ce sont les rares francophones qui étaient bilingues. Deux siècles plus tard, tout s'est inversé.

Ce que le long effort de l'enseignement primaire n'avait pu obtenir, les deux guerres mondiales, l'exode rural, l'allongement de la scolarité, la radio et la télévision l'ont enfin obtenu: aujourd'hui, la totalité des Français parlent et comprennent la langue de la République et le petit nombre d'entre eux qui pratique encore une langue dite régionale l'apprend en plus du français, et le plus souvent en second. Depuis cinquante ans, aucun parler roman, qu'il soit d'oc ou d'oïl, ne se transmet plus de la mère au nourrisson. En métropole, l'usage régulier des langues régionales ne se maintient vraiment que chez les plus de cinquante ans, hormis en Alsace où il y aurait encore 15% des moins de quinze ans à parler alsacien. Mais, là comme ailleurs, la chute est vertigineuse depuis le milieu du siècle.

Le breton, par exemple, comptait environ 1,3 million de locuteurs en 1914, et plus d'1 million encore en 1945. Mais en cinquante ans, il a perdu près de 80% de ses usagers: on estime aujourd'hui à 250 000 le nombre de ceux qui l'utilisent quotidiennement.

La chute dramatique du nombre de locuteurs, et donc de ceux qui transmettent la langue, affecte plus encore les langues romanes, à part le corse dont l'insularité a favorisé la résistance. Les parlers d'oïl, en pleine vigueur sous Grégoire, sont presque tous à la limite de l'extinction, n'ayant pratiquement plus de véritable autonomie à l'oral, et les parlers d'oc, s'ils comptent encore, au total, peut-être deux millions de locuteurs plus ou moins réguliers, sont réduits, eux aussi, aux plus de cinquante ans.

Si le français n'est pas devenu la langue de l'univers, les «patois» sont au bord de ce néant auquel les vouait la Convention. Le dispositif de la loi Deixonne (1951), complété régulièrement depuis lors, concerne maintenant une dizaine de langues, mais il est venu trop tard: 3% seulement des élèves des premier et second degrés reçoivent aujourd'hui un enseignement en langues et cultures régionales.

Certains se réjouissent de cette victoire quasi absolue du français et je sais, comme eux, l'immense avantage que nous tirons tous de la pratique généralisée de la langue nationale. Mais ne pouvait-elle s'accommoder d'un bilinguisme laissant leur place aux langues régionales? Contrairement à ce que croient généralement les Français, le cerveau humain n'est pas fait pour le monolinguisme comme le démontre l'immense majorité de l'humanité, plus souvent encore trilingue ou quadrilingue que bilingue. De fait, une sorte de bilinguisme franco-anglais pourrait s'imposer: près de 9 enfants français sur 10 apprennent l'anglais au secondaire. Je ne doute pas que cette langue leur soit aujourd'hui nécessaire. Elle n'en est pas moins en compétition directe avec la nôtre, qu'elle ne cesse de faire reculer en Europe. L'affaiblissement des langues régionales lui laisse le champ libre en France . . . Qu'on ne vienne pas nous dire que c'est la protection des langues régionales qui menacerait le français! Comment pourrions-nous lutter pour le maintien du plurilinguisme en Europe si nous le refusions en France?

La Charte, en tout cas, ne fait courir aucun risque à notre langue nationale. Les engagements du gouvernement ne mettent pas en cause sa place exceptionnelle, sur laquelle tous les Français sont d'accord. Elle est et restera la langue exclusive de l'État et des services publics; elle est et restera l'unique langue obligatoire dans l'enseignement, la justice, l'administration; elle est et restera la seule langue de France ayant une réalité politique quand les autres n'ont et n'auront de réalité que culturelle. On ne se mariera pas en basque, on ne plaidera pas en breton, on ne légiférera pas en picard . . .

Les langues, ce n'est pas d'abord du politique, c'est de la culture! Ce n'est que secondairement qu'un nombre infime des quatre mille langues du monde peut être associé à la définition d'une entité politique comme c'est le cas du français en France. Les autres langues de France sont un formidable patrimoine culturel national et c'est un devoir national de les défendre.

(Catherine Trautmann, *Le Monde*, 31 July 1999, p.14.)

## Exercices

### *Lexique*

Expliquez les mots et expressions suivants:

| | |
|---|---|
| farouches (l.4) | roman (l.25) |
| anéantir (l.7) | le nourrisson (l.26) |
| les patois (l.7) | hormis (l.28) |
| le patrimoine linguistique (ll.12–13) | les locuteurs (l.31) |
| le dépérissement (l.14) | les parlers d'oïl/d'oc (ll.37–39) |

### *Grammaire et stylistique*

(a) 'depuis que le premier ministre a proposé . . .' (l.1). Traduisez cette phrase et expliquez le temps du verbe. Inventez plusieurs phrases de votre choix dans lesquelles vous utiliserez la préposition 'depuis'.
(b) 'si peu qu'on les reconnaisse' (l.9). Commentez le mode du verbe. Trouvez d'autres phrases commençant par 'si' et construites de la même manière.
(c) 'quand ce n'est pas d'affaiblir le français' (l.10). Paraphrasez cette proposition en français.

### *Compréhension*

(a) 'l'abbé Grégoire'; 'la Convention'; 'Robespierre'; 'Thermidor' (premier paragraphe). De quelle période de l'histoire s'agit-il? Pourquoi ces références sont-elles particulièrement importantes?
(b) Selon l'auteur, quelles influences ont le plus favorisé la progression de la langue française en France?
(c) D'après le texte, des langues régionales ou de la langue anglaise, quelles sont les mieux placées pour concurrencer la langue française?

### *Questions orales ou écrites*

(a) 'Je ne doute pas que [l'anglais] leur soit aujourd'hui nécessaire' (ll.55–56). L'imposition de l'anglais comme langue 'universelle' vous paraît-elle souhaitable?
(b) Faudrait-il protéger les langues régionales et minoritaires ou les laisser disparaître?

TEXT 3.17

## Don Quichotte et les dinosaures

*Dear Bill Clinton,*

Il parait que certains hommes d'État prennent plaisir à déplaire, et en tirent réconfort. Si c'est votre cas, vous devez vous régaler, ces temps-ci, et douter moins que jamais.

Après les Somaliens, qui vous récusent comme gendarme de la planète, voici que d'autres sous-développés, les Français, refusent en bloc de voir «gattifier» leur culture selon vos vœux. Non seulement vous avez réalisé contre vous, à Paris, une union sacrée dont les Gaulois de l'Hexagone ne sont pas coutumiers, mais vous avez obtenu qu'à l'île Maurice nous rejoignent les quarante-sept pays qui s'entêtent à aimer d'amour la langue de Molière, et que la reine d'Angleterre compare volontiers à son Commonwealth.

Vous me direz qu'il aurait mieux valu rallier à nos thèses l'ensemble de nos frères européens, et que nous faisons sans doute figure d' «Américains» pour certains francophones du tiers-monde. Ce qui est sûr, c'est que nos tempêtes d'encrier ont peu de chance de fléchir votre credo, d'autant plus ancré que désormais seul en lice dans le monde, et selon lequel ce qui profite au marché américain est forcément bon pour l'humanité entière.

Quelques libéraux d'autres continents vous suivent, comme Vargas Losa, en faisant semblant de croire que la compétition artistique se joue loyalement entre les meilleurs produits: les «Oscars» et le public trancheront! . . . Vous savez très bien que cette loyauté n'est plus qu'un leurre; pour la simple raison que les conditions matérielles de fabrication et de diffusion des créations de l'esprit ont changé de nature.

Tant que l'émulation entre les œuvres dépendait d'une rame de papier, d'un budget artisanal et d'un conseil de libraire, le jeu était ouvert. La même année 1885, par exemple, les chances étaient comparables entre *Germinal*, le roman, et, mettons, *les Bostoniens*, de James. Entre les deux guerres, Max Linder pouvait encore braver Chaplin. Aujourd'hui, finances et techniques ne permettent plus aux seuls talents de se mesurer.

On a admis, en stratégie, que la capacité nucléaire de désintégrer la planète avait rendu caducs les vieux raisonnements militaires; il y a tromperie à ignorer que la culture de masse a fait un saut qualitatif équivalent.

Si, d'aventure, vous reconnaissez, sur le papier, l'«exception» que nous implorons pour les cultures moins riches que la vôtre, à la façon dont s'organise mondialement l'écologie contre les destructions irréversibles de la logique marchande, vous savez bien que notre marché continuera à plier sous vos conditionnements, que nos systèmes d'aides et de quotas ne favoriseront que rarement des œuvres rivales, et que les satellites se joueront très vite de ces lignes Maginot hertziennes. «*Nous avons les moyens de vous faire câbler!*», auraient dit les Allemands, du temps où ils étaient devenus des Boches.

Le débat sur l'«exception culturelle» oblige à cerner l'incernable. Cette «âme» européenne dont nous craignons la dissolution dans la vôtre pour cause d'infériorité commerciale, qu'a-t-elle de si précieux? C'est quoi, ce bijou de famille promis au clou? Des dizaines de colloques n'ont fait qu'approcher ce qui, par chance, reste un mystère. Nous définissons-nous par le judéo-christianisme, ou par la raison du cinquième siècle grec? De Strindberg à Pirandello, de Joyce à Ritsos, et maintenant de Shakespeare à Tolstoi, en quoi se ressemblent, et diffèrent des vôtres, nos représentations de l'amour, de la mort, de l'argent, de la famille, de la violence, de la pitié? Il existe des réponses pour les savants et, ce qui a plus de prix, pour chacun de nous.

L'Histoire a moins édicté des certitudes, entre Européens, qu'elle n'a esquissé, au-delà des tumultes et des langages, des réseaux de connivences et de beautés, des pôles divers de rayonnement, des musiques, et plus généralement un double sens de la loi et de la transgression, de l'utopie et du doute.

Si nos héros s'appellent Quichotte, Faust et Don Juan (allez, ajoutons-y Woody Allen, européen d'honneur!), c'est qu'ils poursuivent un absolu tout en souriant de leur échec. Plutôt ces Prométhée mal enchaînés que la machine-à-faire-peur-dans-le-noir de *Jurassic Park*! Nous aimerions vraiment, pour nos enfants, que vos dinosaures n'écrasent pas Don Quichotte: passez-nous cette faiblesse!

Mais c'est une des tristesses du débat sur l'«exception» que d'obliger à ces à-peu-près chauvins. On ne devrait pas avoir à se demander qui ou quoi «doit» survivre aux lois de l'argent, de par le monde. La seule conviction à laquelle ne peut que se rallier un homme de liberté comme vous, c'est que si la suprématie économique vaut mieux que les protectionnismes idéologiques défunts, la culture, elle, postule le dialogue, sous peine de barbarie.

Et que pour dialoguer, désolé d'avoir à le rappeler, il faut être au moins deux; ce qu'avant peu les finances et les technologies du plus fort ne toléreront plus, avec la meilleure volonté!

(Bertrand Poirot-Delpech, *Le Monde*, 20 October 1993.)

## Exercices

### *Lexique*

Expliquez les mots et expressions suivants:

nos tempêtes d'encrier (ll.14–15)
votre credo (l.15)
en lice (l.16)
loyalement (l.19)
trancheront (l.20)
un leurre (l.21)
braver (l.28)
se mesurer (l.29)
caducs (l.31)
d'aventure (l.33)
cerner (l.41)
un clou (l.44)
ces à-peu-près (ll.60–61)

### *Grammaire et stylistique*

(a) 'Il aurait mieux valu rallier à nos thèses . . .' (l.12). Expliquez le temps et le mode du verbe.
(b) 'Tant que l'émulation entre les œuvres dépendait d'une rame de papier . . .' (l.24). Trouvez d'autres adverbes de temps dans le texte et expliquez leur fonction.
(c) 'Cette âme européenne (. . .) qu'a-t-elle de si précieux?' (ll.41–43) Cette question en inaugure une série. Commentez l'effet stylistique recherché par l'auteur.

### *Compréhension*

(a) 'les Français refusent de voir "gattifier" leur culture'. Quel processus l'auteur cherche-t-il à définir avec ce néologisme?
(b) 'Strindberg', 'Pirandello', 'Joyce', 'Ritsos', 'Shakespeare', 'Tolstoï'. Identifiez ces écrivains et dites pourquoi ils figurent dans le texte. Auriez-vous fait les mêmes choix que l'auteur?
(c) 'ces lignes Maginot hertziennes' (ll.38–39). En quoi la télévision hertzienne ressemble-t-elle à la ligne Maginot?

### *Questions orales ou écrites*

(a) La culture est-elle 'exceptionnelle' ou doit-elle se plier aux lois du marché?
(b) Les Français ont-ils raison de vouloir défendre leurs cinéma et télévision contre les produits audiovisuels américains?

## TEXT 3.18

# Les foulards de la discorde

Au collège Gabriel-Havez, au cœur de la cité ouvrière de Creil, dans l'Oise, on respire. Samira, Fatima et Leïla, trois jeunes Maghrébines de 13 à 15 ans, nées en France de parents marocains et tunisiens, peuvent à nouveau pénétrer dans leurs salles de classe. A une condition: assister aux cours 'tête nue'. Le principal, Ernest Chenières, réputé homme à poigne, les avait exclues de l'établissement le 18 septembre, estimant que le port du 'hidjeb', le foulard traditionnel coranique, noué sous le menton et cachant les cheveux, représentait 'une atteinte à la laïcité et à la neutralité de l'école publique'. Deux points de vue opposés: pour les familles, leurs filles ne font qu'observer le Coran en portant le voile. 'Peut-être, mais si tout le monde vient à l'école avec son drapeau ou sa bannière religieuse, où s'arrêtera-t-on?' riposte le principal.

Cette histoire de couvre-chef a aussitôt déchaîné les passions, et failli dégénérer en un affrontement entre 'islamistes' et défenseurs de l'école républicaine. Bref, une affaire empoisonnée, qui a plongé dans l'embarras jusqu'au ministre de l'Éducation nationale lui-même, lequel s'est bien gardé de trancher: 'Il s'agit de respecter la laïcité de l'école en n'affichant pas, de façon ostentatoire, les signes de son appartenance religieuse', déclare-t-il, le 8 octobre. Mais il ajoute: 'L'école est faite pour accueillir les enfants et non pour les exclure . . .' Il aura fallu, à Creil, l'intervention d'un inspecteur d'académie et la médiation patiente de l'association culturelle tunisienne locale pour arracher un compromis. Finalement, chacun a mis un peu du sien: les jeunes filles garderont leur hidjeb dans la cour de l'école, mais l'enlèveront en classe.

Affaire terminée? Pas si simple, à entendre témoignages et opinions divergents: 'Le compromis trouvé ne suffira pas à résoudre le problème de l'intégration des musulmans dans notre société', affirment certains enseignants du collège Gabriel-Havez. Là cohabitent, il est vrai, 855 élèves de 25 nationalités différentes, parmi lesquels près de 500 jeunes musulmans: les deux tiers des collégiens ont un retard scolaire. Une situation explosive. Autre question, toujours en suspens: une vingtaine de collégiens israélites refusent de venir en classe le samedi, jour de shabbat. Normal?

Un peu partout en France, des chefs d'établissement se trouvent face à des problèmes similaires. Chacun les résout à sa manière, en jouant les shérifs de la laïcité comme Ernest Chenières, ou, au contraire, en optant pour la 'tolérance'. Ainsi, au collège du Hohberg, à Strasbourg – qui compte 28% de Maghrébins – le principal autorise les jeunes filles à porter le foulard islamique, tout en espérant les convaincre peu à peu de l'abandonner. En revanche, dans le quartier de la Paillade, à Montpellier – un secteur à fort taux d'immigrés – le responsable d'un collège a expulsé récemment deux jeunes élèves qui refusaient d'abandonner leur voile.

Il est temps, en France, de dépoussiérer le concept de laïcité. Une certitude: au Maroc et en Tunisie, le port du voile est interdit à l'école.

(Marie-Laure de Léotard, 'Les foulards de la discorde', *L'Express*, 30 October 1989.)

## Exercices

### *Lexique*

Expliquez les mots et expressions suivants:

un homme à poigne (l.5)
une bannière religieuse (ll.10–11)
un couvre-chef (l.12)
se garder de trancher (l.15)
un inspecteur d'académie (l.19)
chacun y a mis un peu du sien (l.21)
jouer les shérifs de la laïcité (ll.32–33)
dépoussiérer un concept (l.40)

### *Grammaire et stylistique*

(a) Traduisez les lignes 13–15 et 26–28. Précisez les utilisations du relatif 'lequel' et illustrez-les par des phrases de votre cru.
(b) 'assister aux cours' (l.4), 'dégénérer en un affrontement' (ll.12–13), 'refuser de' (ll.29 et 38–39). Faites une liste des verbes construits avec une préposition dans le texte et utilisez-les dans des phrases.

### *Compréhension*

(a) Expliquez comment, du point de vue français, le port du foulard peut constituer 'une atteinte à la laïcité et à la neutralité de l'école publique' (ll.7–8).
(b) 'Chacun y a mis un peu du sien' (l.21). S'agit-il d'une véritable solution? Expliquez la gêne et l'ambiguïté des autorités.
(c) Que comprenez-vous par l'expression 'jouer les shérifs de la laïcité' (ll.32–33)? En quoi peut-on l'opposer au mot 'tolérance' (l.33)? Comparez avec 'islamistes' (l.13) et 'défenseurs de l'école républicaine' (l.13). Avec quel parti la journaliste se range-t-elle? Et que pensez-vous de sa conclusion?
(d) Beaucoup de mots arabes sont passés en français – caoua, toubib, bled. Trouvez-en d'autres.

### *Question orale ou écrite*

(a) Dans 'l'affaire des foulards islamiques' quelle était, selon vous, la véritable querelle entre l'école et les élèves?

TEXT 3.19

## Les limites de la tolérance

Cette excitation pour s'emparer de trois foulards coraniques et y nouer un débat national est-elle déraisonnable? Non! Mais révélatrice, sûrement! On prétendit cacher ces coups de canif de l'islam à l'école laïque, nous en écarter comme des enfants d'un secret de famille. Mais rien n'a pu contenir l'éruption. Pourquoi? Parce que derrière le voile coranique se profilait la question brûlante de l'intégration. Et derrière elle, celle de l'identité nationale. Autant de 'bonnes questions' qui couvaient comme le feu sous la cendre.

Les Français n'ont jamais craint l'immigration, parce qu'ils ont toujours réussi à l'intégrer. Mais, avec plus de trois millions de musulmans, ils voient désormais que la magie du creuset national n'opérera pas comme jadis avec Polonais, Italiens, Espagnols et autres Portugais.

La difficulté nouvelle n'est nullement raciale: elle est culturelle, religieuse et tient à l'islam. Il n'y a aucun 'racisme' à relever, quant à l'islam, quelques vérités qui crèvent les yeux de toute la planète. La première tient à sa propension à mêler le spirituel et le temporel, à régenter les mœurs, le sexe, le vêtement, l'alimentation, à prescrire le rythme des prières, le temps du ramadan, quand ce ne sont pas l'opinion des fidèles et le régime qu'il leur faut. La deuxième est que l'islam maintient la femme dans un statut d'infériorité insupportable à nos mœurs et à nos lois. La troisième est qu'il a développé dans certaines de ses traditions un fanatisme abominable. Ce n'est pas tout à fait un hasard si aucun pays musulman ne pratique encore, à notre manière, la démocratie libérale. Un connaisseur, V.S. Naipaul, met le doigt sur l'essentiel: '*La religion, pour un musulman,* écrit-il, *n'est pas affaire de conscience et de pratiques privées comme le christianisme peut l'être pour un Européen. Accepter l'islam, c'est accepter* (. . .) *un certain ordre social.*' Dans ces quelques mots, tout est dit.

Ce constat déprimant doit-il nous faire trembler? Non. Car il existe, au sein de notre communauté d'origine maghrébine, une majorité de fidèles dont l'islam, heureusement, se fait tiède ou déclinant. On y rencontre un fort courant laïc, et, chez les Beurs, le souci de fuir le Moyen Age. Mais les ferments de l'intégrisme en France, ses capacités de violence, le renfort médiatique du messianisme de la Jihad (pensez à l'affaire Rushdie), le regain de l'islamisme algérien, les aliments que le fanatisme peut trouver en France dans le chômage, le désespoir des ghettos et la détestation d'une société riche et permissive, tout cela justifie en effet que nous fixions des limites claires à notre tolérance.

Entre nous, je fais plutôt confiance au Président tunisien qu'à M. Jospin ou à Mme Mitterrand pour apprécier la symbolique du voile que les musulmans modernistes interdisent dans leurs classes: ils y voient, mieux que nos jobards, l'ostentation d'une règle coranique qui maintient les femmes, au-delà d'une pudeur imposée, dans un asservissement répugnant pour des peuples libres.

C'est une erreur de rêver que, dans une France aplatie de tolérance, l'islam resterait confiné dans la sphère privée. Une autre erreur est de nous monter le bourrichon avec le projet fantasmatique d'une 'nouvelle société multiculturelle' en invoquant l'exemple américain. D'abord, cet exemple n'est guère engageant. Ensuite, pour transposer chez nous la mosaïque américaine, il nous faudrait l'espace, la culture biblique, la morale du shérif et le rêve américains. Chez nous, le mythe intégrateur de la nation reste, via l'école, l'idée républicaine.

Les valeurs de la République ne sont pas neutres. Elles n'appellent pas ces contorsions chèvre-chou pour prescrire aux fillettes de l'islam la gymnastique – où l'on se dévoile – sans proscrire le foulard qui voile. Cette laïcité gagnée par l'esprit jésuite, on dirait le pied de nez de Voltaire à un Bicentenaire flageolant.

(Claude Imbert, 'Les limites de la tolérance', *Le Point*, 30 October 1989, p.29.)

## Exercices

### *Lexique*

Expliquez les mots et expressions suivants:

donner un coup de canif à quelque chose (l.3)
la magie du creuset national (l.10)
un fort courant laïc (l.28)
les Beurs (l.29)
un jobard (l.37)
une France aplatie de tolérance (l.40)
monter le bourrichon (ll.41–42)
une contorsion chèvre-chou (l.48)

### *Grammaire et stylistique*

(a) 'Cette excitation . . . est-elle déraisonnable? Non!' (ll.1–2). Utilisez vous-même des négatives, sur ce modèle et sur d'autres que vous inventerez.

### *Compréhension*

(a) A votre avis, pourquoi 'la magie du creuset national' (l.10) n'opère-t-elle plus?
(b) Qu'appelle-t-on 'l'esprit jésuite' (l.50), et qui est visé? Expliquez la dernière phrase du texte.
(c) 'Chez nous, le mythe intégrateur de la nation reste, via l'école, l'idée républicaine' (ll.45–46). Clarifiez cette idée républicaine et expliquez ce que veut dire l'auteur.

### *Question orale ou écrite*

(a) A l'aide d'une encyclopédie, informez-vous sur l'histoire des relations de la France et de l'islam. L'Occident peut-il 'intégrer' l'islam?

# Chronology

| | | |
|---|---|---|
| **1944** | June | Allies land in Normandy |
| | Aug | Liberation of Paris |
| | Sept | Provisional government set up |
| | Oct | Women obtain right to vote |
| | Dec | Nationalization of coal mines in Nord-Pas-de-Calais |
| **1945** | Jan | Nationalization of Renault |
| | Feb | Law establishes works councils |
| | June | Press censorship ends |
| | Oct | Law establishes social security |
| | Nov | Vote by referendum to end Third Republic |
| | Dec | Creation of *Radiodiffusion-télévision française* (RTF) |
| | | Nationalization of five main retail banks and *Banque de France* |
| | | *Commissariat du Plan* set up |
| | | Bretton-Woods agreements |
| **1946** | Jan | De Gaulle resigns from government |
| | April | Nationalization of gas, electricity and large insurance companies |
| | May | First proposed constitution rejected |
| | | Blum-Byrnes Agreement |
| | June | Nationalization of Air France |
| | July | Law on equal pay for men and women |
| | Aug | Legislation on family allowances |
| | Oct | Constitution of the Fourth Republic accepted by referendum |
| | | Beginning of French military operations in Vietnam |
| | | Renault 4CV launched |
| **1947** | Jan | Vincent Auriol elected President of the Republic |
| | | Social Security Plan begins |
| | March | Creation of *Salaire minimum vital* |
| | April | Gaullist RPF set up |
| | May | Adoption of *Plan Monnet* |
| | | Communist ministers dismissed from government |
| | June | Widespread strikes |
| | | France accepts Marshall Aid |
| | Nov–Dec | Wave of strikes |
| | Dec | CGT splits, CGT-FO established |

| | | |
|---|---|---|
| **1948** | April | Franc devalued twice |
| | May | Hague conference on Europe |
| | Sept | Rent controls implemented |
| | Oct–Nov | Miners' strike, civil servants' strike. Troops intervene |
| | Nov | General strike in Paris region |
| **1949** | Jan | Price freeze |
| | March | Launch of *Paris-Match* |
| | April | North Atlantic Treaty signed in Washington |
| | | Franc devalued |
| | July | France ratifies Atlantic Pact |
| **1950** | Feb | *Salaire minimum interprofessionnel garanti* (SMIG) introduced |
| | June | Korean War begins |
| **1951** | April | Creation of the Coal and Steel Community (CECA) involving France, Germany, Italy and the Benelux countries |
| **1952** | May | Anti-inflation plan by Pinay government |
| | July | Adoption of *échelle mobile des salaires* |
| **1953** | Jan | RPF dissolved |
| | May | *L'Express* launched |
| | July | Pierre Poujade's movement launched |
| | Sept | Vatican condemns worker priests |
| | Dec | René Coty elected President |
| **1954** | April | Introduction of VAT |
| | May | French suffer defeat at Dien Bien Phu |
| | June | New government with Mendès-France as Prime Minister |
| | July | Geneva agreement on Vietnam |
| | Aug | *Assemblée nationale* rejects European Defence Community plan |
| | Nov | Revolt in Algeria |
| **1955** | March | Vote on state of emergency in Algeria |
| | May | Adoption of Second Plan |
| | June | Messina conference on European reconstruction |
| | Nov | Uprising in Algeria |
| **1956** | Jan | Legislative elections in France, Poujadists gain seats |
| | | Atomic energy plant at Marcoule starts operating |
| | Feb | Demonstrations in Algiers against Prime Minister Guy Mollet |
| | | Law passed on third week of paid holiday |
| | March | Tunisia and Morocco gain independence |
| | | Vote in favour of special powers in Algeria |
| | Nov | Franco-British Suez expedition |

| | | |
|---|---|---|
| **1957** | March | Treaty of Rome signed establishing European Community |
| | April | Battle of Algiers begins |
| | Aug | Franc devalued |
| **1958** | Jan | European Community starts functioning |
| | May | French Algerians revolt in Algiers, 'Committee of Public Safety' set up, presided by General Massu |
| | June | De Gaulle becomes head of government and is given full powers |
| | Sept | Overwhelming 'Yes' vote in referendum on new constitution for the Fifth Republic |
| | | Gaullist UNR set up |
| | Nov | Legislative elections, substantial gains for Gaullists |
| | Dec | De Gaulle elected President of the Republic |
| | | Devaluation of the franc |
| **1959** | Jan | Michel Debré becomes Prime Minister |
| | | School leaving age raised to 16 years |
| | | Third Plan adopted |
| | March | French Mediterranean fleet withdrawn from NATO |
| | Nov | Malraux's speech to Assemblée nationale as Minister of Culture promising creation of Maisons de la culture |
| **1960** | Jan | Uprising in Algeria |
| | Feb | Introduction of *nouveau franc* |
| | | French atomic bomb exploded |
| | April | PSU set up |
| | July | *Loi d'orientation agricole* voted which organizes modernization of French agriculture |
| | Jan–July | Francophone African countries and Madagascar granted independence |
| **1961** | Jan | Law on health insurance for farmers |
| | | Large majority vote 'Yes' in referendum over self-determination for Algeria |
| | April | Attempted coup by French generals in Algeria |
| | June | Opening of first Maison de la culture in Le Havre |
| | Sept | Attempt to assassinate de Gaulle at Pont-sur-Seine |
| | Oct | Violent repression of Algerian demonstration in Paris |
| **1962** | Jan | Number of OAS attacks in metropolitan France increases |
| | Feb | Anti-OAS demonstration in Paris: eight killed at metro station Charonne |
| | March | *Accords d'Évian* give Algeria independence |
| | | Pompidou becomes Prime Minister |
| | April | Overwhelming 'Yes' vote in referendum on Évian agreements |

| | | |
|---|---|---|
| | June | Adoption of Fourth Plan |
| | Aug | Attempt to assassinate de Gaulle at Le Petit Clamart |
| | Oct | Assemblée nationale approves motion of censure against Pompidou's government, Assemblée nationale dissolved<br>'Yes' vote in referendum on election of president of the republic by universal suffrage |
| | Nov | Legislative elections, substantial gains for government |
| | Dec | Agreement on four weeks' paid holiday at Renault |
| **1963** | Jan | De Gaulle vetoes British membership of the EEC |
| | March–April | Miners' strike |
| | June | French navy withdrawn from NATO operations in the Channel and Atlantic |
| | July | Franco-German Friendship Treaty signed by de Gaulle and Adenauer |
| | Aug | Collèges d'enseignement secondaire (CES) set up |
| | Sept | Adoption of Giscard d'Estaing's Plan de Stabilisation (anti-inflation measures) |
| | Dec | Second television channel starts broadcasting |
| **1964** | May | Waldeck Rochet becomes general secretary of PCF, Maurice Thorez becomes president |
| | June | Creation of *Office de la Radiodiffusion-télévision française* (ORTF) |
| | July | Death of Maurice Thorez |
| | Nov | Majority of CFTC members leave and form CFDT<br>Launch of *Le Nouvel Observateur* |
| | Dec | Public sector strikes |
| **1965** | May | Agreement between CNPF and unions on extension of four weeks' annual paid holiday to all workers |
| | July | France begins 'empty chair' policy in Brussels (lasts until December) |
| | Sept | *Fédération de la gauche démocratique et socialiste* created (Socialists, Radicals and left clubs) |
| | Nov | Adoption of Fifth Plan |
| | Dec | Presidential elections: De Gaulle wins (55%), Mitterrand beaten (45%) |
| **1966** | Jan | Instituts universitaires de technologie (IUT) established |
| | March | France leaves NATO integrated command |
| | June | Fouchet reform of higher education<br>Extension of health insurance to self-employed |
| **1967** | March | Legislative elections, slim victory for parties of government<br>Wine producers riot over Algerian imports<br>Decrees on participation of workers in the 'benefits of industrial expansion' |

| | | |
|---|---|---|
| | July | Creation of Agence nationale pour l'emploi (ANPE)<br>De Gaulle in Montreal: 'Vive le Québec libre' |
| | Oct | Colour television broadcasting begins |
| | Nov | Gaullist UDVeR set up |
| | Dec | *Loi Neuwirth* legalizes contraception |
| **1968** | Jan | Incidents in *lycées* and at Nanterre University<br>VAT applied across the board |
| | Feb | Demonstrations against US war in Vietnam |
| | May | Student revolt and workers' general strike<br>*Accords de Grenelle* (not subsequently ratified) |
| | June | Legislative elections, increased majority for government |
| | July | Maurice Couve de Murville becomes Prime Minister |
| | Nov | *Loi d'orientation* on higher education approved |
| **1969** | April | 'No' vote in referendum on reform of Senate and regional reforms, de Gaulle resigns |
| | June | Georges Pompidou elected President of the Republic<br>Jacques Chaban-Delmas becomes Prime Minister |
| | July | Parti socialiste (PS) founded |
| | Aug | Devaluation of the franc |
| | Sept | Chaban-Delmas makes speech about 'la nouvelle société' |
| **1970** | Jan | SMIG becomes SMIC (*Salaire minimum interprofessionnel de croissance*) |
| | Nov | Death of de Gaulle |
| **1971** | April | Manifeste des 343 in *Le Nouvel Observateur* in favour of legalizing abortion<br>Launch of *Association Choisir* to campaign for legal abortion |
| | June | Re-unification of socialist movement at Congrès d'Épinay, Mitterrand becomes first secretary of PS |
| **1972** | June | *Programme commun de gouvernement* signed by PS and PCF, creating *Union de la gauche* |
| | July | Pierre Messmer becomes Prime Minister |
| | Sept | Launch of *Le Point* |
| | Nov | Procès de Bobigny |
| **1973** | Jan | Creation of the European Snake |
| | Feb | Manifesto of 331 doctors in favour of abortion<br>Lip watch factory in Besançon occupied |
| | April | Launch of *Libération* |
| | Aug | Demonstration in the Larzac against expansion of army training ground |
| | Sept | *Des femmes* publishing house set up by feminist group *Psychanalyse et politique* |
| | Oct | Huge oil price rise |

| | | |
|---|---|---|
| **1974** | March | Legislative elections: government parties win with a much slimmer majority |
| | April | Death of President Pompidou |
| | May | Presidential elections, Valéry Giscard d'Estaing elected (50.8%), François Mitterrand beaten (49.2%) |
| | June | Jacques Chirac made Prime Minister |
| | | Age of majority lowered to 18 years |
| | July | Immigration suspended |
| | | Françoise Giroud becomes *Secrétaire d'État à la condition féminine* |
| | | ORTF broadcasting network broken up |
| | Dec | Jacques Chirac becomes UDR leader |
| | | Michel Rocard and other Parti socialiste unifié (PSU) leaders join PS |
| **1975** | Jan | *Loi Veil* legalizes abortion |
| | | Reform of broadcasting takes effect. ORTF broken up into seven separate companies: TF1, Antenne 2, FR3, Radio-France, TDF, SFP and INA |
| | April | Giscard d'Estaing visits Algeria in first presidential visit since independence |
| | June | Law allowing divorce by consent and 'no fault' divorce |
| | Sept | Second *Plan Fourcade* aiming to relaunch economic activity |
| **1976** | Feb | PCF congress abandons notion of 'dictatorship of proletariat' |
| | March | Departmental elections: substantial gains for left |
| | | Franc taken out of European Snake for good |
| | Aug | Raymond Barre becomes Prime Minister |
| | Sept | Barre plan to combat inflation, includes price freeze and wage restraint |
| | Dec | Creation of Gaullist RPR |
| **1977** | March | Municipal elections: victory for left |
| | | Creation of *aide au retour* for immigrants |
| | Sept | PS/PCF *Union de la gauche* breaks up |
| **1978** | Feb | UDF set up |
| | March | Legislative elections right wins |
| **1979** | Jan | European Monetary System (EMS) becomes operational |
| | June | European elections: high rate of abstention, left loses ground |
| | July | Second oil crisis |
| **1980** | Jan | Georges Marchais defends Soviet intervention in Afghanistan |
| | Oct | Bomb explodes outside synagogue in Rue Copernic, Paris, killing four |

| | | |
|---|---|---|
| **1981** | Jan | Marguerite Yourcenar first woman elected to Académie française |
| | May | François Mitterrand elected President of the Republic (51.8%), Valéry Giscard d'Estaing beaten (48.2%) |
| | June | Pierre Mauroy becomes Prime Minister |
| | | Minimum wage, pensions and family allowances increased substantially |
| | | PS achieves absolute majority in legislative elections |
| | | Second Mauroy government formed, including four PCF ministers |
| | Aug | 130,000 illegal immigrants given legal status |
| | Sept | Death penalty abolished |
| | | Paris–Lyons TGV opens |
| | Oct | Devaluation of the franc |
| | | Law nationalizing five industrial groups and 38 financial institutions |
| | Nov | Law allowing the creation of private local radio stations |
| | | Unemployment reaches two million, according to ANPE |
| **1982** | Jan | Introduction of 39-hour week and five weeks' holiday |
| | March | Decree on reimbursement of abortion by social security |
| | June | Retirement at 60 introduced |
| | | *Loi Defferre* on decentralization approved |
| | | Devaluation of the franc, pay and price freeze |
| | | Moinot Report on broadcasting creates *Haute Autorité* |
| | Aug | Six killed in attack on Jewish restaurant, rue des Rosiers, Paris |
| | Sept | Demonstration by company directors against socialist economic policy |
| **1983** | March | Defeat for the left in municipal elections |
| | | Devaluation of the franc |
| | | Austerity plan announced |
| | May | Doctors' strike |
| | July | First Airbus flight |
| | Aug | French military intervention in Chad |
| | Sept | In Dreux, victory for united FN-right list in second round of municipal elections |
| | | Government adopts *loi Savary* on private schools |
| **1984** | Jan | Reorganization of the banking system |
| | March | Over half a million demonstrate to defend private schools |
| | April | Financial incentives for immigrants returning to their country of origin |
| | | Demonstration by steel workers in Paris: PCF leaders take part |

| | | |
|---|---|---|
| | June | Over a million demonstrate against *loi Savary* |
| | | European elections: losses for left |
| | July | *Loi Savary* on private schools withdrawn |
| | | Laurent Fabius becomes Prime Minister, PCF withdraws from government |
| | | Violent incidents in New Caledonia |
| | Nov | Unemployment rises above 2.5 million |
| | | Launch of Canal Plus, the first pay TV channel |
| | Dec | Communist deputies vote against budget |
| **1985** | March | Right wins cantonal elections |
| | June | Large *SOS-Racisme* festival, Place de la Concorde, Paris |
| | July | Attack on Greenpeace ship *Rainbow Warrior* in New Zealand |
| | Sept | Defence Minister Charles Hernu resigns |
| | Dec | Law on flexible working time |
| **1986** | Feb | Terrorist attacks in Paris |
| | | Fifth and sixth television channels (*La Cinq, TV6*) begin broadcasting |
| | March | Legislative elections using proportional representation: right wins |
| | | Jacques Chirac becomes Prime Minister and forms RPR-UDF government |
| | June | Abolition of law which obliged companies to consult before making redundancies |
| | July | Law on privatization of 65 companies |
| | | Tighter law on entry of immigrants to France |
| | Sept | Terrorist attacks in Paris |
| | | *Loi Pasqua* on immigration |
| | | *Haute Autorité* replaced by *Commission nationale de la communication et des libertés* (CNCL) |
| | Oct | 'Anti-Hersant' law restricting holdings of any one person in broadcast media |
| | Nov | *Action directe* group kills Georges Besse, director of Renault |
| | | Student and school student strike begins against *loi Devaquet* on higher education |
| | Dec | Minister for Higher Education Alain Devaquet resigns, bill withdrawn |
| | | Public sector strikes |
| **1987** | Jan | Start of deregulation of stock exchange and other financial institutions |
| | Feb | Privatization of TF1 |
| | May | Privatization of Crédit Commercial de France, CGE and l'Agence Havas |
| | | Trial of Klaus Barbie begins |

| | | |
|---|---|---|
| | Sept | Referendum in New Caledonia: 98% in favour of New Caledonia remaining in the French Republic |
| | Oct | World financial crash |
| **1988** | April | First round of presidential elections: Mitterrand and Chirac ahead, Jean-Marie Le Pen receives 14.4% |
| | May | Army assault on cave in New Caledonia to free hostages: two soldiers and 19 pro-independence fighters killed |
| | | François Mitterrand wins presidential election (54.0%), Jacques Chirac beaten (46.0%) |
| | | Michel Rocard becomes Prime Minister |
| | June | Legislative elections: PS wins but has no overall majority |
| | | Government of *ouverture* formed |
| | Nov | *Accord Matignon* on New Caledonia |
| | | Creation of *Revenu minimum d'insertion* (RMI) |
| | | 'Yes' vote in referendum on plans for New Caledonia (63% abstentions) |
| **1989** | Jan | *Conseil supérieur de l'audiovisuel* (CSA) replaces CNCL |
| | March | Municipal elections: gains for PS |
| | June | European elections: right makes gains, high level of abstentions (51.2%) |
| | July | Celebration of bi-centenary of French Revolution |
| | Oct | Beginning of the *affaire des foulards islamiques* |
| | Dec | Creation of *Haut Conseil à l'Intégration* |
| **1990** | March | Opening of *Opéra de la Bastille* |
| | | PS Congrès de Rennes |
| | June | UPF set up, uniting RPR and UDF in opposition |
| | Sept | Jacques Médecin, Mayor of Nice, flees to Argentina |
| | Nov | PCF votes with the right on motion of no confidence in the government |
| **1991** | May | Édith Cresson becomes Prime Minister |
| | Aug | France enters war against Iraq |
| **1992** | March | Pierre Bérégovoy becomes Prime Minister |
| | April | Euro Disney opens |
| | | La Cinq goes bankrupt |
| | | France suspends nuclear tests in the Pacific and signs nuclear non-proliferation treaty |
| | Sept | Referendum on Treaty of Maastricht: 'yes' vote gains small majority (51%) |
| | | Creation of ARTE |
| | Oct | Conviction of Michel Garetta, Jean-Pierre Alain and Jacques Roux in *Affaire du sang contaminé* |

| | | |
|---|---|---|
| **1993** | Jan | Unemployment reaches three million according to ANPE |
| | March | Legislative elections: right wins huge majority of seats |
| | | Édouard Balladur becomes Prime Minister, second period of *cohabitation* begins. Programme of widespread privatizations announced |
| | | Balladur government supports 'franc fort' |
| | May | Pierre Bérégovoy commits suicide |
| | Aug | Franc indirectly devalued through opening of fluctuation margins in ERM |
| | Sept | Speculative attacks against franc in ERM after sterling crisis |
| | | 'Franc fort' policy restated |
| | Dec | GATT negotiations: France secures exclusion of 'audiovisual products' |
| **1994** | Jan | XXVIIIth congress of the PCF. Georges Marchais resigns as general secretary and is replaced by Robert Hue |
| | | Banque de France becomes independent from government |
| | Feb | Assassination of Yann Piat |
| | March | Withdrawal of the *Contrat d'insertion professionnelle* after demonstrations and unrest among students |
| | May | Channel Tunnel opens |
| | June | *Loi Toubon* on French language |
| | | European elections: PS receives only 14.5% and the RPR–UDF list 25.6%. Protest parties do relatively well |
| | | Rocard resigns as first secretary of PS |
| | | French 'humanitarian' campaign in Rwanda |
| | Oct | Alain Carignon, Mayor of Grenoble, sentenced to three years in prison for corruption |
| | Nov | Maastricht Treaty comes into force |
| | Dec | Law on political corruption |
| **1995** | April | First round of presidential elections: Jospin ahead with 23.3%, Chirac receives 18.5%, Le Pen 15%. Two candidates for the RPR |
| | May | Chirac wins presidential elections (52.6%), Jospin beaten (47.4%) |
| | | Alain Juppé becomes Prime Minister |
| | June | Chirac announces new nuclear tests, to last a limited period |
| | | Municipal elections: FN gains Toulon, Marignane and Orange, loses Dreux and Noyon |
| | Sept | France resumes tests in Polynesia |
| | Dec | Widespread strikes and demonstrations, especially in the public sector |
| | | France announces participation in military structure of NATO |

| | | |
|---|---|---|
| **1996** | Jan | Death of François Mitterrand |
| | March | Henri Emmanuelli, former PS treasurer, sentenced to 18 months in prison for involvement in Urba-SAGES affair linked to illegal financing for PS |
| | May | Government announces privatization of Renault |
| | | Chirac announces military service to be phased out by 2002 |
| | June | *Sans papiers* (asylum seekers) occupy Église Saint-Bernard in Paris |
| | | Bernard Tapie sentenced to 18 months in prison for Olympique de Marseille affair |
| | | Police search home of Jean Tibéri, Chirac's former aide at the Mairie de Paris. His wife, Xavière, is implicated |
| | July | Loïk Le Floch-Prigent imprisoned pending investigation of his role in Elf Aquitaine affair |
| | Aug | *Sans papiers* evicted from Église Saint-Bernard |
| | Sept | Law reforming military service |
| | | Juppé announces income tax cuts |
| | Nov | Widespread protests by lorry drivers against working conditions |
| | Dec | *Loi Debré* introduced |
| **1997** | April | Chirac dissolves National Assembly |
| | May | Legislative elections, first round: left receives 44.3%, centre-right 36.2% and FN 14.9% |
| | June | Left wins elections, with 320 seats against the right's 256 |
| | | Juppé resigns as Prime Minister, Jospin replaces him |
| | | New period of *cohabitation* begins. Mainly socialist government also includes ecologists and communists |
| | | Over 20,000 asylum seekers given residence permits |
| | July | *Rapports Weil* on *Code de la nationalité* and on immigration |
| | Sept | Partial privatization of France-Télécom |
| | | Means testing for *allocations familiales* proposed |
| | Dec | New *Code de la nationalité* and *loi Chevènement* adopted |
| **1998** | Jan | Public monopoly on telephone ends |
| | | Demonstrations by unemployed people |
| | March | Regional and cantonal elections: left does better than right in both elections |
| | | Roland Dumas, President of the Conseil Constitutionnel and former Minister for Foreign Affairs, questioned by police in Elf affair |
| | April | Maurice Papon sentenced to ten years in prison for crimes against humanity |
| | June | Law on gradual introduction of 35-hour week, designed to reduce unemployment |

| | | |
|---|---|---|
| | July | Government announces privatization of Aérospatiale |
| | Sept | François Bayrou becomes president of UDF<br>France wins soccer World Cup |
| | Oct | Protests by school students<br>*Journée APD* replaces military service for those born in 1979 |
| **1999** | Jan | Euro becomes legal tender<br>FN split: Le Pen leads the *Front National pour l'Unité Française* (FN-UF) and Bruno Mégret the *Front National – Mouvement National* (later *Mouvement national républicain* (MNR)) |
| | June | Constitutional amendment instituting *la parité*<br>European elections: good result for government parties, extreme right vote drops to under 10% |
| | Oct | *Assemblée nationale* votes in favour of PACS |
| | Nov | RPR splits and Pasqua sets up *Rassemblement pour la France*, with de Villiers as second in command |
| | Dec | RPR becomes first major party to have woman as leader, Michèle Alliot-Marie |

# Index

**Bold** page-numbers denote main treatments; *italic* page-numbers denote figures and tables